International Handbook of Survey Methodology

| | The European Association of Methodology (EAM) serves to promote research and development of empirical research methods in the fields of the Behavioural, Social, Educational, Health and Economic Sciences as well as in the field of Evaluation Research. Homepage: http://www.eam-online.org |

The purpose of the EAM book series is to advance the development and application of methodological and statistical research techniques in social and behavioral research. Each volume in the series presents cutting-edge methodological developments in a way that is accessible to a broad audience. Such books can be authored books, monographs, or edited volumes.

Sponsored by the European Association of Methodology, the EAM book series is open to contributions from the Behavioral, Social, Educational, Health and Economic Sciences. Proposals for volumes in the EAM series should include the following: (1) Title; (2) authors/editors; (3) a brief description of the volume's focus and intended audience; (4) a table of contents; (5) a timeline including planned completion date. Proposals are invited from all interested authors. Feel free to submit a proposal to one of the members of the EAM book series editorial board, by visiting the EAM website http://www.eam-online.org. Members of the EAM editorial board are Joop Hox (Utrecht University), Michael Eid (University of Geneva), Edith de Leeuw (Utrecht University) and Vasja Vehovar (University of Ljubljana).

Volumes in the series include

De Leeuw/Hox/Dillman: International Handbook of Survey Methodology, 2008

Van Montfort/Oud/Satorra: Longitudinal Models in the Behavioral and Related Sciences, 2007

International Handbook of Survey Methodology

Edith D. de Leeuw
Joop J. Hox
Don A. Dillman

Lawrence Erlbaum Associates
Taylor & Francis Group

New York   London

Lawrence Erlbaum Associates
Taylor & Francis Group
270 Madison Avenue
New York, NY 10016

Lawrence Erlbaum Associates
Taylor & Francis Group
2 Park Square
Milton Park, Abingdon
Oxon OX14 4RN

© 2008 by Taylor & Francis Group, LLC
Lawrence Erlbaum Associates is an imprint of Taylor & Francis Group, an Informa business

Printed in the United States of America on acid-free paper
10 9 8 7 6 5 4 3 2 1

International Standard Book Number-13: 978-0-8058-5753-5 (Softcover) 978-0-8058-5752-8 (Hardcover)

Library of Congress Cataloging-in-Publication Data

International handbook of survey methodology / editors, Edith D. de Leeuw, Joop J.
    Hox, and Don A. Dillman.
        p. cm.
    Includes bibliographical references and index.
    ISBN 978-0-8058-5753-5 (pbk.) -- ISBN 978-0-8058-5752-8 (hbk.)
    1. Surveys--Methodology. 2. Social sciences--Statistics--Methodology. 3. Social
sciences--Research--Methodology. I. Leeuw, Edith Desirée de. II. Hox, J. J. III. Dillman,
Don A., 1941- IV. European Association of Methodology.

HA31.2.I565 2008
001.4'33--dc22   2007047297

Visit the Taylor & Francis Web site at
http://www.taylorandfrancis.com

and the LEA and Routledge Web site at
http://www.routledge.com

Contents

Preface

In August, 2003, two of us (De Leeuw and Dillman) met in Berlin at the International Statistical Institute meetings to teach a short course on survey design. The audience consisted of surveyors from most continents of the world. Our first impressions were how different the data collection and analysis problems were that people faced, for example doing face-to-face interviews in rural villages of Uganda and web surveys of the general population in The Netherlands and Denmark. Our second, and more lasting impression, was how much all of the participants had in common. Regardless of country, all of the surveyors in the room had to deal with sample designs, writing questions, turning those questions into meaningful questionnaires, locating sample units, processing data, and analyzing the results.

Procedures we originally thought to be of interest only to those from certain countries, such as visual design for mail and web questionnaires, turned out to be of equal interest to those from developing countries who were concerned with more effective visual layouts for interviewer questionnaires and instructions. The idea for this *International Handbook of Survey Methodology* originated from this experience of two fascinating days with this diverse audience with many common needs and interests.

Our experience there was bolstered further by observations of the difficulties being faced in mounting surveys across national borders, and increased concern that they have to be done. For example, expansion of the European Union from 6 countries in 1957 to 15 countries in 1995 (with 9 candidate-members in 2006), has increased interest in collecting cross-national statistical information, including information from sample surveys. We have also observed with much interest emergent efforts to regularly conduct polls and surveys across continents. These surveys aim to facilitate comparisons of responses across countries widely separated in space, as well as technological development, and economic well-being. All this survey effort has resulted in greater concern about how survey methods unique to one country compare to those used in other countries, and how well questionnaire formats and items translate across cultures. It is also difficult to maintain using the same survey mode in all countries.

Within many countries we have noticed the trend towards mixed-mode surveys that is now occurring. Concerns about coverage and nonresponse in telephone surveys, rising costs for conducting face-to-face interviews, and the emergence of web survey capabilities that only some households have, are all encouraging surveyors to mix modes

We are entering a new era in survey design, in which surveyors throughout the world must think about the fundamentals of survey data collection and methods of turning answers to questions into meaningful results. Increasingly it is a mixed-mode world. Whereas at one time it was possible to learn a single survey mode, e.g., face-to-face interviewing or telephone interviewing, and apply it to all survey situations, doing that is no longer possible. It is now imperative for students and practitioners of surveying to learn the procedures associated with multiple modes of collecting sample survey information and apply the method or combination of methods that fit their specific situation.

This handbook provides expert guidance from acknowledged survey methodologists and statisticians around the world, who bring their experiences to bear on issues faced in their own and other countries. It serves as an excellent text for courses and seminars on survey methodology at the masters and graduate level. It is a key reference for survey researchers and practitioners around the world. The book is also very useful for everyone who regularly collects or uses survey data, such as researchers in psychology, sociology, economics, education, epidemiology, and health studies and professionals in market and public opinion research.

The book consists of five parts: foundations, design, implementation, data analysis, and quality issues. The book begins by focusing on the foundations of all sample surveys, ranging from sources of survey error to ethical issues of design and implementation. It is followed by a design section, which gives building blocks for good survey design, from coverage and sampling to writing and testing questions for multiple survey modes. The third section focuses on five modes of data collection, from the oldest, face-to-face interviews, to the newest, interactive voice response, ending with the special challenges involved in mixing these modes within one survey. The fourth section turns to analyzing survey data, dealing with simple as well as complex surveys, and procedures for nonresponse adjustment through imputation and other means. The fifth and final section focuses on special issues of maintaining quality and of documenting the survey process for future reference. The first chapter of the book, *The cornerstones of survey research*, ends with a more detailed description of the structure and contents of this book. There is a companion website http://www.xs4all.nl/~edithl/surveyhandbook.

As we move further into the 21st century, surveys will become inherently more international in scope and in practice. It is our hope that this book will prove helpful for those who are learning the craft of surveying, which like other life skills, will increasingly be applied beyond one's country of origin.

We thank our colleagues across the world for many lively and stimulating discussions about survey methodology. We also thank our students who inspired us and especially the master class in survey methodology 2006 who enthusiastically and critically discussed the drafts. The final book has profited from close reading and copy-editing by Mallory McBride, Sophie van der Zee, Evert-Jan van Doorn, and Amaranta de Haan. We thank Allison O'Neill for her creative cover design. We also thank Emily Wilkinson and Debra Riegert of Lawrence Erlbaum Associates for their patience and careful prodding in getting this book done.

Edith de Leeuw
Joop Hox
Don Dillman

Chapter 1

The Cornerstones of Survey Research

Edith D. de Leeuw
Joop J. Hox
Department of Methodology & Statistics, Utrecht University

Don A. Dillman
Washington State University

1.1 INTRODUCTION

The idea of conducting a survey is deceptively simple. It involves identifying a specific group or category of people and collecting information from some of them in order to gain insight into what the entire group does or thinks; however, undertaking a survey inevitably raises questions that may be difficult to answer. How many people need to be surveyed in order to be able to describe fairly accurately the entire group? How should the people be selected? What questions should be asked and how should they be posed to respondents? In addition, what data collection methods should one consider using, and are some of those methods of collecting data better than others? And, once one has collected the information, how should it be analyzed and reported? Deciding to do a survey means committing oneself to work through a myriad of issues each of which is critical to the ultimate success of the survey.

Yet, each day, throughout the world, thousands of surveys are being undertaken. Some surveys involve years of planning, require arduous efforts to select and interview respondents in their home and take many months to complete and many more months to report results. Other surveys are conducted with seemingly lightning speed as web survey requests are transmitted simultaneously to people regardless of their location, and completed surveys start being returned a few minutes later; data collection is stopped in a few days and results are reported minutes afterwards. Whereas some surveys use only one mode of data collection such as the telephone, others may involve multiple modes, for example, starting with mail, switching to telephone, and finishing up with face-to-face interviews. In addition, some surveys are quite simple and inexpensive to do, such as a mail survey of members of a small professional association. Others are incredibly complex, such as a survey of the general public across all countries of the European Union in which the same questions need to be answered in multiple languages by people of all educational levels.

In the mid-twentieth century there was a remarkable similarity of survey procedures and methods. Most surveys of significance were done by face-to-face interviews in most countries in the world. Self-administered paper surveys, usually done by mail, were the only alternative. Yet, by the 1980s the telephone had replaced face-to-face interviews as the dominate survey mode in the United States, and in the next decade telephone surveys became the major data collection method in many countries. Yet other methods were emerging and in the 1990s two additional modes of surveying—the Internet and responding by telephone to prerecorded interview questions, known as Interactive Voice Response or IVR, emerged in some countries. Nevertheless, in some countries the face-to-face interview remained the reliable and predominantly used survey mode.

Never in the history of surveying have their been so many alternatives for collecting survey data, nor has there been so much heterogeneity in the use of survey methods across countries. Heterogeneity also exists within countries as surveyors attempt to match survey modes to the difficulties associated with finding and obtaining response to particular survey populations.

Yet, all surveys face a common challenge, which is how to produce precise estimates by surveying only a relatively small proportion of the larger population, within the limits of the social, economic and technological environments associated with countries and survey populations in countries. This chapter is about solving these common problems that we described as the cornerstones of surveying. When understood and responded to, the cornerstone challenges will assure precision in the pursuit of one's survey objectives.

1.2 WHAT IS A SURVEY?

A quick review of the literature will reveal many different definitions of what constitutes a survey. Some handbooks on survey methodology immediately describe the major components of surveys and of survey error instead of giving a definition (e.g., Fowler, Gallagher, Stringfellow, Zalavsky Thompson & Cleary, 2002, p. 4; Groves, 1989, p. 1), others provide definitions, ranging from concise definitions (e.g., Czaja & Blair, 2005, p. 3; Groves, Fowler, Couper, Lepkowski, Singer & Tourangeau, 2004, p. 2; Statistics Canada, 2003, p. 1) to elaborate descriptions of criteria (Biemer & Lyberg, 2003, Table 1.1). What have these definitions in common? The survey research methods section of the American Statistical Association provides on its website an introduction (Scheuren, 2004) that explains survey methodology for survey users, covering the major steps in the survey process and explaining the methodological issues. According to Scheuren (2004, p. 9) the word survey is used most often to describe a method of gathering information from a sample of individuals. Besides sample and gathering information, other recurring terms in definitions and descriptions are systematic or organized and quantitative. So, a survey can be seen as a research strategy in which quantitative information is systematically collected from a relatively large sample taken from a population.

Most books stress that survey methodology is a science and that there are scientific criteria for survey quality. As a result, criteria for survey quality have been widely discussed. One very general definition of quality is fitness for use. This definition was coined by Juran and Gryna in their 1980s book on quality planning and analysis, and has been widely quoted since. How this general definition is further specified depends on the product that is being evaluated and the user. For example, quality can be focusing on construction, on making sturdy and safe furniture, and on testing it. Like Ikea, the Swedish furniture chain, that advertised in its catalogs with production quality and gave examples on how a couch was tested on sturdiness. In survey statistics the main focus has been on accuracy, on reducing the mean squared error or MSE. This is based on the Hansen and Hurwitz model (Hansen, Hurwitz, & Madow, 1953; Hansen, Hurwitz, & Bershad, 1961) that differentiates between random error and systematic bias, and offers a concept of total error (see also Kish, 1965), which is still the basis of current survey error models. The statistical quality indicator is thus the MSE: the sum of all squared variable errors and all squared systematic errors. A more modern approach is total quality, which combines both ideas as Biemer and Lyberg (2003) do in their handbook on survey quality. They apply the concept of fitness for use to the survey process, which leads to the following quality requirements for survey data: accuracy as defined by the mean squared error, timeliness as defined by availability at the time it is needed, and accessibility, that is the data should be accessible to those for whom the survey was conducted.

There are many stages in designing a survey and each influences survey quality. Deming (1944) already gave an early warning of the complexity of the task facing the survey designer, when he listed no less than thirteen factors that affect the ultimate usefulness of a survey. Among those are the relatively well understood effects of sampling variability, but also more difficult to measure effects. Deming incorporates effects of the interviewer, method of data collection, nonresponse, questionnaire imperfections, processing errors and errors of interpretation. Other authors (e.g., Kish, 1965, see also Groves, 1989) basically classify threats to survey quality in two main categories, for instance differentiating between errors of nonobservation (e.g., nonresponse) and observation (e.g., in data collection and processing). Biemer and Lyberg (2003) group errors in sampling error and nonsampling error. Sampling error is due to selecting a sample instead of studying the whole population. Nonsampling errors are due to mistakes and/or system deficiencies, and include all errors that can be made during data collection and data processing, such as coverage, nonresponse, measurement, and coding error (see also Lyberg & Biemer, Chapter 22).

In the ensuing chapters of this handbook we provide concrete tools to incorporate quality when designing a survey. The purpose of this chapter is to sensitize the reader to the importance of designing for quality and to introduce the methodological and statistical principles that play a key role in designing sound quality surveys.

A useful metaphor is the design and construction of a house. When building a house, one carefully prepares the ground and places the cornerstones. This is the foundation on which the whole structure must rest. If this foundation is not designed with care, the house will collapse or sink in the unsafe, swampy underground as many Dutch builders have experienced in the past. In the same way, when designing and constructing a survey, one should also lay a well thought-out foundation. In surveys, one starts with preparing the underground by specifying the concepts to be measured. Then these clearly specified concepts have to be translated, or in technical terms, operationalized into measurable variables. Survey methodologists describe this process in terms of avoiding or reducing specification errors. Social scientists use the term construct validity: the extend to which a measurement method accurately represents the intended construct. This first step is conceptual rather than statistical; the concepts of concern must be defined and specified. On this foundation we place the four cornerstones of survey research: coverage, sampling, response, and measurement (Salant & Dillman, 1994; see also Groves, 1989).

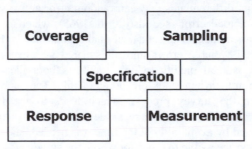

Figure 1.1 The cornerstones of survey research

Figure 1.1 provides a graphical picture of the cornerstone metaphor. Only when these cornerstones are solid, high quality data are collected, which can be used in further processing and analysis. In this chapter we introduce the reader to key issues in survey research.

1.3 BREAKING THE GROUND: SPECIFICATION OF THE RESEARCH AND THE SURVEY QUESTIONS

The first step in the survey process is to determine the research objectives. The researchers have to agree on a well-defined set of research objectives. These are then translated into a set of key research questions. For each research question one or more survey questions are then formulated, depending on the goal of the study. For example, in a general study of the population one or two general questions about well-being are enough to give a global indication of well-being. On the other hand, in a specific study of the influence of social networks on feelings of well-being among the elderly a far more detailed picture of well-being is needed and a series of questions has to be asked, each question measuring a specific aspect of well-being. These different approaches are illustrated in the text boxes noted later.

Example General Well-being Question (Hox, 1986)

Taking all things together, how satisfied or dissatisfied are you with life in general?
- ❑ VERY DISSATISFIED
- ❑ DISSATISFIED
- ❑ NEITHER DISSATISFIED, NOR SATISFIED
- ❑ SATISFIED
- ❑ VERY SATISFIED

Examples General + Specific Well-being Questions (Hox, 1986)

Taking all things together, how satisfied or dissatisfied are you with *life in general*?
- ❑ VERY DISSATISFIED
- ❑ DISSATISFIED
- ❑ NEITHER DISSATISFIED, NOR SATISFIED
- ❑ SATISFIED
- ❑ VERY SATISFIED

Taking all things together, how satisfied or dissatisfied are you with *the home in which you live*?
- ❑ VERY DISSATISFIED
- ❑ DISSATISFIED
- ❑ NEITHER DISSATISFIED, NOR SATISFIED
- ❑ SATISFIED
- ❑ VERY SATISFIED

Taking all things together, how satisfied or dissatisfied are you with *your health*?

Taking all things together, how satisfied or dissatisfied are you with *your social contacts*?

Survey methodologists have given much attention to the problems of formulating the actual questions that go into the survey questionnaire (cf. Fowler & Cosenza, Chapter 8). Problems of question wording, questionnaire flow, question context, and choice of response categories have been the focus of much attention. Much less attention has been directed at clarifying the problems that occur *before* the first survey question is committed to paper: the process that leads from the theoretical construct to the prototype survey item (cf. Hox, 1997). Schwarz (1997) notes that large-scale survey programs often involve a large and heterogeneous group of researchers, where the set of questions finally agreed upon is the result of complex negotiations. As a result, the concepts finally adopted for research are often vaguely defined.

When thinking about the process that leads from theoretical constructs to survey questions, it is useful to distinguish between conceptualization and operationalization. Before questions can be formulated, researchers must decide which concepts they wish to measure. They must define they intend to measure by naming the concept, describing its properties and its scope, and defining important subdomains of its meaning. The subsequent process of operationalization involves choosing empirical indicators for each concept or each subdomain. Theoretical concepts are often referred to as 'constructs' to emphasize that they are theoretical concepts that have been invented or adopted for a specific scientific purpose (Kerlinger, 1986). Fowler and Cosenza's (Chapter 8) discussion of the distinction between constructs and survey questions follows these line of reasoning.

To bridge the gap between theory and measurement, two distinct research strategies are advocated: a theory driven or top down strategy, which starts with constructs and works toward observable variables and a data driven or bottom up strategy, which starts with observations and works towards theoretical constructs (cf. Hox & De Jong-Gierveld, 1990). For examples of such strategies we refer to Hox (1997).

When a final survey question as posed to a respondent fails to ask about what is essential for the research question, we have a specification error. In other words, the construct implied in the survey question differs from the intended construct that should be measured. This is also referred to as a measurement that has low construct validity. As a result, the wrong parameter is estimated and the research objective is not met. A clear example of a specification error is given by Biemer and Lyberg (2003, p. 39). The intended concept to be measured was "…the value of a parcel of land if it were sold on a fair market today." A potential operationalization in a survey question would be "For what price would you sell this parcel of land?" Closer inspection of this question reveals that this question asks what the parcel of land is subjectively worth to the farmer. Perhaps it is worth so much to the farmer that she/he would never sell it at all.

There are several ways in which one can investigate whether specification errors occur. First of all, the questionnaire outline and the concept questionnaire should always be thoroughly discussed by the researchers, and with the client or information users, and explicit checks should be made whether the questions in the questionnaire reflect the study objectives. In the next step, the concept questionnaire should be pretested with a small group of real respondents, using so called cognitive lab methods. These are qualitative techniques to investigate whether and when errors occur in the question-answer process. The first step in the question answer process is understanding the question. Therefore, the first thing that is investigated in a pretest is if the respondents understand the question and the words used in the question as intended by the researcher. Usually questions are adapted and/or reformulated, based on the results of questionnaire pretests. For a good description of pretesting, methods, see Campanelli Chapter 10. Whenever a question is reformulated, there is the danger of changing its original (intended) meaning, and thus introducing a new specification error. Therefore, both the results of the pretests and the final adapted questionnaire should again be thoroughly discussed with the client.

1.4 PLACING THE CORNERSTONES: COVERAGE, SAMPLING, NONRESPONSE, AND MEASUREMENT

As noted earlier, specification of the research question and the drafting of prototype survey questions are conceptual rather than statistical; it concerns the construct validity of the measurement. In other words, does the question measure what it is supposed to measure, does it measure the intended theoretical construct (Cronbach & Meehl, 1955). In contrast, the sources of data collection error summarized in our four cornerstones can be assessed statistically by examining the effect they have on the precision of the estimates. Three of the four cornerstones refer explicitly to the fact that surveys typically collect data from a sample, a fraction of the population of interest. *Coverage error* occurs when some members of the population have a zero probability of being selected in the survey sample. For example, the sample list (frame) may fail to cover all elements of the population to which one wants to generalize results. *Sampling error* occurs because only a subset of all elements (people) in the population is actually surveyed. Sampling error is statistically well understood provided that probability samples are used: in general the amount of sampling error is a direct function of the number of units included the final sample. For a clear discussion of coverage and sampling, see Lohr (Chapter 6). *Nonresponse error* occurs when some of the sampled units do not respond and when these units differ from those who do and in a way relevant to the study. For an introduction into nonresponse and nonresponse error, see Lynn (Chapter 3). The last cornerstone is *measurement error*, which occurs when a respondent's answer to a question is inaccurate, departs from the "true" value (see also Hox, Chapter 20).

A perfect survey would minimize all four sources of errors. Coverage error is avoided when every member of the population has a known and nonzero chance of being selected into the survey. Sampling error is reduced simply by sampling enough randomly selected units to achieve the precision that is needed. Nonresponse error is avoided if everyone responds or if the respondents are just like the nonrespondents in terms of the things we are trying to measure. Measurement error can be prevented by asking clear questions; questions that respondents are capable and willing to answer correctly. In the survey design stage the methodological goal is to prevent or at least reduce potential errors; in the analysis stage the statistical goal is to adjust the analysis for errors in such a way that correct (i.e., unbiased and precise) results are produced. The methodological survey literature suggests a variety of methods for reducing the sources of survey error; however, one should keep in mind that there is more than one source of error and that one has to compromise and choose when attempting to reduce total survey error. And, do this all within a workable budget too; or as Lyberg and Biemer put it in Chapter 22: "the challenge in survey design is to achieve an optimal balance between survey errors and costs." In the remainder we discuss the four cornerstones in more detail and relate these to specific chapters in this book.

1.4.1 Coverage and Coverage Error

When doing a survey one has an intended population in mind: the target population. To draw a sample from the target population, a sample frame is needed. This can be a list of target population members, for instance, a list of all members of a certain organization, or the register of all inhabitants of a certain city. But it may also be a virtual list, or an algorithm, such as in area probability sampling or in Random Digit Dialing (RDD) sampling (cf. Lohr, Chapter 6 on coverage and sampling, and Steeh, Chapter 12 on RDD). In area probability sampling, the population is divided into clusters based on geographical proximity, and then specific areas are selected. In RDD, random telephone numbers are generated using an algorithm that conforms to properties of valid telephone numbers in the country that is being investigated. Frame coverage errors occur when there is a mismatch between the sampling frame and the target population. In other words when there is no one-to-one correspondence between the units in the frame and the units in the target population.

The most common form of coverage error is undercoverage, that is, not all units of the target population are included in the sampling frame. A clear example of undercoverage is persons with an unlisted phone number when the sampling frame is the telephone book. Another form of coverage error is overcoverage; here a unit from the target population appears more than once in the sampling frame. Duplications like this can occur when a sampling frame results from the combination of several lists. For example, on one list a woman is listed under her maiden name, and on a second list under her married name. If these lists are combined, the same person is listed under two different entries. Another example is surveys that use mobile (cell) telephones; these overcover persons who own more than one phone. A third type of coverage error is caused by erroneous inclusions in the frame. For example, a business number is included on a list with household phone numbers.

As a final example, consider the case of web surveys. A common way to attract respondents to a web survey is placing a link to the survey on a popular web site. Basically, this means that the researcher has no control over who responds to the questionnaire. Coverage error for web surveys is related to two different causes (cf. Ramos, Sevedi, & Sweet, 1998). First, it is the respondent who has to make contact with the data collection program. In a web survey, this requires access to a computer and the Internet, plus some degree of computer skill. Individuals who lack these are not covered. In addition, interviewing software is in general not hardware or software independent. Screens look differently in different resolutions, or when different browsers are used to access the survey website, and some combinations of hardware and software may make the survey website inaccessible to some users, resulting in coverage error. For an overview of different types of web surveys and their potential for errors, see Lozar Manfreda and Vehovar (Chapter 14).

The availability of comprehensive lists or algorithms that cover the population differs widely depending on the target population, but also on the country. For instance, in countries like Denmark and The Netherlands the national statistical agency has access to the population registry (see also Bethlehem Chapter 26). This makes it possible for the national statistical agency to draw a probability sample not only of the general population, but also to draw specific subsamples. Some countries have good lists of mobile phone users, whereas others do not. In some areas, the telephone system has a well-defined structure of used and unused number banks, which makes it possible to generate random telephone numbers with good coverage properties. In most areas, the telephone system does not have such a structure or several competing telephone systems are in use, which makes generating random telephone numbers more difficult (cf. Steeh, Chapter 12).

Web surveys are a special challenge to survey methodologists, because the coverage problem is large and difficult to solve. There are no lists of the population that can be used to draw samples with known properties. Email addresses have no common structure that can be used to generate random addresses similar to the way random telephone numbers are generated in RDD. Finally, the often-used volunteer samples are convenience samples, for which coverage cannot be determined (cf. Lozar Manfreda & Vehovar, Chapter 14).

1.4.2 Sampling and Sampling Error

Sampling error occurs because only a sample of the population is investigated instead of the whole population. Sampling and sampling error is treated by Lohr (Chapter 6). Based on the values for the variables in the *probability* sample, the value for the population is estimated using statistical theory. When simple random sampling is used, standard statistical techniques can be used; however, when more complicated sampling schemes are used, such as cluster sampling or stratification, the standard statistical techniques do not provide accurate *p*-values and confidence intervals and more complicated statistical techniques should be used. Methods for analyzing complex survey designs are discussed by Stapleton in Chapter 18.

Sampling error can be controlled by drawing samples that are large enough to produce the precision wanted. Table 1.1 gives an indication of the number of respondents needed for estimated percentages with a specified precision (e.g., Devore & Peck, 2005, pp. 377–378).

Table 1.1 Precision: Number of respondents needed for percentage estimates within 95 percent Confidence Interval (C.I.).

Number of respondents	Width of 95% C.I.
96	± 10%
384	± 5%
1537	± 2.5%
9604	± 1%

Base percentage 50%, 95% Confidence Interval based on normal approximation

The main point of Table 1.1 is that a large precision requires very large samples. The rule of thumb is that to decrease the sampling errors by half we need a completed sample that is four times as large.

The most important issue about sampling is that if our sample is *not* a probability sample, statistical inference is not appropriate. The difference between probability and nonprobability sampling is that nonprobability sampling does *not* use a *random* selection procedure. This does not necessarily mean that nonprobability samples are unrepresentative of the population; however, it does mean that nonprobability samples cannot depend upon statistical probability theory. With a probabilistic sample, we know the probability that we represent the population well and therefore we can estimate confidence intervals and significance tests. With a nonprobability sample, we may or may not represent the population well, but it is not appropriate to apply statistical inference to generalize to a general population. At best, we can use statistical inference to assess the precision with which we can generalize to a population consisting of whoever responded. Whether this is representative for any general population is beyond statistical inference.

1.4.3 Response and Nonresponse Error

Nonresponse is the inability to obtain data for all sampled units on all questions. There are two types of nonresponse in surveys: *unit nonresponse* and *item nonresponse*. Unit nonresponse is the failure to obtain any information from an eligible sample unit. Unit nonresponse can be the result of noncontact or refusal. Lynn (Chapter 3) provides an extensive overview on nonresponse and nonresponse error; for a discussion of nonresponse error in cross-cultural studies, see Couper and de Leeuw (2003); for statistical adjustment and weighting see Biemer and Christ (Chapter 16). Item-nonresponse or item missing data refers to the failure to obtain information for one or more questions in a survey, given that the other questions are completed. For an introduction see de Leeuw, Hox, and Huisman (2003), for statistical approaches to deal with missing data see Chapter 18 by Rässler, Rubin, and Schenker.

Nonresponse error is a function of the response rate and the differences between respondents and nonrespondents. If nonresponse is the result of a pure chance process, in other words if nonresponse is completely at random, then there is no real problem. Of course, the realized sample is smaller, resulting in larger confidence intervals around estimators. But the conclusions will not be biased due to nonresponse. Only when respondents and nonrespondents do differ from each other on the variables of interest in the study, will there be a serious nonresponse problem. The nonresponse is then *selective* nonresponse and certain groups may be underrepresented. In the worst case, there is a substantial association between the nonresponse and an important variable of the study causing biased results. A classic example comes from mobility studies: people who travel a lot are more difficult to contact for an interview on mobility than people who travel rarely. Thus, selective nonresponse caused by specific noncontacts leads to an underestimate of mobility. For more examples, see Lynn (Chapter 3).

Two main approaches are used to cope with nonresponse: *reducing* and *adjusting*. Nonresponse reduction applies strategies that, in general, reduce the number of noncontacts and refusals. Causes of noncontact depend on the specific survey design. For instance, in face-to-face surveys, noncontact can be the result of the inability of the interviewer to reach the respondent within the allotted number of contact attempts. Increasing the number of contact attempts not only increases the number of contacted and thus the response rate, but also the costs. Varying the days and times at which contact is attempted also increases the response rate, without affecting the cost as much. In mail and Internet surveys, noncontacts can be the result of undeliverable mailings due to errors in the address list. Tools to reduce refusals also depend on the data collection mode used. For instance, interview surveys may use specially trained interviewers to convert refusals, while mail and Internet surveys have to rely on incentives or special contacts to counteract explicit refusals. For more detail, see Lynn (Chapter 3).

Nonresponse adjustment refers to statistical adjustments that are applied after the data are collected. If the difference between the respondents and the nonrespondents is known, for instance because we can compare certain characteristics of the respondents to known population values, statistical weighting can be used to make the sample resemble the population with respect to these characteristics. The problem with statistical adjustment is that usually only simple respondent attributes such as age, sex, and education can be used to weigh the sample. This improves the representativeness of the sample with respect to the variables of central substantive interest only if these variables are related to the attributes used in the weighting scheme. Biemer and Christ discuss weighting for survey data in detail in Chapter 17.

Finally, nonresponse figures should be clearly reported in surveys. This often takes the form of a response rate figure. When reporting response rates it is important to state how the response rate was calculated. For details of response rate calculation and a description of sources of nonresponse, see the brochure on standard definitions of the American Association for Public Opinion Research (AAPOR). A regularly updated version and an online response rate calculator can be found on the AAPOR website (www.aapor.org).

1.4.4 Measurement and Measurement Error

Measurement error is also called error of observation. Measurement errors are associated with the data collection process itself. There are three main sources of measurement error: the questionnaire, the respondent, and the method of data collection. When interviewers are used for data collection, the interviewer is a fourth source of error.

A well-designed and well-tested questionnaire is the basis for reducing measurement error. The questions in the questionnaire must be clear, and all respondents must be able to understand the terms used in the same way. With closed questions, the response categories should be well defined, and exhaustive. When a question is not clear, or when the response categories are not clearly defined, respondents will make errors while answering the question or they do not know what to answer. When the data are collected through interviews, interviewers will then try to help out, but in doing this they can make errors too and introduce additional interviewer error (Fowler, 1995). Therefore, improving the *questionnaire* is a good start to improve the total survey quality. For a good introduction into designing and writing effective questions, see Fowler and Cosenza (Chapter 8). It should be emphasized that even carefully designed questionnaires may contain errors and that a questionnaire should always be evaluated and pretested before it may be used in a survey. In Chapter 10 Campanelli provides the reader with information about the different methods for testing survey questions and gives practical guidelines on the implementation of each of the methods.

Respondents can be a source of error in their own right when they provide incorrect information. This may be unintentional, for instance when a respondent does not understand the question or when a respondent has difficulty remembering an event. But a respondent can also give incorrect information on purpose, for instance when sensitive questions are asked (see also Lensvelt-Mulders, Chapter 24). Measurement errors that originate from the respondent are beyond the control of the researcher. A researcher can only try to minimize respondent errors by making the respondent's task as easy and as pleasant as possible. In other words, by writing clear questions that respondents are willing to answer. In Chapter 2, Schwarz, Knäuper, Oyserman, and Stich describe how respondents come up with an answer and review the cognitive and communicative processes underlying survey responses.

The *method of data collection* can be a third source of measurement error. In Chapter 7 of this book, de Leeuw describes the advantages and disadvantages of major data collection techniques. One of the key differences between survey modes is the way in which certain questions can be asked. For instance, in a telephone interview respondents have to rely on auditive cues only: they only hear the question and the response categories. This may cause problems when a long list of potential answers has to be presented. Dillman, in Chapter 9 on the logic and psychology of questionnaire design, describes mode differences in questionnaire design and proposes a unified or uni mode design to overcome differences between modes. This is of major importance when mixed-mode designs are used, either within one survey, or in longitudinal studies (e.g., panel surveys see also Chapter 25 by Sikkel & Hoogendoorn), or between surveys as can be the case in cross-national and comparative studies in which one mode (e.g., telephone) is used in one country an another mode (e.g., face-to-face interviews) is used in another. For important issues in comparative survey research, see Harkness (Chapter 4); for more detail on the challenges of mixed mode surveys, see De Leeuw, Dillman, and Hox (Chapter 16).

A second major difference between modes is the presence versus the absence of an interviewer. There may be very good reasons to choose a method without interviewers and leave the locus of control with the respondents, such as ensuring more privacy and more time to reflect for respondents. Self-administered questionnaires in general are described by De Leeuw and Hox in Chapter 13; technological innovations are described by Lozar Manfreda and Vehovar in Chapter 14 on Internet Surveys and by Miller Steiger and Conroy in Chapter 15 on Interactive Voice Response. On the other hand, using interviewers also has many positive points, especially when very complex questionnaires are used or when special tasks have to be performed. As Loosveldt states in Chapter 11: "...the task of the interviewer is more comprehensive and complex than merely asking questions and recording the respondent's answer. Interviewers implement the contact procedure, persuade the respondents to participate, clarify the respondent's role during the interview and collect information about the respondent."

However, when an interviewer is present, the interviewer can be a source of error too. Interviewers may misinterpret a question, may make errors in administering a questionnaire, or in registering the answers. When posing the question, interviewers may unintentionally change its meaning. By giving additional information or explaining a misunderstood word, they may inappropriately influence a respondent. Even the way interviewers look and dress may influence a respondent in a face-to-face interview. Selecting and training interviewers carefully helps reducing interviewer related errors. For more details, see Chapter 23 on interviewer training by Lessler, Eyerman, and Wang. Interviewers can make genuine mistakes, but they also may intentionally cheat. Interviewers have been known to falsify data, or skip questions to shorten tedious interviews. Monitoring interviewers helps to reduce this. Having a quality controller listening in on telephone interviewers is a widely used method. In face-to-face interviews, recordings can be made and selected tapes can be checked afterwards. Special verification contacts or re-interviews may be used to evaluate interviewer performance in large-scale face-to-face surveys (cf. Lyberg & Biemer, Chapter 22; Japec, 2005, p. 24).

1.5 FROM DATA COLLECTION TO ANALYSIS: HOW THE FOUNDATION AFFECTS THE STRUCTURE

There are several ways in which the design of a survey and the precise data collection procedure affects the subsequent data analysis stage. These also involve the four cornerstones. The most direct influence is the actual *sampling* procedure that is used. As mentioned earlier, standard statistical procedures assume that the data are a simple random sample from the population. In most surveys, other sampling schemes are used because these are more efficient or less expensive, for instance cluster sampling or stratification. When these sampling schemes are used, the analysis must employ special statistical methods (see also Stapleton, Chapter 18). Similarly, when weighting (cf. Biemer & Christ, Chapter 17) is used to compensate for different inclusion probabilities, either by design or because of nonresponse problems, special statistical methods must be used. Standard statistical packages may or may not include these methods. For instance, the package SPSS (version 15 and higher) can analyze complex survey data with weights and complicated sampling schemes, but it includes only selected statistical analyses for such data. The other procedures in SPSS can include weighting, but do not correct the standard errors for the effects of weighting, which produces incorrect statistical tests.

A less obvious way in which the survey design affects the data analysis lies in the adjustment for the combination of coverage error and nonresponse. These may result in data that are not representative for the population, and the most often-used adjustment method is weighting on respondent characteristics for which the population values are known. For more detail, see Biemer and Christ (Chapter 17). Two issues are important here. First, statistical adjustment aims at producing unbiased estimates of population parameters when selection probabilities are not equal; however, no amount of statistical cleverness restores information that we have failed to collect. So, prevention by reducing the problem in the data collection phase is important. Second, the quality of the adjustment depends strongly on the amount and quality of background information that we have available to construct the weights. Collecting this information requires careful planning in the design phase. Auxiliary variables must be included for which the population values are known, for instance for a sample from the general population via the national statistical agency, or for samples from a special population via an existing registry. Because the use of registries is regulated by privacy concerns, in the latter case it may be necessary to obtain prior permission. For more on privacy and ethics in survey research, see Singer (Chapter 5). Finally, to be able to use the information, it is crucial that the data collection procedure uses the same wording and response categories that were used to collect the known population data (cf. Dillman, Chapter 9). Preferably, the same method of data collection should be used, to prevent confounding of selection and measurement errors.

A special case of nonresponse is the failure to obtain information on some of the questions, which leads to incomplete data for some of the respondents. Just as is the case with unit-nonresponse discussed earlier, prevention and the collection of auxiliary information is important with item missing data too (see also de Leeuw, Hox, & Huisman, 2003). The next step is statistical adjustment. In Chapter 19, Rässler, Rubin, and Schenker discuss concepts regarding mechanisms that create missing data, as well as four commonly used approaches to deal with (item) missing data.

Measurement errors, that is discrepancies between the measurement and the true value, influence the analysis in more subtle ways. Again, prevention is the best medicine. Measurement errors originate from the question wording and the questionnaire, from the survey method and the interviewer, from the respondents and from complex interactions between these. Many decisions in the survey design phase have the potential to affect measurement error (cf. Biemer & Lyberg, Chapter 22). Prevention rest on the application of known best practices in survey design; this assumes that these are well documented (cf. Mohler, Pennel, & Hubbard, Chapter 21). Another important step in reducing measurement error as far as possible is thorough pretesting of the survey instrument before it is actually used (cf. Campanelli, Chapter 10). In the analysis phase, some adjustments for the effect of measurement errors can be made; Hox discusses this in Chapter 20. Adjustments for measurement errors can be made when multi-item scales are used, or if auxiliary information is available about the amount of measurement error in specific variables. Again, to be able to adjust in the analysis phase, the design of the survey must make sure that the necessary information is available.

1.6 CAN WE AFFORD IT? BALANCING DESIGN FEATURES AND SURVEY QUALITY

Earlier we discussed the foundation of survey research: breaking the ground (specification) and placing the four cornerstones (coverage, sampling, nonresponse, and measurement). The same fundamental quality criteria are discussed in quality handbooks. For instance, in Eurostat's 2000 publication on the assessment of quality in statistics, the first quality criterion is the relevance of the statistical concept. A statistical product is relevant if it meets user's needs. This implies that user's needs must be established at the start. The concept of relevance is closely related to the specification problem and the construct validity of measurement. Did we correctly translate the substantive research question into a survey question? If not, we have made a specification error, and the statistical product does not meet the needs of the users. Almost all handbooks on survey statistics mention *accuracy* of the estimate as quality criterion. Accuracy depends on all four cornerstones and is discussed at length earlier in this chapter. But, there are additional criteria for quality as well. Biemer and Lyberg (2003) stress the importance of timeliness defined as available at the time it is needed, and accessibility, that is the data should be accessible to those for whom the survey was conducted. Eurostat (2000) distinguishes seven distinct dimensions of statistical quality, adding a.o. comparability, meaning that it should be possible to make reliable comparisons across time and across space. Comparability is extremely important in cross-cultural and cross-national studies (see also Harkness, Chapter 4). For a discussion of quality and procedures for quality assurance and quality control, see Lyberg and Biemer (Chapter 22).

Both Biemer and Lyberg's (2003) quality concepts and Eurostat's (2000) dimensions go beyond the foundation and cornerstones described earlier in this chapter, and are relevant for the quality of the entire survey process and the data it produces. Their criteria were developed mainly for use in large scale survey organizations and governmental statistical offices, but survey quality and quality assurance is an issue that also applies to smaller scale surveys, where the survey researcher is also the survey user. It does not matter if it is a small scale survey or a large survey, whether the survey is using paper and pencil or high technology, quality can and should be built into all surveys. For procedures for quality assessment, see Lyberg and Biemer (Chapter 22).

To come back to the metaphor of building a house: there are many different ways to build a good, quality house. But, there is also a large variety in types of houses, ranging from a simple summer cottage to a luxurious villa, from a houseboat to a monumental 17th century house at a canal, from a working farm to a dream palace. What is a good house depends on the needs of the resident, what is a good survey depends on the survey user (cf. Dippo, 1997). The research objectives determine the population under study and the types of questions that should be asked. Privacy regulations and ethics may restrict the design; other practical restriction may be caused by available time and funds. Countries and survey organizations may differ in available resources, such as skilled labor, administrative capacities, experience with certain procedures or methods, computer hardware and software. It is clear that survey methodologists must balance survey costs and available resources against survey errors, and that any actual survey will be the result of methodological compromises. Surveys are a complex enterprise and many aspects must be considered when the goal is to maximize data quality with the available resources and within a reasonable budget of time and costs.

Finally, surveys are carried out in a specific cultural context, which may also affect the way these aspects influence the survey quality. Survey methodologists need to take this into account when designing a survey. For instance, when a telephone (or Internet) survey is contemplated for an international study, it is important to understand how telephones and Internet are viewed in the different cultures included in the survey. Is it a personal device, such as mobile telephones? Is it a household device, as landline telephones mostly are? Or is it a community device, with one (mobile) telephone or Internet connection shared by an entire village? Survey design means that costs and quality must be optimized, and in a global world this means that they must be optimized within the bounds of cultural and technological resources and differences.

1.7 CONTENTS OF THIS BOOK

The goal of this book is to introduce the readers to the central issues that are important for survey quality, to discuss the decisions that must be made in designing and carrying out a survey, and to present the current methodological and statistical knowledge about the consequences of these decisions for the survey data quality.

The first section of the book, *Foundations*, is a broad introduction in survey methodology. In addition to this introduction, it contains chapters on the psychology of asking questions, the problem of nonresponse, issues and challenges in international surveys, and ethical issues in surveys.

The second section, *Design*, presents a number of issues that are vital in designing a quality survey. It includes chapters on coverage and sampling, choosing the method of data collection, writing effective questions, constructing the questionnaire, and testing survey questions.

The third major section, *Implementation*, discusses the details of a number of procedures to carry out a survey. There are chapters on face-to-face interviews, telephone interviews, self-administered questionnaires, Internet surveys and Interactive Voice Response surveys. Finally, there is a chapter on the challenges that result when different data collection modes are mixed within a survey.

The fourth section, *Data analysis*, discusses a number of statistical subjects that are especially important in analyzing survey data. These include chapters on constructing adjustment weights, analyzing data from complex surveys, coping with incomplete data (item nonresponse), and accommodating measurement errors. The final section, *Special issues*, contains a number of special interest topics for quality surveys. It includes chapters on survey documentation, quality assurance and quality control, interviewer training, collecting data on sensitive topics, and panel surveys including access panels. The final chapter introduces collecting survey-type data without asking questions of respondents, by combining and integrating existing information.

GLOSSARY OF KEY CONCEPTS

Construct validity. The extend to which a measurement instrument measures the intended construct and produces an observation distinct from that produced by a measure of a different construct.
Coverage error. Coverage errors occur when the operational definition of the population includes an omission, duplication, or wrongful inclusion of an element in the population. Omissions lead to undercoverage, and duplications and wrongful inclusions lead to overcoverage.
Measurement error. The extent to which there are discrepancies between a measurement and the true value, that the measurement instrument is designed to

measure. Measurement error refers to both variance and bias, where variance is random variation of a measurement and bias is systematic error. There are a number of potential sources; for example, measurement error can arise from the respondent, questionnaire, mode of data collection, interviewer, and interactions between these.

Nonresponse error. Nonresponse is the failure to collect information from sampled respondents. There are two types of nonresponse: unit nonresponse and item nonresponse. Unit nonresponse occurs when the survey fails to obtain any data from a unit in the selected sample. Item nonresponse (incomplete data) occurs when the unit participates but data on particular items are missing. Nonresponse leads to nonresponse error if the respondents differ from the nonrespondents on the variables of interest.

Sampling error. Error in estimation due to taking a sample instead of measuring every unit in the sampling frame. If probability sampling is used then the amount of sampling error can be estimated from the sample.

Specification error. Specification error occurs when the concept measured by a survey question and the concept that should be measured with that question differ. When this occurs, there is low construct validity.

Chapter 2

The Psychology of Asking Questions

Norbert Schwarz
University of Michigan

Bärbel Knäuper
McGill University

Daphna Oyserman
University of Michigan

Christine Stich
McGill University

2.1 INTRODUCTION

Over the last two decades, psychologists and survey methodologists have made considerable progress in understanding the cognitive and communicative processes underlying survey responses, increasingly turning the "art of asking questions" (Payne, 1951) into an applied science that is grounded in basic psychological research. This chapter reviews key lessons learned from this work (for more extended reviews see Schwarz 1999a; Sirken, Hermann, Schechter, Schwarz, Tanur, & Tourangeau, 1999; Sudman, Bradburn, & Schwarz 1996; Tourangeau, Rips, & Rasinski 2000). We focus on how features of the research instrument shape respondents' answers and illustrate how the underlying processes can change as a function of respondents' age and culture. We first address respondents' tasks and subsequently discuss how respondents make sense of the questions asked. Next, we review how respondents answer behavioral questions and relate these questions to issues of autobiographical memory and estimation. Finally, we address attitude questions and review the conditions that give rise to context effects in attitude measurement.

2.2 RESPONDENTS' TASKS

It is now widely recognized that answering a survey question involves several tasks. Respondents first need to understand the question to determine which information they are asked to provide. Next, they need to recall relevant information from memory. When the question is an opinion question, they will

18

rarely find a ready-for-use answer stored in memory. Instead, they need to form a judgment on the spot, based on whatever relevant information comes to mind at that time. When the question pertains to a behavior, respondents need to retrieve relevant episodes. Unless the behavior is rare and important, this is a difficult task and respondents typically have to rely on inference and estimation strategies to arrive at an answer. Once respondents have formed a judgment in their own minds, they can rarely report it in their own words. Instead, they need to format it to fit the response alternatives provided by the researcher. Finally, respondents may hesitate to communicate their private judgment, because of social desirability and self-presentation. If so, they may edit their judgment before conveying it to the researcher. Accordingly, understanding the question, recalling information, forming a judgment, formatting the judgment to fit the response alternatives, and editing the final answer are the major steps of the question answering process (see Strack & Martin, 1987; Tourangeau, 1984).

Unfortunately, respondents' performance at each of these steps is highly context dependent. From a psychological perspective, this context dependency is part and parcel of human cognition and communication, in daily life as in survey interviews. From a survey methods perspective, however, it presents a formidable problem: To the extent that the answers provided by the sample are shaped by the research instrument, they do not reflect the opinions or behaviors of the population to which the researcher wants to generalize. Complicating things further, a growing body of findings suggests that the underlying processes are age- and culture-sensitive, resulting in differential context effects that can thwart straightforward comparisons across cohorts and cultures.

2.3 UNDERSTANDING THE QUESTION

Survey textbooks typically advise researchers to avoid unfamiliar terms and complex syntax (for helpful guidelines see Bradburn, Sudman, & Wansink, 2004). This is good advice, but it misses a crucial point: Language comprehension is not about words per se, but about speaker meaning (Clark & Schober, 1992). Respondents certainly understand the words when asked, "What have you done today?" But to provide a meaningful answer they need to determine which behaviors the researcher might be interested in. For example, should they report that they took a shower, or not? To infer the intended meaning of the question, respondents rely on the tacit assumptions that govern the conduct of conversation in daily life. These assumptions were described by Paul Grice (1975), a philosopher of language, in the form of four maxims: A *maxim of relation* asks speakers to make their contribution relevant to the aims of the ongoing conversation. A *maxim of quantity* requests speakers to make their contribution as informative as is required, but not more informative than is required. A *maxim of manner* holds that a speaker's contribution should be clear rather than obscure, ambiguous or wordy, and a *maxim of quality* requires speakers not to say anything that's false. In short, speakers should try to be informative, truthful, relevant, and clear and listeners interpret the speakers' utterances "on the assumption that they are trying to live up to these ideals" (Clark & Clark, 1977, p. 122).

Respondents bring these tacit assumptions to the research situation and assume that the researcher "chose his wording so they can understand what he meant—and can do so quickly" (Clark & Schober, 1992, p. 27). To do so, they draw on the context of the ongoing conversation to determine the question's intended meaning, much as they would be expected to do in daily life. In fact, reliance on contextual information is more pronounced under the standardized conditions of survey interviews, where a well trained interviewer may merely reiterate the identical question, than under the less constrained conditions of daily life, which allow for mutual clarifications of the intended meaning. The contextual information provided by the researcher includes formal features of the questionnaire, in addition to the specific wording of the question and the content of preceding questions, as a few examples may illustrate (see Clark & Schober, 1992; Schwarz, 1996; Strack, 1994, for reviews).

2.3.1 Response Alternatives

Returning to the previously mentioned example, suppose respondents are asked in an *open response format*, "What have you done today?" To give a meaningful answer, they have to determine which activities may be of interest to the researcher. In an attempt to be informative, they are likely to omit activities that the researcher is obviously aware of (e.g., "I gave a survey interview") or may take for granted anyway (e.g., "I had breakfast"), thus observing the maxim of quantity. But most respondents would endorse these activities if they were included in a list presented as part of a *closed response format.* On the other hand, a closed response format would reduce the likelihood that respondents report any activities omitted from the list (see Schuman & Presser, 1981; Schwarz & Hippler, 1991, for reviews). This reflects that response alternatives convey what the researcher is interested in, thus limiting the range of "informative" answers. In addition, they may remind respondents of material that they may otherwise not consider.

Even something as innocuous as the *numeric values of rating scales* can elicit pronounced shifts in question interpretation. Schwarz, Knäuper, Hippler, Noelle-Neumann, and Clark (1991) asked respondents how successful they have been in life, using an 11-point rating scale with the endpoints labeled "not at all successful" and "extremely successful." To answer this question, respondents need to determine what is meant by "not at all successful"—the absence of noteworthy achievements or the presence of explicit failures? When the numeric values of the rating sale ranged from 0 to 10, respondents inferred that the question refers to different degrees of success, with "not at all successful" marking the absence of noteworthy achievements. But when the numeric values ranged from -5 to +5, with 0 as the middle alternative, they inferred that the researcher had a bipolar dimension in mind, with "not at all successful" marking the opposite of success, namely the presence of failure. Not surprisingly, this shift in the meaning of the verbal endpoint labels resulted in dramatic shifts in the obtained ratings. Whereas 34% of the respondents endorsed a value between 0 and 5 on the 0 to 10 scale, only 13% endorsed one of the formally equivalent values between -5 and 0 on the -5 to +5 scale 0, reflecting that the absence of great success is more common than the presence of failure. Hence, researchers are well advised to match the numeric values to the intended uni- or bipolarity of the scale.

The numeric values of behavioral *frequency scales* can serve a similar function. For example, Schwarz, Strack, Müller, and Chassein (1988) asked respondents to report how often they are angry along a scale that presented either high or low frequency values. As expected, respondents inferred that the question pertains to more intense anger experiences, which are relatively rare, when accompanied by low frequency values, but to mild anger experiences when accompanied by high frequency values. Throughout, respondents assume that the researcher constructs meaningful response alternatives that are relevant to the specific question asked, consistent with Grice's (1975) maxim of relation.

2.3.2 Question Wording

Similar issues apply to question wording. Minor changes in apparently formal features of the question can result in pronounced meaning shifts, as the case of *reference periods* may illustrate. Winkielman, Knäuper, and Schwarz (1998) asked respondents, in an open response format, either how frequently they had been angry last week or last year. Respondents inferred that the researcher is interested in less frequent and more severe episodes of anger when the question pertained to one year rather than to one week—after all, they could hardly be expected to remember minor anger episodes for a one-year period, whereas major anger may be too rare to make a one-week period plausible. Hence, they reported on rare and intense anger for the one year period, but more frequent and less intense anger for the one week period and their examples reflected this differential question interpretation. Accordingly, it is not surprising that reports across different reference periods do not add up—respondents may not even report on the same type of experience to begin with, thwarting comparisons across reference periods.

2.3.3 Question Context

Respondents' interpretation of a question's intended meaning is further affected by the context in which the question is presented. Hence, a question about drugs acquires a different meaning in the context of health versus a crime survey. Not surprisingly, the influence of *adjacent questions* is more pronounced for more ambiguously worded questions, which force respondents to rely on the context information to infer the intended meaning (e.g., Strack, Schwarz, & Wänke, 1991). Survey researchers have long been aware of this possibility (e.g., Payne, 1951). What is often overlooked, however, is that the *researcher's affiliation*, conveyed in the cover letter, may serve a similar function. For example, Norenzayan and Schwarz (1999) observed that respondents provided more personality focused explanations of a behavior when the questionnaire was printed on the letterhead of an "Institute for Personality Research" rather than an "Institute for Social Research." Such differences highlight the extent to which respondents as cooperative communicators attempt to make their answers relevant to the inferred epistemic interest of the researcher (see Schwarz, 1996).

2.3.4 Age-related Differences

Respondents' extensive use of contextual information requires that they hold the question in mind and relate it to other aspects of the questionnaire to determine its intended meaning. This entails considerable demands on respondents' cognitive resources. Given that these resources decline with increasing age (for a review see Park, 1999), we may expect that older respondents are less likely to use, or less successful in using, contextual information at the question comprehension stage. A limited body of findings supports this conjecture. For example, Schwarz, Park, Knäuper, Davidson, and Smith (1998) observed that older respondents (aged over 70) were less likely than younger respondents to draw on the numeric values of rating scales to interpret the meaning of endpoint labels. Similarly, Knäuper (1999a) observed in secondary analyses that question order effects decrease with age, as addressed in the section on attitude questions. Moreover, children and adolescents, whose cognitive capabilities are not yet fully developed, appear to show a similar deficit in incorporating relevant contextual information into survey responding (Borgers, de Leeuw, & Hox, 2000; Fuchs, 2005).

On theoretical grounds, age-related differences in the use of contextual information should be particularly likely in face-to-face and telephone interviews, where respondents can not look back to earlier questions. In contrast, they may be less pronounced in self-administered questionnaires, where respondents can deliberately return to previous questions when they encounter an ambiguous one (Schwarz & Hippler, 1995). If so, age-related differences in the response process may interact with the mode of data collection, further complicating comparisons across age groups.

2.3.5 Implications for Questionnaire Construction

As the preceding examples illustrate, question comprehension is not solely an issue of understanding the literal meaning of an utterance. Instead, it involves extensive inferences about the speaker's intentions to determine the pragmatic meaning of the question. To safeguard against unintended question interpretations and related complications, psychologists and survey methodologists have developed a number of procedures that can be employed in questionnaire pretesting (see Campanelli, chapter 10; Schwarz & Sudman, 1996). These procedures include the extensive use of probes and think-aloud protocols (summarily referred to as cognitive interviewing; e.g., DeMaio & Rothgeb, 1996), detailed coding of interview transcripts (e.g., Fowler & Cannell, 1996), and the use of expert systems that alert researchers to likely problems (e.g., Lessler & Forsyth, 1996). Without such development efforts, respondents' understanding of the questions asked may differ in important ways from what the researcher had in mind.

2.4 REPORTING ON ONE'S BEHAVIORS

Many survey questions pertain to respondents' behaviors, often asking them to report how frequently they engaged in a given behavior during a specified reference period. Ideally, respondents are supposed to determine the boundaries of the reference period and to recall all instances of the behavior within these boundaries to arrive at the relevant frequency. Unfortunately, respondents are usually unable to follow this recall-and-count strategy, unless the behavior is rare and important and the reference period short and recent (Menon, 1994). Instead, respondents will typically need to rely on estimation strategies to arrive at a plausible approximation. Next, we review key aspects of autobiographical memory and subsequently address respondents' estimation strategies.

2.4.1 Autobiographical Memory

Not surprisingly, people forget events in their lives as time goes by, even when the event is relatively important and distinct. For example, Cannell, Fisher, and Bakker (1965) observed that only 3% of their respondents failed to report an episode of hospitalization when interviewed within ten weeks of the event, yet a full 42% did so when interviewed one year after the event. Moreover, when the question pertains to a frequent behavior, respondents are unlikely to have detailed representations of numerous individual episodes of a behavior stored in memory. Instead, the various instances of closely related behaviors blend into one global, knowledge-like representation that lacks specific time or location markers (Linton, 1982; Strube, 1987). As a result, individual episodes of frequent behaviors become indistinguishable and irretrievable. Throughout, the available research suggests that the recall of individual behavioral episodes is largely limited to rare and unique behaviors of considerable importance, and poor even under these conditions.

Complicating things further, our autobiographical knowledge is not organized by categories of behavior (like drinking alcohol) that map easily onto survey questions. The structure of autobiographical memory can be thought of as a hierarchical network that includes extended periods (like "the years I lived in New York") at the highest level of the hierarchy. Nested within this high-order period are lower-level extended events pertaining to this time, like "my first job" or "the time I was married to Lucy." Further down the hierarchy are summarized events, which correspond to the knowledge-like representations of repeated behaviors noted earlier (e.g., "During that time, Lucy and I quarreled a lot"). Specific events, like a particular episode of disagreement, are represented at the lowest level of the hierarchy. To be represented at this level of specificity, however, the event has to be rather unique. As these examples illustrate, autobiographical memory is primarily organized by time ("the years in New York") and relatively global themes ("first job"; "first marriage") in a hierarchical network (see Belli, 1998, for a review). The search for any specific event in this network takes considerable time and the outcome is somewhat haphazard, depending on the entry point into the network at which the search started. Hence, using multiple entry points and forming connections across different periods and themes improves recall.

2.4.2 Facilitating Recall

Drawing on basic research into the structure of autobiographical memory, researchers have developed a number of strategies to facilitate autobiographical recall (for reviews see Schwarz & Oyserman, 2001; Sudman et al., 1996; Schwarz & Sudman, 1994; Tourangeau et al., 2000).

To some extent, researchers can improve the likelihood of accurate recall by restricting the recall task to a short and recent reference period. This strategy, however, may result in many zero answers from respondents who rarely engage in the behavior, thus limiting later analyses to respondents with high behavioral frequencies. As a second strategy, researchers can provide appropriate recall cues. In general, the date of an event is the poorest cue, whereas cues pertaining to what happened, where it happened, and who was involved are more effective (e.g., Wagenaar, 1986). Note, however, that recall cues share many of the characteristics of closed response formats and can constrain the inferred question meaning. It is therefore important to ensure that the recall cues are relatively exhaustive and compatible with the intended interpretation of the question.

Closely related to the provision of recall cues is the *decomposition* of a complex task into several more specific ones. Although this strategy results in reliable increases in reported frequency (e.g., Blair & Burton, 1987; Sudman & Schwarz, 1989), "more" is not always "better" and decomposition does not necessarily increase the accuracy of the obtained reports (e.g., Belli, Schwarz, Singer, & Talarico, 2000). As many studies documented, frequency estimates are regressive and people commonly overestimate low frequencies, but underestimate high frequencies (see Belli et al., 2000 for a review).

In addition, autobiographical recall will improve when respondents are given sufficient time to search memory. Recalling specific events may take up to several seconds and repeated attempts to recall may result in the retrieval of additional material, even after a considerable number of previous trials (e.g., Williams & Hollan, 1981). Unfortunately, respondents are unlikely to have sufficient time to engage in repeated retrieval attempts in most research situations. Moreover, they may often not be motivated to do so even if they had the time. Accordingly, explicitly instructing respondents that the next question is really important, and that they should do their best and take all the time they may need, has been found to improve recall (e.g., Cannell, Miller, & Oksenberg, 1981). Note, however, that it needs to be employed sparingly and may lose its credibility when used for too many questions within an interview.

Although the previously mentioned strategies improve recall to some extent, they fail to take full advantage of what has been learned about the hierarchical structure of autobiographical memory. A promising alternative approach is offered by the *event history calendar* (see Belli, 1998, for a review), which takes advantage of the hierarchically nested structure of autobiographical memory to facilitate recall. To help respondents recall their alcohol consumption during the last week, for example, they may be given a calendar grid that provides a column for each day of the week, cross-cut by rows that pertain to relevant contexts. They may be asked to enter for each day what they did, who they were with, if they ate out, and so on. Reconstructing the last week in this way provides a rich set of contextual cues for recalling episodes of alcohol consumption.

2.4.3 Estimation Strategies

Given the reviewed memory difficulties, it is not surprising that respondents usually resort to a variety of inference strategies to arrive at a plausible estimate (for a review see Sudman et al., 1996, Chapter 9). Even when they can recall relevant episodic information, the recalled material may not cover the entire reference period or they may be aware that their recall is likely to be incomplete. In such cases, they may base their inferences on the recalled fragments, following a *decomposition* strategy (e.g., Blair & Burton, 1987). In other cases, respondents may draw on *subjective theories* that bear on the behavior in question (for a review see Ross, 1989). When asked about past behavior, for example, they may ask themselves if there is reason to assume that their past behavior was different from their present behavior—if not, they may report their present behavior as an approximation. Schwarz and Oyserman (2001) review these and related strategies. Here, we illustrate the role of estimation strategies by returning to respondents' use of information provided by formal characteristics of the questionnaire.

2.4.4 Response Alternatives

In many studies, respondents are asked to report their behavior by checking the appropriate response alternative on a *numeric frequency scale*. Consistent with Grice's (1975) maxim of relation, respondents assume that the researcher constructed a meaningful scale that is relevant to the task at hand. Specifically, they assume that values in the middle range of the scale reflect the average or "usual" behavior, whereas values at the extremes of the scale correspond to the extremes of the distribution. Given these assumptions, respondents can draw on the range of the response alternatives as a plausible frame of reference in estimating their own behavioral frequency. This results in higher frequency estimates when the scale presents high rather than low frequency values.

For example, Schwarz and Scheuring (1992) asked 60 patients of a German mental health clinic to report the frequency of 17 symptoms along one of the following two scales:

Low Frequency Scale	High Frequency Scale
( ) never	( ) twice a month or less
( ) about once a year	( ) once a week
( ) about twice a year	( ) twice a week
( ) twice a month	( ) daily
( ) more than twice a month	( ) several times a day

Across 17 symptoms, 62% of the respondents reported average frequencies of more than twice a month when presented with the high frequency scale, whereas only 39% did so when presented with the low frequency scale, resulting in a mean difference of 23 percentage points. This influence of frequency scales has been observed across a wide range of different behaviors, including health behaviors, television consumption (e.g., Schwarz, Hippler, Deutsch, & Strack, 1985), sexual behaviors (e.g., Tourangeau & Smith, 1996), and consumer behaviors (e.g., Menon, Rhaghubir, & Schwarz, 1995).

On theoretical grounds, we may expect that the impact of numeric frequency values is more pronounced, the more poorly the behavior is represented in memory, thus forcing respondents to rely on an estimation strategy. Empirically, this is the case. The influence of frequency scales is small when the behavior is rare and important, and hence well represented in memory. Moreover, when a respondent engages in the behavior with high regularity (e.g., every Sunday), its frequency can easily be derived from this rate information, largely eliminating the impact of frequency scales (Menon, 1994; Menon et al., 1995).

2.4.5 Age- and Culture-related Differences in Estimation

Given age-related declines in memory, we may expect that the impact of response alternatives is more pronounced for older than for younger respondents. The available data support this prediction with some qualifications. For example, Knäuper, Schwarz, and Park (2004) observed that the frequency range of the response scale affected older respondents more than younger respondents when the question pertained to mundane behaviors, such as buying a birthday present. On the other hand, older respondents were less affected than younger respondents when the question pertained to the frequency of physical symptoms, which older people are more likely to monitor, resulting in better memory representations.

Similarly, Ji, Schwarz, and Nisbett (2000) observed pronounced cultural differences in respondents' need to estimate. In general, collectivist cultures put a higher premium on "fitting in" than individualist cultures (Oyserman, Coon, & Kemmelmeier, 2002). To "fit in," people need to monitor their own publicly observable behavior as well as the behavior of others to note undesirable deviations. Such monitoring is not required for private, unobservable behaviors. We may therefore expect that public behaviors are better represented in memory for people living in collectivistic rather than individualistic cultures, whereas private behaviors may be equally poorly represented in both cultures. To test these conjectures, Ji and colleagues (2000) asked students in China and the United States to report public and private behaviors along high or low frequency scales, or in an open response format. Replicating earlier findings, American students reported higher frequencies when presented with a high rather than low frequency scale, independent of whether the behavior was private or public. Chinese students' reports were similarly influenced by the frequency scale when the behavior was private, confirming that they relied on the same estimation strategy. In contrast, Chinese students' reports were unaffected by the response format when the behavior was public and hence needed to be monitored to ensure social fit.

As these examples illustrate, social groups differ in the extent to which they pay close attention to a given behavior. These differences in behavioral monitoring, in turn, influence to which extent respondents need to rely on estimation strategies in reporting on their behaviors, rendering them differentially susceptible to contextual influences. Importantly, such differences in respondents' strategies can result in misleading substantive conclusions about behavioral differences across cultures and cohorts.

2.4.6 Subsequent Judgments

In addition to affecting respondents' behavioral reports, frequency scales can also affect respondents' *subsequent judgments*. For example, respondents who check a frequency of twice a month on one of Schwarz and Scheuring's (1992) scales, shown earlier, may infer that their own symptom frequency is above average when presented with the low frequency scale, but below average when presented with the high frequency scale. Empirically, this is the case and the patients in this study reported higher health satisfaction after reporting their symptom frequencies on the high rather than low frequency scale – even though patients given a high frequency scale had reported a higher absolute symptom frequency to begin with. Again, such scale-induced comparison effects have been observed across a wide range of judgments (see Schwarz, 1999b for a review).

2.4.7 Editing the Answer

After respondents arrived at an answer in their own mind, they need to communicate it to the researcher. At this stage, the communicated estimate may deviate from their private estimate due to considerations of social desirability and self-presentation as already mentioned (see DeMaio, 1984, for a review. Not surprisingly, editing on the basis of social desirability is particularly likely in response to threatening questions and is more pronounced in face-to-face interviews than in self-administered questionnaires, which provide a higher degree of confidentiality. All methods designed to reduce socially desirable responding address one of these two factors. Bradburn et al. (2004) review these methods and provide good advice on their use (see also Lensvelt-Mulders, Chapter 24).

2.4.8 Implications for Questionnaire Construction

In sum, respondents will rarely be able to draw on extensive episodic memories when asked to report on the frequency of mundane behaviors. Instead, they need to rely on a variety of estimation strategies to arrive at a reasonable answer. Which strategy they use is often influenced by the research instrument, as the case of frequency scales illustrates. The most basic way to improve behavioral reports is to ensure that respondents have sufficient time to search memory and to encourage respondents to invest the necessary effort (Cannell et al., 1981). Moreover, it is usually advisable to ask frequency questions in an open response format, such as, "How many times a week do you …? ___ times a week." Although the answers will not be accurate, the open response format will at least avoid the systematic biases associated with frequency scales.

Given these memory problems, researchers are often tempted to simplify the task by merely asking respondents if they engage in the behavior "never," "sometimes," or "frequently." Such *vague quantifiers,* however, are come with their own set of problems (see Pepper, 1981, for a review). For example, "frequently" suffering from headaches reflects higher absolute frequencies than "frequently" suffering from heart attacks, and "sometimes" suffering from headaches denotes a higher frequency for respondents with a medical history of migraine than for respondents without that history. In general, the use of vague quantifiers reflects the objective frequency relative to respondents' subjective standard, rendering vague quantifiers inadequate for the assessment of objective frequencies, despite their popularity.

2.5 REPORTING ON ONE'S ATTITUDES

Public opinion researchers have long been aware that attitude measurement is highly context dependent. In this section, we address the two dominant sources of context effects in attitude measurement, namely the order in which questions and response alternatives are presented to respondents.

2.5.1 Question Order Effects

Dating back to the beginning of survey research, numerous studies demonstrated that preceding questions can influence the answers given to later questions (see Schuman & Presser, 1981; Schwarz & Sudman, 1992; Sudman et al., 1996; Tourangeau et al., 2000, for reviews). Moreover, when a self-administered questionnaire is used, respondents can go back and forth between questions, occasionally resulting in influences of later questions on responses to earlier ones (e.g., Schwarz & Hippler, 1995).

Question order effects arise for a number of different reasons. First, preceding questions can affect respondents' inferences about the intended meaning of subsequent questions, as discussed in the section on question comprehension (e.g., Strack, Schwarz, & Wänke, 1991). Second, they can influence respondents' use of rating scales, resulting in less extreme ratings when a given item is preceded by more extreme ones, which serve as scale anchors (e.g., Ostrom & Upshaw, 1968). Third, they can bring general norms to mind that are subsequently applied to other issues (e.g., Schuman & Ludwig, 1983). Finally, preceding questions can influence which information respondents use in forming a mental representation of the attitude object and the standard against which the object is evaluated.

The accumulating evidence suggests that a differential construal of attitude objects and standards is the most common source of question order effects. Hence, we focus on this aspect by following Schwarz and Bless' (1992a) inclusion/exclusion model, which predicts the direction and size of question order effects in attitude measurement, as well as their generalization across related issues.

2.5.2 Mental Construal

Attitude questions assess respondents' evaluations of an attitude object. From a psychological perspective, evaluations require two mental representations: A representation of the to-be-evaluated target and a representation of a standard, against which the target is assessed. Both of these representations are formed on the basis of information that is accessible at the time of judgment. This includes information that may always come to mind when the respondent thinks about this topic (chronically accessible information), as well as information that may only come to mind because of contextual influences, for example information that was used to answer earlier questions (temporarily accessible information). Whereas temporarily accessible information is the basis of most context effects in attitude measurement, chronically accessible information lends some context-independent stability to respondents' judgments.

Independent of whether the information is chronically or temporarily accessible, people truncate the information search as soon as enough information has come to mind to form a judgment with sufficient subjective certainty. Hence, their judgment is rarely based on all information that may bear on the topic, but dominated by the information that comes to mind most easily at that point in time. How this information influences the judgment, depends on how it is used.

2.5.3 Assimilation Effects

Information that is *included* in the temporary representation formed of the target results in *assimilation effects*. That is, including information with positive implications results in a more positive judgment, whereas including information with negative implications results in a more negative judgment. For example, Schwarz, Strack, and Mai (1991) asked respondents to report their marital satisfaction and their general life-satisfaction in different question orders. When the general life-satisfaction question was asked first, it correlated with marital satisfaction $r = .32$. Reversing the question order, however, increased this correlation to $r = .67$. This reflects that the marital satisfaction question brought marriage related information to mind that respondents included in the representation formed of their lives in general. Accordingly, happily married respondents reported higher general life-satisfaction in the marriage-life than in the life-marriage order, whereas unhappily married respondents reported lower life-satisfaction under this condition.

As this pattern indicates, the specific effect of thinking about one's marriage depends on whether it is a happy or unhappy one. Accordingly, no overall mean difference was observed for the sample as a whole, despite pronounced differences in correlation. As a general principle, question order effects are not a function of the preceding question per se, but of the information that the question brings to mind. Hence, pronounced question order effects may occur in the absence of overall mean differences, rendering measures of association more sensitive than examinations of means.

Theoretically, the size of assimilation effects increases with the amount and extremity of the temporarily accessible information, and decreases with the amount and extremity of chronically accessible information, that is included in the representation of the target (e.g., Bless, Schwarz, & Wänke, 2003). To continue with the previously mentioned example, some respondents were asked to report on their job satisfaction, leisure satisfaction, and marital satisfaction prior to reporting on their general life-satisfaction, thus bringing a more varied range of information about their lives to mind. As expected, this decreased the correlation of marital satisfaction and general life-satisfaction from $r = .67$ to $r = .43$. By the same token, we expect that respondents who are experts on a given issue show less pronounced assimilation effects than novices, because experts can draw on a larger set of chronically accessible information, which in turn reduces the impact of adding a given piece of temporarily accessible information. Note, however, that expert status needs to be defined with regard to the specific issue at hand. Global variables, such as years of schooling, are unlikely to moderate the size of assimilation effects, unless they are confounded with the amount of knowledge regarding the issue under consideration. Accordingly, formal education has been found to show inconsistent relationships with the emergence and size of question order effects (Schuman & Presser, 1981).

2.5.4 Contrast Effects

What has long rendered the prediction of question order effects challenging, is that the same piece of information that elicits an assimilation effect may also result in a *contrast effect*. This is the case when the information is excluded from, rather than included in, the cognitive representation formed of the target (Schwarz & Bless, 1992a). As a first possibility, suppose that a given piece of information with positive (negative) implications is excluded from the representation of the target. If so, the representation contains less positive (negative) information, resulting in a less positive (negative) judgment. For example, the Schwarz et al. (1991) life-satisfaction study included a condition in which the marital satisfaction and life-satisfaction questions were introduced with a joint lead-in that read, "We now have two questions about your life. The first pertains to your marriage and the second to your life in general." This lead-in was designed to evoke the conversational maxim of quantity (Grice, 1975), which enjoins speakers to avoid redundancy when answering related questions. Accordingly, respondents who had just reported on their marriage should now disregard this aspect of their lives when answering the general life-satisfaction question. Confirming this prediction, happily married respondents now reported lower general life-satisfaction, whereas unhappily married respondents reported higher life-satisfaction, indicating that they excluded the positive (negative) marital information from the representation formed of their lives in general. These diverging effects reduced the correlation to $r = .18$, from $r = .67$ when the same questions were asked in the same order without a joint lead-in. Finally, a control condition in which the general life-satisfaction question was reworded to, "Aside from your marriage, which you already told us about, how satisfied are you with your life in general?" resulted in a highly similar correlation of $r = .20$. Such *subtraction based* contrast effects are limited to the specific target (here, one's life in general), reflecting that merely subtracting a piece of information (here, one's marriage) does only affect this specific representation. The size of subtraction based contrast effects increases with the amount and extremity of the temporarily accessible information that is excluded from the representation of the target, and decreases with the amount and extremity of the information that remains in the representation of the target.

As a second possibility, respondents may not only exclude accessible information from the representation formed of the target, but may also use this information in constructing a standard of comparison. If the implications of the temporarily accessible information are more extreme than the implications of the chronically accessible information used in constructing a standard, this process results in a more extreme standard, eliciting contrast effects for that reason. The size of these comparison based contrast effects increases with the extremity and amount of temporarily accessible information used in constructing the standard or scale anchor, and decreases with the amount and extremity of chronically accessible information used in making this construction. In contrast to subtraction based comparison effects, which are limited to a specific target, comparison based contrast effects generalize to all targets to which the standard is applicable.

As an example, consider the impact of political scandals on assessments of the trustworthiness of politicians. Not surprisingly, thinking about a politician who was involved in a scandal, say Richard Nixon, decreases trust in politicians in general. This assimilation effect reflects that the exemplar is included in the representation formed of the target politicians in general. If the trustworthiness question pertains to a specific politician, however, say Bill Clinton, the primed exemplar cannot be included in the representation formed of the target—after all, Bill Clinton is not Richard Nixon. In this case, Richard Nixon may serve as a standard of comparison, relative to which Bill Clinton seems very trustworthy. Experiments with German exemplars confirmed these predictions (Schwarz & Bless, 1992b; Bless, Igou, Schwarz, & Wänke, 2000): Thinking about a politician who was involved in a scandal decreased the trustworthiness of politicians in general, but increased the trustworthiness of all specific exemplars assessed. In general, the same information is likely to result in assimilation effects in the evaluation of superordinate target categories (which allow for the inclusion of all information pertaining to subordinate categories), but in contrast effects in the evaluation of lateral target categories (which are mutually exclusive).

2.5.5 Determinants of Inclusion/Exclusion

Given the crucial role of inclusion/exclusion operations in the construction of mental representations, it is important to understand their determinants. When thinking about a topic, people generally assume that whatever comes to mind bears on what they are thinking about—or why else would it come to mind now? Hence, the default information is to include information that comes to mind in the representation of the target. This renders assimilation effects more likely than contrast effects. In fact, assimilation effects (sometimes referred to as carry-over effects) dominate the survey literature and many models intended to account for question order effects don't even offer a mechanism for the conceptualization of contrast effects (e.g., Zaller, 1992), which severely limits their usefulness as general theoretical frameworks. Whereas inclusion is the more common default, the exclusion of information needs to be triggered by salient features of the question answering process. The most relevant variables can be conceptualized as bearing on three implicit decisions that respondents have to make with regard to the information that comes to mind.

Some information that comes to mind may simply be irrelevant, pertaining to issues that are unrelated to the question asked. Other information may potentially be relevant to the task at hand and respondents have to decide what to do with it. The first decision bears on why this information comes to mind. Information that seems to come to mind for the wrong reason, for example because respondents are aware of the potential influence of a preceding question, is likely to be excluded. The second decision bears on whether the information that comes to mind bears on the target of judgment or not. The content of the context question (e.g., Schwarz & Bless, 1992a), the superordinate or lateral nature of the target category (e.g., Schwarz & Bless, 1992b), the extremity of the information (e.g., Herr, 1986), or its representativeness for the target category (e.g., Strack, Schwarz, & Gschneidinger, 1985) are relevant at this stage. Finally, conversational norms of nonredundancy may elicit the exclusion of previously provided information, as seen earlier (Schwarz et al., 1991).

Whenever any of these decisions results in the exclusion of information from the representation formed of the target, it will elicit a contrast effect. Whether this contrast effect is limited to the target, or generalizes across related targets, depends on whether the excluded information is merely subtracted from the representation of the target or used in constructing a standard against which the target is evaluated. Whenever the information that comes to mind is included in the representation formed of the target, on the other hand, it results in an assimilation effect. Hence, the inclusion/exclusion model provides a coherent conceptualization of the emergence, direction, size, and generalization of context effects in attitude measurement (see Schwarz & Bless, 1992a; Sudman et al., 1996, Chapter 5, for more detail).

2.5.6 Age- and Culture-related Differences

To guard against question order effects, survey researchers often separate related questions with buffer items. These buffer items presumably render the previously used information less accessible, thus attenuating the influence of earlier questions (for a review see Wänke & Schwarz, 1997). The same logic suggests that preceding questions should be less likely to influence the judgments of older respondents, due to age-related declines in memory. Empirically this is the case, as Knäuper (1999a) observed in secondary analyses of survey data.

Much as age-related differences in memory performance can elicit age-sensitive context effects, culture-related differences in conversational practice can elicit culture-sensitive context effects. For example, Asian cultures value more indirect forms of communication, which require a higher amount of reading between the lines, based on high sensitivity to subtle conversational cues. Accordingly, Asians are more likely to notice the potential redundancy of related questions, as Haberstroh, Oysermen, Schwarz, Kühnen and Ji (2002) observed in a conceptual replication of the previously mentioned marital satisfaction study (Schwarz et al., 1991) with Chinese respondents. Throughout, such age- and culture-sensitive context effects can invite misleading conclusions about age- and culture-related differences in respondents' attitudes.

2.5.7 Response Order Effects

Another major source of context effects in attitude measurement is the order in which response alternatives are presented. Response order effects are most reliably obtained when a question presents several plausible response options (see Sudman et al., 1996, chapter 6, for a detailed discussion). Suppose, for example, that respondents are asked in a self-administered questionnaire whether divorce should be easier to obtain or more difficult to obtain. When they first think about the easier option, they may quickly come up with a good reason for making divorce easier and may endorse this answer. But had they first thought about the more difficult option, they might as well have come up with a good reason for making divorce more difficult and might have endorsed that answer. In short, the order in which response alternatives are presented can influence the mental representation that respondents form of the issue (see Sudman et al., 1996, for a more detailed discussion).

Which response alternative respondents are more likely to elaborate on first, depends on the presentation order and mode (Krosnick & Alwin, 1987). In a visual format, like a self-administered questionnaire, respondents think about the response alternatives in the order in which they are presented. In this case, a given alternative is more likely to be endorsed when presented first rather than last, resulting in a *primacy effect*. In an auditory format, like a telephone interview, respondents cannot think about the details until the interviewer has read the whole question. In this case, they are likely to begin with the last alternative read to them, which is still in their ear. Under this format, a given alternative is more likely to be endorsed when presented last rather than first, resulting in a recency effect.

2.5.8 Age-related Differences

On theoretical grounds, we may expect that age-related limitations of working memory capacity further enhance respondents' tendency to elaborate mostly on a single response alternative. Empirically this is the case and an extensive meta-analysis documented that response order effects are more pronounced for older and less educated respondents (Knäuper, 1999b). This age-sensitivity of response order effects can again invite misleading conclusions about cohort differences in the reported attitude, suggesting, for example, that older respondents are more liberal than younger respondents under one order condition, but more conservative under the other (Knäuper, 1999a).

The observation that response order effects increase with age, whereas question order effects decrease with age, also highlights that age-sensitive context effects do indeed reflect age-related differences in cognitive capacity, which can plausibly account for both observations. In contrast, attempts to trace these differences to age-related differences in attitude strength (e.g., Sears, 1986) would suggest that question order and response order effects show parallel age patterns, which is not the case.

2.5.9 Implications for Questionnaire Construction

Human judgment is always context dependent, in daily life as in survey interviews. Although attention to the theoretical principles summarized earlier can help researchers to attenuate context effects in attitude measurement, the best safeguard against misleading conclusions is the experimental variation of question and response order within a survey.

2.6 CONCLUDING REMARKS

Survey researchers have long been aware that collecting data by asking questions is an exercise that may yield many surprises. Since the 1980s, psychologists and survey methodologists have made considerable progress in understanding the cognitive and communicative processes underlying question answering, rendering some of these surprises less surprising than they have been in the past. Yet, this does not imply that we can always predict how a given question would behave when colleagues ask us for advice: In many cases, the given question is too mushy an operationalization of theoretical variables to allow for predictions (although we typically feel we know what would happen if the question were tinkered with, in one way or another, to bring it in line with theoretical models). Nevertheless, the accumulating insights (reviewed in Sudman et al., 1996; Tourangeau et al., 2000) alert us to likely problems and help us in identifying questions and question sequences that need systematic experimental testing before they are employed in a large-scale study.

GLOSSARY OF KEY CONCEPTS

Assimilation effect. A catch-all term for any influence that makes the answers to two questions more similar than they otherwise would be; it does not entail specific assumptions about the underlying process.

Backfire effect. See contrast effect.

Carry-over effect. See assimilation effect.

Context effect. A catch-all term for any influence of the context in which a question is asked; it does not entail specific assumptions about the direction of the effect or the underlying process.

Contrast effect. A catch-all term for any influence that makes the answers to two questions more different than they otherwise would be; it does not entail specific assumptions about the underlying process.

Pragmatic meaning. Refers to the intended (rather than literal or semantic) meaning of an utterance and requires inferences about the speaker's knowledge and intentions.

Primacy effect. A given response alternative is more likely to be chosen when presented at the beginning rather than at the end of a list of response alternatives.

Question order effect. The order in which questions are asked influences the obtained answers; different processes can give rise to this influence.

Recency effect. A given response alternative is more likely to be chosen when presented at the end rather than at the beginning of a list of response alternatives.

Response order effect. The order in which response alternatives are presented influences which alternative is endorsed; see primacy effect and recency effect.

Semantic meaning. Refers to the literal meaning of words. Understanding the semantic meaning is insufficient for answering a question, which requires an understanding of the question's pragmatic meaning.

Chapter 3

The Problem of Nonresponse

Peter Lynn
University of Essex

3.1 INTRODUCTION

Many books about survey sampling show how the precision of survey estimates depends on the sample design; however, this assumes that data are obtained for every unit in the selected sample. This is rarely the case; most surveys experience some nonresponse. Consequently, the sample upon which the estimates are based is not the same as the sample that was originally selected. Obviously, it is smaller. But it may also be different in other important ways that affect the estimates.

It may seem rather negative to be discussing nonresponse so early in this book. We haven't yet begun to discuss how to design or implement a survey and yet we are already talking about failure—failure to collect data from all the units in our sample. But this is a fundamental aspect of survey research. If we cannot successfully collect data from a large proportion of the selected units, then it may be a waste of time carrying out a survey at all. And when the data have been collected and we want to make estimates we need to be able to make allowances for the effect of nonresponse. This requires advance planning—even before the sample has been selected. In this chapter, I try to explain how and why nonresponse occurs, why it is important, and what we can do to minimize any undesirable consequences.

3.2 WHY IS NONRESPONSE IMPORTANT?

Even the most well resourced surveys carried out by experienced survey organizations suffer from nonresponse. The level of nonresponse can vary greatly between surveys, depending on the nature of the sample units, the mode of data collection, the fieldwork procedures used and societal and cultural factors. Some of these factors vary between countries and often lead to response rates differing between countries for the same survey. But whatever the circumstances of your survey, you are almost certain to have some nonresponse.

The principles of statistical inference (see Lohr, Chapter 6) allow us to make inferences about a population of interest, provided that the sample has been selected using a known probability mechanism. In other words, we have to know the selection probability of each unit in our sample. But nonresponse disturbs the selection probabilities. The probability of a particular unit being in our final responding sample, sometimes referred to as the inclusion probability, is the product of the original selection probability and the probability of the unit responding once selected. Assuming that we have used a probability sampling design, the first of these is known. But the second is not known. The result is that our sample may no longer be representative of the population.

Consider a simple example of a survey of literacy in a small town. Suppose we want to estimate the proportion of adults classified as low ability, based upon a test that will be administered as part of the survey interview (ignore for the moment the fact that the test may not provide a perfectly accurate measure of ability—see Hox, Chapter 20). Imagine that the population of 14,000 adults in the town consists of 8,000 who would be classified as high ability if the test were administered and 6,000 who would be classified as low ability (though of course we would not know this). The sample design is to randomly select one in every 20 adults (see Table 3.1), so we would expect to find approximately 400 high ability and 300 low ability persons in our sample. Suppose however that the low ability persons are less likely to respond to the survey, with a response probability of only 0.60, compared with 0.80 for the high ability persons. This means that we can expect to find 180 low ability persons in the responding sample of 500, so we might estimate the proportion of low ability persons in the population to be 36%, whereas in fact it is 43% (6,000 out of 14,000). But if we were carrying out this survey for real, we might not be aware that our estimate is too low. We would only observe the numbers highlighted in bold in Table 3.1. In the absence of other information, we would have no way of knowing that low ability persons had been less likely to respond to the survey and no reason to adjust our estimate of 36%.

Table 3.1: The effect of nonresponse on a survey of literacy

	High ability	Low ability	Total
Population	8,000	6,000	**14,000**
Selection probability	**1/20**	**1/20**	**1/20**
Expected sample size	400	300	**700**
Response probability	0.80	0.60	**0.714**
Responding sample size	**320**	**180**	**500**

Note: Figures in bold would be known; other figures not

This error in our estimate has been caused by nonresponse. Specifically, it has been caused by the fact that the response probability is associated with the target variable (literacy ability). If nonresponse had happened completely at random, then we would still have expected to find 43% of the responding sample to be low ability. But nonresponse rarely happens completely at random. There are reasons why some units do not respond and those reasons are typically associated with at least some of the survey variables. In our example, it may be that some residents of the town were away in a different location, engaged in seasonal employment, during the survey field work period. If such people were selected into the sample, it would not have been possible to contact them so they would have been nonrespondents. And if people with low literacy ability were more likely than those with high ability to engage in this seasonal employment, this could lead to exactly the sort of effect shown in Table 3.1.

3.3 HOW DOES NONRESPONSE ARISE?

There are several reasons why nonresponse occurs. If we are to be successful in trying to minimize the extent of nonresponse, we need to understand these reasons and to find ways of combating each of them. A summary classification of reasons for nonresponse appears in Table 3.2. These reflect the stages of the survey data collection process. Once a sample unit is selected, it is first necessary for the data collector to identify the location of that unit. This may prove impossible if, for example, the address information on the sampling frame is incomplete (a). If located successfully, the next step is to make contact with the sample unit. Sometimes, as in the example above, this proves impossible (b). Even if contact is made successfully, it may not prove possible to collect the required data. Reasons for this can be broadly classified into three types: the sample unit may be unwilling to co-operate (c), or unable to co-operate (d), or the data collector and sample unit may be unable to communicate adequately (e). Finally, it sometimes happens that data are successfully collected from the sample unit but subsequently lost–for example if questionnaires go missing in the post or computer files become corrupted (f).

Table 3.2: Reasons for nonresponse

a. Failure of the data collector to locate/identify the sample unit
b. Failure to make contact with the sample unit
c. Refusal of the sample unit to participate
d. Inability of the sample unit to participate (e.g. ill health, absence, etc)
e. Inability of the data collector and sample unit to communicate (e.g. language barriers)
f. Accidental loss of the data/ questionnaire

This simple classification provides a framework for considering reasons for nonresponse but it does not describe the many specific reasons that could apply on any particular survey. Often, reasons for nonresponse will be specific to the topic of the survey, to the types of units from which data are to be collected, and to the way that the survey is designed and carried out. In particular, there are important differences between surveys carried out by face-to-face interviewing, by telephone interviewing, and by self-completion methods. There are also differences between surveys of individuals and households on the one hand and businesses and other establishments on the other. In the case of individuals and households, there is also an important distinction between surveys where the data are collected in the sample member's own home and surveys where the sample member is responding in a different context or in a particular capacity (e.g., as a user of a particular service or as a visitor to a particular place). Let us consider some common types of survey.

3.3.1 Face-to-face Interview Surveys of Households or Individuals

Many surveys of the household population in a country, region or town are carried out using face-to-face interviews in the respondents' own home. For example, most national statistical offices carry out Labor Force Surveys and Household Budget Surveys in this way. The World Bank's series of Living Standards Measurement Surveys (http://www.worldbank.org/lsms/) are also carried out in this way. The sample is usually selected from a list of either persons or addresses (e.g., a population register, a list of postal addresses, or a list of addresses drawn up in the field as part of the survey preparation phase) and the interviewers' first task is to locate each selected address. They must then make contact with the residents, confirm whether any resident is eligible for the survey, possibly make a random selection of one person to interview, contact the selected person, persuade the person to be interviewed, agree a convenient time and place for the interview, administer the interview, and transmit the data to the survey office. At each stage, nonresponse could occur for each of several reasons. To illustrate this, consider the example of surveys of individuals in the United Kingdom, where a sample of addresses is selected from the Post Office list, and one person is subsequently selected for interview at each address. Surveys that use this design include the British Crime Survey, the British Social Attitudes Survey and the UK part of the European Social Survey. Similar designs can be found in several other countries. The fieldwork process is summarized in Figure 3.1. The shaded boxes indicate nonresponse outcomes.

The first stage of the process is to mail an advance letter (or prenotification letter) to each selected address. This notifies the residents that an interviewer will be visiting soon, provides some basic information about the survey, and provides contact details for the survey organization in case the recipient has queries or concerns. Having received this letter, some sample members contact the survey organization to indicate that they do not wish to participate in the survey. Where possible, the survey organization attempts to persuade these sample members to allow the interviewer to visit and to explain the survey in more detail, emphasizing that they will still have the opportunity to decline to take part at that stage if they wish. But this is not always successful; some sample members insist that they do not want an interviewer to visit. These cases are typically referred to as office refusals, as they are refusals noted in the survey office, before the interviewer has had a chance to influence the outcome.

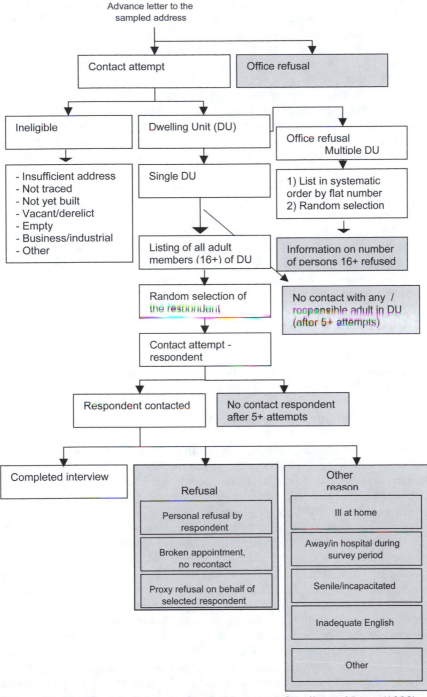

Figure 3.1. The process for a sample of addresses. (cf. Laiho and Lynn (1999).

At all remaining sample addresses, an interviewer attempts to visit the address and make contact with the residents. In the majority of cases, the address will consist of a single dwelling (a house or a flat), in which case the interviewer's task is to list all adult residents and make a random selection of one to interview. Some people refuse to provide the information necessary to list the residents; other people will never be at home when the interviewer visits, resulting in a noncontact. In the small minority of cases where an address contains multiple dwellings, the interviewer has the additional task of selecting one or more dwellings. Once the random selection of a person to interview has taken place, the interviewer must attempt to speak to that person. It may not be the person who provided the information to make the listing, and the selected person may not even be at home, so the interviewer may have to make subsequent visits to the address to find this person. If contact is successfully made, there are still several reasons why an interview may not be achieved. The selected person may refuse, or somebody else may refuse on their behalf (for example, a husband who does not allow the interviewer to speak to his wife, or a parent who does not allow contact with their child—a *proxy refusal*). The selected person may be unable to participate due to illness or incapacity or may not speak adequately the language in which interviews are being conducted. On United Kingdom surveys of this kind, it is often found that around 3% to 6% of sample addresses will result in a noncontact, between 15% and 35% will be a refusal and around 1% to 2% will be a nonresponse for some other reason.

It can be seen that the survey participation process is quite complicated and there are many stages in the process at which there is an opportunity for nonresponse to occur. In general, the more complicated and demanding the process of collecting data is, the more likely it is that nonresponse will occur.

3.3.2 Telephone Surveys of Named Persons

Many surveys are carried out by telephone. In some countries, this is a common method of carrying out surveys of the general population. This usually involves selecting a random sample of phone numbers by a method such as random digit dialling (RDD). Telephone surveys are also often used when the sample is of named persons for whom a telephone number is available, perhaps from the sampling frame or having been collecting in an earlier survey interview. With such surveys, noncontact can occur if the telephone number is incorrect or if the sample member has changed telephone number recently (for example, due to moving home). In some such cases, it will be possible to obtain the new phone number, but not always. If the phone number is correct, noncontacts will occur if the sample member is never at home when the interviewer calls, or if they do not answer the phone. It is increasingly common in some countries for people to use devices that enable them to see the phone number of the person calling them before they answer the phone. They may choose not to answer if they do not recognize the number. And even if contact is made, the sample member may refuse to carry out the interview. It is much easier to refuse on the phone than to an interviewer standing at the door, so it is a big challenge for telephone interviewers to prevent this from happening.

3.3.3 Postal Surveys

Surveys that use self-completion questionnaires administered by post (mail) may seem to be rather simple in terms of the participation process. Either you receive the completed questionnaire or you don't. But in reality the underlying process is still quite complex. The difference is that it is hidden from the view of the survey researcher to a greater extent than with interview surveys. First, there will be some cases where the questionnaire does not reach the intended recipient, because the address is wrong, because of a failure of the postal service, or because someone else at the address intercepts it. Amongst cases where the questionnaire successfully reaches the sample member, there will be several reasons for it not being returned. In some cases this represents a refusal, in the sense that the recipient consciously decides not to complete the questionnaire (but only in a small minority of such cases will the recipient inform the survey organization of this decision), in other cases it may simply be a result of forgetting, as the recipient puts the questionnaire to one side with an intention to complete it later, but then fails to do so. There may be some cases where the respondent is unable to complete the questionnaire due to illness, illiteracy, or inability to read the language of the questionnaire. And some questionnaires may be completed but get lost in the post.

3.3.4 Web Surveys

The nature of nonresponse on web surveys depends heavily on the design of the survey. For invitation-only surveys, where a preselected sample of persons is sent (typically by email) an invitation to complete the questionnaire, noncontact can be considerable. This can be caused by incorrect or out-of-date email addresses, by the recipient's email system judging the email to be spam and therefore not delivering it, or by the recipient judging the email to be spam and not opening it. For web surveys, levels of break-off are typically higher than with other survey modes. This is where a respondent gets a certain way through the questionnaire and then decides not to continue. There are many reasons why this happens and, although the proportion of break-offs can be reduced by good design, it is a considerable challenge. Further discussion of the sources of non-response and what to report can be found on the website of EFAMRO (www.efamro.org), see also de Leeuw, Chapter 7.

3.3.5 Flow Samples

Many surveys involve sampling and collecting data simultaneously from a mobile population that is defined by time and location. Examples include international passenger surveys that sample and interview at ports and airports, surveys of train or bus passengers, and surveys of visitors to a particular location or service such as a national park, a museum, or an employment agency. With this kind of survey, noncontacts are likely to consist solely of cases where the sample person could not be approached as there was no interviewer available to do so. This tends to happen during periods of high flow, as interviewers are still occupied interviewing previously sampled person(s). The extent to which this happens depends on the frequency with which people are sampled at each sample location (determined by the population flow and the sampling interval) and the number of interviewers working at that location. The extent of refusals will largely depend on the time that sample members have available and the circumstances. If you are attempting to interview people while they are waiting in a queue you may get rather low levels of refusal as the sample members do not have many alternative ways to spend the time. But if you are sampling people who have just disembarked from a train, sample members tend to be keen to continue their journey and refusal levels will be higher.

3.3.6 Business Surveys

Surveys of businesses are different from surveys of households in two important ways that affect nonresponse. First, respondents are not answering on their own behalf but on behalf of the business. This raises a different set of concerns regarding confidentiality and sensitivity of responses, which could affect refusals. Second, it is often necessary for more than one person in the business to contribute to the survey answers and the survey organization rarely knows the identity of these people in advance. Consequently, a response will only be obtained if all the necessary people are identified and contacted during fieldwork. Many business surveys are conducted as self-completion surveys, so this often requires a questionnaire to be passed around the business to each relevant person. The ways in which the survey organization controls and facilitates that process are likely to influence the extent of nonresponse due to a failure to reach the relevant person(s)—a form of noncontact.

3.4 WHY DO PEOPLE REFUSE TO PARTICIPATE IN SURVEYS?

Refusals often constitute a large proportion of survey nonresponse. Consequently, they warrant careful attention. A conceptual framework for survey co-operation in the case of interview surveys is presented in Figure 3.2. The decision about whether or not to co-operate is an outcome of the interaction between interviewer and sample member. The behavior and performance of both the sample member and the interviewer during the interaction will be largely influenced by two sets of factors. These can be broadly labeled the social environment and the survey design. (Both actors in this interaction will of course also have their own personal characteristics and predispositions upon which these two sets of factors act.)

The social environment includes the degree of social cohesion, the legitimacy of institutions, and so on. These influence the degree of social responsibility felt by a sample person and the persuasion strategies and decision-making strategies used by interviewers and respondents respectively. Also, the immediate environment in which the survey interview is to take place is likely to affect a sample member's willingness to be interviewed. Relevant factors include comfort and perceived safety.

Many aspects of survey design affect response rates. These are discussed in section 3.5 later. Other, broad, aspects of survey design can be considered as constraints upon the interaction between sample member and interviewer. Mode of interview is very important. Interviewers are much more limited in the ways they can communicate with a sample member if they are talking on the telephone rather than standing in front of them face-to-face. They cannot show the sample member documents or identity cards, they cannot use body language or gestures, and so on. These limitations may contribute to the lower levels of success that interviewers seem to have in avoiding refusals on telephone surveys. How interviewers introduce the survey is also likely to be influenced by the length and content of the interview. For example, if a sample member seems generally willing but appears not to have much time available currently, then faced with a long interview an interviewer may suggest that she returns at a more convenient time ("retreat and return") rather than asking to start the interview immediately. But if the interview is short, she may be more likely to suggest starting the interview immediately. These tactics may have different implications for the survey outcome.

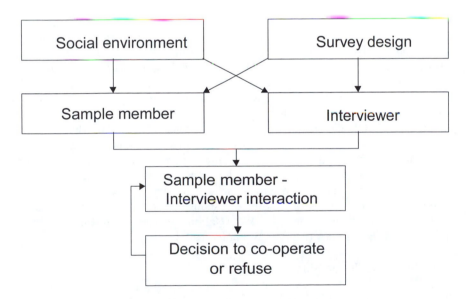

Figure 3.2: A conceptual framework for survey co-operation.
Adapted from Groves and Couper (1998, p. 30).

Groves, Cialdini and Couper (1992) discuss six psychological principles that apply to requests to take part in surveys: reciprocation, authority, consistency, scarcity, social validation and liking. Additionally, three types of attributes of the interviewer may have an important influence on the interaction with the sample member. The interviewer's expectations regarding the likelihood of gaining co-operation is affected by previous experiences but can also be influenced by appropriate training. Their appearance and manner influence sample members' impressions of the interviewer's intentions and whether it is likely to be safe or desirable to talk to them. The more, and more diverse, previous survey experience the interviewer has had, the more likely it is that they will be able to react to particular situations in appropriate ways that will minimize their chances of getting a refusal.

Survey topic influences some sample members' willingness to respond. The more relevant the survey appears, the more likely sample members will agree to be interviewed. But being interviewed can also have negative consequences, often referred to as the burden of taking part in a survey. For many people, the main component of burden is simply the amount of time that it takes. Other aspects of burden include cognitive effort, sensitivity and risk. Cognitive effort essentially relates to how difficult the questions are to answer. Sensitivity refers to embarrassment, stress or pain that may be caused by the questions. Risk acknowledges that being interviewed may (be perceived to) involve a risk to one's personal safety by letting a stranger into one's home, but also that answering questions that may reveal illegal or immoral behavior could result in being punished for that behavior (or at least be perceived to risk such an outcome).

Ultimately, the sample member must rapidly consider the potential benefits and potential drawbacks of agreeing to the interview and make a decision. The benefits and drawbacks will be weighed up against one another and if the drawbacks appear to weigh more heavily, the sample member will refuse. This idea is nicely encapsulated in the leverage-saliency theory of survey participation (Groves, Singer & Corning, 2000). The survey researcher should therefore, through the behavior of the interviewer and the design of survey documents and materials, emphasize to sample members the benefits of taking part and to de-emphasize the disadvantages. Of course, the various considerations will not be equally important to all sample members and that is why interviewers should be able to tailor their approaches (Groves & Couper, 1998, pp. 248-249) to react to the particular circumstances and concerns of each sample member. Various materials are available to assist in training interviewers in techniques to maximize response rates. These include a video with an accompanying trainers' booklet (National Centre for Social Research, 1999) and an earlier book (Morton-Williams, 1993).

3.4.1 Self-completion Surveys

Tailoring is an important tool to reduce the chance of getting a refusal. However, compared with tailoring by interviewers during an introductory conversation, it is much more difficult to tailor documents such as advance letters, as typically little is known in advance about the sample members or their concerns. This is perhaps one reason why self-completion surveys, when not introduced by an interviewer, tend to achieve lower response rates than interview surveys. The framework presented in Figure 3.2 can be applied also to self-completion surveys, simply by replacing interviewer with survey organization in each box. The interaction with the sample member now typically consists of the sample member reading written material. In the case of a postal survey, this will be a letter, a questionnaire, possibly one or more reminder letters, and possibly a survey website. In the case of a web survey, the written material comes in the form of an invitation email or letter plus instructions that accompany the questionnaire on the website. The interaction is therefore much more limited and the survey organization rarely has the opportunity to react to particular concerns or circumstances of sample members. Strategies that can be adopted to minimize refusals on self-completion surveys are discussed in Dillman (2000).

3.5 CALCULATING AND PRESENTING RESPONSE RATES

Response rate is an important indicator of the success of the survey at representing the population of interest (assuming the sample was selected by an appropriate probability method). It can also be used as an indicator of the success of the data collection operation. In fact, response rates and other kinds of outcome rates such as eligibility rates, contact rates and refusal rates provide useful information for many purposes. Consequently, the way they are calculated and presented is important (Lynn, Beerten, Laiho, & Martin, 2002).

Every survey should document the outcome rates achieved. These rates should be calculated in clearly specified ways, so that readers can understand exactly which kinds of units have been included in the numerator and which in the denominator of each rate. Ideally, the method of calculating response rate should be consistent with other similar surveys. Some guidance on how to do this appears in AAPOR (2005) and Lynn, Beerten, Laiho, and Martin (2001); for Internet surveys see EFAMRO. Published response rates are often accepted uncritically, but this is misguided as the rate can be sensitive to the method of calculation. This can make comparisons of published response rates fairly meaningless. It is good practice to publish the number of sample cases in each outcome category (e.g., the kinds of categories in Figure 3.1 mentioned earlier) so that users can calculate whichever rates they wish for themselves. We saw earlier in this chapter that there are many possible ways in which nonresponse can arise on a survey. If we want to learn how to improve response rates next time, it is essential to know how prevalent each reason for nonresponse was. A single response rate does not convey that information—a complete distribution of outcomes is needed.

Even more fundamental is the way in which the outcome categories themselves are defined. This too should be documented explicitly. The guidelines referred to earlier provide a set of standard definitions of outcome categories that can be applied to most surveys.

3.6 MINIMIZING NONRESPONSE

A consequence of the diversity of ways in which nonresponse arises is that we need a range of techniques and tactics to prevent nonresponse. No single technique is likely to have a large impact on response rate. We need to combine many techniques, applied to different stages of the design and implementation process. The classification in Table 3.2 can serve as a useful starting point for thinking about what we should do.

3.6.1 Identifying/Locating Sample Units

Success at identifying or locating sample units largely depends on the quality of information on the sampling frame. Sometimes, it may be possible to augment sampling frame information by matching sample units to other data bases or sources of information. The researcher should consider at an early stage whether this is likely to be necessary and, if so, to set up systems in advance of field work. During field work, it may be appropriate to have systems for locating new contact details for sample members who have moved. This may require interviewers to travel to different areas. Again, such systems require advance planning.

3.6.2 Making Contact

Often, considerable efforts are needed to make contact with sample members. This is particularly true for face-to-face and telephone interview surveys. The necessary extent of the efforts, and the best way to make them, depends on the nature of the sample units and the nature of the survey task. The researcher should consider carefully how, when and where the sample members are most likely to be available to be contacted and to develop field work procedures appropriately. I outline below some techniques that have been found to work well in some common survey situations, but you must think critically about the extent to which these findings are relevant to your survey.

In some countries, particularly industrialized ones, the amount of time that people spend in their home has been decreasing in recent years. Some population subgroups—for example, young single professionals living in big cities—spend very little time at home. This presents challenges for at-home interview surveys. Interviewers can reduce noncontact rates by making more call attempts and by varying the times of day and days of the week of their call attempts. Both of these dimensions of interviewers' calling patterns (number of calls and time/day of calls) are important. In the case of face-to-face surveys, many survey organizations stipulate that an interviewer must visit an address at least 4 (or 5) times, including at least once on a weekday evening and at least once at the weekend, before it can be classified as a noncontact. Often, considerably more attempts are made. With a clustered sample (see Lohr, Chapter 6), each time an interviewer visits the sample area, he or she can make a further call at each address where contact has not yet been made. With a more dispersed sample, the noncontact rate is likely to be higher unless special measures are taken. It is important to provide interviewers with motivation to make extra calls, especially at evenings and weekends. This can partly be achieved by good training, but financial reward will also be needed. Paying a fixed hourly rate provides no incentive for interviewers to call at times when people are more likely to be at home rather than times when they themselves prefer to work. Paying a modest bonus for achieving a target contact rate could be effective. All these counter measures are, unfortunately, likely to increase the costs of fieldwork and the length of the data collection period.

The marginal cost of making extra call attempts is relatively low on a telephone survey so many attempts can be made. It is not uncommon for survey organizations to stipulate that a sample telephone number must be attempted at least 12 or 15 times before it can be classified as a noncontact. If sample members are being telephoned at their homes, it will be important, as with face-to-face interviewing, for interviewers to work evenings and weekends. As some people can be away from home for long periods (on holiday, on business, etc.), contact rates will be higher the longer the fieldwork period.

If contact is made with someone other than the sample member, it is important to obtain and record information about when the sample member is likely to be available, and subsequently to phone again at that time. This requires a carefully planned call scheduling system. The system should ensure that an interviewer (it may not necessarily be the same interviewer) calls back at an appropriate time if an appointment is made or if an indication is given of when the sample member is likely to be available. Even if no contact at all is made, the call scheduling system should aim to ensure that future calls are made at different times and on different days to the previous unsuccessful calls. On a modest sized survey, the interviewers may do the scheduling using paper based diary systems. On a larger survey, it may be more efficient for a supervisor (perhaps themselves a senior interviewer) to do the scheduling using a spreadsheet or other computer based system. If the work is being carried out from a telephone unit or other central office location, this is particularly likely to be the best solution. Many survey organizations use computer assisted systems for telephone surveys, and these incorporate automatic call scheduling facilities.

If self-completion questionnaires are to be posted to sample members, contact will only be made if the sample member actually receives the mailing, opens the envelope and looks at the contents. The most important determinant of noncontact rate is therefore likely to be the quality of the address information used for the mailings. Once the mailing has arrived at the correct address, the sample member must be motivated to open it. A plain envelope may be best, to avoid it looking like junk mail. The design of postal survey packages is discussed by de Leeuw in Chapter 13.

On web surveys, to make contact typically requires both that a valid email address is available for each sample member (i.e., one that relates to an account that the sample member checks regularly) and that the recipient is motivated to open the invitation email and read it. The subject line of the message and the 'ender are therefore important. For further discussion of making contact on web surveys, see Lozar-Manfreda and Vehovar (Chapter 14).

Surveys that aim to sample from a flow (as described earlier) are rather different from other surveys in terms of strategies to minimize noncontacts. The important thing is to ensure that field workers are able to deal adequately with periods of high flow. The appropriate strategy depends on the rate of flow, how well the flow can be predicted in advance, and the time taken for field workers to hand out each questionnaire or administer each interview. It may involve having different numbers of field workers in each sample location, or at different times of day, or using different sampling fractions at different times.

3.6.3 Obtaining Cooperation

To minimize refusals, the survey researcher should: (a) increase (and emphasize) the benefits of taking part, (b) reduce (and de-emphasize) the drawbacks, and (c) address legitimate concerns of sample members.

The survey should be introduced in a way that makes participation seem likely to be interesting and enjoyable. Emphasize the aspects of the interview that people are more likely to find interesting. Explain that the survey serves useful purposes. Provision of payment or a small gift can also help. There is considerable experimental evidence that such incentives can reduce survey refusal rates, though the extent of the reduction depends on the nature of the incentive, the study population and other features of the survey. Offering survey respondents a token of our appreciation helps to establish the *bona fide* nature of the survey and makes them feel better disposed to reciprocate by offering their co-operation in return; however, providing an incentive to each respondent raises costs and survey funders may need to be convinced that it is likely to be cost effective.

For many people, the main drawback of taking part in a survey is the amount of their time that it will take. This should be minimized by keeping questionnaires as short as possible – ask only questions that are necessary; do not ask an open ended question (which might take a minute or two) if a closed question (taking a few seconds) provides equivalent information. People might be more willing to take part at certain times than others. Be flexible and allow them to take part when it is most convenient for them. On interview surveys, the interviewer should be prepared, when it is clear that she has called at an awkward time, to call back later when it is more convenient for the sample member. Otherwise, there is a high risk that a refusal will result. Offer to make an appointment. Some sample members may think that taking part will be too difficult for them, or that the survey is not relevant to them. Tell them that the questions are not difficult and that no specialist knowledge is required. Tell them that you are interested in the views and experiences of *all* kinds of people—that the survey results must represent everyone, not just the people with strong views or expert knowledge.

Sample members may be concerned that their answers should not become known to anyone else. Tell them that the survey is confidential and that nobody outside the research team will be able to link their answers to their name or address (you must, of course, have systems in place to ensure this). Explain that results will be made available only in the form of statistical summaries—no individuals will be identified. Tell them that they will not receive any direct mail as a result of taking part and that they will not be asked to take part in any further surveys (if this is true). On an in-home interview survey, sample members—especially older people—may be reluctant to invite a stranger into their home. Be sure that interviewers carry identification and that sample members are given the name and telephone number of someone who can verify that the survey is genuine. It is good practice to notify the local police station in areas where you are carrying out in-home interviews. Interviewers can tell wary respondents that the police know about the survey and suggest that they contact the police station to check this if they wish. Interviewers should be prepared to offer to come back when there will be someone else there too, if a sample member is reluctant to let them in while they are alone.

The method of communicating all these messages to sample members depends on the survey. On interview surveys, you will be heavily dependent on the interviewers to explain the survey and answer questions. It is therefore important that interviewers are well trained in what to say to avoid getting a refusal. Depending on the nature of your sample, you may also be able to send an advance letter to sample members. If the letter has an official letterhead, that helps to establish the credibility of the survey. The letter should also provide the name and phone number of someone to whom queries can be directed. (This person, of course, must also be trained in refusal avoidance techniques and must be provided with information necessary to answer most of the sorts of queries and concerns that sample members are likely to raise). The letter should also briefly outline the nature of the survey and explain that answers will be treated confidentially. It should explain that an interviewer will be in touch shortly. It is generally best to avoid mentioning how long the interview will take in the advance letter—leave this to the interviewer to explain.

On a postal survey, the survey documents must convey all the important messages to sample members. Typically, the documents consist of a covering letter and the questionnaire itself. You may also include a leaflet containing further information about the survey or about the organization for whom the survey is being carried out. Sample members will decide, based upon their perceptions of these documents alone, whether or not to take part. Similarly, for web surveys the respondent's perception of the information presented on screen determines whether or not they decide to proceed with the survey.

3.6.4 Minimizing Other Reasons for Nonresponse

To reduce the number of interviews that are lost due to the sample member being too ill or temporarily away, a compromise solution can be to accept a proxy interview from a spouse or other household member, answering on behalf of the sample member. This can sometimes be appropriate, depending on the nature of the survey questions. There is no point asking a proxy respondent about things that they do not know. And it is certainly not possible to ask opinions or attitudes by proxy. In general, if you choose to accept proxy interviews in certain circumstances, there is likely to be a trade-off between response rate and measurement error. Other ways of reducing the number of temporarily absent sample members include extending the field work period and offering alternative modes of response, although these may have other disadvantages.

For many surveys, people who do not speak (in the case of an interview survey) or read and write (in the case of a self-completion survey) the main language (or one of the main languages) of the country are an important subgroup. Excluding them would certainly introduce nonresponse bias. But including them is likely to be expensive. It is necessary to provide translated materials and, in the case of an interview survey, trained interviewers who speak each language. And translation of survey materials is not a simple matter (see Harkness, Chapter 4), so the translation process must be a careful one.

3.7 NONRESPONSE ERROR

Ultimately, nonresponse is important because it affects estimates. In our earlier example, nonresponse caused us to estimate that 36% of people had low literacy ability when the true figure in the population was 43%. In general, nonresponse introduces error to our estimates if the nonrespondents differ from the respondents in terms of the things we are trying to measure (unless we can fully correct for these differences at the analysis stage—see section 3.8). Suppose we want to estimate a characteristic Y. This could be any kind of population parameter: a mean, a proportion, a measure of association, and so forth. We estimate Y by the corresponding sample statistic y. But we only observe y for the respondents in the sample, so the value we observe might differ from the value we would have observed if we had complete response. We can express this as follows:

$$y_r = y_n + \frac{nr}{n}(y_r - y_{nr}), \tag{3.1}$$

where n is the (selected) sample size; there are r respondents and nr nonrespondents (so $r + nr = n$); y_r is the value of y for the respondents (observed); y_{nr} is the value of y for the nonrespondents (not observed); and y_n is the value of y for the complete sample (not observed).

The amount by which the estimate y_r differs from y_n is the nonresponse error. This is the product of two components. The first, nr/n, is the nonresponse rate. The second, $(y_r - y_{nr})$, is the difference between respondents and nonrespondents in our variable of interest. We therefore need to pay attention to *both* these components. The nonresponse error or bias is given by

$$y_r - y_n = \frac{nr}{n}(y_r - y_{nr}). \tag{3.2}$$

Note that knowledge of the response rate alone does not tell us anything about nonresponse error. It is possible to have a high response rate (small nr/n) but have large nonresponse error (if $(y_r - y_{nr})$ is large); it is also possible to have a low response rate (large nr/n) but have little or no nonresponse error (if $(y_r - y_{nr})$ is small). To estimate the extent of nonresponse error, we need to find a way to estimate $(y_r - y_{nr})$ (see section 3.7). And to minimize nonresponse error we need to minimize *both* nr/n and $(y_r - y_{nr})$. The previous section discussed how we can minimize nr/n, but minimizing $(y_r - y_{nr})$ can be more challenging. Essentially, we need to concentrate on increasing response rates amongst the sample groups who would otherwise be unlikely to respond.

To illustrate the use of this expression for nonresponse error, we return to our literacy example (Table 1). We have $y_r = 180/500 = 0.36$ and $y_n = 300/700 = 0.43$; the nonresponse error $y_r - y_n = -0.07$ is based on $(y_r - y_{nr}) = (0.36 - (120/200)) = -0.24$ and $nr/n = 200/700 = 0.286$, alternatively calculated as $0.286 \times (-0.24) = -0.07$.

3.8 ESTIMATING NONRESPONSE ERROR

Estimating $(y_r - y_{nr})$ is a big challenge as y_{nr} is, by definition, not observed. But there are several possible approaches. Often, more than one of them is possible. It is a good idea to look at every available source of information about nonresponse as this helps you to build up a picture of the nature of nonresponse on your survey.

3.8.1 Use sampling frame information

Many sampling frames are a useful source of auxiliary information about each unit. If we include this information on the sample file, we can use it to compare respondents and nonrespondents.

Table 3.3: Estimating nonresponse error using sampling frame data

Highest qualification	Response rate	Selected sample %	Responding sample %
1. 5+ Higher grades	91.1%	18.0	21.4
2. 3-4 Higher grades	85.1%	13.0	14.5
3. 1-2 Higher grades	81.7%	15.0	16.1
4. 5+ Standard grades 1-3	76.4%	8.1	8.1
5. 3-4 Standard grades 1-3	74.1%	9.1	8.8
6. 1-2 Standard grades 1-3	69.1%	14.5	13.1
7. Standard grades 4-7 only	62.6%	14.4	11.8
8. No qualifications	59.6%	7.8	6.1
N		4,542	3,469

Source: Lynn (1996)

Table 3.3 presents an example, using data from the Scottish School Leavers Survey, a postal self-completion survey of young people aged 16 to 18 in

Scotland. The sampling frame for this survey includes a record of examination passes achieved at school. This information has been used to derive an ordinal variable with eight categories, shown as rows in Table 3.3.

Because we know the level of qualification achieved by each sample member, whether or not they responded to the survey, we can calculate response rates separately for each group. The response rate is highest amongst the most highly qualified sample members (91.1%) and lowest amongst those who left school with no qualifications (59.6%). Thus, we can obtain a direct measure of nonresponse error in, say, the percentage of people leaving school with very low qualifications: $y_r - y_n = 17.9 - 22.2 = -4.3$. However, it is not immediately helpful to know that nonresponse would cause us to underestimate this percentage by 4.3 if we used the responding sample, because we already know the percentage for the complete sample. The usefulness of the statistic lies in the fact that leaving school with very low qualifications is correlated with other parameters that we might wish to estimate using the survey data, such as labour market outcomes. We could be fairly sure that nonresponse error would cause us to underestimate the proportion of young people who are unemployed at age 20, for example, although we would not know by how much. Using sampling frame data thus has the advantage that nonresponse error can be calculated directly, but the disadvantage that this can only be done for the auxiliary variables and not for survey variables. Typically, it requires advance planning as we need to capture the auxiliary data during the process of sample selection.

3.8.2 Using Linked Data

It may be possible to link data from other sources to the sample records (see Bethlehem, Chapter 26). Only rarely is this possible for individuals, as in most contexts this requires the individuals' consent (which cannot be obtained for nonrespondents). But linkage is often possible at some higher level of aggregation. For example, in many countries a range of population statistics are published for small areas, either from a Census or from administrative data (e.g., on zip code level). The sample for a general population survey can be linked to such auxiliary data provided that suitable geographic identifiers exist on the sample file. The data can then be used in the same way as for sampling frame data.

3.8.3 Interviewer Observation

For an in-home face-to-face interview survey (and some other types of survey) it can be possible to ask interviewers to record certain characteristics of each sample unit from observation. For example, this might include the type of dwelling, the construction materials, the age of the dwelling, the nature of the surrounding area, and so on (e.g., Lynn, 2003b). The data on these characteristics can then be used in the same way as for sampling frame or linked data. A variation on interviewer observation is to collect data about nonrespondents by proxy, for example from neighbors or work colleagues. This is rarely very satisfactory as a means of studying nonresponse, as the data are typically far from complete and it cannot be assumed that measures are comparable with those collected from the respondents themselves.

3.8.4 Comparison with External Data

Sometimes there exist aggregate data about the population under study from some external source such as a recent Census or administrative data. If these data relate to one or more of the same variables about which data have been collected by the survey, then the responding sample can be compared with the population data; however, there are two important things to note about such comparisons. First, any differences between the two sources may not be due (solely) to nonresponse. Other factors affecting the comparison include coverage error and sampling error. These factors are confounded. Second, the data themselves may not be strictly comparable. There may be differences in the time period to which they refer, in the reference population to which they relate, and in the way they have been collected. Some data items may be more sensitive than others to such differences. In consequence, some observed differences between the responding sample and the external data may not reflect any real difference at all—rather, they may simply be due to differences in the way the variables have been measured. If you are planning an external comparison, consider carefully which variables are likely to be least sensitive to differences in the way the data were collected.

3.8.5 Using Process Data

Often, survey researchers can learn a lot from information about the process of collecting the survey data. For example, for an in-home survey, it is possible to record the number, timing, and outcome of all visits made to each sample unit before the interview was achieved; for a telephone survey you can record the number, timing, and outcome of all calls; for a postal survey you can record the number of days until the questionnaire was received or the number of reminder mailings that had to be sent to each unit. Process data of this kind, also often referred to as para data (see also Mohler et al, Chapter 21), can be available for all sample units. You can then observe how these data relate to the survey variables to obtain an indication of the likely direction and magnitude of nonresponse bias.

3.8.6 Survey of Nonrespondents

After a survey is complete, a sample of the nonrespondents can be selected for intensive follow up. This can be enlightening, but it is very hard to get a good response rate to a survey of nonrespondents. Ultimately, the follow up survey only tells us something about the relatively more accessible and less unwilling nonrespondents and we will not know how representative they are of all nonrespondents. In short, this survey too suffers from nonresponse error.

3.8.7 Panel Dropouts

In the case of panel surveys and other follow up surveys, we are in a strong position to understand the nature of nonresponse subsequent to the first wave. For the first wave, we still have to use one or more of the methods described earlier. But for subsequent waves, we can use all of the survey data collected at the first wave, and any other wave prior to the one being studied, as auxiliary data. The advantage of this is that we typically have a rich range of variables available and at least some of them are likely to be highly correlated with the survey variables of interest. Often, they are measures of exactly the same concept, relating to an earlier point in time.

3.9 ADJUSTMENT FOR NONRESPONSE

Understanding something about the nature of nonresponse and the likely impact of nonresponse error on survey estimates is important. But rather than simply describing it, it is better to adjust the estimates for it. This can be done quite simply using weighting. However, although it is simple to implement nonresponse weighting, it is not necessarily so easy to identify a *good* way of weighting amongst the possible ways that present themselves. Care is needed.

Consider again the data of Table 3.3. The response rate amongst sample members in category 1 was 91.1%. If we give each respondent in category 1 a weight of 100/91.1 (i.e. 1.098) in our analysis, and applied a similarly constructed weight to respondents in each of the other seven categories, then the categories would be represented in their correct (selected sample) proportions in the analysis. This makes intuitive sense, as every 91.1 respondents in category are in some sense representing 100 selected sample members, so they must be given extra weight to represent the additional missing 8.9 sample members. The weights will be greater the lower the response rate: in our example the largest weight is 1.678 for respondents in category 8.

After weighting has been applied, the nonresponse error that remains in a weighted estimator can be expressed as follows:

$$y_{rw} - y_n = \frac{1}{n} \sum_{h=1}^{H} nr_h \left(y_{r_h} - y_{nr_h} \right)$$

where there are H weighting classes, denoted $h = 1, \ldots , H$ ($H = 8$ in our example).

It can be seen that the error is now a weighted sum across the weighting classes of the difference in y between respondents and nonrespondents. In other words, the error no longer depends on differences *between* the classes, as this is what the weighting has corrected. The definition of the classes is therefore important. For nonresponse weighting to be successful, four criteria should be met: (a) Response rates should vary over the classes; (b) Values of target variables (y) should vary over the classes; (c) Respondents and nonrespondents should be similar to one another *within* each class (i.e. $y_{r_h} - y_{nr_h}$ should be small); (d) Class sample sizes should not be too small. When choosing between alternative ways of creating weighting classes, these criteria should provide guidance. Weighting is discussed in more detail by Biemer and Christ in Chapter 17. An important point to remember at this stage is that it will not be possible to implement effective weighting unless you have planned ahead and collected some of the kinds of data outlined in the previous section.

3.10 CONCLUSION

Nonresponse is important and there are many different ways in which it can arise. Equally importantly, there are many different things that we as survey researchers can do to combat the undesirable consequences of nonresponse. Almost every stage of the survey design and implementation process has the potential to affect nonresponse error. Consequently, we must keep the issue of nonresponse in mind at all times. When specifying the sample selection method, we should consider whether there are useful data that can be captured from the sampling frame and that will help us later with nonresponse analysis and possibly weighting. When designing field control documents and sample control systems, we should consider whether there are useful data that can be collected by interviewer observation or as indicators of the difficulty of obtaining a response from each unit. When recruiting and training interviewers, we should place an emphasis on the kind of social skills needed to avoid refusals and on working patterns that will minimize noncontacts. Data collection procedures should incorporate appropriate reminders or multiple attempts to contact sample members. Questionnaires should be attractive, interesting, and not too demanding or intrusive. And so on. There are many things we can do to minimize the impact of nonresponse and there are many success stories of surveys that have successfully improved response by reviewing their procedures and implementing a coherent set of changes.

Nonresponse will therefore be a theme throughout this book. In almost every chapter you will find references to it. Tackling nonresponse involves carrying out every stage of the survey in a thoughtful, careful and thorough manner. In short, good survey practice.

GLOSSARY OF KEY CONCEPTS

Adjustment. A term applied to a number of post fieldwork procedures, such as weighting and imputation, that can be used to reduce nonresponse error.
Noncontact. Failure to communicate with a selected sample unit and to inform the unit of their selection for the survey.
Nonresponse. Failure to obtain useable survey data from an eligible selected sample unit.
Nonresponse error. The difference between a survey estimate and the equivalent estimate that would have been obtained if all selected units had responded.
Refusal. A decision by a selected sample unit not to respond to the survey.

Chapter 4

Comparative Survey Research: Goals and Challenges

Janet A. Harkness

Director Survey Research and Methodology Program,
Director Gallup Research Center,
University of Nebraska-Lincoln, USA
Senior Scientist at ZUMA, Mannheim, Germanyy

4.1 INTRODUCTION

This chapter considers some of the key challenges to achieving comparability in deliberately designed cross-cultural and cross-national surveys. As the word challenge reflects, we focus on topics for which theoretical frameworks or current solutions are less than perfect. We spend some time therefore on issues of standardization and implementation, on question design and on question adaptation and translation. Among the topics not dealt with here, but of obvious relevance for comparative survey research, are sampling, analysis, instrument testing, study documentation, and ethical considerations. See Häder and Gabler (2003), Lynn, Häder, Gabler & Laaksonen (2007), Lepkowski (2005) on sampling in cross-national contexts; Saris (2003a, 2003b), Billiet (2003), van de Vijver (2003), and contributions in Hambleton, Merenda, & Spielberger (2005) cover important issues in instrument testing; on documentation see Mohler, Pennell & Hubbard (Chapter 21) and Mohler and Uher (2003) and on ethical considerations see Singer (Chapter 5).

Because numerous terms used in the chapter are understood in a variety of ways in different disciplines, we explain how these are used here. The term *comparative* is used to refer to any research that is designed to compare populations. The term *cross-cultural* is used to refer to research across cultural groups either within or across countries. *Cross-national* will be used as a general term for research involving more than one country or nation. Throughout the chapter the emphasis is on *multinational* surveys, that is, surveys across multiple countries or nations. In many instances multinational surveys are more complex than within-country cross-cultural research, but they have many basic challenges in common. *Multilingual* surveys are surveys conducted in numerous languages. These can obviously be cross-national studies but may also be national studies. For example, to collect data from multiple immigrant groups, the 2000 US Census was conducted in 6 languages and support was provided for 49 languages (www.facts.com/wusp3006y5.htm). In the Philippines, a country currently reckoned to have about 170 languages, International Social Survey Program (ISSP) modules are fielded using questionnaires in five languages. In South Africa, ISSP modules are fielded using five written translations and several orally translated versions (see Harkness, Schoebi, Joye, Mahler, Faass, & Behr, 2007, on quality issues in orally translated interviews). Multilingual surveys may or not be comparative with respect to questionnaire design; some may merely be translations of a survey designed for a single context. *Multiregional* surveys collect data at regional levels. The regions may be within-country regions but can also cover regions above the country level, such as southern Mesoamerica (including Nicaragua, Costa Rica, and Panama) versus northern Mesoamerica (covering Belize, Guatemala, and Mexico).

In the course of the chapter we refer to *source* questionnaires or languages and *target* questionnaires or languages. Following usage in the translation sciences, the source language is the language translated out, and the target language is the language translated into. *Questionnaire* is used here to refer to the set of questions that make up a study. This might consist of several sub-sets of questions. In some disciplines these would be called *instruments*, in others, *modules*. In this chapter, however, *instrument* is used as an alternative to *questionnaire*. Distinctions are also possible between *questions* and *items* and between *item scales* and question *batteries*. Thus a Likert-type format of a question might contain multiple statements (the items) that would be assumed to form a scale. Items grouped together for other reasons would simply form a set or battery. Finally, we use the term *general survey research* to refer to research and research methods in which (cross) cultural considerations play no deliberate, active role with regard to design or implementation.

4.2 GROWTH OF MULTINATIONAL, MULTILINGUAL SURVEYS

Into the 1970s, cross-national analyses were still often based on data collected at national level for national purposes that were recoded according to a comparative scheme developed ex post (cf. Gauthier, 2000; Rokkan, 1969). In the intervening decades, deliberately designed cross-national research has burgeoned in every field that uses survey data, with marked growth in the number, size and diversity of studies undertaken, the disciplines involved, the kinds of instruments used, and the cultures and languages accommodated. Twenty years ago, Parameswaran and Yaprak (1987, p35) emphasized the need for better cross-national measurements in consumer research in the face of "explosive growth in the multinationalization of business."

Data collected at national level for national purposes are also still used to make analyses at the supra-national level. Indeed, in developing countries, national data may be all that are available. Comparative uses of national data raise their own particular sets of problems. Mejer (2003), for example, discusses efforts to harmonize social statistics in the European Union; Smid and Hess (2003) discuss challenges related to cross-national market research, and Barnay, Jusot, Rochereau, & Sermet (2005) discuss the problems faced in trying to compare health data across different studies.

Multinational survey data are used both as primary sources of information and in combination with data from other sources such as official statistics, records, and specimens from people, places, or animals. Large-scale surveys and harmonized data studies provide cross-national data for key public domains; education and psychological testing, health, labor statistics, population demographics, and short and longer term economic indicators across multinational regions. In the private sector, data from global marketing studies, consumer surveys, establishment surveys, and media research inform production, planning, and resource allocation.

Changing patterns of immigration have increased cultural diversity in many developed countries and the need to collect accurate and reliable information has resulted in an increase in within-country multilingual research. Sometimes these studies aim to produce national estimates that are as unaffected as possible by bias related to culture and/or language differences. At other times, minority populations are deliberately targeted to gain insight into their living conditions, access to facilities, or family composition. In the coming decades, ensuring adequate language coverage in national surveys may become a pressing issue in some countries, as different linguistic communities do or do not gain high fluency in the country's majority language(s) and as the majority languages possibly cease to be that.

As in national research (cf. Converse and Presser, 1986), questions or questionnaires developed for one context are frequently used elsewhere. Sometimes the goal is to compare findings across studies. In other cases, questions are re-used simply because they have already proved themselves useful. As a result, translated questions may be used verbatim or in translation around the globe. Examples can be found in every discipline: indicators of economic development, of well-being, of product or service satisfaction, of socioeconomic status or human values, as well as medical diagnostic instruments, pain indexes, human skills and competence measurements, and personality assessment are used repeatedly in different contexts and languages throughout the world.

The need for global data has led to a new surge of interest in how best to undertake cross-cultural and cross-national survey research. Similar developments can be noted in the 1940s, in the 1960s and again in the 1980s (cf. for example, Hantrais & Mangen, 1996; Scheuch, 1990; Peschar, 1982; Armer & Grimshaw, 1973; Rokkan & Szczerba-Likiernik, 1968; Rokkan, 1962). Researchers entering the field of general survey research can draw on an array of guidelines, best practice standards, protocols for key procedures, and a rich survey methods literature. Unfortunately, there is not a correspondingly comprehensive and accessible set of tools and guidelines available for multinational survey research. It is therefore not easy for researchers entering comparative research to be sure how best to proceed. In the editors' preface to a book considering qualitative and quantitative research, Hantrais and Mangen note: "Notwithstanding this impressive outburst of research activity, it remains true that few social scientists have been trained to conduct studies that cross national boundaries and compare different cultures" (1996, p. 16).

Can researchers follow best practices as advocated in the general survey context? If so, why do these not always produce the results expected?

Must researchers be informed about the countries, cultures, and languages involved in order to conduct comparative research? What can they do to try to ensure that data collected are valid and reliable? Who can collect the data and how should this be done? Are there informed networks to approach for help? The remaining pages of the chapter address these and other questions.

4.3 TOWARD A COMPARATIVE RESEARCH METHODOLOGY

Discussions of comparative survey research often remark that all social science research is comparative and researchers have often debated whether there was anything particular or different about cross-national research (cf. Lynn, Lyberg & Japec, 2006; Øyen, 1990; Teune, 1990; Lipset, 1986; Grimshaw, 1973).

Acknowledging that social science research is based on comparison does not resolve the question whether different methods are needed for different forms of this research. As Johnson (1998, p. 1) notes: "A major source of the criticism directed at cross-cultural research, in fact, has been the uncritical adaptation of the highly successful techniques developed for monocultural surveys."

Multinational survey research has much in common with other survey research and researchers entering the field should therefore have a solid understanding of general survey research methods and the principles of research in their respective discipline. Nonetheless, we suggest that the methods and the perspectives required for comparative research differ in some respects from those of non-comparative research. In mono-cultural research, for example, questions mirroring the culture, containing culturally tailored language and content and possibly tapping culture-specific concepts, are likely to be the *successful* items. In comparative research, such questions would count as culturally biased and would require to be modified, or accommodated or possibly excluded in the analysis. In non-comparative research, valid and reliable data are critical. In comparative research, data must be valid and reliable for the given national context but must also be comparable across contexts.

At the same time, one can design and analyze comparative research without deciding whether the differences are truly qualitative or not. Grimshaw (1973, p. 4), for example, bridges the divide as follows: "My argument is that while the problems involved are no different in kind from those involved in domestic research, they are of such great magnitude as to constitute an almost qualitative difference for comparative, as compared to non-comparative research."

There *is* general agreement in the literature that multinational research is complex (e.g., Lynn et al, 2006; Øyen, 1990; Kohn, 1987; Grimshaw, 1973; Verba, 1971; Zeldich, 1971). In addition, as Kohn (1987) points out, it is also expensive. Nevertheless, the increased complexity and costs of multinational research are not always matched by an increased sophistication of methods. In fact, the methods adopted in multinational survey research frequently do not reflect more recent developments in general survey methodology. With the exception of Quality of Life research (cf. Skevington, 2002; Murphy, Schofield & Herrman, 1999), few comparative studies report using cognitive testing, focus group input, expert consultations or extensive pre-testing to develop questions (cf. Smith, 2004). In addition, standards accepted as best practice in survey research at the national level, are often not targeted in multinational research (Harkness, 1999; Johnson, 1998; Jowell, 1998). It may be difficult in the multinational context to find sufficient funding to meet such standards, in that everything has to be paid for multiple times. Many multinational studies certainly do not pre-test *draft* versions of the source questionnaire in multiple countries because of the costs this would incur for translation of questions that might never be used. Translated versions of the *finalized* source questionnaire may be pre-tested, as in the European Social Survey, but such pre-tests are not intended to contribute to source questionnaire development. In addition, as Lynn (2003a) notes, the variability of features in the cross-national context makes it more difficult to set common standards. Documentation of procedures may also be poor (see, for example, Herdman, Fox-Rushbie & Badia, 1997, on translation procedures and their documentation; Harkness, 1999, on quality monitoring; Mohler and Uher, 2003, on general documentation in the comparative context).

4.4 COMPARABILITY AND EQUIVALENCE

In cross-national research, the pursuit of data quality is simultaneously the pursuit of data comparability. Comparability is often discussed in the literature in terms of equivalence. Johnson (1998) counts 52 definitions of equivalence within the social and behavioral sciences. In many instances, functional equivalence, understood as having questions perform in the same way across different populations is targeted through question translation, and numerous kinds of translation equivalence are referred to in survey literature. However, as Snell-Hornby (1988) indicates, the translation sciences also use the term equivalence in multiple ways. In this chapter, when referring to the fact that properties of data, questions, meanings or populations, and so forth admit and justify comparison, we prefer to use the term *comparability*.

Researchers use whatever means are available to try to ensure that data from different populations do permit comparison. A strategy frequently adopted is to keep as much in the project as similar as possible, for example, to ask the same questions, to use the same method of data collection, to standardize interviewing methods with a view to reducing variance in interviewer effects, and to use probability sampling designs. In practice, it is neither possible nor always desirable to implement the same detailed protocols everywhere. For instance, the legal definition of what counts as a refusal and whether refusals can be converted varies from location to location. Properly speaking, anyone declining to participate in Germany is a refusal. Once coded as such, the person should not be re-approached. In other locations, saying no need not immediately count as a final refusal, hence the concept of refusal conversion. The greater restrictions in some locations on interaction with targeted sample units can obviously affect response rates considerably.

4.5 STANDARDIZATION AND STUDY SPECIFICATIONS

The goal of standardization is to enhance comparability; inappropriate standardization may do just the opposite. Appropriate standardization is thus crucial. Because it is neither desirable nor feasible to keep everything the same, study designers have to identify what must be standardized to ensure comparability and at what level this standardization should take place. However, standardization, in particular with respect to data collection procedures and protocols, is an area in which much must still be shared and learned. The following examples illustrate some of the problems.

Some places are inaccessible in winter, others again only properly accessible during winter; Chile is only one example of a country with many climate zones. Thus deciding to standardize fielding periods rigidly can be impractical and disadvantageous. Cultures also differ in the times at which they eat, sleep, work, and so forth. As a result, fixing contact times rigidly across countries would be counterproductive. Thus decisions about the best time, say, to contact sample units must take local conditions into account.

At the same time, awareness of strategies to optimize contact attempts may differ from survey culture to survey culture. It may therefore be important to negotiate minimum contact requirements for every location and to discuss and share tactics known to have worked for other locations. In this way, local conditions can be taken into account and information also shared about strategies that have been used in various contexts. Since procedures that are unfamiliar may at first be declared unsuitable or impractical, it is also important to strike a balance between recognizing local constraints and encouraging local actors to adopt or adapt useful techniques.

A complicating factor in this is that one and the same procedure may produce different effects in different contexts. The Swedish participants in the 2002 European Social Survey (ESS) were convinced they could increase response by making advance telephone contact. French agencies sometimes make the same point. Blohm and Koch (2004), on the other hand, found that advance contact by telephone in the German context reduced the propensity of people to participate. Such findings may reflect cultural differences in norms of communication or in the use of the telephone, or simply reflect interviewer proficiency or preferences.

Decisions about standardization determine the specifications for a study. *Study specifications* are intended to be explicit descriptions of the design and implementation requirements that hold for all participants. They can also specify the means by which different steps are to be achieved (e.g., whether contact can be made by mail, phone, or only in person). Examples of mostly top-down specifications for a European social science study can be found on the ESS web site (European Social Survey site: www.europeansocialsurvey.org).

The challenges involved in implementing decisions and in monitoring compliance with specifications should not be underestimated. Misunderstanding of specifications, or the goal of these specifications, is likely to lead to non-compliance. Intensive discussion of the meaning of specifications and the steps needed to implement them will often be the only route to full understanding.

The desire to excel and to be seen as excelling, often coupled with a lack of expertise in one or more areas, may also encourage non-compliance with required specifications. Here too, we lack a general handbook of shared experience, lessons learned and of "how-to-do-despites."

In top-down designs, external design requirements are fixed first (e.g., face-to-face interviewing) and specifications at national levels articulated later. In a bottom-up approach, conditions at local levels shape the formulation of the general study specifications (e.g., the likelihood of third party presence in interviews determines the design). The most viable mix will often lie somewhere between, with general requirements deciding critical specifications (e.g., that multiple contact attempts are made) although local constraints inform how specific these requirements are and shape the protocols for local elaborations or deviations. Special efforts may be needed to ensure that accurate information about local constraints is collected. Some studies are fortunate enough to be able to finance international meetings of participating teams or visits by information-gathering teams to local sites. Less well-funded projects need to exchange information by other means. Some form of E-conferencing could be useful here. Distributing information collected to all involved can actually stimulate further input. Indeed, some participating units (countries or minorities) may only fully recognize it is appropriate for them to contribute once they see input from other participants. Here too, unfamiliarity can foster uncertainty and rejection, a point to be considered in deciding which specifications are truly viable and which not.

4.6 DESIGNING QUESTIONS

This section describes basic approaches used to design questions in comparative research. At present, we lack an overarching framework for how to apply what we know about question design from general survey research to comparative contexts. The literature on specifics of question design in the comparative context is thus somewhat fragmentary. Moreover, approaches differ depending on the discipline and on the type of instrument involved.

Although he does not address the issue of a general framework, Smith (2003, 2004) provides numerous useful examples and extensive references for individual aspects of questions that may be affected by cultural and linguistic issues, from response scale design, to layout and visual aids, to wording, ambiguity and social desirability. A number of health and education projects also outline their particular models of question design in some detail (e.g., the EORTC Quality of Life guidelines described by Blazeby, Sprangers, Cull, Groenvold, & Bottomley, 2002 and the TIMMS and PISA websites[1]). Harkness, van de VIjver, and Johnson (2003) provide a general overview of question design models that is in part followed in this chapter. Braun and

---

[1] Trends in International Mathematics and Science Study (TIMSS) site: http://timss.bc.edu;_Programme for International Student Assessment (PISA) site: http://www.pisa.org.

Harkness (2005) discuss the interdependence of meaning and context, indicating how differences in socio-cultural context affect how a respondent perceives what a question means. Culture can determine whether information is considered relevant (cf. Smith, Christofer & McCormick, 2004 for health issues among American Indian women). Schwarz (2003) reports differences across cultures in response to the same response scale stimuli; and Haberstroh, Oyserman, Schwarz, Kühnen, and Ji (2001) illustrate how design modifications can affect what is often assumed to be cultural response behavior. Anderson (1967) and Tanzer (2005) illustrate how comparative design needs to consider visual aspects of instrument design. Authors in Hoffmeyer-Zlotnik and Wolf (2003) and in Hoffmeyer-Zlotnik and Harkness (2005) discuss design and comparability issues for so-called background variables such as income, education, religion, occupation, and race and ethnicity.

Response scales and response styles are more frequently discussed topics. Authors such as Lee, Rancourt, & Särndal (2002) and Chen, Lee, & Stevenson (1995) discuss difficulties encountered in trying to replicate features of Likert-type scales in Asian languages. Ewing et al (2002) discusses four different response scales in the cross-national advertising context; Skevington and Tucker (1999) describe the WHOQOL approach to answer scale development; Johnson, Kulesa, Cho, & Shavitt (2005), Johnson and van de Vijver (2003), Gibbons et al (1999), Baumgartner and Steenkamp (2001), and Javeline (1999) discuss different aspects of social desirability, response styles, and acquiescence in cross-cultural contexts.

Pre-testing is part of questionnaire design refinement. Smith (2004, p. 450f) reviews current practices in cross-national testing and notes that "most cross-national studies fail to devote adequate time and resources to pretesting." When pretesting is conducted, techniques developed in general survey research are applied to instruments intended for cross-cultural implementation. In various places we discussed the interdependence of cultural context and cultural meaning and how this determines whether questions are understood or understood in the same way across cultures. Such cultural differences carry over into discourse. We must therefore be wary about assuming that pragmatic features of discourse are also shared across contexts, assuming, for example, that a sensitive question calling for covert disclosure in context A is sensitive and requires covert disclosure in context B (cf. Kim, 1994, Smith et al, 2004). Recent descriptions of cognitive pretesting, mainly for minority populations in the United States context, are Warnecke & Schwarz (1997), Miller (2003), Willis (2004) and Goerman (2006). Schmidt and Bullinger (2003) point to perceived inequalities in QoL research with regard to within-country testing for minorities. Harkness, van de Vijver, & Johnson (2003) and Harkness and Schoua-Glusberg (1998) outline various techniques used in different disciplines for testing translated questions.

4.6.1 Basic Options for Design

In producing questions for multinational implementation, question design teams have three basic decisions to make. First, they can decide to ask the *same* questions of every population or they can decide to ask *different* questions of each. A mixed approach based on these choices can combine a set of country-common questions with other country-specific questions. This is sometimes called an emic-etic approach (see 4.6.3). A second and related decision is whether researchers want to *adopt* existing questions (i.e., replicate), *adapt* existing questions (i.e., modify) or, alternatively, *develop new* questions for their study. In many instances, all three strategies may be used in one study. Harkness, van de Vijver, & Johnson (2003) outline the advantages and disadvantages associated with each option: adapting, adopting and writing new questions. Thirdly, researchers also implicitly or explicitly decide on the degree of cross-cultural input they intend to target in their instrument development (see 4.6.2).

    Much survey research, comparative or not, is based on using existing questions verbatim for new studies or in modified, adapted form. Questions are often replicated, for example, to compare measurement across time. However, questions may also be modified to accommodate new needs or new contexts. For example, instruments developed for adults can be adapted for children (cf. de Leeuw & Hox, 2004); questions that have become out-dated can be up-dated (Porst and Jers, 2005); or instruments designed for business and commerce can be tailored for use in an academic setting.

    In the cross-cultural context, researchers also prefer to use existing questions verbatim or, if this is not possible, in an adapted form. Close translation has traditionally been preferred to more free translation. In each case the assumption is that closely translated questions will succeed in conveying the same stimulus for a new population. Harkness (2003) and Harkness, Pennell, & Schoua-Glusberg (2004) discuss the general challenges of such close translation. As Peschar (1982, p. 65) notes: "However, a literal translation of items and questionnaires does not guarantee the equivalence of instruments…Therefore *functional equivalence* is a much more important objective in comparative research" (emphasis original). Greenfield (1997), Herdman et al (1997), and Herdman, Fox-Rushby, & Badia (1998) are skeptical about how suitable translated survey instruments are for new contexts.

4.6.2 Simultaneous, Parallel and Sequential Approaches

Cross-cultural Quality of Life (QoL) research distinguishes between *sequential*, *parallel* and *simultaneous* approaches to question design. Differences can be found in the way the terms are used and explained in the QoL literature (cf. Skevington 2002; Bullinger, 2004; Anderson , Aronson & Wilkin, 1993; van Widenfelt, Treffers, de Beurs, Siebelink & Koudijs, 2005; the Medical Outcomes Trust Bulletin, 1997) and we do not attempt to resolve these here.

    Generally speaking, the terms reflect something about when cultural considerations are considered in questionnaire design, how these are taken into account, and whether the questionnaires in different languages that aim to be functionally equivalent are translations of a source instrument or developed by other means. Simultaneous development targets the highest degree of cross-cultural involvement and sequential development the least. The simultaneous approaches described in QoL literature may aim to have each culture develop its own questions or to have repeated and considerable cross-cultural discussion of a common set of items. The initial draft items may stem from different cultures and languages. Descriptions of elaborate QoL multi-stage approaches can be found, for example, in Bullinger (2004), Skevington (2002, 2004) and the WHOQOL Group (1994). Parallel designs target cross-cultural input early in the conceptual and question development stages or a common instrument. This is sometimes achieved by collecting items from all the participating countries (cf. Bullinger, 2004) or, as in the ISSP, by having a multi-cultural drafting group develop a set of questions of less varied origin. Sequential models focus on having different populations asked the same questions, with little emphasis at the question development stage on cross-cultural input. Further details are provided later.

4.6.3 Ask-Different-Questions Models

One of the great appeals of asking different questions is that one does not need to translate. Another attractive feature of Ask-Different-Questions (ADQ) models is that the country-specific questions used can relate directly to the issues, terminology and perspectives salient for a given culture and language. A third advantage is that the development of a questionnaire can be undertaken as and when needed. Countries might therefore develop their instruments at the same time (in a sense, simultaneously) or, if joining an existing project at a later date, develop their own country-specific and country-relevant questions as these are required. ADQ approaches are sometimes described as functional equivalence strategies. However, because the questions in any kind of comparative study are required to be functionally equivalent, we have coined the term ADQ. A basic procedure is as follows:

- The design team decides on the concepts and constructs to be investigated and any other design specifications they might make;
- Country– or population-specific questions are designed that collect the locally relevant information for a given construct;
- Versions for different countries and languages can be produced in a collective effort or developed by different teams as the need arises.

A practical example illustrates how ADQ might work and also highlights challenges incipient in the approach. (British) *trousers*, (Scottish) *kilt*, and (Indian) *dhoti* could be considered to be functionally equivalent articles of male apparel, all being coverings for the lower part of the body. Distinctions among them exist nonetheless, such as the contexts in which the garment might be worn (everyday wear vs. festive occasions) or the degree of leg coverage afforded. Such differences might be relevant for some comparisons and irrelevant for others. In similar fashion, the following questions might all be effective indicators of the concept of intelligence for individual populations: Is she quick-witted?, Does she give considered responses?, Is she good at knowing whom to ask for help?, and Is she good at finding solutions to urgent problems? However, in formulating the most salient questions for each local context and thereby focusing on different kinds of intelligence, the degree of overlap in the construct of intelligence across populations might be greatly reduced (cf.

Brislin, 1986). A further drawback is that ADQ designs do not permit the item-for-item comparison that underlies full scalar equivalence. As a result, demonstrating equivalence across populations at pretesting stages and in analysis is more complicated, in particular if multiple countries are involved.

The notions of *emic* and *etic* concepts and emic and etic indicators (questions) are basic to much of the discussion of ADQ models. We note that the terms emic and etic are used differently in different fields (cf. Headland, Pike & Harris, 1990; Serpell, 1990). Simply put, emic questions are population-specific in relevance and etic questions are universal in relevance. In similar fashion, emic concepts are concepts considered salient for one population and etic concepts are considered to be universal. If an ADQ study uses emic questions to tap a construct/concept assumed to be etic and analysis demonstrates this is the case, the literature speaks of a *"derived* etic". When researchers decide to ask the *same* question of different populations, they assume the question has etic status. Here the literature speaks of an imposed etic, reflecting the top-down approach taken. Prominent early advocates of emic-etic approaches were the psychologist Triandis (1972) and the political scientists Przeworski and Teune (cf. 1966, 1970). Brislin (1980) provides a useful discussion of the advantages and potential drawbacks to early emic-etic approaches. Johnson (1998) refers to a number of studies using variations of the emic-etic approach; van Deth (1998) advocates a functionally equivalent approach in deciding which questions to analyze. A recent two-language application is described in Potaka and Cochrane (2004).

Sometimes a mixed emic-etic approach is used, in which a common core of etic questions, shared across countries, is combined with country-specific emic questions to provide better country-specific coverage of the concepts of interest (see, for example, Berry, 1969; van de Vijver, 2003). Finally, we note that ADQ formats are involved in collecting socio-demographic information whenever population-specific formulations are the best option. Sometimes such questions are blends of translation and country-specific formulations. Educational questions asking for highest qualifications, for example, might begin with the same question text (translated) and continue with a list of the qualifications or school types pertinent for a given educational system.

4.6.4 Ask the Same Question

One general drawback in trying to develop shared questions for multiple populations is that the questions may become less specific than would questions designed for a national study. This may result in inadequate coverage of the construct to be measured and in construct bias (cf. van de Vijver, 2003). Country-specific questions can sometimes be added to counteract this, as mentioned earlier in connection with the emic-etic mixed approach. Ask the same question (ASQ) approaches can differ in the degree of cultural input targeted during development. In terms of QoL literature, they might then be described as simultaneous, parallel, or sequential models.

Sequential ASQ approaches: In a sequential ASQ approach, a source questionnaire is developed and finalized before other versions are produced as translations of the source questions. In this approach, multicultural considerations are basically addressed at the translation stage. The success or failure of an ASQ sequential approach is largely determined by the suitability of the source questions for all the cultures for which versions will be produced. Without cross-cultural input, however, the questions chosen may be culturally biased. Not surprisingly, criticism of sequential ASQ models focuses on the lack of cross-cultural input at the initial stages of development (for example, Skevington 2002; Camfield, 2003; Ponce, Lavarreda, Yen, Brown, DiSagra, & Satter, 2004). Despite such criticism, sequential ASQ procedures are those most frequently adopted in multinational surveys. Questionnaires developed for one context that are translated at some later date for fielding with a population requiring a different language do not count as *designed* for comparative use; they are simply used in different contexts and languages.

Simultaneous ASQ approaches: In a simultaneous ASQ approach, the questions in different languages are generated together. Classic *decentring* is a procedure that produces questionnaires in two languages more or less at the same time. The goal is to arrive ultimately at items in two languages that are felt to correspond without allowing any one language or culture to dominate. Decentring as a question design procedure is not used widely in survey research. However, the term is also sometimes used to refer to adaptation procedures such as discussed in 4.8. Decentring is one of several design procedures that involves the use of translation. Uses of translation to *develop* questions are distinct from translations made simply to produce new language versions needed. These last are discussed in 4.7.

Decentring can begin with existing questions or, alternatively, with a list of concepts for which questions are to be devised. If questions are the starting point, these will change in the process of decentring. As a result, questions cannot be replicated and simultaneously decentred. There are various ways to proceed within classic decentring; we describe only one option here. The procedure for each question can begin in either language:

- A question is devised or chosen in language A and translated into language B. This translation is only the first step towards removing cultural anchoring; thus no emphasis is placed on close translation;
- Multiple paraphrases or further translations are generated for the translated item in language B;
- Paraphrases for the first item are also produced in language A;
- Anything that causes problems in either language with regard to matching or producing a paraphrase or translation is altered or removed. In this way, culturally anchored obstacles are eliminated from the sets of items generated;
- The sets in each language are appraised and the two items considered to match best are chosen as the comparable questions.

Decentring provides researchers with a means of avoiding language and cultural dominance. However, because it removes culturally specific material, it may result in a loss of specificity and saliency. As a result, questions may be less appropriate for fielding in both contexts than emic items would be. As may be apparent, classic decentring is not suitable for simultaneous production of multiple translations. Apart from the practical difficulty of attempting this process across twelve languages and cultures, construct coverage, indicator saliency and comparability would be at risk.

Parallel ASQ approaches: Parallel models incorporate cross-cultural input in formulating and selecting draft questions. This input can take the form of advance consultation with local experts, their involvement in the drafting group, or strategies such as incorporating questions from all participating countries in the item pool from which source questions are selected. In other respects, the parallel ASQ approach may resemble the sequential ASQ; a source questionnaire is finalized and any other versions needed are produced on the basis of translation.

Parallel ASQ approaches that ensure adequate cross-cultural co-operation at the conceptualization, drafting, and testing stages may offer a viable compromise between the lack of cultural input in sequential approaches and the complex and expensive demands of simultaneous approaches. At the same time, if discussion and testing of the material and questions is conducted in only one language, problems for cross-cultural implementation may be overlooked. Harkness and Schoua-Glusberg (1998), Braun and Harkness (2005) and Harkness, Schoebi, Joye, Mohler, Faass, & Behr (2007) discuss using advance translation as a means to counteract source questionnaire language dominance.

4.7 TRANSLATING SURVEY INSTRUMENTS

Translation plays a key role in most cross-lingual survey projects. Poor translations can rob researchers of the chance to ask the questions they intend and need to ask. At the same time, projects are often reluctant to invest effort, time or funds in translation procedures. This reluctance is sometimes encouraged by bad past experience with professional translators who proved unable to produce the kind of translations needed. Moreover, because survey questions often look deceptively simple, the temptation to do-it-yourself may also be high. A strategy sometimes adopted does without a written translation and instead has bilingual interviewers translate orally whenever necessary.

The important thing to note is that the effort and cost of producing and testing translations are small, compared to the financial investment made in developing and fielding instruments. In contrast, the price to be paid for poor translations can be high. If poorly translated or adapted questions must be discarded at the analysis stage for even one country, these are lost for analysis across all countries.

4.7.1 Current Good Practice for Translation

In the last decade or so, conceptions of best and good practice regarding survey translation have changed noticeably, as have preferred strategies and the technology used. Translation guidelines published by the US Bureau of Census

(Pan & de la Puente, 2005; de la Puente, Pan, & Rose, 2003), by the European Social Survey (Harkness, 2002/2007) and by Eurostat for health surveys (Tafforeau, López Cobo, Tolonen, Scheid-Nave, & Tinto,, 2005) reflect considerable agreement on how to produce and test translated questions. We summarize here key points on which there is growing consensus:

- A range of expertise is needed to produce a successful survey translation product. This includes expertise in survey questionnaire design, substantive understanding of the subject, source and target language competence, translation training and expertise, and knowledge of the local fielding situation. Translators cannot provide all of these;

- Team approaches, such as described below, have been increasingly advocated as a practical way to bring together the necessary competence;

- Translation teams should consist of those who translate, those who review translations and those who take the final decisions on versions (adjudicators). Consultants for specific aspects can be brought in as required (e.g., on adaptation issues).

- Translators should be skilled practitioners who have received training on translating questionnaires and should normally translate out of the source language into their strongest language. Reviewers need to have at least as good translation skills as the translators but should be familiar with questionnaire design principles, as well as the study design and topic. Adjudicators make final decisions about which translation options to adopt. They do this in cooperation with reviewer and translators, or at least in discussion with a reviewer. Adjudicators must (a) understand the research subject, (b) know about the survey design, and (c) be proficient in the languages involved;

- It is better to use several translators rather than just one, not only in projects where regional variation is expected within the translated language. (cf. Harkness, 2002/2007);

- Wherever feasible, each translator should make a draft translation. The alternative is to have each translator do a section. (See Harkness, 2002/2007; Harkness & Schoua-Glusberg, 1998 on such "split" translation techniques.);

- Translators should be part of the review team and not only employed as translators;

- Translation and adaptation go hand-in-hand (see 4.8);

- Translated questionnaires should be assessed using both quantitative and qualitative procedures (cf. suggestions in Harkness et al, 2004; Harkness & Schoua-Glusberg, 1998; Smith, 2004);

- Translated questionnaires should be pre-tested for the intended population;

- Performance and output should be checked at an early stage in the project when feedback can lead to improvement and save time;

- Team members should be briefed on tasks and responsibilities.

For translators this may include briefing on questionnaires and applications, the mode of data collection, the target audience and required level of vocabulary (see Harkness, 2002/2007). Reviewers should be briefed on their role in reconciling the requirements of question design and those of translation as well as on monitoring translation output. Adjudicators may need to be briefed on the potential and the limitations of translation as a procedure. All may need clarification on types of adaptation (see 4.8):

- Translators and reviewers should take notes on any points of deliberation to inform review and adjudication and to facilitate version documentation;
- Documentation tools should be used to facilitate review and adjudication. These tools often combine translations, source text and note-taking in one document. Examples are provided on the web;
- Translation costs and time should be explicitly included in the study design and budget;
- The planning for translation should identify all the components that may require translation.

Apart from instruments themselves, descriptions of research projects, information leaflets, interviewer manuals, technical fielding reports, pretesting schedules, focus group reports or schedules, and responses to open-coded questions may require translation.

4.7.2 How A Team Approach Works: The Example Of TRAPD

Translation procedures in the ESS comprise a five-step iterative process of **T**ranslation, **R**eview, **A**djudication, **P**re-testing and **D**ocumentation (TRAPD)[1]. Much of the work leading to a final translation is a team effort. Those involved take one or more of the three different roles mentioned earlier: translator, reviewer, and adjudicator. Consultants are recruited as necessary. Approaches of this sort often merge review and adjudication wholly or in part, depending on the expertise of the team and on practical and logistical considerations. The main steps and strategies are presented later; a detailed account, also dealing with sharing languages and splitting translations, is available on the ESS website provided earlier.

- ESS countries are usually required to produce two draft translations. Each translator produces a draft translation independently;
- At a review meeting, translators and a reviewer go through the questionnaire question by question, discussing translated versions and agreeing on a review version;
- Translators and reviewers take notes on unresolved issues and on any compromise decisions;

---

[1] Pretesting and documentation steps of TRAPD are not fully implemented in the ESS. Participating countries do not pretest the draft source questionnaire, only their translated versions of the finalized source questionnaire. The opportunity to change source questions is thus restricted. The degree of documentation provided by countries on translation also varies in the ESS.

- Adjudication can be part of the review process, in which case the adjudicator attends the review session. Alternatively, adjudication is undertaken at a further meeting between reviewer and adjudicator, possibly with consultants and translators attending;
- Adaptations a country wishes to make in its translation have to be approved by the central co-ordinator of the ESS;
- Countries sharing a language are encouraged to collaborate after they produce their national draft translation(s). In this way, country A can benefit from solutions found by country B. Unnecessary differences can also be avoided.

For more information on team approaches to translation see Harkness and Schoua-Glusberg (1998), Harkness et al (2004) and, explicitly on the ESS, Harkness (2002/2007).

4.7.3 Back Translation

The homepage of the Australian Institute of Interpreters and Translators (AUSIT[1], 2007), the Australian national association for the translating and interpreting professions, has this to say about back translation: "Contrary to popular opinion, having someone translate a translation back into its original tells you nothing about the quality of the first translation. There are better ways to find out whether you're getting what you paid for." The history of back translation and how it came to be the most frequently mentioned survey translation assessment procedure is complex. As described in 4.6.4, decentring uses a form of back and forth translation and paraphrase to develop questions, although not to assess translations as such. This may explain why back translation is often but incorrectly referred to as a translation approach. Whatever the reason, in the social and behavioral sciences back translation is used primarily as a procedure to assess translations.

At its very simplest, the idea is that by translating the target translation back into the source language researchers can compare two versions in a language they understand (the source language version produced in the back translation and the original source language version) and decide on that basis about the quality of a translation in a language they do not understand.

Currently, back translation is the issue on which guidelines possibly differ most. The ESS only mentions back translation in passing, whereas the US Bureau of Census explicitly states it does not recommend back translation. The International Test Commission is less positive about back translation, as reflected in keynote presentations at the 2006 International Test Commission conference in Brussels. The Eurostat guidelines on health surveys mentioned earlier (Tafforeau et al., 2005) recommend back translation but also note that views on its usefulness differ. Somers (2005) discusses how even back translated machine translations do not indicate whether the quality of the first translation is good or not. One example of commercial company statements on the pitfalls of back translation can be found on the Barinas Translation

---

[1] http://www.ausit.org/eng/showpage.php3?id=648. Accessed July 2007.

Consultants website.[1]

Early advocates of back translation suggested it was a useful assessment tool but were careful to also mention that it had limitations, even if, in our view, such comments reassert a basic usefulness (e.g., Brislin 1970, 1976 and 1986). Throughout the years researchers have expressed misgivings about back translation (Geisinger, 1994; McKenna and Doward, 2005). Recent criticism has emphasized that, since the target language text is the real object of interest, review procedures should focus on this text and not source language texts (Harkness & Schoua-Glusberg, 1998). At the same time, the frequency with which back translation is mentioned in the literature makes it difficult for researchers not to be seen adhering to what has become received practice. As a result, quite elaborate procedures have developed around back translation; either further detailing back translation procedures or adding other assessment procedures before and after back translation (e.g., Sperber , DeVellis, & Boehlecke, 1994; de Mello Alves, Chor, Faerstein, De Lopes,, & Guilherme, 2004).

Although back translation is not a procedure suited to finding subtle but important differences between questions, only targeted research can properly identify which assessment procedures are most useful in which contexts. Targeted research projects comparing back translation with other strategies will doubtless be needed to clarify the effectiveness and costs of alternatives available.

4.8 ADAPTING SOURCE QUESTIONS IN COMPARATIVE CONTEXTS

In terms of source question design, adaptation is the second most popular strategy after replication. In this instance, existing questions are modified and used as the source questions for translations. Such adapted questions are new questions and need to be treated and tested as such.

While translation always involves some kinds of adaptation, adaptation does not necessarily involve translation. In this section, we discuss adaptations of translated questions, not adaptations to source questions. These adaptations are triggered by the act of switching languages, and not by differences in the sociocultural settings and populations.

Educational testing and health research have paid more attention to certain forms of instrument adaptation than have other disciplines (see, for example, Hambleton, 2005; Cook, Schmitt-Cascallar, & Brown, 2005; Chrostowski & Malak, 2003). In fact, the International Testing Commission Guidelines for test adaptation prefer the term adaptation rather than translation because it is "broader and more reflective of what should happen in practice when preparing a test that is constructed in one language and culture for use in a second language and culture. …Test translation is only one of the steps…and…adaptation is often a more suitable term than translation to

---

[1] http://www.barinas.com/myths.htm

describe the actual process…" (Hambleton, 2005, p. 4). At the same time, no discipline has developed either a systematic analysis of the kinds of adaptation needed for instruments or a detailed description of the strategies that can be used to adapt and test appropriately. In the following paragraphs we present simple examples of some the basic forms of adaptation encountered in comparative instrument-based research (cf. Harkness, 2004, 2006).

Language-driven adaptation: Because translation entails change, all translated questions are in some sense adapted questions. Thus recommendations to keep things the same in translation are bound to fail. Words change, sentence structure changes, the organization of information changes, sound systems change, alphabets change, and the frequency of occurrence of sounds letters and words changes. Comparative linguistics abounds with discussion of differences and similarities between languages. Strictly language-driven changes are fairly predictable instances of adaptation. For example, the English *twenty-eight* is "eight and twenty" in German. Such lexical and structural differences across languages can pose problems for comparability. Thus achieving a good rendering of a source question that accommodates language-driven change and maintains required measurement properties is often a major challenge.

Sociocultural, system-driven adaptation: Measurement systems are a good example of this kind of adaptation (yards, pounds, fahrenheit vs. metres, kilos, centigrade), as are functionally equivalent institutions (parliamentary elections, primary school, Value Added Tax vs. presidential elections, grade school, and purchase tax). Depending on the purpose of a question, adaptations might be simple or complex. Some, such as distance measurements in inches or centimeters, could be directly calibrated if that were necessary or roughly matched if that were sufficient. Hanh et al. (2005) report that the Adolescent Duke Health Profile question *Can you run 100 metres?* was adapted for Vietnam to ask *Can you run 100 metres or the distance between 3 light poles?* The Vietnamese researchers were uncertain that respondents would understand the distance correctly and offered a locally salient approximation. Whereas light poles were the adaptation for Vietnam, something different might be required for rural Africa (for further examples, see Harkness, 2004).

Adaptation to maintain or reduce level of difficulty: Educational tests are biased if it is easier for one population to have access to the knowledge tested or perform the task required than it is for another population of equal ability. Knowledge questions are thus sometimes adapted to maintain the same level of difficulty across different populations. Language-based memory and vocabulary tests also need to accommodate differing average lengths of words and the relative frequency and difficulty of words chosen across languages. Depending on the test, other aspects, such as ease of pronunciation or visual complexity, might bias recall, repetition or interpretation. In social science, reducing respondent burden is more the issue; adjustments are thus often made to the level of vocabulary used in a translation for populations with expected low levels of education.

Adaptation to ensure local coverage of a concept: Health research has become increasingly cognizant of the fact that translated questions may not ask for the local information needed to ascertain the presence of a given medical condition (Rogler, 1999; Cheng, 2001; Bolton, 2001; Andary, Stolk, & Klimidid, 2003). The 2000 version of the Diagnostic and Statistical Manual of Mental Diseases, for example, includes localized indicators for depression not present in earlier versions (Cheung, 2004). Similar needs of local or localized questions to improve construct or concept coverage could be identified for many areas—for political or social commitment, religious identification or environmental perceptions and behaviors.

Adaptation to ensure questions are understood as intended: Vision assessment questions are sometimes formulated along the lines of *Do you have difficulty reading a newspaper, even with spectacles?* Such questions assume that respondents are literate, that is, can read, have access to newspapers and, if their vision is impaired, also have access to corrective aids. Someone who is illiterate, for example, might understand the questions as one about whether they know how to read. If newspapers or access to eye care are not readily accessible, other unintended readings of the question could become salient. The question would thus need to be adapted or possibly reframed entirely.

Adaptation related to cultural norms of communication and disclosure: Speech communities differ in how they frame and conduct communication. Depending on cultural expectations regarding politeness, more or less overt expressions of politeness may be required (polite imperatives, apologies for asking a question, etc). A question about female personal hygiene, for example, begins in Asian countries with an apology for asking the question. This is not found in the corresponding English question. In a similar fashion, populations unfamiliar with the survey question and answer game may need more explanation and more directions about what to do than survey-savvy populations would.

Adapting design features: Changes in the design of an instrument can be motivated by many factors including a number mentioned earlier. The direction languages are read or written in, familiarity with certain visual representations (thermometers, faces) and an array of culturally anchored conventions related to visual presentation including color symbolism may call for design adaptation (cf. Tanzer, 2005 on diagram processing). Lexicon (a language's vocabulary) and grammar may also motivate a change in design. For example, the English mid-scale response category *neither agree nor disagree* is rendered in Hebrew ISSP questionnaires as "in the middle". A word-for-word equivalent of the English *neither agree or disagree* in Hebrew would produce "no agree no no agree". Because this means as little in Hebrew as it does in English, a functionally equivalent label is used instead. As things stand, little is known about the effects of changing response scale formats across languages.

The examples presented here are simple; adaptation issues can quickly become quite complex. If information about adaptations and the rationale behind them were drawn together in a databank, it would be possible to learn more about regularities in adaptation needs. In this way a typology could gradually be developed for different disciplines. A cognitive testing report databank called Q-Bank that is being developed by U.S. government agencies could serve as a model for such work. Longer term, such information on adaptations could inform revision and adaptation practices.

4.9 CONCLUSION AND OUTLOOK

The volume of comparative survey research has been growing for decades and the need for global data has never been greater. It is hard to imagine a field which does not use survey data in one form or another. As comparative research projects become increasingly ambitious, technological developments in applications and documentation have increased the power of tools and reduced the effort involved. At the same time, the methodological research needed to inform essential procedures for comparative research has not yet been systematically addressed. As Harkness and colleagues (2003) note, comparative research challenges described in literature of vintage date have still not been systematically addressed.

This chapter focused on important issues for which answers, partial or not, must still be found. There is a good sense in some sections of the research community about what the key comparative methodological issues are and how these might be tackled. A number of the problems faced are, in fact, problems shared across disciplines. On these fronts an increase in cross-disciplinary exchange and collaboration could markedly accelerate progress. Initiatives on different aspects of comparative research could, for example, pool findings, and benefit mutually.

Research on modes in survey research programs such as the ESS and the ISSP could also be shared, as could the work in the ISSP methods work groups on demographic variables, on translation, and on question design. By testing hypotheses and methodological procedures empirically and by ensuring that knowledge and skills accrued are widely shared, progress can be made on issues discussed for over three decades. Joining forces would help groups to find resources to conduct much-needed methodological research. The guideline initiatives in the International Workshop for Comparative Survey Design and Implementation (www.csdi-workshop.org) and the International Test Commission spring to mind as examples.

Standards and protocols developed in one project can serve as models for others. The funding provided by the European Union and participating countries for the ESS, for example, has made it possible to develop protocols and good practice procedures that can benefit other projects, irrespective of whether they adopt the same tactics. In fact, some of the procedures developed in the ESS can be traced back to experience gained in the ISSP. The EU clearly recognizes the importance of evidence-based methods for comparative research. An infrastructure grant to the ESS, for example, has funded training, research, and dissemination projects. As research becomes available that will change expectations and establish new standards, it is critical that research communities collaborate and share their individually developed techniques and expertise. It is also important to avoid a situation in which deserving but modestly funded projects find their achievements overshadowed by the prominence of better-funded projects.

Awareness of the need for research on and refinements of comparative survey methodologies is uneven across disciplines and geographical areas. Lyberg (2006) indicates that official statistics in Europe, for example, has not yet shown a sustained interest in comparative survey methodology or cooperation with other fields. Certain parts of the world have only very modest survey infrastructures and limited access to training, literature, or basic tools for their work. Survey research is also not welcomed in every part of the world, although national needs for data on topics such as household composition, migration, education, health, and human capital encourage governments to promote data collection and dissemination.

There are also areas in which cross-national, cross-cultural research very much needs to recognize and incorporate methodological advances made in national centers of excellence. At the same time, research across countries or within countries has its own special requirements and procedures. Comparative research is not simply an elaborate extension of general survey research. Certain core challenges, such as question design, are both complex and in some respects politically charged. Commitments to existing instruments, for example, and the time series these represent make it at times difficult to introduce new questions or new design approaches.

Notwithstanding, recent developments, this suggests that considerable methodological progress is likely in the coming decade. These include the ESS infrastructure projects, the ongoing success of the ISSP program and its methodological activities, the emergence of CSDI and CSDI work groups and the international methods conference and monograph planned by that group for 2008, the growth in thematic sessions on comparative research at conferences, the increase in the number of courses taught on comparative survey research in a variety of places, the establishment of the European Survey Research Association (ESRA) and the appearance in 2006 of *Survey Research Methods*, an online journal focusing on methodological issues. Comparatively speaking, the future is most, encouraging.

GLOSSARY OF KEY CONCEPTS

Adaptation. Adapted questions are derived from existing questions by deliberately changing some content or design component to make a question more suitable for a new sociocultural context or for a particular population. Adaptation can be necessary without translation being involved (e.g., adapting a questionnaire for children). However, whenever translation is necessary, some forms of adaptation are also generally required. Adaptations may be substantive, relate to question design, or consist of slight formulation and wording changes. Regardless of the form or the degree of change, it is wise to consider adapted questions as new questions and to test them accordingly.

Ask-Different-Questions Approach (ADQ). In ADQ approaches, researchers collect data across populations/countries using the most salient population-specific questions on a given topic that are felt or demonstrated to tap a construct that is germane or shared across populations.

Ask-the-Same-Question Approach (ASQ). With the exception of *decentring*, researchers adopting ASQ approaches collect data across populations/countries by first deciding on a common source questionnaire in one language and then producing whatever other language versions are needed on the basis of translation. Although *close translation* is often preferred, adaptations of several kinds may nonetheless be necessary.

Back Translation. Back translation is a procedure which can be sued for several purposes but in survey research is now most often used to assess translations. The translated questionnaire is translated back into the source questionnaire language. Then these two versions in the source language are compared for difference or similarity. Good similarity between these two is taken to indicate that the translated text, which is not itself examined, is faithful to the original source questionnaire.

Close translation. A variety of terms, including close translation, are sometimes used to express that a translation tries to stay as close as possible to the original text in content, presentation and in the case of surveys, format and design. In practical terms, a close translation policy often stands at odds to an approach embracing *adaptation*.

Decentring. In classical decentring models, two different cultures are asked the same questions but the questions are developed simultaneously in each language. Thus there is no source questionnaire or target language questionnaire. The decentring process removes culture-specific elements from both versions. Decentring can thus be seen to stand between *ADQ* models and models based on *ASQ* source questionnaire and translation models.

Etic-Emic. Following distinctions developed by Pike, etic concepts or constructs are universal and therefore shared across multiple cultures, whereas emic concepts or constructs are culture-specific in constellation or significance and cannot be assumed to be shared across populations.

Functional Equivalence. Multiple definitions of functional equivalence exist within and across disciplines. When used in this chapter, it refers to the comparability of the function of a question in a specific context with that of another question in a different specific context.

Team translation. A team translation approach as used in this chapter, combines translation with translation review. It (a) uses more than one translator (b) involves the translators in the review process and not just for the first stage of draft translation (c) brings other expertise to the review process (e. g., survey design and implementation, substantive) and (d) reiterates translation, review, adjudication, and testing as necessary. Thus a good part of the work is carried out by members of the team working as a group.

Chapter 5

Ethical Issues in Surveys[1]

Eleanor Singer
Survey Research Center, Institute for Social Research
University of Michigan

5.1 INTRODUCTION

Although the Romans conducted population censuses for purposes of taxation and military recruitment even before the beginning of the Christian era, and although the ancestors of the contemporary social survey can be traced, to, among others, Le Play in France and Booth in England in the 19th century, survey research as a profession is less than a hundred years old.

One defining characteristic of a profession is the existence of a recognized, specialized body of knowledge specific to the profession; another is a code of ethics regulating the conduct of its members, on the basis of which the profession claims the right to regulate itself (cf. Goode, 1973, ch. 14). Codes of professional ethics have a very long history, but those for survey researchers are relatively recent, emerging in the United States in 1947 and in Europe in 1948. The existence of a recognized body of knowledge specific to survey research is of even more recent origin. The first Ph.D. program in survey methodology was created in the United States at the University of Maryland in College Park, Maryland, in 1997; the first textbook explicitly devoted to survey methodology was published in 2004 (Groves, Fowler, Couper, Lepkowski, Singer, & Tourangeau, 2004), though many earlier textbooks had dealt with various aspects of survey methods, such as sampling, survey design and analysis, and questionnaire design, and (e.g., Kish 1965; Hyman 1955; Fowler 1995).

Most features of the ethics codes of survey researchers are common to the ethics codes of other professions: for example, most such codes contain prescriptions concerning the relationship between the professional and the client, between the professional and the public, and among professionals. Even those sections dealing with the relationship between researchers and their subjects (or respondents, in the case of survey research) are common to the ethics codes of other professions engaged in research involving human subjects, for example, physicians, sociologists, psychologists, and anthropologists.

Although codes of ethics came into being because professions claimed

---

[1] This chapter draws heavily on the author's chapter on ethics in Groves *et al.*, *Survey Methodology* (New York: Wiley, 2004).

the right to regulate themselves, many of these ethical prescriptions are currently embodied not only in professional codes, but also in government laws and regulations that vary somewhat from one country to another. Thus, depending on the kind of research in which they are engaged, survey researchers may be subject not only to the ethics code of their professional organization, which may or may not carry enforcement penalties, but also to regulations enforceable by government agencies. For example, academic survey researchers in the United States must abide by the Code of Federal Regulations for the Protection of Human Subjects (45 FCR 46) in addition to the Code of Ethics of the American Association for Public Opinion Research, whereas survey researchers engaged in market research are so far exempt from the federal regulations. If they carry out research involving respondents in more than one country, they may be subject to the laws governing survey research in all of these countries. Some professional codes of ethics have a long history, especially in the medical professions (cf. Baker. 1999). However, codes of ethics governing relations between researchers and their subjects are more recent in origin, arising from specific historical contexts in which abuses of subjects occurred. It is these principles, and their application to the relationship between survey researchers and respondents, which are the focus of this chapter. Along the way, however, we touch on other provisions of professional codes of ethics for survey research as they apply to relations between survey researchers and clients, the public, and other researchers.

5.2 GENERAL PRINCIPLES FOR THE TREATMENT OF SUBJECTS: THE HELSINKI DECLARATION AND THE BELMONT REPORT

The ethical, as distinct from the legal, principles for protecting the rights of respondents and other subjects of social, behavioral, and biomedical research are rooted in the Helsinki Declaration and the Belmont Report. The Helsinki Declaration (and the earlier Declaration of Geneva, adopted by the General Assembly of the World Medical Association in 1948), originally adopted by the World Medical Assembly in 1964, was a direct response to gross violations of subjects' rights by biomedical scientists during the Nazi era, and defined the ethical responsibilities of physicians to their patients as well as to the subjects of biomedical research. The Helsinki Declaration asserts the need for special protection for "those who cannot give or refuse consent themselves, for those who may be subject to giving consent under duress, for those who do not benefit personally from the research and for those for whom the research is combined with treatment." It also recognizes the special needs of those who are "economically and medically disadvantaged," and specifically asserts that "in medical research on human subjects, considerations related to the well-being of the individual subject should take precedence over the interests of science and society." Many other stipulations finding their way into current regulations for the protection of human subjects can be found in the Helsinki Declaration—for example, the requirement to obtain assent from a minor child.

The Belmont Report, issued in the United States in 1979, was the work of the National Commission for the Protection of Human Subjects of Biomedical and Behavioral Research, created under the National Research Act of 1974. It advanced three principles for the conduct of all research involving human subjects: beneficence, justice, and respect for persons. The principle of beneficence requires researchers to minimize possible harms and maximize possible benefits for the subject, and to decide when it is justifiable to seek certain benefits in spite of the risks involved or when the benefits should be foregone because of the risks. The extensive attention to risks and harms in the Code of Federal Regulations reflects this principle of beneficence.

The principle of justice aims at some fair balance between those who bear the burdens of research and those who benefit from it. In the 19th and early 20th centuries, for example, indigent patients largely bore the burdens of medical research, whereas the benefits of improved medical care went largely to affluent private patients. Eventually, research on prisoners was severely curtailed in the United States because this population, too, was seen as a convenient subject pool for a variety of medical experiments. Subpart C of the Federal Code of Regulations (45 CFR 46), protecting prisoners as subjects of biomedical and behavioral research, was adopted in 1978.

The third principle, respect for persons, gives rise to the ethical requirement for informed consent, which is defined in the Code of Regulations as the "knowing consent of an individual or his legally authorized representative . . . without undue inducement or any element of force, fraud, deceit, duress, or any other form of constraint or coercion."

5.3 CODES OF ETHICS FOR SURVEY PROFESSIONALS

As professionals, survey researchers have relationships not only with participants or respondents but also with three other important groups: clients or sponsors, the public, and other researchers. The codes of ethics of professional organizations define the norms of these relationships and have created mechanisms for dealing with norm violations. The World Association for Public Opinion Research, has a code (http://www.unl.edu/wapor/ethics.html), as does the American Association for Public Opinion Research (http://www.aapor.org/pdfs/aapor_code_2005.pdf). And ESOMAR, the World Organization for Market Research, as well as market research organizations in the United States and other countries, have developed similar codes for their members, many of whom are survey researchers. An individual who is a member of several, or all, of these organizations may be subject to the prescriptions of all of these codes. ESOMAR recognizes this and on its website provides information on national market research, marketing, and advertising associations per country worldwide, including the codes of ethics used (http://www.esomar.org). For an European view see also the RESPECT code of practice, which is a voluntary code covering the conduct of socio-economic research in Europe (see http://www.respectproject.org/code/).

Not surprisingly, there is a great deal of overlap among these codes of ethics. We focus here on the text of the WAPOR code, which is directly relevant to survey researchers all over the world. It contains prescriptions in four areas: Responsibilities to sponsors, and sponsors' responsibilities to researchers; reporting responsibilities; responsibilities to respondents; and responsibilities to other researchers.

Because much public opinion research is carried out for private sponsors, the code's provisions protect the sponsor's interests as well as those of the researcher and the public. So, for example, researchers are enjoined not to deviate from agreed-on specifications without advance consultation, to hold confidential materials and information provided by the sponsor, to inform sponsors if data from a single survey are to be provided to more than one sponsor. At the same time, sponsors are discouraged from using one researcher's proposals to drive down another one's bid, and forbidden to use the researcher's name on a report without explicit permission.

Both the WAPOR and the AAPOR codes stress the need to protect the respondent from possible harm resulting from the interviewing process or the answers given. WAPOR emphasizes the respondent's right to refuse to answer and to withdraw at any time. Both codes emphasize the need for maintaining confidentiality. We return to this issue, which is central to the research profession, later in the chapter.

By far the most elaborate of the codes of conduct that apply to survey researchers is the ICC/ESOMAR International Code of Marketing and Social Research Practice (see http://www.esomar.org/). First promulgated in 1948 by ESOMAR for European market research organizations, the code was subsequently revised to include provisions of the International Chamber of Commerce (ICC). It has been adopted by many other countries, including Australia. The current revision dates from 1994, and "sets out . . . the basic ethical and business principles which govern the practice or marketing and social research. It specifies the rules which are to be followed in dealing with the general public and with the business community, including clients and other members of the profession." The code specifically refers to national legislation, which, when it differs from the code, takes precedence in research carried out in that country, and the ICC/ESOMAR code instructs researchers always to consult such laws before embarking on a study. For example, although the ESOMAR Code specifies that survey researchers must obtain parental consent when doing research with children under 14, in England the law specifies that consent must be obtained for children under 16, and in Sweden, for those under 18 (De Leeuw, Borgers, & Smits, 2004).

Close examination of the ICC/ESOMAR code reveals striking similarities with both of the codes already discussed. It differs in its greater specificity—for example, requiring the researcher to notify the client "as soon as possible in advance when any part of the work for that client is to be subcontracted outside the researcher's own organization." It also differs in providing elaborate details of how the code is to be implemented, providing for variations required by the laws of different countries. ESOMAR also provides guidelines for specific research situation, such as, interviewing children, the use of internet panels, pharmaceutical research, and customer satisfaction studies (for more details see the section on professional standards at the ESOMAR website).

Like the AAPOR Code, and for similar reasons, the WAPOR and ESOMAR Code take no position on standards of survey practice. It does not, for example, take a position on probability sampling, on pretesting, on appropriate follow-up procedures, or on the response rates that should be achieved. Instead, the codes rely on a requirement for reporting the methods used in carrying out the survey. So, for example, the codes stipulate that every report on a survey should contain information about the sponsor, the organization carrying out the fieldwork, the universe to which findings are to be generalized, the sample size and the method by which the sample was selected, a copy of the questionnaire, a description of the precision of the findings, and similar items. In theory, such reporting permits consumers of the research to judge its quality, though there is surely much variability in this regard.

Interestingly enough, none of the codes refers to certain general standards of research conduct, perhaps because adherence to them is taken for granted. In the United States, the federal executive branch department that funds most research on human subjects (much of it biomedical) is the Department of Health and Human Services. Within that department, the Office of Research Integrity (ORI) oversees scientific misconduct, which consists of plagiarism, falsification, or fabrication in proposing, performing, reviewing research, or in reporting research results. These terms have been defined by ORI as follows: (a) Fabrication: Making up data or results and recording or reporting them; (b) Falsification: Manipulating research materials, equipment, or processes, or changing or omitting results so that the research is not accurately represented in the research record; (c) Plagiarism: Theft of misappropriation of intellectual property, and the substantial unattributed copying of another's work.

5.4 THE ROLE OF LEGISLATION IN THE ETHICAL CONDUCT OF RESEARCH

Although it is impossible to discuss all laws that have a bearing on the ethical conduct of research with human subjects, it is necessary to at least mention some that translate the principles already discussed into binding rules of conduct, enforceable by national laws. Prominent among these are the Federal Regulations for the Protection of Human Subjects of Research in the United States (45 Code of Federal Regulations 46), most recently revised in 1991, and the European Union Directive on Data Protection (see http://europa.eu.int/comm/justice_home/fsj/privacy/).

Canada and Australia have guidelines for research on human subjects that are similar to those in the United States. In Canada, all research involving human subjects must be reviewed by Research Ethics Boards (http://www.pre.ethics.gc.ca/english/policystatement/section1.cfm#1A); in Australia, such review boards are known as Human Research Ethics Committees (*http://www.health.gov.au/nhmrc/issues/researchethics.htm*).

5.4.1 Regulations for the Protection of Human Subjects of Research

As already noted, the early violations of subjects' rights occurred in biomedical studies, and the Helsinki Declaration defined the ethical responsibilities of physicians to their patients as well as to the subjects of biomedical research. A well-known example of violation of subjects rights in the United States is the Tuskegee syphilis study (Faden & Beauchamp, 1986; Katz, 1972; Tuskegee Syphilis Study Ad Hoc Advisory Panel, 1973). The Tuskegee study, which continued from about 1932 to the early 1970s, enrolled poor black men in a longitudinal study of syphilis whose aim was to observe the natural course of the disease. The subjects were led to believe that they were receiving treatment; in fact, no treatment was offered them even after penicillin, a highly effective treatment, became available, and most of them died. This study remains a symbol of exploitation by the medical establishment for many African Americans, and continues to engender distrust of research among them.

But some social science studies (e.g., research by Humphreys observing homosexual acts in public toilets, Humphreys, 1970), as well as other social psychological research involving deception (e.g., Zimbardo's studies of simulated prison settings (Haney, Banks, & Zimbardo, 1973) and Milgram's studies of obedience to authority (Milgram, 1963) also aroused public concern. These varied concerns led in the United States to the creation of the National Research Act and to the codification and adoption of the Federal Regulations for the Protection of Human Subjects in the same year. In 1991, the various rules of seventeen federal agencies were harmonized as Subpart A of 45 Code of Federal Regulations (CFR) 46—otherwise known as the Common Rule. From the outset, social and behavioral as well as biomedical research were encompassed by these regulations.

The regulations require colleges, universities, and other institutions in the USA who receive federal funds to establish Institutional Review Boards (IRBs) to safeguard the rights of research volunteers, including respondents to surveys. IRBs are committees of researchers and local community representatives that review proposed research on human subjects and decide whether they meet the ethical standards laid out in the regulations. Now, only surveys conducted at United States institutions that receive federal funding for research are subject to the Regulations for the Protection of Human Subjects. Thus, most commercial surveys are currently exempt from their provisions.

Earlier, we talked about the principles articulated in the Belmont Report, stressing two of them especially: beneficence, and respect for persons. The principle of beneficence is translated, in the Regulations, into the requirement that researchers strive for a favorable risk-benefit balance by minimizing the risks of harm to which subjects are exposed. Greater than minimal risk must be justified by potential benefits either to the individual or to society. Minimal risk is defined as meaning "that the probability and magnitude of the harm or discomfort anticipated in the research are not greater in and of themselves than those ordinarily encountered in daily life or during the performance of routine physical or psychological examinations or tests" [45 CFR 46.102i]. Understandably, because people's lives differ, and the risks to which they are exposed also vary accordingly, this requirement has led to some difficulties and inconsistencies in the interpretation of the Regulations. We return later in the chapter to the particular risks of harm to which subjects of social research are exposed, and some of the efforts required minimizing them.

The second key principle articulated in the Belmont Report, respect for persons, is translated in the Regulations into the requirement for obtaining informed consent from research subjects. This requirement at times conflicts with the requirement for assuring a favorable risk-benefit ratio, because it asserts that if individuals are adequately informed about the conditions of the research and its potential risks of harm, and if they are able to make a voluntary decision about participation, they can choose both to expose themselves to greater risks than is warranted by the potential benefits of the research, and, conversely, to decline to expose themselves even to minimal risks.

Included among the elements of informed consent are a description of the purposes of the research, the benefits and potential harm of participation, confidentiality protections provided, and the voluntary nature of participation. Under specified circumstances, IRBs may waive some or all of these elements, or even waive the requirement to obtain informed consent entirely.

Unfortunately, in practice, the requirement for informed consent is often treated merely as a requirement for obtaining a signed consent form, rather than as an opportunity for assuring that subjects understand the risks and opportunities to which they will be exposed by the research. Much research suggests that the informed consent statements typically employed in social as well as biomedical research are poorly understood by respondents and subjects, thus violating the principle of beneficence as well as that of autonomy. Procedures well known to survey researchers—cognitive interviewing and pretesting, for example—should be used to remedy this. We return to a fuller consideration of the implications of informed consent for research later.

5.4.2 European Union Directive on Data Protection

Although the European Union has no regulations comparable to those described in the preceding section for the United States, it has a very detailed set of regulations designed to protect the confidentiality of the information provided by survey respondents. The European Union Directive on Data Protection, passed in 1995, required member countries to incorporate its provisions into national legislation by 1998, although not every country had complied by that date. The directive established a regulatory framework to ensure both a high level of protection for the confidentiality of individual information in all member states and the free movement of personal data within the European Union. Because it prevents the transfer of personal data to countries that do not meet its data protection standards, the directive is a potent force for raising these standards even stretching beyond the borders of the European Union (http://www.europa.eu.int/comm/internal_market/privacy/index_en.htm.). But because it alters established ways of doing things in some countries—for example, the use of health registers as sampling frames without the consent of participants—it has raised concerns on the part of market research and other survey organizations, as well as among some government and academic researchers, about the directive's effect on the ability to carry out needed research (see, e.g., Angus, Entwistle, Emslie, Walker, & Andres, 2003; Coleman, Evans, & Barrett, 2003).

5.4.3 International Regulations

Recognizing the continued growth of international research, the Office for Human Research Protections has developed an International Compilation of Human Subject Research Protections. The Compilation lists the laws, regulations, and guidelines of over 50 countries where DHHS funded or supported research is conducted. The Compilation provides direct web links to each country's Key Organizations and laws, whenever available. OHRP believes this Compilation will help IRBs, researchers, and others to meet regulatory requirements to assure that research studies comply with applicable law. (http://www.hhs.gov/ohrp/international/index.html#NatlPol).

5.5 KEY ISSUES IN THE ETHICAL TREATMENT OF HUMAN SUBJECTS OF RESEARCH

Two issues are key to the ethical treatment of human subjects in social research: informed consent, and confidentiality protection. Up to now we have considered the roots of informed consent and confidentiality in general ethical principles, professional codes of ethics, and codes of law. In this section, we examine how application of the principles in specific situations complicates their apparently clear-cut prescriptions for behavior.

5.5.1 Informed Consent

Informed consent requires (a) providing enough information about potential benefits and risks of harm to permit subjects to make informed participation decisions; (b) assuring that the information is understood; and (c) creating an environment that is free from undue influence and coercion. In addition, (d) research organizations ordinarily need some evidence that subjects have, in fact, been adequately informed and have agreed to participate. How easy is it to create these conditions in the context of real-life research?

5.5.2 Providing Enough Information and Assuring Comprehension

Although codes of ethics of some major professional associations (for example, the American Statistical Association and the American Sociological Association) mention the requirement for informed consent, the AAPOR, WAPOR, and ESOMAR codes do not. Unlike much biomedical research, the quality of surveys depends on the response rates they achieve. As a result, the need to gain the respondent's cooperation puts a premium on brief, engaging survey introductions that make it difficult to convey all the required elements of informed consent. And because the studies carried out by members of these organizations often pose only minimal risks for respondents, many of the elements of informed consent stipulated in the Regulations simply do not apply.

But studies of opinions and marketing preferences are not the only studies carried out by survey researchers. Many surveys are carried out by government statistical agencies, such as the Census Bureau, or by academic or other nonprofit research organizations acting on their behalf, and inquire into topics that might well put respondents at risk of harm if their answers were disclosed to others. As we have seen, the Regulations for the Protection of Human Subjects specify eight pieces of information that must be provided to potential research participants in such surveys ahead of time. Because these can seem daunting to survey researchers, changes in the way survey data are disseminated have prompted a National Academy of Sciences panel (National Research Council, 2005) to recommend the following additional information about planned future uses of the data:

- Planned or anticipated record linkages for research purposes.
- Planned and possible future uses of the data for research purposes.
- The possible future uses of the data by researchers other than those collecting the data.
- Any planned or potential nonstatistical uses of the data.
- A clear statement of the level of confidentiality protection that can be legally and technically assured, recognizing that a zero risk of disclosure is not possible.

To help researchers apply the recommendation, the panel offered a model paragraph incorporating this additional information:

Your information is being collected for research purposes and for statistical analysis by researchers in our agency and in other institutions. Your data will not be used for any legal or enforcement purpose [unless required by the Patriot Act]. The researchers who have access to your data are pledged to protect its confidentiality and are subject to fines and prison terms if they violate it. Data will only be provided to researchers outside our agency in a form that protects your identity as an individual. Some uses of your data may require linking your responses to other records, always in a manner that honors our pledge to protect your confidentiality (National Research Council, 2005).

One question that can be raised about this paragraph, as well as other attempts to convey information to research participants, is how much detail should be communicated in order to inform them adequately—should they, for example, be told in advance that they are going to be asked about their income near the end of the interview, or is it enough to tell them that they need not answer a question if they choose not to? Is it enough to mention "researchers in other institutions," or is it necessary to go into detail about the ways in which the data will be made available?

Surveys that rely on face-to-face interviewing, and self-administered surveys, such as mail surveys or Web surveys, have the ability to convey fairly lengthy information about the study to respondents, and even telephone surveys that have addresses available for potential respondents can do so by means of advance letters. But providing the information to respondents does not assure that it is either read or understood. On the contrary, research suggests that many informed consent statements are written at a level far beyond the literacy of the average respondent (Paasche-Orlow, Taylor, & Brancati, 2003). Researchers rarely test what respondents actually understand on the basis of the informed consent statement, and IRBs rarely require such empirical evidence of comprehension. One practice recommended by some researchers to increase the likelihood that participants will actually understand what they are getting into is to present them with a list of frequently asked questions and answers as a supplement to the consent document itself. Interactive versions of such question-and-answer sequences have the advantage of tailoring the amount of information provided to the tastes of individual respondents. The potential disadvantage of such an approach is that, as a result, the context in which different people answer the questions will vary; however, this kind of variation in context can, in principle, be measured and controlled for in the analysis.

5.5.3 What if Information Cannot Be Provided?

Survey researchers rarely carry out the kind of experiments that require the temporary withholding of information in order to obtain valid experimental results. Such experiments are much more often carried out in the laboratory by psychologists, who debrief subjects—that is, share the real purpose of the experimental manipulation—at the conclusion of the experiment (Goodwin, 2005). But research carried out in the 1970's by Berscheid and her colleagues (1973) suggests very strongly that for experiments involving more than minimal stress for participants, such as the Asch (1951) or Milgram (1963) experiments on conformity, withholding this information recruits participants who would have refused had they been fully informed. Under what circumstances, if ever, it is ethical to deceive respondents, even if temporarily, is a matter of continuing debate among researchers and ethicists (cf. Faden & Beaumont, 1986, esp. 362ff. and the references cited there; see also the ethics code of the American Psychological Association, http://www.apa.org/ethics/). The codes of ethics for survey organizations are generally mute on the issue of deception, although the AAPOR code says that survey researchers should strive to not seriously mislead survey respondents.

Survey researchers do, of course, often carry out experiments to find out what effect different ways of asking a question, or different survey introductions, have on respondents' answers or willingness to participate in the survey. They don't inform people about these experiments, which are often embedded in a larger survey context; nor do they necessarily "debrief" them at the conclusion of the survey. Because these kinds of experiments involve minimal risk, Berscheid's research suggests that withholding such information does not influence respondents' willingness to participate. Whether researchers should tell respondents, either before or after the survey, that one of its purposes is to find out how best to ask certain kinds of questions is an issue for discussion.

Another solution to the dilemma of giving subjects enough information to make an informed, voluntary decision about participation without sacrificing scientific validity is to tell them about the different experimental conditions but obtain their consent to randomize them into one or another condition. This approach is often used in studies of alternative treatment therapies, but can be adapted to other experimental situations, as well.

5.5.4 Undue Influence: Vulnerable Populations and Incentives

That there are populations in need of special protection as research subjects is generally recognized in biomedical research. Understandably, the professional codes of AAPOR and WAPOR make no mention of such populations, because little opinion research is carried out with these groups, but the ESOMAR code singles out children and young people as requiring special care, and notes that the consent of a parent or responsible adult must be obtained before children can be interviewed. The Regulations for the Protection of Human Subjects, intended as they are for biomedical as well as social research, go further, stipulating special precautions and procedures for several "vulnerable" populations, including children and young people under 18, prisoners, and people with diminished mental capacity who cannot give truly informed consent.

The concerns with all of these groups are similar: Because of age, incapacity, or situation, they are believed to be unable to make fully informed, voluntary choices about research participation, and therefore require special procedures either to prevent coercion or to protect them from risk of harm, or both.

The concepts of coercion and undue influence arise especially in the context of these three vulnerable populations, but some writers believe that the use of incentives, especially large monetary incentives, constitutes undue influence with respect to other population subgroups, such as those being asked certain kinds of sensitive questions or those who have very low incomes or few resources (cf. Dunn & Gordon, 2005). The ethical questions are under what circumstances an incentive becomes so large that it distorts respondents' perceptions of the risk-benefit ratio, leading them to assume risks that a rational person would otherwise refuse, and whether groups low in economic or social power are especially likely to be influenced in this way. Both questions are susceptible of empirical research, but very little research has so far been done in this area.

5.5.5 Documenting Consent

In biomedical studies, information about the risks and benefits of the research is ordinarily communicated in writing, and the subject signs a copy of the consent form, which is retained by the researcher. Clearly, there are situations in which a consent form should be required from participants in survey research. These situations have the following characteristics:

- The participant is at more than minimal risk of harm.
- Without the requirement for a signed consent form, participants may not receive adequate information about these risks.

- The researcher and/or the institution undertaking the research require proof that the legally required information has been communicated to participants.

Although many surveys are not characterized by these three features, some clearly are. For example, surveys that ask questions about illegal or stigmatizing behavior may put participants at risk of harm if the information is disclosed, either inadvertently or deliberately. Respondents have the right to be informed about these risks before they decide whether or not to participate. In these circumstances, it is appropriate to provide respondents with a written document describing the risks, as well as protections against them and recourse in case of injury. It is also appropriate for researchers to obtain documentation that such information has actually been provided to respondents before their participation. The question is whether such documentation must be in the form of a signed consent statement.

Evidence from several studies documents the harmful consequences of requiring signed consent forms for survey participation. The earliest such study was done by Singer (1978), in which the request for a signature to document consent reduced the response rate to a national face-to-face survey by some 7 percentage points. But most respondents who refused to sign the form were, in fact, willing to participate in the survey; it was the request for a signature that deterred them from participation. Similar findings are reported by Trice (1987), who found that subjects asked to sign a consent form responded at a lower rate than when no signature was required. More recently, an experiment by Singer (2003) found that some 13% of respondents who said they would be willing to participate in a survey were not willing to sign the consent form that would have been required for their participation.

Groves et al. (2004, p. 365) argue that, "Given these deleterious effects on response rates of requiring a respondent's signature to document consent, we would argue that such a signature should almost never be required. Such a signed consent form protects the institution rather than the respondent. Instead, a functional alternative should be used. For example, the interviewer can be required to sign a form indicating that an informed consent statement has been read to the respondent and a copy given to him or her to keep." Because this poses an inherent conflict for interviewers, whose job it is to get the highest possible response rates, Groves and his colleagues recommend that "survey firms should be required to audit the truthfulness of these affidavits, just as they are required to audit whether or not an interview has been conducted."

5.5.6 Does the Content of Consent Forms Affect Participation?

What evidence do we have for the effect of informed consent statements on willingness to cooperate, and on the quality of cooperation?

The mid-seventies saw the first two studies on this topic, one sponsored by the National Science Foundation and carried out by the National Opinion Research Center, the other sponsored and carried out by the Census Bureau. The first study was motivated explicitly by the newly promulgated Federal Regulations for the Protection of Human Subjects of Research. The second study was motivated by worries that privacy and confidentiality concerns might reduce cooperation with the 1980 census.

The first study (Singer, 1978) used the survey introduction to investigate how variations in the assurance of confidentiality and in the amount of information provided about the sensitive content of the survey affected response rates as well as response quality. Although the assurance of confidentiality had no consistent impact on willingness to participate in the survey, it did affect willingness to answer the most sensitive questions—in this case, those having to do with sexual behavior and drug use. The study also varied the amount of information respondents were given about the content of the survey. Some respondents were told only that the survey was about leisure time activities, and about how they were feeling; others were told that the survey included questions about alcohol, drugs, and sexual behavior. This manipulation had no significant impact on the response rate, either. But those respondents told ahead of time to expect questions about drinking and sexual behavior expressed less embarrassment and upset in self-administered retrospective questions after the interview than those who were not given this information.

The second study (National Research Council, 1979) was designed to see whether information about the confidentiality of answers provided to the Census Bureau would affect willingness to return the census form and to answer census questions (the questionnaire itself was intermediate between the long and short census forms). The introduction to the survey varied the information respondents were given about the length of time for which their answers to the census would remain confidential—from a statement that answers would remain confidential in perpetuity to a statement that they might be shared with the public or other agencies.

Refusals to the survey showed a linear relationship with the length of time for which confidentiality was promised, and although the differences were very small, they were statistically significant. Furthermore, those respondents promised the longest period of confidentiality were most likely to answer the most sensitive questions on the survey, those having to do with income.

The effects of variations in the information provided to potential respondents about the content and purpose of the study have received little attention from survey researchers in the intervening years. This is clearly an area in which more research is needed.

5.5.7 Confidentiality Protection

5.5.7.1 Why confidentiality matters
Arguably, the most serious risks of harm to which participants in social research are exposed are breaches of confidentiality, and the consequences that may follow from such breaches. Temporary embarrassment or upset arising from survey questions about sexual or other sensitive behaviors seems trivial by comparison.

Many surveys sponsored by government agencies ask about sensitive, stigmatizing, and even illegal behavior, knowledge of which by unauthorized others (family and friends, employers, insurers, or law enforcement agencies, for example) could subject the respondent to loss of reputation, employment, or civil or criminal penalties. Not surprisingly, recent experiments with hypothetical introductions to such surveys show that concerns about privacy and confidentiality are among the reasons most often given by potential respondents for their unwillingness to participate (Singer, 2003).

A variety of threats to the confidentiality of survey data exist. Probably the most common is simple carelessness—not removing names, addresses, or telephone numbers from questionnaires or electronic data files, leaving cabinets unlocked, not encrypting files containing identifying information.

Potentially more serious threats to confidentiality are legal demands for identified data, either in the form of a subpoena or as a result of a Freedom of Information Act (FOIA) request.

In addition to the legal attempts to obtain confidential information described earlier, confidentiality may also be breached as a result of illegal intrusions into the data, for example in order to perpetrate theft or fraud. For example, in 2005, the Choice Point Corporation, a data warehouse, was duped by thieves posing as businessmen into selling hundreds of thousands of confidential records containing sensitive personal information. Also of concern are instances of intrusion into government statistics by other government agencies for law enforcement purposes. Anderson and Seltzer (2004) have recently documented a number of such attempts to use Census Bureau data for such purposes between 1910 and 1963.

A final threat to data confidentiality that is receiving increasing attention is the possibility of statistical disclosure, which refers to the re-identification of individuals (or their attributes) as a result of an outsider's matching of survey data that has been stripped of explicit identifying information, such as names and addresses, with information available outside the survey. Although there are no known instances of the confidentiality of survey data having been breached as a result of statistical disclosure except in a research context, government data collection agencies and other survey organizations are increasingly taking steps to protect against this possibility, either by restricting the data (altering the raw data by collapsing categories, rounding numbers, adding random noise, or withholding certain variables, such as birth date and small geographic detail, which increase the likelihood that individuals in the data file can be identified) or by restricting access to the data by making them available only through license agreements or in secure research data centers (see National Research Council, 2005).

Not only do potential breaches of confidentiality pose a risk of harm to survey participants; but they also pose a risk of harm to the survey enterprise itself. There is evidence, for example, that concern about privacy and confidentiality reduces people's willingness to participate in surveys. In Germany, the 1983 census had to be postponed for four years because of concerns about inadequate data protection (Flaherty, 1989, p. 83), and in the United States, concerns about privacy and confidentiality significantly reduced participation in the decennial censuses of 1990 and 2003 (Singer, Mathiowetz, & Couper, 1993; Singer, Van Hoewyk, & Neugebauer, 2003).

Both of these are observational studies. But recent experiments also show that potential subjects do, in fact, process the information they are given in the way intended by the ethics of the informed consent process: that is, their perception of the risks and benefits of a hypothetical study are significantly related to their expressed willingness to participate in the study, in the expected direction, although they overestimated the size of the risks involved (Singer, 2003). In this experiment, risk was defined as the likelihood that other people would see their answers to the survey, along with their name and address; and harm was defined as how much they would mind if this in fact occurred.

5.5.7.2 Ethical and legal standards
All of the ethics codes reviewed earlier in this chapter specifically mention the researcher's obligation to maintain the confidentiality of the respondent's answers. Of the three, the ESOMAR code is the most explicit, and it is the only one of the three to take note of the potential for breaching both anonymity and confidentiality when audio and, especially, video recordings are used. The ESOMAR code states that respondents must be told, "normally at the beginning of the interview," if recording or observation equipment is being used (except when these are used in a public place, where respondents have no reasonable expectation of privacy). The code requires that these recordings, or the relevant portions, must be deleted if the respondent requests it.

Like the European ethics codes, European laws have until now been more responsive to privacy and confidentiality concerns than those in the United States. Detailed examination of the provisions of the European Directive on Data Privacy is clearly beyond the scope of this chapter, especially because countries that implement the directive are free to increase (though not reduce) the protections afforded the data. Some guidance on how the Directive affects market research is provided on the ESOMAR website (http://www.esomar.org/esomar/show/id=65961); this includes a discussion by Diane Bowers, of the Council of American Survey Research Organizations, of the "safe harbor" provisions that permit organizations in the United States to receive data from countries that have signed on to the directive. (See (http://europa.eu.int/comm/internal_market/privacy/index_en.htm).

5.5.7.3 What should researchers do to protect confidentiality?
The confidentiality of individual respondents may be breached as a result of carelessness, legal and illegal intrusions into the data, and law enforcement activities. What can researchers do to protect against these threats? Here we briefly discuss four strategies: training employees and investigators in confidentiality protection practices; reinforcing norms of confidentiality protection among researchers and staff; obtaining or using legal protections for confidential data; and research on statistical disclosure limitation.

Training employees and investigators in confidentiality protection practices, and reinforcing norms. Survey organizations that collect individually identifiable data should provide training in confidentiality practices and data management for all staff who work with or have access to such data. A list of 14 simple principles that apply to both paper-and-pencil instruments and electronic files appears in Box 5.1. For a fuller discussion of each of these, see the Principles and Practices for Research Staff of the University of Michigan ISR Standing Committee on Confidentiality and Data Security at the website accompanying this book (Chapter 5).

Box 5.1 Principles and Practices for Protection of Confidential Data	
1.	Evaluate risks. Materials containing direct identifiers require a great deal of care; files containing edited and aggregated data may or may not need to be treated as confidential.
2.	Assess the sensitivity of all data under your control.
3.	Apply appropriate security measures. Remove direct identifiers such as name, address, and Social Security number. Questionnaires or tapes containing personally sensitive information, for example about drug use or medical conditions, should be stored in locked cabinets, as should questionnaires containing responses to open-ended questions that may reveal the identity of the respondent or others.
4.	Do not include identifying personal information on self-administered questionnaires. Provide a separate return envelope for such information.
5.	Store cover sheets with personal information about respondents in locked cabinets.
6.	Physically secure electronic files just as you do their paper copies.
7.	Take special care to secure hard disks containing sensitive material.
8.	Segregate sensitive from nonsensitive material on your hard disk.
9.	Consider encryption of sensitive material.
10.	Consider the costs and benefits of security measures.
11.	Know the physical locations of all your electronic files.
12.	Know the backup status of all storage systems you use.
13.	Be aware that email can be observed in transit.
14.	Take care when you erase files—most such files can be recovered unless special precautions are taken.
Source: ISR Survey Research Center, *Center Survey*, April 1999, pp. 1,3. Reprinted with permission from Groves *et al.*, 2004, p. 369.	

Training alone is not enough; survey organizations must foster an awareness of the importance of confidentiality, and be willing to use sanctions for violations of the guidelines for protecting it. For an example of the Confidentiality procedures of the Social and Economic Sciences Research Center (SESRC) of Washington State University see this book's website (Chapter 5).

In the United States and elsewhere, survey organizations are increasingly requiring interviewers and other employees to sign confidentiality pledges, and to renew those pledges yearly. For an example of such a pledge see this book's website (Chapter 5).

Use certificates of confidentiality and knowledge of relevant legal protections. To protect against potential subpoena of individual records for law enforcement purposes or civil litigation, U.S. researchers studying sensitive topics, whether federally funded or not, may apply for certificates of confidentiality from the U.S. Department of Health and Human Services. The National Institute of Justice (in the U.S. Department of Justice) also makes confidentiality certificates available for criminal justice research supported by agencies of the U.S. Department of Justice. Such certificates, which remain in effect for the duration of a study, protect researchers in most circumstances from being compelled to disclose names or other identifying characteristics of survey respondents in federal, state, or local proceedings (42 *Code of Federal Regulations* Section 2a.7, "Effect of Confidentiality Certificate").

In 2002, the U.S. Congress passed the Confidential Information Protection and Statistical Efficiency Act, which protects information collected by statistical agencies (or others working for them) for exclusively statistical purposes under a pledge of confidentiality from being disclosed in identifiable form without explicit permission from the respondent. This law extends to all agencies collecting such data, as well as organizations or individual researchers acting as their agents, protections previously enjoyed only by the US Census Bureau. The European Directive has a similar, even broader, function.

Use statistical disclosure limitation. It is necessary to mention briefly a final threat to confidentiality that is increasingly preoccupying government statistical agencies and other researchers—namely, the problem of statistical disclosure. Re-identification of respondents in data files from which direct identifiers such as names and addresses have been removed is increasingly possible because of high-speed computers, external data files containing names and addresses or other direct identifiers as well as information about a variety of individual characteristics, and sophisticated software for matching survey and other files. There is also a growing concern by data collection agencies that wider dissemination of research data may itself increase disclosure risk (National Research Council, 2005).

Discussion of the techniques currently being used to avoid statistical disclosure, which are constantly changing in response to new research, is beyond the scope of this chapter. In general, they involve one or more of the following: data swapping; recoding to avoid outliers and small cell sizes; adding noise to observations, for example by adding the value of a randomly generated variable to each data record's value on some items; and multiple imputation methods, which use a statistical model to generate synthetic values for each variable in a data set. For an introduction to the techniques of disclosure limitation, see Subcommittee on Disclosure Limitation Methodology (1994). For more recent examinations of the problem, see Doyle, Lane, Theeuwes, & Zayatz (2001) and Volume 14, No. 4 of the *Journal of Official Statistics* (1998), edited by Stephen Fienberg and Leon Willenborg. Because of the skills and resources required to limit statistical disclosure, a National Academy of Sciences panel (2005) has recommended that data archives should be encouraged to assume this function on behalf of individual researchers.

5.6 EMERGING ETHICAL ISSUES

5.6.1 Ethical Standards in Web Surveys

All of the ethical standards that have been discussed to this point—for example the need for protecting confidentiality and for securing informed consent— apply to Web-based surveys just as they do to all other modes of data collection. Surveys conducted using the Internet also pose some additional problems in connection with those standards. For example, maintenance of privacy and confidentiality in such surveys requires technological innovations (secure Web sites, encryption of responses) beyond those required by older modes of data collection. Other ethical issues simply do not arise with older modes of conducting surveys—for example, the possibility that a respondent might submit multiple answers, thus deliberately biasing the results. For still other ethical issues, such as obtaining informed consent, surveys on the Web both pose new challenges (how can one be sure that no minors are participating in a survey?) and new possibilities for solutions (e.g., an interactive consent process in which the respondent is asked to demonstrate understanding of a module before going on to the next one). For a comprehensive discussion of these issues, see American Psychological Association (2003) and the chapter on Web surveys by Katja Lozar Manfreda and Vasja Vehovar in this volume.

5.6.2 Survey Standards as Ethical Standards

One interesting consequence of the requirement that researchers strive for a favorable risk-benefit ratio is that the quality of the research becomes relevant to the ethical judgment of whether the research should be permitted to go forward. If the design of an experiment, or the quality of sampling, questionnaire construction, or field work of a survey is so poor as to yield no meaningful results, then it becomes fair to ask whether it would be unethical to permit the research to proceed, especially if subjects will be exposed to greater than minimal risk.

Institutional Review Boards in the United States increasingly argue that unless the research methods used will yield the information desired, it is unethical to conduct research with human subjects that puts them at greater than minimal risk. As a result, there is increasing pressure on survey researchers to justify the validity and reliability of the information obtained through surveys. Response rates and nonresponse bias, for example, are coming under increasing scrutiny (e.g., Groves, forthcoming), as is the ability of surveys to elicit honest responses to questions about sensitive behaviors (e.g., Currivan, Nyman, Turner, & Biener, 2004; Couper, Singer, & Tourangeau, 2003; see also Lensvelt, chapter 24). Respondents' willingness and ability to recall events and feelings long in the past is another area of continuing concern (e.g., Tourangeau, Rips, & Rasinski, 2000), and so is the influence of the interviewer on both cooperation rates and the content of the responses (e.g., Schober & Conrad, 2002).

The investigations stimulated by these challenges are, in fact, salutary for the growth of survey research as a profession. Although economic and intellectual pressures might have prompted such investigations in any case, the linkage of methodological with ethical concerns provides another critical stimulus for continued research on these problems.

5.7 SUMMARY AND CONCLUSIONS

This chapter has traced the ethical standards for survey research back to the more general ethical principles underlying those standards and examined their expression in the ethics codes of the major international survey organizations as well as in laws governing research in the United States and in Europe. The chapter argues that in the case of survey research, the most serious risk of harm to which participants are subject is a breach of confidentiality and the consequences that may flow from such a breach, for example the loss of reputation or employment or the risk of civil or criminal prosecution. Much of the chapter is devoted to ways of avoiding such breaches, through the training of interviewers and other employees in appropriate means of protecting data confidentiality and through careful scrutiny of the data released to other researchers and the public. The chapter also reviews research on public attitudes toward ethical issues, especially confidentiality and privacy. It reviews research on the effects of ethical requirements, for example the requirement for obtaining informed consent, on the quality of survey research. In conclusion, the chapter points to some emerging issues in the area of ethics and survey research, including the fact that the quality of the research is itself increasingly being regarded as an ethical issue. Throughout, the chapter has tried to integrate three aspects of ethical concerns: principles, practices, and research on the consequences of ethical concerns and practices for survey participation.

GLOSSARY OF KEY CONCEPTS

Autonomy. The right of self government.
Beneficence. In Belmont Report, the requirement to minimize possible harms and maximize possible benefits for the subjects of research, and to decide when research may be permissible in spite of the risk of harm, and when it may not.
Confidentiality. The safeguarding, by a recipient, of information about another individual.
Fabrication. Making up data or results and recording or reporting them.
Falsification. Manipulating research materials, equipment, or processes, or changing or omitting results such that the research is not accurately represented in the research record.
Informed consent. The "knowing consent of an individual or his legally authorized representative…without undue inducement or any element of force, fraud, deceit, duress, or any other form of constraint or coercion."
Justice. In Belmont Report, the requirement to achieve some fair balance between those who bear the burdens of research and those who benefit from it.
Plagiarism. The theft or misappropriation of intellectual property or the substantial unattributed copying of another's work.
Privacy. The right to determine when, and under what conditions, to reveal information about oneself to others.
Respect for persons. The basis for the informed consent requirement.

Chapter 6

Coverage and Sampling

Sharon L. Lohr
Arizona State University

6.1 INTRODUCTION

R.A. Fisher (1938) once wrote: "To consult a statistician after an experiment is finished is often merely to ask him to conduct a *post mortem* examination. He can perhaps say what the experiment died of." Fisher's words apply equally well to surveys: implementing a badly designed survey can be worse than collecting no data at all. Conclusions drawn from a poorly designed survey, such as a call-in poll in which individuals volunteer to be in the survey, can be completely misleading: all that a survey statistician can do after the deed is point out the design flaws that make the results questionable or false.

One example where lack of attention to survey design relative to intended use led to possibly erroneous conclusions occurred in 2002 when CBS News told Americans that "Sleeping longer—like getting eight hours or more a night—could shorten your life" (http://www.cbsnews.com/stories/2002/02/14/-health/main329440.shtml).

Kripke, Garfinkel, Wingard, Klauber & Marler (2002), using the 1982 Cancer Prevention Study II of the American Cancer Society, concluded that persons who sleep eight or more hours per night have higher risk of mortality than persons who sleep six or seven hours. This conclusion was widely reported in the news media at the time (*USA Today* reported that "People who sleep less might live longer"), and has been stated as scientific fact since then in such diverse popular magazines as *Time, Forbes,* and *Woman's Day.* Most news accounts reported that the results were based on a nationwide survey of 1.1 million people, but they did not report *how* those people were selected. In fact, the participants consisted mostly of friends and relatives of American Cancer Society volunteers. Although the sample contained Americans of diverse ages and backgrounds, and the sample may have provided valuable information for exploring factors associated with development of cancer, its validity for investigating the relationship between amount of sleep and mortality is questionable. The questions about amount of sleep and insomnia were not the focus of the original study, and the survey was not designed to obtain accurate responses to those questions. The design did not allow researchers to assess whether the sample was representative of the target population of all Americans. Because of the shortcomings in the survey design, it is impossible to know whether the conclusions in Kripke et al. (2002) about sleep and mortality are valid or not.

 This chapter presents the issues of coverage and sampling as elements in survey design. From a statistical point of view, a good survey design satisfies four characteristics: (a) every individual in the population of interest can potentially be selected in the sample, (b) results can be generalized to the population of interest, (c) quantities of interest can be estimated accurately and cost-effectively, and (d) the survey is flexible for some unanticipated uses.

6.2 THE IMPORTANCE OF SURVEY DESIGN

It is virtually impossible to design a survey or even a census where the statistics calculated from the sample will exactly equal the characteristics of interest in the population. Errors arise in almost every data collection effort. But a good survey design tries to minimize and quantify the different types of errors than can affect the survey results. Linacre and Trewin (1993) argued that a survey design should attempt to minimize the total survey error. The total error for estimating a quantity of interest from a survey, as described in Groves et al. (2004), is the sum of four components:

 total survey error = coverage error + sampling error + nonresponse error + measurement error.

For accurate coverage, the sampling frame must include all units in the population of interest. Coverage error occurs when the sampling frame does not include parts of the population of interest, for example when a frame of telephone numbers does not include nontelephone households. The survey used in Kripke et al. (2002), consisting mostly of friends and relatives of their volunteers, did not sample the parts of the target population with no connection to those volunteers; it thus had undercoverage of the U.S. adult population.

 Nonresponse error occurs when units are contacted for the survey but provide no data or only partial data. Both undercoverage and nonresponse lead to missing data from units that should be in the survey, and can result in biased estimates if those units differ systematically from units that are in the sampling frame and that respond to the survey.

 Although undercoverage and nonresponse can both lead to missing data, undercoverage may be more difficult to assess and treat. The survey taker often knows which units in the selected sample are nonrespondents, and may have some information about them that can be used in attempting to adjust estimates for the nonresponse (Biemer & Christ, Chapter 17). Persons or businesses not in the sampling frame, however, have zero probability of being selected for the sample. They are never given the opportunity to even be a nonrespondent, and the survey taker may be unaware that important parts of the population are excluded from the survey.

 Measurement errors result from inaccurate responses to questions or inaccurate measurements. For example, in a telephone survey on AIDS, persons with AIDS might not know that they have it and therefore give an inaccurate response, or they might be fearful that their condition would become known and deliberately not report it. In other surveys, interviewers may prompt respondents for a desired answer, or even falsify responses. In the Kripke et al. (2002) study, the survey instrument was designed for studying cancer, not for obtaining accurate measurements of amount of sleep. Measurement errors may have resulted because respondents may understate or have inaccurate recall of how much they sleep; the survey also did not ask about naps.

The last of the four types of errors, sampling error, is the error that occurs because a sample is taken instead of measuring the entire population. If the sampling procedure were repeated, a different set of persons would be selected for the sample and the estimates would differ from the estimates obtained from the first sample; both sets of estimates differ from the quantities that would be obtained if the entire population were observed. The sampling error is often the only type of error that is reported in survey results, even though sampling error may be small relative to the other three sources of error. Dalenius (1977, p. 21) referred to the all-too-common practice of acting as though sampling error is the only component of survey error as "'strain at a gnat and swallow a camel'; this characterization applies especially to the practice with respect to the accuracy: the sampling error plays the role of the gnat, sometimes malformed, while the non-sampling error plays the role of the camel, often of unknown size and always of unwieldy shape."

Many people believe that a census, in which every member of the target population is contacted, is more accurate than a sample survey. This is generally not true; even if the census has no sampling error, it is subject to the other three types of error in data collection. Budgets are limited for any data collection effort, and the resources directed toward collecting information from every member of the population cannot be used train interviewers, follow up on nonrespondents, or reduce measurement error. A well-designed sample, with careful attention to controlling all sources of error, will have higher accuracy than a sloppy census.

A survey should give accurate estimates of a number of quantities. Measurement error and nonresponse error, and ways of reducing or compensating for these, are discussed in this book by Lynn (Chapter 3), Biemer and Christ (Chapter 17), Stapleton (Chapter 18), Rässler, Rubin, and Schenker (Chapter 19) and Hox (Chapter 20). In this chapter, we focus on survey design features that can be used to help control coverage and sampling errors.

6.3 COVERAGE

Coverage may be defined as the percentage of the population of interest that is included in the sampling frame. The main concern about undercoverage, which occurs when the sampling frame is incomplete, is that it can lead to misleading or biased estimates of population quantities. If a segment of the target population is missed that differs on key measurements from the surveyed population, then the resulting estimators are biased. If wealthier households are more likely to have internet access, then a survey about household assets that is conducted exclusively on the internet will produce estimates that are too high.

Overcoverage can be a problem as well. In some circumstances, individuals not in the target population are included in the sampling frame and are not screened out of the sample. These ineligibles can also systematically differ from the members of the target population. A telephone survey asking adults their radio listening habits may end up including persons under age 18, who may listen to different stations than their elders.

The main concern about undercoverage or overcoverage is that they may result in biased estimates. Coverage bias is the error caused by the difference between the frame and the entire target population. Let $\overline{Y}$ denote the mean of all units in the population, and let $\overline{Y}_F$ denote the mean of all units in the sampling frame. Then the coverage bias is $\overline{Y}_F - \overline{Y}$. If the units not in the sampling frame are similar to those in the sampling frame on characteristics of interest, then the coverage bias is small. The problem is that the survey researcher will not know whether this similarity exists unless data are collected on the persons not in the sampling frame. Thus, in many surveys, the amount of coverage bias is unknown.

6.3.1 Survey Mode and Coverage

Different modes of survey administration (in-person, telephone, mail, email, fax, internet, or other mode) exert great influence on the coverage properties, and choice of mode should be influenced in part by the coverage that can be obtained. Dillman (2006) provides an excellent discussion of coverage issues in sample surveys. Other considerations for choice of mode, such as response rate and accuracy of responses for various modes, are discussed in this book by De Leeuw (Chapter 7).

Area frames are generally considered to have the best coverage properties, and are often used in conjunction with in-person surveys. The region of interest is divided into areas; a list of housing units is constructed for the areas chosen to be in the sample and a sample of housing units is selected from that list. Area frames provide a current listing of the population in the area and include households without telephones. Even area frames may have coverage problems, however. Some housing units may be excluded from the frames because they are difficult to find, for example, a housing unit may be located above a business or may have an entrance on an alley. Other housing units may be missed because the enumerator may not be aware of multiple housing units within a structure. There may also be problems when constructing a list of persons within selected households; some persons may not be listed whereas others such as students not in residence may be erroneously included.

Mail surveys require a list of addresses to be used as a sampling frame. Some lists may be complete enumerations of the population, for example, a university's list of all graduates of a certain year for an alumni survey; however, even if the list is complete, the contact information might not be accurate. The list of alumni from a university may not have current addresses of persons who move frequently, are in the military, or are in prison. Other list frames may be incomplete or out of date. The list of faculty in a university may not include visiting or adjunct faculty members, or a list of employees of a corporation may not include independent contractors or recent arrivals. Some list frames, available from commercial organizations in the United States and other countries, are assembled from various public databases. The coverage of these lists is not known.

Email surveys, though attractive because of their low cost, may have coverage problems similar to those of mail surveys. They are suitable for surveys in which the entire population has and uses email accounts, and they require a list of accurate email addresses. It may be challenging in practice to verify that using the listed email addresses will actually reach the persons selected for the sample. In a survey of university students, a student may have an official email address from the university but may never check the account and instead use one from a private internet service provider in practice. Other students may have filters on their accounts that only permit selected messages to be delivered to their mailboxes.

Telephone surveys may use list frames from electronic or printed directories, or may use random digit dialing, which does not require a list of telephone numbers. Telephone list frames, like list frames for mail surveys, may be incomplete or may have incorrect contact information. In the United States, many persons choose to have an unlisted number and thus do not appear in directories, and the proportion of unlisted numbers varies with region of the country and age of the householder. Persons who move frequently often cannot be contacted through a list frame of telephone numbers.

Random digit dialing takes a probability sample of possible telephone numbers, and thus theoretically covers the entire population of households with telephones. But random digit dialing methods may also have problems with coverage. The telephone survey frames do not include households without telephones, estimated to be about 5–6% of the U.S. population, with higher figures in many other countries. In the United States, most telephone survey frames currently do not include households whose only telephone is a cellular phone, and thus often have undercoverage of younger age groups.

The Behavioral Risk Factor Surveillance System survey (BRFSS; described at www.cdc.gov) provides an example of some of the coverage problems that occur in a telephone survey. It is designed to measure preventive health practices and risk behaviors associated with health problems. The survey collects data from a sample of adults aged 18 and older in the United States through a household telephone survey. If the target population is all U.S. residents, some undercoverage results because persons in institutions such as nursing homes or prisons are excluded from the survey. Additional undercoverage occurs because it is a telephone survey. Telephone coverage overall is about 95%, but varies from 87% to 98% across states. Telephone coverage is also lower for households in the southern part of the United States, for minority households, and for households in lower socioeconomic groups. Random digit dialing is used to select telephone numbers for inclusion in the survey, but there is additional undercoverage in the survey because only blocks of numbers with a minimum number of listed household telephone numbers are included in the sampling frame. Households that have only a cellular telephone are currently not included in the sampling frame.

Coverage of the population is a crucial issue in election polls. Ideally, the target population is all persons who will vote on Election Day. Polls use different methods to try to sample from all of, and only from, the set of persons who will vote. In the United States, a sampling frame of all adults, or even of all registered voters, includes many persons who will not vote on election day. In fact, the target population technically does not exist at the time the sample is taken; it is only formed on election day. Most pollsters use models to predict likely voters from a series of screening questions, and there is misclassification. As with other telephone samples, election polls in the United States currently do not cover nontelephone or cellular telephone households.

Internet surveys present new challenges to the survey taker. Couper (2000b, p. 467) states that coverage error is "the biggest threat to the representativeness of sample surveys conducted via the Internet." The obvious coverage problem for internet surveys is that only a portion of the population has access to the internet to participate in surveys, and it is difficult at present to say exactly who the sampling frame population is. In the United States, persons who have high incomes and are college educated are much more likely to have internet access than persons with low incomes or less education. Even if internet users matched the target population on demographic characteristics such as age, sex, income, and education, there is still likely coverage bias because they may well differ on other characteristics. Thus, for internet surveys, the target population must be a carefully defined subset of persons who have access to the internet. Couper (2000b) describes several methods that can be used to conduct internet surveys with good coverage properties; many of these methods involve contacting persons through some other mode such as telephone or email, then asking them to fill out the survey on the internet.

Coverage cannot be determined in samples that consist of volunteers, such as an internet survey in which a web site invites visitors to "click here to participate in our online survey." One typically has no knowledge of characteristics of the survey participants; indeed, the survey respondents may consist of only a handful of separate persons who each participate multiple times. Nonresponse rates also cannot be calculated for such surveys, because the denominator of number of persons who had the opportunity to respond is unknown. In general, samples that rely on respondents volunteering to participate cannot be used to make inferences about a population, no matter how large the sample size is. At best, they are entertainment; at worst, they give misleading statistics, regardless of mode used to collect the data.

6.3.2 Assessing Coverage of a Survey

How can one tell if there is under- or overcoverage of a population? Because by definition undercoverage occurs because persons are missing from the sampling frame, one must use a data source external to the frame to assess the coverage of the population.

For some surveys, it is obvious that there is undercoverage. An email survey, for example, will not cover population members without email accounts. But it is not necessarily known how many such people there are. In some instances, one can consult an external database to see if members of the target population found in the database are missing from the frame.

One method that is sometimes used to assess both undercoverage and nonresponse is to compare estimates of demographic characteristics with known values of those characteristics for the population. If the estimated number of 18–24 year-old males in the population is far lower than a census or population register count of 18–24 year-old males, then there is likely undercoverage of that subpopulation. Note, though, that even if the demographic estimates are close to the population values, undercoverage may still be a problem. A telephone election poll may sample persons from demographic groups in proportion to their representation in the population, but it may happen that supporters of one candidate are less likely to have a telephone and thus will be underrepresented in the poll.

Poststratification can partially alleviate coverage bias, but, as with all after-the-fact adjustments for nonresponse or coverage errors, one does not know whether the adjustment truly compensates for coverage bias unless one obtains data on the persons not covered by the sampling frame. To implement poststratification in the BRFSS, the weight for each respondent in the survey is multiplied by a poststratification adjustment factor. The adjustment factor is the ratio of the number of people in an age-by-sex or age-by-race-by-sex category in the population of a state to the estimate of the number of people in that category based on the sample. Thus, if the sample gives an estimate of 20,000 18–24 year-old males in a region, and the census count of 18–24 year-old males in that region is 25,000, the weight for each 18–24 year-old male in the sample would be multiplied by 25,000/20,000. Those individuals would then also be representing persons in the same category who were not included in the sampling frame. The poststratification adjustment forces the estimates from the reweighted sample to equal the population estimates for the different demographic classes in the region.

Coverage is the critical issue for population censuses, and in that setting it is generally assessed through post-enumeration surveys. Citro, Cork, & Norwood (2004, Chapters 5-6) describe procedures that were used to assess coverage of the year 2000 U.S. Census. The dual-systems estimation procedures used to assess coverage are related to the technique of capture-recapture estimation, which is commonly used for estimating sizes of wildlife populations (Lohr, 1999, Chapter 12). Capture-recapture methods estimate the number of fish in a lake by taking two samples from the same population. In the simplest form of the method, a simple random sample of, say, 100 fish is taken from the lake. These fish are tagged, released, and allowed to mix with the other fish in the lake. A second simple random sample of, say, 200 fish is then taken, and the number of tagged fish in that second sample are counted. If the second sample has 50 tagged fish, then the total number of fish in the lake would be estimated to be $(200/50)(100) = 400$.

Dual systems estimation for assessing coverage works much the same way, by determining how many people in one survey are also counted in a second survey that is conducted independently. A sample of census blocks is chosen for assessing coverage. The original census enumeration in those selected blocks is considered to be the first survey, called the E-sample. Then a second comprehensive sample, called the P-sample, is taken independently in the same blocks. Individuals in the two samples are matched (this is analogous to tagging fish in capture-recapture methods), and the concordance or discordance between the two samples is used to assess the accuracy and possible duplication of E-sample records and to estimate the proportion of the population missing in the E-sample.

6.3.3 Multiple Frame Surveys

As we saw in Section 6.2.2, almost any type of sampling frame or mode of survey administration can present challenges for obtaining full coverage of the target population. In some situations, coverage can be improved by using more than one sampling frame. In a *multiple frame survey,* several sampling frames are employed. Ideally, the target population is the union of the sampling frames; even if the frames taken together do not cover the entire population, however, they often have better coverage than a single frame. In a survey of persons with HIV, one frame might be a list of doctors who treat HIV patients, another frame might be a list of recipients of government-sponsored treatment, and a third frame might be hospitals. Together, the three frames would cover a larger part of the HIV-positive population than any of the frames used individually. Even better population coverage could be obtained by including a fourth frame used for a general population health survey; the fourth frame would include persons missed by the other three frames.

Multiple frame surveys can also be used to reduce survey costs when one sampling frame is inexpensive to use but has incomplete coverage, whereas another frame is more expensive to sample from but covers more of the population. Typically, an area frame has good coverage properties, but is used in conjunction with an in-person survey. A list frame is likely incomplete, but can be sampled more inexpensively, perhaps by using a mail survey. With a dual-frame survey, one takes independent probability samples from the two frames, then combines the information after the data are collected to take advantage of the cost savings from the list frame and the complete coverage from the area frame. If it is possible to remove members of the list frame from the area frame before the samples are taken, then the two frames cover complementary subsets of the population, and population totals can be estimated by summing the estimated population totals from the two samples. If such prescreening cannot be done, several methods have been developed for combining the information from the surveys; some of these methods are summarized in Lohr and Rao (2000).

Often cost savings are realized in multiple frame surveys through using different modes of survey administration in the different frames. Even if the same general mode is used, there may be some differences in the frames that require different treatment: for example, one frame may cover residential telephones, and a second may sample cellular telephones. Thus, the general procedures and concerns described for mixed mode surveys by Dillman, de Leeuw and Hox (Chapter 16) need to be considered for multiple frame surveys.

6.4 PROBABILITY SAMPLING

Probability sampling is the most widely accepted method for allowing quantification of the sampling error, the error that is ascribed to observing only a sample of the population rather than the entire population. In any finite population, there are only a finite number of possible samples (although that number may be very large); with probability sampling, the survey designer explicitly or implicitly assigns a probability that each possible sample will be the one that is actually taken for the survey. Units are then selected for the sample using random numbers generated in accordance with the assigned probabilities. In probability sampling, the probabilities of selection are used to make inferences to the population. This section presents a general overview of probability sampling designs; more comprehensive reviews and methods for estimation may be found in Cochran (1977), Lohr (1999), Thompson (2002), or Lehtonen and Pahkinen (2004).

6.4.1 Why Use Probability Sampling?

Most surveys have a goal of being able to make inferences about quantities of interest in the target population. One may want to estimate the amount of unemployment, illiteracy, or criminal victimization in the population, or one may want to study relationships between these variables. If the persons in a survey on employment status are chosen because they are convenient to reach, or because they volunteer to be in the sample, the survey taker has no way of knowing whether they are representative of persons in the general population or not. With a nonprobability sample, one can compare estimates of demographic characteristics to the general population in an attempt to assess the quality of the sample—if the proportion of young men in the sample differs substantially from the proportion of young men in the population, one may be concerned that the sample is unrepresentative on other characteristics as well—but even if the demographics match the sample could still be unrepresentative for characteristics of interest such as HIV prevalence. In general, one must make strong (and usually untestable) assumptions that the persons in a nonprobability sample are similar on the characteristics of interest to persons not in the sample in order to make inferences about the population. A model-based approach must be adopted for inference with non-probability samples, and the model adopted must be appropriate for units in the population that are not observed in the sample. Chambers and Skinner (2003, Chapters 2–5) have an excellent overview of inferential methods in probability and non-probability samples.

Nonprobability samples are often used for market research or for preliminary work such as testing questionnaires on focus groups, but for official statistics and reliable scientific work, a probability sample is preferred. With a probability sample, the survey taker has less discretion over which individual units in the population appear in the sample. This can remove many of the sources of possible bias in the results. Taking a probability sample particularly helps with reducing some types of coverage error, becausae every unit in the sampling frame has a positive probability of being selected to be in the sample.

Many in the scientific community viewed the results on sleep and mortality in Kripke et al. (2002) with skepticism because the results were based on a convenience sample rather than a probability sample. Even if the sample matched the population on certain demographic characteristics such as age, sex, and income, there is no reason to believe that the sample mirrors the population on the sleep and mortality variables. It may be, in fact, that volunteers and their relatives sleep less (or say they sleep less) than persons in the general population or that they may have been motivated to volunteer in the American Cancer Society because of cancer prevalence in their families.

6.4.2 Types of Probability Sampling

There are many possible methods for designing a probability sample; all of them involve setting out the probabilities that different subsets of the population may be selected as the sample. In this chapter, we briefly describe the main probability sampling designs in common use; methods used for analyzing data collected using these designs are outlined in Chapter 18. The choice of design often depends on the mode of survey administration.

Simple random sampling is the simplest form of probability sampling, and forms the building block for many of the other sampling designs. Every possible subset of size n from a population of size N has the same probability of being selected as the sample. In particular, this means that every unit in the population has the same probability ($= n/N$) of being in the sample, every pair of units has the same probability of being in the sample, and so forth.

A simple random sample is a good choice for a design if little is known about the population being studied. For example, if the sampling frame is a list of email addresses of university students with no additional information about the students, a simple random sample will be easy to select and implement. It has the additional advantage that persons with little background in statistics often consider a simple random sample to be fair.

Because every possible subset of the population has a positive probability of being selected as the sample, it is possible that the actual simple random sample selected will have unusual properties. A simple random sample of students from a university might contain no or only a few women, or no engineering majors, or no students from a certain region of the country. If the sample size is large, it is less likely that these unusual samples will occur, but they are still theoretically possible.

Stratified random sampling provides a means of ensuring that the sample contains representation from population subgroups of interest. The population is divided into groups called *strata* so that each population unit belongs to exactly one stratum. Thus, if additional information such as gender and major is known for the sampling frame of university students, one can divide the population into, say, 20 strata based on these two variables: male engineering majors, female engineering majors, male humanities majors, female humanities majors, and so forth. Then 20 independent simple random samples are taken, one from each of the 20 strata.

The stratified design ensures that the sample will have members from each stratum, so it is impossible to select a sample that contains no engineering majors. The survey taker can also select the sample size for each stratum, which gives a great deal of control over the survey design. If a main purpose of the survey is to compare male engineering majors with female engineering majors, the survey taker can set equal sample sizes for these two strata, which gives the greatest precision for such comparisons. Thus if there are 1000 male engineering majors and 100 female engineering majors, the sample design might specify sampling 50 persons from each category. In this case, the probability that a male engineering major would be selected for the sample is 1/10, and the probability that a female engineering major would be selected for the sample is ½. To estimate population characteristics such as the average number of hours spent studying by all students at the university; these unequal probabilities of selection are incorporated into the estimation procedure through weighting (Biemer & Christ, Chapter 17).

If a sample that reflects the overall characteristics of the population is desired, the survey taker can use a stratified design with *proportional allocation,* in which the same proportion of population units is sampled in each stratum. With proportional allocation, if 5% of the population is to be sampled overall, the design would specify sampling 5% of the male engineering majors, 5% of the female engineering majors, and so forth. Because undesirable samples (such as those with no engineering majors) are eliminated from the set of all possible samples, and because often persons within the same stratum are similar to each other, estimates of population quantities based on a stratified sample with proportional allocation are almost always more accurate (have smaller variance) than estimates based on a simple random sample from the population of the same total sample size.

Simple random sampling and stratified random sampling work well when there is a list frame of persons in the population, such as a list of addresses or telephone numbers of all customers or a list of email addresses of all students. When the list contains additional information such as number of purchases or college major, that information can be used to stratify the population to gain more efficiency in the sampling. In either case, a random number generator can be used to select the units to be included in the sample from the list.

Cluster sampling. With some of the other modes of survey administration, though, it may be difficult to obtain a sampling frame of individuals, or it may be expensive to take a simple random sample. With an in-person survey, a simple random sample from a country would be prohibitively expensive because it would entail traveling to certain villages just to interview one or two persons. Instead of using a simple random sample, cluster sampling methods would typically be employed in this situation. Two or more sizes of sampling units are used in cluster sampling: first, larger units called *clusters* or *primary sampling units* (psu's) are selected for the sample using a probability sampling design, then some or all of the smaller units, called *secondary sampling units* (ssu's) are selected from each psu in the sample. To take a cluster sample of persons in a region where everyone lived in villages, one would first select a probability sample of villages (the psu's); from the selected villages, one would then construct a list of the households or persons in that village and take a probability sample of households or persons from that list. This design would be less expensive to implement than a simple random sample of persons because the interviewing is restricted to the sample of villages. It also does not require a list of households or persons for the entire region; that list only needs to be constructed for the villages selected to be in the sample.

Cluster sampling is frequently used with other modes of survey administration as well. A mail survey asking all employees of each business in a simple random sample of businesses to fill out a questionnaire gives a cluster sample of employees; the psu in this case is the business, and the ssu is the employee. In a telephone survey, the interviewer may ask questions of several members of a household once a household is reached for the survey, so that a cluster sample of persons is taken. To conduct an email survey of university students in a country, the investigator may take a sample of universities, then obtain a list of email addresses of students from each selected universities; each university is a psu, and the students are the ssu's.

The psu's often occur naturally in the population, for example, the villages in a region, the employees in a business, or the students in a university. Because ssu's in the same psu generally have environmental factors in common, they are often more similar to each other than would be the case if they were randomly selected from the entire population. Some villages are primarily agricultural, and others have more industry: one would expect that persons selected from the agricultural villages would be more likely to report an agriculturally related primary occupation. Students attending a university specializing in engineering are likely to report more scientific training than students attending a liberal arts university. Because of this similarity, sampling five students from the same university generally would not provide as much information about the population of all university students as would sampling five students at random from the population. Thus, although cluster sampling may be less expensive per person interviewed, persons in the same psu often provide somewhat overlapping information. In general, more persons must be interviewed in a cluster sampling design to obtain comparable precision with a simple random sample.

Unequal probability sample. Psu's may be of disparate size. Some universities may have 500 students; others may have 45,000 students. If a simple random sample of universities is taken at the first stage of cluster sampling, it is possible that many of the large universities, accounting for most of the students in the country, will not appear in the sample. An unequal probability sample design could be employed instead to avoid this problem. Instead of having the same probability of selection for every university, the probability that a university would be selected for the sample could be set in proportion to the number of students, so that the larger universities would have higher probabilities of being included in the sample. If it is desired that every student has the same probability of being selected for the sample, then one could specify sampling k students from each sampled university. Then, if M_i is the number of students in university i and M is the total number of students in all universities in the population, the probability that a given student at university i is selected for the sample would be $(M_i/M)(k/M_i) = k/M$.

Unequal probability sampling can occur in practice even though at first glance it might be thought that all units have an equal chance of being included in the sample. Random digit dialing is often recommended for telephone surveys in order to have better coverage than can be obtained using a list frame of telephone numbers from a directory. In its simplest form, random digit dialing could be carried out be taking a simple random sample of all possible telephone numbers. However, this is a simple random sample of telephone numbers, not necessarily a simple random sample of households with telephones. Some households have multiple residential telephone lines, and these households are more likely to be included in the sample than are households with only one telephone number. Even in its simplest form, random digit dialing results in an unequal probability sample, where households are selected with probability proportional to the number of telephone lines.

In many countries, the simplest form of random digit dialing is inefficient for telephone surveys because a relatively low proportion of possible numbers are actually assigned to a household. The Mitofsky-Waksberg method of random digit dialing employs cluster sampling with unequal probabilities: in the first stage of sampling, psu's of blocks of 100 telephone numbers are selected with probabilities proportional to the number of residential telephone numbers in the block. In the second stage of sampling, k individual telephone numbers are selected from each block of numbers. Tucker, Lepkowski, & Piekarski (2002) discuss Mitofsky-Waksberg sampling and compare its efficiency to stratified telephone sampling designs.

Stratified multistage samples. Many large surveys use both stratification and clustering, often with several stages of clustering. Stratified multistage samples are common for large national surveys, such as surveys taken to estimate unemployment, income, or public health. First, the country is divided into strata, often based on geographic regions. Such stratification is done because (a) one wants separate estimates of unemployment in the different regions, and the stratification guarantees a specified sample size in each region and (b) it is likely that unemployment differs in the regions, and stratification can lead to gains in efficiency. Then, within each stratum, psu's (often smaller regions such as metropolitan areas or counties) are sampled; often the psu's are sampled with probability proportional to population. The psu's may themselves be too large for all the households to be enumerated, so smaller enumeration areas (ssu's) may be subsampled from the sampled psu's. At the last stage of sampling, individual households are selected to be interviewed.

A stratified multistage sampling design uses auxiliary information from a source such as a census or population register in forming the strata and setting the selection probabilities for psu's; however, it also allows for better coverage of the population than if the census or population register were used as the sampling frame. When an enumeration area is selected for the sample, the area is visited and an up-to-date sampling frame of the households in that area is constructed prior to selecting the households to be interviewed. Consequently, recent migrants to that area are included in the sampling frame, although they would be part of the uncovered population if the census list were used.

When analyzing the data from any probability sampling design, the estimation procedures must be appropriate for the design. It is, unfortunately, not uncommon to see standard error formulas for a simple random sample used, even when a complex design is used. This is particularly prevalent in the reporting of political polls in the United States, where the margin of error reported is usually simply based on the observed sample size, and does not reflect any of the sampling design. Stratification, clustering, and unequal probability sampling are powerful techniques for the sampling toolbox, but these design features must be incorporated into the data analysis, as described by Biemer and Christ (Chapter 17) and Stapleton (Chapter 18).

6.5 SAMPLING RARE POPULATIONS

Many surveys are taken to study characteristics of a subpopulation that may be numerous but does not constitute a large proportion of the overall population, or is widely dispersed in that population. An agency might want to take a survey of persons who are unemployed; there may be millions of unemployed persons in a country, but many general population surveys would consist mostly of employed persons and yield relatively small samples of unemployed persons. Several of the methods described above may be used to take a probability sample of a rare population. These, and other methods, are described in more detail in Kalton and Anderson (1986).

Stratification with disproportional allocation may be used to increase representation of the rare population in the sample. In some cases, strata can be constructed so that persons in the subpopulation of interest are concentrated in some of the strata, and then one can take larger sample sizes from the strata with high concentrations of the subpopulation. To get more unemployed persons in the sample, one can take higher sampling fractions within strata where it is thought the unemployment rate is higher. To obtain coverage of the entire population, though, one also needs to sample observations from the strata thought to have low concentrations of the population of interest, even if those strata are sampled with lower sampling fractions. Unemployed persons in regions of high unemployment may have very different characteristics from unemployed persons in areas with low unemployment, and need to be included in the sample.

Similarly, if the persons in the rare population are clustered geographically, one can select psu's for the sample with probabilities proportional to the estimated concentration of members of the rare population. If that concentration cannot be estimated in advance, a two-stage procedure similar to the Mitofsky-Waksberg random digit dialing design may be used, where one household from the cluster is selected in the first stage. If that household has a member from the rare population, the cluster is included in the sample and more households from that cluster contacted; otherwise, the cluster is rejected. With this procedure, clusters containing no members of the rare population are excluded from the sample at the first stage.

Adaptive cluster sampling (see Thompson, 2002) may also be used to sample rare populations that are geographically clustered. An initial probability sample of psu's is selected, and the number of members of the rare population is estimated for each sampled psu. From that point, sampled psu's are chosen sequentially: a psu not in the sample is assigned a higher probability of selection if it is next to a psu from the original sample with a high concentration of the rare population. The modification of the selection probabilities in the sequential sampling is accounted for when estimates of population quantities are calculated.

Screening can be used with any probability sampling design. A preliminary contact is made with a household selected for a large screening sample, and a household member may be asked if anyone in that household is unemployed. If the answer is yes, the household is included in the sample for more in-depth questions; if no, the household is discarded from the sample. Screening must be done carefully so that households are not misclassified as being out of the rare population when in fact they belong to it. This is a particular danger in surveys involving a public health component or sensitive information, where persons in a household may be unaware that someone in the household has cancer or is HIV positive. If misclassification is a concern, a sample may be divided into two parts: one in which all households are interviewed, and a second part in which households are screened and only the households that pass the screening test are interviewed.

Multiple frame surveys, described in Section 6.2.4, are particularly useful for sampling rare populations. The survey taker may have one or more list frames of potential members of the rare population, for example, a list of persons currently collecting unemployment benefits. The list is inexpensive to sample from but does not necessarily cover all of the population of interest; with a multiple frame survey a separate sample can be taken from an area frame so that the entire rare population is covered.

6.6 CONCLUSION

Probability samples are widely regarded as the gold standard for sampling, because they allow quantification of the sampling error and may reduce coverage error as well. Stratification can be used to decrease the sampling error. Cluster sampling, although it generally increases sampling error, often results in cost savings and better coverage for a survey. Probability sampling methods have been used with face-to-face, mail, email, and telephone surveys with great success. One current challenge is development of methods for using probability sampling with internet surveys; at this writing, many internet surveys use convenience samples and are not reliable for making inferences to the population. For populations with internet access, an internet survey may be a low-cost method of collecting survey data; however, in most instances one does not know who will be accessing a web site and thus one currently cannot quantify probabilities of inclusion in the sample.

The design of a survey is crucial to its success and all potential sources of survey error— coverage error, nonresponse error, measurement error, and sampling error—must be considered at the design stage. A design that achieves a small sampling error, for example a stratified random sample from a list of e-mail addresses of customers, may have severe undercoverage problems. The features of a survey design are interconnected, and the survey design must be fitted to the statistical priorities (Dalenius, 1985). With careful attention and resources devoted to the survey design, one can anticipate and prevent many of the possible errors in the survey.

GLOSSARY OF KEY CONCEPTS

Cluster sample. A sample in which the sampling units are groups (clusters) of population units.

Coverage. The percentage of the population of interest that is included in the sampling frame.

Multiple frame survey. A survey in which samples are selected separately from two or more sampling frames.

Probability sampling. Probability sampling methods give a known probability of selection for all possible samples from the sampling frame. They thus provide protection against selection bias, and give a means of quantifying sampling error.

Rare population. A subpopulation that does not constitute a large proportion of the overall population, and is often widely dispersed in that population.

Sampling error. Error in estimation due to taking a sample instead of measuring every unit in the sampling frame.

Sampling frame. A list, map, or other specification of units in the population from which a sample may be selected. Examples include a list of all university students, or a telephone directory.

Stratified sample. A sample in which the population is divided into groups called strata, and independent probability samples are taken separately in every stratum.

Chapter 7

Choosing the Method of Data Collection

Edith D. de Leeuw

Department of Methodology & Statistics, Utrecht University/MethodikA

7.1 INTRODUCTION

Essentially there are two basic forms of data collection: those with and those without an interviewer, in other words: interviews and self-administered questionnaires. Interview surveys can either be in person or over the telephone, and there is a large variation across countries in the usage of these methods. Countries with a high telephone penetration, like the United States, Canada and Scandinavia, use mainly telephone interviews and face-to-face interviews are only implemented when needed for special surveys or special populations. Other countries, which have a lower telephone penetration, rely on face-to-face surveys for the general population and employ telephone surveys successfully for special groups (e.g., elites). For a more in-depth discussion of face-to-face interviews, see Loosveldt (Chapter 11); for telephone interviews, see Steeh (Chapter 12). Self-administered questionnaires take many forms. They can be used in group settings, such as classrooms in educational research, or they can be used in more individual settings, such as the respondent's home or office (see de Leeuw & Hox, Chapter 13). A well-known and frequently used self-administered method is the mail survey (Dillman, 1978), but its computerized version the Internet survey (Lozar Manfreda & Vehovar, Chapter 14) is gaining rapidly in popularity.

Different methods can also be combined in one mixed mode design (see de Leeuw, Dillman, & Hox, Chapter 16). A good example is a procedure for asking sensitive questions during an interview. At a certain point the interviewer hands over a paper questionnaire that the respondent completes in private without direct participation of the interviewer. After completion the respondent may seal the questionnaire in an envelope and mail it back or return it directly to the interviewer (de Leeuw, Hox, & Kef, 2003).

All methods described earlier are respondent oriented. There are also data collection methods that do not involve active participation of respondents (Biemer & Lyberg, 2003). Examples are direct observation, which is often used in biology and qualitative research, and the linking of administrative records and existing data files in official statistics (see Bethlehem, Chapter 26).

Computer-assisted procedures for data collection methods have been developed in the last 40 years and computer-assisted methods are replacing paper-and-pen methods at an increasing pace. In Western Europe and North

America many government survey organizations now employ computer-assisted methods for their surveys and large market research organizations and academic research organizations have followed. Characteristic of all forms of computer assisted data collection is that questions are read from the computer screen, and that responses are entered directly in the computer, either by an interviewer or by the respondent. An interactive program presents the questions in the proper order; in more advanced forms this order may be different for different (groups of) respondents. For each paper-and-pen data collection method there is now a computer-assisted form available. (For a detailed review and summary see this book's website, Chapter 7). Computer-assisted methods have many advantages, but I want to emphasize that it is possible to do high quality paper-and-pen surveys too, as the history of survey research proves.

In theory, when designing a survey there are many data collection methods to choose from: face-to-face and telephone interviews, mail questionnaires, Internet surveys, and all kinds of combinations. One may use paper-and-pen forms, in which an interviewer writes down the answers, or one may use sophisticated computer-assisted forms. All forms can result in high quality data and the choice for a particular data collection method is dictated by the research objectives, the concepts to be measured, and the population under study. For instance, if one needs data quickly as in election studies, telephone interviews are a good choice. But, only in theory; in practice, there may be limitations to the choice, which vary across and within countries. For instance, in a developing country, telephone penetration may still be low and the general population may not be adequately covered. However, in that same country, telephone penetration may be high for special groups and quality telephone interviews for those groups may be feasible. This chapter guides researchers from different countries in the complex decision about which mode to choose for a particular survey. I concentrate on four main modes of data collection: face-to-to-face, telephone, mail, and Internet surveys. The next sections provide material for a well-informed choice, based on both theoretical and practical considerations and taking into account empirical research on mode comparison.

7.2. WHY EXPECT DIFFERENCES BETWEEN MODES

In the literature several theoretical factors are identified that differentiate between survey modes. These factors can be grouped in three classes: interviewer effects, media related factors, and factors influencing information transmission (de Leeuw, 1992, this book's website Chapter 7). Understanding why and how data collection modes differ will *both* help researchers to choose the mode, which is best for their research objective, *and* help researchers to implement the chosen mode optimally.

7.2.1 Interviewer Impact

Modes of data collection clearly differ in how much they restrict interviewer impact. In a mail or Internet survey the interviewer is absent and cannot play a role—either positive or negative—in the question-answer process. In a telephone interview, which is aural only and has a limited channel capacity (e.g., no nonverbal communication see 7.2.3.), interviewers have potentially less impact on respondent behaviour than in a face-to-face interview.

Interviewers have several responsibilities during an interview: they have to motivate respondents, to deliver and when necessary clarify questions, to answer respondent's queries, and to probe after inadequate answers (cf. Loosveldt, Chapter 11; Lessler, Eyerman & Wang, Chapter 23). In face-to-face situations interviewers can use nonverbal cues (e.g., smiles, nods) to motivate respondents and keep the flow of information going. Furthermore, interviewers can monitor and react to respondents' nonverbal expressions. In telephone interviews these tasks are more difficult; nonverbal communication is impossible and interviewers must be alert to attend to auditory information (cf. Conrad, Schober, & Dijkstra, forthcoming). But, in both modes interviewers are present to answer questions, solve problems, and give additional information. In mail and Internet surveys the respondent is totally dependent on the questions as stated and on the instructions in the questionnaire. Internet surveys have more opportunities (e.g., help keys, pop-up screens) to give additional information than paper mail questionnaires.

Interviewers clearly have advantages, but they also have disadvantages, for instance by inhibiting socially undesirable answers. Therefore the more limited impact of interviewers in telephone surveys may also have a positive influence on respondents. After all, the interviewer is only a voice over the phone, and as a consequence the respondent is less restricted in his/her personal space and can be more relaxed. In face-to-face surveys, respondents often fall back on the 'receiving a guest' script, and their self-imposed role as a host may influence their reactions. The total absence of an interviewer in a mail or Internet survey allows respondents even more personal space than a telephone interview and may introduce a greater feeling of anonymity in the respondent. A more anonymous and private setting reduces the tendency of respondents to present themselves in a favourable light and induces fewer problems of self-presentation, which is a great asset when sensitive questions are asked.

The simple presence of an interviewer may influence answers, but interviewers can affect respondent behavior in many ways; not only through what they say and do, but even by how they look and sound (cf. Loosveldt, Chapter 11). This interviewer effect increases the total variance of the statistics under study leading to more measurement error (cf. Kish, 1962). The restricted channel capacity, sound only, of the telephone interview gives telephone interviewer characteristics less chance to influence respondents. Furthermore, the central setting of most telephone interviews allows for a stricter control over interviewers and thereby for smaller interviewer effects; however, as interviewers in telephone surveys usually have larger workloads than in face-to-face interviews, the total effect on the data may still be large. For an overview of interviewer effects see Hox, de Leeuw, & Kreft (1991) and Japec (2005).

7.2.2 Media Related Factors

Besides the presence or absence of the interviewer, there are other factors related to the data collection mode that affect survey data, such as media related factors. Media related factors are concerned with the social conventions and customs associated with the media used in different survey methods, such as familiarity with a medium and use of a medium. Media related factors are mainly sociocultural factors, but they do influence the cognitive processing factors in the question-answer process (cf. Schwarz, Knäuper, Oyserman & Stich, Chapter 2; Campanelli, Chapter 10), and thereby may cause mode effects. Media related factors may differ between data collection modes; they may also differ between countries and cultures, just as familiarity with surveys in general and with the respondent role may differ between countries and cultures (cf. Loosveldt, Chapter 11).

7.2.2.1 Familiarity with medium
The first media related difference between data collection modes concerns the degree to which people are acquainted with the media concerned. In general, people are used to all kinds of face-to-face interactions in which information is being gathered, for example, conversations with medical doctors, teachers, and supervisors. Face-to-face contacts in surveys are therefore seen as appropriate and have acquired a place in society.

The first use of the telephone was as an instrument of business for short communications. Later, the telephone became an instrument for private conversations with family and friends, enabling people to maintain close contacts over larger distances. Social customs concerning this private use may differ between cultures; but everywhere telephone calls received at home from strangers are typically expected to be for a business purpose (e.g., selling), and not for an exchange of personal information, and this has consequences for both cooperation and data quality in telephone surveys (de Leeuw & Hox, 2004). Also, there may be a marked difference in use. In the western world a mobile phone is a very personal device, like a wristwatch, and is used to stay in constant contact with the outside world. There is also a trend to have more than one mobile phone, one for the job with a number that is generally known, and one with a secret number for friends and family only. In contrast, in several non-western countries, mobile phones are seen as a community device, when whole villages share one or two mobile phones.

The medium for mail surveys is the self-administered form. Most people in western society are familiar with forms, such as immigration forms, school tests, or tax forms. But, completing these types of self-administered forms is not the most exciting or pleasant thing to do. Also, the completion of self-administered forms demands literacy and a relative high level of active command of a language. People may feel more compelled to avoid grammatical errors in written communications, which may inhibit the freedom of expression and the amount of details in written answers as compared to spoken answers. In many countries, the younger generation is now growing up with Internet. There are special web sites for young children, for adolescents and for special interest groups, and especially chatting online is very popular. Also, the text facilities of mobile phones are being used intensely and a special 'texting' language has developed, for instance using D8, when making a date. It may be expected that young people, growing up with new technology, will freely use Internet and related media in answering questions and will give more information in 'typed' answers than in spoken ones.

How familiar people are with Internet depends on the Internet penetration within a country and the computer literacy within a specific culture. Although Internet access is growing and in 2007 almost 70% of the U.S. population had access to the net, the picture is diverse ranging from 76% in Sweden and 74% in the Netherlands to 4% for Africa (www.internetworldstats.com). But even within highly computerized societies there are differences in computer literacy, related to age, sex, education, and socioeconomic class, just as within developing countries special highly computer literate subgroups can be identified and used in surveys.

7.2.2.2 Locus of control

The second media related factor focuses on the locus of control during data collection, that is, who has the most control over the question-answer process. In a face-to-face interview both respondent and interviewer share the locus of control. As initiator of the conversation the initiative is given to the interviewer, but the social rules of good behavior during a personal visit prescribe that the pace of the interview and the communication flow are determined by both parties involved. In a telephone interview the interviewer is more in control, as traditional rules of behavior dictate that the initiator of a telephone conversation, here the interviewer, controls the channel and the regulation of the communication flow. This may lead to more superficial cognitive processing by respondents, leading to more top-of-the-head answers, and more satisficing in responses to telephone questions (see also Schwarz et al., Chapter 2).

In a mail or Internet survey the respondent is in control and the respondent is the one who determines when and where the questions are being answered and at what pace. This gives respondents the opportunity to look up information and consult other members of the household when proxy information about household members is being asked for. Furthermore, in a self-administered questionnaire the respondent and not the interviewer notes down the answer, which gives an extra check on the correctness of the recorded answer and emphasizes the total control of the respondent on the pace of the question-answer sequence. The Internet is a much more dynamic medium than a paper form, allowing for multitasking and quickly skipping from one topic to the next. Also, Internet users are more impatient with the web than they are with paper; they may have more screens open at one time, and may very quickly terminate an online survey whenever they want to do so. Just as in telephone interviews, this may lead to more superficial cognitive processing and more satisficing; in addition Internet surveys may be prone to more early break-offs.

7.2.2.3 Silences

The third media related factor involves the social conventions regarding the acceptability of silences in a conversation. This factor sharply distinguishes the face-to-face interview from the telephone interview. There is a marked tendency to avoid silences in a telephone conversation and long silences over the telephone are considered improper and rude. In a face-to-face situation, both respondent and interviewer see what is happening and can use nonverbal communication to make silences acceptable. In telephone conversations one solely relies on the auditory channel and an interviewer has to be trained to bridge silences and, for instance, say explicitly "I am noting your answer down" to make a long silence acceptable.

7.2.2.4 Sincerity of purpose

The fourth media related factor refers to the differences in the ability of media to convey sincerity of purpose. This is extremely important for soliciting cooperation and for trustworthiness and quality of answers. The personal contact in a face-to-face situation gives an interviewer far more opportunities to convince a respondent of the legitimacy of the study in question. The behavior of an interviewer and even the way they dress can communicate trustworthiness; furthermore, they can show official identification cards, brochures, and survey related material. A telephone interviewer, without any clear means of identification, has far less chances to communicate trust and legitimacy, and that is why the initial text spoken in a telephone interview is so important. In order to establish legitimacy, survey organizations may send an advance letter explaining the survey, or have a special toll-free telephone number available for inquiries (cf. de Leeuw & Hox, 2004, de Leeuw, Hox, Lensvelt-Mulders & Callegaro, 2006). Establishing sincerity of purpose is even a greater problem in general web surveys. The increasing rate of misuse, such as, SPAM, phishing and identity spoofing, makes Internet users distrustful of general email invitations to click on a provided link, especially when no previous relation with the sender exists. Only in the case of a well-established and trusted relationship with the surveying company is a general email invitation workable; for instance, when an established (access) panel is being used. In other cases, trustworthiness should be communicated in other ways, for example with a paper mail advance letter, or telephone invitation, or by using the Internet in a mixed-mode setting (de Leeuw et al., Chapter 16). When special populations are surveyed, one may use special methods to establish trustworthiness, such as an email sent through the secure intranet of a specific company, or an announcement in the company's (electronic) newsletter. A mail survey can use a logo, a valid return address, and other visual means to emphasize the trustworthiness of the survey. Furthermore, mail surveys do not have to be answered immediately and offer the respondent the possibility to check out the survey organization first.

7.2.3 Information Transmission

As has been discussed, the presence or absence of an interviewer and general medium related factors can influence the data collected. Related to these factors is the way the information is transmitted through the interviewer or through the medium of choice. This determines the cognitive stimulus respondents receive and differs across various modes of data collection. Important factors in information transmission are presentation of information, channels of communication, and regulation of communication flow.

7.2.3.1 Presentation of information

Information can be presented visually, or aurally (auditory), or both. When information is presented only aurally, for instance in a telephone survey, this demands more of the memory capacity of the respondent and may lead to recency effects in longer lists. As a consequence, in telephone interviews respondents may have a tendency to choose the last response category more often than earlier categories on the list. Visual presentation of information, both in self-administered questionnaires or via special show cards during a face-to-face interview, relieves the cognitive burden and may lead to fewer response effects. However, for web surveys the situation is different; social customs in Internet surveys differ and this may interact with cognitive burden. For example, Internet users may be more impatient and use satisficing strategies more often, as a consequence, they may not process the whole list of response categories fully and opt for the ones early in the list: a primacy effect.

7.2.3.2 Channels of communication

Three types of communication are traditionally distinguished: verbal communication, nonverbal communication, and paralinguistic communication. Verbal communication is only concerned with the spoken words or the printed text, nonverbal communication is concerned with the meaning of gestures, expressions and body posture, and paralinguistic communication is concerned with (nonverbal) auditory signals, like emotional tone, timing, emphasis, and utterances like "mhm-hmm" (cf. Argyle, 1973). These channels of communication are important for posing and answering questions; for instance, paralinguistic information, such as putting emphasis on a word conveys to the respondent the importance of this term. But, these channels are also used to give 'para-information' about the question-answer process. During an interview, just like during an ordinary conversation, the participants give each other nonverbal cues like nods, paralinguistic cues, like "uh-uh," and verbal cues, like "what do you mean by…". Therefore, these communication channels are extremely important for sending and receiving cues of (mis)understanding by interviewer and respondent, and thus for the quality of the final answer.

A fourth way of communication is through graphical language, such as different fonts, italics, use of arrows, shades, and other graphical and lay-out tools. This graphical language is all-important for the visual design in self-administered questionnaires, and can be seen as a mix form of nonverbal and paralinguistic communication to transmit additional information to the respondent without the help of an interviewer (de Leeuw, 1992, Redline & Dillman, 2002).

In face-to-face interviews verbal, nonverbal and paralinguistic communication is used to transmit information between respondent and interviewer; when visual material, such as a show card, is presented graphical communication plays a role too. Telephone interviews have a far more limited channel capacity; only verbal and paralinguistic means of communication are available in telephone conversations, although modern technology (e.g., multimedia cell phones) may change this (see Steeh, Chapter 12). The absence of a channel for nonverbal communication in telephone surveys makes the transmission of all kinds of information harder for both interviewer and respondent, and interviewers have to be specially trained to use verbal communication as a compensation for the lack of nonverbal communication. For instance, telephone interviewers have to learn to say explicitly yes and thank you instead of using a nonverbal nod or smile. In mail surveys all information is conveyed by the printed word and, besides the verbal text itself, the main tool of communication is through visual design. For instance, the lay-out of a questionnaire and the use of graphical devices and illustrations can partly take over the role of the nonverbal and paralinguistic channels to add extra emphasis to a term or to clarify parts of a text (see also Dillman, Chapter 9). The Internet is a mixture, it mainly uses text and graphical information, but the multimedia potential (both audio and video) can and sometimes is used. Visual design is especially important in Internet surveys. Not only does the software provide more possibilities for using graphical language in Internet than in paper surveys, but users have also learned to use graphical language on the web. Clear examples are the use of font types for emphasis (e.g., CAPITALS indicate shouting), and special words (e.g., LOL indicating Laughing Out Loud) and emoticons (e.g., smileys ☺) to convey emotions.

7.2.3.3 Regulation of communication flow

Telephone and face-to-face surveys differ clearly in the regulation of the communication flow between interviewer and respondent. In face-to-face interactions nonverbal cues are very important for channel control (e.g., to determine turn taking). Argyle (1973, p. 72) points out that channel control is an important factor to make verbal exchanges possible. "Interactors have to take it in turns to speak and listen, and speech itself cannot be used to decide who shall speak or for how long … channel control is effected by small nonverbal signals, mainly head-nods and eye movements. These signals are presumably learnt." In telephone conversation mainly paralinguistic cues are used to regulate the communication flow. For instance, prolonged silence means "your turn," and mhm-hmm means "continue, I am listening to you." Also, contrary to the custom in face-to-face interactions, explicit spoken signals are allowed in a telephone conversation. For instance, in a telephone conversation, an explicit yes or okay replaces the nonverbal nod. In mail and Internet surveys no explicit turn taking takes place. The respondent is the locus of control over the information flow and can decide when to stop or to continue the question-answer process (pause and resume). However it is feasible that new technology may be used to simulate interviewers and to control the interview process more (cf. Couper, 2002), thereby changing the communication process in Internet surveys into a more dynamic one.

Why Expect Differences?

Data collection modes differ in availability of communication channels, in media related factors, and in interviewer effects. It is important to realize that these factors are related; for instance, in a face-to-face situation an interviewer can use more channels of communication than in a telephone situation, thus information transmission and interviewer impact are related. Also, the factors locus of control and interviewer impact are correlated and differ across modes, thereby influencing privacy of disclosure. Thus, the more control respondents have, the more privacy, the more willingness to disclose on sensitive matters and the less social desirability. On the other hand, the greater the control on the part of the respondent, the less chance that they can be persuaded to answer and the fewer opportunities to motivate them or give additional information and explanation. Finally, different modes make use of different communication channels. This in turn influences the type of questions that can be asked *and* the way questions and questionnaires are constructed. The implication of mode choice for questionnaire construction is more fully discussed by Dillman in Chapter 9.

7.3 MODE OF DATA COLLECTION AND MEASUREMENT

7.3.1 Questions and Questionnaire

7.3.1.1 Questionnaire length and duration of interview
Regarding the duration of the interview and the amount of questions asked, the face-to-face interview has the most potential. Face-to-face interviews can last longer than telephone, mail, or Internet surveys. When an interviewer is physically present, it takes a highly assertive respondent to end an overly long face-to-face interview. It is much easier to hang up a phone in mid-interview or stop completing a long mail survey. Terminating a web survey is easiest of all, a break-off is just one mouse-click away. As a rule, successful telephone surveys can be conducted with an average length of twenty to thirty minutes. Longer telephone interviews generally lead to either a higher nonresponse rate or a higher probability of premature termination of the interview. Still, successful telephone interviews have been reported which took over 50 minutes. A small negative effect of questionnaire length on the response rates has been found for mail surveys (e.g., Heberlein & Baumgartner, 1978). According to Dillman (1978, p. 55) mail questionnaires up to 12 pages, which contain less than 125 items, can be used without adverse effects on the response. Internet surveys must be relatively short; 10–15 minutes is already a long time for an Internet survey (Czaja & Blair, 2005). But, longer web surveys may successfully be implemented for special groups, panel members, and/or when a salient topic is surveyed.

7.3.1.2 Differences in question format and complexity

Face-to-face interviews are the most flexible form of data collection method. Visual and auditory stimuli may be used, all channels of communication are available for information transmission and feedback, and an interviewer is present as intermediary between researcher and respondent. The presence of a well-trained interviewer enables the researcher to use a large variety of measurement instruments. Structured or partly structured questionnaires can be used, and open questions needing detailed answers are possible, because interviewers may prompt respondents to add more details. With specially trained interviewers even specific measurements are possible, such as physical measurements in health surveys or reading and other tests in literacy surveys. Also, respondents can be presented with all kinds of visual stimuli, ranging from simple show cards listing the answer categories of a question, to pictures, advertisement copy, or video clips. Furthermore, highly complex questionnaires can be successfully implemented as a trained interviewer takes care of the navigation through the questionnaire. In computer-assisted face-to-face interviews (CAPI), the interviewer is guided through the (complex) questionnaire by a computer program. This lowers error rates even more and gives the interviewer more opportunities to concentrate on the interviewer-respondent interaction and the respondent tasks.

Telephone interviews are less flexible. Their major drawback is the absence of visual cues during the interview; telephone is auditory only. No show cards with lists of answer categories are available; the interviewer reads the question out aloud with the available response categories and the respondent has to rely solely on memory. Therefore, only questions with a limited number of response categories can be used. In general, questions must be short and easily understandable over the phone. Just as in face-to-face interviews, well-trained interviewers are an advantage. In telephone surveys the interviewer can assist respondents in understanding questions, administer questionnaires with a large number of screening questions, control the question sequence, and probe for answers on open questions. But nonverbal communication is not possible, and interviewer and respondent must rely on what they hear; therefore fewer cues about misunderstanding or errors in communication are available (cf. Conrad, Schober & Dijkstra, in press). Again like in CAPI, the use of computer-assisted telephone interviewing (CATI) facilitates the handling of complex questionnaires (e.g., questionnaires with many routings or skips) for the interviewer.

The absence of an interviewer makes mail surveys the least flexible data collection technique when complexity of questionnaires is considered. All questions must be presented in a fixed order, and only a limited number of simple skips and branches can be used. For routings, like skips and branches, special written instructions and graphical language tools, such as arrows and colors, have to be provided. In a mail survey, all respondents receive the same instruction and are presented with the questions without added interviewer probing or help in individual cases. In short, a mail questionnaire must be totally self-explanatory. A big advantage is that visual cues and graphical language can be used, and with well-developed instructions fairly complex questions and attitude scales can be asked. The visual presentation of the questions makes it possible to use graphical questions (e.g., ladder, thermometer), and to use questions with seven or more response categories. Also, information booklets or product samples can be sent by mail with an accompanying questionnaire for their evaluation. Another advantage is that mail surveys can be completed when and where the respondent wants. A respondent may consult records if needed, which may improve accuracy, and the greater privacy is an advantage with sensitive topics.

Internet surveys share the advantages of mail surveys regarding visual aids. Also, just as in mail surveys, the respondent is in charge and the situation may offer more privacy. Because an interview program determines the order of the questions, more complex questionnaires can be used than in a paper mail survey. In this sense (complexity of questionnaire structure) an Internet or web survey is equivalent to an interview survey. But, Internet also has a drawback, it is a more perfunctory medium and people often just pay a flying visit. Respondents may have a stronger tendency to satisfice and give top-of-the head answers (cf. Schwarz, Knäuper, Hippler, Noelle-Neuman, & Clark., 1991).

Question Format and Complexity of Questionnaire

When an interviewer is present more complex structured questionnaires can be used. Besides handling the questionnaire routing, interviewers may offer help or additional explanations when respondents misunderstand parts of questions or questionnaire. In face-to-face interviews, where interviewer and respondent not only hear but also see each other, there are more opportunities for avoiding and repairing mistakes and misunderstandings. Available communication channels and the way stimuli may be presented also influence the format of the questions. If questions are only presented aurally (auditory), as is the case in telephone interviews and in practice often in face-to-face interviews, simpler questions with fewer response categories can be asked than when full visual presentation of questions and response formats is possible. For a detailed discussion of data collection method and question format, see Dillman, Chapter 9.

7.3.2 Empirical Evidence of Mode Effects on Measurement Error

The influence of data collection method on data quality has been extensively studied for face-to-face interviews, telephone surveys, and self-administered mail questionnaires. De Leeuw (1992) performed a meta-analysis of 67 articles and papers reporting mode comparisons. The resulting overview showed consistent but usually small differences between methods, suggesting a dichotomy of survey modes in modes with and modes without an interviewer. Comparing mail surveys with both telephone and face-to-face interviews, de Leeuw found that it is indeed somewhat harder to have people answer questions in mail surveys. Both the overall nonresponse and the item nonresponse are higher in mail self-administered questionnaires when compared with interviews. But when questions are answered, the resulting data tend to be of better quality. Especially with more sensitive questions, self-administered mail surveys performed better with, in general, less social desirability in responses, more reporting of sensitive behavior like drinking, and less item nonresponse on income questions. When face-to-face and telephone surveys were compared, small differences in data quality were discovered. Face-to-face interviews resulted in data with slightly less item nonresponse. No differences were found concerning response validity (record checks) and social desirability. In general, similar conclusions can be drawn from *well-conducted* face to face and telephone interview surveys (de Leeuw, 1992).

In a carefully designed experiment, de Leeuw (1992) investigated additional aspects of data quality, such as consistency and reliability of answers, response tendencies, and responses to open questions. Again, the main differences were between the mail survey on the one hand and the two interview surveys on the other hand. The self-administered questionnaire, where the respondent has most control and can read the questions and answer at leisure, resulted in more reliable and consistent responses and less acquiescence. Face-to-face interviews performed slightly better than telephone interviews, but the differences are relatively minor. Regarding responses to open questions, the results were mixed. When short open questions are asked on well-defined topics, the differences between mail and interview mode are small. With more complex questions, the assistance and probing of an interviewer is necessary to get more detailed answers.

When interviewers are explicitly studied, larger interviewer variances are generally found in face-to-face interviews than in telephone interviews. This is usually attributed to the closer interviewer supervision in centralized telephone surveys compared to face-to-face interviews. On the other hand, in centralized telephone interviews usually a small number of interviewers conduct a large number of interviews, while in face-to-face interviews this is just the opposite. Therefore, as the total effect of the interviewers on the overall variance of the survey statistic is a function of both interviewer variance and interviewer workload, the overall effect may be larger in telephone surveys than in face-to-face surveys (e.g., Groves, 1989; Japec, 2005).

A limited number of studies have studied specific response effects, such as recency and primacy effects, acquiescence, and extremeness. Although some studies found more acquiescence and extremeness for telephone interviews than in face-to-face surveys and mail surveys, the results are not strong and completely consistent (for an overview, see de Leeuw, 1992). Evidence for recency and primacy effects is mixed; in a large number of experiments and using a variety of question structures, Dillman, Brown, Carlson, Carpenter, Lorenz, Mason, et al. (1995) found inconsistent evidence for primacy effects in mail and recency effects in telephone surveys. These inconsistent findings could be due to interaction effects; for instance mail surveys will in general produce less social desirable answers, whereas in telephone surveys recency effects occur and the last options is favored. When the last response option of a question is also the less social desirable answer, the two mechanisms counteract each other, resulting in no large overall differences between the methods.

Internet is a relatively new medium for surveys, and as a result systematic mode comparisons are still scarce (for an overview see de Leeuw, 2005; see also Couper, 2000; Lozar Manfreda & Vehovar, Chapter 14). There is some indication that Internet surveys are more like mail than like telephone surveys, with more extreme answers in telephone surveys than in Internet surveys. More extremeness in telephone interviews was earlier found in comparisons with paper mail surveys and is attributed to visual versus aural information transmission; the same mechanism may be responsible for differences between telephone and Internet surveys. Comparisons between web and mail surveys give mixed results, some studies find more partial nonresponse and more item nonresponse in web surveys, others report less item nonresponse in web surveys than in mail surveys. To fully understand if and how Internet differs from other modes, controlled mode comparisons with Internet are needed in different situations and using a variety of topics to enhance the generalizability of findings. This should be preferably be followed by a systematic overview of mode effects or a meta-analysis.

Mode Effect on Data Quality

When comparable surveys with equivalent questionnaires are investigated, no data collection mode is superior on all criteria. The most pronounced differences have been found with more sensitive topics. Modes with an interviewer produced more socially desirable answers and less consistent answers, but also more detailed responses to open questions. Differences between face-to-face and telephone interviews were small, with the face-to-face interview doing slightly better than the telephone.

7.4 DIFFERENCES IN COVERAGE AND SAMPLING

Provided that a complete list of the individual members of the target population is available and the list contains full contact information, there is no difference between the modes. A random sample of the target population can be drawn regardless of the data collection method used, and coverage and sampling will not be a decisive issue in the choice of data collection. Examples are surveys of special groups, surveys of members of an organization, in-company surveys, and surveys of students or alumni of a university.

When one is interested in studying the general population and no up-to-date population registers are available as sampling frame, the face-to-face survey has the greatest potential. Sophisticated sampling designs for face-to-face surveys have been developed that do not require a detailed sampling frame or a list of persons or households. For instance, area probability sampling selects geographically defined units (e.g., streets or blocks of houses) as primary units and households within these areas. Therefore, a main advantage of face-to-face interviews is its *potential* for a high coverage of the intended population. Elaborate techniques based on household listings (e.g., inventories of all household members derived by an interviewer) can then be used to randomly select one respondent from those eligible in a household; for an overview, see Gaziano (2005). Face-to-face interviewing has the highest potential regarding coverage and sampling, but it can be very costly, especially if the country is large and sparsely populated. Cluster sampling may be needed, and if the sample dispersion is very high telephone surveys are often employed. For coverage and sampling see Lohr (Chapter 6).

Telephone interviews are feasible if telephone coverage is high, in other words if the nontelephone part of the population can be ignored. To be sure that persons with unlisted telephones are also included, one can employ Random Digit Dialing (RDD). Random digit dialing techniques, which are based on the sampling frame of all possible telephone numbers, make it possible to use telephone interviews in investigations of the general population. A new challenge to telephone survey coverage is the increasing popularity of mobile (cell) phones. If mobile phones are additional to fixed landline phones, that is, a household has a landline phone and the individual household members also have mobile phones, this will not pose a major problem for (under)coverage. But, there is evidence that certain groups (e.g., the young, lower income, urban, more mobile) are overrepresented in the mobile-phone-only part of the population, and are not covered when landline only phones are sampled. For more detail see Steeh, (Chapter 12). In telephone interviews, as in face-to-face interviews, elaborate procedures can potentially be used to select respondents within a household; however, asking for a complete household listing at the start of a telephone interview is a complex and time consuming procedure and increases the risk of break-offs. Good alternatives are the next birthday and the last birthday method. In the last birthday method, the interviewer asks to speak with that household member who most recently had a birthday.

Mail surveys require an explicit sampling frame of names and addresses. Often, telephone directories are used for mail surveys of the general population. Using the telephone directory as a sampling frame has the drawback that people without a telephone and people with an unlisted telephone cannot be reached. The reason for the frequent use of the telephone directory as sampling frame is the relative ease and the low costs associated with this method. A drawback of mail surveys is the limited control the researcher has over the choice of the specific individual within a household who in fact completes the survey. There is no interviewer available to apply respondent selection techniques within a household and all instructions for respondent selection have to be included in the accompanying letter. As a consequence, only simple procedures such as the male/female/youngest/oldest alternation or the last (most recent) birthday method can be successfully used. The male/female/youngest/oldest alteration asks in a random 25% of the accompanying letters for the youngest female in the household to fill in the questionnaire, in 25% of the letters the youngest male is requested to fill in the questionnaire, et cetera.

In Internet or web surveys, coverage is still a major problem when surveying the general population. Not all people have access to the Internet, and Internet penetration varies from country to country. But Web surveys can be successfully used for special subgroups or subpopulations or be applied in a mixed mode design. Just as in paper-mail surveys the control of the web interview situation is low. A wife may fill in a survey in the name of her husband or vice versa, people can fill in a questionnaire together and so forth.

In market and applied research access panels are becoming increasingly popular for web surveys. An access panel is basically a rich database of *willing* respondents, which is used as a sampling frame for Internet studies, but also may be used for other data collection procedures (e.g., a subsample may be approached by phone). When used for Internet surveys, samples of access panel members are sent requests to fill in web questionnaires at regular intervals. Panel research is not new, and the advantages and disadvantages of panel research have been well described (e.g., Kasprzyk, Duncan, Kalton, & Singh, 1989), what is new is the potential of Internet to select and survey huge panels at low costs. A major quality criterion for Internet panels is how the Internet panels were composed. Is the panel based on a probability sample (e.g., RDD telephone invitation), or is it a nonprobability sample, in other words is it based on self-selection (e.g., through banners or invitations on a website inviting people to become a panel member). Only probability-based panels allow for sound statistical analysis. Nonprobability panels may result in very large numbers of respondents, but beware those respondents are a convenience sample. As all statistics are based on the assumption of probability sampling, statistics (e.g., margin of errors, p-values) computed on nonprobability samples, such as self-selected Internet panels, make no sense at all. Recently, propensity score adjustment has been suggested to reduce the biases due to noncoverage, self-selection, and nonresponse (Lee, 2006). In propensity weighting one ideally has access to a reference sample with high quality data and low nonresponse. As in all weighting schemes it is important that good auxiliary variables are available and that the variables used in the adjustment are both highly related to the outcome variable and to the self selection mechanism. If this is the case, is the question. Therefore, it is the researchers' duty to be transparent on the weighting procedures used and the predictive power of the propensity model.

Coverage and Sampling

If telephone penetration in a country is low, a telephone survey of the general population will lead to serious coverage error. But a telephone survey of special groups who are accessible by phone will still be feasible. The same goes for Web surveys and Internet penetration. Internet surveys of special groups may be highly successful. For mail surveys lists of postal addresses are needed. If these are not available, trained persons may be used to sample names and addresses through a random walk method, comparable to the face-to-face interview situation. The difference is that no interview is attempted, but that questionnaires are sent to the persons sampled, thereby saving time and money. Face-to-face surveys are the most flexible method regarding coverage and sampling, but may be very difficult or costly to apply in large and sparsely populated countries

---

7.5 DATA COLLECTION MODES AND NONRESPONSE

Survey nonresponse is the failure to obtain measurements on sampled units. Nonresponse can be distinguished from coverage error by the fact that not-responding units are selected into the sample, but not measured, whereas noncovered units have no chance of being selected in the sample (e.g., no known address, no telephone number) and thus cannot be measured. For a detailed discussion of nonresponse see Lynn (Chapter 3). There are two major sources of nonresponse: noncontact in which no request for cooperation can be made, and explicit refusal. A third source is incapacity to cooperate. Examples of method-specific incapacities to answer are illiteracy in mail and web surveys, and deafness and language problems in telephone and face-to-face surveys.

Survey response can be influenced by many factors: the topic of the questionnaire, the length of the questionnaire, the survey organization, the number of callbacks or the number of reminders, and other design features. One should distinguish between so called cold surveys, that is, surveys for which a fresh sample is drawn, and surveys that use a panel design or a respondent pool or access panel of respondents. The latter are based on respondents who responded positively to an earlier request for participation and are willing to take part in subsequent studies. In general, (access) panels have a much higher response rate than cold surveys. The reason for this higher response is that the hard-core nonrespondents have already been filtered out in the acquisition stage. For a fair comparison between surveys based on fresh samples and on (access) panels, the initial nonresponse in the panel acquisition phase should be taken into account too.

In general, nonresponse has increased over time. For instance, de Leeuw and de Heer (2001) showed that response rates have been declining internationally. They analyzed data from national statistical agencies of 16 different countries over the period 1980–1998 and found an increase in both noncontacts and refusals over the years. The de Leeuw and de Heer international study investigated mainly non-response in face-to-face situations. Curtin, Presser, and Singer (2005) studied trends for telephone surveys in the United States, focusing on the Survey of Consumer Attitudes, which is university based. They also found a distinct increase in nonresponse over the past 25 years. These studies point in the same directions as earlier explicit mode comparisons. In general, face-to-face surveys tend to obtain higher response rates than comparable telephone surveys, and mail surveys tend to have a lower response rate than comparable face-to-face and in lesser degree to telephone surveys. In addition, the response rates for both telephone and face-to-face surveys are declining, although such a trend is not as evident for mail surveys. Goyder (1987) published one of the first systematic overviews on differences in nonresponse among modes. He collected data on 385 mail surveys, 112 face-to-face surveys and 53 telephone surveys in the United States and Canada between 1930 and 1980. On average the response rate for the face-to-face interview was 67.3%, for the telephone interview 60.2%, and for the mailed questionnaire 58.4%. Goyder (1987) also notes a pronounced increase in nonresponse for the face-to-face interview over the years, whereas the nonresponse for mail surveys remains stable. Hox and de Leeuw (1994) came to similar conclusions. Their meta-analysis summarized the results of 45 studies that explicitly compared the response obtained in mail, telephone, and face-to-face surveys. The data for these 45 mode comparisons were collected in several countries in Europe, in the United States, and in Canada. Again, on average face-to-face interviews produced the highest response (70.3%), telephone interviews the next highest (67.2%), and mail surveys the lowest (61.3%). The trend remarked upon by Goyder (1987), is clearly visible in the data of Hox & de Leeuw (1994). Both the face-to-face and telephone surveys show a decrease in response over time, while the response of mail surveys remains stable over time. Similar results were found in Germany for the time period 1960-1995 (Bretschneider & Schumacher, 1996). It should be noted that all figures cited were based on official (government) surveys and on semi-official and academic surveys at the end of the twentieth century. Response figures for commercial and market research surveys are in general even much lower. To our knowledge, no recent and systematic mode comparisons are available.

Systematic overviews of response rates in Internet surveys are scarce. For nonscientific pop-up web surveys, where an invitation to complete a survey pops-up on a web portal, the response rate can not be determined. The reason why the response rate can not be computed for pop-up web surveys is that the total number of eligible respondents is not known and the population not well-defined. When a good sampling frame is available and a sample is drawn, response rates for web surveys can be computed. The first results for such probability based web surveys are promising (Vehovar, Batagelj, Lozar Manfreda & Zaletel, 2002), although studies comparing response rates among Internet, mail and telephone surveys suggest that response rates are generally lower for online surveys (Matsuo, McIntyre, Tomazic & Katz, 2004). Empirical comparisons between e-mail and paper mail surveys of the same population indicate that response rates on e-mail surveys are lower than for comparable paper mail surveys (Couper, 2000b); similar results are found for list based web surveys (Couper, 2001). It should be noted that with special populations and extra effort comparable response rates are feasible (Kaplowitz, Hadlock, & Levine, 2004),

Data collection methods differ not only in response rates, but also in opportunities to reach not-at-homes and to convince reluctant respondents. Furthermore, there are differences in richness of available information on nonrespondents and the why and how of nonresponse. Face-to-face interviewers, standing on the doorstep, have most opportunities to convince respondents and to gather additional information on nonrespondents. Due to the absence of a visual communication channel, telephone interviewers have far less opportunities to convince reluctant respondents and to gather additional data. But, an advantage of the telephone is that it is very easy and inexpensive to reapproach not-at-homes until a contact is being made, whereas in face-to-face surveys, only a very limited number of contact attempts is affordable. Due to the absence of an interviewer in mail and web surveys, strategies to convince potential respondents are usually limited to written text. Research has shown that personalization, prenotifications, and reminders do have a positive influence on response in mail and web surveys. Also, mail and web surveys have far less access problems than interviews, the mail survey is delivered on the doormat and the announcement of a web survey is either delivered through email or by ordinary mail. But, due to the lack of personal contact both mail and web surveys are very limited in detecting reasons for nonresponse. The exception is when access panels are used for web surveys; inherent in access panels is that a rich database with background characteristics is available for all panel members (see also Hoogendoorn & Sikkel, Chapter 25). This allows nonresponse analysis for specific surveys based on this panel. It should be noted that in general no information is available about the initial nonrespondents in the panel formation stage.

Nonresponse

Each method has its own strength and weaknesses. The telephone makes it very easy and affordable to contact potential respondents often and at different times of the day and week, while in a face-to-face situation an interviewer has more time and more opportunities to persuade. When the postal services in a country are reliable, a mailing will reach the respondent so noncontact is low, whereas security systems and answering machines may hinder contact in face-to-face and telephone interviews. Therefore, mixed-mode strategies are often employed to contact and persuade respondents. For instance, an advance letter before an interview or a telephone follow-up after a mail survey.

7.6 TIMELINESS, COSTS, AND LOGISTICS

In general, Internet and telephone surveys are the fastest to complete for a survey organization. Mail surveys are usually locked into a definite time interval of mailing dates with rigidly scheduled follow-ups, although large geographically dispersed face-to-face interviews take the longest. When speed of completion is important and data are needed very quickly, telephone and Internet surveys are best. If the data are needed in a couple of weeks, mail surveys are also feasible. Dillman (1978, p. 68) gives an example in which a survey unit of 15 telephones can complete roughly 3000 interviews during the 8 weeks it takes to do a complete mail survey with carefully timed reminders. Only if the telephone unit is smaller than 15 interviewers, or the number of needed completed interviews larger than 3000, a quality mail survey will be faster.

Each data collection technique requires that certain organizational conditions are met. The implementation of a successful, large scale, face-to-face survey demands most from an organization and its personnel. Interviewers have to be selected and trained; not only in standard interview techniques, but also in how to implement sampling and respondent selection rules and in how to solve various problems that can arise when they are working in the field. In addition, a supervisory network is necessary to maintain quality control. Finally, an administrative manager is needed to make sure that new addresses and interview material are mailed to the interviewers on a regular base.

The personnel requirements for a telephone survey are less demanding. As interviewers do not have to travel considerable distances to respondents less interviewers are needed. Also because of the centralized setting and centralized quality control, fewer highly trained supervisors are needed. Interviewers should, of course, always be well trained in standard interview techniques. But, because of the close supervision the variety of skills needed is less in telephone interviews. The majority of the interviewers no longer have to be prepared for every possible emergency and can concentrate on standard good quality interviewing. Difficult respondents or problem cases can be dealt with by the available supervisor or can be allocated to more experienced or specially trained interviewers.

Organizational and personnel requirements for a mail survey are even less demanding. Most of the workers are not required to deal directly with respondents, and the necessary skills are mainly generalized clerical skills (e.g., typing, sorting, response administration, and correspondence processing). Of course, a trained staff member must be available to deal with requests for information, questions, and refusals of respondents. Finally, the number of different persons needed to conduct a mail survey is far less than that required for face- to-face or telephone surveys with equivalent sample sizes. For instance, one person can single-handedly successfully complete a mail survey with reminders of a sample of 1000 persons in the prescribed 8 week Dillman schedule (cf. de Leeuw, 1992). However, to design and implement an Internet survey skilled and specialized personnel is needed. To design a successful Internet survey both technical knowledge is needed (e.g., operating systems, browsers, etc.) and knowledge on usability and visual design. In addition help-desk personnel must be available to address questions or problems of respondents (see also Lozar Manfreda & Vehovar, Chapter 14).

Timeliness, Costs, and Logistics

Requirements for the organization and personnel do influence the cost of data collection. Mail and Internet surveys have relatively low costs and may be the only modes affordable in certain situations. Both web and e-mail surveys are less costly than comparable mail surveys, but they do require highly skilled personnel, which mail surveys don't. Telephone surveys are less expensive than face-to-face modes, especially for widely geographically dispersed surveys. Telephone surveys also need a smaller staff than comparable face-to-face surveys. When interviewer assistance is essential, but the survey is a large national or international study and

---

7.7 WHICH METHODS TO CHOOSE

In some situations, circumstances decide which mode is to be used. In a country where telephone penetration is low, telephone surveys cannot be used. If speed is important, as in election polls, mail surveys are too slow to be useful. If a large number of respondents is needed and cost is of extreme importance, an Internet survey will have the lowest costs per completed questionnaire. Also, sometimes traditions or in-house expertise within research organizations decide the mode. If a research organization has much experience with telephone surveys and an efficient telephone interview facility, telephone surveys will be the preferred mode. On the other hand, if a research organization has invested in large Internet panels and has years of experience with online research, Internet surveys will probably be their first choice.

However, in most situations there is a genuine choice and advantages and disadvantages must be weighted against each other to reach a decision. The first set of factors to consider is the research objective, that is the concepts to be measured and the target population. These influence the characteristics of the sample and the types of question that will be used, and are therefore important factors to think about in choosing the survey mode.

The second set of factors to consider are characteristics of the survey mode itself. First, as discussed earlier in this chapter, there are two main forms of survey data collection: self-administered questionnaires and standardized interviews, mainly characterized by the absence versus presence of an interviewer. Secondly, it is important to know whether paper or computer administration will be used. As a consequence, there are many possible variations to choose from, such as face-to-face and telephone interviews with their computer-assisted equivalents CAPI and CATI, self-administered mail questionnaires, and Internet surveys. Each method has its advantages and disadvantages. Box 7.1 summarizes the main advantages and disadvantages of questionnaires and interviews. Although Internet surveys are in fact self-administered questionnaires, they are sufficiently different from their paper counterpart that they merit a separate comparison in Box 7.1.

Ideally, the choice for a specific survey mode is made on the basis of the intrinsic value given the research question and population, in actual fact the decision will also be based on expected response rate, financial cost, and timeliness. The survey costs depend strongly on the particular survey situation and the available organizational facilities; it is impossible to give general guidelines, especially when differences between countries are involved. To facilitate the cost appraisal, it is convenient to divide survey costs into front-end, fieldwork, and back-end costs. Front-end costs are costs that are encountered before the survey is put in the field. These include for example the time needed to devise the questionnaire, design the lay-out and/or program the questionnaire, print questionnaires, hire interviewers and train them, and design the sampling plan. Fieldwork costs are the costs of the actual data collection, such as interviewer reimbursement and travel costs, postage, and telephone costs. Back-end costs are the costs made in data coding and entry, and in correcting data errors. With computer-assisted data collection, back-end costs tend to move to the front-end. Computers increase the effort at the front-end, because questionnaires need to be programmed and tested before the data collection starts. Questionnaires can also be made more complex, which often leads to several revisions before the final questionnaire is available to be fielded. On the other side, during the fieldwork interviewer and respondent errors are diminished, so that at the back-end substantial time and cost savings occur because data coding, entering and correcting are greatly reduced. More time is spent at the front-end, and less at the back-end, so the data are available more rapidly after the fieldwork itself has ended.

7.8 CONCLUSION

It is clear that deciding which data collection mode is best in a certain situation is a complex decision. Which data collection mode or mix of modes is chosen is the result of a careful consideration of quality and costs. Using multiple modes or mixed modes of data collection, in an effort to obtain the best of different modes, has become increasingly popular. In mixed-mode surveys, two or more modes of data collection are combined in such a way that the disadvantages of one method are counterbalanced by the advantages of another. For instance, combining a web survey with a telephone interview to compensate for undercoverage of the elderly and lower educated on the Internet, or combining a face-to-face interview for the general part of the questionnaire with a self-administered method for the more sensitive questions and topics of the questionnaire. Of course, when modes are mixed, particular attention should be paid to equivalence of question format and comparability of answers (cf. Dillman, Chapter 9). For a discussion of issues in mixed-mode surveys see de Leeuw, Dillman, & Hox (Chapter 16).

Box 7.1 Advantages and Disadvantages of Four Data Collection Modes

Mail Surveys:
1. Mail surveys lack the flexibility and interviewer support of interview surveys, which limits the complexity of the questionnaire. This is partly mitigated because visual stimuli, such as pictures or graphics can be used.
2. Mail surveys are less intrusive than interviews: respondents may answer at leisure in their own time and there is no interviewer present who may inhibit free answers to more sensitive topics.
3. Lists with addresses of the target population should be available, but telephone numbers are not necessary.
4. Mail surveys have a longer turn-around than telephone surveys, but face-to-face interviewing usually takes even longer.
5. Mail surveys are less costly than both face-to-face and telephone interview surveys, and require a much smaller field staff.

Internet Surveys:
1. Internet access varies strongly between countries and within countries. As a consequence, coverage and sampling may be sub-optimal. Lists with email addresses of the target population should be available, and depending on the population under investigation large coverage problems may arise.
2. In Internet surveys complex questionnaires and visual stimuli can be applied, but questionnaires must be short.
3. Like mail surveys Internet surveys are less intrusive and more private.
4. Large numbers of completed questionnaires can be collected in a very short time and at low cost.
5. Internet surveys can easily reach international populations.
6. Almost all Internet surveys run on the respondents' computer, and questionnaire implementation must consider potential differences in computer systems and browsers used.

Box 7.1 Advantages and Disadvantages of Four Data Collection Modes (continued)

Face-to-Face Interviews:

1. Face-to-face interviewing has the highest potential with respect to types of questions and questionnaire complexity. To realize this potential one needs both well-trained interviewers and well-tested questionnaires, and a qualified field staff is needed to take care of the logistics. This is very costly and time consuming and only worth it in some situations; researchers should carefully consider if all that potential is really needed to answer the research objective.

2. Face-to-face interviewing has also the highest potential regarding coverage and sampling, but again it can be very costly, especially if the country is large and sparsely populated. Cluster sampling may be needed, and if the sample dispersion is very high telephone surveys are often employed.

3. The greatest asset of the face-to-face interview—the presence of an interviewer—is also its greatest weakness. Their presence may influence the answers respondents give, especially when sensitive questions are being asked, and in general they may contribute to the total survey error, due to variance in interviewer skill.

Telephone Interviews:

1. Telephone interviews have less potential with respect to types of questions than face-to-face interviews, because there is no visual communication. But interviewers are available to assist the respondent and complex questionnaires may be used. However, fewer questions can be asked. A good rule of thumb is 20–30 minutes although longer telephone interviews can and have successfully been completed.

2. Due to households that have no telephone, unlisted numbers, and mobile phones, coverage may be sub-optimal. However, if good lists are available, telephone interviewing is, from a sampling point of view, comparable to face-to-face interviewing. If the sample dispersion is very high, telephone surveys are often the only *interview* mode feasible.

3. In telephone interviews quality control is high as interviewers can be closely monitored and immediate feedback is possible.

4. Many interviews can be completed in a relative short time using a smaller number of interviewers than face-to-face. Also telephone interviews are less costly than face-to-face interviews.

GLOSSARY OF KEY CONCEPTS

Access Panel. An access panel is basically a rich database of willing respondents, which is used as a sampling frame for Internet studies, but may be used for other data collection procedures too. Panel members are invited and selected in various ways, through self-selection via websites, through acquisition by other panel members, at the end of successful face-to-face or telephone interviews, and so forth. Quality panels use a probability sample (e.g., RDD telephone interview) to approach and invite potential panel members.

Computer Assisted Self Interviewing (CASI). Also known as **Computer Assisted Self Administered Questionnaires (CSAQ).** Defining characteristic is that the respondent operates the computer: questions are read from the computer screen and responses are entered directly in the computer. One of the most well-known forms of CASI is the web survey. Other forms are Disk-by-mail (DBM) and Interactive Voice Response (IVR).

Face-to-face interview. In a face-to-face interview an interviewer administers a (partly) structured questionnaire to a respondent within a limited period of time and in the physical presence of the respondent (often at the respondent's home).

Internet (Web) Survey. Internet surveys are a form of self-administered questionnaires, in which a computer administers a questionnaire on a web site. Survey questions are viewed and answered using a standard web browser on a PC. The responses are transferred through the Internet to the server.

Mail (postal) survey. When a mail questionnaire is used, a respondent receives a structured questionnaire and an introductory letter by mail, answers the questions in her/his own time, without any assistance from the researcher or her/his representative except for any written instructions in the questionnaire or in the accompanying letter, and finally sends the questionnaire back.

Mixed-mode survey. A survey where multiple and different data collection modes are used to make contact with the respondents or to complete the total questionnaire.

Satisficing. When the cognitive tasks required to answer a question is quite burdensome, respondents may look for ways to avoid expending all the effort required to optimally process the information, while still maintaining the appearance of answering adequately and responsibly; they try to find a heuristic. This is called satisficing. The opposite, respondents attempt to be fully diligent, is called **optimizing**.

Self-Administered Questionnaire (SAQ). Questions are administered and answered without the assistance of an interviewer. There are several forms of SAQ, such as paper questionnaires in mail surveys, group administered questionnaire in schools (e.g., tests), individual questionnaires filled in during an interview to ensure privacy, and drop off questionnaires, where surveyors personally deliver questionnaires, but the respondents fills in the questionnaire on their own and either mail it back or keep them for the surveyor to collect.

Telephone interview. In a telephone interview the interviewer administers the questions (from a structured questionnaire and within a limited period of time) via a telephone. Telephone interviewing is often centralized; that is, all interviewers work from a central location under direct supervision of a field manager or a quality controller.

Chapter 8

Writing Effective Questions

Floyd J. Fowler, Jr.
Carol Cosenza
University of Massachusetts

8.1 INTRODUCTION

In surveys, the answers to questions are measures. Researchers define the constructs that they want to measure. They ask respondents questions, and they want the answers to those questions to be measures of those constructs. The degree of association between the construct and the answers is the way we know how well the question has been designed. The purpose of this chapter is to describe what we know about how to design questions, the answers to which are good measures of constructs.

8.1.1 What Is a Construct?

For those familiar with the philosophy of Plato, the idea of a construct will be easy. Every reality can be thought of as an abstract concept, which we refer to as a construct. Some constructs involve very little abstraction. The color of a person's hair or how much a person weighs, for example, can be easily observed or measured. In contrast, constructs such as wealth or distress may be more complicated to define and, as a result, pose more difficult challenges for question design. Wealth can include how much money people make on their jobs, how much money they have accumulated in the past, the value of the things they own, and even the assets of other family members who may share with them. A first, important step in designing a measure of wealth is deciding what the construct is, what one really means by wealth, for the particular research project.

Distress poses similar problems. Distress can be physical or mental; it can be short-lived or continuous. Distress may not be observable directly by others. It is not easy to think about how to measure distress independently of asking people questions.

Survey researchers do design questions to measure all of these things: Hair color, weight, wealth and distress. This chapter helps readers understand the threats to good question design, the reasons that questions may not be good measures of constructs, and techniques for overcoming those challenges.

8.1.2 Reliability and Validity

Reliability and validity are the standards by which we measure how well a question performs. The validity of measurement refers to how well the answer to a question corresponds with the true value for the construct that is being measured (Cronbach & Meehl, 1955). Reliability has two meanings. First, a given respondent whose value on a construct has not changed should give the same answer to the same question at different points in time. In a parallel way, two respondents whose true value on a construct is the same should answer the question in the same way. To the extent that there is inconsistency, we say that the measurement is to some degree unreliable; that is, it does not always give the same result when the true value is the same.

Reliability is a desirable characteristic in a measure, and less reliable measures will also be less valid. However, reliable answers are not necessarily valid. A question can produce reliable results that do not correspond very well with the "true value" of a construct. Validity is the ultimate measure of how good our questions are as measures.

For constructs such as weight, it is theoretically easy to assess validity by comparing respondents' reports of their weight with the readings from a scale. In a similar way, objective raters could describe a person's hair color, and those ratings could be compared with the answers provided by respondents.

For constructs such as distress, which cannot be measured directly, the way in which we assess validity is less direct, but the goal is basically the same: to assess how closely our measure corresponds to evidence about the true score or value of our target construct (Cronbach & Meehl, 1955; Ware, 1987). If we could identify two groups of people whom we thought, on average, differed in distress, we could find out if our measure of distress reflected the same kind of difference between the groups. If we have some valid, independent way of assessing the extent to which individuals are distressed, our measure of distress should get higher as our various indications of distress go up; it should be lower to the extent that our independent measure of distress goes down.

8.1.3 Goals of Question Design

One useful framework for thinking about question design is provided by Roger Tourangeau and colleagues (Jabine, Strac, Tanur, & Tourangeau, 1984; Tourangeau, Rips, & Rasinski, 2000, see also Schwarz, chapter 2). The following is an adaptation of this framework to the question-and-answer process in a survey.

To answer a question, a respondent must: (a) Understand the question. If respondents do not understand a question in the way the researcher intended, that is one obvious reason that answers may not be good measures of the target construct. (b) Have or retrieve information needed to answer the question. (c) Translate relevant information into the form required to answer the question. (d) Provide the answer by writing it on a form, entering it into a computer, or telling an interviewer.

This chapter is largely organized around these steps. However, before getting to the issues related to how to design questions, we want to discuss the choice of questions to ask.

8.2 ASKING THE RIGHT QUESTION

When designing survey instruments, researchers first have to decide which constructs they want to measure, the ones that will meet their analytic needs, then decide what questions they can ask people in order to get good measures of those constructs.

Example construct:
How people feel about universal health insurance.
Example question:
Do you favor or oppose health insurance for all people in the United States?
Comment:
It does not take much testing to learn that this question as designed measures the wrong construct. Almost no one is opposed to the idea of everyone in the United States having health insurance. If someone answers "oppose," probing reveals that most will be opposed to a particular way of providing health insurance, not the idea of insurance itself. The controversy is around who is going to pay for it and who is going to provide it: the Federal government, state governments, private insurance companies, or some combination thereof. Thus, the researchers have to rethink their analysis goals and redefine their target constructs.

Example construct:
The quality of medical care provided by physicians.
Example question:
How would you rate the ability of your doctor to diagnose what is wrong and recommend the right treatments?
Comment:
When this question was tested, researchers found that most patients could not answer this question (Fowler, 1997). In many cases, when patients see doctors, the doctor does not even get a chance to demonstrate how well he or she can diagnose and choose treatments. The problem is obvious, the treatment options are limited, or perhaps no treatment is needed at all. Moreover, when respondents who did have the experience of needing diagnosis and treatment were probed about their answers, they typically had little confidence in their ability to judge how well physicians carried out these tasks. The researchers concluded that there were no questions to which respondents could give meaningful answers that would constitute good measures of the technical ability of physicians. In some occasions, asking questions is not the best way to measure a construct. Measuring the technical quality of physicians is one such construct.

If constructs are not well chosen and properly defined, or if researchers do not identify questions people can answer that will be good measures of the constructs, good question wording or other aspects of question design cannot produce valuable data. On the other hand, once the right question objectives are chosen, how those objectives are turned into questions will make all the difference in the validity and reliability of the resulting data.

8.3 ASKING QUESTIONS THAT ARE CONSISTENTLY UNDERSTOOD

A core concept in using questions as standardized measures is that every respondent is supposed to be answering the same question. When two or more respondents could have different understandings of what a question is asking, answers might differ due to the way the question was understood rather than because respondents had something different to say. One important goal when designing effective questions is to reduce the potential for misunderstandings. In short, we want to reduce ambiguity: the potential to be open to more than one interpretation.

Choice of vocabulary is a very important part of how respondents understand questions. Researchers should take into account the reading level of potential respondents and take steps to write clear and simple questions. In addition, there are several other features of a question that have the potential to create ambiguity:

1. The use of unfamiliar, complex, or technical words and phrases, abstract nouns and verbs, and ambiguous adjectives and adverbs;
2. Lack of a time frame;
3. Imbedded assumptions about the respondent's situation or the way he/she views things;
4. Asking multiple questions at the same time.

8.3.1 Choice of Vocabulary

8.3.1.1 Unfamiliar or technical terms
Questions that contain unfamiliar or technical terms are often difficult for respondents to answer because they do not know or understand some of the words. When respondents do not understand the words used in the question, they might ask for clarification, might refuse to answer it, or might guess at the meaning of the unknown phrase and answer the question anyway. All three of these options decrease the reliability of the measurement. By writing questions using simple words and defining uncommon or technical phrases, the potential for problems because of vocabulary greatly decreases. This is especially important in health studies, where specific names of diseases and diagnoses are often asked about. For example, respondents may know they have particular symptoms (such as pain or stiffness in the joints) but may not know the name of the actual diagnosis (for example, arthritis). If a survey simply asked about the diagnosis, respondents might incorrectly respond that they do not have that problem. All fields of inquiry have words that are used by the experts that are not familiar to the general public; such words do not belong in survey questions without being defined.

Example:
Have you ever had a pneumonia shot?
Alternative:
The pneumonia shot, also called the pneumococcal vaccine, is a shot usually given only once or twice in a person's lifetime and is different from the flu shot. Have you ever had a pneumonia shot?
Comment:
By providing additional information about what a pneumonia shot is, the alternative increases the likelihood that the question is better understood and that it will provide reliable data.

Some topics remain difficult, even after definitions are provided.

Example:
Do you think the United States should or should not sign the Kyoto Protocol?
Alternative:
The Kyoto Protocol is a proposed international agreement to try to reduce the amount of gases that are emitted by cars, factories, and other fuel burning activities. Do you think the United States should or should not sign the Kyoto Protocol?
Comment:
It is unreasonable to think that most people would know what the Kyoto Protocol is. Including a description gives all respondents the same minimum level of information and may increase the chances that this question is being understood consistently. Still, because it is likely that familiarity with the Kyoto Protocol is low, a brief description like this is probably no insurance that respondents will be providing meaningful answers.

8.3.1.2 Abstract nouns & verbs
Abstract nouns are words that describe a class of more specific items. Abstract verbs describe a class of more specific actions. A question that contains abstract nouns or verbs without including a definition, places the burden on the respondent to decide what to include or not include.

Example:
In the last week, did you exercise?
Comment:
Respondents could include many different activities as exercise. Whether or not walking is included as exercise and for how long one has to do the activity to count as exercise are left open for the individual to decide. Depending on what construct the question is intended to measure, it could be modified to specifically include, or exclude, walking and to mention any specific time implications.
Alternative:
In the last week, did you exercise or participate in any physical activity for at least 20 minutes that made you sweat and breathe hard, such as basketball, soccer, running, swimming, bicycling, or similar activities?

When abstract words and phrases are defined, the question becomes less ambiguous and the answers become more reliable (see Fowler, 1992).

8.3.1.3 Ambiguous adjectives or adverbs
Another potential source of unreliability is the use of ambiguous adjectives or adverbs. Like abstract nouns and verbs, the use of words that are ambiguous, such as "strenuous," or "when," force respondents to make their own decisions about how to think about the question and what their task actually is.

> *Example*:
> When did you move to London?
> *Comment*:
> A respondent could answer "when I was 20" "in 1985" or "when I left college." All are legitimate answers to the question of "when." A better question would be clear about the kind of answer that was needed. (See Fowler, 1995, for more examples.)
> *Alternative*:
> In what year did you move to London?

8.3.2 Lacking a Time Frame

Ambiguity can also arise when a question does not have a reference period or time frame. Time frames provide respondents with the boundaries of how to think about the question—it tells them when to start including things and when to stop. With no reference period, respondents can answer a question about today, the past year, their entire lives, or answer about how things usually are. It is obvious that concepts such as feelings, mood, health, and participation in activities can vary. Interestingly, some things that at first appear that they do not need any time frame, for example, hair color or place of residence, actually can and do change over time. Any question for which the answer could reasonably be expected to vary from day to day, week to week, or month to month should have a time reference.

> *Example*:
> How often are you sad?
> *Comment*:
> Respondents could interpret this question generally ("Am I generally a sad person?") or randomly pick some reference period to answer about ("In the last week have I been sad, regardless of how I usually feel?") A specific time reference makes sure that respondents are answering the same question.
> *Alternative*:
> In the past 4 weeks, how often have you felt sad - all the time, most of the time, some of the time, a little of the time, or not at all?

8.3.3 Imbedded Assumptions

Questions sometimes contain assumptions about the respondent's situation, or the way the respondent thinks about things, that are not necessarily true but that are critical to answering the question. When a question makes an assumption about a respondent's situation, and that assumption is not true, the respondent must choose how to handle the situation

Example:
When riding in the back seat of a car, do you wear a seat belt all of the time, most of the time, some of the time, once in a while, or never?
Comment:
This question assumes that at some point, all respondents ride in the back seat (Fowler, 2004). However, this is not true. There is no option provided for respondents who never ride in the back seat. They could offer that they did not ride in the back seat, or they could report what they think they would do if they did ride in the back seat. "Never" would be another possibility, since they never did use a seat belt in the back seat (because they were never there). A better way to measure this construct would be to first ask if a person rides in the back seat, then ask about seatbelt use.
Alternative:
In the past year, did you ever ride in the back seat of a car? (IF YES) When riding in the back seat of a car, how often do you wear a seat belt—all of the time, most of the time, some of the time, once in a while, or never?

Questions might also include assumptions about how respondents think about the world. If respondents do not agree with the imbedded assumption, it makes the question more confusing and thus more difficult to answer.

Example:
Because of the increase in juvenile crime, do you think that the school day should be longer?
Comment:
This question assumes that respondents think juvenile crime is rising and that longer school days would reduce juvenile crime. A respondent could agree with the main part of the question (school day should be longer) but not the assumptions that go along with it. For example, a respondent might feel that the school day should be longer because it is educationally better. In this situation, the respondent could either answer "no" (because juvenile crime is not a consideration for the respondent) or ignore the "juvenile crime" phrase and say "yes" (which means a different question is being answered). Depending on the construct, a less ambiguous series of questions could first ask the main question (should the school day be longer) and then, if affirmed by the respondent, follow-up by asking why.
Alternative:
Do you think that the school day should be longer? (IF YES) Do you think test scores will increase if the school day is longer? Do you think there will be less juvenile crime if the school day is longer?

8.3.4 Multiple Questions

Asking more than one question at the same time is a cognitively complex task for the respondent. It is also another source of ambiguity, and thus unreliability. Like a question with imbedded assumptions, respondents have to decide on their own how to deal with this ambiguity. The simplest solution is to ask each question separately.

Example:
Do you want to be rich and famous?
Example:
How helpful were your friends and family while you were sick?
Comment:
These are classic examples of double-barreled questions. In the first example, a person might want to be one but not the other. In the second, friends and family could offer different amounts of help. If the answers are different, the respondent has to decide which part of the question to answer and which to ignore.

It is the responsibility of the researcher to write clear and unambiguous questions. By asking one question at a time, defining abstract and ambiguous concepts, including time frames and not making assumptions about the respondent's situation, the chances are greatly improved that all respondents are trying to answer essentially the same question.

8.4 QUESTIONS TO WHICH RESPONDENTS CAN RETRIEVE ANSWERS

The second step in the question-answer process is for the respondent to retrieve, usually from memory, the information needed to answer the question. Researchers who hope to write effective questions should be interested in how this recall process works. Two variables that influence a person's ability to retrieve information are: (a) not having the needed information, and (b) problems with recalling information that is known.

8.4.1 Lack of Information

Though it seems obvious, it is worth keeping in mind that respondents can only answer questions to which they know the answers. Yet, we have ample evidence that respondents will try to answer questions about which they have no information (Schuman & Presser, 1981). There are several ways that researchers can unintentionally ask a question for which respondents do not have the information needed to provide an answer.

8.4.1.1 Asking about a construct for which a respondent does not have the information needed to answer the question

As discussed earlier in the chapter, for some constructs, such as measuring the technical quality of a health provider, asking a respondent may not be appropriate. The researcher needs to carefully examine the construct to be measured and evaluate whether most respondent are likely to know enough to be able to answer it.

Example:
How much is your house currently worth?
Comment:
Although some people may know the answer to this, many people will not. Depending on the actual construct the researcher is trying to measure, there is information that a respondent could provide that might help. For example, if a respondent provides the zip code or area in which they live and the size of the house, a researcher may be able to estimate the worth of the house based on recent home sales information.

8.4.1.2 Asking about a construct in a way that the respondent may not usually think about

Sometimes researchers will write questions that they feel will provide the information they need for their analysis without considering whether it is in a form that makes sense to respondents.

Example 1:
How many calories did you eat yesterday?
Example 2:
How many miles from your home is the nearest hospital?
Comment:
These might be the question objectives (what the researcher wants to measure), but they are not questions that respondents are likely to be able answer. Respondents certainly have relevant information, but as questions they are asking for answers in terms that respondents will not usually be able to report. The first example could be changed to a series of questions (perhaps using some kind of diary) to try to capture what foods a respondent ate yesterday (from which a calorie count could be created). For the second example, there are several things about where the nearest hospital is that respondents might be able to report accurately. For example, they may be able to report how long it takes to get to the hospital—which might serve the analysis goals as well as distance. They also might be able to provide information about the hospital's location, which could permit actual distance to be computed by the researcher.

8.4.1.3 Asking about other people

Asking respondents to provide information about other people should be done with caution. When the person of interest is unable to respond to the survey, for example, being deceased or incapacitated, or is not available during the study period, having proxy reports may be better than having no information at all. It is also cost-effective to ask one person in the household to answer about other household members. Researchers should understand the risks of asking questions about someone else. The literature on when proxy reports are more or less accurate than self reports is not definitive at all (Groves, 1989; O'Muircheartaigh, 1991).

If a researcher must use a proxy respondent, it is best to ask questions that are factual or observable. It is also best to do some cognitive testing to be certain that proxy respondents generally have the needed information. Proxies usually are not reliable reporters of the internal states or beliefs of other people. Respondents are not mind readers and should not be asked about how others feel or about the subjective states of other people.

Example 1:
How many of your neighbors oppose building the new playground?
Example 2:
How much does your mother enjoy the activities in the nursing home?
Comment:
Because people cannot reliably report on how others feel, if the intent of asking these questions is a measure other people's beliefs, it may not be possible when using proxy respondents. There may be some information the respondent can provide. By revising the goals of the questions, the researcher may be able to measure the same or similar constructs.
Alternative 1:
How many of your neighbors have signs in their yard opposing the new playground?
Alternative 2:
Does your mother participate in any activities in the nursing home?

8.4.2 Recall Problems

There are many things that affect a person's ability to recall and retrieve the information needed to answer a question. Psychologists and other researchers continue to study memory and how people store and retrieve information. In The Psychology of Survey Response, Tourangeau, Rips & Rasinski (2000) present a detailed discussion of what issues influence recall and how a respondent goes about retrieving different kinds of information based on what is needed in the question. The accuracy of information provided by the respondent is a combination of two things—elapsed time and impact.

Table 8.1 was created from a study in which people selected from records of automobile accidents were interviewed about accidents they had experienced. The table reports the percentages of known accidents that were and were not reported to the interviewers. The greater the time period between the accident and the interview, the less likely the accident was reported in the interview. Accidents that resulted in a personal injury were more likely to be reported than those without. Thus, recent accidents with a personal injury were reported almost perfectly, whereas 37% of those that happened 9–12 months before the interview without any personal injury were not reported.

Table 8.1 Number of recorded automobile accidents, both involving personal injury or not, and percent not reported in interviews, by time elapse between accident and interview.

Time Elapsed	Accidents with NO personal injury		Accidents WITH personal injury	
	Recorded Numbers	Percent NOT Reported	Recorded Numbers	Percent NOT Reported
Less than 3 months	48	6	71	1
3-6 months	68	12	141	10
6-9 months	48	22	71	10
9-12 months	49	37	94	22

(Summary of Studies, Cannell, Marquis & Laurent, 1977)

Although there are not any definitive solutions that will eliminate the problems associated with memory and recall, we offer several approaches that might make it easier for respondents to recall information:
1. Make the reference period consistent with the significance of the events to be asked about; the more minor the event, the shorter the reference period should be;
2. Decompose a large complex question by asking several smaller questions. This not only makes it easier for respondents to answer, but it also allows respondents to spend more time on each element of the question.

Example:
How many different doctors have you seen in the last 12 months?
Alternative:
I'd like to ask about the number of doctors you've seen in the past year. Have you seen any primary care doctors or general practitioners? (IF YES, how many doctors like that did you see?)
Have you seen any specialists? (IF YES: How many?)
Have you seen any psychiatrists? (IF YES: How many?)
How many other doctors that you have not mentioned have you seen in the last 12 months?

Finally, retrieval cues can aid recall. For example, asking respondents to think of actions often associated with seeing a doctor (e.g., taking a prescription medicine, missing work, staying in bed) may improve the recall of visits to doctors.

8.5 QUESTIONS TO WHICH RESPONDENTS CAN PROVIDE AN APPROPRIATE RESPONSE

The next step in the question-answer process is for respondents to take the information they have gathered in the retrieval process and translate it into an answer. In order for a question to be effective, the form of the answer must give respondents a way to accurately report what they have to say. Some questions are closed-ended and provide a list of alternatives from which the respondent chooses an answer. Other questions do not provide a set of responses, but rather allow respondents to answer in their own words. These open-ended questions could require the answer to be in the form of a number, a word or phrase, or sometimes a more complex narrative answer. The task could also be a direct or an indirect rating.

Characteristics of an effective response task include:
1. The way the question is supposed to be answered should be clear to the respondent.
2. The response task must be appropriate to the question.
3. If the question is closed-ended, the response options should be mutually exclusive and exhaustive.
4. For ratings, the question form should be direct rather than indirect.

8.5.1 Clear Response Task

In order for a response task to be clear to the respondent, the question must be clear about what kind of answer is required and what level of detail is required for an appropriate response.

Example:
Ho long ago did you leave your job?
Comment:
Although the intent is obvious, the task is not clear. The question does not explicitly tell the respondent in what terms to answer. The respondents could report in months or years, or they could also say "Not long ago."
Alternative:
How many months ago did you leave your job?

8.5.2 Response Tasks for Open-ended Questions

Both closed-ended and open-ended questions have their own challenges in terms of providing a clear response task to the respondent. For open-ended questions, it is often not clear to the respondent how to categorize their answers.

Example:
Why did you go to the doctor last time?
Comment:
Questions that ask "why" something happened are problematic for several reasons. For the respondent, this question gives no clue about the kind of response or the level of specificity that the researcher is looking for. Respondents could answer that they came because of a specific health problem, for a check-up, or because someone else encouraged them to go. The question even could be interpreted as asking why someone visited a "doctor" rather than another kind of health professional. Depending on the

research goal, a better alternative would be to tell the respondent what the parameters of the question should be.

Alternative:

When you last went to your doctor, was there one particular health problem or condition that was the reason for your seeing the doctor? What was it?

8.5.3 Response Tasks for Closed-ended Questions

An advantage of fixed response questions is that respondents get to choose from a list of allowable answers. There nonetheless are challenges to providing good response options. For example, the response options should not be multibarreled.

Example:

In the last 12 months, did your child's doctors talk with you about how to feed your child?

        ☐ YES and my questions were answered
        ☐ YES but my questions were not answered completely
        ☐ NO but I wish we had talked about that
        ☐ NO but I already had information in this topic and did not need to talk about it any more

Comment:

The question itself is a yes/no question. But the researcher attempted to get additional information from the respondent that was not part of the question. In this situation, although the question is clear and asks about a single concept, there are at least 3 different concepts in the response choices: (a) Did the doctor talk to the respondent, (b) Did the respondent have questions about this, and (c) Were the respondent's questions answered? By asking about each of these concepts separately, the researcher obtains better data.

Alternative:

In the last 12 months, did you have any questions about how to feed your child?

(IF YES) In the last 12 months, did your child's doctors talk with you about your questions on how to feed your child?

(IF YES) How well were your questions answered - very well, fairly well, or not well at all?

Another problem for closed-ended response tasks occurs when the situation could be variable, but responses are dichotomous.

Example:

In the past 12 months, did your doctors treat you with respect? (Yes/No)
Comment:

In this example, a doctor could sometimes treat the respondent with respect. Or, perhaps, some doctors treated the respondent respectfully and others did not. But the response options only allow 2 choices, yes or no. These choices

do not provide respondents with a way to describe their actual situations, which could be considered a "sometimes".
Alternative:
In the last 12 months, how often did your doctors treat you with respect? (Always, Sometimes, Rarely, Never)

8.5.4 Response task should be appropriate to the question that is being answered

8.5.4.1 Response options should match the question
Sometimes the response options provided do not match the question. This type of problem can usually be caught before a survey is fielded, either through presurvey testing or by carefully reading the questions *and* answer categories.

> *Example*:
> Can you name some of these benefits?
> *Comment*:
> This question is written in a yes/no format, but the researcher probably expects that when a respondent says "yes" it will lead to a narrative response of what these benefits are.
> *Alternative 1*:
> Can you name some of these benefits? (IF YES) What are they?
> *Alternative 2*:
> What are some of the benefits?

> *Example*:
> If this class were available at a location convenient to you, how likely would you be to participate—definitely would, probably would, not sure, or probably would not?
> *Comment*:
> In this example, the question asks about how likely the respondent would be to participate. The responses offered are on the same topic, but they do not match what is asked.
> *Alternative*:
> If this class were available in your area, how likely would you be to participate—very likely, somewhat likely, a little likely, or not likely at all?

8.5.4.2 Response options should be obvious from the question
A similar problem occurs when the responses categories are not obvious from the question. This is most often a problem for interviewer-administered surveys, when the respondent may not be able to see answer options.

> *Example*:
> Do you have any concerns about your operation? (Yes a lot, Yes some, No)
> *Comment*:
> From the question, there is no way for the respondent to know that what appears to be a simple yes/no question has an added component of how

many concerns in the response task. A better question would alert the respondent to this in the question itself.
Alternative:
How many concerns do you have about your operation—a lot, some, only a few, or none?

8.5.4.3 Response options should not assume regularity

Some response tasks assume that the behaviors or events being asked about happen on a set schedule. This assumption of regularity makes the question more complex for respondents, who may not be able to find an option that fits their particular situation.

Example:
How frequently do you, or someone in your household, take your trash to the dump or landfill - Once per week, Twice per week, Every other week, Once per month, or Less often?
Comment:
These response options assume that trash is taken to the dump on some sort of weekly schedule. However, it could be done on an as-needed basis. The options, as they are written, do not allow for that. Asking for a specific number of events in the reference period gathers frequency information with no assumption of regularity.
Alternative:
In the last month, about how many times did you or someone in your household take your trash to the dump or landfill?

8.5.5 Answers Should be Mutually Exclusive and Exhaustive

For questions that are closed-ended, answer categories should be mutually exclusive and exhaustive. This refers to the idea that all respondents should have only one response option that best describes their situation and that there is a response option for everyone. If respondents can legitimately put themselves into more than one category, the measurement will not be reliable because people in the same situation could answer differently.

Example:
Are you currently married, separated, divorced, widowed, living with a partner, or have you never been married?
Comment:
In this classic example, the researcher is combining two concepts: the legal marital status of respondents and their living arrangement. A person could be living with a partner and also fit into any of the other categories. In this situation, the researcher needs to decide the purpose of the question and which of those two constructs this question is intended to measure.
Alternative:
What is your current marital status? Are you married, separated, divorced, widowed, or have you never been married? Are you currently living with (a partner/your spouse)?

8.5.6 Direct Rating Tasks

Many survey questions are designed to have respondents place their perceptions or evaluations on some kind on continuum. Possibly the most common such task it to evaluate ideas, people, or objects by placing them on a rating scale from very positive to very negative. Continua are defined by adjectives. Table 8.2 provides three examples of how this could be done.

Table 8.2 Some Alternative Rating Scales

As bad as possible 0	1	2	3	4	5	6	7	8	9	As good as possible 10
☐	☐	☐	☐	☐	☐	☐	☐	☐	☐	☐

Poor	Fair	Good	Very Good	Excellent
☐	☐	☐	☐	☐

Not Good At All	Not So Good	Good Enough	Very Good
☐	☐	☐	☐

The typical task is to ask respondents to choose the number or the adjective on the scale that best describes their assessments.

Although evaluations based on good to bad may be the most common uses of such rating tasks, parallel ratings can be made of promptness, ability, energy levels, or political conservatism. In each of these cases and many more, a continuum can be defined and respondents can be asked where on that continuum they think something lies. Questions like that are considered direct ratings.

When designing rating tasks, two issues face the researcher: how many categories should be presented and whether categories should be labeled with words or numbers.

In general, it has been found that increasing the number of categories in a rating scale up to at least seven improves the quality of measurement (Krosnik & Fabrigar, 1997; Andrews, 1984). Beyond that, more categories do not improve measurement on average. The psychometric value of numerous categories must be balanced against ease of administration. Fewer response categories tend to be easier for respondents to use. Telephone respondents in particular benefit from having to retain fewer categories (de Leeuw, Chapter 7).

There is evidence that respondents give more consistent (and hence reliable) ratings when all the categories are labeled with words, rather than just labeling the end points or using numbers (Krosnick & Fagrigar, 1997). Numbered categories have several interesting strengths: For many questions, it is hard to think up more than four or five adjectives to define a continuum, but numbers can be used to label an infinite number of categories with unambiguous order. It is also easier for respondents to remember all the options when numbers are used. On the telephone, respondents can easily retain all the eleven answer possibilities from zero to ten, whereas it is almost impossible to retain ten, or even six or seven, adjectives (Harris-Kojetin, Fowler, Brown, Schnaider, & Sweeney, 1999). Finally, numbers translate across languages much better than adjectives. So, although one may pay a small reliability price, when more than three or four categories are desired, there is a good case to be made for using numbered categories for ratings rather than labeling all the categories with adjectives.

8.5.7 Indirect Rating Tasks

There is another approach to measurement that seems to accomplish the same thing. We call this an indirect approach to rating. The defining characteristic of questions like this is that the stem of the question itself defines a spot on a continuum. Respondents are then asked some question such as how close that spot is to the way they see things.

Alternative 1:
Would you describe your health as very good?

This question can be answered with a "yes" or "no." Let us consider briefly, as shown in Figure 8.1, what respondents have to do cognitively in order to answer a question like that:

1. Respondents have to decide where on the continuum from excellent to poor to rate their health (R).
2. They have to calculate where on the same continuum "very good" lies, the point on the healthy continuum specified by the stem of the questions (VG).
3. They have to evaluate the distance between the rating they would give (R) and "very good" (VG) and decide if they are close enough to the same that they are willing to give a "yes" answer.

From a cognitive point of view, it is obvious that such a question is much harder than the original example. In essence, respondents have to formulate the answer to the original question and then go through two further cognitive steps in order to provide answers.

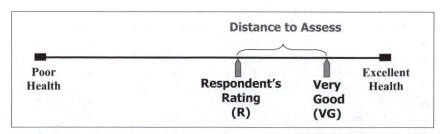

Figure 8.1 Cognitive Processes of Indirect Rating Task Visualized

From a psychometric point of view, consider the basic equation: $x = t + e$, where x is the answer given, t is the true score (the real answer) and e is the error, the amount that x deviates from t. Error results from anything other than variation in the true score that affects the answer the respondent gives. Anytime a respondent is asked to give a rating, there is the potential for error associated with how the question is understood and how the respondent uses the response scale. In addition, the indirect rating approach adds a further source of potential error because of differences in how close respondents require the spot defined in the question stem to be to their preferred answer in order to be considered a match. We could put that in notation form as: $X = t + e_d + e_i$, where e_d refers to the error in performing the basic task of placing the stimulus on a rating scale and e_i refers to the error introduced by the additional task of integrating that direct rating into the new, unrelated format.

Example:
In the past 30 days, how often have you felt anxious—very often, often, sometimes, rarely, or never?

There are several ways that same question could be asked:

Alternative 1:
In the past 30 days, have you often felt anxious?
Alternative 2:
Consider the statement, "In the past 30 days I have often felt anxious."
(a) Would you say that is very true, somewhat true, somewhat untrue, or very untrue?
(b) Would you say you strongly agree, agree, disagree, or strongly disagree?

Alternative 1 can be answered "yes" or "no". Alternative 2 sets up either response task A or B. All of these approaches introduce indirect measurement error in addition to the error associated with making the basic rating in the original example.

   The agree-disagree form of the question raises two other concerns. First, it is difficult to pose agree-disagree alternatives that constitute an unambiguous monotonic continuum. It is not clear that the "strongly agree" responses mean they are closer than simply "agree" to the respondent's view, and it is common to analyze the results as a dichotomy: agree vs. disagree. There are other forms of the response categories (for example, completely agree, somewhat agree, somewhat disagree, completely disagree), but they all raise problems of whether or not they are really ordered and what the distance is between responses. For example, what is the difference between "somewhat agreeing" and "somewhat disagreeing"?

   Another concern with such questions is acquiescence. Krosnick's (1991) concept of satisficing is a kindred idea that has similar effects. When questions are put in the form of a statement, it has been shown that some respondents are more likely to agree than disagree. Those who are less educated, have less knowledge of the topic or are less interested are particularly likely to show this pattern. Acquiescence thus becomes another source of error variance, something that affects answers that has nothing to do with the true answer to the question.

The built-in cognitive complexity, the difficulty of creating meaningful monotonic scaling categories, and the introduction of acquiescence bias all should lead researchers to avoid indirect rating tasks, particularly agree-disagree questions, and choose direct rating tasks when designing questions.

8.6 QUESTIONS THAT RESPONDENTS ARE WILLING TO ANSWER ACCURATELY

Respondents do not always want to provide the literally accurate answer to a question (see also Lensvelt-Mulders, Chapter 24). When Locander et al (1976) compared survey reports of drunk driving arrests with official records, they found considerable underreporting. Similarly, when Cannell, Oksenberg and Converse (1977) compared survey reports with hospital records, they found that hospitalizations associated with conditions that were rated as embarrassing were less likely than average to be reported.

There are three main forces the lead respondents to distort their answers:

1. Sometimes respondents do not want certain information disclosed to anyone because of real risks of disclosure. The information that respondents have used illegal drugs, stolen money, or committed an assault could keep them from getting jobs or, literally, lead them to be prosecuted.

2. A much more common force is the natural desire of people to want to present a good image to others—to put themselves in a favorable light. This leads them not only to avoid reporting embarrassing events, like being arrested for drunk driving. It also leads them to over report socially desirable things like having a library card or voting in elections.

3. A more subtle, but still real, third force that can lead to distorted answers is the desire for respondents to be properly classified, regardless of the social desirability of the classification. If the literally correct answer is seen as potentially leading to an incorrect conclusion, respondents feel pressure to distort their answers to produce a more accurate classification.

Two of the approaches to reducing these forces have nothing to do with designing questions. First, assuring respondents that their answers will be kept confidential and not analyzed in ways that they can associated with their answers is a standard part of most survey protocols—particularly if the survey asks questions covering potentially sensitive topics. Second, there is an extensive literature that shows that when interviewers ask questions, answers are more likely to be distorted in a socially desirable direction than when respondents give answers by filling out a self-administered form or entering their answers into a computer (e.g., Tourangeau & Smith, 1998; Turner et al.,

1998; de Leeuw, Chapter 7 & 13). In addition to those steps, there are a number of features of the design of questions that have been shown to affect answers that are subject to the forces outlined earlier.

Most of the strategies are designed to assuage respondent concerns about how their answers will be interpreted. There are four interrelated but different approaches that are used:

1. An introduction to the question can help reassure respondents.
Example:
Many people find they do not exercise as much as they want to because of their family responsibilities, their work, or because they do not have exercise facilities that are convenient for them to use. How about you, would you say you do or do not exercise as much as you would like to?
Comment:
The idea is that by providing respondents with some socially acceptable reasons why people do not exercise, respondent concerns that a "no" answer will be interpreted as reflecting sloth or a lack of interest in exercise will be reduced, thereby possibly making it easier to truthfully answer the question.

2. Prior questions can allow respondents to provide context that may reduce concerns about how their answers will be interpreted. Loftus, Smith, Klinger, & Fiedler (1991) report on an experiment to understand why respondents over reported medical tests. When respondents were asked if they had various medical tests (mammograms, pap smears, having blood pressure measured) in the two months before the interview, respondents overreported tests. Loftus devised an experiment in which respondents were first asked about tests in the preceding six months, then asked how many of those tests occurred in the preceding two months. With that protocol, over reporting of tests in the preceding two months was greatly reduced. Presumably the reasons were two. First, cognitively, the question series made it quite clear the question was really asking literally about those two months, not about some more general time period, such as "recently." Second, the series gave respondents a chance to report the tests that occurred more than two months previously, so they did not have to worry about not being correctly classified as people who have recently had medical tests.

3. Context can affect the sense of how answers will be interpreted. In the United States, drinking alcohol is subject to stigma in some circles. It is also known to have health benefits. Think how different a question about alcohol consumption would be if it was tucked in a list of substances one could abuse, such as marijuana, cocaine, or heroin, compared with being in a list of healthy behaviors, such as frequency of exercise, eating low-fat foods, or having regular health check ups.

4. The response alternatives that respondents are given to use can also affect respondents' willingness to give accurate answers. A good example comes from work by Schwartz, Hippler, Deutsch, & Strack (1985) on reports of how many hours per day respondents watched television. Two scales were compared:

Scale A:	<½ hr	½-1 hrs	1-1½ hrs	1½-2 hrs	2-2½ hrs	>2½ hrs
Scale B:	<2½ hrs	2½-3 hrs	3-3½ hrs	3½-4 hrs	4-4½ hrs	>4½ hrs

In this experiment 84% of those who answered using Scale A reported watching less that 2 ½ hours of television per day, while only 63% of those who used Scale B reported watching less than 2.5 hours of television per day. The scale provides information to people about what the investigators think is the distribution. In the first scale, obviously 2 ½ hours is a lot, whereas in the second one it appears the investigators think that most answers will be higher than that. From a respondent's perspective, if one does not want to be classified as a very high television viewer, higher answers would seem more socially acceptable if the investigators think the distribution looks like the second scale than if they think it looks like the first scale.

If a survey is aimed at highly embarrassing or illegal behaviors, steps that go well beyond standard question design issues, such as making responses anonymous in some way, will be needed to collect credible data. For more typical survey objectives, it still is important to be attentive to question features that might lead respondents to distort their answers. The most important general principle is to minimize respondent concerns that the accurate answer will result in their being misclassified or correctly classified in a category that is seen as socially undesirable.

8.7 DESIGNING QUESTIONS FOR INTERVIEWER ADMINISTRATION

When a survey is self-administered, with the respondent reading questions and entering answers in some way, the only communication between the researcher and the respondents is via the wording of the questions and the way they are formatted (see Dillman, Chapter 9). If there are unclear questions or if instructions are unclear, respondents are on their own to figure out what to do, with the resulting consequences for data quality. When an interviewer asks questions and records answers, the interviewer can intervene when respondents are unclear about what a question means or how to answer. From a measurement point of view, this can be both good and bad. On the positive side, the interviewer can repeat a question when there is evidence that the respondent did not fully grasp its meaning. The interviewer can make sure that all questions are answered and that answers meet the question objectives. If respondents are answering in their own words, interviewers can probe for more details when answers are not clear or are incomplete.

On the negative side, interviewers can introduce unreliability, and potentially error, into the measurement process by not being consistent in the way that questions are asked or by probing in ways that change the question's meaning or the way it is answered. It is obvious that the true value of a construct is unrelated to who is asking the questions in a survey. Therefore, to the extent that interviewers affect answers, there is error in the measurement of constructs (Loosveldt, Chapter 11).

The way interviewers are trained and supervised can help to reduce interviewers' effects on data (Fowler & Mangione, 1990; Billiet & Loosveldt, 1988, see also Lessler et al., Chapter 23). However, research has shown that the way questions are designed can also have an important effect on how much interviewers affect the answers they obtain (Mangione, Fowler & Louis, 1992). There are two main question features that are critical to minimizing interviewer effects on data.

First, design questions that can be read exactly as worded. If respondents are not answering the exact same question, there is reason for concern that their answers might differ for that reason alone. Fowler and Cannell (1996) report studies showing that some questions are consistently read as worded, while others are consistently misread. This means that whether or not a question is read correctly is largely determined by how the question is worded. Using behavior coding in pretests (Campanelli, Chapter 10) to find those that are consistently misread is one way to help interviewers read questions consistently.

Second, questions should be designed to minimize the extent to which interviewers have to probe in order to obtain adequate answers (Mangione Fowler, & Louis, 1992). One way to do this is to minimize ambiguous words and provide definitions of key words, to reduce the rates at which respondents are confused and the rates at which interviewers will have to answer questions about the meaning of questions. Perhaps the most important step, however, is to make it is as clear as possible how to answer the questions. Studies show that the most common reason for probing is that the kind of answer that will meet the question objectives is not clear in the question itself. Again, a way to identify questions that require a lot of interviewer probing is through behavior coding pretest interviews (Campanelli, Chapter 10).

The precision of survey estimates is reduced if interviewers affect the answers respondents give. Designing questions that can be read exactly as written and that minimize the need for probing are two of the best ways to minimize interviewer effects on data.

8.8 CONCLUSION

As we have written elsewhere, (Fowler, 1995; Fowler, 2001), there is no substitute for good question evaluation prior to launching a survey. No matter how expert the question designer, there will be things to learn from cognitive testing and field testing questions. Researchers will know better how to respond to problems they identify if they have a firm grasp of the principles articulated in this chapter.

Asking the right question is one of the most subtle and important issues. If the researcher does not identify the right question objective to measure the target construct, then there is little that question design and testing can do to produce the desired measurement.

Beyond that, researchers need to be attentive to all the aspects of the question and answer process where measurement can go wrong. In order for the answer to a question to produce a valid measure of a construct, respondents have to: (a) understand the question as intended, so they know what is being asked of them; (b) have, or be able to retrieve, the information needed to form an answer; (c) be able to fit what they have to say into the form in which they are required to answer; and (d) be willing to provide what they deem to be the most literally accurate answer they can.

Failure to attend to any one of these issues can have a major effect on the validity of the data collected. These issues and some of the approaches to question design discussed in this chapter are summarized in Figure 8.2.

There is considerable judgment in survey question design. Much of the judgment requires balancing competing demands that affect questions (Fowler, 2001). So, a researcher might like to ask respondents to report events occurring during the past year, to increase the number of events reported. That goal may conflict with the respondents' ability to provide accurate, detailed information about the events they report. A shorter reference period might produce more accurate information, albeit about fewer events. A researcher might have to choose between asking a single summary question, such as total combined income for a year, or a series of questions about individual components of income. The latter approach might be more accurate, but it requires more interview time.

There also is the potential for judgment because sometimes there is more than one way to design a question that will measure a target construct equally well. "How old were you on your last birthday?" and "What is your date of birth?" produce results that are not identical, but are quite similar in quality.

Researchers should not be confused between the judgment about what the question objectives should be or the choice between two questions nearly equal in quality and the scientific principles about how to write questions to achieve those objectives. How well questions meet the standards articulated earlier can be measured through question testing and psychometric evaluation. Questions that prove to have significant flaws based on those standards will not produce good measurement of target constructs. That is the core message to take away from this chapter on how to write effective survey questions.

Ask the right question:
- Constructs that the question measures should meet analysis objectives
- The question to measure the construct should be one that respondents can answer
- Answers to the question should be a measure of the chosen construct

Ask questions that are consistently understood:
- Avoid unfamiliar and technical terms
- Define abstract nouns and verbs
- Avoid ambiguous adjectives and adverbs
- Use a time reference for any question that reasonably might vary over time
- Avoid imbedded assumptions
- Ask one question at a time (avoid multi-barreled questions)

Ask questions that respondents can retrieve answers to:
- Respondents should have the information needed to answer the question
- Questions should ask about information respondents have access to
- Questions should ask about constructs in terms that respondents use
- Questions should be about respondents and not about other people (Avoid proxy questions)
- If proxy questions must be asked, ask about factual and behavioral issues, not internal states
- Length of the reference period should be consistent with the significance of the event
- Decompose complex questions to make questions easier to answer and give respondents more time to think about the topic
- Provide retrieval cues to aid memory

Ask questions for which respondents can provide appropriate responses:
- Response task should be clear and obvious from the question
- Response options should match the questions
- Response options should not assume regularity
- For closed-ended questions, response options should be exhaustive and mutually exclusive
- Direct rating tasks are better than indirect ratings

Ask questions that respondents are willing to answer accurately:
- Minimize respondent concerns about being seen in a negative light or having their answers interpreted inaccurately
- Give attention to:
  - " Introductions
  - " Vocabulary
  - " Context
  - " Response alternatives

Figure 8.2. Designing Effective Questions: A Summary

GLOSSARY OF KEY CONCEPTS

Acquiescence. The tendency for respondents to agree or say *yes* (rather than disagree or say *no* to questions that are put in the form of statements.

Closed-ended questions. Provide the respondent with a set of response alternatives from which to choose an answer.

Construct. The abstract conception of the reality that a question is designed to measure.

Direct rating. A type of question that asks respondents to locate their views of an idea, a person or something else on an abstract continuum.

Indirect rating. A type of question that asks respondents to answer questions that are not themselves direct ratings but from which the values of direct ratings may be inferred.

Multibarreled questions. Questions phrased so that they, in fact, are asking two or more questions at once. As a result, there potentially is more than one answer that the same person could give that would be an accurate answer to one or another part of the question.

Mutually exclusive and exhaustive. Describes response choices for closed-ended questions that provide all respondents with at least one, but only one, option that answers the question.

Open-ended questions. Ask respondents to answer in their own words.

Reliability. The extent to which answers to a question provide consistent results at different times or for different respondents when the values of a construct are the same.

Validity. The extent to which the answer to a question corresponds to the true value for the construct that is being measured.

Chapter 9

The Logic and Psychology
of Constructing Questionnaires

Don A. Dillman
Washington State University

9.1 INTRODUCTION

A questionnaire is more than a simple list of questions. Well-written questions
that are composed according to the principles outlined in Chapter 8 by Fowler
and Consenza may need further modification as they are ordered and placed in
questionnaires suited for a particular survey mode or a particular population of
respondents. Turning a collection of questions into a questionnaire brings into
consideration nonresponse concerns as well as measurement concerns. It raises
issues of how communicating with respondents, visually, in mail and web
surveys versus aurally in interviews, requires that adaptations be made. The
design process may also encourage reordering of questions and the writing of
connective language to help respondents grasp the intent of questions and how
to respond to them. The logic and psychology of this process of turning a list of
proposed survey questions into an acceptable questionnaire is the focus of this
chapter.

9.2 GOOD QUESTIONS ARE NOT ENOUGH

The transition from questions to questionnaire is illustrated by a recent general
public mail survey (Stern & Dillman, 2006). Considerable time had been spent
by the investigators writing a series of questions to ascertain the names of each
respondent's closest friends and relatives plus the frequency and means of
communication with each of them. Our purpose was to collect necessary
information for a network analysis of close social ties. The result of our writing
effort was a series of seven questions that would be repeated in sequence for
each of the five closest friends and the same number of relatives. Informal tests
suggested that each of the questions could be answered accurately by
respondents and would provide meaningful data for the proposed analysis;
however, it was also apparent that some people would find the questions
intrusive, and were likely not to answer them.

Thus, a second round of question writing was begun. Here, the focus was
on how to place the questions into the proposed mail questionnaire in a way that
would improve the likelihood of responses being given, while also achieving

161

our measurement objectives. First, we relocated the questions so that instead of being asked first in the questionnaire, they would be asked near the end after the questions we thought the respondents were more likely to find interesting. We also reduced the response burden by asking about only three friends and three relatives instead of five. In addition a way was found to eliminate the repetitiveness of asking the same questions sequentially for one person at a time while also reducing the number of pages needed from four to two. The objection of some respondents to identifying persons close to them to the researcher was responded to by asking only for first names and making even that optional. We also decided that the total questionnaire length would be no more than 12 pages, of which 10 pages of questions, in a further attempt to reduce overall nonresponse.

When the survey was implemented a few weeks later, 69% of the households that received the questionnaire completed and returned it. The social network questions in their final form, which appear for friends in Figure 9.1, were answered by nearly all of the respondents. The result of this question transformation was to achieve an overall response rate as well as item response that exceeded the expectations set when the decision to collect detailed social network data was made.

32. Thinking about your three closest friends who do not live with you please answer these questions.

	Friend 1 ▼	Friend 2 ▼	Friend 3 ▼
First name/Initials (optional)	(name)	(name)	(name)
Does this friend live in the Lewiston/ Clarkston area?..........	❏ Yes ❏ No	❏ Yes ❏ No	❏ Yes ❏ No
If no: About how far away from Lewiston/Clarkston do they live?	____Miles	____Miles	____Miles
About how old is this friend?......................	____years	____years	____years
Approximately, how often do you communicate with this friend?......................	❏ Less than once a month ❏ Once a month ❏ Every week ❏ Everyday	❏ Less than once a month ❏ Once a month ❏ Every week ❏ Everyday	❏ Less than once a month ❏ Once a month ❏ Every week ❏ Everyday
When you want to communicate with this friend, which of the following do you use most often?...............	❏ Personal visit ❏ Postal mail ❏ Email ❏ Cell phone ❏ Other telephone	❏ Personal visit ❏ Postal mail ❏ Email ❏ Cell phone ❏ Other telephone	❏ Personal visit ❏ Postal mail ❏ Email ❏ Cell phone ❏ Other telephone
Is this friend in any of the same organizations, clubs or groups as you?	❏ Yes ❏ No ❏ Don't know	❏ Yes ❏ No ❏ Don't know	❏ Yes ❏ No ❏ Don't know

Figure 9.1. Example of redesigned social network question

9.3 RESOLVING CONFLICTING NEEDS

First time designers of surveys are often surprised when data collection professionals propose changes in questions or even the elimination from surveys of questions that have already been judged acceptable. The challenge faced in constructing questionnaires is to develop them in ways that achieve accurate measurement, while also mitigating effects of individual questions on item nonresponse and premature termination. As discussed by de Leeuw in Chapter 7 these twin concerns often lead to the selection of one survey mode over another. They may also lead to unanticipated compromises.

Often the desire for precise measurement results in the use of many questions to measure a particular construct. For example, the desire for a good measure of total annual income might lead to asking a series of questions that ask for the amounts of income one receives from each of many different sources (interest, wages, pension, etc.). To reduce burden, as well as objections, it may be preferable to ask only the overall amount of income one receives each year. Another example of ideal measurement might be to ask people to agree or disagree with dozens of statements designed to precisely measure a single attribute, such as socially conservative versus liberal, rather than ask a single question of what one considers him or herself to be. As Hox explains in Chapter 20, longer scales based on more information from respondents, are generally considered more reliable. On the other hand, when questionnaires become long and detailed the likelihood of item nonresponse and/or complete nonresponse tends to increase, regardless of mode. Thus the trade-off that one may face is to accept less precise measurement versus no measurement at all.

In addition, the order in which questions are placed in a questionnaire may itself suggest that questions be reworded. In Chapter 2, Schwarz, Knäuper, Oyserman and Stich argue that questionnaires should be viewed as a conversation in which norms are invoked as the participants attempt to be cooperative communicators. For example, the general norms of conversations suggest that each contribution be relevant and that neither party be redundant. Thus, when a researcher asks a series of questions about one's first employment after receiving a college degree, one does not need to repeat before each and every item the same words, for example, "In your first position after receiving graduating from college...," but instead might begin follow-up questions with, "In this position...."

Nor does the respondent want her answer to a question to be redundant with previously provided information. An example of this effect was observed by Mason, Carlson and Tourangeau (1994) in a survey that asked respondents how they felt about economic conditions in their state and another question that asked about economic conditions in their community. When the community question followed the state question they observed a subtraction effect, whereby respondents tended to compare the situation in their community to how they viewed the state situation, a process that resulted in their offering a somewhat different answer than when the questions were asked in reverse order. In essence the respondent tries to add new information in light of the first response. It may be possible to reduce effects that some questions have on other items by separating them, but even that may not eliminate them. The main conclusion is that effects of questions on answers to other questions cannot simply be ignored (Schwarz et al., Chapter 2).

The process of designing questionnaires varies significantly depending upon the mode chosen. It also involves making decisions that respond to the unique opportunities offered by that mode, while minimizing adverse affects. Thus, the structuring process can be described as finding an optimal compromise among the opportunities and needs specified in the study objectives, the nature of which varies greatly by survey mode.

9.4 TAKING SURVEY MODE INTO ACCOUNT

9.4.1 Face-to-Face Interviews

Because of the increased availability of other survey modes, face-to-face interviews are typically reserved for the most difficult and longest surveys that place the greatest burden on respondents. These are the kinds of surveys for which the other modes are not so likely to perform well. Face-to-face surveys also tend to be reserved for surveys that are most important to society, for which sponsors are willing to pay the cost.

Face-to-face interviews provide the opportunity to use both aural and visual channels of communication for communicating with respondents (de Leeuw, Chapter 7). Some information can best be communicated visually, such as pictures, and questions with many parts, such as asking people to rank answer choices. Such interviews are often designed with show cards. Questions, parts of questions, and/or answer choices are displayed on individual cards and the respondent is referred to those cards when the question is read to them, for example, "Looking at Card A, which of those five choices best describes the organizational goal that you feel should be your employer's highest priority?" To insure equal exposure to the categories, interviewers are commonly instructed to read each category, although having all categories exposed visually helps respondents to compare them, and choose their answer.

Observation of show-card construction practices across organizations suggests that no standards have been developed for what should or should not be placed on show cards. One common use of such cards is to present scale labels for opinion questions. Another use is to present particularly complex questions or visual images. Still another way how show cards have been employed is to make them nearly the same as the interview form, with all information to be read to the respondent, appearing there.

It should not be surprising that when writing a face-to-face interview instrument, questions may change substantially from the wording used when constructing questions for possible use in other survey modes. The human interaction that is involved in face-to-face interviews gives interviewers an opportunity to observe body language and facial expressions. When these nonverbal communication cues suggest that a question is not being understood, the interviewer can then reread the question, possibly with an informal statement, "Let me read the question again, just to be sure that it is clear." One of the big assets of interviewers is that they may assist respondents and help out, whenever a difficulty in the question-answer process occurs. This may also have biasing effects; therefore one aspect of designing face-to-face interviews is to specify the kinds of phrases that should be used by the interviewer in these situations, along with when and how they should be used.

It is also common to build in transitional statements into questionnaires, to help orient both the respondent and the interviewer to the new topics, for example, "Next I am going to ask several questions about any recent visits you have had to see a medical care provider." In an interview situation, such phrases are also used to help respondents understand a change in type of question and what the role of both the interviewer and respondent should be, for example, "Now, I am going to read some statements to you and ask you to indicate the extent to which you agree or disagree with each of them."

Instructions that may be needed by respondents when completing the interview are often listed sparingly on face-to-face interview forms, leaving it up to the interviewer to correct a respondent if it appears they need a particular definition or question clarification. Preferably, definitions and instructions are available to interviewers when needed and interviewers should be trained to use these. Thus, an important aspect of making a face-to-face questionnaire work is to complement what is on the page with interviewer training and support that shows Interviewers how to handle unusual situations, while maintaining the flow of questions and answers. Once, while accompanying an interviewer who was conducting employment status interviews for the U.S. Census Bureau, I noticed a pet iguana resting on a branch of a large houseplant that was near the interviewer's shoulder. It moved slightly so that she detected its presence, a fact observed by the respondent. The interviewer momentarily stopped asking questions, while looking at the iguana and had a short but pleasant conversation with the homeowner about his pet. She then went back to the interview, backing up with an impromptu reminder of the previous two questions about the person's current job. She then proceeded to re-ask the question that had been posed just before the interview was interrupted. Situations of this nature illustrate how the asking and answering of questions in face-to-face interviews depend on much more than words on the page or computer screen and cannot be arbitrarily separated from interviewing training for handling interruptions and making sure each question is understood by respondents.

Turning the questionnaire into a detailed interview form requires textual and graphical additions. Face-to-face interview questions are commonly written with certain words to be read by the interviewer and words NOT to be read (e.g., "Be sure to probe if respondent does not answer"). In addition, certain answer categories are often listed that interviewers are instructed not to provide to respondents (no opinion, refuse, does not apply) unless the respondent is unwilling to choose one of the categories.

One of the techniques designed to help interviewers read the appropriate information and not read aloud information for their use only is described by Dillman, Gersteva and Mahon-Haft (2005). This technique is based on visual processing behavior described by Ware (2004). Central to it is the consistent use of graphical variations, such as placing questions in **bold**, instructions in *italics*, text not to be read in CAPITALS, and interviewer instructions in (parentheses). Although such consistency has been advocated primarily for respondent self-administered questionnaires, the need for appropriate visual communication to interviewers as a means of encouraging consistent interviewing has been stated by Smith (1995). It is similarly important for the design of computer screens for telephone interviewing.

Additional materials must be written to guide respondents when developing answers to likely questions, and preparing show cards to supplement the interview form. The effort required for completing all of these tasks may exceed the effort required for writing the questions, themselves. Occasionally, first time designers of face-to-face surveys respond to the complexity of these tasks by ignoring the need for supporting materials, thinking that each interviewer and respondent can figure out what or what not to do. To ignore these needs is as unthinkable as ignoring the need to carefully word each question; these directions are as integral to the process of obtaining good measurement in surveys, as the wording of the questions themselves.

Finally, the mere presence of an interviewer makes termination in the middle of the questionnaire less likely. In addition, there is often less concern about overall length, and as a consequence, reducing the number of questions to be asked. All in all, there is little pressure on survey designers to order questions in ways that will place questions that are of more interest to the respondent early in the interview, although this is still advisable in face-to-face interviews as it makes for a pleasant introduction and interviewers often use the first questions as an illustration of the survey to persuade reluctant respondents.

9.4.2 Telephone Interviews

The major construction challenge faced with telephone interviews might be summed up by noting the policy of one major data collection organization in the United States. For many years it has refused to conduct any telephone survey that is expected to be more than 18 minutes long. Thirty years ago, in the early days of telephone interviewing, people were far less likely to refuse an interview request, and once begun, the interview was unlikely to end until all of the questions have been asked (Dillman, 1978). At that time, it was not uncommon to conduct telephone interviews as long as 30–60 minutes. The culture surrounding use of the telephone has changed dramatically since that time, as discussed by Steeh in Chapter 12, and respondents are far less likely in the United States to tolerate long telephone interviews.

The construction pressures this situation places on designers of telephone questionnaires are considerable (e.g., Frey, 1989). It is important to begin interviews with questions that are likely to engage people rather than items that are complicated, difficult to answer, quite personal, and/or likely to be uninteresting to most respondents. The first minute or so of an interview is critical for conveying to respondents what it is about and providing them with a sense of being able to give useful answers. For this reason, an order for questions may be proposed that is different than that used in a face-to-face interview.

Besides length and question order other issues are important in designing telephone questionnaires. The telephone depends entirely upon aural communication. The absence of show cards means that designers often feel pressured to shorten questions compared to formats used in the face-to-face situation. For example, numbers are often substituted for verbal labels in scalar questions, in order to simplify communication. For example a question that asks whether someone is completely satisfied, mostly satisfied, somewhat satisfied, only slightly satisfied or not at all satisfied may be changed to: "On a scale of 5 to 1 where 5 means 'Very Satisfied' and 1 means 'Not At All Satisfied' and you can use a number from 5 to 1, how satisfied are you?" (Dillman & Christian, 2005). A tendency also exists to reduce the number of words and sentences used to formulate questions, and some of the informal connective phrases are often deleted.

At the same time, telephone interviews may require building in redundancy to help respondents visualize and remember information. For example, if one is asked the extent to which they agree or disagree with each item in a series that uses the same response categories, the scale may be repeated for the first two-three items, and then omitted unless the interviewer senses the respondent has forgotten the categories. Such wording typically gets built into the questionnaire itself so that all interviews will be similarly done.

In response to the difficulties people have remembering and using substantial amounts of information, designers of telephone questionnaires may also use a variety of other shortening techniques; such as, rewording response categories so that they contain fewer words, eliminating categories by shortening eleven or seven point scales to five or even three categories. In addition, designers sometimes add visual analogues; for instance, "Imagine a thermometer with a scale between 0 and 100 in which 100 represents the best possible quality of life and zero the worse, where would you consider yourself to be on this thermometer?" Yet another technique is to unfold scales, asking direction of an opinion (e.g., favor or oppose) and following that with how intensely one feels that way, (e.g., strongly, somewhat or slightly).

In sum, the switch from aural communication that in personal interviews can be augmented with visual show cards and observations of the respondent's apparent understanding or lack of understanding of questions, places significant limitations on the telephone as a means of collecting data. The dependence solely on aural communication often results in significant changes for many survey items.

Yet, many features of carefully structured telephone questionnaires remain very similar to those used in face-to-face interviews. The interviewer is relied upon to provide specific instructions or interpretations when requested by the respondent, and certain response categories available on the interviewer's questionnaire may not be given to respondents (e.g., no opinion, don't know, refuse).

As with face-to-face interviews, much of the questionnaire construction effort gets devoted to preparing auxiliary materials to help with conducting the interview, and giving interviewers the needed tools for probing and answering questions in appropriate ways. Just as described earlier for the face-to-face interview, it is of the utmost importance that the final interview schedule has a layout that helps interviewers avoid mistakes and read out aloud the appropriate information only. As telephone interviews are often done using computer-assisted interviewing or CATI-systems, attention to screen design helps in reducing interviewer errors too (e.g., Edwards, Schneider & Dean Brick, in press).

9.4.3 Interactive Voice Response

Interactive Voice Response (IVR), a third survey mode depending on aural communication, poses even more stringent question structure requirements, as described by Steiger-Miller and Conroy in Chapter 15. An even greater premium is placed on avoiding unnecessary words. Not only must respondents remember questions, but also they must simultaneously absorb and use information on how to respond. Thus, answering instructions on which number to push becomes an integral part of each question, for example, "To answer yes, press 1 and to answer no, press 2."

The need to make room in peoples' minds for which digit corresponds to each answer choices, while remembering the question and choices, contributes further to the desire to simplify questions. Whereas one might decide to ask a mail or web survey respondents to choose which of five different criteria they consider most important in choosing a personal physician, such questions may not work well for IVR surveys (Dillman, 2000).

One effect of choosing IVR may be to limit the variations across questions. For example, I have observed IVR questionnaire designers make a decision to convert all of their opinion questions to the same scale format, for example, using agree–disagree items, thus eliminating such formats as satisfaction scales or even yes no questions in order to avoid having to convey to respondents, changes in answer formats.

Another way of reducing the amount of information that IVR respondents need to process is to make greater use of branching than is done in other surveys, for example, asking whether respondents are satisfied or dissatisfied (allowing them to press a 1 or 2), and then, for example, to ask the satisfied respondents whether they are very or somewhat satisfied.

One of the most critical construction procedures, as described by Miller Steiger and Conroy in Chapter 15, is to anticipate problems respondents have and prerecord appropriate reminders on what numbers to use when answering, how and when to repeat questions, and so forth. These reminders thus become integral aspects of the questionnaire stimulus.

It is evident that making the transition from face-to-face, voice telephone and IVR successively represents a narrowing of the communication channel. Questions that work fine for face-to-face interviews, may not work as well for telephone interviews, and even less well for IVR where no live interviewer is present. As a result, the questionnaire construction process may require designers to return to their original survey questions and change them significantly so they will work for this survey mode.

9.4.4 Self-Administered Paper Questionnaires

The decision to use self-administered paper questionnaires raises issues seldom considered by designers of face-to-face and telephone interview surveys. There is no interviewer to answer respondent questions or to correct different respondent interpretations of questions. The pace of answering is entirely up to the respondent. In addition, much of the design effort focuses on questionnaire appearance and its likely effects on convincing recipients to answer the survey questions.

Thus, making the questionnaire appeal to respondents—a nice cover and interesting first questions—is often a dominant concern of those who decide to use mail questionnaires. Development of an appeal also raises the prospect that whatever is chosen attracts some respondents, but repels others. An example might be to develop a cover page with a title, "How Can our Environment be Protected," rather than something more neutral, such as "Opinions on Environmental Issues." In addition, the general appearance of a questionnaire and whether it looks long and difficult may affect respondent decisions to continue. Once, when working with an economist on a mail survey, he insisted that the first question in the survey should be about the respondent's income, reasoning that if only one question was to be answered it should be the income question. Doing that would have increased the likelihood of receiving no response at all (Dillman, 2000)

Use of the mail survey encourages surveyors to develop themes to questionnaires that are likely to spark respondent interest in ways that are most likely to encourage respondents to begin answering and keep going. Typically, this means placing income and other sensitive questions near the end. It also means that one should place questions near the end that are uninteresting or objectionable to respondents. Location of items may to some extent change the way a question is viewed. The friends' and relatives' network questions mentioned at the beginning of this chapter represent such an example. Whereas asking these questions first seemed likely to raise objections from respondents, asking them late in the questionnaire following many community questions, probably diminished those objections. Placing them late in the questionnaire was aimed at making them seem less intrusive to respondents.

In self-administered questionnaires, individual questions may be edited so that answer choices no longer appear in the query, as is done for interview surveys. Instead, the answer choices appear as categories with appropriate answer boxes beside each category. Designers of mail questionnaires also face a different challenge in presenting the hidden answer choices (Do Not Know, Refuse, No Opinion) that in interview surveys are often reserved on the form for interviewer use, but not explicitly articulated to respondents. In mail surveys, either the categories need to be presented explicitly or entirely withheld. The middle ground of providing them only when needed is difficult to emulate. One possibility for achieving that may be to use visual design principles of separating these categories slightly from the substantive ones and presenting them in a smaller type, but to our knowledge this possibility has not been carefully tested. Designers face the same problems with detailed instructions and definitions. Pretesting questions and using this information to place instructions directly before they may be needed seems a good strategy. Again visual design principles may help respondents to identify instructions from questions and guide respondents successfully through questionnaires.

It has become evident that, when relying on visual communication, the meaning of questions and how to answer them is communicated through more than words (Jenkins & Dillman, 1997; Redline & Dillman, 2002; Christian & Dillman, 2004; Dillman, 2006). Numbers, symbols, and graphical layout (e.g., spacing, location, brightness, contrast, and figure/ground arrangements) communicate meaning to respondents that may be consistent or inconsistent with the words used. Thus, a major concern of mail questionnaire construction is designing pages so that respondents can quickly determine its elemental organization, detect the pattern of organization and take the appropriate response action (Ware, 2004; Dillman, Gertseva & Mahon-Haft, 2005). The multiple aspects of the answering process from correctly figuring out the location and arrangement of questions to following a carefully prescribed navigational path are summarized in Dillman (2006).

In the past, designers of mail questionnaires often rewrote questions in order to avoid branching instructions by combining items together that would be asked sequentially in a telephone or IVR questionnaire. An example might be asking people which of these categories best describes their housing situation: (a) own with a mortgage, (b) own without a mortgage, (c) rent with payment by check or cash, (d) rent without payment. A telephone surveyor is likely to use a branching strategy and ask first whether people own or rent and get the greater detail with an appropriate follow-up question. It has now been shown that using graphical and symbolic instructions greatly increases the likelihood that people will follow branching instructions correctly (Redline, Dillman, Dajani & Scaggs, 2003), thus reducing the temptation to bundle multiple concepts within a single answer choice in self-administered questionnaires. This is especially important, when questionnaires for mixed-mode surveys (e.g., telephone + mail) are designed (see also de Leeuw, Dillman, & Hox, Chapter 16).

In sum, the designer of mail surveys faces a variety of questionnaire construction decisions that are not aspects of the construction process for interview modes. These choices also include deciding on the questionnaire format (booklet vs. some other format), what to do about cover pages designed to develop interest in responding, ordering questions to overcome possible resistance, avoiding page breaks in the midst of questions, placing answer spaces consistently on pages so they are unlikely to be missed, and a host of other decisions. In addition, it is imperative that the designer be consistent in the use of graphics, symbols and numbers, which in essence become rules of presentation in much the same way that highway signs exhibit consistency in color, shape, and use for particular purposes. Each of the decisions on building such consistency becomes an integral part of the question stimuli posed to respondent, either directly or indirectly, and thus a potential influence on answers. Research reporting a number of those influences is summarized elsewhere (Dillman, 2007, 472-493).

9.4.5 Web Surveys

Surveys on the Internet provide opportunities for measurement not available in any other mode, including a seemingly infinite array of colors, shapes, and graphics available on demand (Best & Krueger, 2004). Sounds, animation, and video can also be added. Measurement devices not available for other modes, e.g., slider bars whereby one physically moves an answer indicator between extreme points on a scale and drop down menus that display on demand all possible answers to a question, such as a list of all countries in which one might have residence. These features open the way to creative measurement of concepts not previously used in survey research.

These potential features of web survey design appear to cut two ways. On one hand, the use of some of these features may unintentionally change the intended measurement of survey questions, for instance, pictures that bias peoples' answers (Couper, Tourangeau, Conrad, & Singer, 2006). In addition, web features, may slow down the process of responding, thus adding burden without improving measurement (Thomas, 2002). Couper, Tourangeau, Conrad and Singer (2006) report no greater time being required for responding to visual analogue scales, and also no measurement advantages. Furthermore, research has shown that graphical enhancements on web page design do not result in a corresponding increase in response rates (Coates, 2004).

On the other hand, the web also provides an opportunity to utilize some of the most desirable features of aural and visual surveys. Branching instructions can be built in automatically as in computer assisted interview surveys. Detailed instructions that interviewers provide can be made available to respondents who are willing to go to the web page on which they are located. Designers can also keep control over the sequence in which questions are read and answered. At the same time, visual displays of maps and longer questions asked with the help of interviewer show cards and in mail surveys can be used without difficulty on web surveys (Crawford, McCabe & Pope, 2005). Also, when desirable, one can be allowed to look backwards as well as forwards to get a better understanding of question context. Thus, the web has the potential of providing the best of both the telephone and mail survey world.

Thus, it is now apparent that a web survey can be designed in ways that bring it closer to interviews, such as one question per screen, providing instructions when requested, using fill-ins from answers to previous questions to pose later questions. Web surveys can also be designed in ways that bring them closer to mail surveys (pages that scroll, and making the visual layout look the same). It is the versatility of web that adds significantly to its advantages as a survey mode.

However, designers of web questionnaires also face significant problems. Web surveys are often terminated before completion, as inhibitions to breaking off a conversation are likely to be greater in interview surveys than in web surveys. It has now become common practice in web surveys to examine carefully where break-offs occur, and consider whether questions can be restructured in some way to present such break-offs. The web survey designer must also make certain decisions, for example, whether to require or not require responses to each question, which can be a major source of break-offs for items that respondents prefer not to answer. The pressure to keep web questionnaires short is greater than for mail and even telephone surveys.

Technical restrictions may cause break-offs, but may also threaten data quality. Because people have telecommunication lines with different transmission speeds, certain question formats may take a long time to load on some respondents' computer, thus discouraging completion of the survey. The quality of connections, ranging from slow dial-up modems to Ethernet access, means that survey features that work for some people will not work for others. In addition, some potential respondents may not have the software required to make some features of surveys work. Respondents also use different browsers and have different screen configurations that may lead to questions looking differently on one person's computer screen than on the monitor used by another person. The questionnaire construction process must take these considerations as represented in their survey population. In these early days of web design, less may be more, as designers attempt to widen access to the entire population of Internet users in countries throughout the world.

One of the major challenges of web survey design is to help respondents retain a sense of where they are in the questionnaire. When individual pages are used for each question, wording sometimes needs to be changed to help respondents maintain context for each succeeding question. For example, a sequence of questions about previously held jobs needs to maintain a reference which job is being referred to as one proceeds through those items.

For these reasons, it should not be surprising that the activities involved in questionnaire construction differ significantly for web surveys and encourage the use of different question formats, question wordings, and even question order than that used for any other mode. Like the other survey modes, the web also has unique construction requirements.

9.5 COMPETING PHILOSOPHIES OF QUESTIONNAIRE CONSTRUCTION

Faced with the potential for questionnaire construction efforts to change significantly the wording and ordering of individual questions, it is not surprising that two distinct philosophies of questionnaire construction have emerged.

9.5.1 Mode-specific Design

One prominent philosophy is to do what is best for the particular mode, regardless of what might be done in another mode. We refer to this as mode-specific design (Dillman, 2006). Examples include:

- Deciding to use show cards in face-to-face interviews even though they cannot be used in a follow-up telephone survey.
- Changing telephone scalar questions from fully labeled seven point scales used in face-to-face, mail and web surveys, to five point scales with only the endpoints labeled in order to make the telephone interviewing task easier.
- Changing a series of attitude items from individual questions posed one at a time to respondents as done for a telephone survey to a visual set of items with queries to the left and categories to the right, thus encouraging respondents to think of them as related items rather than separate items.

- Limiting respondents to IVR surveys to choosing from among no more than two or three response categories, and converting all items to only one or two basic structures (e.g., yes/no), rather than using a variety of scalar question formats as done for the telephone.
- Using slider scales for web surveys even though that format cannot be used in the same way for scalar items in other survey modes.

The perspective underlying this approach to questionnaire construction appears partly to be encouraged by the desire to use as many communication channels and senses as possible, thinking this will help produce the best data that can be achieved by a particular mode. The justification offered for this approach emphasizes trying to obtain the best measurement and/or response rate possible. Sometimes however, such changes are motivated primarily by tradition, personal preferences of designers who tend to be specialized in working with a particular mode, and what is easiest for those who implement the mode.

Especially for web surveys, a compelling case can be made for changing questionnaire stimuli across modes, as web surveys present a large number of possibilities for improving questions that do not exist in other modes. An example is to provide hotlinks that allow for the possibility of obtaining virtually limitless additional information or instructions. In addition, drop-down menus can be used to provide large numbers of answers to questions like, "Please click the state in which you now live?" that would likely be asked in a mail survey as: "Please write the name of the state in which you now live."

9.5.2 Unified Mode Design

A different philosophical approach to questionnaire design is to find ways of constructing questionnaires that provide the same stimulus in all survey modes. Unified mode design, or unimode mode design, as it has been described elsewhere (Dillman, 2007, Chapter 6), seeks to avoid unnecessary divergence across modes by keeping construction the same.

An example of striving for unimode construction, in a situation where it counts, is the use of forced choice versus check-all question formats. When respondents to interview surveys are asked to indicate which of a list of items describe them or their opinions in some way, they are almost always asked to reply to each item immediately after it is read to them. On the other hand, when such questions are posed in mail or web surveys, they tend to be posed in a way that asks respondents to mark only the items that apply to them. A comparison of the check-all and web surveys shows that respondents consistently mark more items on web and mail surveys when the items are posed in a forced choice manner (Smyth, Dillman, Christian & Stern, 2006). In addition, it has been found that answers to web and telephone surveys differ very little when the forced-choice format is used in both web and telephone, but exhibit more differences when forced-choice is used for the telephone and check-all for the web. (Smyth, Dillman, & Christian, 2006). The practical implication of these findings is that use of the forced-choice format for both modes is more likely to produce equivalent answers, and should therefore be used.

Unified mode construction would seem to be desirable for other question formats as well. For example, if no opinion or don't know options are offered in visual surveys they can also be explicitly offered in interview surveys. Also, if a question on something as simple as marital status is asked by presenting categories to choose from in one mode, then it would seem desirable to present it in the same way in other modes. For example, as reported by Dillman and Christian (2005), asking peoples' marital status in an open-ended fashion in a telephone survey produced fewer single, divorced, widowed and separated people than married people, compared to a comparable web survey question that presented those categories. In this case, the decisions, each made independently, to ask the question differently in the two modes, changed the question stimulus. When confronted with whether one is single or married, people can easily respond by indicating they are married or not, without realizing that the surveyor is interested in a more detailed description.

One of the main applications of these findings is for panel studies in which surveyors are attempting to measure change over time. Frequently, survey conditions lead to changing survey modes between the initial data collection and the follow-up. Unless unimode principles construction are adhered to, then the chances of producing differences as a result of changed questionnaire construction practices would seem to exist for many types of questions (Dillman & Christian, 2005).

Increasingly, modes are likely to be mixed for conducting surveys in order to overcome coverage, nonresponse, and cost concerns (see also de Leeuw et al., Chapter 16). Thus, we expect pressures towards unimode construction for surveys to increase in importance. However, it is unlikely that unimode construction will assure consistency in answers across all survey modes. This problem is illustrated by findings from Christian, Dillman, and Smyth (in press), which revealed that answers to scalar questions across modes persistently produced more extreme responses on the positive end of the scale in telephone surveys than was produced in web surveys.

It seems unlikely that the tension between mode-specific design and unimode construction will be resolved anytime soon. There is no shortage of advocates in the survey research community for each of these perspectives on questionnaire design. In addition it is important to recognize that should one mode produce better data because of being designed differently than a less adequate question structure used in another mode, the overall quality of the resulting data set may be improved as a result of using mode-specific design. Nonetheless, it is important to realize that when multiple modes are used to conduct a particular survey, a topic we return to in Chapter 16, it is critical that unnecessary or unusual divergence across survey modes be avoided.

9.6 CONCLUSION

The process of producing a questionnaire from a list of well-written questionnaire items makes evident many underlying tensions in survey design. Reconciling the needs for precise measurement with the ability to obtain good response rates is an important part of the questionnaire construction process.

The choice of survey mode is likely to produce concerns about questionnaire length, the order of questions, the exact wording of questions and other issues that tend to pull the questionnaire construction process in different directions for different modes. It is also important that response rates not be obtained at the expense of increasing nonresponse error, because the persuasion techniques used to convince people to respond differ across modes.

Different modes also pull designers in the direction of different question formats, often chosen, for example in the case of Figure 9.1, without knowing the exact measurement consequences, that is, knowing whether presenting questions in a table rather than sequentially person by person, produced better or worse measurement. Although research has addressed and continues to address issues of this nature, the need for experimental testing is never ending as survey topics and issues introduce new survey questions that need to be asked.

The fact that survey modes use different modes of communication, verbal versus visual, brings with it the recognition that different visual layouts may produce different answers than other visual layouts, both of which may produce different results than verbal questionnaires.

Finally, the questionnaire construction process also forces survey designers to come to grips with which of two competing design philosophies, mode-specific vs. unified mode, that is, designing in a unique way for each mode, attempting to use all the capability a mode offers to produce the best possible measurement versus holding back on some of the features of individual modes in an attempt to get common survey measurement across modes. Issues of this nature have no easy solutions and promise to hold the attention of survey methodologists for decades to come. Meantime these perspectives may be seen as a continuum, with survey designers being left to decide which is optimal for their survey.

GLOSSARY OF KEY CONCEPTS

Aural Communication. The method of providing information to another person that depends upon speaking and listening, through which questions are communicated by entirely in telephone interviews and to a large extent in face-to-face interviews.

Mode-specific Questionnaire Design. Writing questions and implementing a questionnaire in the best way for a mode, regardless of what might be done in another mode. That is, the questionnaire is optimized for each mode separately in an effort to improve the performance of individual survey modes, even if that results in different question formats across modes.

Unified Mode Questionnaire Design. Designing questions and questionnaires to provide the same stimulus in all survey modes in order to reduce differences in the way respondents respond to the survey questions in the different modes.

Visual Communication. The method of providing information to another person that depends upon what one sees, which is the means by which questions are mostly communicated to respondents in mail and web surveys.

Chapter 10

Testing Survey Questions

Pamela Campanelli
Independent Consultant

10.1 INTRODUCTION

*"Even after years of experience, no expert can write a perfect questionnaire...
If you do not have the resources to pilot-test your questionnaire,
don't do the study."*
(Sudman & Bradburn, 1982, p. 283)

Why test survey questions? This question is well answered by the quote of Sudman and Bradburn. It is true that no expert can write the perfect questionnaire simply sitting in his or her office. Respondents' experiences and attitudes are too multitudinous in nature. Survey questions created without thorough testing on members of the population for whom the questionnaire is intended will always miss these complexities. This is summarized well by van der Zouwen and Smit (2004, p. 128) who state that an expert review of a questionnaire "differs from field testing as next week's weather forecast differs from today's weather report."

Testing is the only way of assuring that the survey questions written, do indeed communicate to respondents as intended. A useful way to study this process is through the four cognitive steps of comprehension, recall, judgment, and response (Tourangeau, 1984). Under this framework, error results if respondents misunderstand the survey questions or key concepts, do not know or cannot recall the needed information from memory, use an inappropriate shortcut for making a judgment, or prefer to hide or distort certain information and provide a socially desirable answer (see also Schwarz et al., Chapter 2, and Fowler & Cosenza, Chapter 8).

Comprehension in itself is quite an extensive concern (see Sudman, Bradburn & Schwarz, 1996; Tourangeau, Rips, & Rasinski, 2000). It involves respondents' ability to understand the "literal meaning" of individual terms and phrases as well as any grammatical ambiguity. Take, for example, this humorous item from DeVellis (2003, p. 68) "Murderers and rapists should not seek pardons from politicians because they are the scum of the earth." More problematic is respondents' understanding of the pragmatic meaning of the survey question that goes beyond the literal meaning. The survey can be seen as a type of conversation, either between interviewer and respondent in interview surveys or between researcher and respondent in self-completion surveys (see also Loosveldt, Chapter 11; de Leeuw, Chapter 13). In normal conversation, if something a speaker says is ambiguous or incomplete, the listener makes an inference drawn from the original sentence about what the speaker really meant. What respondents assume the question means or implies, may cause errors in their responses. Respondents, for example, will infer the meaning of the question from the words within the question, the answer categories, numeric values given on a rating scale, the surrounding questions, and their own previous answers (see Sudman, Bradburn and Schwarz, 1996; Tourangeau, Rips, & Rasinski, 2000). This may lead to many of the response effects observed in surveys.

In this chapter, the four cognitive steps of comprehension, recall, judgment, and response are used as a general framework. Within this framework, I first discuss the traditional methods for pretesting, followed by modern developments and new methods. I end with a summary section on combining methods into a successful testing plan.

10.2 TRADITIONAL FIELD

10.2.1 The 3 Stages of Testing

On the road from theoretical concepts to finalized questionnaire, one can identify 3 stages of testing: The Developmental stage, the Question Testing stage and the Dress Rehearsal stage.

The Developmental stage is the time for preparatory and background work prior to actually writing any survey questions. It is a time to thoroughly explore (1) the subject matter through reading the existing literature and, if necessary, consulting experts and (2) various cultural and language issues that may affect how proposed respondents will comprehend and process survey questions. For example, "before questions can be prepared, it is necessary to know the level of respondent knowledge that can be assumed and something of the terminology that respondents will understand" (Cannell, Oksenberg, Kalton, Bischoping, & Fowler, 1989, p. 1). Methods at this stage are typically qualitative. The length of the developmental phase will depend on the complexity of the topic as well as on previous experience with that topic and the proposed research population.

The Question Testing stage involves the testing of survey questions, whether this is just some initial questions or a full draft questionnaire. The aim of this phrase is to ensure that each individual question meets all the principles of good questionnaire design (see also Schwarz et al., Chapter 2, Fowler & Cosenza, Chapter 8; Dillman, Chapter 9). If a complete draft questionnaire is being tested it is equally important to check the flow of the questionnaire as a whole and be alert of any unexpected effects of context.

The third stage is the Dress Rehearsal where the goal is to test the questionnaire as a whole under real survey conditions (or as close as possible) with a much larger sample size than the Question Testing stage. It's focus in not on the viability of individual questions, but rather on assuring the smooth co-ordination of procedures and establishing correct survey routines. It also allows one to get an estimate of first contact (rather than final) response rates, to check timings of the length of the questionnaire and to develop precodes for open-ended questions.

Note that a large Dress Rehearsal is not essential in most cases. A lot depends on the complexity of the survey, the budget, and the confidence and experience of the research and interviewing teams. For example, when the British Household Panel Study first started, the team at the University of Essex felt somewhat uneasy in that they had few experienced survey personal, were out-sourcing the interviewing rather than having direct control, and had a very complex set of tasks for interviewers to complete. In addition, because it was the beginning of what they hoped to be a long panel survey, it was important to start with a good response rate to help balance the inevitable panel attrition. They felt it was essential to have a dress rehearsal study large enough to fully analyse the results.

Unless a large Dress Rehearsal is explicitly needed, a better third stage is to conduct a second test at the Question Testing level. In the first test, problems are identified and fixed. Ideally, the revised questions should be re-tested. Revisions can be prone to unseen errors. In an experiment, Forsyth, Rothgeb, and Willis (2004) found that some of their improved questions were better for respondents but worse for interviewers. If major revisions have been made in the second Question Testing phase, this same logic would suggest the need for a third test. Ideally, the goal is that the final survey should not contain any untested questions. But obviously there may be practical constraints. Researchers conducting surveys in professional survey organizations are typically very hard pressed for time. Students doing a survey for their Masters or PhD degree have more flexibility in time, but are typically more restricted in resources.

In the literature, the terms pretesting and piloting are used. There is international ambiguity around these terms. Generally in the United States and several European countries, stage 2 is called a pretest and the full dress rehearsal at stage 3 is called a pilot. In contrast, in the United Kingdom, both stages 2 and 3 would be called pilots. This is the reason for the avoidance of these terms in this chapter.

The remainder of this chapter focuses exclusively on the Question Testing stage.

10.2.2 Informal Methods

There are several informal methods that can and should be used just before the Question Testing stage. These suggestions may seem very simple and unscientific, but they are very effective for quickly finding errors *early* in the questionnaire design process. Nevertheless, this step is not a substitute for an actual test with real respondents!

One of the first things to do is to read the questionnaire aloud to yourself. This highlights the differences between written and spoken language. A question that looks great on paper can still be difficult to read aloud. This is extremely important in questionnaires for face-to-face and telephone interviews.

Another very useful informal method is to try interviewing yourself. Play the role of the respondent, read through the questionnaire and try to answer each question yourself. What aspects of the question make it easy or difficult to answer? Are terms ambiguous, or questions or answers sensitive? Is it too difficult to remember exact information? This method helps to identify difficulties in the question-answer process and is useful for both interview questionnaires and self-administered ones.

Other options are to have a mock interview with a colleague, listen to another person conducting the mock interview, interview friends/family, and so forth, as these methods allow a researcher to hear the questions aloud and see how they are answered. Similarly, colleagues and friends can be asked to complete a self-administered questionnaire and subsequently be interviewed about how they came up with their answers.

10.2.3 Traditional Field Test for Interview Surveys

In a professional survey organization a typical question-testing phase for face-to-face surveys would involve a small number of interviewers doing a few interviews each. This would be accomplished in a 1 to 2 weeks time period. A quota sample, aligned to match the final survey population, would be used. After all interviews are completed the interviewers are called in for a group debriefing session. A quota sample is typically used because it is cheaper and quicker to implement than a probability sample and considered adequate for a test, though often not for the main survey (see also Lohr, Chapter 6).

In centralized telephone facilities a similar format can be used, except that the test interviews can be accomplished much more quickly and it is easier to employ a probability sample.

There are various other decisions that need to be made about the test. I made a distinction between what applies to researchers in a larger organization who have access to a team of interviewers and individuals who may be doing all of their interviewing themselves.

10.2.3.1 Sample sizes
A range of sizes has been recommended. Converse and Presser (1986) suggest a sample size from 25 to 75 persons (units). This is quite large compared to other authors. Fowler (1995), for example suggests a sample size of 15–35. Sheatsley (1983) suggests 10–25 and Sudman (1983) suggests 20 to 50. Your final sample size depends on your time and budget. Note that a small test is much better than no test.

All questions in the questionnaire should receive an equal amount of testing. Thus, if there are some questions that are only asked of certain subgroups then provision needs to be made to ensure there are an adequate number of persons from that subgroup in the test sample.

Another concern is when the overall population is small. One may not want to waste members of the population on the test. For example, a student who wanted to do a census of farmers in a particular region had to test her questionnaire among farmers from an adjacent region who had similar farming conditions. Note that it is not advisable to include the test interviews as part of the main survey as questions are always revised after the test.

10.2.3.2 Interviewer selection (organization)
Should one use only the highly experienced interviewers, as they will be the ones most able to diagnose problems (see, Converse & Presser, 1986)? Or should a mix of experienced and novice interviewers be used (see, DeMaio, 1984)? The concern here is that experienced interviewers are also good at making poor questions work and therefore some problems may be bypassed that will cause difficulties for novice interviewers on the main survey.

10.2.3.3 Briefing interviewers (organization)
This is better done in person, although some pretraining self-completion exercises could be distributed in advance. Unless there is a standard and well-enforced question testing policy at a company, don't assume that interviewers know how to conduct a test. They need to be told what to do. See, for example, a questionnaire for interviewers as suggested by Converse and Presser (1986).

10.2.3.4 Informing respondents that it is a pilot (organization and individual)
Should this be done before the interview, afterwards, or will you not inform respondents? Converse and Presser (1986) call the first option a participating pretest and the last option an undeclared pretest. Before using an undeclared test, be sure that it is acceptable within any informed consent policy that governs research in your country (see also Singer, Chapter 5.)

The arguments for a participating pretest are that the respondent can become a conscious ally in the testing process. The reverse concern is that the respondent who knows that the survey is only a test will take it less seriously and be less motivated to provide optimum answers.

A compromise position is to tell the respondent at the beginning that there will be two parts. After the survey is conducted, they will be asked some questions about the survey questions to help determine how well the survey questions are working. This is a "Respondent Debriefing" session. Instead of asking respondents what they think of the questions, respondent debriefing sessions focus on how respondents came up with their answers. Respondent Debriefing will be discussed in depth in Section 10.3 of this chapter.

10.2.3.5 Re-wording questions? (organization and individual)
Should interviewers be allowed to re-word problem questions on the pilot (as Cannell, et al., 1989, would suggest) or discouraged from doing this? The argument for allowing test interviewers to reword questions is that after just one or two test interviews, good interviewers will know that a question isn't working and will often have an idea about how the question could be changed to make it work better. Allowing interviewers to reword questions during the test gives them the opportunity to try out new wordings and see how they work before returning to the researcher. The argument against this practice is that standardized interviewers may start to find that they like re-wording questions and become unstandardized. Secondly, unless the interviewer is well briefed in

the objective of the question, his or her new revisions may be useless. The scenario is obviously different for the individual working on his or her own, who has written the questionnaire and is doing his or her own testing. Such individuals can easily try out new versions of a question when the signs of a problem are clear.

10.2.3.6 Observing and taking part (organization)
Too often the researcher in the organization only receives the testing news indirectly from the interviewers (Converse & Presser, 1986). Some ways to remedy this are to accompany an interviewer, to do some testing yourself, or to have interviewers tape-record some test interviews.

10.2.3.7 Debriefing interviewers (organization)
This is better done in person rather than over the phone or by post.

10.2.3.8 Examining results (organization and individual)
After the test, the researcher should look through the test questionnaires. If there is only a small number (say 20 or less) the review can simply be a visual review of the actual questionnaires. If there are a larger number of questionnaires, it could be useful to actually key in the data and examine it using statistical software (Converse & Presser, 1986). In either case look for patterns in the substantive answers (Are they what you expect? Is there enough discrimination?) and for patterns in item nonresponse (Are there certain questions that receive large amounts of don't know's or refusals?)

10.2.3.9 Course of action
Deciding upon a course of action is based upon the researcher's judgment. Each question needs to be reviewed in turn. Look for problems that are dominant trends across all interviews and well as discoveries. Even if problems occur in only one interview, they may uncover an obvious flaw or an important problem with the question for certain sub-groups, and so forth. Furthermore, the nature of the problem has to be identified before it can be fixed. Is it an issue of an ambiguous term or concept, is the task requested by the survey question too difficult, is it too sensitive, and so forth. Also be aware that the problem may not lay solely with the survey question. It could be that the research objective needs to be revised or be made more specific.

There are always difficult decisions to be made. We aim for all respondents to be able to easily answer each question with perfect accuracy. But sometimes one is faced with a difficult trade off. For example, having one simple and clear question that works for 98% of respondents or replacing this with a complex series of ten questions that works for 100% of respondents.

10.2.4 Limitations of the Traditional Field Test for Interview Surveys

The traditional field test as described earlier is not capable of identifying all of the problems, which can exist with the individual questions and the questionnaire as a whole. For example, National Center for Health Statistics (1989, p. 9) research suggests: "Respondents often answered the questions confidently without noticeable delay and did not reveal their underlying confusion... Respondents may not themselves be aware that they have misinterpreted a question, and are apparently reluctant to volunteer lack of knowledge."

For standard field tests of interview surveys, the presence of the interviewer is both an advantage and disadvantage. As Fowler (1995, p. 115) suggests, describing the views of Presser (1989), the ability of interviewers to diagnose questions is confounded by their dual role as implementer and observer. Good interviewers are good at making poor questions work and therefore could be less sensitive to question problems. Unless well briefed in question objectives, interviewers are likely to differ from the researcher in their perceptions of what constitutes a question problem. In addition, by only interviewing a few respondents it may be difficult for the interviewer to judge if the problem is with the question or with the particular respondent's idiosyncrasies. And finally there is the problem with the group debriefing format, itself. "Some interviewers speak out more often and eloquently than others, not necessarily in proportion to the quality of the things they have to say" (Fowler, 1995, p. 116). To minimize this final problem, one can use an Interviewer Rating form (see Exhibit 1 on the website accompanying this book, Chapter 10), which forces each interviewer to rate each question. An alternative, which is less burdensome on interviewers, is the flexible set of questions proposed by Converse and Presser (1986, p. 72).

10.2.5 Traditional Field Test for Self-completion Surveys and Limitations

The U.S. Census Bureau called their postal survey tests a "Mail-out/Mail-back test." Essentially, questionnaires are mailed out and respondents mail them back. The questionnaires can then be examined for patterns of substantive answers and patterns of item nonresponse (as described in the *Examining Results* subsection for interview surveys mentioned earlier). In addition, it is useful to look for any indicators of confusion, such as not following the answering task correctly or missing skip patterns. Finally, it gives an idea of initial response rates, before reminders.

This type of test is severely limited. Researchers learn about the problems, but have to speculate on why they occurred. Much more information is available in tests of interview surveys. So at the early stages of self-completion survey construction, one could test the questionnaire as if it were an interview questionnaire. But this is not ideal because respondents need to be able to cope with a self-completion questionnaire on their own and correctly perceive and comprehend its visual aspects as well as its verbal aspects (see Jenkins & Dillman, 1997; Dillman, 2000; Dillman & Redline, 2004). Large improvements in the quality of the testing of self-completion questionnaires are to be had with several of the methods discussed in Section 3.

10.3 NEW METHODS

Described are six new methods for the testing of survey questions: Making use of experts, Systematic reviews of questionnaires, Respondent debriefing, Behavior coding, Cognitive interviewing, and Focus groups. These methods are also known under the label 'cognitive laboratory methods' or pretest methods.

10.3.1 Making Use of Experts[1] for Interview and Self-completion Questionnaires

As suggested by Thomas (2002), experts are researchers with good knowledge of the particular substantive topic, fieldwork issues, questionnaire design, cognitive perspectives, and so on. Consulting with experts offers good feedback to the original questionnaire designer, can help stimulate the designer's own critical thinking, and can help generate hypotheses to be used with other testing methods. In survey organizations or research institutes, experts are other colleagues in the organization. In other work environments that contain no other survey researchers, outside experts can be brought in. If you are working on your Masters or PhD, other university staff can serve as experts.

10.3.1.1 Number of experts
Consulting even one expert is a good thing. If time and budget allow, consulting several can be very useful, because experts may vary in what they notice and what they recommend. Experts can be consulted independently or brought together in the form of an expert panel. Although logistically difficult to form, an expert panel is advantageous in that it allows differences in recommendations to be debated.

A panel of 3–4 experts plus the questionnaire designer(s) can be convened in the manner of a focus group (see Section 10.3.6). Note that ideally, experts should have no personal stake in the project, so that their judgments are objective. The group discussion should be informal and free flowing, but needs to be monitored to stay on topic and within time-constraints. The questionnaire designer should participate in the discussion, but should aim to be receptive, rather than directive or defensive (which is sometimes not easy). Tape-recording or having a designated note-taker is essential.

If it is not possible for experts to meet, for instance in an international survey where experts are scattered over different countries, other options are open. For instance, experts can type in their comments directly in the questionnaire in a different color, or by using the track changes option in word or its equivalents. Other forms are having experts send in a short written report, or have a telephone conference, or Internet chat.

10.3.1.2 Preparation
The researcher or research team needs to provide a brief to the expert(s) that

---

[1] This section is from our work in developing expert panels at the UK National Centre for Social Research and is adapted from a summary by Thomas, 2002.

sets out the key aims and objectives of the survey and draws attention to questionnaire design problems and issues on which advice is sought. The brief also needs to points out any immovable constraints on the scope and design of the questionnaire (e.g., mode of administration, length, questions inserted for comparability with other surveys, etc.). The brief plus the draft questionnaire should be given to the expert with adequate time for the expert to respond (if consulted independently) or prepare for the expert panel.

10.3.1.3 Timing

Like any kind of question testing, timing is critical. Time pressures often make the window for consultation very narrow. If consultation is too early, the questionnaire designer may not have got far enough to set up a well-focused discussion. But it is better to consult too early than too late, because preparation and discussion stimulate design thinking. If consultation is done too late it may no longer be possible to put suggested changes into effect, so that the input of the expert(s) is wasted.

10.3.1.4 Within an organization

Within an organization, an expert review is based on the idea that researchers can learn from each other's experience in designing questionnaires and avoid repeating mistakes: Creating a regular forum for using the expertise within an organization is no easy matter. All researchers need to be eligible to be experts. A roster system is needed so that all researchers are used and none are over-burdened. Institutional support and understanding are very important in establishing a framework for routinely generated expert panels. Management needs to be not just permissive, but positively supportive. Senior staff needs to understand the value of panels as a cost-effective way of raising survey quality standards and understand what support is required. All staff needs to accept that acting occasionally as a panel member is part of a researcher's responsibilities. More junior staff needs assurance that asking for the time of busy experts to sit on panels is acceptable. A fairly senior person, who consistently acts as the champion of expert panels within the organization, is also needed.

10.3.2 Systematic Reviews of Questionnaires for Interview and Self-completion Questionnaires

The expert reviews discussed earlier are free flowing and informal. In contrast, there exist a number of check lists that can be used to evaluate a questionnaire. Some of these were designed to be used by cognitive experts, such as the detailed schemes from the Research Triangle Institute (RTI) developed by Forsyth & Hubbard (1992) and Lessler & Forsyth (1996), which are called Cognitive Forms Appraisals. (c.f. Exhibit 2 on this book's website, Chapter 10). More recent is RTI's Questionnaire Appraisal System (QAS–99) (Willis & Lessler, 1999), which is designed with the survey practitioner in mind. It has 26 categories grouped into 8 steps and a 37-page manual on how to use the form. The most accessible checklists are those developed by staff at Statistics Netherlands (see Example 10.1 here, and Exhibit 3 on this book's website, Chapter 10).

Example 10.1: Condensed Expert Questionnaire Appraisal Coding System

Problems in questionnaire with regard to:		
Question comprehension	Information processing	Reporting
o Difficult wording → o Unclear wording → o Difficult syntax → o Long question with list of items o Double-barreled questions o Double-negative questions o Question/answer mismatch o Reference set (perspective) change → o Response task → o …	o Retrieval task → o Long period of recall o Much information needed to answer question o Judgment task → o Difficult task (complex calculation, estimation) → o Social desirability o …	o Difficult wording in answering categories → o Unclear wording → o Boundary problems → o Overlapping categories → o Missing categories → o …

→ Indicates a description of the problem, and suggestions for improvement.
Source: Snijkers, G. (2002). Cognitive laboratory experiences on pre-testing computerised questionnaires and data quality. Heerlen: Statistics Netherlands.

It is also possible to develop your own scheme from existing ones. The reader may also be interested in "QUEST" which is a computational model of human question answering and proposes a number of categories for a checklist (see Graesser, Bommareddy, Swaner, & Golding, 1996; Graesser, Kennedy, Wiemer-Hasting, & Ottati, 1999).

10.3.3 Respondent Debriefing for Interview and Self-completion Questionnaires

Respondent debriefing questions are special follow-up questions used to determine respondents' understanding of the original survey question, sometimes referred to in the literature as special probes (Oksenberg, Cannell, & Kalton, 1991) or frame of reference probing (DeMaio, 1984). This technique was originally developed by Belson (1981). After administering the survey, Belson's interviewers worked through each survey question in turn, reading back the question and the respondent's answer and then asking specific follow-up questions to determine how respondents had understood individual terms and phrases as well as the overall meaning of the survey question. After reading the section on Cognitive Interviewing (10.3.5), you will see there is a great similarity between cognitive probes and respondent debriefing questions. Respondent debriefing questions came first, but both techniques can borrow from each other.

Respondent Debriefing Questions are often used to determine respondents' understanding of terms and phrases in survey questions and the extent to which these are in line with what the questionnaire designer had in mind. Example 10.2 shows the use of a respondent debriefing question to ascertain how respondents interpreted a particular phrase (in this case, "last week"). In the old version of the Current Population Study (CPS, i.e., the U.S. Labour Force Survey) before the major redesign in the late 1980's/1990's, "last week" was not defined for respondents. Yet it is a critical time period for many of the survey's questions. As you can see from Example 10.2, there is a good deal of variation in interpretation.

Example 10.2:

Respondent Debriefing Question
At the start of the questions about work, I asked you what (name) was doing most of LAST WEEK. When you answered that question, which days did you think LAST WEEK was supposed to cover?
Interpretations of LAST WEEK
Sunday–Saturday   17% (CPS Definition)
Monday–Friday   54%
Monday–Saturday   9%
Monday–Sunday   6%
Sunday–Sunday   4%
Other   10%
Total cases with complete data n=2091

Source: Campanelli, P.C., Martin, E.A. & Rothgeb, J.M. (1991). The Use of respondent and interviewer debriefing studies as a way to study response error in survey data. *The Statistician*, 40, 253-264.

In contrast, it is also possible to use debriefing questions that specifically focus on what a respondent included or excluded in the answer. During the redesign of the CPS there was concern that informal work arrangements, such as unpaid work as part of family business, would be incorrectly excluded by the respondent. A debriefing question asked directly about informal work done (see Esposito, Campanelli, Rothgeb, & Polivka, 1991; Fowler, 1995, p. 126) shows a useful series where an initial question about how many times you have seen a medical doctor is followed up by categories likely to be missed such as telephone advice from a physician or visits to psychiatrists.

Respondent debriefing questions can also be used to explore memory and judgment issues. Take, for example, this question from the old version of the CPS: "How many hours did (name) work last week, at all jobs?" Asking "How did you come up with your answer?" will yield a variety of memory and judgment issues. Invariably, some simply choose the number of hours for which they are paid (an available answer), others ignore the reference period and say what they typically do (a representative answer) and others may use an available/representative answer as a base and actually try to adjust it for what happened last week. Memory and judgment issues can be blended with comprehension issues. If at all jobs includes housework, then some answers take the form of the total number of hours in a week minus hours for sleep.

Some authors suggest that respondent debriefing questions can also be used to explore the sensitivity of the final response. Sudman and Bradburn (1982) found that asking people "Which questions, if any, were too personal?" was not useful. Such a direct question about threat was actually threatening to respondents. They had better success with this indirect method: "Questions sometimes have different kinds of effects on people. We'd like your opinions about some of the questions in this interview. As I mention groups of questions, please tell me whether you think those questions would make most people very uneasy, moderately uneasy, slightly uneasy, or not at all uneasy?" (p. 72)

Other types of respondent debriefing questions may be problematic if they make a respondent appear unknowledgeable. Answers to the questions in Example 10.3 were generally uninformative because the vast majority of respondents answered No to the first two questions and Certain or Fairly Certain to the last. More importantly, Campanelli, Martin, and Rothgeb (1991) found that there was no correlation between how confident respondents were and how well their classification of various situations coincided with CPS definitions. Oksenberg and Cannell (1989, p. 26) summed this up nicely when they noted that: "Respondents did not appear to doubt their own, often mistaken, interpretations."

Example 10.3:

Uninformative Debriefing Questions

1. "Which questions, if any, were unclear or hard to understand?"
2. "For any of the questions, were you unsure about the type of information we wanted you to provide?"
3. "In general, how certain are you about the accuracy of your answers for other members of your household? Would you say that you are very certain, fairly certain, not very certain, or guessing?"

Source question 1: Sudman, S. and Bradburn, N.M. (1982). *Asking questions: A practical guide to questionnaire design*. San Francisco: Jossey-Bass.
Source questions 2 and 3: Campanelli, P.C., Martin, E.A. & Rothgeb, J.M. (1991). The use of respondent and interviewer debriefing studies as a way to study response error in survey data. *The Statistician*, 40, 253-264.

It is also very important to avoid questions that are too general. For example, simply asking respondents what they thought of the questionnaire is not useful. Members of the general public are not good judges of poor survey questions. As discussed in Section 10.2.3, Hunt, Sparkman, & Wilcox (1982) discovered that respondents evaluating a survey questionnaire failed to notice loaded words, double-barreled questions, ambiguous questions, and so forth. *Rather than asking their opinions, focus on respondents' understanding of terms and phrases and how they came up with their answers.*

10.3.3.1 Implementation

Respondent debriefing typically takes place immediately after the standard survey has been completed. It is exceedingly important to inform the respondents at the beginning of the interview that the exercise will be in two parts. Otherwise, when you finish the survey questionnaire, they will think they are done and be irritated by the need for additional questions.

After the standard survey interview, you can instruct your respondent to assume a new role by giving a new introduction. Perhaps something like the following, which was used by Oksenberg, Cannell, and Kalton (1991, p. 357) "The questions we've been asking you are important for finding out about people's [. . .]. We want to make sure these questions are as clear and easy to answer as possible. We would like your help in making them better. To do this, I'd like to read some of the questions I asked you earlier and get some of your thoughts about them."

The easiest situation for implementing a respondent debriefing study is when doing your own interviewing and debriefing. The debriefing can be standardized or more qualitative and in-depth in nature depending on what you are most comfortable with. The more challenging situation is implementing respondent debriefing in the context of a team of quantitative survey interviewers. The debriefing questions need to be written out as standard survey questions and ideally the interviewers should be given special coaching about how to do the debriefing.

10.3.4 Behavior Coding for Interview Questionnaires

Behavior coding was originally developed to monitor the performance of standardized interviewers and was later adopted as a way to evaluate survey questions. For example, if an interviewer does not read a question as worded, the interviewer may be a poor interviewer, but if several interviewers all misread the same question, it is probably a poor question. Similarly, if one respondent interrupts a question, this may be due to the respondent, but if several respondents all interrupt the interviewer before he or she finishes the question, the question is probably too long or has a dangling modifying clause after what appears to be the completion of the question. If several respondents on a particular question request clarification, then it could be that the question had unclear, undefined terms, or presented an unclear response task (see Fowler, 1995).

"Behavior coding documents the way in which a survey was actually carried out as no other procedure can" (Fowler & Cannell, 1996, p. 169). Therefore, behavior coding is used to understand the question-answer process more generally and is included in many survey methods experiments to document improvements in survey questions. It has great popularity, particularly in the United States and the Netherlands.

A strength of behavior coding is that it is a quantitative method. It is particularly useful when others have insisted that a certain question must be included in the questionnaire, but you feel that it is of poor quality. It is hard to argue with a quantitative result such as, "40 percent of respondents asked for clarification on Question 3". Its quantitative advantage is also seen in subsequent tests. For example, you believe you have improved Question 3, but have you? Let's say the behavior coding from a test of the new questionnaire now indicates that only 10 percent of respondents asked for clarification on Question 3, a definite improvement.

Another strength of behavior coding is that it can be easily combined with the traditional field test and used to enhance it. The behavior coding data are collected and "a question by question summary of the frequencies of each coded behavior is tabulated before a debriefing meeting. The behavior coding results themselves become a subject for discussion, with input from coders and interviewers" (Fowler & Cannell, 1996, p. 171).

There are several issues in setting up behavior coding; each will be examined below.

10.3.4.1 Which behaviors to code?

There are a variety of options in terms of what behaviors to code. Cannell and his colleagues (Oksenberg, Cannell, & Kalton, 1991) used the scheme shown in Example 10.4.

Example 10.4: Behavior Code Categories

Interviewer Question-Reading Codes	
Exact	Interviewer reads the question exactly as printed.
Slight change*	Interviewer reads the question changing a minor word that does not alter the question meaning.
Major change*	Interviewer changes the question such that the meaning is altered. Interviewer does not complete reading the question.
Respondent behavior codes	
Interruption with answer*	Respondent interrupts initial question-reading with answer.
Clarification*	Respondent asks for repeat or clarification of question, or makes statement indicating uncertainty about question meaning.
Adequate answer	Respondent gives answer that meets question objective.
Qualified answer*	Respondent gives answer that meets question objective, but is qualified to indicate uncertainty about accuracy.
Inadequate answer*	Respondent gives answer that does not meet question objective.
Don't know*	Respondent gives a "don't know" or equivalent answer.
Refusal to answer*	Respondent refuses to answer the question.
* Indicates a potential problem with the question.	

This scheme was later adopted for the re-design of the CPS (see Campanelli, et al., 1991; Esposito, et al., 1991). Some studies have used a large number of codes. For example, Sykes and Collins (1992), van der Zouwen and Smit (2004).

10.3.4.2 Coding live or taped?
Using a tape recorder to record the interview and then doing the behavior coding afterwards is the preferred method as it allows one to re-listen to confusing interactions. Some authors have opted for a live coding of the interview while it is in process (e.g., Campanelli, et al., 1991; Esposito, et al, 1991 who were coding CPS interviews which averaged about 10 minutes each).

10.3.4.3 Behavior coding form
There are no standardized forms for doing behavior coding. Each team of researchers have tended to create their own, designed to capture the codes they are most interested in. An example of the paper form used in the CPS behavior coding work is found on this book's website, Chapter 10, Exhibit 4. Creating your form directly in a database package to facilitate data entry, would be an advantage (see Fowler & Cannell, 1996).

10.3.4.4 What data to analyze?
Behavior coding provides an abundance of data. In the CPS test, behavior coding data were collected for 229 households. This translates into 483 people and 4,646 first-level exchanges. In this instance, an exchange is a verbalization from the interviewer and then one from the respondent. The ideal scenario is one exchange per question: interviewer reads the survey question as worded and the respondent provides an adequate answer. But depending on the question, there may be several exchanges, hopefully culminating in an adequate answer by the respondent. Some researchers see the behavior of the respondent in the initial exchange as the most important (e.g., Campanelli, et al., 1991; Esposito, et al., 1991). In contrast, some researchers actually study the sequence of language, not just a given verbal behavior, across all exchanges (see, Sykes & Collins, 1992; van der Zouwen & Smit, 2004).

10.3.4.5 How much of a problem is a problem?
If 10% of interviewers misread a question is that a problem? Or does it have to be 20%? There is no standard criterion in the literature. Different teams of researchers have used different criteria. A number of authors have considered anything below 85% exact readings of a question by interviewers as a problem and anything below 85% adequate answers by respondents as a problem (see, for example, Marquis & Cannell, 1969; Morton-Williams, 1979, Hess, Singer, & Bushery, 1999, among others).

10.3.4.6 Simplified behavior coding
If you are working on your own or are concerned about the time investment needed to collect and code the behavior coding data, an option would be to use simplified behavior coding to code respondent behavior while you are interviewing. Set up your questionnaire so that the survey questions and

answers only cover the left hand half of the page. On the right hand half of the page, you include a behavior coding grid with respondent behaviors at the top. After asking each survey question and recording the respondent's answer, you put an "X" next to their behavior. For example, you could only record the respondent's behavior from the first exchange and then proceed to the next survey question. This process may seem awkward at first, but the more comfortable you are with interviewing and the more familiar you are with the behavior coding categories, the easier the task becomes. The behavior codes provide a handy summary of which questions had which problems, something that is not always easy to remember after an interview.

10.3.4.7 Summary
Exhibit 5 on this book's website (Chapter 10) is a very useful table from van der Zouwen and Smit (2002) which summarizes the behavior coding literature with respect to various key points such as coding procedure, number of codes, frequency analysis of codes versus a study of sequences, criterion used, and so forth.

10.3.5 Cognitive Interviewing for Interview and Self-completion Questionnaires

Cognitive interviewing is a type of in-depth interviewing which pays explicit attention to the mental processes respondents use to answer survey questions. It grew out of systematic collaboration between cognitive scientists and survey researchers. The Advanced Research Seminar on Cognitive Aspects of Survey Methodology (CASM) in 1983–1984 was the clearest example of such collaboration. Since then, cognitive interviews have been used extensively in the United States and Europe.

Studies have found that "many problems that were identified in the first field test were pinpointed in the laboratory in less time, with fewer respondents, with less professional effort, and at a lower cost. The laboratory setting can also be used to gain greater insight into the source of respondent difficulties" (National Center for Health Statistics, 1989, p. 29).

Cognitive interviewing is specially designed to uncover respondents' thought processes in answering a survey question, covering the four cognitive steps of comprehension, recall, judgment and response. It is an in-depth type of interview very similar to a good qualitative interview: flexible and interactive in style with the use of open-ended probing questions. The main difference between qualitative interviewing and cognitive interviewing is the subject matter. The qualitative interviewer wants to know the details of the respondent's answer, the details of the respondent's life-experiences. The cognitive interview is not interested directly in the answers to the survey questions, but rather wants to understand how the respondent comes up with his or her answer and what difficulties or ambiguities are created for the respondent during that cognitive process.

This makes conducting a cognitive interview a unique skill, as it is neither a quantitative nor a qualitative interview. Thus at some organizations, the cognitive interviewer is a cognitive psychologist or cognitive specialist who is a member of the research team. But at other organizations the cognitive interviewers are specially trained quantitative interviewers. Some organizations use specially trained qualitative interviewers. For example, the U.K. National Centre for Social Research, at different points in time, has used all three.

10.3.5.1 Sampling and recruitment
The purpose of the cognitive interview is to identify problems in the survey questions and their causes, and hopefully suggest solutions. It is not designed to quantify the problem. Sampling is therefore purposive and numbers are often small, 10–12 per round of testing (Collins, 2002). Having said that, one needs to recruit participants who reflect the population of interest as closely as possible. Actually it may be advisable to over-recruit from the less literate or less educated portion of the sample (Caspar, 2004). Recruitment can proceed through the use of flyers (this book's website, Chapter 10, Exhibit 6), word of mouth, and snowball sampling (where your first respondent tells you about other eligible individuals who in turn tell you about yet others). As in qualitative interviewing, you will need to give the respondent a small financial incentive for their time.

10.3.5.2 The setting and length
Initially cognitive interviews were designed to take place in a laboratory setting. Such labs were equipped with video/audio recording equipment and one-way mirror. And more recently with eye tracking equipment, rigorous timing mechanisms, and so on (Caspar, 2004). But cognitive interviews do not have to be constrained to this type of environment. Any quiet and private interview setting that is free from interruptions and interference will do. Some cognitive interviewing is actually conducted in field settings such as respondents' homes. In any case, tape-recording is essential. More on structuring and conducting a cognitive interview is found on the website, Chapter 10, Exhibit 7.

Aim for between 1 and 1½ hours. Note that because the special techniques used in cognitive interviewing lengthen the interview, you may only be able to test part of a questionnaire or focus on selected questions in any one cognitive interview.

10.3.5.3 Special techniques
To uncover the respondents' cognitive processes, special techniques are used. These are divided into core techniques (think-alouds, probes, and observation), which are discussed in this chapter and other techniques (paraphrasing, rating tasks, response latency, qualitative timing, and free-sort and dimensional sort classification tasks), which are described on this book's website, Chapter 10, Exhibit 8.

The think-aloud procedure is derived from the work of Ericsson and Simon (1984) where verbal reports are seen as data. For this task, respondents are encouraged to say out loud all of the thoughts that go through their mind in answering a survey question. These verbal reports are understood to demonstrate respondents' cognitive processes while they are answering the survey questions. As thinking out loud is not a typical everyday activity. It is useful to train respondents in the think-aloud task before the actual interview. For example, a useful exercise developed by Mingay and reported by Willis (1994, p. 7) is to instruct respondents to "Try to visualise the place where you live, and think about how many window there in that place. As you count up the windows, tell me what you are seeing and thinking about." Respondents typically require frequent neutral probes to encourage them to keep thinking aloud (such as, "remember to tell me what you are thinking" and "you look puzzled, tell me what you are thinking." Further think-aloud probes are given on the website, Chapter 10, Exhibit 9.

Think-alouds can be concurrent with the respondent thinking aloud as he or she answers every survey question (see Example 10.5) or think-alouds can be retrospective where all of the questions are administered first and then the respondent is reminded of each survey question, in turn and asked to think aloud about his or her previous answers. The disadvantage of the concurrent approach is that it breaks up the flow of the survey and becomes less like a real interview. This is avoided in the retrospective approach. But on the other hand, the concurrent approach in more likely to capture what the respondent is thinking at the time he/she answers the question, which is more problematic in the retrospective approach. Sudman, Bradburn, and Schwarz (1996) suggest doing the retrospective think-alouds after each question, that is, have respondents first provide their answer to the survey question and then think-aloud to the interviewer about how they came up with their answer. This minimizes the memory error of the standard retrospective approach.

Example 10.5:

Concurrent Think-Aloud for Interview Survey Question
Question: In your main job are you… (READ OUT)…
    … an employee   1
    or self-employed?   2

Think Aloud Response: Oh, this is difficult. I want to say self-employed, but then technically I'm not completely self-employed because some of my clients withhold tax from my wages like they do for employees. But they don't consider me to be an employee and I don't feel like an employee, but when I fill in my tax form, the income with the tax withheld needs to be listed on the employed pages, not the self-employed pages. I'm not sure how to answer this question. A few years ago I was interviewed in a survey and I said I was self-employed, but then all my other income wasn't listed on the questionnaire as there was no option to be both an employee and self-employed.

In self-completion questionnaires, prior to the four cognitive steps, the respondent needs to perceive and comprehend the layout prior to comprehending the actual questions (Dillman & Redline, 2004). Cognitive interviews are very useful for ascertaining how respondents utilize and interpret such information. Some researchers see the concurrent think-aloud approach as particularly useful for self-completion. Note that when using think aloud in this mode, you need to instruct your respondent to read out loud (anything they are reading) as well as think out loud. But note that others feel that observation of self-completion may be preferred (see Dillman, 2000).

   Probes are special questions used to explore the responses provided by respondents; they are grouped under the four cognitive steps of comprehension, recall, judgment, and response. Example 10.6 illustrates the use of probes.

Example 10.6:

Probes for Use AFTER a Think-Aloud in Self-Completion

Question: Please indicate which of the following facilities you use in the area?

	Use	Don't Use
Childcare	☐	☐
Employment advice	☐	☐
Literacy and numeracy classes	☐	☐
Arts and crafts classes	☐	☐
Lone parent support group	☐	☐
Credit union	☐	☐
Chiropodist	☐	☐

Think-aloud Response: Let's see… Please indicate which of the following facilities you use in this area? Sounds simple enough. I don't use childcare. I don't use employment advice. I don't have any problems with literacy or numeracy. I wonder who would want to admit to needing those types of classes. Most people who have those types of problems try to cover that up. Aaah, arts and crafts classes… I did do a stained glass course a few months back, but I'm not taking anything at the moment. Should I say "use" or "don't use?" I guess I would assume that "use" means "current use." I'll answer "don't use". Lone parent support group… Nope, definitely don't need that. Credit union, no. Chiropodist… Chiropodist… Chiropodist. Didn't use.

Pre-prepared probe:
The question used the phrase "in the area." What to you, is "in the area"?

Spontaneous Probe:
You repeated the word Chiropodist. What were you thinking about?

These probes greatly resemble respondent debriefing questions. Probes can be used during a concurrent or retrospective think-aloud. Probes can be pre-prepared before the cognitive interview in the same way as respondent debriefing questions or they can be spontaneously created during the interview in response to something the respondent has said or done which the cognitive interviewer wants to investigate further. Note that in Example 10.6, if the respondent had thought aloud about the issue of what in the area meant, the interviewer wouldn't need to ask the pre-prepared probe. Further examples of probes are found on this book's website, Chapter 10, Exhibit 10.

10.3.5.4 Think-aloud versus probes

It is useful to think of the contrasting strengths and weaknesses of the think-aloud versus specific probe approaches. Think-alouds are respondent driven, with low burden on the interviewer. In fact, if the respondent is thinking aloud well and staying on topic, the interviewer doesn't have to do anything but listen attentively. In contrast, specific probes are interviewer driven with much lower burden on the respondent, not requiring any special training for the respondent.

10.3.5.5 Observation

Throughout the interview it is useful to observe the respondent; his or her reactions and behavior while answering survey questions or filling in a self-completion form. Observation and good listening supply cues for your spontaneous probes.

Other documents such as advance letters or instruction sheets can be tested too. For example, it is useful to observe how respondents respond to an instruction sheet. Do they systematically read all of it, skim it quickly, or ignore it completely?

10.3.5.6 Combining cognitive techniques

In practice, cognitive interviewing techniques are not used in isolation. Pre-prepared and spontaneous probes and observation can all be used as part of a concurrent or retrospective think-aloud interview. But, note that you don't want to use think-aloud and probes at exactly the same time. Asking a probe in the middle of a respondents' think-aloud can be distracting to his or her thought processes. The probes should be reserved for after the think-aloud is finished (this is true for both concurrent and retrospective). The exception is the occasional thinking-aloud probes to keep the flow going (e.g., you look puzzled; tell me what you are thinking, etc.).

Example 10.7:

Cognitive Interviewing Plan for testing the 1996 Survey of Teachers' Workloads Diary, U.K. National Centre for Social Research
1) Introduction to respondents, outlining who we are and the objectives of the session
2) Background questions about respondent
3) Observation of respondent reading instruction booklet
4) Introduce think-aloud task; and do practice
5) Respondent thinks aloud while completing the diary (only think-aloud probes)
6) Specific probes about the diary exercise

An example of a study plan is shown as Example 10.7. This was part of a test conducted by the U.K. National Centre for Social Research of a very complicated time-use diary that was proposed for use by U.K. teachers.

10.3.5.7 Practice
Becoming a good cognitive interviewer requires a lot of practice. Knowledge and experience of qualitative in-depth interviewing offer a good platform on which to lay the cognitive techniques (see, for example, Rubin & Rubin, 1995; Kvale, 1996; Ritchie & Lewis, 2003 about in-depth interviewing). Ideally it would also be advisable to have an experienced cognitive interviewer listen to tapes of novice cognitive interviewers and give feedback. As an initial start, try some of the practice scenarios on this book's website, Chapter 10, Exhibit 11.

Interviewers' skill at cognitive interviewing also benefits from good knowledge and experience of questionnaire design and being "familiar with the ways in which fundamental cognitive processes may influence the survey response" (Willis, 1994, p. 28).

10.3.5.8 Writing notes
Cognitive interviewers can write down a few short keywords and notes during the interview, but these should be kept to a minimum so that full attention can be paid to the respondent.

As soon as the interview is finished, it is time to sit down and write more extensive notes about the key points from the interview. Do not go for a walk or do something else, write your notes first. And under no circumstances start another interview until the previous interview is documented. The notes can be written in the form of short phrases, but need to be clearly identifiable upon later reading. Some note taking advice and an example page are shown in Exhibits 12 and 13 on the website accompanying this book.

10.3.5.9 Analysis
Now that the interviews are over, what should be done next? Once again, there is no standardized practice. An ideal scenario would be to thoroughly listen to each tape (or thoroughly read a transcription). Statistics Netherlands goes beyond this by having each transcript reviewed by at least two staff members. In contrast, the practical scenario used by some organizations is to read through all notes and listen to tapes where necessary. At the extreme this can become simply a review of notes. Also, coding schemes have also been suggested (see Sudman, Bradburn, & Schwarz, 1996).

10.3.5.10 Cognitive interviewing in current perspective
As suggested at the beginning of this chapter, many question test techniques are still being refined. At the time of this writing, cognitive interview practice is far from standardized. "The fact that cognitive interviewing is widely practiced is indisputable, but it is not always completely clear what the practice entails" (Beatty, 2004, p. 45). For example, some organizations use predominantly think-aloud (see Forsyth & Lessler, 1991—Research Triangle Institute), others, predominantly probes (see Willis, 1994—U.S. National Center for Health Statistics), and others a balance of both (DeMaio & Rothgeb, 1996—U.S. Bureau of the Census). To give you further idea about the variants in practice see DeMaio & Landreth (2004).

10.3.6 Focus Groups for Interview and Self-completion Questionnaires

A focus group is a small group discussion under the direction of a moderator who promotes interaction and assures that the discussion remains on topic. Focus groups are particularly useful where it is important to highlight shared or common experience, to identify different or polarized views, or to stimulate debate amongst participants. There are lots of excellent texts on how to conduct a focus group. A good place to start could be Morgan (1988) or Stewart and Shamdasani (1990).

Focus groups provide an ideal forum for exploring new ideas or concepts for the developmental stage of testing, but also provide a forum to ascertain reactions to prepared written or visual stimuli such as draft survey questions, a complete draft questionnaire or advance letters.

Focus groups can be particularly useful for self-completion questionnaires. A possible scenario is for the focus group participants to be handed the self-completion questionnaire as they first arrive for the group. When everyone has finished, a break is declared and the moderator collects and reviews the questionnaires for indicators of confusion and patterns of response, and so forth. It can be useful to have an assistant present who assists in this process. After the break, the moderator debriefs the respondents using both preplanned debriefing questions and spontaneous ones based on the review of the completed questionnaires and observations of participants. As you plan the probes for your focus group, review the Section 10.3.3 on Respondent Debriefing questions as all the suggestions from that section apply here as well.

10.4 CONCLUSION

Comparative research found that the different methods often make different contributions toward identifying problem questions. Presser and Blair (1994), for example, found that the traditional field test identified virtually no analysis problems and cognitive interviews and expert reviews yielded almost no interviewer problems. They also explored issues of reliability and cost. All of these studies argue for the use of more than one method in order to get a complete picture of question problems.

Taking what we know, it is best to combine methods and take advantage of the strong points of each method. This would suggest an extremely thorough approach with four steps. The first step would be to start with informal testing (Section 10.2.2). This would be followed by a method using experts, that is, either expert review (Section 10.3.1) or a systematic review of the questionnaire (Section 10.3.2). Step three would be cognitive interviews (Section 10.3.5) or focus groups (Section 10.3.6). The fourth would involve the test of the questionnaire in actual field conditions (Section 10.2). This can be done with the addition of both respondent debriefing (Section 10.3.3) and behavior coding (Section 10.3.4). If there are still major changes after this fourth step, yet more testing would be needed.

Obviously there may be practical constraints to implementing this extremely thorough four-step approach. As noted in Section 10.2.1, for researchers conducting surveys in professional survey organizations, time is often the main constraint whereas for students doing their Masters or PhD degree the main constraint is resources. Thus a more moderate solution would be to have three steps. Informal testing followed some type of in-depth testing such as expert review, expert systematic review of the questionnaire, cognitive interviews, or focus groups. Finally a field test with either respondent debriefing or behavior coding.

Under severe constraints, it is good to remember that any form of question testing is better than none at all. Under such conditions, one can still do the informal testing and could consider doing a self-systematic review of the questionnaire without involving experts. I would then say that it is essential to use a method that accesses members of the target population who are strangers to the researcher. So this could be cognitive interviews, focus groups, or a small-scale traditional test with respondent debriefing. I would probably not opt for behavior coding in this last scenario, as it will provide no information on respondent problems that are invisible.

GLOSSARY OF KEY CONCEPTS

Behavior Coding. The systematic coding of both interviewer and respondent behavior as a way of diagnosing problem questions.

Cognitive Interviewing. A type of *in-depth or intensive* interview that pays explicit attention to the mental processes respondents use to answer survey questions and uses specialized techniques, such as thinking aloud.

Expert Reviews/Panels. A way of making use of the advice of an expert or panel of experts to identify potential problems in the questionnaire. No respondents are involved.

Focus Groups. Small group discussions under the guidance of a moderator. Focus Groups are used extensively in qualitative research, but they can also be used to test a survey questionnaire.

Respondent Debriefing Questions. Special follow-up questions used to determine respondents' understanding of the original survey question. Similar to probes used in cognitive interviewing.

Systematic Review of Questionnaire. The review of a questionnaire by an expert using a specific checklist, often based on cognitive principles.

Traditional Field Test. For interview surveys this involves a small number of interviewers doing a few interviews each followed by an interviewer debriefing session with the researcher. For postal surveys this involves posting the questionnaires to respondents and reviewing the questionnaires that are returned.

Advantages and Disadvantages of Different Question Testing Methods

	Advantages	Disadvantages
The Traditional Field Test	• Can be an aid to identify — *Troublesome questions* — *Difficult concepts* — *Respondent reactions to new data collection techniques* — *Etc.*	• Yet, many problems can go by unnoticed • Respondents may — *Misunderstand questions* — *Use inappropriate judgment strategies* — *Provide socially desirable answers* — *Etc.* without giving off any signals that these error sources are occurring
Expert Review/Systematic Reviews of Questionnaires	• Quick • Cost effective • Can uncover a wide range of potential problems from typos and skip pattern logic errors to problems in how concepts have been operationalized, plus — *Covers cognitive aspects for respondent* — *Can uncover possible difficulties for the interviewer* — *Can uncover possible problems for analysis* • Can generate hypotheses for testing with other methods • If a specific appraisal form is used, the method yields quantitative data	• Depends on abilities of the experts • No respondents involved, so less convincing
Respondent Debriefing	• Comments are received directly from the respondent • Question-specific comments can be used to fix the survey question • Field setting • Larger sample sizes permit greater confidence in the results • Can be used to diagnose problems in continuous surveys. • In continuous survey — *Large N facilitates statistical analysis* — *Rare groups can be debriefed*	• Potential main survey problems have to be identified in advance • Subject to its own sources of response error • Difficult to write good debriefing questions

	Advantages	Disadvantages
Behavior Coding	• Direct observation of the question-answering process • Quantitative indicator • Standard codes enhances comparability • Replicable • Flexible, codes can be tailored to the specific needs of the study	• Standard method is time consuming • Coders must be well-trained and use the codes consistently • Gives no information about why problem occurs • Additional investigation is needed to follow up on those questions that receive many problem codes
Cognitive Interviewing	• Studies have found that "many problems that were identified in the first field pretest were pinpointed in the laboratory in less time, with fewer respondents, with less professional effort, and at lower cost. The laboratory setting can also be used to gain greater insight into the source of respondent difficulties" (NCHS, 1989, p. 29)	• How to generalize — *Small sample size* — *Often a convenience sample* — *Often non-field setting* • Need highly trained interviewers • Full analysis can be very time consuming
Focus Groups	• The approach is flexible enough that unexpected information can be immediately followed up on by the moderator • Information is obtained directly from the types of individuals who will participate in the study eventually • Speed and cost saving as compared to one-on-one interview	• Small group dynamics must be appropriately controlled or results will have limited value • Preparing the data for analysis and analyzing the results can be time-consuming — *Qualitative review of the transcript* — *Information is not as detailed or as systematic as from a one-on-one interview* • Results from a small number of subjects must be interpreted with care

Chapter 11

Face-To-Face Interviews

Geert Loosveldt
Katholieke Universiteit Leuven

11.1 INTRODUCTION

Broadly speaking, a face-to-face interview in the context of survey research can be defined as a face-to-face interaction between two persons in which one person (interviewer) asks questions by means of a questionnaire and the other person (respondent) answers these questions. The essential characteristics of a face-to-face interview are the direct personal contact between interviewer and respondent, the specific division of tasks between them (asking and responding questions) and the use of a questionnaire in which the wording and the order of the questions are fixed. In fact the questionnaire guides and standardizes the interaction between the interviewer and the respondent. The direct contact between interviewer and respondent is an important difference with telephone interviews. The presence of an interviewer not only offers some additional opportunities but also creates risks. The most important opportunity is the fact that an interviewer can give direct support to the task performance of the respondent. Face-to-face interviews are therefore more suitable for longer interviews with more complex tasks. On the other hand, the most important risk of the presence of an interviewer is the influence or effect that the interviewer may have on the respondent's answers.

The general objective of an interview can be defined as obtaining correct information about characteristics (measurements) from a large number of persons so that research questions can be answered in a valid way. Correct information or high quality data means that every type of errors is absent or at least minimized. The collection of high quality data through face-to-face interviews must be considered as the shared responsibility of the researcher, the interviewer and the respondent. The researcher is responsible for the quality of the questionnaire, and the selection and training of the interviewers. The well-trained interviewer is the link between the researcher and the respondent and must perform his or her job in an adequate way. This is easier with a well-developed questionnaire and when interviewers receive intensive and adequate training. Finally, the respondent must be capable and motivated to answer the questions properly. A well-trained professional interviewer can support respondents. It is clear that when one of the three actors (researcher, interviewer and respondent) does not perform his or her tasks adequately, it will have a negative effect on the data quality.

Sticking to the key principle of standardized interviewing is deemed to be the best way to minimize errors and to realize the general objective of an interview: obtaining high quality data. The key principle of standardized interviewing specifies that all the questions are asked in the same way and that the respondents' interpretation of these questions is the same (Groves et al., 2004). It should be noticed that this key principle is sometimes disputed. Some argue that a standardized interview is not an indispensable, nor fail-proof condition to obtain valid information, for a discussion see Schober and Conrad (2002). Instead, our starting point will be the implementation of the key principle of standardized interviewing.

The general definition and objective of a face-to-face interview indicate that research with face-to-face interviews is a rather complex operation incorporating several activities. The translation of the research questions into a questionnaire (development of a questionnaire) is one of these activities and it can be considered as the first step in the organization of a survey research project. Rules about question wording and question order are presented in Writing Effective Questions (Fowler, Chapter 8). Drawing a sample of research units (e.g., persons, households) is another important component of the research process. Sampling procedures are discussed in Lohr, Chapter 6. Prior to the start of the fieldwork, the interviewers must also be selected and trained (Lessler, Eyerman, & Wang, Chapter 23). In this chapter, we focus on the basic task of the interviewer, some interviewing techniques, and on problems in face-to-face interviews.

11.2 BASIC TASK OF THE INTERVIEWER

During the briefing of a survey research project, interviewers receive specific information and instructions about the project. The active role of the interviewer in the survey research process starts after the briefing. The task of the interviewer is more comprehensive and complex than merely asking questions and recording the respondent's answer. Interviewers implement the contact procedure, persuade the respondents to participate, clarify the respondent's role during the interview and collect information about the respondent. Each of these basic tasks can be divided into subtasks (e.g., collecting information from the respondent: asking questions, clarifying questions, probing) and must be carried out according to some instructions (e.g., contact procedure: at least four contact attempts at different times of the day). In the following sections of this chapter, we elaborate and discuss the interviewer's job responsibilities.

Related to the basic task description it must be noted that interviewers must perform their tasks in such a manner that interviewer-related errors are avoided or at least minimized. The principle of minimizing interviewer-related error must guide interviewers during their task performance. Interviewer bias and interviewer variance are two components of the interviewer error. Interviewer bias occurs when interviewers have a systematic effect on the respondents' answers. This means that interviewers could be (partially) responsible for systematic measurement error. Interviewer variance is produced when different interviewers have a different effect on the answers. It is part of variable measurement error. Both types of errors are discussed in great depth in section 5. In the next section the most striking characteristics of a face-to-face interview are described.

11.3 ESSENTIAL CHARACTERISTICS OF A FACE-TO-FACE INTERVIEW

Listening to a few audio-taped interviews must be a compulsory part of each course in survey research and interviewer training. It is an excellent first introduction to the essential characteristics of a face-to-face interview and a very appropriate method for gaining a first understanding of the main problems in face-to-face interviews. Audio-taped interviews illustrate that the basic interaction structure of interviewer reads a question of the questionnaire and the respondent gives an answer to that question, is only a small part of the interaction between an interviewer and a respondent. Sometimes an interview resembles an ordinary conversation in which the interviewer has an effect on the obtained answers. These characteristics of face-to-face interviews are discussed in the following sections.

11.3.1 The Complexity of the Interviewer-Respondent Interaction

Although the interviewer's task in standardized interviewing is comprehensive, it is possible to describe all subtasks in detail and to provide instructions for each part of the task. With such a detailed list of tasks and instructions, one could assume that most of the problems arising during a face-to-face interview can be resolved; however, this is a rather naïve idea, not taking into account the *complexity of the interaction between the interviewer and the respondent*, which is an essential characteristic of a face-to-face interview. In other words, the job of the interviewer is complex because of the interaction with the respondent. A lot of the interviewers' task performance problems occur because respondents not always react in an adequate way. Most interviewers do not spontaneously produce problematic behavior but they may be triggered by problematic behavior of the respondent (Ongena, 2005, p.101). Negative reactions during the doorstep interaction to the request to participate in the interview (e.g., I'm not interested, I have no time) and the fact that respondents during the interview do not immediately answer all the questions complicate the task of the interviewer. Interviewers must react adequately to this kind of inadequate respondent behavior. The following (fictitious) example illustrates this situation: the interviewer reads the question as worded in the questionnaire (adequate interviewer behavior), the respondent doesn't select one of the response categories, and there is an inadequate reaction of the interviewer (interviewer expresses his or her own opinion about the topic of the question).

Example 11.1: Interviewer respondent interaction with an inadequate reaction of the interviewer to inadequate respondent behavior.

> **I:** Thinking about the housework you usually do, how much do you agree or disagree with the statement "I find my housework monotonous." Do you strongly agree, agree, neither agree nor disagree, disagree, or strongly disagree?
>
> **R:** I don't like housework.
>
> **I:** Neither do I.

With an interviewer-respondent interaction analysis, one can gain a clear insight in the interaction complexity. An interviewer-respondent interaction analysis related to a particular question is a description of the successive utterances of the interviewer and the respondent during a question answer sequence (see example 11.2).

Example 11.2: Interviewer respondent interaction analysis: Utterances of the interviewer and respondent with a description.

Utterances of interviewer and respondent	Description
I: Thinking about the housework you usually do, how much do you agree or disagree with the statement "I find my housework monotonous." Do you strongly agree, agree, neither agree nor disagree, disagree, or strongly disagree?	Interviewer asks the question as required.
R: I don't like housework.	Respondent gives an inadequate answer.
I: Can you select one of the response categories: strongly agree, agree, neither agree nor disagree, disagree or strongly disagree?	Interviewer asks the respondent to give an adequate answer and repeats the response categories.
R: Strongly agree.	Respondent gives an adequate answer.
I: OK.	Interviewer gives positive feedback.

In the early eighties, Brenner presented results from such an interaction analysis. In one of his examples, he shows that in only 63.4% of all sequences related to a closed question that was asked as required, the question was immediately followed by an adequate answer. In 18.47% of the sequences, respondents provided, at least initially, inadequate information. "In dealing with inadequate answers, feedback was most frequently deployed (18.47%), followed by leading probing (17.83), directive probing based on respondent's information (15.92%), answering for respondent (12.1%) and repeating respondents' inadequate information (4.46%)" (Brenner, 1981, p. 150). This example illustrates that a standardized interview cannot be considered as a simple interaction in which a question is immediately followed by an adequate response. The results of interaction analysis also clearly show that interviewers do not always have enough interviewing skills to correct inadequate response behavior and that interviewer behavior during a complex interaction can have an effect on the respondent's answer. The understanding of the interviewer respondent interaction is extremely useful to develop interviewer training with interviewing techniques that can be used to deal adequately with inadequate respondent behavior.

The initial doorstep interaction between an interviewer and a respondent can also be complex. Interaction analysis of doorstep interactions show that 'too busy', 'not interested', and 'bad timing' are frequently used reactions. In an interesting experiment in scripting interviewers' survey introductions, Morton-Williams uses interaction analysis to get information about the doorstep conversations. She demonstrates that a prepared script hindered rather than helped (Morton-Williams, 1993, p. 82). The response rate for interviewers using the script was significantly lower than interviewers using their own introductions. The results of the analysis elucidate that standardizing interviewer behavior is not always an adequate preventative treatment for complex interviewer respondent interactions. Interviewers have problems with the script when they are forced to depart from it to deal with a question or expression of respondent's reluctance. They are unable to adapt the script to the new situation. This illustrates once again that reactions or utterances of the respondent cause complex interactions patterns, which the interviewer has problems dealing with. In Chapter 3 about the problem of nonresponse (Peter Lynn) a more complex conceptual framework for survey co-operation is presented. In this framework the interaction between interviewer and respondent (sample member) is the central component.

11.3.2 The Similarity of an Interview with a Conversation

As shown in the previous section, the interaction between interviewer and respondent is sometimes more complex than the ideas and principles of the standardized interview would lead us to expect. Sometime the interaction during an interview resembles the interaction in an ordinary conversation. Some of the interaction problems during a face-to-face interview result from the similarity of an interview to a normal conversation and the requirements of standardized interviewing.

Because asking and answering questions are important components of everyday conversation and conversational skills are used in face-to-face interviews, the face-to-face interview bears some similarity to a normal conversation. Still, survey researchers emphasize that a standardized interview is not a conversation, nor is it meant to be (Schaefer, 1991, p. 367). As early as 1924 this similarity on one hand and the difference on the other hand were expressed by characterizing a standardized interview as a "conversation with a purpose" (Bingham & Moore, 1924, cited by Cannell & Kahn, 1968).

Although a face-to-face interview is not a normal conversation, it is important to know which principles and tacit assumptions are used in everyday conversations. After all the best starting point to understand the way a respondent reacts during an interview is to assume that the respondent is not familiar with his or her respondent's task and that respondents use a normal conversation as a frame of reference. This means that they use the general conversational principles during an interview.

Grice (1989) formulates four basic principles of conversation: (a) Speakers should not say things that they believe to be false (Truthfulness); (b) Speakers should make comments that are relevant to the purposes of the conversation (Relevance); (c) Speakers should make their contributions as informative as possible and not repeat themselves (No redundancy); (d) Speakers should express themselves as clearly as possible (Clarity). In fact a collaborative model of communication can or must be used to understand the conduct of conversations in everyday life. In this model, speakers and addressees collaborate to create a pragmatic meaning of utterances. They are cooperative communicators. Speakers monitor their addressees for evidence of understanding or misunderstanding and they adjust their contributions to ensure that their addressees understand them well enough. Addressees' reactions display such evidence. This interaction results in a grounded utterance; this means that both participants accept that they understand the utterance. (Schober & Conrad, 2002, p. 69–70). This fundamental process of creating grounded utterances makes clear that the interaction between the interviewer and respondent will be more complex than the simple interaction model which specifies that the interviewer asks questions and the respondent answers these questions. The task of both interviewer and respondent is more complex. The general conversational principles must be used during the questionnaire development and the specification of the interview rules and the instructions for the interviewers. These basic task rules for the interviewer and interviewing techniques are presented in the next section.

11.4 BASIC TASK RULES AND INTERVIEWING TECHNIQUES

Given the general objective and the essential characteristics of an interview discussed in the previous sections, interviewers must do their job according to some basic task rules and they can use some interviewing techniques. The task rules are the instructions the interviewer must follow while carrying out the basic tasks. For example, one of his basic tasks is to ask questions. The associated rule is to read questions as worded in the questionnaire. The techniques relate to the manner in which the interviewer must deal with the respondent in order for the respondent to carry out his task well. A classic example of this is to give positive feedback when the respondent gives an accurate answer. The rules and techniques have two important objectives.

Firstly, they clarify what is expected of the respondent during a structured interview and how he can adequately accomplish his task. Secondly, they aim to avoid interviewer effects. If the first objective is met, the interview will obviously proceed more smoothly, reducing the risk of interviewer effects.

11.4.1 The Respondent's Role Must Be Clarified

When a respondent is asked to participate in a survey interview, one can assume that he or she has no clear idea about his or her task and role during this "conversation with a purpose". This assumption is supported by an old study about the respondent's understanding of the interview (Cannell, Fowler & Marquis, 1968). In this study, respondents were interviewed a second time about the (health) survey which they had participated in on the previous day. The results of this study show that most respondents knew neither the agency carrying out the survey nor the agency commissioning it. In the health survey, the researchers wanted specific and complete information. About half of the respondents had a correct perception of this goal whereas the others thought that general responses were sufficient. Over half of the respondents had no idea why the information was being collected. The conclusion is that respondents tolerate the interview but do not necessarily have a clear understanding of their task. These results also suggest that respondents use a normal conversation as a frame of reference and that they apply the basic principles of conversation. To solve the problem of the respondent's ignorance and to create a conversation with a purpose the respondent must be trained as a respondent and the basic conversational principles must be met with additional instructions for the respondent. The specific purpose of the interview must be made clear and the respondent must be told what is expected during this special conversation. Interviewers must explain why it is necessary to do the interview in a standardized rather than a nonstandardized way (Fowler & Mangione, 1990).

Although one can assume that currently in a lot of countries standardized interviewing became more established and some groups of respondents (e.g., high educated persons) are already familiar with it, one may not overestimate the respondent's experience with interviews. The best starting point is still to assume that a respondent doesn't know what is expected. All kind of instructions about respondent's task performance are useful and usually less trivial than they seem at first glance.

Clarifying the respondent's role is an important aspect of the interviewer's task. We argue that it is not only the interviewer's responsibility but also the responsibility of the researcher. An introduction letter, general and specific instructions during the interview and feedback can all be used to clarify the respondent's role.

11.4.2 Introductory Letter

In the subject index of Jean Morton-Williams' book 'Interviewer Approaches', the subject "Introductory letter" is followed by a referral to "see Explanatory Letter" (Morton-Williams, 1993, p. 235). This illustrates the basic requirements of an introduction letter. An introductory or advance letter is sent to the respondent before the interviewer contacts the respondent, explaining the general objectives of the survey as well as why and how the information will be used. Based on a content analysis of advance letters from seven expenditure surveys, Luppes (1995) concludes that advance letters rarely touch on the reflections a respondent may make while deciding whether to take part in an interview. His analysis demonstrated that the advance letters do not throw any light on the precise role of the respondent during an interview. An introductory letter should explain in broad terms that the respondent will be expected to answer some questions. It should also be made clear that anyone is capable of answering the questions and that no special skills or knowledge is required.

To summarize, an explanatory letter must include a general explanation of the role of the respondent and it must reassure de respondent that he will be able to accomplish that role without problems.

11.4.3 General Instruction

At the start of the interview, the interviewer must tell the respondent that he seeks to collect accurate and complete information and what the respondent must do to adequately perform his or her role. The interviewer must therefore use general instructions. These instructions generally clarify the purpose of the interview and the respondent's actions involved in achieving the goals of the interview. An example of such a general instruction is: "In order for your answers to be most helpful to us, it is important that you try to be as accurate as you can. Since we need complete and accurate information from this research, we hope you will think hard to provide the information we need" (Cannell, Miller & Oksenberg, 1981). In this example, the purpose of the interview is described as "we need complete and accurate information" and the respondent's behavior related to this goal "you will think hard". Sometimes these kinds of general instructions contain other general specifications about what should and should not be the goal of the interview. For example "we are interested in your personal situation and opinions" and that the respondent must not give "social desirable answers". In a general instruction, one can also explain an overview of the different types of questions, for example: "You will be asked to answer two kinds of questions. In some cases, you will be asked to answer in your own words; I will have to write down your answers word for word. In other cases, you will be given a list of answers and asked to choose the one that fits best." (Fowler & Mangione, 1990, p. 51). Instructions about how to perform the respondent's role are: carefully consider each question, ask for clarification if a question is not clear and take time to reflect and to answer adequately.

This kind of general instructions must be part of the questionnaire. The explicit referral to a general instruction at the beginning of the questionnaire provides support for the interviewer performing his task. This introductory, general instruction also illustrates that clarifying the respondent's role is the responsibility of the researcher as well as that of the interviewer. It is clear that general instructions will not be sufficient to guarantee that respondents perform their role adequately during the entire interview. The questionnaire should therefore also contain specific instructions.

Example 11.3: An example in which several elements of a general instruction are integrated.

> Some people want to know what they can do to give accurate and complete information. We know that people do better when they think carefully about each question, search their memory, and take their time in answering. People also do better if they give exact answers and give as much information as they can. This includes important things as well as things which may seem small or unimportant. Please tell me when a question is not clear, and I will read it again. For some questions you may want to take time out and look for the answer by checking whatever is available to you in the house, so we can be sure we get complete and accurate answers.

Source: Cannel, Miller & Oksenberg, 1981, p. 408

11.4.4 Specific Instructions

One general introduction at the start of the interview is insufficient to ensure that the interview progresses smoothly. Each new part of the interview or each new task for the respondent must be introduced with specific instructions. For example, many questionnaires contain lists of attitude items with five point scales. It is not a normal practice during a conversation to express his or her opinion on a five-point scale. The respondent must therefore be given specific instructions about this task, for example: "I will read a list of statements about .... After each statement, you are asked to answer with one of the response possibilities on this show card. Choose the one that best matches your personal opinion." For questions about facts and events, one can emphasize the need for exact information: "Please be as complete and as accurate as you can about this." The respondent can be told to take his time to reply and that he should ask for clarification if needed. In summary, the instructions must clarify what is expected of the respondent and what he has to do to meet those expectations.

In a face-to-face survey interview, a questionnaire must be a list with standardized questions and general and specific instructions. Accordingly, a questionnaire is much more than a list of questions. Constructing the questionnaire is part of the researcher's job; using the instructions during the interview is a task of the interviewer. This illustrates that clarifying the respondent's role in a face-to-face interview is a responsibility shared between the interviewer and the respondent.

11.4.5 Reinforcement and Feedback

Using reinforcement and feedback is the logical continuation of instructions. This kind of interviewer reactions must inform the respondent about how well (or badly) he or she is performing his or her role. Feedback is the interviewer's assessment and appreciation of the way the respondents follows the instructions. Examples of positive feedback are: "OK", "Thanks"; "That is the kind of exact information we want"; "I appreciate your accuracy/frankness".

Examples of negative feedback are: "May I ask you to select one of the response categories"; "You answered that quickly; could you give it some more thought? We need exact information". In a face-to-face interview, feedback can also be nonverbal. Just a nod of the head, which indicates that the interviewer accepts the respondent's answer, can also be considered as an important expression of positive feedback. It is clear that all types of feedback must be consistent with the specific instructions and must be considered as an instrument to motivate the respondent. The feedback must relate to the way the respondent accomplishes his task and it should not express appreciation of the answer given by the respondent. The distinction seems obvious but is not always clear-cut in practice.

Results of experimental research about feedback procedure showed that feedback was effective in producing more complete information (Cannell, Miller, & Oksenberg, 1981). Interaction analysis also showed that interviewers spontaneously give little positive feedback and that they also give positive feedback to inadequate respondent behavior (e.g., refusal to answer a question). It is not unfeasible to indicate for certain questions in the questionnaire when and what feedback should be given. But this is not possible for all questions and not self-evident either. Reinforcement and feedback are important components of the behavior repertory of the interviewer that are not usually supported by instructions in the questionnaire. Accordingly, these elements of interviewer behavior should be given sufficient emphasis during interviewer training.

11.5 COLLECTING INFORMATION

The main objective of an interview is to collect data, suitable for answering the research questions. The prime concern of the interviewer carrying out his main task is to avoid or at least minimize the aforementioned interviewer bias and variability. A few ground rules are needed to accomplish this.

11.5.1 Reading Questions as Worded in the Questionnaire

A question-answer sequence in an interview can be considered as a simple stimulus response model. Reactions to a stimulus are only comparable if they are reactions to the same stimulus. This implies that answers to a question can only be compared if they are answers to the same question. Answers to the question "On average, how many hours a day do you watch television during the week, not counting the weekend?" are not comparable to answers on: "On average, how many hours a day do you watch television?"

A great deal of research into the effect of the wording of questions has demonstrated that small changes in phrasing a question can actually have an effect on the answers received (Schuman & Presser, 1981). An important prerequisite for ensuring that the replies to the questions are comparable is therefore the requirement that all interviewers read the questions precisely as worded in the questionnaire. Reading questions as worded in the questionnaire can be considered as the ground rule of standardized interviewing.

It could be assumed that interviewers would have no problems in applying this rule. Moreover, applying the rule is likely to facilitate the interviewer's job. Nevertheless, interaction analysis shows that interviewers do not always observe this ground rule (Groves, 1989). Interviewers deviate from the wording for several reasons. One reason, undoubtedly, is that the questions as they are worded and recorded in the questionnaire do not flow easily off the tongue. Once again, this point illustrates how the researcher shares responsibility for the way the interviewer performs his task.

In a number of cases, the respondent already answers the question before the interviewer has read out the question in full, resulting in a partially read out question. For closed questions that incorporate the different response options, it may happen that the response options cannot (fully) be read out. The latter is usually also considered as failing to read a question as worded in the questionnaire. It also happens that the interviewer adjusts the wording of the question because he knows from previous interviews that the adjusted version poses fewer problems to the respondent. Extensive general interview experience and experience with the specific questionnaire involved are definitely no guarantee that the ground rule will be applied. After all, experienced interviewers tend to be more laid-back about the wording of the questions (Bradburn, Sudman, Blair, & Locander, 1979). When assessing interviewers, it is important to verify whether interviewers actually apply this principal ground rule (pose question as worded) of the structured interview. One way of doing this is by asking interviewers to record their interviews on tape at regular intervals.

11.5.2 Clarifying Questions

Reading the questions as they are worded in the questionnaire offers no fail-proof guarantee that all respondents immediately understand the questions. A respondent's failure to understand a question may be deduced from an irrelevant answer or from the respondent's explicit request for clarification. Clarifying questions is usually a difficult issue for interviewers. Clarifying a question cannot be done in a directive manner and it must be in line with the objectives of the question. In other words, the reply of the respondent should not be steered into a particular direction and the interviewer cannot alter the frame of reference of the question. The recommendation is therefore that interviewers provide clarification in the first instance by repeating the question clearly and precisely. When this does not help—and only then—can they explain the basic idea and concepts behind the question in their own words. It is critical that the questionnaire is thoroughly analyzed during the survey briefing, so that all interviewers are clear about the exact meaning of the questions. Also the questionnaire should be extensively pretested (Campanelli, Chapter 10) to avoid as much problems as possible. In questions using specific concepts, the researcher is advised to include standard definitions and specifications in the questionnaire that can be used for providing explanation. What must in any case be prevented is that interviewers, asked to clarify a question, interpret it their own, but systematic manner. If this would happen, it would obviously be a significant cause of interviewer bias or interviewer variability.

11.5.3 Probing

Not all respondents' answers are immediately adequate and complete, and ready to be recorded by the interviewer. If respondents give an inadequate answer, the interviewer must ask additional questions. Asking those additional questions with the purpose of getting an adequate answer is called probing. Just as with clarifying the question, probing cannot be done in a directive manner. In this context, it is useful to distinguish between open and closed questions.

With a closed question, the respondent is asked to select one of the response options proposed to him. If he does not do so, his response is inadequate. This situation may arise with a list of statements on a certain subject with an answer scale, for example: "strongly agree, agree, agree nor disagree, disagree, strongly disagree" and the respondent replies with "Yes" or "No". In this situation, the interviewer must insist that the respondent selects one of the response options. The adequate probing question is: "Please choose one of the given response options (on the show card)?" At this point, the interviewer is free to repeat the response options. Repeating only a limited number of response options is considered as inadequate probing because it disturbs the calibration of the response scale, changing the significance of the response options. A respondent may also reply to a closed question with: "don't know" when this is not one of the response options provided. In a number of cases, it may be a well-considered answer and it is inappropriate for the interviewer to persist. If the "don't know" can be considered as an evasive answer, the interviewer can repeat the question and response options and ask the respondent to take his time to think it over and to select one of the options. He may remark that it is critical for the survey that the respondent expresses his view. The response options with closed questions are fairly limited. Probing can therefore be done in a fairly standardized way.

Compared with closed questions, open questions can be met with a wider variety of inadequate response behavior requiring probing. Asking probing questions with open questions is hence also more varied. Broadly speaking, the answers may be too general, too vague or incomplete. The answer may also lie outside the frame of reference of the question and in fact not be an answer to the question at all. The question: "Can you list a few advantages of the environment you live in?" may meet with the response "It is very pleasant to live here". On receiving such a general and vague response, the interviewer must do some probing. He can ask: "Why is it pleasant to live here, and what are the advantages of your environment?" In this manner, he asks the respondent to explain his answer and also repeats the question to reactivate the frame of reference of the question. Other typical probing questions are: "What do you mean exactly?" and "Can you tell me a little more about this?"

If the reply falls outside the frame of reference of the question, the question must be clarified and repeated. For example, to the question regarding the advantages of the environment he lives in, the respondent may reply that he is living in a comfortable home. With this answer, the respondent demonstrates that he has misunderstood the question. The interviewer must clarify the reference frame of the question by pointing out that the question relates to the environment and not the home. It would be best to repeat the question afterwards. Also after respondents have given clear, adequate answers, the interviewer can probe for more information. The standard question for this is "Anything else?"

Adequate probing is a critical skill for interviewers. When interviewers probe well, it benefits the quality of the data and gathers more and also more relevant information. In probing, interviewers must take care not to alter the question's frame of reference and not to steer the answer in any way. If they fail to do so, probing becomes a prime source of distortion and interviewer effects. Fowler and Mangione conclude that "the most important correlate of questions which are prone to interviewer effects is the likelihood that they will require interviewer probing" (Fowler & Mangione, 1990, p. 45). For all these reasons, learning to probe is an essential element of interviewer training.

11.5.4 Recording Answers

The rule for recording answers is just as self-evident and simple as the rule about reading questions. It is crucial that the interviewer accurately records the respondent's replies to open questions or selected response option to closed questions. This rule can only be applied when the respondent gives an adequate answer. In that sense, the skill of recording answers is closely associated with being able to probe when necessary. Recording answers accurately is in particular an issue when the respondent is expected to respond with a figure (amounts, hours, distances, etc.). The interviewer must record the units associated with the figures (i.e., minutes or hours). Particularly with CAPI questionnaires, it is easy to make typing errors in numbers (missing or excess zero, digital point in the wrong place, etc.). This sort of mistakes result in improbably values and the responses may subsequently be classified as missing. This can cause a considerable loss of data.

The interviewer must also be given clear instructions that the answer recorded or selected should under no circumstances be his interpretation of an inadequate answer. After all, an interviewer may resort to solving the problems a respondent has with a particular question by selecting a response option or to record his interpretation of a vague response. To him, it may wrongly seem a good solution ending a question-answer sequence when the respondent is struggling, and then proceed with the next question.

Interpreting responses is also an issue for the field coding. For field coding, the interviewer is asked to assign the respondent's reply to an open question to one of several response categories, provided in the questionnaire. It is therefore the interviewer who interprets the reply and who determines in which response category the answer can be placed. In view of the principal role played by the interviewer and the fact that the original answers of the respondent are subsequently no longer available, field coding is generally not considered to be a good interview method. Only for open questions where the diversity of the replies is limited and where a rather limited yet exhaustive list of response options can be provided or with intelligent computer assisted methods, field coding is an option.

Recording answers may seem an easy task. Nonetheless, the manner in which the interviewer fulfils this task may impact the data obtained.

11.6 INTERVIEWER BIAS AND INTERVIEWER VARIANCE

Given the characteristics of a face-to-face interview and the comprehensive and complex task of the interviewer, it is possible that an interviewer is a source of measurement error. This means that interviewers are not always improving data quality but sometimes they can have a negative effect on the data quality. In this sections interviewer related errors are discussed.

In general, there are two types of measurement error: systematic error and variable error. The distinction between both types is straightforward. For example the question: "In general, how many hours of spare time do you have during the weekend?" One can assume that some respondents overestimate their hours of spare time and that others underestimate the amount of spare time. If one assumes that both processes are random, these processes are variable errors. Variable errors can be positive or negative and they neutralize each other; they cancel each other out and the effect on the estimated mean will be zero. This does not mean that variable errors are irrelevant and that they do not have an effect at all. After all, variable errors cause some noise in the data and they have an effect on the variance of the estimate. Systematic errors occur when positive and negative errors do not neutralize or compensate each other. This means that some types of error (positive or negative) are more dominant, causing a systematic effect. As a consequence of these systematic errors the survey estimates are biased: the survey estimate of the population parameter differs from the true value in the population.

We consider the systematic and/or variable impact of interviewers on the precision of a survey estimate as an interviewer effect. The presence of an interviewer in a face-to-face interview in itself and the way an interviewer performs his task during the interview can cause interviewer effects. This means that interviewers can be responsible for variable errors as well as systematic errors. Systematic errors caused by interviewers are labeled interviewer bias. When the interviewer is a source of variable errors, the term used is interviewer variability. On the face of it, the distinction between interviewer bias and variability seems straightforward. Still, both types of interviewer error are entangled and must be considered together. This can be illustrated with one of the first publication about interviewer bias.

For a long time, interviewer bias has been recognized as a problem in face-to-face interviews. In 1929, Stuart Rice published a methodological note about "Contagious Bias in the interview". In this note data collected in 1914 are presented to illustrate the danger of "a constant distorting factor in the data". The data are related to the physical, mental, and social characteristics of 2000 homeless people. Rice observed some systematic patterns in the obtained answers to questions about the homeless' own explanation of his or her destitution and the interviewer's explanations. One interviewer considered an alcohol problem as the main cause of most of the homeless respondents he interviewed. Another interviewer ascribed the problems of most respondents to impersonal, industrial causes. Further examination disclosed that the first interviewer was an ardent believer in prohibition; the second interviewer was regarded as a socialist. Interviewers use their own frame of reference when they interpret the respondent's answer. Rice also demonstrates that the respondents' interpretation of their own situation is influenced by the interviewers' frame of reference. The percentage of respondents ascribing their own problems to liquor is higher for the prohibition interviewer than for the socialist interviewer. The latter obtained a higher percentage of respondents who considered industrial factors as the main reason for their problems. These results illustrate that interviewers also communicate their frame of reference to the respondent.

In Rice's note, the systematic effect at interviewer level is considered as the central element of bias. Both interviewers produce their own systematic effect or bias. But there are also differences between these systematic effects. In such a situation, we get interviewer variance or variability. According to Biemer and Lyberg, interviewer variance refers to the variability between systematic biases of interviewers (Biemer & Lyberg, 2003). Using this definition, Rice's note about bias is in fact a note about interviewer variance.

To recapitulate in plain terms: When there is a dominant and systematic effect of all interviewers, we get interviewer bias. When these systematic effects differ between interviewers, interviewer variability or variance occurs. This means that interviewer variability or variance cannot be considered as variable error at the interviewer level. Variable errors occur when, within the data collected by one and the same interviewer, errors vary from respondent to respondent. In this situation interviewers do not produce bias but they are responsible for additional variance or noise in the data. Note that pure bias (same bias for each interviewer) and variable error do not result in differences between interviewers and cannot be observed by comparing interviewers. Comparison of interviewers can reveal interviewer variance.

11.6.1 Interviewer Bias

Interviewer bias results from dominant and systematic effects of all interviewers on the obtained answers. Sometimes, the presence of the interviewer in itself is sufficient to create bias. Social desirability bias is an example of this type of bias. Social desirability bias is the systematic under-reporting of undesirable attitudes or behavior (e.g., drug use) and the systematic over-reporting of desirable ones (e.g., voting behavior). To explain this response tendency, one assumes that the presence of the interviewer activates social norms in the answering process and that respondents use these norms to produce socially acceptable responses. Respondents try to make themselves look better in the eyes of the interviewer by expressing opinions and behavior that conform to societal norms. Respondents use these norms regardless of the way interviewers behave during the interview. In fact, the general consensus about social norms is responsible for the systematic effect. Interviewers cause this kind of bias but it is out of their control and they cannot avoid it. Questions concerning topics, for which social norms are clear, are sensitive to social desirability.

It is also possible that particular groups of interviewers characterized by some observable traits cause some systematic effects. Especially observable interviewer characteristics with a specific social meaning related to the topics of the questionnaire, are important. A typical example of the systematic effect of such interviewer characteristics is presented in the study of Schuman and

Converse (1971) on the effects of black and white interviewers on black responses. In this study, black heads of households or their spouses were interviewed by black or white interviewers. The results show that for attitudinal questions with racial content, black interviewers—compared to white interviewers—obtained answers that expressed a more negative attitude towards whites. Systematic effects of race of interviewers are not restricted to attitudinal and face-to-face interviews. Davis and Silver found that black respondents, asked a battery of questions about political knowledge in a telephone survey, scored worse when interviewed by a black interviewer (Davis & Silver, 2003, p. 43).

11.6.2 Interviewer Variance

Interviewer variability refers in general to differences between interviewers in the way they do their job and/or in the answers they obtain. In the spare time question, for example, some interviewers can use a broad definition of spare time and others a limited one. Due to these different interpretations of spare time, some interviewers overestimate the amount of spare time and other interviewers make an underestimation. As a consequence, interviewers introduce additional variance in the survey estimate of spare time. This means that the interviewers are responsible for part of the variance of this variable. Interviewer variance is the proportion of variance due to the interviewers. In other words, part of the variance in the estimate can be explained by the interviewer. It is clear that interviewer variance is not supposed to happen and can be considered as an indicator for the poor quality of the measurement of a substantive variable.

The general assumption is that when all interviewers do their job in a standardized way and adhere to the interview rules, and when they interview a comparable group of respondents, they will get comparable answers. Comparable answers means that there are only random differences between interviewers in the obtained response distributions.

The central point of interviewer variance is differences between interviewers. These differences can be observed and evaluated by comparing the answers obtained by the interviewers. This kind of comparison of interviewers is only meaningful when one can assume that each interviewer interviews a comparable group of respondents. Otherwise differences between interviewers can arise from the differences between groups of respondents interviewed by each interviewer. The evaluation of interviewer variance therefore implies that the workload of each interviewer can be considered as a subsample of the total sample. This can be realized by interpenetrated sample assignments. This means that respondents in an area are randomly assigned to the interviewers working in that area. The random assignment creates comparable interviewer's workloads. Most often these interpenetrated sample assignments are not realized in a survey. Because of cost savings (e.g., minimizing travel costs), survey organizations allocate interviewers to a particular geographical area (e.g., a city, a village, etc.). In this situation, it is not possible to make the distinction between areas and interviewers. When differences between these areas are substantively relevant (e.g., differences between urban and rural areas), the groups of respondents interviewed by different interviewers are not comparable. In this situation, the evaluation of interviewer variance is more complicated because one must control for the substantively relevant differences between interviewers.

The intra class correlation coefficient, ρ_{int} (rho-int), is a frequently used measure of the interviewer variance of a variable (Kish, 1962). In the chapter about analysis of data from complex surveys (Stapleton, Chapter 18), the intra class correlation is also introduced. There it is a measure of the amount of variability in a response variable that can be accounted for by the clustering of respondents when cluster sampling is used. The link with interviewer variance is straightforward. The interviewers can be considered as clusters and respondents are clustered within the interviewers. Here we use the subscript *int* to indicate that the classes or clusters are formed by the interviewers. In fact, we calculate the intra-interviewer correlation coefficient. This coefficient is used as an indication of the degree to which interviewers influence survey responses. To calculate this coefficient we need the between-interviewer variance and within-interviewer variance. The coefficient equals the following expression:

$$\rho_{int} = \frac{between - interviewer\ variance}{between - interviewer\ variance + within - interviewer\ variance}$$

The between-interviewer variance expresses the differences or variability between the interviewers. It is part of the variance of a variable that can be allocated to the differences *between* the interviewers. The within-interviewer variance is the expression of the scatter of a variable *within* each interviewer. It is part of the variance of a variable that can be allocated to the differences between respondents within each interviewer. The sum of the between and the within variances equals the total variance of the variable. As a consequence, the formula shows that the intra-interviewer correlation is the ratio of the interviewer variance to the total variance or the proportion of the total variance of a variable due to or explained by the interviewer. Given this definition, it is clear that the values of the intra interviewer correlation are in the interval $[0,1]$[1]. When ρ_{int} for a particular variable equals 0 there is no interviewer variance. In that event, there is no effect or impact of the interviewers on the variance of the obtained answers to a particular question of the interview. The larger the value of ρ_{int} the larger the effect of the interviewers on the variance of a variable. The estimates of the between and the within-interviewer variance can be obtained by using a multilevel model in which respondents at first level are nested in the interviewer or second level (Hox, 2002).

The presence of interviewer variance means that interviewers add some additional variance to the sample responses. The extent to which the variance of a sample mean of a simple random sample is increased due to interviewer

---

[1] With small numbers of interviewers or cases the estimates of ρ_{int} can be negative. The usual way to deal with such negative values is to replace them by zero and interpret them as absence of interviewer variance (Biemer & Lyberg, 2003).

variance is the interviewer design effect = deff$_{int}$. Deff$_{int}$ is the inflation factor of this variance. In the expression given here, we see that the intra-interviewer correlation in interaction with the average number of interviews per interviewer (m) is an important component of this interviewer design effect.

$$deff_{int} = 1 + \rho_{int}(m-1)$$

There is no inflation of the variance when deff$_{int}$ equals 1. A deff$_{int}$ of 1.6 means a 60% increase in the variance or 26% (sqrt 1.6 = 1.26) increase in the standard error of a mean. Note that one can realize a deff$_{int}$ of 1.6 with a rather small intra-interviewer correlation of 0.015 and a normal workload of 41. This illustrates that even a small interviewer variance in interaction with the *size* of the workload can have a considerable effect on the precision of a survey estimate. This is also important in telephone interviews, where a limited number of well-supervised interviewers reach a large number of respondents.

The structure of the expression of interviewer design effect suggests a few practical strategies to reduce the interviewer design effect. Deff$_{int}$ equals 1 when each interviewer interviews only 1 respondent ($m=1$). This means that the number of interviewers equals the number of respondents. Although this option is not realistic, it demonstrates that under the assumption that the interviewer variance remains constant, increasing the number of interviewers or decreasing the number of interviews for each interviewer reduces the interviewer design effect. This is an argument in favor of using as many interviewers as possible to improve the accuracy of the survey. Increasing the number of interviewers off course also increases the training and supervising cost and the likelihood of differences between interviewers (interviewer variance).

Another strategy to reduce the interviewer design effect concentrates on the minimization of the intra-interviewer correlation. Additional investment in training to standardized interviewer behavior, thereby minimizing the differences between interviewers, is an important aspect of this approach. Follow-up of the interviewers and feedback during the fieldwork offer additional possibilities to improve interviewer behavior. Evaluation of the intra-interviewer correlation during the fieldwork is another aspect of the strategy. It is therefore necessary to split up the workload (e.g., 30 interviews) of an interviewer into different sets (e.g., 3 x 10 interviews) and to calculate the intra-interviewer correlation after all or nearly all interviewers completed a set. This procedure makes it possible to detect which interviewers contribute to a considerable extent to the intra-interviewer correlations.

This discussion makes clear that the workload of an interviewer is an important element of a survey design and that there is no standard optimal workload. The workload must be within reasonable limits (rule of thumb in face-to-face: a minimum of 10 and a maximum of 50). In a survey with well-trained and experienced interviewers with positive evaluations in previous surveys, the workload can be higher than in a survey with less skilled and less competent interviewers. In surveys with a rather large average workload, the evaluation of the intra-interviewer correlations for all important substantive variables is an extremely relevant aspect of the evaluation of the data quality.

11.7 CONCLUSION

Face-to-face interviews can be considered as an important and efficient manner for gathering data in social science research. In comparison with other data collection methods using questionnaires (surveys by mail, through the Internet, by telephone), the personal presence of the interviewer offers the researcher additional opportunities to explain to the respondent what is expected, and to observe the respondent's reaction. He can clarify how the interview differs from a normal conversation. If required, he can explain questions and tasks, and if the respondent fails to formulate an adequate answer, he can do the necessary probing. In brief, the interviewer can guide the respondent in his task and encourage him to accomplish that task as well as possible. This direct support makes a face-to-face interview particularly suitable for longer and more complex interviews. On the other hand, the interviewer presence also entails a risk that he or she has an effect on the answers obtained. In order to minimize the risk, it is preferable for the interview to be conducted in a standardized manner. It implies that the interviewers must observe the structure and content of the questionnaire and that they must apply a few ground rules when conducting interviews. The researcher is responsible for constructing a questionnaire that is suitable for such a standardized interview. In addition, the researcher is responsible for providing appropriate training, giving interviewers the necessary interviewing skills and giving them the competence to apply the ground rules without significant problems. Results of an experimental study show that an interviewer training with a strong emphasis on the interviewing techniques discussed in this chapter, can improve survey data quality (Billiet & Loosveldt, 1988).

GLOSSARY OF KEY CONCEPTS

Bias. The difference between the survey estimate of the population parameter and the true value in the population.

General instruction for the respondent. General instructions clarify the purpose of the interview and the respondent's actions involved in achieving the goals of the interview.

Grounded utterances in a conversation. Utterance in a conversation for which the participants in the conversation accept that they understand the meaning of the utterance.

Interviewer bias. Bias caused by interviewers due to systematic interviewer effects (error).

Interviewer design effect (Deff$_{int}$). The extent to which the variance of a sample mean of a simple random sample is increased due to interviewer variance.

Interviewer-related error. Systematic or variable measurement errors for which interviewers are responsible.

Interviewer respondent interaction analysis. Description of the successive utterances of the interviewer and the respondent during a question answer sequence.

Interviewer variability or variance. Differences between interviewers in their systematic effects. The intra class coefficient, ρ_{int} (rho-int), can be used to measure the amount of variability in a response variable that can be accounted for by the interviewers.

Probing. Asking additional questions with the purpose of getting more and adequate information.

Reinforcement and feedback. Reactions of an interviewer which inform the respondent about how well (or badly) he/she is performing his or her role.

Specific instructions for the respondent. Specific instructions for a particular question or task clarify what is expected of the respondent and what he has to do to meet those expectations.

Standardized interviewing. Interviewers use a questionnaire in which the wording and the order of the questions are fixed and they ask the all the questions in the same way so that the respondent's interpretation of the questions is the same.

Chapter 12

Telephone Surveys

Charlotte Steeh
Independent Consultant

12.1 INTRODUCTION

In a review of what he calls telesurvey methodologies, Gad Nathan calls the telephone survey "the major mode of collection in the sample survey field" (2001, p. 7). Although this may be true overall, the generalization needs considerable modification in specific cases. Despite the apparent simplicity of using the telephone to conduct surveys of the general population, the conditions that foster this mode of data collection vary considerably across countries. For the telephone to be a reasonably feasible and cost-efficient survey method by itself, service must be available to large proportions of a country's population, ideally as high as eighty to ninety percent. Short of this kind of penetration, telephones may be used in surveys but only as supplements to other types of data collection methods or when a subset of the general population with nearly universal access to telephone service is the target population. In addition, there must be an accurate and comprehensive list of telephone numbers that serves as a sample frame or a reasonable way to construct such a list. Finally telephone devices must be so woven into the transactions of daily life that sample members are familiar with their operation and are at least somewhat willing to use them to engage in an extended conversation with a stranger. Obviously, these conditions are satisfied to different degrees in countries around the world.

In Table 12.1, we see the range of situations survey researchers face. In 2004, the number of fixed main line telephones was as low as three per one hundred inhabitants in Africa but as high as forty in Europe and forty-one in Oceania. Among countries the spread is equally dramatic going from twenty-four per one hundred inhabitants in China to eighty in Luxembourg. The table also illustrates the complicated nature of telephone surveys in the twenty-first century. Throughout the world, there were more mobile telephones per one hundred inhabitants in 2004 than there were fixed line telephones. Five countries actually had more cellular telephones than residents. Thus depending on the location of the target population, the survey could be conducted by telephone in a number of different ways—by mobile telephone only, by landline telephone only, or by some combination of the two. In Africa or Central America where neither fixed line nor mobile telephones have reached the required penetration threshold (Denton, 2005), it is probably not feasible to do a telephone survey at all. Several European countries—for example,

Hungary, Portugal, and Spain—rely mainly on face-to-face interviews. As a result of these varying circumstances, the telephone survey has taken many forms in the past twenty-five years, just as it continues to evolve for the foreseeable future. After briefly discussing the factors, both technological and social, that are now affecting telephone use, this chapter describes the different types of scientifically respectable telephone surveys noting the advantages and disadvantages of the most prominent.

Table 12.1   Telephone Penetration by Continent and Selected Countries, 2004

Area	Number of Fixed Line Telephones/ 100 Inhabitants	Number of Mobile Telephones/ 100 Inhabitants	Percent of Telephones that are Mobile Telephones
Regions			
Africa	3.1	9.0	74.6
Americas	33.9	42.4	55.6
Asia	14.4	18.9	56.9
Europe	40.4	71.5	63.9
Oceania	41.1	62.7	60.4
Countries/Cities			
United States	59.9	61.0	50.4
Canada	*63.2*[a]	47.2	42.7
Finland	45.4	95.6	67.8
Japan	46.0	71.6	60.9
Russia	*25.3*[a]	51.6	66.8
China	23.8	25.5	51.7
Australia	54.6	82.6	60.2
Israel	43.7	104.7	70.6
Hong Kong	53.1	114.5	68.3
Taiwan, China	59.4	100.0	62.7
Italy	45.3	109.4	70.7
Luxembourg	*79.8*[a]	*119.4*[a]	*60.0*[a]

[a]Figures in italics are estimates or refer to years other than 2004—usually 2003.
Source: International Telecommunication Union (ITU),
http://www.itu.int/ITU-D/ ict/statistics/index.html

12.2 THE IMPACT OF TECHNOLOGICAL AND ATTITUDINAL CHANGE

In the first decade of the twenty-first century the telephone survey stands at a perilous crossroad. During the 1980s, it seemed a model of efficiency and speed when compared to the alternatives of a face-to-face or a mail survey. In his text on telephone survey methods first published in 1987, Paul Lavrakas remarked that the telephone stands "as the preferred approach to surveying" (p. 12) due primarily to its centralized administration and its cost effectiveness. The similarity of most results to those obtained in personal interview surveys helped account for this ascendancy (Groves & Kahn, 1979; de Leeuw & van der Zouwen, 1988). By 2000, however, well-known survey methodologists wondered whether or not the telephone survey had a future in the new century (de Leeuw, Lepkowski, & Kim, 2002) with some declaring that, unless the trend of declining response rates could be reversed, the telephone survey would disappear (Kalton, 2000; Tortora, 2004). The rapid rise and anticipated downfall of telephone interviewing is a phenomenon that requires explanation.

First of all, no other traditional mode of data collection has felt the impact of changing technologies and social conditions more than the telephone survey. In the 1970s and 1980s, it was relatively straightforward to contact sample units by dialing a number. People seemed willing to answer their phones and participate in surveys. By the end of the 1980s, however, new technologies and shifting social milieus began to make it more difficult to contact and interview respondents at reasonable costs. Because each of the new technologies appeared first in the United States, I frame the discussion largely in terms of the United States. However, just as the spread of telephony itself has occurred at different rates throughout the world, the diffusion of subsequent innovations has also been uneven resulting in constellations of services that are unique across countries and regions.

> It is the first task of the survey researcher planning a telephone survey to understand the particular national or regional setting in which the survey will be carried out.

12.2.1 Technological Innovations

Answering machines were the first in a line of technologies that have limited access to potential respondents. Answering machines very soon became ubiquitous with nearly 80% of U.S. telephone households acquiring one by 2003 (Pew Research Center for the People and the Press, 2004). Telephone companies in the United States also began to let customers block incoming calls from all numbers except a specified few. Call blocking has never been widespread in the United States despite the advertising efforts of major companies, but every telephone survey has a small percentage of numbers that can not be contacted due to call blocking. With the arrival of caller-id, which displays the name or telephone number of the caller, individuals could screen incoming calls for themselves and decide which ones to answer. Caller-id for home telephones has never attained the popularity of answering machines (only 50% ownership according to the 2003 survey cited earlier), but it is now standard on most mobile phones where it is much more conspicuous and harder to ignore. Although the exact impact of these technological developments on telephone surveys has been extensively debated (Link & Oldendick, 1999; Tuckel & O'Neill, 2002), most researchers agree that, taken together, they have increased the number of call attempts necessary to reach a household and therefore the expense of conducting a telephone survey (Steeh, Kirgis, Cannon, & DeWitt, 2001; Curtin, Presser, & Singer, 2005). The rapid growth of wireless telecommunications and internet telephony during the late 1990s and early 2000s promises to alter the methodology of telephone surveys in more dramatic ways. As noted earlier, in most of the countries of the world mobile telephones outnumber traditional fixed line telephones (see Table 12.1). This means that the telephone survey of the twenty-first century is most likely going to be conducted over a wireless device rather than a landline telephone. However, the precise nature of this wireless device is evolving rapidly and we discuss the possibilities in Section 12.4.

12.2.2 Survey Environment

In addition to adjusting to technological innovations, telephone interviewers have had to face an increasingly hostile environment for conducting surveys, and response rates have declined in most western countries (de Leeuw & de Heer, 2002). With the expansion of the work force to include women, fewer and fewer adults are home to accept an interviewer's call. Furthermore, public willingness to be interviewed, always less over the telephone than in face-to-face surveys, has declined dramatically over the last twenty years as telemarketing calls increasingly interrupted the daily activities of individuals. The creation of the U.S. National Do-Not-Call Registry in June 2003 revealed the extent of the public's resistance. Within four days, the list contained ten million numbers (Ho, 2003) and, after one year, the total had reached sixty-two million (Mayer, 2004). Although the legislation creating the U.S. Do-Not-Call List does not specifically prohibit calls for survey research, the Federal Trade Commission has, nevertheless, issued an advisory that explicitly recognizes its exempt status. It appears that the existence of the list has been reasonably effective in limiting telemarketing calls (Mayer, 2004; Link & Mokdad, 2004; Lavrakas, 2004), and the strictness of current law concerning cellular telephones suggests that antagonism to unannounced calls from survey interviewers may further decline as people increasingly rely on wireless devices. On the other hand, the mobile phone presents its own barriers to survey participation, at least in the United States.

> The first decades of the twenty-first century will be a period of transition for the telephone survey. During this transitional period the level of strain as well as the negativity of survey environments will vary by country, being greater in the United States and Canada and less in Europe and Asia.

12.3 TYPES OF TELEPHONE SURVEYS

Two cross-cutting dimensions define the major types of telephone surveys that are currently being conducted—the sample design and whether or not an interviewer reads the questions and records the answers. Samples are drawn either from lists or through a procedure known as random digit dialing. In both cases the questionnaire may be interviewer-administered or self-administered depending on the topic, survey costs, and other features of the study. Of the self-administered telephone surveys, only one, Touchtone Data Entry (TDE) or Interactive Voice Response (IVR) (see also Miller Steiger, Chapter 15) does not involve an interviewer at all. The others, which we discuss later, use an interviewer to introduce the survey and gain the cooperation of the respondent. The website to this book (section Chapter 12) provides links to an example of each type of survey. For example, the surveys of welfare recipients who left the program after the passage of the 1996 Welfare Reform Act are illustrations of telephone surveys using list samples.

12.3.1 Surveys Using List Samples

The process of selecting sample units is usually straightforward in surveys using list samples. The first step is to sort the list by relevant characteristics and then employ systematic sampling methods to draw the sample units (see Lohr, Chapter 6). Almost any list that contains telephone numbers can serve as the sample frame so long as it is comprehensive, accurate, and sufficiently large. Generally the target populations for these kinds of studies are individuals, that is, members of organizations, clients of government programs, students enrolled at a university, or registered voters, to name only a few of the possibilities. Countries with a population register or a well-maintained and comprehensive telephone directory can use list samples for general population surveys. When the list is a population registry, as in Finland and Japan, the sample unit for the survey is the individual rather than the household. When the list is a comprehensive telephone directory with small percentages of unlisted numbers, the sample unit can be the household. In this case, a respondent must be chosen from among the eligible household members. Until recently, these kinds of general population telephone surveys were common in Australia and are still being used in Italy. The future survival of directories as sample frames depends on whether or not the directories systematically include numbers that access new technologies such as mobile phones.

12.3.1.1 Benefits of list samples
The benefits of list samples are many. Because the list usually contains auxiliary information, such as names and addresses, personalization of the interview makes the survey seem more like a face-to-face interview than the random digit dial survey that we shortly describe. Advance letters explaining the purpose of the study and alerting the recipient to the interviewer's call can be mailed to all sample members or sample households if a directory constitutes the sample frame. When the list sample is made up of individuals, asking for a specific person during the introductory call avoids the awkwardness of respondent selection and makes it easier to obtain cooperation. Furthermore, the legitimacy of the call is not in doubt because the potential respondent will most likely recognize the sponsor of the survey and be predisposed to participate.

As a result, response rates to telephone surveys using list samples, even household surveys drawn from directories, have acceptably high response rates, such as 75% in the case of the Massachusetts welfare leavers study listed on this book's website, Chapter 12. It makes no difference what type of telephone device is associated with the listed number. It could be a mobile phone, a fixed line phone, or even a computer through Voice over Internet Protocol (VoIP). Self-administered telephone surveys, described in Section 12.3.3 can also be based on list samples. These myriad advantages of list samples have led scholars to view national IDs as the perfect frame for future sample surveys of the general population (Nathan, 2001).

12.3.1.2 Disadvantages of list samples

As the discussion in Chapter 6 makes clear, the condition of the list controls the survey outcome. If the list is current and well-maintained, the telephone survey based on it will be of high quality. If, however, the list is out-of-date, incomplete, or inaccurate, problems abound. When a list does not include the telephone number or a name and address, commercial services in the United States attempt to locate the missing information for a fee, but successful matches occur for only 40–50% of the selected sample (Curtin et al., 2005). In Finland, however, where the Population Register does not include a telephone number, the match is in the 90% range due largely to the database of mobile and fixed line numbers maintained jointly by the telephone companies and made available through the internet (Kuusela & Simpanen, 2002; Kuusela, 2003). Nevertheless, the inability to match a sufficient number of names with telephone numbers deprives this type of telephone survey of many of its advantages.

A pre-existing frame that lists members of a target population by their names, addresses, and telephone numbers, presents the ideal condition for conducting a telephone survey either by interviewer- or self-administration. As long as there are such lists, telephones will be used to contact and interview a sample drawn from them.

12.3.2 Surveys Using Random Digit Dial Samples

Hand wringing about the viability of telephone surveys (Tuckel & O'Neill, 2002; Kalton, 2000) has occurred primarily over surveys for which there is no comprehensive and accurate list of the target population even in countries where the penetration rate for fixed line phones is greater than 90%. Although a telephone directory exists in the United States, over the last twenty years larger and larger percentages of subscribers have decided not to publish their numbers. According to the website of Survey Sampling International Inc, the unlisted rate has risen to 30% in 2005. When this rate is combined with the 12–15% of residential numbers that are disconnected each year because subscribers move, it is obvious that the United States telephone directory does not cover a large enough proportion of fixed line telephone subscribers to warrant its use as a frame for a general population survey (http://www.ssisamples.com). In addition to other omissions, the directories in the U.S. do not include mobile telephone numbers. Finland's database, which includes both fixed line and mobile numbers, provides a contrasting example. Only 5% of numbers are secret there (Callegaro et al., 2004). In other countries, the percentage of unlisted numbers varies considerably (Nathan, 2001). As a result, some countries more than others need an alternative to the list sample.

12.3.2.1 The evolution of random digit dialing designs

Just as the area probability sample design overcomes the obstacles to general population surveys in the face-to-face mode, random digit dial procedures overcome the problems that an inadequate directory poses for general population telephone surveys. In his 2001 review article, Gad Nathan charts the various permutations of random digit dial (RDD) methods that have been proposed since the 1970s and ends with a full description of the list-assisted design that currently dominates general population sampling for telephone surveys in some countries, particularly the United States and Canada. Basically the random digit dial technique takes the information that we know for certain about a telephone system and combines it with random computer generation of the last digits of the number. In the United States, for example, a master list of telephone prefixes (a three digit area code plus a three digit exchange code) that have been assigned for distribution to customers can be purchased and sampled systematically. A computer then generates the last four digits of a ten digit number. In this example, the area code/exchange combinations would represent groups, known as banks, of 10,000 numbers. Most RDD surveys use banks that are much smaller, usually consisting of only one hundred numbers. These smaller banks are created by adding to the six digit prefix all possible combinations of two digits and then drawing a sample. As the final step, the last two digits are chosen by computer to complete the telephone number (Nathan, 2001; Lepkowski, 1988; Casady & Lepkowski, 1999).

The major problem with this basic procedure is its inefficiency. Although it gives each number an equal chance of being selected, it also leads to a large percentage of numbers that have not yet been assigned to customers or that are not working for some other reason. In one of the first major national surveys using random digit dial methods, the residential working rate was as low as 21% (Groves & Kahn, 1979). Thus interviewers in these early applications of RDD had to engage in excessive dialing to identify working residential numbers, and the costs of conducting the survey went up accordingly. Later iterations of random digit dial procedures sought more effective means of identifying working numbers at the sampling stage in order to lower the interviewer burden during the actual field period.

The first such procedure to gain wide acceptance is known as the Mitofsky-Waksberg sample design. From its beginning in the mid-1970s until approximately ten years ago, this design dominated telephone sampling. Its purpose was to identify banks that probably contained many working residential numbers. Although the Mitofsky-Waksberg design was a definite improvement over the simple element designs of earlier telephone samples, it had two basic inefficiencies. It was a two-stage sample design, and it required interviewer effort at the first stage to eliminate nonworking, nonresidential sample numbers. As a result, survey methodologists devised other less cumbersome ways to improve the efficiency of RDD samples. Chief among these is the list-assisted method that has now come to dominate sampling for general population telephone surveys.

Contrary to the Mitofsky-Waksberg design, list-assisted designs identify working residential numbers without involving interviewers. Instead the method utilizes information contained in the standard telephone directory. Banks of one hundred numbers can be separated into two groups or strata, those that have at least one of their numbers listed in the white pages of the telephone book and those that have no listing whatsoever. Drawing the sample primarily from the strata made up of banks with at least one working residential number greatly increases efficiency so that now approximately 50% of the sample selections turn out to be working residential numbers. It is even considered acceptable to truncate the frame by excluding the banks with no listed numbers since the yield from sampling and interviewing in these banks is not substantial enough to justify the costs (Tucker, Casady, & Lepkowski, 1992; Casady & Lepkowski, 1991 & 1993; Brick, Waksberg, Kulp, & Starer, 1995).

12.3.2.2 General applicability of random digit dialing designs
RDD designs cannot easily be used in many countries to sample telephone subscribers. First of all, coverage of the general population has to be nearly universal, as we have reiterated. In addition, telephone numbering schemes do not necessarily follow the United States' ten digit pattern (Nathan, 2001). For example, in Germany the procedure had to be modified to accommodate telephone numbers of varying lengths since the area codes there range from 2–5 digits (Gabler & Häder, 2000). RDD frames are provided by one U.S. sampling organization for twenty-one developed countries where fixed line telephone ownership is widespread and comprehensive information about area codes and exchanges is available (http://www.surveysampling.com). As we have noted, however, the existence of a frame does not mean that RDD sampling should be the design of choice even when telephone penetration is high. For example, in Japan it is possible to draw a random digit dial sample of numbers, but the existence of the National Residents Registry System, even though controlled by local municipalities that may withhold access, makes RDD seem second best. Similarly, when compared to other survey modes of administration, RDD may still be deemed less desirable. In 1999, the British General Election Studies explored the possibility of changing from personal interviews to random digit dial telephone surveys. The results of the experiments in the Welsh Assembly Election Study convinced survey methodologists that such a change would "compromise the British General Election Study" despite the fact that personal interviews cost five times as much (Thomson, Nicolaas, Bromley, & Park, 2001).

12.3.2.3 Benefits of RDD surveys
The primary benefit of an RDD survey is that it offers a cost-efficient method for gaining access to the general population. In some countries where residents are geographically dispersed, it may be the only way to gauge public opinion or collect vital statistics for government reports. Unlike the list sample telephone survey, however, the primary unit in an RDD survey is the household. Usually one household member is randomly selected to be the respondent although some surveys attempt to interview all adults. In addition, RDD surveys are conducted under relatively uniform standards, and certain procedures, such as

post-survey adjustments to the data, are well-established, straightforward, and widely used.

Screening for rare subgroups within the general population is an advantage of RDD surveys that is not often discussed. For example, the National Immunization Survey (NIS) conducted in the United States since 1994 would be impossible to carry out using any other mode of administration. The target population for the survey consists of infants in the age range of 19 to 35 months. In 1994 this group made up only 5% of the U.S. population (Massey, 1995). Thus, to obtain 30,974 interviews in 2002, over two million numbers were called during the screening stage (Smith, Hoaglin, & Battaglia, 2005).

12.3.2.4 Disadvantages of RDD surveys

Despite these benefits, the RDD telephone survey has always had problems that have been difficult to overcome and that seem to have worsened with time. The two most serious are noncoverage and nonresponse. Fixed line telephone penetration that grew substantially in several western countries during the 1970s and 1980s reversed course in the late 1990s as mobile phones came into general use. This trend means that a standard random digit dial sample based on fixed line numbers is becoming less and less representative of the general adult population even in countries where RDD surveys are commonplace.

Regardless of the potential seriousness of the coverage problem, the principal difficulty has been maintaining adequate response rates (see Lynn, Chapter 3). Systematic studies of trends across general population surveys conducted at regular intervals show that response rates dropped significantly when the data collection method changed from face-to-face interviewing to the RDD telephone mode in the late 1970s (Steeh, 1981). At present, response rates in the U.S. tend to fall in the 30% range or below (Council for Marketing and Opinion Research, 2001). Response rates in RDD studies conducted in other countries appear to be a bit higher, rising above 40% (Vehovar Belak, Batagelj, & Čikić, 2003; Lau, 2004; Callegaro et. al., 2004), but empirical data on trends abroad are sparse (de Heer, 1999; de Leeuw & de Heer, 2002). Thus, it is difficult to categorically state that RDD response rates have declined in Europe and Asia as they have in the U.S.

It is not clear how much of the decline in response rates for RDD surveys in the United States is due to growing individual hostility to telephone surveys. There are many other contributing factors. Let's look first at some of the conditions common to almost all random digit dial studies that lead to lower response rates.

Because the only information interviewers have in a typical RDD survey is the telephone number, calls to a large portion, if not all, of a telephone sample are unannounced. As a result, random digit dial surveys begin under less than ideal circumstances. Because there is no address, it is not possible to alert a household by sending a letter in advance of the interviewer's call. These cold calls inevitably produce a large number of refusals. The legitimacy of the sponsoring organization thus assumes more importance in an RDD survey than in either a personal interview survey or a telephone survey based on a list sample.

> Even under nearly ideal conditions, the RDD survey places interviewers in an awkward position and often leads to respondent resistance that requires special skills, training, and patience to overcome.

Because the conventional RDD survey is based on households rather than individuals, another disadvantage that comes up quite soon in the interview involves the respondent selection process. The impersonal nature of the initial contact makes the process of taking a household listing seem more intrusive than in a face-to-face survey (Groves & Kahn, 1979). As a result over the years, researchers have proposed and tested many different procedures that usually sacrifice strict probability for speed and ease of administration. The many methods that have been tried are ably described by Gaziano (2005), but the latest procedure was advanced too recently to be included in the review (Rizzo, Brisk, & Park, 2004).

> After years of experimentation and study there is still no general agreement among survey methodologists about the best method for choosing a respondent in a traditional RDD survey.

Changes in the calculation of response and other outcome rates have surely accentuated the decline. Over time, the formulas and the definitions of call dispositions on which the formulas are based have evolved from being overly broad to being more structured and standardized. This means that a response rate calculated by today's equations cannot be validly compared with a rate calculated in the 1950s or 1960s. The standardization effort in the United States was initiated by the Council of American Survey Research Organizations (CASRO) in 1979 and culminated in the definitions established by the American Association for Public Opinion Research (AAPOR). These AAPOR codes and formulas are continuously updated and are now widely accepted as authoritative within the U.S. survey research community (http://www.aapor.org/pdfs/standarddefs_3.1.pdf). The AAPOR standards acknowledge that not all numbers in an RDD sample can be identified as either eligible or ineligible. To minimize the impact of this reality on response rates, they allow the base of the rate to be adjusted by the factor 'e' following the original formula developed by the CASRO task force (Frankel, 1983). Despite the fact that all survey modes have sample units of undetermined eligibility; the problem is the most serious for RDD surveys where the size of this component is likely to be large. How to decide what value to give this adjustment factor has become a major issue in discussions of RDD response rates (see Brick et al., 2002).

The AAPOR standard definitions, however, do not cover all the situations that may arise in international surveys. Admitting that the variation in calculating response rates has been as chaotic in the United Kingdom and Europe as in the United States, Lynn, Beerten, Laiho, and Martin (2001) developed definitions that seemed to fit the European survey environment somewhat better. The informative disposition codes that Lynn and colleagues have published under the auspices of the Institute for Social and Economic Research (ISER) refer to the outcomes in face-to-face surveys that are administered by interviewers. By 2006 the definitions and formulas had been extended to telephone surveys that use RRD or list samples.

> As of 2005, United States and European survey methodologists generally classify call outcomes and calculate response rates in the same way. Nevertheless, there are differences of emphasis that take into account conditions in the various countries.

12.3.3 Self-administered Telephone Surveys

Recent technological advances now make it possible to conduct self-administered surveys over the telephone. Using IVR (Interactive Voice Response) or T-ACASI (Telephone Audio Computer Assisted Self Interviewing), interviewers dial the sample number, choose the appropriate respondent, and explain the purpose of the survey (see Miller-Steiger, chapter 15). The interviewer then switches the respondent to a recording that administers the questionnaire. The respondent answers by speaking into the phone or using the telephone keypad. IVR/T-ACASI surveys provide respondents maximum privacy when answering sensitive questions without sacrificing the speed and efficiency of interviewer administration (Turner et al., 1998; Tourangeau, Steiger, & Wilson, 2002). Another self-administered telephone survey, TDE (Touchtone Data Entry) is used primarily in establishment surveys to collect statistics on an organization's performance. In this case, the designated respondent dials a toll-free number and responds to recorded requests for data items by entering the figures on the telephone keypad (Groves et al., 2004).

Several laboratory experiments have suggested that IVR/T-ACASI studies do not remove the social presence of the interviewer from the question and answer process. Initial field experiments have revealed that respondents are fairly immune to the characteristics of the voice of the interviewer (Couper, Tourangeau, & Kenyon, 2004). On the other hand, two recent studies found that, although IVR/T-ACASI did produce more reports of smoking behavior among teenagers than a conventional CATI survey, it did not equal the reports obtained in school-based surveys that are completely self-administered (Currivan, Nyman, Turner, & Biener, 2004; Moskowitz, 2004).

12.3.4 The Telephone as a Supplement to Other Modes

Although this use of the telephone does not qualify as a survey, it is at least worth mentioning that the telephone often combines with other modes to accomplish various purposes. Nonrespondents to self-administered surveys are followed up over the telephone by interviewers in attempts to increase participation. In addition, coverage of households without telephone lines has sometimes been obtained by supplementing telephone interviews with personal interviews. Thus many surveys were multi-mode long before the multi-mode approach came into vogue. Presently multi-mode designs are most likely to mix the telephone with the web (De Leeuw, 2005).

In most surveys that combine the telephone with another mode, the sample is either a list sample or an area probability sample, not random digit dial. Government agencies in the United States, for example, make systematic use of multi-mode surveys when the sample is a rotating panel design. In these cases, the first interview is conducted face-to-face but subsequent interviews are carried out over the telephone. The most prominent example of this is the Current Population Survey (CPS) conducted by the U.S. Census Bureau on a monthly basis.

Many of these methods have been used for many years, but the number of surveys administered in more than one mode has greatly increased (De Leeuw, 2005). When the modes employ the same channel of communication—voice, for example, there appears to be little danger of distorting results by combining them (de Leeuw & van der Zouwen, 1988). However, when the modes employ different channels of communication, such as voice and self-administration by mail or the internet, compatibility may be at issue. There is evidence that respondents react differently to modes depending on whether they are visual or auditory although no definitive conclusions have been reached (Tourangeau & Smith, 1996; Schwarz & Sudman, 1996). Many survey experiments are now being conducted that should indicate the consequences of combining the telephone with self-administered forms of data collection. Chapter 15 by Miller-Steiger and Conroy has an extended discussion of multi-mode surveys and their difficulties.

> Increasingly, the telephone mode will be used in combination with other modes to increase coverage and reduce nonresponse.

12.4 NEW FORMS OF TELEPHONY AND THEIR IMPACT

In the introduction, we noted that mobile telephones outnumber fixed line telephones either in highly developed, technology oriented countries or in countries at the other extreme where the fixed line telephone system hardly exists. Although in most of these latter countries telephone penetration of any kind is still too sparse to make telephone surveys feasible, it is evident that worldwide the telephone survey of the future will be conducted by mobile phone or a multi-mode off-spring. Using mobile phones for surveys will require substantial changes in the procedures and methods we have just outlined. Research is only now beginning to suggest what these changes may entail, but it is clear that at least two further developments will have to be taken into account. Mobile phones are becoming more than just devices that allow voice communications. The newest models are web-enabled, can download music, tune in radio stations, take photographs, and broadcast television programs. In addition, telephone calls are being routed over the internet in a process known as Voice over Internet Protocol (VoIP). Mostly used in businesses until the last few years, VoIP now seems to be gathering momentum and will rival fixed line and mobile devices for private and residential use. Although the precise impact of these advances on telephone survey methodology cannot be accurately accessed at the present time, they will most probably result in the convergence of telephone, television, and the internet in one handheld device. Thus, the scope of the telephone survey will expand, taking on a myriad of different forms that allow multiple modes to mix with interviewer and self administration in novel and unexpected ways. The following discussion of findings from the work that has been completed to-date on mobile phones provides a first glance at the contours of the twenty-first century telephone survey

12.4.1 Mobile Phones

Despite the preeminence of mobile phones in most parts of the world, very few surveys have actually been conducted using them except in Finland. In the United States, cellular telephones first appeared in the literature during the mid-1990s as adjuncts to surveys where sizeable proportions of the population had no telephone service of any kind. For example, interviewers for the National Survey of America's Families (NSAF) carried cellular telephones to households without telephones so that the interview could be conducted using the same CATI system and the same interviewers as the standard component of the study. Since then, the emphasis has changed to actively employing these wireless devices directly in the survey process, a development that is occurring faster in Europe than in the United States where legal restrictions have hindered development.

Surveys using list samples may already include mobile numbers because the listed number can belong either to a cellular or a fixed line telephone. General population telephone surveys in Finland systematically contain cellular and fixed line numbers (see the survey discussed by Kuusela and Simpanen on this book's website, Chapter 12) because the sample is selected from a population registry rather than by random digit dial methods. Lists of numbers in telephone directories, even those that are up-to-date such as in Australia, are comprehensive only for fixed line numbers and either exclude mobile numbers altogether or include only a selected proportion of them, usually businesses that want their mobile number listed. Although RDD procedures can be used to select a sample from a cellular number frame, the results are not yet representative of the general population (Steeh, 2004). Furthermore, it is still not clear how to design a sample that includes both fixed line and mobile numbers. The reason for this lies in the definition of the sample unit. For the fixed line telephone frame the household is the sample unit. For the mobile number frame, the individual subscriber is the sample unit although there is some evidence that household members share a mobile phone (Tucker, Brick, Meekins, & Esposito, 2005). As a result of this basic incompatibility, most traditional RDD surveys exclude cellular numbers from sample frames. Mixed designs would, however, compensate for the coverage problems that plague each frame independently and would offer the possibility of increasing response rates. How to bridge this gap—through either weighting procedures or sample designs or both--is currently the object of intense investigation (see the papers presented at a session of the 2005 Joint Statistical Meetings in Minneapolis and referenced on the website, Chapter 12).

Although the mobile phone surveys discussed earlier have involved interviewers, the text messaging capabilities of most current mobile phones raise the prospect of self-administered surveys. Market researchers in the United Kingdom and Norway have taken the lead in developing this alternative (Widman & Vogelius, 2002). In Norway, survey methodologists think of the new smart G3 phones as small computers that allow a form of survey administration they call MCASI, that is, online data collection through a mobile phone (Tjostheim, 2005; Tjostheim & Thalberg, 2005; see also Friedrich-Freksa & Liebelt, 2005 for a similar proposal). These kinds of self-administered mobile phone surveys are more likely to be accepted first in Europe rather than in the United States where mobile phone users have not adopted text messaging as quickly (SIBIS, 2003; see http://www.pewinternet.org/press_release.asp?r=99).

12.4.2 Internet Telephony

In this first decade of the new century, Voice over Internet Protocol (VoIP) or Internet telephony has a relatively small number of private subscribers. IDC, a global market intelligence firm for the information technology and telecommunications industries, estimates only three million subscribers in the United States during 2005 with a growth projected to only twenty-seven million by 2009 (Sharma, 2005). When compared to the approximately 198,700,000 mobile phone owners as of November 2005 (http://www.ctia.org), these totals seem paltry at best. The ratio of VoIP subscribers to mobile phone subscribers is probably also skewed in other countries where VoIP options exist. Summary international data on the spread of this technology are currently unavailable.

The big advantage of VoIP telephony is its seemingly low cost. Sending calls over the internet rather than through ordinary telephone lines currently eliminates many fees that are part of fixed line billing practices. Thus the service is cheap provided that the subscriber has a computer and broadband access. For telephone surveys, VoIP poses major problems comparable to those of mobile phones. First, the assigned area code can be chosen by the subscriber and may have no relationship to the person's geographic place of residence. In addition, the number may be listed in a telephone directory, but chances are greater that it will not be. Such omissions undermine list-assisted RDD sampling methods. Finally, VoIP allows individuals to purchase virtual numbers for family members or friends who live great distances away. These virtual numbers allow long distance calls from a traditional fixed line phone at local telephone rates. Thus, the individual of the future may have a series of numbers—one for a fixed line phone, another for a cellular phone, and two or three virtual numbers for family members or close friends. Beginning now and increasingly over time, telephone surveys of whatever type are going to have to adjust for the differing probabilities of selection that result when individuals can be reached by multiple numbers. These adjustments will be necessary until voice communication is no longer tied to telephone numbers.

Currently there is no methodological research that would help to evaluate the effects of VoIP on telephone surveys. The great need at this point is for these studies to begin. IP telephony does appear to have one certain advantage for survey organizations. Large call centers with multiple locations can achieve considerable savings and implement streamlined calling procedures by switching to VoIP for their telephone service.

12.5 THE TELEPHONE SURVEY IN THE TWENTY-FIRST CENTURY

Given the pace of change in telephony that we have experienced since the turn of the twenty-first century, it may seem folly to try to predict what the telephone survey of the future will be like, especially when variations across countries and telephone systems are large even now. Some features seem inevitable even though time lines are uncertain and technological change among countries will proceed unevenly. The telephony device used to conduct interviews in the future will be web-enhanced, digital, and wireless, allowing VoIP, the web, and text messaging to be seamlessly combined in one instrument. Over time telephone samples will be less and less reflective of geographic location as well. In countries that currently do not have sufficient coverage to support a telephone survey, the increased penetration of wireless technology will make systematic data collection possible in sparsely populated areas.

In addition to sketching this broad portrait, we now suggest which specific factors will be most important over the next five to ten years. These are the issues that must be confronted regardless of the variation across countries in telephone systems and social customs. The choice of sample design ranks highest. Using a preexisting list as the sample frame minimizes many of the problems that random digit dial frames present (see Section 12.3.1). With a list sample there is usually enough auxiliary information about sample units to substantially improve the chances of making contact and gaining participation. As a result, response rates are generally quite acceptable (in the 6--70% range in the United States). The quality of the list is paramount, however. It must provide adequate coverage of the target population and contain the requisite auxiliary information for most of the sample units. In many countries, however, preexisting lists are available only for specialized populations—members of professional organizations, for example, and so a list sample is simply not feasible for general population surveys. Countries with population registries, such as Finland and Japan, are able to enjoy the benefits of list sampling.

Planning and executing a random digit dial telephone survey, on the other hand, will be particularly complicated for the next decade or so. The first step, of course, will involve deciding which sample frame to use—only fixed line numbers, only mobile numbers, or a mix of the two. Because it is not clear which of these numbers access individuals and which access households, the decision is not easy. As we stated previously, there is some evidence that mobile phones, which appear to exemplify individual ownership, are used by more than one person and perhaps even by entire households (Tucker et al., 2005). Current research indicates that the fixed line frame still produces a demographically representative sample of households, but it is difficult to estimate how much longer this finding will be valid. Of the remaining options the better alternative will probably differ by country. In the United States mixing fixed line and mobile frames seems more reasonable than using only a mobile frame, but in many European and Asian nations a mobile only frame may work quite well. The mixed option raises a number of difficult sampling and weighting dilemmas that have not yet been resolved. For a short while, multiple frame sampling procedures may suffice, but the first efforts to compare weighted dual frame estimates of telephone use with similar estimates from personal interview surveys were not encouraging (Brick, Dipko, Tucker, & Yuan, 2005).

Whichever frame is chosen, however, survey practitioners and methodologists will have to deal with more complicated probabilities of selection than in the standard fixed line survey (see Section 12.4.2). Individuals and households may now be reached through multiple numbers—for example, a fixed line number, a mobile phone number, and a VoIP number or a fixed line number and two or more mobile numbers. The rather casual adjustment for number of telephones carried out in past surveys must be replaced by a more rigorous accounting. To calculate correct probabilities of selection, surveys have to collect more specific information about an individual's and a household's telephone use. Including additional questions of this kind will take more time in an interview that already must be relatively short. Technological developments that we can scarcely imagine may overcome some of these problems. For example, new software allows fixed/mobile convergence, which gives phone users one point of contact no matter how many different devices and different numbers they have (Reuters, 2005).

On a lesser scale and in every telephone survey regardless of sample design, methodologists will have to pay particular attention to question wording and interviewer training. Although it seems quite likely that the question formats used in fixed line telephone surveys will also apply when the mode is a cellular or VoIP (see Fowler, Chapter 8), this principle has not been confirmed by empirical research. We have learned, however, that survey introductions need to be very carefully crafted when the mode is a mobile phone (Steeh & Piekarski, 2006). Although all telephone devices have limited channel capacity compared to personal interview and web surveys, this limitation may disappear as mobile telephony and the internet merge, and open exciting opportunities for graphic and textual displays. These opportunities plus the continued proliferation of telephony devices requiring different methodological procedures will tax the skills of survey interviewers, alter the organization of call centers and telephone laboratories, and cause major changes in computer assisted interviewing software. Standard training will need to cover all the types of telephone along with their unique demands. In addition, interviewers may specialize in conducting interviews primarily over either mobile phones or VoIP. Expertise in using text messaging, most probably through a provider website, will also be necessary. Thus future interviewers will tend to be full-time and well-paid professionals rather than students or part-time employees.

Whatever outcome all of these factors may ultimately produce, it seems likely that the telephone survey throughout the twenty-first century will assume many different forms due to the varying speeds with which new developments will be adopted. Despite—or perhaps because of—this variety, the telephone survey continues to be a viable mode of administration. Whenever list samples can be employed, it may even be the mode of choice.

12.6 CONCLUSION

Despite the variety of options provided by current telephony, all telephone surveys have certain features that distinguish them from other survey modes. Interviewer-administered questionnaires can be carried out not only using paper-and-pencil, but all forms of telephone survey, whether self-administered or interviewer-administered, can be computer-assisted, thereby assuring more uniform and error free data collection, and instant and continuous data entry. Although most computer-assisted (CATI) systems require a substantial monetary investment, telephone surveys can be inexpensively conducted using paper-and-pencil technology and ordinary telephones, either fixed line or mobile. One clear advantage of computer assistance is the centralized administration CATI systems provide even when an organization's interviewing facilities are in different locations. As a result, survey lab directors and supervisors can exert complete control over all aspects of the interviewing process including the careful monitoring and evaluation of interviewer performance.

Telephones surveys put greater distance between the interviewer and the respondent than do face-to-face surveys. Without access to much auxiliary information about the household or respondent, interviewers have much less opportunity to tailor their introductions to specific concerns (Groves & Couper, 1998). Although an interviewer is not able to establish as good rapport over a telephone as in person, this distancing characteristic has the effect of reducing error due to interviewer styles. Also the personal features of the interviewer such as age and race, which cannot be viewed by the respondent, do not have as great an impact on answers as in the personal interview mode. Thus we do not expect pronounced interviewer effects in telephone surveys, but in telephone interviewers usually have a larger workload than face-to-face interviewers, which still may add up to sizable interviewer error (see Loosveldt, Chapter 11).

Perhaps the most prominent commonalities are those that involve the format of the questionnaire. Because telephones are restricted to auditory channels of communication, it is difficult to keep the average respondent involved in a question and answering process on a topic that may be of little interest. As a result, interviews must be considerably shorter than in personal interview surveys. This is especially true of interviews conducted over mobile phones where the respondent's situation may be fraught with numerous distractions, such as being in a restaurant or driving a car. The narrow channel of communication of telephones requires that questions be as uncomplicated as possible and contain only a limited number of straightforward response categories. Often it is necessary to break down a question into parts, a formatting technique known as branching, in order to ensure that the respondent fully comprehends what is being asked. Because open questions elicit much shorter responses in telephone surveys, they are used much less often, and again this disadvantage may be exacerbated in a survey conducted via mobile phone. Dillman (Chapter 16) provides a comparison of these issues across different survey modes.

RDD telephone surveys usually need post-survey weights, discussed more fully in Biemer and Christ (Chapter 17). At the most basic level, researchers adjust for the number of separate telephone lines that access a household or an individual. With the proliferation in the forms of voice communication, this need will not go away. Instead it will become even more critical to gather all of the information necessary to calculate a proper weight during the interview. In the conventional RDD survey of the 1980s, most households had only one telephone line. The situation changed in the 1990s as people ordered new lines to dedicate to computers and fax machines. Even if the sample unit for future telephone surveys becomes the individual person rather than the household, the line weight, as it is usually called, will still be critical. It is also common for telephone surveys to calculate post-stratification weights to bring such sample demographics as age, race, and gender into agreement with U.S. Census estimates for the general population. Design effects that are necessary post-survey adjustments when the sample is clustered are not required in most RDD telephone surveys.

GLOSSARY OF KEY CONCEPTS

CATI. Computer Assisted Telephone Interviewing systems allow centralized survey administration, instant and relatively error free data entry, and automatic dialing. Questionnaires must be programmed and loaded into the system. Interviewers then read the survey questions from a computer screen and instantaneously record the respondent's answer on the computer keyboard.

IVR. Interactive Voice Response designates a self-administered telephone survey. See T-ACASI.

List-Assisted. A list-assisted design increases the chances of selecting a working residential number for a telephone sample. It eases the interviewer burden of calling nonworking, ineligible numbers and increases the efficiency of the sample, thus also lowering costs.

RDD. Random Digit Dial denotes a procedure for drawing probability sample of the general population using computer generated telephone numbers.

SMS. Text messaging on mobile phones is made possible by the Short Message Service. Thus SMS has become shorthand for text messaging.

T-ACASI. This mnemonic refers to a telephone survey that is self-administered. The letters stand for Telephone Audio Computer Assisted Self Interviewing. See IVR.

TDE. Touchtone Data Entry is a form of self-administered telephone survey that does not require interviewer assistance.

VoIP. Voice over IP (VoIP) is the family of technologies that allow the internet to be used for voice applications, such as telephony, voice instant messaging, and teleconferencing.

Chapter 13

Self-Administered Questionnaires:
Mail Surveys and Other Applications

Edith D. de Leeuw
Joop J. Hox
Department of Methodology & Statistics, Utrecht University

13.1 INTRODUCTION

The essence of self-administered surveys is that there is no interviewer to administer the survey, pose the questions, and record the answers. The respondent administers the questionnaire, reads the questions, and records the answers and there is no interviewer to assist or explain. The question-answer process (see Schwarz et al., Chapter 2) is totally self-administered. Self-administered questionnaires can be used in an individual setting (such as a mail survey) or in a group setting (for example, surveys of pupils in classrooms). Computer-assisted equivalents are available for different types of self-administered questionnaires. For example, in educational research the school computers and computer labs can be used to administer questionnaires and tests, whereas in establishment surveys web applications are becoming popular. Sometimes, for special topic surveys, a laptop is brought to respondents and the respondent answers the questions using this laptop without any interviewer interference. This form is called CASI or computer assisted self-interviewing. Finally, Internet surveys for population surveys and web panel research are the latest development. For an introduction and overview see de Leeuw, Hox, & Kef, 2003; de Leeuw, (2006), this book's website Chapter 13.

Postal or paper mail surveys and Internet surveys are the two best known forms of self-administered questionnaires, especially in social sciences and in polling. In these surveys, there is no personal contact with the respondent, and all information (for example, instructions, explanations, the questionnaire itself) has to be transmitted through paper or via a computer interface. There are also forms of self-administered questionnaires, in which an intermediary or representative of the researcher contacts the respondent and introduces the questionnaire, but the question-answer process itself is totally self-administered. Examples are drop-off questionnaires, where an enumerator hands out questionnaires to specific households or persons, but the respondents complete the questionnaire on their own and Interactive Voice Response, where a telephone interviewer introduces the technique and then switches over to a computer (see also Miller Steiger & Conroy, Chapter 15). Finally, there are hybrid forms in which an intermediary introduces the questionnaire, gives additional instructions and provides help when needed. Although in these hybrid forms the question-answer process is in principle self-administered, the intermediary of the researcher may provide help when problems arise. A good example is computer-assisted self-interviewing, in which a laptop computer is brought to the respondent and a trained interviewer gives instructions and provides help when necessary. Other examples are educational surveys in the classroom, or (computer-assisted) self-administered questionnaires tailored to special groups who may need extra assistance (de Leeuw, Hox, and Kef, 2003).

Besides the absence (or very limited presence) of an interviewer, there is another important difference between self-administered questionnaires and structured interviews. In a self-administered questionnaire, be it a psychological test, a postal survey or a web questionnaire, the respondent *sees* the questions with the associated answer categories, but in structured interviews respondents usually do not, although show material such as flash cards with response categories may occasionally be used. As a consequence, the visual presentation of questions and the general layout of the questionnaire are far more important in self-administered questionnaires, both on paper and on the computer screen (see also de Leeuw, Chapter 7 and Dillman, Chapter 9).

This chapter briefly discusses the effects of interviewer absence and of visual presentation of a questionnaire on the data. We then present five main types of self administered questionnaires: (a) the mail survey, (b) internet surveys and panels, (c) interactive voice response, (d) interviewer introduced self-administered questionnaire, and (e) group administration. The major part of this chapter is devoted to mail surveys of the general population, because this application demonstrates all the important issues. Web surveys and interactive voice response are of course also self-administered methods, but they need to deal with a number of specific issues and challenges, and they are therefore discussed briefly in this chapter and at greater length by Lozar Manfreda and Vehovar (Chapter 14) and Miller Steiger and Conroy (Chapter 15). Interviewer mediated self-administered questionnaires are only discussed on those points that differ from general self-administered questionnaires as discussed under mail surveys. Although group self-administered questionnaires are less known in general survey research, they are a major tool in educational surveys and have some special issues associated with them, which we discuss here.

13.2 EFFECTS OF THE ABSENCE OF INTERVIEWERS

13.2.1 Response Rate

When respondents are approached with a request to participate in a survey, interviewers may convince reluctant respondents, motivate respondents, and provide additional information about the survey. As a result, response rates in face-to-face and telephone interviews are in general higher than in self-administered surveys (Groves & Couper, 1998; de Leeuw, Chapter 7, section 5). Although interviewers differ in their individual success rate, all interviewers can be trained to do a good job of convincing respondents to cooperate, both for face-to-face surveys (National Centre for Social Research, 1999; Snijkers, Hox, & de

Leeuw, 1999) and for telephone interviews (Groves & McGonagle, 2001); for a general overview see Lessler, Eyerman & Wang (Chapter 23).

To achieve a high response rate in self-administered surveys requires special efforts in the contact phase of the survey. What needs to be done differs according to the specific type of survey that is conducted. For instance, in mail surveys an attractive questionnaire and cover letter in combination with well-timed reminders are necessary (Dillman, 1978, 2007). Internet surveys need a well-written invitation, in combination with timed reminders and a good layout and web interface (Dillman, 2007, see also Lozar Manfreda & Vehovar, Chapter 14). In drop-off questionnaires and other types of interviewer-mediated self-administered questionnaires, special training in nonresponse conversion helps the mediator to persuade reluctant respondents (see also Lessler et al., Chapter 23). Finally, in all types of surveys advance letters or prenotifications have a positive influence on the response (de Leeuw, Callegaro, Hox, Korendijk, & Lensvelt-Mulders, 2007).

13.2.2 Data Quality

In interview studies, interviewers can provide instruction or explanations when needed during the data collection. When responses are required from specific members of the household, interviewers can control who completes the questionnaire. But the presence of the interviewer can also influence responses, and cause unwanted interviewer effects, especially when sensitive issues are being discussed. In other words, the presence of an interviewer is at the same time an asset and a liability, and it is important that interviewers are trained well (cf. Loosveldt, Chapter 11; Lessler, Eyerman & Wang, Chapter 23).

In contrast, in self-administered questionnaires, *all information* about the study and the questionnaire must be carried by the questionnaire itself and the accompanying cover letter or instructions. This includes the questions and response categories, but also *meta-information*: explanations on the goal and content of the study, and instructions on how to respond to specific questions. In Web-surveys and other forms of computer-assisted self-interviewing, meta-information also includes the information available in the help system. In some cases (such as Internet panels), explicit instructions may be added requesting a specific person in the household to respond.

In addition, there is *para-information*, which is all information implicit in the questionnaire by layout and visual design, independent of the textual information. In self-administered questionnaires graphical language can take over the role of nonverbal and paralinguistic communication, which is so important to convey meaning in interviews (see also Redline & Dillman, 2002; de Leeuw, Chapter 7). For instance, a question mark gives the same information in graphical form as the higher tone of voice of the interviewer communicates paralinguistically. Using different fonts conveys graphically that a specific word is important, whereas interviewers use their voice to emphasize important terms paralinguistically. Visual design is more than graphical language; it also concerns, among others, spatial arrangement of text and response categories, background, especially figure/ground contrasts, and use of color. These visual cues are extremely important for respondents and help them to navigate through a questionnaire and focus on relevant information, resulting in fewer errors. For an introduction into visual design and questionnaires, see Dillman, Gersteva, & Mahon-Haft, 2005).

To enhance data quality pretesting is necessary in all survey modes, but pretesting is extremely important for self-administered questionnaires, because no interviewer is present to correct mistakes or problems in the questionnaire. Much depends on the correct understanding of the wording of questions and pretesting these is an integral part of professional questionnaire construction. Just pretesting the questions is not enough. A self-administered questionnaire is more than a collection of questions, and all other texts, such as instructions and verbal transitions to new parts of the questionnaire should also be tested (for an introduction and overview on pretesting, see Campanelli, Chapter 10).

> An important task in designing and implementing a self-administered survey is to ensure that the respondent receives all information that would otherwise be conveyed by the interviewer. In the contact phase, for example in advance letters or calls, this information relates to the survey itself and its function is to encourage the respondent to participate in the survey. In the data collection phase, this information mainly addresses the question-answer process and its function is to support the respondent in understanding the questions and providing adequate answers.

13.3 EFFECTS OF THE VISUAL PRESENTATION OF THE QUESTIONNAIRE

In a self-administered questionnaire the respondent is the center of everything and consequently everything must be tailored to the respondent. Good visual design is of fundamental importance here, as the main interface between the researcher and the respondent is the questionnaire. A respondent-oriented questionnaire starts with the consistent use of typographical language, such as different fonts. For example, using darker (bold) print for the questions and lighter (normal print for the answers, draws the eye to the question first. For other types of information, other styles should be used, for example, instructions to the respondent in italics, transitional texts between blocks of questions in a box or with a shaded background. Salant and Dillman (1995) and Dillman (2000, 2007) give clear instructions and numerous examples how to construct and order questions, how to give special instructions, how to guide the respondent successfully through the questionnaire, and how to use an attractive lay-out to keep respondents motivated.

Numbers, symbols and graphical layout (for example, spacing, location, brightness, contrast, and figure/ground arrangements) all communicate meaning, and should be used to optimize a questionnaire for self-administered use (for a theoretical background see Redline, Dillman, Dajani, & Scruggs, 2003; for clear examples and a case study see Dillman, Gertseva, & Mahon-Haft, 2005). In addition to consistent graphical layout, there are more general issues of visual design as visual design concerns the general appearance of the total questionnaire on paper or on the screen. The general appearance of a self-administered questionnaire evokes reactions. In a respondent-oriented design the researcher tries to make the respondent's task as easy, pleasant and interesting as possible, and visual design is a very effective tool when used systematically and sparingly.

Especially with computer assisted methods and Web surveys there are many design options. The easy availability of fonts, styles, templates, not too mention animations, tempts the novice designers to use too many graphical elements. This may easily lead to a visual overload distracting from the questions to be answered. The resulting visual distraction caused by graphics makes the tasks of the respondents actually more difficult, when they try to focus on the questions and search for relevant information.

> Professional visual design should facilitate communication, and support the question-answer process in a way that is relevant for the audience and the content of the survey. In this sense, the old designers rule stating that less is more is also valid for questionnaire design.

13.4 MAIL SURVEYS

13.4.1 General Characteristics of Mail Surveys

Mail surveys consist of questionnaires that are sent by postal mail to a sampled individual, who is requested to complete the questionnaire and send it back; no interviewer is present and the survey is completely self-administered. The questionnaire may be on paper or on computer disk (Disk by Mail); a special format used in establishment surveys is a questionnaire by fax. Main advantages of mail surveys are low costs, no time pressure, use of visual stimuli, absence of interviewer bias and more privacy for respondents. Disadvantages are: potential low response rate, and limited capabilities for complex and open questions.

Mail surveys require an explicit sampling frame of names and addresses. Telephone directories or other lists are often used for mail surveys of the general population. Using the telephone directory as a sampling frame has the drawback that people without a telephone and people with an unlisted telephone cannot be reached. It has the advantage that telephone numbers are available for all sample units and telephone reminders or follow-ups can be implemented quickly and smoothly. Another reason for the frequent use of the telephone directory as sampling frame is the relative ease and the low costs associated with this method. Some countries (such as Denmark) have excellent administrative records with names and addresses that may be used as sampling frame, in other countries (such as the Netherlands) the central post office provides lists of official postal delivery addresses which is used as sampling frame for the general population. In the United States, a postal delivery sequence file (DSF) is now available, which makes it possible to get a good postal general public frame for sampling.

A distinct drawback of mail surveys is the limited control the researcher has over the choice of the specific individual within a household who in fact completes the survey. There is no interviewer available to apply respondent selection techniques within a household, and all instructions for respondent selection have to be included in the accompanying letter. As a consequence only simple procedures such as the male/female/youngest/oldest alternation or the first or last birthday method can be used successfully. The male/female/youngest/oldest alteration asks in a random 25% of the accompanying letters for the youngest female in the household to fill in the questionnaire, in a second random 25% of the letters the youngest male is requested to fill in the questionnaire, and so on.

When a complete list of the individual members of the target population is available, as is the case in surveys of special interest groups or in countries with good administrative records, a random sample of names and addresses of the target population can be drawn. In this case, coverage and sampling are as good in mail surveys as in interview methods.

The absence of an interviewer also makes mail surveys the least flexible data collection technique when complexity of questionnaire is considered. In a mail survey, all respondents receive the same instruction and are presented with the same questionnaire, without added interviewer probing or help in individual cases. Thus, a mail questionnaire must be totally self-explanatory. All questions must be presented in a fixed order and only a limited number of simple skips and branches may be used. For routings special written instruction and graphical aids, such as arrows and colors have to be used. Principles of visual design and layout must be used to create a navigational path and guide the respondents through the questionnaire and to ensure that respondents receive the same question stimulus in the same way (see section 13.3, and Dillman, Chapter 9).

An advantage of mail surveys is that visual cues and stimuli are available, and with well-developed instructions fairly complex questions and attitude scales can be implemented. Even rank-ordering lists or sorting items are possible in mail surveys. The visual presentation of the questions makes it possible to use all types of graphical questions (for example, ladder, smiley faces, thermometer), and to use questions with seven, nine, or more response categories. In addition to the questionnaire itself, information booklets or product samples may be included in the mailing. In sum, self-administered questionnaire are very flexible regarding question type and format, only open-ended questions are difficult to ask in a mail survey, as no interviewer is present to probe for more details.

In general, self-administered questionnaires are less intrusive and allow for more privacy and induce less time pressure. The absence of an interviewer can be a real advantage in certain situation, especially when sensitive or socially desirable questions are being asked. Another advantage is that mail surveys can be completed when and where the respondent wants. Respondents can consult records if needed, which may improve accuracy especially in household surveys on income and health. For an overview see de Leeuw (1992) and Dillman (2000).

From a logistics point of view mail surveys have two drawbacks: questionnaire length and turnaround time. The personal presence of interviewers in face-to-face interviews prohibits break-offs and allows for longer questionnaires than in mail surveys, although telephone interviews or web surveys do not have this advantage and also have to be short. Turnaround time in mail surveys may take several weeks as mail surveys are locked into a definite time interval of mailing dates with a scheduled series of follow-up reminders, and therefore may take longer than telephone and web surveys (see also de Leeuw, Chapter 7).

Logistically, mail surveys also have two huge advantages: small staff and low costs. Organizational and personnel requirements for a mail survey are far less demanding then in interviews: the necessary skills are mainly generalized clerical skills and no interviewers are needed, although a trained staff member is needed to answer respondents' queries. Thus, the number of persons necessary to conduct a mail survey is far less than that required for interview surveys with equal sample sizes. Requirements for the organization and personnel do influence the cost of data collection; as a consequence mail surveys are among the least expensive and may be the only affordable mode in certain situations.

13.4.2 The Total Design Method

Most research into mail surveys has concentrated on improving the response rate. An early systematic overview is Heberlein and Baumgartner's (1978) meta-analysis; more recent overviews can be found in Kanso, 2000; Groves, Dillman, Eltinge & Little (2001). To enhance response, Dillman (1978) has developed an approach called the Total Design Method (TDM). In Dillman (2000, 2007) the TDM is renamed Tailored Design Method to emphasize the need to tailor the approach to the specific situations where it is employed. The TDM is based on Social Exchange theory, a social psychological perspective that explains social actions by the returns these are expected to bring; in other words it is based on the exchange and reciprocation of favors. Three elements are central in social exchange theory: (a) rewards, that is what one expects to gain from a certain action, (b) costs, what one expects to spend or give up, and (c) trust, the belief that the rewards will indeed come forward and will outweigh the costs (Dillman, 2000). Figure 13.1 portrays social exchange theory. The terms reward and cost are more general than just the monetary meaning; psychological costs, such as expecting a future obligation, and rewards, such as feeling important, are also included.

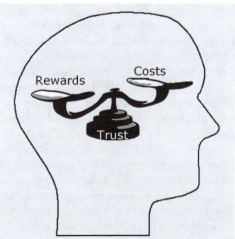

Figure 13.1 Graphical Example of Social Exchange Theory

The TDM gives detailed instructions for the design and implementation of a mail survey all based on a theoretical orientation. The theoretical underpinning of the TDM facilitates translating the principles and prescriptions into different situations and different cultural environments and allows for tailoring the approach to the specific needs of target populations in different countries. The intercultural generalizability of the TDM is high and it has been successfully applied to mail surveys not only in the United States and Europe, but also in Japan and other countries (cf. de Leeuw & Hox, 1988; Hippler & Seidel, 1985; Jussaume & Yamada, 1990; de Rada, 2001; Dewar, 2006).

The TDM organizes the design and implementation of a mail survey around the principles of maximizing the rewards, minimizing the costs, and maximizing the trust of the respondent that the rewards will indeed come to pass and that there are no hidden costs. The TDM comprises the following measures to attain these goals:

1. *Rewards*: These may be psychological and material. The respondents are shown positive regard and made to feel that they are important for the study and that their particular opinions are really needed. An individual appeal is made to the respondents and the value of their contribution is explicitly recognized. A special effort is made to make the questionnaire look interesting and pleasant to respond to. An explicit thank you is conveyed, and a token of appreciation or reward is provided, such as a summary of the results, or an explicit (monetary) incentive. The inclusion of a small token incentive in the mailing is one of the factors that increase response rates in mail surveys. The incentive should be included in the first mailing with the questionnaire because a prepaid incentive evokes the norm of reciprocation more than a promised incentive that may or not may be delivered. Only if there is a longer and /or trusted relation with the survey organization or sponsor, such as in a panel survey, a promised incentive works as well as a prepaid.

2. *Costs*: Again these may be psychological or material; costs in effort, time and money are minimized. The questionnaire is designed to seem easy to complete and the task is made to look small and undemanding, requiring little effort from the respondent. If sensitive questions are included, negative feelings or embarrassment are avoided as far as possible by an appropriate introduction and wording. Requests for personal information are minimized. Monetary costs are absent: the questionnaire can be sent back in a special stamped and preaddressed return envelope.

3. *Trust*: The letter with the questionnaire is explicitly made to look different from the usual advertising materials. Official letterhead is used to identify the study with a *legitimate* survey organization, such as a university or a government body. Contact information, such as a telephone number and address, underline the legitimacy. Associating the survey with an existing relationship can also enhance the trust relationship, for example when the members of an existing organization are surveyed. Finally, any association with junk mail, advertising, and SUGGING (Selling Under the Guise of a survey)

must be avoided. A rule of thumb is to take a good look at recently received mass mailings and advertisements and avoid this image.

Because a mailed questionnaire can easily be lost, or thrown away, or lie for days unnoticed and forgotten on a desk or kitchen table, a carefully planned system of reminders and follow-up mailings is necessary. In fact, previous research has shown that the number of reminders is one of the most powerful determinants of a high response in mail surveys (Heberlein and Baumgartner, 1978; de Leeuw & Hox, 1988; Dillman, 1991). These repeated contacts are tailored to the situation, should look different from each other, and each has to add something new. In the TDM approximately a week after the initial mailing a thank you postcard is sent to all sampled units. The purpose of this postcard is to thank all those who have responded and gently prod those who have not. Two weeks after this postcard a second mailing is sent to the nonrespondents only. This mailing includes a replacement questionnaire and return envelope, and a new cover letter that is especially composed to encourage nonrespondents to reply. This new letter is more insistent than previous communications, and explicitly states that around three weeks ago a questionnaire has been sent, which is not returned yet. It also addresses questions some respondents may have, based on questions and problems encountered in already returned questionnaires (cf Dillman, 2007, p.181-2). In his 1978 book, Dillman advices a third and last reminder by special, registered or certified mail, seven weeks after the first mailing of the questionnaire. This lengthens the time slot for a complete TDM to 8 weeks. To shorten this, variations have been suggested, such as leaving out the last reminder altogether or replacing it by a telephone call one or two weeks after the second reminder. A telephone call makes it also possible to communicate with respondents personally and inquire if they need help with or have concerns about the questionnaire.

The system of follow-ups is designed to emulate certain aspects of successful interviewer behavior in getting cooperation and refusal conversion. Therefore each follow-up mailing, and especially the cover letter text, is tailored to the phase of the survey (for example, first reminder, second reminder, for annotated examples see Dillman, 1978, 2007). Sending an advance letter also increases the response and works almost as well as a follow-up; this prenotification should be sent out to all sampled units a few days to a week before the first mailing (Dillman, 2000, 2007). Although an advance letter works in all cases, it is especially recommended when a shortened TDM is used, that is, when a third reminder is left out.

To implement reminders efficiently, a good sample status administration, either on paper or computerized, is necessary. A simple table with respondent numbers as rows and type of mailing/follow up as columns together with a straightforward code (response, nonresponse, address unknown, etc.) suffices. The TDM system of special reminders to nonrespondents also makes it necessary to identify the questionnaires with an individual respondent number. Dillman (1978, 2007) advises to be quite straightforward about this, and state in the cover letter "You may be assured of complete confidentiality. The questionnaire has an identification number for mailing purposes only…Your name will never be placed on the questionnaire (Dillman, 1978, p. 169; Salant & Dillman, 1994, p. 143). This statement is followed almost immediately by a paragraph stating that the researchers would be happy to answer any questions about the study, explicitly giving a telephone number and other contact information. In doing so, the principle of reciprocation is used to establish trust. To underscore the confidentiality a special procedure is used when respondents wish to receive a summary of results. A separate post card is added to the mailing on which respondents may fill in a contact address and mail this back to the survey organization separately from the completed questionnaire (Dillman, 1978, p. 179). When questions about a very sensitive topic are asked, it may be advisable to omit an identification number altogether. For this situation Dillman (2007, p. 166) proposes a procedure in which a separate return postcard with identification number is enclosed. In the cover letter it is stated that the questionnaire is complete anonymous and there is no identification on the questionnaire. The respondent is also requested to sign and return the enclosed postcard separately to let the researchers know that the questionnaire is returned. The respondent is assured that after returning this postcard, his or her name is deleted from the mailing list to make sure that no further reminders are sent.

For all types of surveys the pretesting of questionnaire plays an important role in professional survey design (cf., Campanelli, Chapter 10). In professional mail survey design, the pretesting of *all* survey material is important. This includes pretesting the text of the questionnaire (are the questions understood, are the answers categories sufficient, can all answers be marked, etc.), but also pretesting the advance and cover letters (are the words understood, does it create a positive image, do respondents have questions regarding the text), the attractiveness of the cover design, and the attractiveness and general image of the complete mailing-out package (would one open the envelope, read the letter, respond to the questionnaire and why (not)).

Box 13.1 Summary of construction and implementation of a mail survey following the TDM (after Hippler & Seidel, 1985; Dillman 2007).

CONSTRUCTION

Questionnaire Small neat booklet. Attractive cover with interesting title and a drawing or picture. Name and address of research organization. Backside has a box for comments and at the bottom a thank you.

Question order Start with simple and interesting questions. Order questions in a logical sequence *for the respondent*. Difficult or sensitive questions and biographical questions at the very end.

Layout Compact. Questions in bold typescript, answer categories in normal (lighter) letters. Transitions are marked with a small introduction. Instructions at the place were needed in questionnaire and if necessary repeated on next pages. Skips and branches are clearly indicated using graphical aids such as arrows.

Box 13.1 Summary of construction and implementation of a mail survey following the TDM (continued).

IMPLEMENTATION

Advance letter   Official letterhead. Full name and address of respondent in letter. Correct full date. Announce questionnaire. Tell what it is about. Thank you and Real signature. If incentive will be used, announce this in p.s.

Cover letter   Official letterhead. Full name and address of respondent in letter. Correct full date. Request and introduction topic and its importance. Emphasize importance of participation, express appreciation. Confidentiality guarantee. Provide contact information. Thank you and Real signature.

Package   Envelope contains questionnaire, cover letter, (pre stamped) return envelope, and separate card to ask for summary.

Schedule   If advance letter is used mail this a couple of days to a week before the mail out of complete package. Mail complete package out in the middle of the week. Avoid official holidays and summer holiday. After one week thank you reminder postcard. Two weeks later a firm reminder with full package. Four weeks later, so seven weeks after the initial mailing, a gentle reminder with full package by special (e.g., certified) mail.

Variations are: (1) sending an advance letter a week before the first mailing, (2) replacing the last reminder (after 7 weeks) by a telephone call four weeks after the initial mailing, that is two weeks after the firm reminder, or (3) leaving the third reminder out altogether.

Important facets of the TDM are summarized in box 13.1. For practical examples of questionnaire construction and text of accompanying letter see Salant and Dillman, 1994; Dillman, 2007.

13.4.3 Mail Surveys: Summing Up

Mail surveys are very suitable to surveys situations where a low budget and limited staff is available. Mail surveys require a reliable postal system and accurate address lists for the sampled population. To achieve a high response rate, multiple contacts are essential, including a special contact either be special mail or telephone. This system of planned reminders implies that the turn-around time for mail surveys is fixed to 5–7 weeks, independent of the sample size. In addition, the researcher should make the task of responding as attractive as possible. In

Dillman's TDM intangibles are used, such as, respect, appreciation, and a promised summary of results; in addition the use of a prepaid token monetary incentive is recommended. If the budget allows it a small incentive helps to raise the response even further.

Mail surveys have no interviewer support, which limits the complexity of the questionnaire. Good graphical design is important to guide respondents through a more complex questionnaire. As all self-administered questionnaires, mail surveys have the advantage that they are less intrusive than interview surveys. Dillman (1978, 2007) stresses that there is not one magic trick to ensure a high response and that TDM should be viewed as a system, meaning that it is important to pay attention to detail and remain consistent in approaching the respondents. The letters should be carefully drafted and the layout of the questionnaire should be well designed with consistent use of graphical tools. Provided that sufficient effort is given to get all of the details right, mail surveys can provide acceptable response rates (cf. Dillman, 1991) and data of good quality (de Leeuw, 1992).

13.5 INTERNET SURVEYS AND ACCESS PANELS

Internet surveys face many of the challenges of mail surveys. In web-based surveys, there is little control over who responds to the questionnaire, and although the web through computer assisted self interviewing (CASI) provides a much more flexible interface than a paper questionnaire and allows for complicated skip patterns, there is again no interviewer present to resolve difficulties. All problems that a respondent may encounter must be anticipated when the questionnaire is programmed, and a solution must be devised in advance. On the other hand, Internet surveys have the great advantage of all self-administered forms: that of eliminating unwanted interviewer effects and providing more privacy when answering sensitive questions. Other advantages of web surveys are timeliness and low costs. Internet surveys are discussed in detail in Chapter 14; this section provides a brief description and points out methodological issues web surveys have in common with other self-administered surveys.

Chapter 1 lists four topics as cornerstones of survey research: coverage, sampling, measurement, and nonresponse. Internet surveys encounter major obstacles in the areas of coverage, sampling and nonresponse, which are discussed first; measurement issues are discussed later.

13.5.1 Coverage, Sampling and Nonresponse in Internet Surveys

Coverage is still very problematic in web surveys of the general population: not everyone has easy Internet access, and the proportion of persons who do have Internet access varies strongly from country to country. Still, Internet access is growing world-wide and it is likely that the (under-) coverage problem will decrease in the future. A more critical problem is that Internet is not structured in a way that allows researchers to construct well defined sampling frames, that is, complete lists of Internet users that can be used to draw probability samples with known characteristics. Also, the widely varying structure of email addresses does not allow random generation of addresses, analogous to the telephone numbers generated in random digit dialing.

Sampling does not have to be a major issue in Internet surveys, provided the population can be defined and a good sampling frame is available sampling is straight forward. If the target population is the membership of an organization, and a list of email addresses is available, then computer methods for drawing probability samples are easy to implement. In some applications, such as a customer satisfaction study for an online shop, the target population is whoever visits the shop's website. Drawing a probability sample, for instance by offering a questionnaire to every 100th visitor of that website, is again simple to implement. But in general, well-defined sampling frames are not available for most Internet surveys.

In reaction to coverage and sampling problems, many commercial research organizations now maintain standing Internet-based *access panels*. An access panel is a rich database of willing respondents that is used as a sampling frame for Internet studies. As in all panels, members are requested to complete questionnaires on a regular basis. The problem is that most access panels consist of volunteers, and it is impossible to determine how well these volunteers represent the general population. If one basically lets anyone who wants to respond to a questionnaire do so, one can obtain very large samples at a relatively low cost. Sometimes this large sample size is mistakenly seen as an indication of representativeness, mostly on the argument that a large sample has a better chance of including all segments of the population. A famous example is a statement made on *National Geographic's* Survey2000 Website: "We received more than 50,000 responses—twice the minimum required for scientific validity...". This statement was enthusiastically ridiculed by survey methodologists, and was soon withdrawn from the website (Macer, 2001).

Statistical inference applies only to probability surveys, where each element of the population has a known and nonzero probability of being included in the sample (see de Leeuw, Hox, Dillman, Chapter 1, and Lohr, Chapter 6 for a more thorough discussion of this issue). Volunteer (opt-in) panels are not probability samples and applying statistical inference to non-probability samples is questionable. The American Association of Public Opinion Research provides an unambiguous standard on how to report on non-probability samples and how to avoid misleading references to margins of error (AAPOR, 2007). A good solution to the coverage and sampling problems of most access panels is to use a different data collection mode and probability samples (for example, RDD telephone interviews) for the recruitment of panel members and provide a computer and Internet access to those without. This method was successfully pioneered by Willem Saris and his group (Saris, 1998). At present there are several panels, which operate on this principle, such as CENTERdata and MESS in the Netherlands and Knowledge Networks in the United States.

Nonresponse is a serious problem for Internet surveys. In a carefully conducted meta-analysis, Lozar Manfreda (in press) studied 45 empirical comparisons and found that on average web surveys yield an 11% lower response rate than comparable paper mail and telephone surveys. Cook, Heath,

& Thompson (2000) did a meta-analysis on the response of 68 web surveys and found an average response of 35% with a standard deviation of 16%. Nonresponse not only lowers the number of available questionnaires, but it may also bias probability samples (cf. Lynn, Chapter 3). For instance, assume that we do carry out a customer satisfaction survey for a website. Every 100th visitor gets a pop-up survey, and we have a response rate of 20%. We are interested in the satisfaction with the website just visited. Nonresponse bias is a function of the nonresponse rate and the difference between the respondents and the nonrespondents on the variable of interest. If we assume that the probability of responding to the survey is larger for satisfied visitors (frustrated visitors leave the website altogether), our survey overestimates visitor satisfaction.

Dillman (2007) recommends following a Tailored Design Method (TDM), meaning to tailor what we know about increasing response rates in mail surveys to the Internet environment. Thus, principles of social exchange theory can be applied in Internet surveys too. Tailoring to the Internet means translating these principles into Internet equivalents, taking into account the specific features of the survey situation such as content, target population, and survey sponsor. Given inexpensive communications, one may be tempted to increase the number of email contacts, but overburdening respondents must be avoided because this can easily be conceived as *spamming*, which is one of the biggest irritations on the web. In a social exchange context irritation and negative feelings are a cost factor, which may lead to lower response rates as Lozar et al (in press) point out. Some evidence for this is given in the review by Cook, Heath, & Thompson (2000) who found that reminders do have a positive effect on the response compared to no reminders, but there is a diminishing effect of number of contacts.

Also, the timing of reminders should be tailored to the customs of the web. A typical pattern for web surveys is that completed surveys are returned almost immediately, but the returns diminish at a fast pace, whereas in paper mail surveys the returns build up more slowly and start to decline after 3–5 days. Internet is a more dynamic medium and Internet users read many messages a day. A survey emailed to a respondent yesterday is forgotten and deleted tomorrow, but an attractive paper questionnaire usually lies around the house for a week. Therefore, web surveys may need a shorter time lag between request and reminder than paper mail surveys. A study by Crawford, Couper, and Lamias (2001), indeed showed that a quick reminder after two days works better than a reminder after five days. How many reminders are most effective in Internet surveys and how these should be timed is still an open question; empirical research is necessary to settle this important question.

Personalization, reminders and incentives are effective response inducers in paper mail surveys, and may be successfully translated to an Internet environment as the meta-analysis of Cook et al (2000) suggests. For example, assume that a university wants to survey employee satisfaction. It has a good list of the employees email addresses, so coverage and sampling are not a problem, but nonresponse still is, and the following measures are taken to raise the response. Employees receive a paper letter on official letterhead with a small incentive. Next, they receive an email that invites them to respond to a web-based survey, using an access code (included as a clickable link for easy access, again to reduce respondent costs) included in a personalized email. Schaefer and Dillman (1998; see also Dillman, Tortora, & Bowker, 1998) discuss opportunities for personalization in Internet surveys. Box 13.2 shows an example of a personalized and a nonpersonalized email contact.

Box 13.2 Example of personalized vs. nonpersonalized contact email.

PERSONALIZED

From: John Doe [jdoe@uni.edu]   Sent: Wed 8/9/2007

To: Joop de Leeuw [jdlw@uni.edu]

Subject: Please help us with our employee survey!

Message: Dear Joop
          < cover letter including individual access code >

NONPERSONALIZED

From: surveyinfo@uni.edu   Sent: Wed 8/9/2007

To: jdlw@uni.edu

Subject: Employee survey

Message: Dear employee
          < cover letter including individual access code >

After this first email contact, follow-up emails may be used. Dillman (2007) advises a tailored thank you-reminder by email. Contrarily to the thank-you reminder with paper mail surveys, where no replacement questionnaire is added, a thank-you reminder for a web survey should always contain an explicit invitation and active link to the questionnaire as the risk is too high that good-willing respondents have already lost the original email invitation and link. Also contrary to paper mail surveys, it seems wise not to wait for a full week, but send the reminder earlier.

13.5.2 Measurement in Internet Surveys

Internet surveys are self-administered, so there is no interviewer present to assist the respondent when difficulties arise. Internet surveys are by definition computer-assisted and share all the advantages of computer-assisted surveys, which means that complex questionnaires with controlled routing (skipping and branching) can be used. In addition, Web-based surveys are based on a rich visual medium, which allows adding color and texture to the page layout, graphical elements, pictures, sounds, and other multimedia content. Internet questionnaires, like all self-administered questionnaires, have to be respondent friendly, and the visual potential of the Internet as medium can at the same time be an advantage and a disadvantage. Respondents vary in computer skills, and at least some respondents have minimal computer skills. Thus, not all respondents know how to operate drop-down menu boxes or how to mark (or correct) responses using radio buttons. Scrolling is generally awkward. All problems that develop from lack of computer skills translate to a greater effort required from the respondents, and thus increase the respondent costs. This not only increases the probability of abandoning the survey, resulting in (partial) nonresponse, it also takes away from the attention given to the actual questions, and so decreases the quality of the question-response process.

Effects of variations in visual design on responses in Web surveys have been reported a.o. by Dillman (2000), Christian, Dillman, and Smyth (2007), Couper, Traugott and Lamias (2001), and DeRouvray and Couper (2002). The position taken here is that Web surveys use a medium that leads to questionnaire formats that are distinctly different from paper questionnaires (cf. Couper, 2000). All the same, many of the design principles that apply to paper questionnaires also apply to Web questionnaires (Dillman, 2007). For instance, Schwarz et al. (Chapter 2: The Psychology of Asking Questions) note that respondents use verbal and numerical labels of scales as a reference point to evaluate their answer. Dillman (2007) argues that the graphical language that is used in Web surveys interacts with the verbal and numerical meaning of the question and response categories. He emphasizes respondent friendly design. This refers to both technical and psychological issues. Respondent-friendly design must be concerned with the problems some respondents may experience with advanced web questionnaires, which cannot be received or easily responded to because of limitations in equipment, browser, or data transmission. In addition, respondent-friendly design must bear in mind the logic of how people expect questionnaires and computers to operate. This requires attention and careful thinking about the interplay of verbal and numerical stimuli and the graphical language used in the Web questionnaire. For details we refer to Dillman (Chapter 9) and Lozar Manfreda and Vehovar (Chapter 14).

Finally, web questionnaire designers should anticipate that their questionnaires are likely to be used in mixed mode survey situations. This could introduce new sources of measurement error when different question formats are used in different modes. We refer to de Leeuw, Hox, and Dillman (Chapter 16) for a discussion of the issues involved in questionnaire design and measurement in mixed mode surveys.

13.5.3 Internet Surveys: Summing Up

Internet surveys are fast and have low cost. Being self-administered there are no interviewer effects, although the use of pictures and visual illustrations may influence respondents answers. The largest problems in Internet surveys are coverage and nonresponse. Often, the sample in a Web survey is not a probability sample from a general population, and there is no good method for generating random samples of email addresses. In addition, measurement problems arise because questionnaires may look different in different browsers and on different monitors, and respondents may have different levels of computer expertise. Data traffic speed may also still be an issue, as fast Internet access is not universally available. Despite these problems, Internet offers great opportunities for survey research. Because this is a relatively new mode of data collection, and both the technology and its dissemination in various societies is changing fast, much methodological research is needed to understand its impact on the quality of surveys.

13.6 INTERACTIVE VOICE RESPONSE

Basically, Interactive Voice Response (IVR) is a self-administered form of a telephone interview. It is a telephone-based system that accepts voice telephone input or touchtone telephone keypad entry, to collect information without using a live interviewer. Typically, an IVR system plays prerecorded voice prompts to which the respondent can reply by pressing a number on the telephone keypad to select a response option, or by speaking clearly simple answers such as "yes," "no," or simple numbers. When used in surveys, a live interviewer may introduce IVR and then connect willing respondents to the computer and its virtual IVR interviewer. Other names for IVR are T-ACASI (Telephone-Audio Computer Assisted Self Interview), TDE (Touch Tone Data Entry), VRE (Voice Recognition Entry) and ASR (Automatic Speech Response). For a detailed introduction see Miller Steiger and Conroy (Chapter 15).

The main advantage of IVR is the low cost structure: no interviewer is necessary, and contrary to a mail survey, no printing costs are made. These costs advantages are precisely why IVR has become popular in marketing and market research. Statistical offices use IVR techniques, usually referred to as TDE, for call-in panel surveys of establishments, when short questionnaires on the business structure have to be answered on a regular basis (cf. Nicholls, Baker, & Martin, 1997).

Self-administered data collection techniques have the advantage that they evoke a greater sense of privacy and lead to more openness and self-disclosure. To improve the quality of responses to sensitive questions in telephone interviews T-ACASI was developed, which can be seen as an interviewer initiated form of IVR. Because for specific questions, respondents do not have to report to an interviewer, they are more likely to report sensitive data more accurately (Turner, Forsyth, O'Reilly, Cooley, Smith, Rogers & Miller, 1998).

A major difference with other forms of self-administered questionnaires (for example, mail and Internet surveys) is that the information channel employed by IVR is aural only. In IVR, as in ordinary telephone interviews, the only available communication channels are the verbal (spoken words) and the para-linguistic channel (timing, emphasis, emotional tone) and all forms of nonverbal and visual communication are excluded. In addition, the aural channel is sequential and transitory, which places larger demands on the respondents' memory capacity (cf. Schwarz et al., Chapter 2; de Leeuw, Chapter 7). As a result only short questionnaires with simple questions and reduced response categories can be used.

IVR is a hybrid form between telephone and self-administered surveys. IVR requires high quality telephone connections and touch-tone telephone sets, which may lead to coverage problems in international surveys. As IVR technology is widely used for sales, marketing and customer support, an IVR approach may evoke the wrong script and associations in respondents, and thereby lead to a very low response rate or premature break-offs. Interviewer initiated forms, such as T-ACASI, resemble in their introduction ordinary telephone interviews, which results in similar response rates. Because questions can only be presented aurally and because of limitations of touch-tone data entry and speech recognition software, there are restrictions to the type of questions that can be asked. Interviewer effects are eliminated which is an advantage when sensitive questions are being asked over the telephone.

13.7 INTERVIEWER INITIATED SELF-ADMINISTERED QUESTIONNAIRES

In an effort to combine the advantages of interviewer administered and self-administered data collection techniques, various forms of interviewer initiated self-administered surveys have been developed which differ in the amount of interviewer involvement.

In the first form, interviewers are used as intermediaries to sample and select respondents, explain the purpose of the questionnaire, and encourage cooperation, although the data collection itself is totally self-administered. Examples are forms of IVR, drop-off mail-back questionnaires, and questionnaires on location. For instance, if no sampling frame is available, interviewers can be used for elaborate sampling techniques, such as area probability sampling, and deliver questionnaires at the selected addresses. This makes mail survey procedures possible even when names or addresses of the target sample are unknown. The completed questionnaires can be mailed back by the respondents, or picked up by the interviewers on an agreed upon date to enhance response. Visitors to a museum or national park can be asked to fill in a questionnaire and mail it back, or even may be asked to complete a computer-assisted self-administered questionnaire on the spot. Parents of newborn babies may be asked to complete a questionnaire on their first visit to a baby health service, and so forth.

Using the personal approach in combination with social exchange principles improves the response rate (cf Dillman, Dolson, & Machlis, 1995), and the question-answer process remains totally self-administered. Once when visiting the Getty museum with young children, we were asked by a friendly young woman to evaluate the child-friendliness of the museum. We were given a paper questionnaire to mail back, a postcard of the Getty museum and coloring books for the children, to guarantee said the interviewer with a smile that we could fill in the questionnaire in peace. This illustrates how interviewer approach and incentives can be tailored to the survey situation.

In the second form of interviewer initiated self-administered questionnaires, the question-answer process is still self-administered, but the interviewer is available whenever assistance is needed. This is the case when a second more private mode is used for a subset of special questions to ensure more self-disclosure and less social desirability. For example, a paper questionnaire is handed over by an interviewer and filled in by the respondent in private, without direct participation of the interviewer. After completion the respondent can seal the questionnaire in an envelope and mail it back or return it to the interviewer. In a computer-assisted personal interview a similar procedure is used. The interviewer hands over the computer to the respondent when sensitive questions have to be asked, and the respondent can answer in all privacy while the interviewer remains at a respectful distance, but remains available for instructions and assistance. When a large number of sensitive questions have to be asked, the role of the interviewer is restricted to selecting and engaging the respondent, start-up the computer and remain available for assistance. For example, the US National Survey on Drug Use and Health (NSDUH) now uses computer-assisted self-interviewing (CASI), where respondents answer the question privately by directly entering the answer in the computer, and only a few nonthreatening questions are posed by an interviewer (NSDUH, 2005). When special populations (for example, visually handicapped, hospitalized patients) are investigated, tailored interviewer assisted self-administered methods may be used. For an overview see de Leeuw, Hox, Kef, 2003.

> Interviewer-initiated self-administered questionnaires combine advantages of trained interviewers (for example, respondent selection, offering assistance when needed) with advantages of self-administered questionnaires (for example, more self disclosure, less social desirability).

13.8 GROUP ADMINISTRATION

Interviewer initiated self-administered questionnaires are more costly than mail and Internet surveys, and in some cases may be almost as costly as an interview. Substantial cost savings can be made when self-administered questionnaires are given to larger groups of people simultaneously, such as school children, students, patients at hospitals, or health testing centers. Group administration of self-administered surveys is mainly used in the context of organizational or educational research, where the population contains natural groups of respondents, which makes it a very efficient way of data collection. Besides for reasons of efficiency or costs, group-administered surveys, are also used when special groups are surveyed, who may need extra attention and time, and the design asks for a self-administered approach. For example, when studying loneliness and friendships among deaf adolescents, the researchers can used a combination of a self-administered questionnaire and a trained sign-language interpreter as group administrator, to explain the procedure and answer questions.

13.8.1 Logistics of Group Administration.

Group administration of self-administered questionnaires is a special situation than needs to be organized well. Exactly how the questionnaire administration is organized depends on the specific group that is surveyed. Group administration of a survey of the general population is unusual. The typical use of group administration is targeted at existing natural groups that can be approached as such. Self-administered-questionnaires are then administered to the group as a whole, with a live person present to deliver the introduction, to clarify problems, and to assist in the survey process.

Survey administrators need not be fully qualified interviewers, for instance, in classroom research it could be the teacher, and in a health clinic it could be a nurse. Of course, administration procedures do matter to motivate respondents and increase response quality. Therefore, administration procedures must be carefully designed, and survey administrators need to have enough information about the aims of the study and the research question to administer the survey correctly. The researcher should prepare an introduction of the survey that the administrators use in their introductory speech. This introduction basically contains the same topics that a good cover letter does: a friendly introduction, explaining who is doing the survey, what the purpose and usefulness of the study is, why the respondents are selected, and an assurance of confidentiality. In addition, an estimate of the usual duration can be given and the administrator may ask if there are any questions (Dornyei, 2003). An incentive may be mentioned and in all cases an explicit thank you is necessary. Also survey administrators must understand the questionnaire well, so they can assist respondents when problems arise, and it is wise to prepare a help booklet for the administrators with specific instructions, not unlike an interviewer guide with (frequently asked) questions and answers.

When a specific group is targeted for group administration of a self-administered questionnaire, it is important to tailor not only the questionnaire but also the survey procedure to the specific situation. For instance, when corporate units are surveyed in a work satisfaction study, the researchers could contact the head of each organizational group or administrative unit to set a date for the data collection and recruit the respondents. Then, they would presumably send a survey administrator to the organization to actually collect the data, on the assumption that if the head of the organizational group or department carries out the data collection, privacy issues could arise. Even if the confidentiality of the respondents' answers is assured, the respondents may still feel intimidated, and provide socially desirable answers to the survey questions. The issue here is not only whether the confidentiality is protected, but also whether the respondents themselves feel assured that the confidentiality is protected.

A good example of tailoring is a study by Molitor, Kravitz, To, and Fink (2001). Molitor and colleagues carried out a longitudinal survey of homeless individuals living in transitional housing. The first survey administration used a face-to-face interview, and for cost reasons the second data collection used group administration. For the second data collection, residents were recruited to meet at specified locations (such as a shelter's dining hall). The data collection used a self-administered questionnaire. Given this special group, where reading problems may be expected, the survey administrator read aloud each question and the answer categories, while a copy of the current page was displayed with an overhead projector. In this study, there were no indications that the group administration affected the quality of the data.

Instead of paper-and-pencil questionnaires, computer assisted self-interviews (CASI) are often used in group settings, such as computer labs at schools (Beebe, Davern, McAlpine, Call, & Rockwood, 2005). In health studies on sensitive topics, such as alcohol and drug use, sexual behavior, HIV, computer assisted self-interviews are often administered at a central site outside the home of the respondent (for example, in a clinic, a health center, a mobile van). Again the administration can be tailored successfully to the respondents, as Thornberry, Bhaskar, Krulewitch,Wesley, Hubbard, Das, Foudin & Adamson (2002) show. In their study they combined audio and touch screen technologies in computer-assisted self-interviews of young, low educated, pregnant women. The computer administered the recorded questions via headphones and at the same time displayed them on the screen. The response choices were highlighted on the screen when heard on the headphones and the respondents answered by touching the response of their choice on the computer screen.

When group administration is used, researchers should consider the nature of the research problem together with the salient group characteristics and tailor the logistics and survey procedure to these. The essential first step is an analysis of the research problem and of the group to be surveyed. What makes the research problem special? Why is the group under study special? For a discussion of these issues, see de Leeuw et al, (2003).

13.8.2 Surveying Schools

School research often uses self-administered questionnaires, and these are frequently in the form of group administration where a whole class fills out a questionnaire or an educational test at the same time. Most school studies that are carried out this way share a number of methodological characteristics.

When designing the questionnaire the researcher should take care that the length of the questionnaire fits in the normal time frame of the class. One should keep the slowest readers in mind when estimating the time, and one should also take into account the time needed for instruction, handing out and collecting questionnaires. In school research, researchers also need to tailor their questionnaire towards the special age groups. The age of seven can be seen as a major turning point in the development of children; at this age language expands, reading skills are acquired, and children start to distinguish different points of view. In middle childhood (age 7–12) children acquire the ability for concrete mental operations; they have still problems with abstract thinking, and lack the capacity for formal logical thinking, but given appropriate tailoring they can be interviewed and given sufficient reading skills they can fill out a questionnaire. In early adolescence (12–16) cognitive functioning is already well developed and it is possible to use standardized questionnaires similar to questionnaires for adults. Memory capacity is now fully grown, but memory speed is not. Even in this older age group ample time for answering questions should be allowed. Besides cognitive development, the emotional and social development of the intended age group should be taken into account, especially in adolescence when peer pressure and self-presentation are becoming important. From 16 years onwards, adolescents can be regarded as adults with respect to cognitive development and information processing. But resistance to peer pressure is still very low and older adolescents have their own group norms and social norms. For an overview of issues in surveying children and adolescents, see de Leeuw, 2005. Pretesting survey procedures and questionnaires is especially important when surveying children and adolescents, and the pretesters need to take into account that the pretesting methods should also be tailored to the age group in question. We refer to de Leeuw, Borgers, and Smits (2004) for a more thorough discussion of survey design and pretesting questionnaires for children and adolescents.

Before the actual data collection can take place important steps should be taken to ensure full cooperation. Getting cooperation of a school is extremely important, if one school does not cooperate, this can mean a loss of hundreds of respondents. Schools are hierarchical systems, and the motivated cooperation on all levels is important, starting with the head of the school and the administration, the teachers involved, and finally the pupils themselves. In addition, in several countries a researcher must also obtain parental consent to survey children. The approach of each actor should be tailored to the specific group. For instance, when approaching parents for parental consent, a letter of recommendation of the head of the school, and the cooperation of the pupils' teacher helps. When approaching the head of the school and the teachers, a letter of introduction from a well-known person together with specific information about the study itself helps. Teachers are often very busy and a personal approach together with emphasizing the usefulness for the teacher itself helps. Promising and delivering feedback to the actors involved is a good incentive for cooperation. For the head master this could be the overall result of the school compared to (anonymous) overall survey results; for teachers this could take the form of a profile of the class in comparison to similar classes or to test standards. The cooperation of teachers is crucial to the success of the survey and the attitude of the teachers is very important to motivate the pupils, so it pays off to invest time in the teachers.

After permission has been obtained, the researcher delivers material at schools with instructions, as a kind of drop-off-pick-up questionnaire and the teachers act as intermediary between the researcher and the pupils. This has implications for the logistics of the study. First, there must be some procedure to drop of the survey package (including questionnaires and instructions) and these must be distributed, collected again, and returned. In large schools it may be advisable to have a site coordinator who is responsible for this process, either one of the teachers or an assistant of the researcher. Second, if teachers are the questionnaire administrators, they must be motivated and briefed to strive for a high return rate and data of good quality. A carefully written guideline with instructions is necessary, and when possible a personal meeting with the teachers is advised to explain the procedures, discuss the guideline, and motivate the teachers. During the field period, there must be a helpdesk available to deal with any problems that may arise. Finally, when sensitive topics are investigated or when both pupils and teachers are respondents, privacy issues need to be resolved. For a discussion of confidentiality and other ethical issues, see Dorneyi (2003), and de Leeuw, Borgers, and Smits (2004)

A good example of the issues involved in researching schools is reported by van Hattum and de Leeuw (1999). A disk-by-mail survey was implemented in a random sample of 106 primary schools in the Netherlands. The respondents were 6428 pupils aged 8–12 years, and the topic of the study was bullying. Because this is a sensitive topic, the researchers looked for a method to combine the cost effectiveness of group administration with the privacy provided by self-administration. In addition, given the age range of the pupils in the sample, the questionnaire had to be easy to fill out. The procedure they used was computer-assisted self-interviewing with the teachers acting as intermediary. The teachers received a disk that contained an automated setup procedure for the survey software. A second disk contained the automatic procedure to collect the data files from the computers' hard disk. The teachers had to install the software on one or more of the school's computers and to allocate the pupils to answer the questionnaires on the computer, fitting this in the normal class schedule. At the end of each week, the second disk was used to copy the data and this was sent back to the researchers. If the data collection was still going on, the teachers received a new data collection disk. The pupils had one yellow card with instructions, mainly the use of the Enter and Backspace keys, and the instruction to type in a 9 if they did not know the answer (this response option was not shown on the screen). The pupils got positive feedback by the system at regular intervals to keep them motivated ("you are doing fine"). A telephone helpdesk was available during the entire data collection period, and a number of university laptops were available as backup. The study was preceded by a pilot study to pretest both the questionnaire and the data collection procedures

13.9 CONCLUSION

There are many types of self-administered questionnaires, of which mail and Internet surveys are the best known. Self-administered questionnaires can be administered individually (such as at home by mail survey), or group-wise (such as in a class room at school). A second dimension on which self-administered questionnaires can differ is the level of interviewer availability; this varies from none at al (mail survey) to interviewer-assisted (for example, a self-administered questionnaire handed out during an interview of hospitalized patients). Box 13.3 contains a schematic overview of the different types of self-administered questionnaires.

Common to all self-administered questionnaires is that the respondents are the locus of control and complete the questions without interviewer involvement in the question-answer process. As a result, not only the questions and answer categories, but also *all information* about the study and the questionnaire must be carried by the questionnaire itself and the accompanying cover letter or the instructions. The general data collection strategy is to make the demands on the respondent as low as possibly by making the questionnaire simple and attractive, and easy to fill in, and providing the respondents with appropriate rewards. To be successful, all these elements must be tailored to the population under study and all elements (such as invitation, instructions, questionnaire, reminders) need to be pretested for the specific survey situation.

Box 13.3 Typology of Self Administered Questionnaires		
	Administration	
Level of interviewer involvement	Individual	Group
None No interviewer, or intermediary of researcher present	Postal mail survey Internet survey	—
Some Interviewer selects respondent and introduces survey, but question-answer process is self administered	IVR Drop off–pick up questionnaires SAQ on location, e.g., mall or airport intercept	Psychological or educational testing
Restricted interviewer assisted Question-answer in principle self administered, but assistance available if needed	Paper questionnaire handed out during interview A-CASI Video- A-CASI	School surveys Special groups

GLOSSARY OF KEY POINTS

Access Panel. An access panel is basically a rich data base of willing respondents, that is used as a sampling frame for Internet studies, but may be used for other data collection procedures too. Panel members are invited and selected in various ways, through self-selection via websites, through acquisition by other panel members, at the end of successful face-to-face or telephone interviews, etc.

Aural Communication. The method of providing information to another person that depends upon speaking and listening, through which questions are communicated by entirely in telephone interviews and to a large extent in face-to-face interviews.

Computer Assisted Self Interviewing (CASI). Also known as Computer Assisted Self Administered Questionnaires (CSAQ). Defining characteristic is that the respondent operates the computer: questions are read from the computer screen and responses are entered directly in the computer. One of the most well-known forms of CASI is the web survey.

IVR. The acronym for Interactive Voice Response, which is a data collection technology in which the computer plays a recording of the question to the respondent over the telephone, and the respondent indicates the response by pressing the appropriate keys on his or her touchtone telephone keypad.

Meta information in surveys. Information about the survey and the questions. This includes explanations on the goal and content of the study, and instructions on how to respond to specific questions. In interview surveys this is mostly conveyed by the interviewer. In self-administered questionnaires this has to be done explicitly in written form. In Web surveys and other forms of computer-assisted self interviewing this information may also be (partly) available in the help system.

Para information. Information that goes alongside the textual information and adds meaning to the textual information. For example, to emphasize a word in order to give it more importance para-information is necessary. In interviews this is achieved through para-linguistic information (for example, tone of voice); in self-administered questionnaires through graphical language (for example, fonts, lay-out).

Self-Administered Questionnaire (SAQ). Questions are administered and answered without the assistance of an interviewer. There are several forms of SAQ, for instance paper questionnaires in mail surveys, group administered questionnaire in schools (tests), individual questionnaires that are filled in during an interview to ensure privacy, and drop off questionnaires, where surveyors personally deliver questionnaires, but the respondents fills in the questionnaire on their own and either mail it back or keep them for the surveyor to collect.

Sensitive questions. Questions are considered sensitive when they are about private, stressful or sacred issues, and when answering them tends to generate emotional responses, or potential fear of stigmatization on the part of the person or his/her social group.

Social Exchange Theory. A social psychological theory that states that actions of individuals are motivated by the returns these actions are expected to bring.

Visual Communication. The method of providing information to another person that depends upon what one sees, which is the means by which questions are mostly communicated to respondents in mail and web surveys.

Visual design. Using graphical language and lay-out in a planned and consistent way to facilitate (visual) communication and convey the information needed. Visual design incorporates graphical language tools, such as, figure-ground composition, location and spacing, size changes, brightness variations, and changes in similarity and regularity.

Web (Internet) Survey. Web surveys are a form of self-administered questionnaires, in which a computer administers a questionnaire on a web site. Survey questions are viewed and answered using a standard web browser on a PC. The responses are transferred through the Internet to the server.

Chapter 14

Internet Surveys

Katja Lozar Manfreda
Vasja Vehovar
University of Ljubljana

14.1 INTRODUCTION

Internet survey data collection was introduced at the end of 1980s with email surveys. In the mid 1990s, the World Wide Web (WWW) began to be used for survey data collection and this is the most widely spread form today. In the last few years, we face the integration of technologies resulting in WebTV or digital TV surveys, M-CASI—computer assisted self-interviewing using mobile phone devices, and other integrated solutions (e.g., integrated CATI—computer assisted telephone interviewing systems).

In this chapter, we refer to the form of Internet surveys that are most often used today, which is web surveys that are computerized, self-administered questionnaires (CSAQ) answered without the presence of an interviewer. Survey questions are viewed and answered using a standard web browser on a PC. The responses are transferred through the Internet to the server. Today, *these interactive surveys* (in contrast to *initial email surveys* or *static web surveys*, used till the mid 1990s) allow the respondent–researcher interaction during the questionnaire completion and enable all the features of computer-assisted survey data collection required by sophisticated questionnaires. Automatic skipping and conditional branching, random question/item order, randomization of questionnaires to participants, adaptive questionnaires (assigning questionnaire items based on earlier answers of a participant), control for item nonresponse, consistency and range, quota controls for accessing the questionnaire, time measuring, etcetera can all be handled in a manner similar to that in CATI. For a general review of computer assisted interviewing, see De Leeuw (Chapter 7) and this book's website (Chapter 14).

Several of the presented issues can be applied also to other forms of Internet surveys. The main intention of this chapter is to present the problems and solutions when conducting interactive web surveys that prevail today. Further reading regarding the emerging forms of surveys using the Internet technology is presented in the accompanying website to this book.

A comprehensive source of information regarding the implementation of Internet surveys can be found at the WebSM site, an academic website dedicated to the methodology of Internet surveys (http://www.websm.org). The WebSM site contains an extensive bibliography and Internet survey software information, for details on WebSM see this book's website (Chapter 14).

14.2 TAXONOMY AND TERMINOLOGY

Internet surveys are often perceived as a questionnable survey mode. Any discussion of Internet surveys should always be made in the context of their type and function, because there exist a wide variety of Internet survey methods with different technological approaches, purposes, populations, and methodologies. A particular type of Internet survey may give results of high quality for a certain purpose, but have no scientific value for another purpose.

14.2.1 Probability and Nonprobability Web surveys

From the aspect of sample selection we can distinguish between several types of probability and non-probability web surveys (Couper, 2000).

Probability web surveys (often perceived as scientific surveys) are performed on a probability sample of units that is obtained from a sampling frame satisfactory covering the target population. If a sampling frame is available and a representative sample is needed, sampling methods can be rather simple, such as simple random or systematic sampling because there are no additional cost considerations due to geographical dispersion of units (see Lohr, Chapter 6). There are several types of probability web surveys:

1. *List-based surveys of high-coverage populations.* These surveys are implemented on samples of students, members of organizations or associations, employees, clients, etcetera which all can access the World Wide Web (WWW) or other needed technology and where a sampling frame with satisfactory contact information is available.
2. *Surveys on probability pre-recruited lists or panels of Internet users.* These surveys are implemented on samples of Internet users that were pre-recruited with another probability sampling method, most often with a telephone survey on a random sample of households or using random-digit-dialing. Pre-recruitment may be used for a one-time only survey or in order to develop a probability panel of Internet users willing to participate in several web surveys.
3. *Surveys on probability panels of the general population.* These surveys are implemented on samples from panels of the general population that are not only pre-recruited with a probability sampling method, but are also given hardware and software equipment needed to participate in several web surveys. Due to high costs considerations such surveys are rather rare. In addition, we should mention that despite the initial representative sampling frame used to recruit the panel and opportunities to use probability sampling to select respondents from the panel, the final sample of respondents might not necessarily be a representative sample of the target population due to the cumulative

nonresponse at several stages of such a survey procedure.

4. Probability web surveying can be used also in *mixed-mode survey designs*. A probability sample of respondents can be given the opportunity to choose a web questionnaire among the available survey modes or the researchers allocate part of the sample (usually those respondents known to use the Internet) to the web mode. The purpose is to reduce the respondents' burden, decrease survey costs or overcome the problem of non-coverage. In using these procedures one should be aware of the possible differences in data quality and substantive responses among the used modes due to eventual mode effect (see Chapter 16 on Mixed Mode Surveys in this book).

5. A special type of probability web surveys is *intercept surveys*. Here, systematic sampling is used to intercept visitors of a particular website(s) (see Comley, 2000 for a discussion of available sampling techniques). Respondents are supposed to be representative of visitors to that site, who constitute the target population. However, the non-response bias may be large in this case since we can expect that those who decide to complete the survey may have different views about websites—the usual topic of these surveys—from those who ignore the request (Couper, 2000b, p. 485).

Nonprobability web surveys (often perceived as nonscientific surveys) do not have a probability sample of units obtained from a sampling frame covering the target population satisfactory. In some cases (e.g. volunteer opt-in panels) probability sampling may be used, however the sampling frame is not representative of the target population. There are several types of such web surveys.

1. *Web surveys using volunteer opt-in panel* (also called *access panels*) are the most common non-probability web surveys, used especially in market research. Some controlled selection (sometimes probability, but most often quota sampling methods) of units from lists of panel participants is used for a particular survey project. These lists are usually maintained by a professional market research agency and are basically a large database of volunteer respondents. These lists are obtained through participants' self-inclusion (opt-in) and therefore are not representative of any population and inference from such panel web surveys is questionable.

2. *Web surveys using purchased lists* (lists of email addresses purchased by a commercial provider, usually obtained either by specific computer programs searching for email addresses on websites or by participants self-inclusion) are similar to volunteer opt-in panels as regards the sample nonrepresentativeness. In addition, when no specific opt-in procedure is used their use is rather unethical and as such either prohibited or at least not recommended by professional research associations and in some countries also legal regulations.

3. *Unrestricted self-selected web surveys* use open invitations on different websites, but also in online discussion groups and traditional

media. Usually, they have neither access restrictions nor control over multiple completions. The obtained sample of respondents is again nonrepresentative of any population due to lack of a sampling frame and probability sampling and due to self-selection. It is problematic when such a survey claims legitimization based on the large number of obtained responses, which happens rather often (Couper, 2000b, p. 479).

4. *Online polls* are similar to the previous category as regards the self-selection and non-representativeness of respondents. They are intended primarily for entertainment purposes and as forums for exchanging opinions. Examples of such surveys are *'Public' polls* that are published on websites dedicated to the posting and completion of polls. Anyone can post any survey question on these sites and there is no control over who responds. Another example are *'Question of the day' polls* which are not really surveys because usually only one question regarding a current issue of interest is asked. They are often published on media websites or major portals and other high-traffic websites. They reflect only the opinions of those Internet users who visited such a website and chose to participate. In both cases, results are usually published simultaneously with the questionnaire. Newcomers can eventually see what others have responded, a feature that might increase response, but may also affect their responses.

14.2.2 Solicitation

Web surveys can also be classified into several types with regards to the solicitation procedures used, that is, the methods of contacting and inviting respondents to participate. We can basically distinguish between list-based (which have parallels within traditional survey modes) and nonlist based web surveys (which are rather specific and rarely having parallels in the off-line world).

List-based web surveys use individual invitations to units from a list. This list can be a probability sample from a representative sampling frame, thus a probability web survey is performed (such as types (1), (2), (3) from section X.2.1). It can also be a probability or non-probability sample from a sampling frame that is not representative of some target population, thus a nonprobability web survey is performed (such as types (6), (7) from X.2.1). The implementation is similar in all cases. Participants from the list get an individual (personalized) invitation to the survey by email or regular mail (sometimes even by fax or SMS—Short Messages Services, also known as TEXT-message, on mobile phones). The survey's URL address is included in the invitation. The access to the survey can be restricted and tracking of respondents (for nonresponse conversion) can be performed. Incentives can also be used.

Non list-based web surveys are also known as w*eb surveys with general invitations* because no list of potential participants exists prior to the survey. Only a general plea for participation is published, either on Internet or in other media. Anyone on the Internet who notices the invitation may complete the questionnaire. These surveys are by definition nonprobability (types (8) and (9) from 14.2.1) and no generalization can be made beyond the sample universe that participated in the survey. They are similar to polls where questionnaires are printed in newspapers or magazines and readers are asked to return the completed forms, or to call-in polls' on television or radio stations. These surveys are inexpensive and offer the potential to reach a large number of persons in a short period of time.

Intercept web surveys are a special type also regarding implementation. No list of participants is prepared beforehand, but one is generated during web users' sessions when the data collection is performed. Sampled visitors are invited to complete a survey by banner ads or pop-up windows.

14.2.3 Areas of Applications

The Internet is used for survey research in many different ways and in many different fields. For instance, web surveys on either probability or nonprobability panels are used for *market research* on a wide range of topics, not necessarily connected with information-communication technologies or the web. The results of such surveys are statistically adjusted to compensate for demographic differences between Internet users and the target (usually the general) population.

A special type of Internet usage surveys is *websites' evaluations*. The target population—web visitors—can be easily contacted when they visit the site. Most often intercept surveys, list-based samples (if visitors of the site are registered), or unrestricted, self-selected web surveys with ads on the targeted site are used. Their aim is mostly to measure visitors' characteristics (determining their sociodemographic background, lifestyle-related activities, how they view the site, and what other sites they frequently visit) and usability of the website.

Web surveys are also often used for *customer satisfaction studies* in Internet-based businesses and services and other businesses where most customers have access to the Internet. In this case, most often email (or mail) invitations are sent to customers from the lists of business' clients. In addition, intercept surveys are also used.

Internet technology is often used also for *web experiments*, for example in psychological research (see this book's website, Chapter 14 for examples) or for the purpose of testing questionnaire design or some other aspect of web survey implementation procedures (e.g., incentives, content of invitation letter). Here, random assignment of participants to experimental conditions is used. Both probability and nonprobability samples of participants can be used.

In addition to targeting individuals, web surveys are used in *establishment research*, due to a higher Internet penetration in establishments in comparison to households. In establishment research, lists of target units (establishments) are usually available; therefore list-based samples are used. Either all units are administered a web questionnaire, or a web questionnaire is used in a mixed-mode design.

We should mention that surveys, either web or other modes, are not the only means of studying the behavior of Internet users. Although some research questions require asking respondents directly for information, there are several topics that can be addressed in different ways. For example, online behavior can be tracked using monitoring technologies, thus decreasing the need for asking Internet users to describe their online behavior through a web questionnaire.

14.3 CONDUCTING WEB SURVEYS

14.3.1 Coverage

Coverage error is the most often mentioned limitation of web surveys. When discussing coverage error (see also Lohr, Chapter 6) of web surveys, this should be done in the context of the Web survey *target population*. Coverage error is a severe problem for web surveys aimed at the general population, but less critical for web surveys aimed at Internet users only and for web surveys of special populations where all or most of the members have Internet access.

Web surveys aimed at the general population have the largest noncoverage problem because to date there is no country of the world where all or most people use the Internet. The percentage of Internet users is extremely low in some countries of the underdeveloped world, but even in the most developed countries (e.g., Scandinavian countries, United States, South Korea, Hong Kong) it is at most three quarters of the general population (ClickZ Stats, http://www.clickz.com, retrieved August 2007). This is still below the telephone coverage in the 1970s when telephone interviews were widely introduced in survey research. Furthermore, Internet users are different from nonusers in their sociodemographic characteristics and lifestyle-related activities (see the book's website, Chapter 14 for further reading on the digital divide) which makes it difficult to generalize to the general population.

Despite severe coverage problems, web surveys are sometimes used to draw conclusions about the general population, especially in market research. Surveys on probability panels of the general population, who are provided with the needed hardware and software equipment by the research agency, are a legitimate approach (see Saris, 1998 or Krotki, 2001 for examples). In this case, the coverage problem is almost eliminated by offering Internet access to all selected participants. Noncoverage is not completely eliminated, for instance, when some households are without phones (needed for telephone pre-recruitment of the probability panel), and/or some areas are not covered by sufficient bandwidth infrastructure (needed for offering adequate equipment). In addition, the high non-response in the pre-recruitment stage and subsequent stages of the survey process, in addition to the relative high equipment and maintenance costs associated with these panels further decreases the usefulness of this approach.

Sometimes, surveys of Internet users only are used to make inferences to the general population. In these cases, quota sampling or weighting (for example, propensity score adjustment, Bremer Terhanian, & Strange, 2004, Schonlau, van Soest, Kapteun, Couper, & Winter, 2004) are used to reproduce the distribution of known characteristics of the target population (e.g., age, education, sex). This is used especially with volunteer opt-in panel web surveys where large databases of potential participants are available. The problem with this approach is that only certain characteristics (most often demographic parameters) are taken into account when weighting procedures are developed, and these may not be the only differentiating characteristics between Internet users and nonusers.

A mixed-mode approach may also be used to overcome the coverage problem. Respondents may be offered a web survey as one of the possible alternative methods for answering survey questions or the researcher can allocate only part of the sample (those known to use the Internet) to the web survey while other parts are allocated to other modes (e.g., telephone, paper mail survey).

14.3.2 Survey Invitations and Contacts with Respondents

There are different practices in using survey invitations depending on whether individual invitations to the participants are sent from a list (i.e., list-based surveys) or only general invitations are made (i.e., nonlist based surveys and intercept surveys).

For web surveys with *general invitations* (nonlist based survey and intercept surveys) researchers rely on invitations on websites or in traditional (printed) media, and on general invitations in online mailing lists and discussion groups. Such invitations often have little success (around a few percents response) (e.g., Schillewaert, Langerak, & Duhamel, 1998; Tuten, Bosnjak, & Bandilla, 1999/2000). The success of this practice is influenced by where (on which websites, discussion groups, media), on how many places, and when to post the invitation. In addition, the researcher has to decide whether to use a pop-up window, a banner ad, or simple hypertext link. A pop-up window is the most intrusive and potentially the most effective; however, the latest developments in browser's software makes pop-ups unusable by blocking them. A banner ad or hyperlink, on the other hand, is more passive and may easily be overlooked. Still, a well-designed graphical banner ad will be more noticeable than a simple hyperlink. On the other hand, the intrusiveness of graphically more fancy invitations may also irritate visitors and deter them from participation. Nevertheless, one study (Bauman, Jobity, Airey, & Atak, 2000) found that more dynamic banner ads (with more colors and flashing content) are more successful in attracting visitors than more static images.

Sending out *individual invitations* to participants is far more effective than general invitations. A prerequisite is that up-to-date contact information is available for units of the sampling frame. In that case, the method of utilizing multiple and carefully timed contacts, such as, prenotification, main invitation and several follow-ups for nonrespondents is recommended (Dillman, 2000).

Prenotifications are used to inform participants about incoming web surveys, to stress the importance and legitimacy of the survey, and by this to increase response rates. Prenotifications are recommended especially when email is used for sending-out survey invitations in order to prevent that participants perceive the survey invitation as spam. A prenotification "…should be brief, personalized, positively worded, and aimed at building anticipation rather than providing the details or conditions for participation in the survey"

(Dillman, 2000, p. 156) and should be sent only a few days ahead of the main survey invitation (Dillman, 2000, p. 156). Pre-notifications for web surveys have been shown to be effective in increasing response rates (Cook, Heath, & Thompson, 2000, p. 828–829, 831; Kaplowitz, Hadlock, & Levine, 2004).

The goal of the *main survey invitation* is to motivate respondents and provide them with necessary information for answering the survey questionnaire. The invitation should be personalized (Cook et al., 2000), although when email is used, one study showed that personalization might not have such an impact as in other survey modes (Porter & Whitcomb, 2003). The text should be short and getting to the point, the purpose of the study, quickly; clearly identify the survey sponsor or research organization; provide additional contact information, beside the reply email address, so that participants can check the source; provide an option to opt out of the list; provide information on how inclusion in the list occurred, and give a deadline for response.

Follow-up contacts, that is, reminders sent to non-respondents, are also a standard practice in self-administered surveys (Dillman, 1991, 2000) and their purpose is to increase response rate. Their effectiveness in increasing response rates (Enander and Sajti, 1999, p. 42; Kwak & Radler, 1999; Lozar Manfreda, 1999, p. 81; Lozar Manfreda, Vehovar, & Batagelj, 2001) and decreasing non-response bias (Batagelj & Vehovar, 1998; Enander & Sajti, 1999; White, 1996, p. 49–50; Willke, Adams, & Ginnius, 1999, p. 150) has been shown for web surveys too.

The medium of communication used to send out invitations depends on the information available from the sampling frame; usually the researcher chooses between email, paper mail and fax invitations. Lately, attempts have been made to use SMS or texting on mobile phones (e.g., Neubarth et al., 2005). Considering survey costs and speed of response, email invitations are preferable: messages are sent and received immediately; costs are low; there are no mediators in the communication; nonexistent email addresses are known immediately; time/distance problems do not exist, and it is easily to offer or dispose of additional information. But, looking at response rates, the situation is not that clear. There are several pro and con arguments on the use of email invitations, especially in comparison with paper mail invitations. The problems with email invitations lie in the frequent change of email addresses and the need for exact addresses as no misspelling is excused.

Address changes and misspellings increase the percentage of undeliverable invitations. In addition problems with email invitations are associated with the threat of viruses delivered by email, decreased perceived legitimacy of the survey (e.g., lack of detailed text in the sender's letterhead and signature), deletion of invitations due to automatic spam filters; and not noticed invitations from unidentified senders. On the other hand, the main argument in favor of the use of email invitations is a decreased burden on respondents. When email invitations are used, the web questionnaire is already at hand, only a single click is needed to move from the email message to the survey questionnaire in a web browser, especially when respondents have a permanent Internet connection (and not use a dial-up). Many more actions are needed in the case of mail or fax invitation (from switching on the computer, login to the Internet, opening a web browser and typing in the URL address of the questionnaire). The few empirical studies that actually compared the effectiveness of email versus mail invitation letter (Lesser & Newton, 2001; Vehovar et al., 2000), found mixed evidence, not giving a definite answer o the question which approach is best. For pre-notifications it has been shown that a paper mail pre-notification is more efficient than an email one (Harmon, WSestin, & Levin, 2005).

In Internet surveys time intervals between contacts may be compressed compared to standard paper mail TDM method (Dillman, 1978), especially when contacts by email are used. Respondents react to email very quickly, with a characteristic decrease in response soon after an email invitation.

Intuitively one would assume that the larger the number of contacts with respondents, the larger the response rates. But, the large number of reminders may also have a negative impact due to individuals reaching a saturation point in reading their messages or becoming resistant to being reminded more than once about the survey (Kittleson, 1997, p. 196). This diminishing return from numbers of contacts was actually observed in a meta-analysis of Internet surveys (Cook et al., 2000, p. 827, 831); they found that average response rates increased with number of contacts up to three contacts (pre- and follow-up contacts were counted), but decreased with four and five contacts.

The visual design of invitations may also have an impact on respondents' participation. For instance, a clear indication of research organization (letterhead, use of logotypes) is needed. Extremely fancy graphical design (extensive use of colors, photographs and graphics) is not recommended, especially if email invitations are used (Whitcomb & Porter, 2004).

To conclude, the communication mode for sending out individual invitations to web surveys depends mostly on the available contact information in the sampling frame. If both email and paper mail addresses are available, an email invitation is preferable since it is faster and cheaper. Email invitations are most suitable for respondents that have some bond with the research organization and provided email is the typical communication mode for this group. For example, when a university is surveying its students or when an organization that is accustomed to organizational email is surveying its members. When respondents do not have such a bond with the research organization, paper mail invitations are more suitable because it is important to emphasize the legitimacy of the study. In both email and paper mail invitations, it is important to personalize the invitation, and clearly mention the research organization and the method of inclusion in the sample. In addition, a combination of several contacts (prenotification, main invitation, follow-ups), potentially sent by different communication media and their carefully timing is important. When general invitations to web surveys are used (pop-ups, banner ads, hypertext links) more dynamic invitations should attract more respondents.

14.3.3 Other Researcher—Respondent Interaction

Once respondents have been invited and have found their way to the survey site, the task of the survey introductory page is to persuade them to take time to complete the survey, to motivate, to emphasize the ease of responding, and to instruct respondents. This page is even more important for surveys that use general invitations, such as banner ads and pop-ups, as in that case very little information can be given in the invitation itself. It is useful that the text and graphics on the web survey introductory page are organized in such a way that respondents can quickly understand what the researcher is asking for and how this benefits the respondent.

Several elements of the introductory page have actually been found to significantly influence response rates in web surveys. For example, Bauman, et al. (2000) report that the traditional cover letter style of introduction is not successful. It is too lengthy for a web introduction, and the text is too dense and not clearly communicating the web introduction and instructions, the confidentiality assurances and information on incentives. In contrast, a visually more appealing introduction tailored to the web and designed to facilitate reading and getting the salient points across quickly has been found to be more successful. In such an introduction only the critical information is first conveyed after which the visitor can proceed to the survey. Survey instructions are laid out on a separate page after the visitor has agreed to participate. Other key words (such as FAQs: Frequently Asked Questions) are also highlighted.

Another aspect of researcher-respondent interaction that may influence web survey participation is a more facilitated communication with the research organization (Lichman, 1999a, p. 72). This may be done in the form of a Help Desk or simply with a reply address for comments or questions, with for instance an additional website containing the result of an incentive lottery (if used), by sending results, and so forth.

Offering contact information and thus enabling survey participants to send their questions, complaints, comments, and so on, is important for several reasons. By understanding the respondents' problems, the researcher can immediately see what is not functioning properly with the questionnaire and correct it. In addition, participants can express their opinions, which might make them feel involved and more positive about cooperating. This is in line with the nature of Internet as an open forum for exchanging ideas and information (Woodall, 1998). For the same reason, Woodall (1998) suggests adding some open-ended questions to the questionnaire to allow respondents to expound on their experiences and offer their insights on the subject (cf. Dillman, 1978, for paper mail surveys).

Offering results to participants can be used as an incentive for their participation. Results may be available immediately after respondents complete the questionnaire or mailed to them after the data collection is finished. The later is relatively easy in web surveys where respondents' email addresses are known. In addition, other information can be added. For example, Batagelj and Vehovar (1998, p. 217) report that in one of their web surveys, each respondent leaving his/her email address received an email message with thanks and the URL address where results were available. The letter was made individually for each respondent, with the exact duration time of each interview stated (for example, "Thank you for 5 minutes and 35 seconds of your time on May 15 at 10.35 …"), which impressed the respondents. The intention of this is to motivate the respondents to participate again in the next survey.

14.3.4 Data Security, Confidentiality, and Anonymity

In order to obtain respondents' trust and cooperation, they should be assured that their data will be kept secure (i.e., data are secured during transport and when they are stored on the server), confidential (a response may be linked to a person's name, but only by the survey researcher for the purpose of the survey management and not by others), or sometimes even anonymous (a response cannot be linked to a person's name). To secure the data, research organizations should assure adequate cryptographic protection during the transfer of the data and protect the server against unauthorized invasions. To assure confidentiality, they should behave in accordance to ethical principles of conducting survey research on the Internet. Full anonymity, on the other hand, cannot always be assured for administrative reasons. The researcher usually needs respondents' identification to limit access only to those selected in the sample, to prevent multiple responses of the same person, to follow up nonrespondents, to compare results over time, or to maintain the responses when an interruption occurs during the web session. In practice there are several possible ways of identifying respondents in web surveys: from 'cookies' through manual or automatic logins to a combination of all.

Cookies are usually used for nonlist based web surveys in order to prevent multiple responses by the same persons. This does not prevent multiple accesses from the same persons using different Personal Computers or persons who reject or delete cookies. On the other hand, it prevents access to different persons using the same (public) PC.

Manual and automatic logins are used in list-based web surveys. In manual login participants need to enter a previously provided username/password, whereas in automatic login the URL link provided to them already includes an identification code and serves as the password for entering the web survey page.

Control of survey access may influence response rates and data quality. The automatic login procedure may generate higher response rates as the respondent burden is reduced. The explicit request to enter the password in the manual login procedure may remind participants that their participation is not anonymous and thus affect their answers. On the other hand, a manual login may lead to a sense of confidentiality (Crawford, Couper, & Lamias, 2001, p. 148) resulting in more accurate and truthful responses. Empirical evidence for these hypotheses is rather mixed. For example, Crawford, et al. (2001, p. 154) found that the response rate for automatic login was higher. Heerwegh and Loosveldt (2002), on the other hand, found a higher response rate with manual login, although the difference was not statistically significant. In this second study the manual login procedure was simplified (a four digit PIN number instead of codes in two input fields in the first case) resulting in a smaller respondents' burden. This suggests that a simplified code decreases the burden, and thereby increases response. However, a simplified code limits the possible codes for a larger number of respondents, and a combined automatic and manual login condition is suggested (Heerwegh and Loosveldt, 2001). None of these studies found evidence that respondents would give more thought to their responses in the manual login condition.

Ethical guidelines and principles dealing with web surveys (see 14.3.7) pose large emphasis on problems of data security, confidentiality, and anonymity. The general best practice is that procedures are explicitly explained to reassure respondents. This may positively influence their decision to participate in the survey and result in answers of the desired quality.

14.3.5 Incentives

In web surveys, just as in other survey modes, incentives increase response rates and motivate respondents to complete the whole questionnaire, as both experimental research and experience from practice have shown. Much research is still needed on the type of incentive used and its effect on survey errors and survey costs for web surveys.

Certainly, the impact of incentives depends on the type and value of the incentive. Incentives used in web surveys are actually very variable, from incentives offered to each respondent, through lotteries with only a chance on winning, to various combinations of both. Sometimes, material incentives, such as theatre tickets, posters, products, or simple payments, are sent to respondents. These can be prepaid if sufficient contact information is available from the sampling frame, or promised and sent afterwards, when respondents have completed the survey and revealed their contact or bank data. Given the Internet environment, some virtual incentives are often used. These can be monetary (e.g., cash prizes in the form of electronic money—depositing money on Internet accounts, gift certificates, redeemable loyalty points—points collected to spend on online services or in online shops) or non-monetary (e.g., access to free software, free online time, free delivery for online orders, donation to charity, stock options, listing of company logo for establishment surveys). Additionally, survey results can be offered as an incentive.

Beside the type and value of incentives, their impact depends on the whole context of the web survey, especially on the population targeted and the type of survey information sought. For instance, students may be motivated by a (mobile) phone card or Amazon gift certificate, whereas experienced professionals will need a more valuable incentive. In addition, short and simple surveys (e.g., visitor profiles) may not need incentives, while longer surveys do.

Using incentives in web surveys may also create problems, for instance, when some participants try to complete the survey several times, or answer under false pretences. In addition, incentives may emphasize self-selection: the final sample may be biased to certain types of people, for example, those with less income, more time than most, younger, etcetera. Incentives may also affect response quality, such as more missing items, shorter open-ended response, and filling in rubbish data. Finally, researchers also need to take into account legal regulations regarding incentives in participants' countries; for example, in some countries monetary incentives for surveys or lotteries are not allowed.

The use of incentives usually increases survey costs and researchers should find the right balance between costs for incentives, their effect on data quality, and possible costs and effects of other design measures. For example, would the use of incentives have a more positive impact than sending a third reminder to nonrespondents, and what are the consequences for the survey costs in both situations? Of course, finding the right balance is difficult and a thorough appraisal is needed.

In sum, incentives increase response rates, also in web surveys. The types and value of incentives need to be tailored to the population in question. In addition, a compromise in the form of an affordable increase in response rate and available survey funds for distribution of incentives needs to be found. See Goeritz (2005) for more detail.

14.3.6 Questionnaire Design

There are several reasons why web questionnaires may produce larger errors than other survey modes. Web questionnaires are often designed by people with no survey methodological skills (Couper, 2000, p. 465), resulting in badly designed questionnaires. In addition, Internet users tend to read more quickly, are more impatient, and they scan rather than carefully read the text. This suggests that mistakes in questionnaire design, which would be considered of minor importance in other survey modes, may be very significant in web surveys.

The specific wording of the questions itself does not introduce any major problems in web questionnaires in comparison to other modes as long as the same standards for the correct formulation of questions in survey research in general are borne in mind (see Fowler & Cosenza, Chapter 8; Dillman, Chapter 9). However, it has been suggested (Gräf, 2002, p. 79) that the question/answer texts should be kept short, concise, and clearly presented because Internet users seldom read the text carefully, but rather scan it.

The nonverbal aspect of the web questionnaire is far more important and specific. First, the questionnaire's visual design, such as flow, form, layout, is the only instrument that the researcher has to communicate with the respondents during the questionnaire completion. There is no interviewer who can motivate respondents, explain misunderstandings, correct mistakes, and so on. In addition, Internet technology greatly extends the possibilities of questionnaire design. This sometimes leads to exaggerations in visual layout, which do not necessarily contribute to the data quality. Research on web questionnaire design is thus very important and the basic principles for designing web questionnaires are actively being pursued.

When designing a web questionnaire, it is important to use a design that mimics the conventional format similar to that normally used on self-administered paper questionnaires (Dillman, 2000), and at the same time to take into account that the web is a very special medium with special design options, visual features and required respondents' actions – all of which require special treatment of the questionnaire (Couper, 2000b, p. 476).

14.3.7 Form of Questions and Response Options

When designing web questionnaires, we should keep in mind that respondents will complete the questionnaire using different technologies, for instance, different web browsers, operation systems, screen configurations, and hardware. This may influence how the questions and response options appear on the screen, which in turn may influence the responses. For example, in grid questions (see example on this book's website, Chapter 14) items are presented in a matrix form, where several items with the same answer categories or response scale are positioned together in a table. These grid questions may be problematic since change in physical distances between points on the response scale can occur under different web configurations, or answer categories are not seen if the list of items in the grid is too long (Dillman & Bowker, 2001: 65). Additional testing of the layout is therefore always advaisable.

In web questionnaires, grid questions (table, matrix) are often used to make the questionnaire look shorter. Grid questions also eliminate redundancy in questions, as response categories are not repeated after each item, and require less effort with keyboard and mouse actions. Also smaller cognitive effort is needed as the same response categories are used for all items in a grid and respondents do not need to read the response labels every time. All this should decrease respondents' burden and result in better data quality for grid questions. On the other hand, grid questions may be unsuitable because respondents, especially the less interested, more tired or inattentive, tend to answer the questions uniformly in order to decrease cognitive effort (Gräf, 2002, p. 80). In addition, the grid format may also change the nature of questions. The items are to some extent placed in a comparative framework. The visual structure encourages respondents to think of them as a unit. This may result in context effects, that is, that respondents when answering one question think about it in relation to other questions increasing the correlation among them (Couper, Traugott, & Lamias, 2001). Experimental research regarding the effect of grid questions gives mixed results. None or very few differences in effects on substantive results were found (Couper et al., 2001; Lozar Manfreda, Koren, & Heblek, 2004; Peytchev, Crawford, McCabe, Conrad, & Couper, 2003). However there was some effect—although mixed—on indicators of data quality. Knapp and Heidingsfelder (2001) found increased dropout rates and Peytchev et al. (2003) more non-substantive responses when grid questions were used. On the other hand, Lozar Manfreda et al. (2004) found no difference in item non-response, and Couper, et al. (2001) even found lower item-nonresponse in grid questions. Higher correlations among the items in the grid design were found by Couper, et al. (2001) and Peytchet, et al. (2003), but not by Lozar Manfreda et al. (2004). Although Gockenbych, Bosnjak, and Goeritz (2004) found more uniform answers in the grid design, Couper, et al. (2001) and Lozar Manfreda, et al. (2004) found no such effect. This suggests that grid questions may be used successfully in order to give the respondents the perception of lower burden. Uniform answers to grids, which are suspected to be an error and not proper answers, can be eliminated later in the data editing and cleaning phase. However, one should be cautious in using grids if particular sensitivity to context effect is expected and needs to be avoided.

Another feature used to make the web questionnaire appear shorter is to list answers in the form of drop-down menus, which have no alternative in a paper self-administered form, instead of radio buttons, which are equivalent to circles or squares to cross in a paper-questionnaire (see example on this book's website, chapter 14). Drop-down menus are especially useful when very long lists of answers are needed (e.g., age, country, list of products). On the other hand, drop-down menus are more burdensome for respondents, potentially resulting in skipping questions or even abandoning the questionnaire. Empirical evidence regarding the effect of using drop-down menus are mixed. One experiment showed no influence on answering behavior when drop-down menus or radio buttons were used (Reips, 2001a, p. 102). On the other hand, exchanging a drop-down menu for a question on age with a radio button response option significantly changed respondents' answers (Couper, 2001). Anyway, when using drop-down menus it is important that the response label that is seen on the screen is not one of the substantive answers, but rather blank or answer such as "Don't want to answer." Otherwise, item nonresponse cannot be separated from answers using the first offered response option.

Open-ended questions are another question form that seems promising in web surveys. The relative ease of typing a longer response, as compared to handwriting, made researchers believe that Internet surveys would generate richer open-ended responses (Schaefer & Dillman, 1998). On the other hand, answering open-ended questions is considered high-cost behavior, increasing respondents' burden and as such open questions are only sufficiently answered by those with strong attitudes (Bosnjak, 2001). The impact of open-ended questions on respondents' burden was indirectly shown to be important; in a review of several web surveys increased dropout rates were observed when open-ended questions were used (Knapp & Heidingsfelder, 2001). With regard to the richness of open-ended responses, results from experimental studies are again mixed. Comley (1996), Gonier (1999), Kwak and Radler (1999), Mehta and Sivadas (1995), Schaeffer and Dillman (1998), Sturgeon and Winter (1999), and Willke, et al. (1999) showed that answers to open-ended questions in email and web surveys are much richer than in other survey modes. Lozar Manfreda, et al. (2001) found no difference in item response to open-ended questions in a web and a mail questionnaire. Aoki and Elasmar (2000), on the other hand, showed that a mail questionnaire resulted in statistically significantly more answers to open-ended questions than a web one. The above studies did not report on the size of the box provided for open-ended questions. However, larger text boxes may convey to respondents the message that longer, more detailed responses are needed. This was shown in several studies where offering a larger text box in the web questionnaire resulted in a significantly higher number of characters typed in (Couper, 2001; Kwak & Radler, 1999: Lozar Manfreda et al., 2004). However, a larger number of characters does not necessarily mean higher data quality; Lozar Manfreda et al. (2005) found there was no effect on substantive answers and Couper et al. (2001) showed that long text boxes where numerical answers were requested resulted in more invalid entries than did short text boxes.

Computer-assisted data collection allow for quality checks and quality check reminders. This should be handled and programmed with care. In principle, forcing respondents to answer questions properly can prevent any item non-responses or inconsistent responses. However, respondents' frustration associated with this likely leads to premature terminations or answering a question without due consideration (Dillman, 2000; Dillman, Tortora, & Bowker, 1998; Zukerberg, Nichols, & Tedesko, 1999). Soft reminders—when the program allows one to proceed even if the error was not corrected—or providing prefer not to answer and/or don't know categories are a reasonable alternative to hard (forced) reminders.

14.3.8 Overall Questionnaire Visual Layout

The available graphical interface of Web browsers allows advanced graphics and multimedia features to be easily implemented in Web questionnaires. The aim is to improve respondents' motivation and satisfaction, and generate a valuable feeling of having a good time or fun while answering a web questionnaire. They can also decrease respondents' burden if designed to ease the navigation through the questionnaire. In the early days of web surveys, technological limitations created problems because not all respondents could access or clearly see the questionnaire using multimedia features, or because transfer of data was too slow (Dillman et al., 1998; Gräf, 2001; Vehovar, Lozar-Manfreda, & Batagelj 2000a). These problems have been eliminated for respondents in the countries with a developed Internet infrastructure, allowing large bandwidth for people using ADSL, VDSL, and cable connection or at least ISDN modems. Now the research focus has shifted to the effect of using multimedia on measurement error. For example, Vehovar, et al. (2000a) showed that responses differ when answers are illustrated with graphics.

An issue in questionnaire design that still waits for a definite answer is the use of a progress indicator. This can be textual or graphic (see the accompanying website for examples). When a web questionnaire consists of one HTML page only, a progress indicator is not needed because the scroll bar at the right hand of the browser window already serves as one. For web questionnaires spread over several HTML pages, a progress indicator may be needed, but a progress indicator is difficult to implement in questionnaires with complicated skip patterns and/or self-selected or randomly assigned modules (Kaczmirek, Neubarth, Bosnjak, & Bandilla, 2005).

The progress indicator shows how the respondent is proceeding with completing the questionnaire and conveys a sense of orientation in the questionnaire completion process. According to Dillman (2000), letting respondents know how close they are to the end, prevents them from becoming discouraged or quitting when they are nearly finished. It has actually been shown that its application decreases dropout rates (Couper et al., 2000b). On the other hand, in lengthy surveys the progress indicator may remind people of the length and cause them to abandon the survey prematurely. In certain circumstances, depending on the graphic used, it may also increase the download times for each page (Couper et al., 2000b).

There are other questionnaire design options that are not mentioned here. We limit our discussion to those issues that are specific for web questionnaires and have been tested and developed in the last ten years of using web questionnaire. Also some other issues were extensively researched (such as number of questions per page, differences in respondents' screens, etcetera) at the early days of using web surveys, but were correlated with the development of technical solutions and have already been solved in the last years. For issues regarding the design of survey questionnaires in general see Fowler and Consenza, Chapter 8 and Dillman, Chapter 9.

14.3.9 Ethical Issues

In general, web surveys are not inherently more difficult to conduct or inherently riskier to subjects than more traditional survey modes. Nevertheless, there are several reasons why issues that have been long settled in more convential survey research settings are raised again and need to be highlighted. For a general discussion of survey ethics, see Singer (Chapter 5).

First, because of low marginal costs, simple software solutions, simple access to large samples of human subjects, and the nonregulative nature of the Internet, web surveys may be performed by less experienced or less scrupulous individuals and organizations, often based outside the research industry. This may result in web surveys that fall below the high standards promoted by professional research organization and such misuses make it more difficult for legitimate researchers to use the Internet for research and may abuse of the goodwill of Internet users in general.

In addition, privacy concerns of participants in Internet surveys are larger than in more conventional survey research settings, which may result in lower willingness to participate. For exampe, an email invitation to a web survey is often percieved as an invasion of privacy and unethical, whereas a telephone call or even a visit of an interviewer at home is not. Privacy concerns may also influence data quality, and concerned respondents may give different answers online than they would give offline. There are several reasons for increased privacy concerns in web surveys. The first is the novelty of the survey mode and potential suspisions regarding the new method. A second concerns the increased possiblity of combining data from different sources on the Internet, which increases concern of web respondents that their answers will be matched with other data sources. A third focusses on additional information that is collected during the questionnaire completing without respondents' consent or even awarness; for instance, time, software used, type of Internet connection. The fourth centers around the general extreme reactions to privacy violations on the Internet, mail boxes being filled-up with spam, the possibility of false identity on the Internet (e.g. with all false bank messages and lottery wins that we get every day by email why would not one suspect that also the identify of the researcher is false), and the associated fear of identy theft.

Ethical concerns regarding Internet surveys will probably diminish with time, owing to better technology ensuring security, legal and professional ethical regulation, and familiarity of the Internet environment. As people become more comfortable buying goods, filling out application forms and transmitting private communications over the Internet, they will also be less troubled by submitting survey responses. Nevertheless, at the moment there are severe ethical issues in implementing Internet surveys that in practice receive or should receive special attention.

Several professional research associations developed codes of ethics and ethical guidelines dealing with Internet research (see the list on this book's website, Chapter 14). The following issues are addressed in these documents:

- Need of the survey organization to request informed consent from respondents and to allow them to opt-out from the sample list;

- Surveying children and minors where parental consent is needed;
- Ethical ways of collecting email addresses and sending out email invitations;
- Need that respondents are always offered alternative response options if they do not want to complete a web questionnaire;
- Use of cookies should be avoided. And if used, the respondents should be explicitly told about them and having the opportunity not to allow them while nevertheless participating in the survey;
- Discloser of researcher's identify, contact information, purpose of the study, how the data will be used and stored etcetera;
- Need to separate the email address and other information that can be used to identify respondens from the survey responses when archiving the data;
- Providing technical solutions for adequate data security;
- Allowing respondents to access their own data collected with the Web survey and having the opportunity to modify or even delete it;
- Reporting of data;
- Cross-cultural awarness in cross-cultural studies;
- Questionnaire design and not offending respondents, not increasing their burden if not really neoessairy, not to make them fell embaraced when answering the questions etcetera.

14.4 SOFTWARE PACKAGES

Several software packages for implementing web surveys can be found on the market. A list can be found at the WebSM site (http://www.websm.org). In general, software can be classified into two groups: (a) packages which are downloaded and the researcher or research organization needs to take care of the whole implementation process from questionnaire design, through sample management, hosting the survey, to transfer of responses and data storage; (b) solutions which are hosted on the software provider's server enabling the researcher to design the questionnaire online, having the sample managed, the survey hosted and responses collected and stored by the software provider. The decision on what kind of software to use depends on the resources (e.g., budget, human resources, hardware/software equipment) available, and on the needs (e.g., if one or several regular survey project will be implemented).

In any case, a professional survey software package should support the following features:

- Sample management allowing the researcher to send out pre-notifications, initial invitations and follow-ups for nonrespondents;
- User-friendly Interface for questionnaire design, with several help features. For instance, manuals, online help, tutorials, but also question/questionnaire libraries, and export from other software packages;
- Flexible questionnaire design regarding layout (e.g., background color/pattern, fonts, multimedia, progress indicator), question forms

(e.g., open, close, grid, semantic differential, yes/no questions), and features of computer-assisted survey information collection (e.g., complex branching, variable stimuli based on previous respondent's selections, range controls, missing data and consistency checks);

- Reliable and secure transfer and storage of data.

The latest trends in software developments move toward the integration of survey modes, that is, software package not only for implementing web surveys, but allowing for implementation of surveys in any mode. Once the questions and response options are written and their forms and flow are determined, the software automatically converts the questionnaire as needed, either to a web questionnaire, a paper self-administered questionnaire or questionnaire for a CATI or a CAPI system.

14.5 COST ISSUES

Internet surveys are often praised as being cheaper than other survey modes. Compared to mail surveys there are lower or even no costs for paper, printing, envelopes, postage, and related administrative work. Compared to paper-and-pencil questionnaires (mail, telephone, or face-to-face), the web survey mode spares the costs of data entry and editing procedures. Compared to any interviewer-administered survey (telephone or face-to-face), additional cost reductions arise from the absence of interviewers. On the other hand, start-up costs for equipment, web page design, and usability testing are needed. Nevertheless, the costs per response decrease with the number of questionnaires completed. The larger the sample size, the greater the differences in cost effectiveness between web and traditional surveys and the greater the advantages of the web over the traditional approaches.

Cost comparisons of web surveys to other survey modes depend very much on the type and implementation procedures of the web survey conducted. For example, costs are higher for list-based web surveys where participants receive invitations by mail. Costs are also higher for unrestricted self-selected surveys for which banner ads are located on frequently visited websites that charge for this service. Costs are also very high for pre-recruited samples. In addition, costs are higher if incentives are used.

The importance of lower costs of web surveys lies not only in higher profits for the survey research industry, but also in the potential for higher data quality. Low costs enable larger sample sizes, providing an increased potential for subgroup analysis and decreased sampling variance. In addition, they enable additional resources, which can be directed to the decrease of measurement error concerns.

14.6 CONCLUSION

In this chapter, we present different types of Internet surveys. We concentrate on interactive web surveys that are the prevailing form of Internet surveys. We present best practices and some solutions for implementation of these surveys, particularly issues in the sampling and solicitation stage of the survey process and in the questionnaire design stage. We also introduced the characteristics of professional software packages for conducting web surveys. We critically presented the cost issues regarding web surveys by diminishing the myth of web surveys being the cheapest survey mode.

GLOSSARY OF KEY CONCEPTS

Banner ad. A graphical part of a web page usually used for advertisements. In case of web surveys it can be used to invite visitors of a web page to participate in a survey. It provides link to a web survey.

Check box. Design element used to present response options in computerized questionnaires. Check boxes are usually used to present response options for questions with multiple possible answers. A respondent can select individual response options by clicking on them.

Cookie. A file that is sent from a web server to a web browser to be stored on user's disk for later retrieval. It contains data that enable the web server to recognize returning visitor of a web page, though it cannot reveal user's identity. This enables some control over multiple responses to web surveys by potentially recognizing persons who have already completed the survey.

Data security. Protection of data against loss and unauthorized access. It applies to the protection of data during the collection process and when stored at the server. Problem of data security is salient for web surveys since sufficient protection (e.g., encryption) of communication between respondent and server and also data server itself is necessary.

Drop-down menu. A design element used to present response options for single-answer question in web questionnaires. When a respondent clicks on a drop-down menu a list of available response options is opened. The respondents can choose one of them by scrolling down the list and select it.

Dropout rate. Proportion of respondents who only partially complete the questionnaire and preliminary abandon it. It is calculated as the ratio between number of respondents who abandoned the questionnaire prior its completion and number of all respondents to survey.

Interactive web survey. A web survey using an interactive survey questionnaire – a questionnaire where interaction with the server occurs during its completion. It enables interactive features such as conditional branching, randomization of items, inclusion of multimedia elements, control of answers, and so forth.

Intercept web survey. A web survey in which respondents are recruited by intercepting them during their visit to a specific web page. This is usually done using pop-up windows or banner ads on web page.

Internet survey. Broad term for all surveying modes implemented through one or more Internet services. These include World Wide Web (web surveys), email (email surveys), and WebTV (WebTV surveys).

List-based web survey. A type of web survey where a list of units from the target population (sampling frame) is available.

Login procedure (to web survey). A procedure used in web surveys with restricted access to authenticate respondent's permission of entering the web questionnaire. We speak about automatic login procedure when respondent's identification is part of the survey's URL address provided to him/her to access survey. We speak about manual login when respondent is asked to manually enter his/her username and password to access the survey questionnaire.

Opt-out (in web panels). Feature usually available in web panels. It enables participant to opt out from the panel, that is, to leave the panel when convenient to them.

Progress indicator. A graphical or textual element of computerized questionnaires that informs respondent about the proportion of the questionnaire that he/ she has already completed. It is usually implemented in web surveys.

Radio button. Design element used to present response options in computerized questionnaires. Radio buttons are usually used to present response options for questions with single possible answer. A respondent can select an individual response option by clicking on it.

Static web survey. Web survey based on simple HTML form without interactive features (in contrast to *Interactive web survey*). The web questionnaire is static – the same for all respondents.

Volunteer opt-in panel. A panel of units which self-selected themselves to it (inclusion in the panel is voluntary, not based on a probability sample from a certain sampling frame). It is a common approach in web surveys where such panels assure large number of participants of desired characteristics. Because such panels are not based on a representative sampling frame, statistical inference from such surveys is questionable.

Chapter 15

IVR: Interactive Voice Response

Darby Miller Steiger
Beverly Conroy
The Gallup Organization

15.1 INTRODUCTION

Over the past 25 years, western culture has experienced a dramatic shift in the conduct of daily functional transactions, replacing traditional interpersonal contact at places like banks, stores, and post offices with electronic self-administration such as ATMs, self check-out, and automated postal centers Online and automated telephone systems are now the norm rather than the exception for transactions such as catalog purchases, airline reservations, bill payments, and banking. Another powerful example of this shift is the increasing popularity and usage of electronic self-administered surveys such as Web-based data collection and telephone computer-automated data collection (also known as IVR, or Interactive Voice Response). These new methods of data collection offer the power and complexity of computerization combined with the privacy of self-administration. Web and IVR technologies have become increasingly popular for studying populations that have easy access to the technology and that have a high level of willingness to interact directly with computers.

15.2 WHAT IS IVR, AND HOW DOES IT FIT INTO THE FAMILY OF DATA COLLECTION METHODOLOGIES?

15.2.1 What is IVR?

IVR is a data collection technology in which the computer plays a recording of the question to the respondent over the telephone, and the respondent indicates the response by pressing the appropriate keys on his or her touch-tone (global) telephone keypad. IVR is also referred to as T-ACASI (Telephone-Audio Computer-Assisted Self-Interviewing), TDE (Touch-tone Data Entry), and VRE (Voice Recognition Entry).

IVR is created by programming the computer to play prerecorded prompts to the respondent based on the respondent's answers. A typical survey begins with a greeting to the caller, asking for an entry to prove identity such as a personal identification number (PIN) or password. The IVR system accesses the computer-stored data and verifies the caller's identity and password before any additional information is spoken. Only callers who are validated are permitted to continue. The survey items are then read to the caller.

IVR technology is widely used for sales and marketing, market research, customer satisfaction, employee assessment, and personnel selection, among other purposes. IVR is ideally used when the data desired are numeric or can easily be linked to a numeric code, such as "press 1 if yes, press 2 if no" (though open-ended data can also be collected via IVR), and is especially appropriate for surveys that are short and repetitive (Weeks, 1992).

IVR research can be executed in a number of different ways. The main distinctions are between *inbound* IVR studies, in which the sample member dials into an IVR system at his or her convenience, and *outbound* IVR studies, in which an interviewer dials out to the sample member to recruit respondents to participate and then transfers them directly into the IVR system. Some examples of these methods include:

- *Inbound mail recruit*: The U.S. Bureau of Labor Statistics uses IVR (referred to as TDE) for the Current Employment Statistics (CES) survey. Respondents receive a monthly advance postcard or fax reminding them to call in to the TDE system to provide payroll data. Nonrespondents receive telephone or fax prompts. (Phipps & Tupek, 1991).

- *Inbound recruit and transfer:* Using IVR (referred to as T-ACASI), customers calling in to the National Energy Information Center are transferred to an IVR system to get their feedback on the Energy Information Administration's products and services (Weir, Laurence, & Blessing, 2000).

- *Outbound CATI recruit*: Recent customers at a bank are recruited by live interviewers to provide customer feedback and are transferred to an IVR survey to provide their responses (Tourangeau, Rips, & Rasinski, 2000).

- *Inbound customer receipt recruit*: A national discount retail chain prints a toll-free number on a random sample of customer receipts to solicit feedback on their retail experience. Customers are asked to dial in within 24 hours of their store visit to provide feedback on their visit.

- *On-site inbound recruit*: Outreach workers visiting sites serving homeless adults offer them a cellular phone to take a survey about substance abuse treatment needs (Alemagno, Cochran, Feucht, Stephens, & Wolfe, 1996).

IVR has a number of strengths and limitations, which are discussed next.

15.2.1.1 Strengths

The key advantage to conducting research using IVR technology is that no human intervention is needed during data collection. Thus, the costs of data collection tend to be lower for IVR studies than for comparable studies employing live interviewers. Furthermore, inbound IVR data can be collected at any time of day or night, at the discretion of the survey respondent. Outbound

IVR studies are generally conducted during regular hours, because a live interviewer is typically present to transfer the respondent into the IVR survey.

IVR is best suited for surveys consisting primarily of closed-ended questions with a small set of response choices. IVR is an extremely efficient methodology for cross-cultural studies being conducted in multiple languages, since it is relatively inexpensive to translate and program a survey into additional languages.

15.2.1.2 Limitations

Because IVR technology relies on the usage of a touch-tone telephone in order to transmit the information, IVR is not a viable method of data collection among populations lacking a high prevalence of touch-tone telephones.

The company hosting the IVR system must have the capacity to accept a large volume of incoming calls. See this book's website, Chapter 15, Exhibit A, for a list of key features and components of a successful IVR system.

Respondent burden is an important issue to consider with IVR surveys. Without an interviewer to motivate the respondent to carry through to the end of the survey, long IVR surveys can suffer from high break-off rates. IVR should thus be limited in its usage to shorter questionnaires. IVR is less suitable for questions with more than five to seven response categories and many open-ended items. The IVR researcher must be very cautious in designing an IVR questionnaire to ensure that the respondent has a clear understanding of how to navigate the system, including how to have a question repeated, and how to skip an item.

15.2.2 How Does IVR Fit into the Family of Data Collection Methodologies?

IVR is somewhat of a hybrid data collection method. It is comparable to a CATI (computer-assisted telephone interviewing) survey in that it is administered by telephone, but is also similar to Web or other self-administered surveys, because no live interviewer is present to collect the data.

15.2.2.1 IVR vs. CATI

Like computer-assisted telephone interviewing (CATI), IVR is administered by telephone and requires the respondent to rely on an aural presentation of the survey questions. It also uses programming technology similar to CATI to allow for skip patterns and the use of sample frame information to feed into the way questions are asked. Furthermore, IVR data collection can produce an instant data file, as does CATI, upon completion of the interview, unlike paper surveys that need to be scanned or manually data entered upon receipt. Finally, like CATI, a responder to an IVR survey does not know how far along he or she is in the survey instrument unless the recorded voice gives some indication of that progress. This is a key difference from a paper survey, in which the respondent can physically see how many questions are left. If the IVR respondent senses that the survey is long and has no indication of how many questions are left, he or she may be more likely to break off the interview. The same could occur in a CATI interview, though the interviewer can easily provide an indication of progress to the respondent.

In spite of these similarities to CATI interviewing, a key difference between CATI and IVR interviewing is the presence of a live interviewer. Live CATI interviewing can be subject to interviewer discrepancies in how interviewers read the questions, such as speed, tone, and personality that may come through as the questions are being read. Though CATI interviewers are trained to read every question exactly as worded, they sometimes do not, which may affect the quality of data collected. IVR interviewing, in contrast, uses a single recorded voice to deliver exactly the same reading of the questions every time. In addition to the potential for interviewer variability, there has been much research conducted to examine the impact of an interviewer's presence on survey statistics. The removal of the live interviewer in the IVR mode can potentially lead to more accurate reporting, particularly for items of a sensitive nature. In these respects, IVR interviewing is vastly different from CATI.

To summarize, the key advantages of IVR over CATI include: (a) for inbound IVR studies, respondents can complete the interview at their convenience, at any time of day or night; (b) IVR provides significant cost savings by eliminating the need for an interviewing workforce; (c) IVR provides consistent delivery of survey questions without any interviewer variability or unintended influence; and (d) IVR may provide more honest reporting on sensitive items.

Important disadvantages of IVR relative to CATI are: (a) for inbound IVR studies a reliance on the respondent to initiate the call, resulting in diminished response rates; (b) a lack of interviewer presence to motivate respondents to complete the interview, resulting in higher break-off rates and item nonresponse rates; (c) IVR is not suitable for lengthy or complex surveys; and (d) some respondents do not have access to a touch-tone phone.

15.2.2.2 IVR vs. paper-and-pencil

The main similarity between IVR data collection and traditional paper-and-pencil mail surveying (PAPI) is the absence of a live interviewer. Both of these modes are apt to produce less socially desirable responses than modes employing live interviewers. Inbound IVR studies are similar to paper mail surveys in that the respondents can complete the survey at any time of day at their convenience. Outbound recruit-and-switch IVR surveys, however, require the sample member to be available at the time of the interviewer's call.

In contrast, the key difference between IVR and PAPI is the method of delivery of the questions. The aural format of IVR requires a much different set of questionnaire design techniques than the visual format of paper surveys, and does not require respondents to be able to read or see. IVR questions must generally be shorter, with fewer response categories.

The main advantage of IVR over PAPI is that data are collected electronically and can be immediately processed with no delay from mail time or scan time.

Some disadvantages of IVR relative to PAPI are: (a) IVR is not suitable for lengthy surveys; (b) IVR may be more subject to context effects, since there is no visual presentation of survey items; (c) some respondents do not have access to a touch-tone phone; and (d) the respondent generally must complete the IVR survey all in one sitting, whereas the paper survey can be done over time.

15.2.2.3 IVR versus Web

Both IVR and Web-based data collection allow computer-programmed delivery of questions without the presence of an interviewer. Skip-pattern logic can be employed and both methods are appropriate for asking sensitive items. They are also similar in that they are both relatively new data collection technologies that are still being explored and experimented with in order to determine the most effective way to use the technologies.

The key difference between IVR and Web-based data collection, again, is the aural versus visual format. IVR typically requires shorter question wording and shorter response categories than Web surveys.

Some advantages of IVR over Web-based data collection include: (a) with outbound interviewer recruiting, respondents can be immediately transferred into the IVR system, with no delay (as opposed to waiting for the respondent to log onto the Web survey); and (b) touch-tone telephone penetration is typically higher than computer penetration among households.

Key disadvantages of IVR relative to Web are: (a) IVR is not suitable for lengthy or complex surveys; (b) IVR may be more prone to context effects, since there is no visual presentation of survey items; and (c) some respondents do not have access to a touch-tone phone.

15.3 IVR AND SOURCES OF SURVEY ERROR

Surveys are subject to various types of errors (Groves, 1989). *Observational* errors are measurement errors that arise when survey responses differ from the true statistic, stemming from interviewer bias, bias in question wording, or bias related to the mode of data collection. *Nonobservational* errors arise because part of the population failed to be measured, for reasons such as being excluded from the sample frame, not having the technology to participate in the survey, or choosing not to respond (cf. de Leeuw, Hox, and Dillman, Chapter 1).

This section lays out the potential for these types of errors in IVR surveys as compared to other modes of data collection in order to aid the IVR researcher in making careful decisions about when and how to best use IVR as a data collection method.

15.3.1 Measurement Error

Measurement error can occur from a variety of sources, including the interviewer, the questionnaire, the respondent, and the mode of data collection.

15.3.1.1 Interviewer bias

Although IVR interviewing does not use live interviewers, it can still be subject to bias if the choice of voice somehow influences response. The voice can be the key factor that keeps the respondent's interest for a sufficiently long time to complete the survey. There have been a number of studies to experiment with the use of voice in IVR research. The prevailing hypothesis in those studies was that the gender of an automated voice in an IVR survey can lead to stereotyping and thus influence responses. Tourangeau, Couper and Steiger (2001) tested this hypothesis in a series of Web and IVR experiments, varying the gender of the "presence" of an interviewer. In the IVR setting, respondents were assigned to hear either a male voice reading the questions, a female voice, or a blend of male and female voices reading questions and response options. The survey asked questions about gender attitudes, sensitive items about drug use, and other questions known to elicit socially desirable reporting. The authors found no impact of the voices on gender attitude scales or on reporting of embarrassing behaviors.

Similarly, other studies have failed to find any effect of the choice of voice on reporting levels and response rates (see Turner, et al., 1998). In a further twist on the use of voice in IVR research, Tourangeau, et al., (2001) experimented with personalization of question wording in an IVR setting, varying whether respondents heard "Now I will ask you…" to more closely mimic an interviewer-administered survey as opposed to "Next, please answer…" as a more generic application. They found that personalization of question wording in an IVR survey resulted in significantly fewer embarrassing admissions. This suggests that even though IVR is a standardized method of delivering survey questions, the level of personalization in the way questions are recorded can influence responses.

Couper, Singer, and Tourangeau (2004) also experimented with the use of a human versus a synthetic voice in an IVR experiment and found no differences in break-off rates or in reporting of embarrassing admissions between the human recording and the synthetic voice recording, in spite of respondents clearly being able to distinguish between the human and machine-generated voice. The authors concluded that synthetic voice recordings in an IVR application are a feasible alternative to human recordings.

> **Recommendations**: IVR research calls for a straightforward and serious recording that is easy to understand. This generally is best achieved by a human voice because it is recorded in a way to achieve a higher quality of conversation with the respondent than is true for a synthesized voice. IVR survey designers should minimize the level of personalization in the IVR script, especially for surveys covering sensitive topics. Respondents can detect age and locality in the voice of the IVR interviewer; thus, choose a voice that emulates trust and commitment with respondents. Finally, given the mixed findings in the literature, researchers should carefully consider the gender of the voice being used to read the questions, as well as whether a synthetic or a human voice should be used.

15.3.1.2 Questionnaire bias/error

According to Dillman (2007), different modes of data collection require different standards for designing questions (See also Dillman, Chapter 9). CATI favors shorter scales, scales with only the endpoints labeled, unfolding of questions, yes/no items instead of mark all that apply, and generally short questionnaires. IVR, according to Dillman, favors even shorter wording formats than telephone, even shorter scales, and even shorter questionnaires. Exhibit B (this book's website, Chapter 15) presents some examples of how questions are often constructed differently across modes, demonstrating the complexities of administering certain items in IVR.

Recommendations: There are many factors to consider when choosing wording for an IVR script. Complete sentences should be kept brief, simple, and to the point. Parentheses, slashes, or abbreviations cannot be used in an IVR script, because these items will not be read by the voice talent. All questions will be recorded exactly as the script is written. Also, clearly and consistently indicate in the script how respondents should provide their response. Response options are typically presented in ascending order, with the content mentioned first, then the key value. For example, "If you are male, press '1,' if you are female, press '2.'" When choosing words, consider how they sound and their meaning. For example, it is difficult to hear the difference between "literate" and "illiterate" on a recording.

15.3.1.3 Respondent Bias/Error

There are several respondent-driven factors that may lead to errors in an IVR setting. First, respondents may not be comfortable or familiar with the technology. Second, the use of a synthetic voice may be more difficult to understand than natural speech and may lead to problems with comprehension and memory as the respondent tries to understand the question. Some of these errors will subside as respondents become more familiar with the technology. In a study to identify respondent problems using a touch-tone system, Phipps and Tupek (1991) asked respondents to respond both by TDE as well as by returning a paper survey form. They compared the TDE data with the survey forms and found the largest number of errors in TDE item nonresponse (82/177). An additional 18 respondents typed in too few or too many digits, and 17 slipped on the keypad and mistyped their responses. They also found that errors were reduced with experience and suggest that a panel survey may be the most appropriate for this method of data collection.

The design of some telephones may be another potential source of error. Many households have touch-tone telephones with the keys on the handset rather than the base, so the respondent needs to pull the phone away from his or her ear to press the response. Participants report higher difficulty answering the questions because of this constant moving of the handset away from their ears to press their responses (Mingay, 2000).

Recommendations: It is critical to include a practice item at the beginning of the IVR script to help respondents get accustomed to the methodology. The IVR system should allow a sufficient number of seconds for the respondent to enter their response, which accounts for the physical movement of the phone from ear to data entry. All IVR instruments should be pretested to ensure a smooth, error-free administration of the instrument.

When asking questions that are very personal to the respondent, such as income or age, it is usually best to ask these questions at the end of the survey, and to give an option to the caller who chooses not to respond. For example, "If you choose not to respond, press '0.'" This same type of option can also be given for open-ended questions, such as "If you would like to provide a response, press '1.' If not, press '0.'"

Designate a standard key to be used to repeat the question and inform the respondent of this option at the beginning of the survey. Typically, this is the asterisk (*) on the keypad. For sample IVR default scenarios and suggestions for conveying instructions to the respondent, see Exhibit C, this book's website (Chapter 15).

15.3.1.4 Bias Resulting From Mode of Administration

Respondents may be more willing to honestly respond to sensitive questions if they believe their responses will be anonymous or confidential (see also Lensvelt-Mulders, Chapter 24). A large body of studies, in fact, shows that more embarrassing (or less socially desirable) behaviors are reported at a higher rate in a self-administered survey environment than in an interviewer-administered environment (Turner, Miller, & Smith, 1996; Tourangeau & Smith, 1998; Gribble, Miller, Codey, Catania, Pollack, & Turner, 2000; Cooley, Miller, Gribble, & Turner, 2000; Currivan, Nyman, Turner, & Biener, 2004).

Table 15.1 Respondent preferences for T-ACASI versus standard telephone interview using a human interviewer

Dimension	Preferences for			ODDS RATIO (a)
	T-ACASI	Human	Indifferent	
	%	%	%	
Best at protecting your privacy	49	11	40	4.53
Best for getting honest answers	73	17	10	4.39
Best for asking about sensitive topics like sexual behavior	66	23	11	2.88
More comfortable giving your answers	44	24	31	1.82
Easier to use	30	59	11	.51
Most interesting to use	27	50	23	.54
Easiest to change answer (b)	1	61	37	.02

(a) Odds ratio for choice of T-ACASI. Indifferent responses were excluded.
(b) This question asked respondents to rate, which was the "hardest" mode in which to change answers. Authors report responses for the "easiest" mode in order to make them consistent with the coding of other dimensions in the table.
Source: Turner et al. (1996).

According to Turner, et al. (1996), respondents thought T-ACASI was better than CATI at protecting privacy, was a better environment for answering sensitive questions, made them more likely to report sexual behaviors, and was a more comfortable environment for giving answers. They also felt CATI interviewing was easier and more interesting to use, and was easier for changing answers.

With slightly less sensitive items that may still be subject to some social desirability bias, mode comparison experiments have shown mixed results, with some showing lower and perhaps more honest satisfaction ratings on IVR than CATI (Tourangeau, Steiger, & Wilson, 2002; Weir, Laurence, & Blessing, 2000). Other studies have suggested that IVR and CATI produce similar responses (Dillman, Phelps, Tortora, Swift, Kohrell, & Berck, 2002) but that IVR and CATI both produce more extreme responses than visual modes of Web and paper (see also Srinivasan & Hanway, 1999). The theory is that in a visual environment, respondents are more likely to consider the entire scale of response options than in an aural mode when factors such as primacy, recency, acquiescence bias, and social desirability may be at play.

Not all survey questions are subject to social desirability bias. For less sensitive items, IVR is considered to be an excellent alternative to the costly CATI method of data collection. The Bureau of Labor Statistics has been collecting reliable employment statistics using IVR technology since 1987. Businesses are asked to provide straightforward statistics each month in a survey that usually takes less than two minutes. Record check studies show the average error rate is less than 1.8% (Phipps & Tupek, 1990). Mingay (2000) shows several other studies that suggest that the reliability and validity of IVR as a method to collect nonsensitive information is no different from modes using a live interviewer.

> **Recommendations**: Researchers should generally be cautious about using more than one methodology to collect survey data, especially for topics that may be sensitive in nature. IVR data can be significantly different from interviewer-collected or visually administered survey data.

15.3.2 Nonresponse Error

Nonresponse error occurs when some sample members cannot be located, refuse to participate, or are otherwise unavailable to participate in the survey during the data collection period. When nonrespondents are different from respondents, this can affect the survey statistics. Nonresponse can occur at the unit level, meaning no response is obtained from that sample member, or at the item level, meaning questions on the survey are skipped or do not have a legitimate response.

15.3.2.1 Unit nonresponse
When considering the choice of mode, one must consider respondents' willingness to participate using that method of data collection (cf. Lynn, Chapter 3). For example, sample members may be much more likely to

participate in a survey if called by a live interviewer who persuades them of the importance of participation than if handed a receipt at a store with an 800 number to dial to complete a survey. There certainly is a tradeoff with costs, because using interviewers to dial out can increase the cost of what should otherwise be a less expensive methodology than interviewer-administered CATI surveys. Exhibit D (this book's website, Chapter 15) summarizes recent research into differential response rates by mode of data collection. IVR typically produces lower response rates than CATI, but can also achieve extremely high response rates if executed carefully.

15.3.2.2 Item nonresponse

Item nonresponse in a CATI survey arises when the respondent notifies the interviewer that he or she does not have an answer to the question or would like to refuse to provide a response. In a visual environment such as Web or paper-and-pencil, the respondent may simply leave an item blank or mark off a "don't know" box if he or she chooses not to provide a legitimate response. IVR respondents, however, must become familiar with the norms of the technology in order to perform these basic functions.

In a recent study, Mingay and Kim (1998) found that in spite of reporting that they understand how to respond to an automated interview, respondents might not recall or realize how to repeat questions, change answers, or indicate they would like to skip a question. Indeed, Couper, Singer, & Tourangeau (2004) found that with no human present to prompt the respondent to provide an answer and with the possibility of technical errors (e.g., pressing an out-of-range key), missing data rates were significantly higher for the IVR conditions than for CATI (more than 2% of the answers were missing in the three IVR conditions versus about 0.5% in the CATI condition).

> **Recommendations**: In order to minimize item nonresponse, two guiding principles are: keep the questionnaire short, and ask short questions with a short list of response categories. Additionally, the survey designer should write simple instructions into the IVR script about how to skip a question. This may be necessary to do more than once, but not too often or else respondents may be encouraged to skip items.

15.3.2.3 Break-off rates compared to other modes

IVR can provide some easy opportunities for respondents to hang up without having completed the interview. If the data collection method is outbound interviewer recruit with a transfer into the IVR system, the transfer period affords an easy opportunity for the respondent, who has already agreed to participate, to change his or her mind and hang up. This can be an especially vulnerable period if it takes more than a few seconds to complete the transfer to the automated interview. For example, Gribble, et al. (2000) found that about 18% of the sample disconnected during the transfer to IVR. Dillman, et al. (2002) portrays a typical transfer success rate of 69% when the transfer time to the IVR system is about 10 seconds long. As technology improves and this transfer time is reduced, this type of break-off rate should decline.

Tourangeau, et al. (2002) conducted an experiment in a recruit-and-switch IVR survey whereby the interviewers asked half the sample a few innocuous questions before switching them to IVR, and the other half were switched to IVR immediately upon agreeing to participate. The hypothesis was that respondents would be less likely to break off during the transfer if they had already begun the survey with the interviewer. Indeed, respondents who were asked the additional questions before the switch were significantly more likely to complete the IVR questions (68.5% versus 59.6%, $p < .001$).

Even if the transfer is successful, it is all too easy for the respondent to break off part of the way through the questionnaire if he or she finds the topic to be boring, the survey too long, or for some other distraction such as call waiting to occupy their time. Tourangeau, et al. (2002) found that most break offs occurred at two points in their survey: (a) when a lengthy explanation of a response scale was read, and (b) when a message indicated that the respondent was "now about halfway done with the interview." These findings are consistent with earlier results that break offs are likely when respondents believe there are still many items to come (Tourangeau & Steiger, 1999).

Break offs can be computer- or respondent-generated. Nyman, Roman, & Turner (2001) recontacted respondents who had broken off the survey to find the reason for the break-off. Reasons were split between computer problems and respondents being the source of the break off. Computer break offs were mainly because the computer disconnected (51%), and call waiting (20%). Respondent break offs were mainly because the interview was too long (33%) and they did not like the questions (28%).

Break-off rates can be extremely high with a long IVR survey. Tourangeau, et al. (2002) measured a 40% break-off rate in a survey averaging 30 minutes. Cooley, et al. (2000) reported a break-off rate of 24% in a similarly long questionnaire.

Recommendations: For outbound recruiting with an immediate transfer to IVR, it is important to use an IVR system that can minimize the number of seconds to complete the transfer. It may help to engage the respondent before the transfer by having the live interviewer ask a few nonsensitive survey items. When transferring a respondent to the IVR system, it is important that the live interviewer: thanks the respondents, tells them how long the survey lasts, explains they may experience a delay in transfer (don't hang up), and confirms their willingness to complete the survey before the transfer.

15.3.3 Coverage Error

Coverage error occurs when some people are not included on the frame or are not given an opportunity to participate in the survey. Examples include lack of telephone in a CATI survey, lack of Web access on a Web survey, or lack of a touch-tone phone in an IVR survey.

15.3.3.1 Proliferation of Touch-Tone Phones, Phone Coverage

The feasibility of using IVR depends upon the number of target respondents who have access to a touch-tone telephone. According to Turner, et al. (1998), touch-tone phone ownership in the United States is over 90%, but is less common among elderly households (i.e., those without an 18- to 49-year-old) and households with people with lower levels of income and education. These rates will obviously differ across nations, and can be a source of error if the technology does not support this method.

Rotary dial registers are an option for IVR data collection, by detecting a series of clicks that are written to the data set. The cost of rotary detection depends on the penetration of rotary phones in the sample area.

15.3.3.2 Regional and Global Reach

It is important to recognize the cost of long-distance telephone calls when deciding how to manage an IVR system. For multiple incoming calls from a region, it may make sense to centralize the termination of calls to a regional hub. For example, calls from Japan may be terminated in Australia even though this is a higher rate per minute call because there may not be enough volume to warrant the expense of another system in Japan. Or given the business reasons, there may need to be several points of call termination to meet the research needs because the volume of calls to each termination point is high enough that the cost of the systems placed will offset or be less than the long distance per-minute costs.

In general, multi-nation IVR studies are often more complicated than single-nation studies. In addition to an international toll-free number (which depends on the local telephone companies working together), there is the added challenge of writing the script, translating, and recording to accommodate all respondents. And all combinations of respondents need to be considered (physically impaired or rotary phones) or based on the area, which may be technologically less advanced than other areas being sampled for the survey.

Recommendations: The rate of touch-tone phone penetration in your area should be examined before a decision is made to use this mode of data collection. For multi-nation surveys, it will be important to assess the costs of international phone calls versus adding the cost of additional IVR systems to be placed in each country.

15.4 CONCLUSIONS

15.4.1 Summary of IVR Technical Specifications

When setting up a new IVR system, the survey organization must first determine the scope of the projects likely to be using the system. Larger projects require more extensive hardware, either in-house, or supplied by a vendor. Some examples of commercial IVR software in the United States and globally include Voxeo Voice Center IVR Platform (global), Amcat IVR (U.S.,

Europe), Cyber Futuristics IVR Go4 (India), CT Developer Studio (North America), VoiceGuide IVR (Australia, U.S.), and EasyIVR (U.S.). The projected number of simultaneous callers is the main factor in determining the size of the IVR installation. It is usually wise to create a buffer in case the volume of callers goes over the planned maximum. The number and type of phone lines that will be needed will also be determined by the number of simultaneous callers. The IVR system itself is a self-contained computer server that functions much like any other computer on the network. It needs to be located in close proximity to the incoming phone lines, preferably in a climate-controlled environment.

Once the hardware has been installed and the phone lines have been tested, the system is ready for use. The IVR application must be programmed according to the company's best practices. It is usually best to develop an IVR script that contains all the questions that are required as well as the survey flow logic. Additionally, the script should contain any error messages and other instructional messages the system might need to respond with in the event that the respondent makes a mistake or needs special guidance. Remember that respondents are guided through the system by voice prompts, so the prompts need to be specific and succinct. The IVR voice prompts will need to be recorded by the chosen voice talent and the application will need to be tested for functionality prior to taking live callers. Pay close attention to the exact wording of the recorded prompts and specific pronunciations of more difficult words in the script. It is useful to have difficult words spelled phonetically on the IVR script. After it has been properly tested and the resulting data has been checked for accuracy, the survey is ready for live callers.

Since the IVR system is unattended and available 24 hours a day, it is recommended that the system be monitored for continuous operation. The survey should have a specific field period so the respondents know when they are able to call in and let their opinions be heard. Creating a successful IVR system requires a solid understanding of your project scope and attention to detail to make a robust IVR system.

15.4.2 Future of IVR

IVR is a cost-efficient way to collect data, and continues to be recognized as such in the future. As the penetration of touch-tone telephones grows within areas around the globe, IVR will become increasingly feasible as a data collection method, particularly for niche surveys in which the population of interest is known to have access to touch-tone phones.

In the United States specifically, there exists a steady stream of activity toward this method. It is particularly popular for targeting a sample with a research collection and solution product that is known to have easy access to telephones. The international survey researcher must consider the rate of touch-tone penetration and the availability of good commercial IVR systems before deciding upon IVR as a method of data collection.

GLOSSARY OF KEY CONCEPTS

Break offs. Occur when a respondent fails to complete the survey request. The break off is determined to be at the last question the respondent answered before hanging up or exiting the survey. This results in a partial interview that may or may not be counted towards the final dataset, depending on the researcher's decision.

CATI. The acronym for Computer Assisted Telephone Interviewing, in which a questionnaire to be administered by telephone interviewers is programmed into a computer system that manages the data collection and eliminates the need for interviewers to use paper and pencil to record responses.

Coverage error. Occurs when some people are systematically excluded from the sampling frame or are not given an opportunity to participate in the survey. Examples include lack of telephone in a CATI survey, lack of Web access on a Web survey, or lack of a touchtone phone in an IVR survey.

Inbound studies. Those in which the sample member dials into an IVR system at his or her convenience.

IVR. The acronym for Interactive Voice Response, which is a data collection technology in which the computer plays a recording of the question to the respondent over the telephone, and the respondent indicates the response by pressing the appropriate keys on his or her touchtone telephone keypad.

Outbound studies. Those in which an interviewer dials out to the sample member to recruit respondents to participate and then transfers them directly into the IVR system.

PAPI. The acronym for Paper and Pencil Interviewing, which can take several forms, but is typically a mailed questionnaire in which the respondent is asked to write in their responses and mail their completed questionnaire back to the data collection organization.

Respondent burden. A measure of the amount of time and effort it takes a respondent to respond to a question or a survey.

Social desirability bias. Occurs when the respondent attempts to portray himself or herself in a positive light to the interviewer.

T-ACASI. The acronym for Touchtone-Audio Computer Assisted Self-Interviewing (see IVR).

TDE. The acronym for Touchtone Data Entry (see IVR).

VRE. The acronym for Voice Recognition Entry (see IVR).

Chapter 16

Mixed-mode Surveys: When and Why[1]

Edith D. de Leeuw
Joop J. Hox
Department of Methodology & Statistics, Utrecht University

Don A. Dillman
Washington State University

16.1 INTRODUCTION

Data collection in surveys can be carried out using several methods. In Chapters 11–15, five different choices for survey mode — face-to-face, telephone, mail, Interactive Voice Response and web—were described as possibilities for implementing a survey. With all these possibilities, the choice for a specific mode is difficult and involves trade-offs between the strong and weak points of each mode (de Leeuw, Chapter 7). Sometimes a survey sponsor is better advised to use more than one data collection mode for implementing a proposed study and to conduct a multi-mode or mixed-mode survey. Mixed-mode surveys are appealing because one can attempt to combine the strong points of each individual mode; however, such a decision should not be made without careful thought and planning. Introducing a second, or even a third or fourth survey mode into the data collection plan, implies a more complicated, more expensive, longer, and more challenging survey implementation. It also means that the strong and weak points of each mode may need to be reconsidered to take advantage of each mode's relative strengths, compensating for each mode's weaknesses.

An initial consideration is that doing a mixed-mode study does not necessarily mean that some respondents are going to be asked to complete a questionnaire in a different mode than are other respondents. Multiple modes can be used in different stages of the survey: in the initial screening and contact stage, in the main data collection stage, or in the follow-up stage. Thus a second mode may be limited to initial contacts used to initiate the data collection process or perhaps used as a follow-up reminder to encourage completion of the questionnaire in another mode.

---

[1] This Chapter draws on E.D. de Leeuw (2005). To mix or not to mix: Data collection modes in surveys, which appeared in *Journal of Official Statistics*, *21*, 2, 1-23.

When multiple modes are implemented in the data collection phase and different modes are used to obtain answers, survey costs may have figured into the design decisions. For example, in surveys that require a high response, it is customary to follow-up nonrespondents. In those cases, it is attractive to start the first round of data collection with an inexpensive survey mode (e.g., a mail survey), which is then followed by more expensive methods (e.g., telephone or even face-to-face). A different approach is to give respondents the option to respond in the survey mode they prefer. Cost considerations can play an important role here too, when researchers try to make the least expensive mode more attractive. Offering respondents a choice of ways of responding can also build goodwill and improve the attitude toward survey taking, though not necessarily increase overall response. Another reason for using different modes for different respondents is calling for a telephone interview those respondents who cannot be contacted through the Internet: a telephone-web mix is then used to reduce undercoverage of those who have no web access.

There are many reasons and many possibilities for implementing mixed-mode surveys. According to Biemer and Lyberg (2003), mixed-mode surveys are now the norm in the United States and parts of Western Europe. Still, methodological publications on how to secure methodological quality in mixed-mode surveys are scarce, and most handbooks do not even discuss mixed-mode designs. Exceptions are Biemer and Lyberg (2003), Czaja and Blair (2004), and Groves, Fowler, Couper, Lepkowski, Singer, and Tourangeau (2004), who all include a section on mixed-mode designs in their chapters on data collection, and Dillman (2007).

A significant drawback with mixing modes in one study is that the survey mode may have an effect on the data that are collected, as described earlier in Chapters 7 and 9. Different modes have different ways of contacting potential respondents and may result in different contact or cooperation rates, which may result in dissimilar compositions of the realized sample in the different modes. Second, different modes may have an effect on the question-answer process, and so lead to different answers to the survey questions. In sum, the question is whether data collected with different survey modes can be combined and compared. This is especially important in comparative surveys, when data are collected using one mode in Scandinavia, and using a different mode in a number of Mediterranean countries. What does it mean when we find a north-south difference on some survey question? Is it real, or could it be a mode effect? Similarly, if respondents may choose their preferred mode, what happens if that preference changes over time? If in a longitudinal study the proportion of respondents who use Internet to send in their answers increases, can the data still be compared over time?

These are important methodological issues. De Leeuw (Chapter 7) discusses the theoretical reasons why mode effects are to be expected and summarizes the empirical research on mode effects. In short: mode effects do exist but tend to be small in well-conducted surveys. Social researchers tend to regard face-to-face interviews as the queen of data collection, but in fact, when comparable surveys with *equivalent* questionnaires are investigated none of the data collection modes is superior on all criteria. The most pronounced differences are found with sensitive topics. Modes with an interviewer produced more socially desirable answers and less consistent answers, but also more detailed responses to open questions. Differences between face-to-face and telephone interviews were small, with the face-to-face interview doing slightly better than the telephone (see also de Leeuw, 1992).

16.2 WHY MIX SURVEY MODES?

Survey designers choose a mixed-mode approach because using multiple data collection modes in one study gives an opportunity to take advantage of the strengths and compensate for the weaknesses of each individual mode at affordable costs. The most cost-effective data collection method may not be optimal for a specific study, but by combining this least expensive method with a second more expensive method in a mixed-mode design the researcher has the best of both worlds: less costs and less error than in a single-mode approach. In mixed-mode designs there is an explicit trade-off of cost and errors, focusing on non-sampling errors, that is, frame or coverage error, nonresponse error, and measurement error (Biemer & Lyberg, 2003; Groves, 1989; de Leeuw, Hox & Dillman, Chapter 1).

The usual goal is to find an optimal mix of modes for data collection given the research question and the population under study, within certain restrictions (Biemer & Lyberg, 2003). The basic research question defines the population under study, the topic and type of questions that should be asked, and the complexity of the survey instrument. Survey ethics and privacy regulations may restrict the design, just as practical restrictions like available time and budget do. When designing a survey the goal is to optimize data collection procedures and reduce total survey error within these restrictions; that is, to find the best *affordable* method, and sometimes the best affordable method is a mixed-mode design.

For instance, to reduce coverage bias in the early days of telephone surveys, dual frame mixed-mode surveys were employed. Coverage bias occurred because part of the population did not have a telephone and the nontelephone households differed from the telephone households on sociodemographic variables such as age and socioeconomic status. Thus, part of the sample was approached using a telephone survey, and another part was approached using a face-to-face procedure, in which area probability sampling was often used (cf. Lohr, Chapter 6). This dual frame mixed-mode combines the advantage of the cost savings of telephone interviewing and the better coverage of area probability sampling: the best affordable method from a coverage-costs point of view. For a comprehensive discussion of dual frame surveys, see Groves and Lepkowski (1985).

A comparable issue exists in modern web surveys. Although Internet access is growing and around 70% of the US population has access to the net, the picture is diverse with percentages ranging from 76% coverage for Sweden to 3.6% in Africa (www.internetworldstats.com, data from August 2007). Thus, many countries have a considerable coverage problem when Internet surveys are used. Furthermore, those covered differ from those not covered, with older people, lower educated, lower income, and minorities less well represented online. To compensate for coverage error in web surveys, mixed-mode strategies are employed. For example, in a survey on mobile phones and interest in WAP technology, Parackal (2003) anticipated coverage bias with more innovative and technological advanced individuals in the Internet population. Parackal therefore used a mixed-mode or hybrid survey approach, in which all sampled units were contacted with a paper letter and given the choice to either use Internet or to request a paper questionnaire. In market research, telephone and web hybrids are become increasingly popular as the development of special multi mode CATI/CAWI software is also indicating (for a critical overview, see Macer, 2003).

Most literature on mixed-mode applications refers to the reduction of nonresponse error. Response rates have been declining over the years (de Leeuw & de Heer, 2002); see also Lynn (Chapter 3). To achieve higher response rates, while keeping the overall costs low, mixed-mode data collection strategies are used, starting with the less costly method first. A good example is the American Community Survey, which is a mail survey with follow-up telephone interviews for nonrespondents, followed by face-to-face interviews for a subsample of the remaining non-respondents. Another example of a large mail survey with an interview follow-up is the National Mortality Followback Survey of the US National Center of Health Statistics. Telephone follow-ups appear to be effective in raising response and may even reduce nonresponse bias in mail surveys (cf. Fowler, Gallagher, Stringfellow, Zalavsky, Thompson, & Cleary, 2002). To reduce selective nonresponse, Beebe, Davern, McAlpine, Call, and Rockwood (2005) even went a step further. To include ethnic groups, their mail survey—that was in English only—had an explicit statement on the cover in several languages, urging respondents interested in completing a telephone survey to contact the survey center where bilingual interviewers were available. Both incentives and mail and telephone follow-ups were employed to raise response.

Another well-documented application of mixed-mode research is research into sensitive topics. One of the most consistent findings in mode comparisons is that self-administered forms of data collection perform better than interview-modes when sensitive questions are asked (for an overview, see de Leeuw, 1992). Therefore, mixed-mode approaches using a paper self-administered form for a subset of questions to elicit sensitive information in a face-to-face interview have been standard good practice for a long time. In this approach a questionnaire containing the sensitive questions is handed out during the interview and the respondent has the opportunity to answer in all privacy. Methodological studies comparing data quality in computer-assisted forms of data collection also found that the more private computer-assisted self-administered forms led to more accurate reporting of socially undesirable attributes (e.g., Tourangeau & Smith, 1996; Tourangeau, Rasinski, Jobe, Smith, & Pratt, 1997). Therefore the U.S. National Survey on Drug Use and Health (NSDUH) now uses computer-assisted self-interviewing (CASI), where respondents answer the questions privately by directly entering the answer in the computer, and only a few non-threatening questions are posed directly by an interviewer.

16.3 TYPES OF MIXED-MODE DESIGNS

There are many forms of mixed-mode designs and many ways of summarizing them. Dillman (2000) and Dillman and Tarnai (1988) focus on the data collection and its objectives, whereas Balden (2004) uses timing of interacting with respondents (i.e., contact phase, response phase, and follow-up phase) as organizing principle. These overviews can be integrated and expanded by taking into account both actual *data collection mixtures* and mixtures of *means of communication.* It is important to realize that survey researchers communicate with sample members at different points in time and that they may use different modes of communication at each point to do so. Prime examples are prenotifications, screening procedures and reminders. This goes beyond the data collection itself, and it is better to use the term *mixed or multi mode system.* A clear example of such a mixed-mode system is the Nielsen media research methodology (Bennett & Trussell, 2001; Trussell & Lavrakas, 2004). This mixed-mode system uses an RDD-selected sample of households to which addresses are matched. The mixed-mode system consists of seven steps: first a prerecruitment postcard is mailed to all homes for which addresses are available; this is followed by a recruitment phone call; the third contact attempt is again by mail and in an advance postcard announcing the diary; next the diary survey packet is mailed to all homes for which an address is now available (regardless of the result of the recruitment call). This diary survey packet includes a cover letter, diaries, a cash incentive, a return envelope, and a brochure. A reminder postcard in step 5, a reminder phone call in step 6, and again a reminder postcard in step 7 follow. Although the actual data collection is using a single mode (diaries), the data collection system uses multiple modes with mail and telephone advance notifications and reminders. Figure 16.1 presents an overview of mixed-mode systems.

Mixed-Mode Survey System	*Rationale for Implementation*	*Effect on Survey Quality*
Contact Phase Mode Change		
Advance notification in different mode than **data collection**	▪ Correct sampling frame ▪ Raise response ▪ Enhance credibility/trust	▪ Reduce coverage and nonresponse error ▪ No threats to measurement if data collection single-mode
Recruitment / Screening / Selection in different mode than **data collection**	▪ Reduce cost ▪ Enhance efficiency ▪ Update / expand contact information for main mode	▪ Timeliness ▪ If pure screening, no threats to measurement ▪ If screening plus first part data collection in other mode potential mode effects on measurement

Figure 16.1. Types of mixed-mode systems (source de Leeuw, 2005, Figure 1)

Mixed-Mode Survey System	Rationale for Implementation	Effect on Survey Quality
Response Phase Mode Change		
Different (sample) persons by different modes when surveying **one sample** at one time period with one questionnaire	▪ Reduce costs ▪ Improve coverage ▪ Improve response	▪ Reduction of coverage and nonresponse error ▪ Mode effects on measurement confounded with subgroups
Different parts of a questionnaire by different modes when surveying one sample at one time point	▪ Improve privacy of measurement ▪ Reduce social desirability	▪ Improved data quality, especially with very sensitive questions
Same person with different modes at multiple time points (panel)	▪ Reduce costs	▪ Measurement differences causing confounding of time and mode effects
Different (whole) samples by different modes, often at different times with different questionnaires	▪ Comparative research ▪ Different research traditions ▪ Different coverage ▪ Different cost structure	▪ Coverage error ▪ Nonresponse error ▪ Measurement error ▪ Incomparability
Follow-up Phase Mode Change		
Reminders in different modes from mode in which all respondents are asked to complete questionnaire.	▪ Raise response	▪ Reduce nonresponse error ▪ If pure reminder no threats to measurement ▪ If reminder plus part data collection in other mode risk of potential mode effects on measurement
Partly based on:	Dillman (2000)	Balden (2004)

Figure 16.1. (Continued) Types of mixed-mode systems

16.3.1 Contact Phase Mode Change

16.3.1.1 Advanced notification in different mode than data collection
In the contact phase, modes may be mixed or changed entirely to accomplish prenotification and recruitment. A classical example is the use of paper advance

letters in telephone surveys. This mix is chosen, because it is easier to establish legitimacy and trust in an official letter that has a letterhead, contact information and signature, than with just a voice over the phone. That advance letters indeed work to reduce nonresponse in telephone surveys is shown by De Leeuw, Callegaro, Hox, Korendijk, and Lensvelt-Mulders (2007), who used meta-analysis to review a large number of prenotification experiments. In establishment surveys the opposite mix—a telephone precontact before a mail or web survey—has been found to be effective (Paxson, Dillman, & Tarnai, 1995). Business surveys face different methodological issues than household surveys, and a telephone conversation is far more efficient than a letter in getting past gate keepers and in identifying the targeted most knowledgeable respondent in the establishment. Another mix is a telephone invitation from a life interviewer for an IVR (Interactive Voice Response Survey, see Steiger Miller, & Conroy, Chapter 15). Finally, people may also be contacted by postal mail to deliver an incentive and/or encourage sampled individuals to go to the Internet and complete a questionnaire. As the actual data collection in these cases is *single-mode*, the mixed-mode system has no implication for measurement error, but will reduce nonresponse error: a win-win situation.

16.3.1.2 Advance notification to offer choice of mode

A quite different situation occurs when an advance notification is used to invite sample members to complete a questionnaire and leave it to the respondent to choose a specific data collection mode. This could be a paper mail advance letter with an invitation to complete a web survey, but also offering the opportunity to ask for a paper questionnaire. This is a form of concurrent multiple modes: both modes are being implemented at the same time (Balden, 2004). Another example of concurrent mixed-modes is the American lung association survey of asthma awareness among school nurses. In this survey postcards are sent to a random sample inviting them to participate online via an indicated web site or by telephone via a toll free number. A procedure like this is often used to reduce coverage error, but because the data collection itself is now multiple-mode, other errors come into the picture. First of all, self-selection may cause differences in socio-demographic variables and secondly the mode itself may cause measurement differences. The researcher has to decide which scenario is the best: multiple-mode with reduced coverage error at the price of increased measurement error or a single-mode approach with a larger coverage error component. In web surveys, where the risk of coverage error is still very high, researchers often opt for the multi-mode approach and take the risk of mode effects on measurements. Because self-selection and mode-effects are completely confounded in such designs, it is difficult to correct for mode effects in these cases.

16.3.1.3 Mode change to recruit or screen for eligibility

The same reasoning can also be applied to screening and selection. For reasons of time efficiency and costs, screening and selection is often done over the telephone. If the telephone conversation is *only* used for screening and recruitment purposes and the subsequent data collection is done in one single mode that is different from the screening mode, then again there is a win-win situation of increased efficiency without added mode effects in the main measurement phase. Examples are a telephone screening on health issues, followed by an in depth face-to-face interview, or a telephone screening followed by a mail survey. Sometimes a screening procedure is used to get additional address information to facilitate the main study. Again, if the data collection in the main study is by one single mode, there is a win-win situation. But with the increased interest in web surveys, the subsequent main study is often multiple-mode: a web survey for those with Internet access and a telephone survey for the remainder. Both modes are implemented at the same time, so a concurrent multiple mode system is used.

Often the screening and/or recruitment are part of a longer interview. If a respondent is eligible, an interview takes place and ends with a request for participation in coming surveys. This is quite common in longitudinal studies, but also in recruitment for Internet panels and access panels (Hoogendoorn & Sikkel, Chapter 25). In those cases more often than not different modes are used for the subsequent data collection periods: a form of sequential multiple-mode. Here the danger of mode effects on measurement is a serious risk, as it is hard to decide whether a change over time is a real change in the person surveyed or if it is caused by a change in mode. Time effects and mode effects in the results are then fully confounded.

16.3.2 Response Phase Mode Change

During the *response phase* both concurrent and sequential multiple-mode systems can be used. In a concurrent multiple mode design, two or more modes are implemented parallel within a certain time period; in a sequential design the different modes are implemented in sequential order during the data collection period. There are several situations in which these multiple mode systems can be employed.

16.3.2.1 Different persons by different modes within one sample
The first situation mentioned in Figure 16.1 is where one mode of data collection is used for some respondents of a sample and another mode for others in that same sample in order to collect the same data in the same time period. An example of a concurrent mixed-mode design for this situation is a paper mail survey with a web option. Another example is the asthma awareness survey among school nurses mentioned earlier that offers a choice for web or telephone. The aim of these designs is to reduce coverage bias and still complete the survey at reasonable costs. It is also assumed that giving a sample member a choice may reduce nonresponse, as certain persons may have specific mode preferences. There is no firm empirical evidence for this; Dillman, Clark, and West (1995) did not detect any improvement in response rate when respondents were given a choice between sending in a mail questionnaire and phoning in their answers. A similar conclusion was reached by Lozar Manfreda, Vehovar, and Batagelj (2001) who offered a choice of web and paper mail to respondents. Balden (2004) also reports that in his experience providing respondents in market research with choices does in general not improve the overall response rates; this includes choice combinations of mail/web,

mail/IVR, and phone/web. Still, giving respondent a choice may be a good option, as it may create goodwill and can save costs. In establishment surveys it is more usual than in household surveys to allow response by a chosen favorite method (i.e., paper, fax, Disk-by-Mail, web, Electronic Data Interchange or EDI).

Far more common than concurrent multiple-mode designs are sequential multiple-mode systems. Here the main goal is to reduce survey nonresponse. Usually an inexpensive mode is used as the main data collection mode for the whole sample and then a more expensive data collection mode is used for the nonresponse follow-up to improve response rates. This approach originates from the empirical work of Hochstim (1967), who compared three strategies of mixed-mode data collection: one starting with the expensive face-to-face interview, one starting with the less expensive telephone survey, and one starting with the modest mail survey. In two independent studies, Hochstim found that the three mixed-mode strategies were highly comparable regarding final response rate and completeness of questionnaires, and that substantive findings were virtually interchangeable. The only important difference was costs per interview, which varied considerably by strategy. These findings were corroborated by Siemiatycky (1979), who concluded that strategies beginning with mail and telephone and following-up with other methods, provided response rates as high as face-to-face, for only half of the costs.

In later years various studies used sequential mixed-mode strategies and showed that switching to a second and even third mode is an effective means of improving survey response, even for newer data collection methods such as IVR and the Internet (Dillman, Phelps, Tortorra, Swift, Kohrell, & Berck, 2002). Sequential mixed-mode surveys will increase response both for the general population (Brambilla & McKinlay, 1987; Fowler et al, 2002; Jackson & Boyle, 1991), for different racial and ethnic groupings (Beebe, Davern, McAlpine, Call, & Rockwood, 2005), for special groups like mothers with Medicaid-eligible children of different ethnic/racial background (Grembowski & Phillips, 2005), and for professionals, such as scientists (Wilkinson & Hines, 1991), paediatricians (McMahon, et al., 2003), and veterinarians (Wilkins, Hueston, Crawford, Steele, & Gerken, 1997). There is also evidence that a sequential mixed-mode design raises the response in establishment surveys (e.g., Jackson, 1993; Werking & Clayton, 1993).

Sequential mixed or multiple-mode data collection methods are effective in reducing nonresponse, but a coin has two sides and there is a potential for measurement error as the modes used may cause measurement differences. As different groups (e.g., early vs. late respondents) are measured using different modes, this may cause data comparability problems for these groups. Hochstim (1967) in his early study reported that substantive findings were virtually interchangeable and this study had much influence in accepting mixed-mode strategies. Later studies are less optimistic and emphasize the difference between visual communication and aural or auditory communication for interview versus mail and web surveys and its influence on measurement (e.g., Dillman & Christian, 2005; see also de Leeuw, Chapter 7).

16.3.2.2 Different parts of a questionnaire by different modes
A second form of mixed-mode is when different modes are used for a *subset* of questions in a questionnaire implemented for the whole sample during a single data collection period. Usually a mix of interview and self-administered forms is used to exploit the strong points of both methods. For instance, within an interview a self-administered form of data collection such as a paper questionnaire is used for sensitive questions to reduce social desirability and enhance privacy, as neither the interviewer nor any other person present will know the answers given. When a computer-assisted interview (CAPI) is used the computer may be handed over to the respondent to complete the sensitive questions in privacy using a CASI or Audio-CASI method. This situation has only positive points and is not a case for concern.

Other multiple mode designs for surveys of sensitive topics should be avoided. For instance, when one part of a sample is interviewed by a self-administered form (e.g., mail or web) and another part by telephone, mode effects with more self-disclosure in the self-administered form are to be expected (e.g., de Leeuw, 1992; Tourangeau & Smith, 1996; Tourangeau, Rasinski, Jobe, Smith, & Pratt, 1997). As a consequence, the two parts of the sample will not be comparable. Thus, general multiple mode approaches mixing interview and self-administered forms (e.g., in a sequential mixed-mode design, or offering a choice between web and telephone) are not recommended for surveys on sensitive topics.

16.3.2.3 Same persons with different modes at multiple time points
A third form of multiple modes in the data collection phase is a longitudinal study or a panel in which the same respondents are surveyed at different time points whereas different modes are used at these different time points. Here practical considerations and costs are the main reasons for this multiple mode approach. For example, the practical availability of contact information in the sampling frame. Sometimes addresses are available, but telephone numbers or email addresses are not and have to be collected first; sometimes no sampling frame is available and area probability sampling is the only option. This means that an initial contact with sampling units should be made using a face-to-face method.

Together with the greater flexibility of an interviewer to gain cooperation at the doorstep and the opportunities for optimal screening, a face-to-face interview is often the favorite choice for the base-line study of a panel. During this base-line interview, additional contact information (e.g., telephone number, e-mail address) is collected and where possible a less expensive method is used after the first wave to reduce overall survey costs. For instance, a combination of face-to-face interviews for the first wave and telephone surveys for the next is used for labor force surveys in several countries. Another example of a mixed-mode panel combines an initial face-to-face interview with mail surveys in the following waves. Sometimes modes alternate and after an initial face-to-face survey, telephone and mail surveys are employed with an occasional face-to-face survey interspaced at crucial points. For example, in longitudinal health surveys or in growth studies it may be necessary to include simple medical tests at regular times, which need a face-to-face contact.

There are many practical advantages for sequential mixed-mode studies in a panel design. On the other hand, there are problems from a data integrity point of view: time and mode effects are fully confounded and it is difficult to decide if a change over time is a real change over time or the result of a change of mode.

16.3.2.4 Different samples studied by different modes

The fourth and last variation in multiple mode data collection uses different modes for different populations or sub-groups. Reasons for this vary: different countries may have different survey traditions and/or different practical restraints. In a densely populated country face-to-face surveys are feasible, but in sparsely populated areas this may not be the case. Some countries have detailed registers and address information to ensure successful mail surveys, while in other countries area probability based samples are the only option. Low literacy levels can preclude mail surveys and in poor regions electronic equipment may be difficult to use. Furthermore, different data collection agencies may have different survey traditions and thus may differ in availability of experienced and trained staff needed for specific modes and other required resources. To enhance comparability, design factors should be kept constant as far as possible. For example, the International Social Survey Programme (ISSP) operates on the principle of 'keep as much the same as possible' across implementations. At the start of the ISSP the required mode was self-completion, but as new members joined in, the self-completion format proved unsuitable for populations with low literacy and face-to-face interviews were allowed (Skjåk & Harkness, 2003). An example from the United States is the Behavioral Risk Factor Surveillance System (BRFSS) of the Centers for Disease Control and Prevention (CDC) in which 15 states participate in monthly data collection. A standard core questionnaire was developed by CDC for the states to use and to provide data that could be compared across states. Data collection varies by state, which results in a single-mode approach within one state, but a mixed-mode design for the total study.

Although mode effects may cause apparent differences between countries, a single-mode approach is nevertheless not always feasible in international research. One may even argue that keeping modes the same across countries is enhancing the differences between countries, as a mode that is optimal for one country, may be a very poor choice for another country. For instance, selective nonresponse caused by large numbers of noncontacts (in face-to-face interviews) in secluded rural regions, may enhance small or nonexisting differences between countries. In planning cross-cultural and international studies a careful consideration should be made of the relative risk of mode effects in a mixed-mode approach compared to differential effects of other error sources in a single-mode approach.

In secondary analysis regularly different countries or cultures are compared on a variety of variables. Different populations are compared, using data that were collected for other purposes. Different data collection methods may have been used, but other and more serious differences may play a role too and threaten the internal validity of the conclusions. For instance, the studies that are combined may suffer from differential nonresponse, nonequivalence of questionnaires, and time differences in data collection. Here the predominant issue is not mixed-mode, but nonequivalence of design. A problem is that the primary data sources used in secondary research often do not report such differences in sufficient detail.

16.3.3 Follow-up Phase Mode Change

Reminders are an efficient tool to increase response, and as a consequence reminders are commonly used. Sometimes reminders employ the same mode of contact as the main data collection, for instance a postcard in a mail survey, an email in an Internet survey, or a telephone reminder in a telephone survey. Sometimes a different mode of contact is used for the follow-up contact. For example, time and costs constraints may prohibit in-person follow-ups in a face-to-face survey. A second, different mode for the follow-up may also lead to additional information about the sampling frame or improved contact information, (e.g., a telephone reminder to an internet or mail survey) and changing communication modes may improve the attention or novelty value of the reminder.

Persuasion letters are another form of a mixed-mode follow-up contact. Reluctant respondents in face-to-face and telephone surveys are sometimes sent a special persuasion letter, emphasizing the importance of complete measurement for the survey. In general persuasion letters should communicate the legitimacy and importance of the study to the reluctant respondent, and wherever possible, persuasion letters should be tailored to subgroups of refusers.

If the mode change only involves the follow-up reminder itself, potential measurement errors through mode effects are avoided, whereas the potential benefits of a second mode of communication can be exploited: a win-win situation just as when using prenotifications. When the follow-up is also used to collect additional data, then a potential mode effect may occur. If the follow-up takes the form of administering the full questionnaire in another mode to reduce nonresponse, it is a sequential mixed-mode approach; this was discussed in section 16.3.2.1. A special case is when a reduced questionnaire is used to reduce response burden and collect at least some data from nonrespondents. These data may shed light on selectiveness of nonresponse and can be used for weighting and adjustment. Preferably, this is done in the same mode as the main study, but practical constraints may force the researcher to use another mode. In this case the researcher should again decide which sources of error are the most important, and whether mode effects or nonresponse is the worst of two evils.

16.4 IMPLICATIONS

Depending on the survey situation one has to decide upon the optimum design, while appraising the different sources of error. Only after careful consideration can one decide if the expected mode effects are serious enough to avoid mixed-mode designs or if the advantages of mixing modes outweigh the risks. If a researcher opts for multiple data collection modes there are certain safeguards one can and should implement in the data collection procedure.

16.4.1 Designing for Mixed-Mode

Mode effects are important, and should be reduced in the design phase of the survey as far as possible. If multiple modes are used, it is useful to distinguish between two different situations: (a) there is one main data collection method and in addition one or more auxiliary data collection methods (e.g., a different method for nonresponse follow-up, a longitudinal survey with only recruitment face-to-face, but the data collection in all follow-up waves is by telephone), and,)b) there is a truly multiple mode design in which the different methods are equally important (e.g., a web/mail or web/telephone mix in which respondents are given the choice).

16.4.1.1 One preferred mode

In the first case, one main mode is chosen that accommodates the survey situation the best. This main or preferred mode is used to its maximum potential (see also Dillman, Chapter 9); the other modes are used as auxiliary or complementary modes only. As a consequence, the study design is optimized for that specific mode and the other modes are adapted to the preferred mode, and may therefore be suboptimal and not used to their fullest potential. This is the mixed-mode condition that Biemer and Lyberg (2003, p. 208–210) describe. An example is using a limited number of response categories for questions in a telephone survey with face-to-face follow-up. Potentially face-to-face surveys may use visual stimuli, such as response cards, which facilitate using longer lists of answer categories than in a telephone survey (e.g., seven- or nine-point scales in stead three- or five-point response scales). However, using different question formats may result in differences in response distributions (e.g., Sudman & Bradburn, 1974). Therefore, to ensure equivalence of answers the preferred or main telephone mode gets priority in questionnaire design and the auxiliary face-to-face follow-up interview is not used to its fullest potential. This is a special form of a mode-specific design (cf. Dillman, Chapter 9), and can best be described as a preferred-mode-specific design where the design is optimized for the main or preferred mode only. In a mixed-mode study that uses a preferred-mode-specific design one presents the same questions in the same layout, optimized for the preferred mode, with the risk of not using the auxiliary modes to their fullest potential.

16.4.1.2 Equivalent multiple modes

In the second case, there is not really a preferred versus an auxiliary mode, but all modes are equally important. For this specific situation two completely different strategies of questionnaire construction are in use: mode-specific design and unified mode design (Dillman, Chapter 9; Dillman 2000, 2007).

In a mode-specific design, the questionnaire is optimized for each mode separately, even if that results in different question formats between data collection modes. A classic example is using a seven-point answer scale with show card in a face-to-face interview, while using a two step unfolding format in a telephone survey, that is, first presenting a respondent with a three point scale, and in the second step asking for more detail. For example, the first question asks "are you satisfied, dissatisfied or somewhat in the middle," and after the answer "satisfied" the second question asks if this is "completely satisfied, mostly satisfied, or somewhat satisfied" (Groves, 1989). The same principle is frequently used in mixed-mode web and telephone surveys. In these mode specific designs the goal is to obtain the best possible data for each mode separately with the rationale that the combined data set will have the smallest overall error. This is justified only if one is interested in estimates for the *entire* sample. However, when subgroups (e.g., young vs. old) are to be compared, group membership may be confounded with mode effects (e.g., young mainly questioned by web survey whereas older people are interviewed by telephone) and group comparisons may be biased.

Therefore, the preferred strategy is to use *unified-mode* or *uni-mode design*. The goal of unified-mode or uni-mode design is to construct the questions and the questionnaire in such a way that the survey is not sensitive to mode effects. Examples of uni-mode design principles are to make response options the same across modes, not to use category labels in a visual mode if they cannot be used in the aural mode, not to use a 'check all that apply' format for a set of questions on an Internet survey if there is a telephone mode where all these questions are asked as a sequence of yes/no questions. Dillman (2000, 2007: p.232-240) presents a number of principles for unified-mode design that are helpful in minimizing mode differences both in specific mode designs with one preferred or main mode (preferred-mode-specific design) and in uni-mode designs. For a practical example of how these principles were used in constructing equivalent questionnaires for different modes, see de Leeuw (1992, pp 36-38),

16.4.1.3 Beyond unified mode design

Finally, one can go beyond designs that force different modes to use the same questions, by considering questions as stimuli that initiate a response process in the heads of the respondents. Thus, the perspective changes from offered stimulus to perceived stimulus. Using the same stimulus in different modes does not always guarantee that the same response process will be initiated. Schwarz (Chapter 2) discusses differences in the response process between aural and visual modes, which lead to different response biases, and therefore may lead to different countermeasures. For example, a question in a telephone survey remains not necessarily the same *perceived* stimulus to a respondent if that same question is posed in a web survey, since the visual mode may change the meaning of the question and may therefore present a different perceived stimulus to the respondent than the aural mode. Thus, in designing questions for a mixed-mode study, one should go one step further and aim at achieving cognitive equivalence, rather than literal uniformity of questions across modes. De Leeuw (2005) coined this *general mode design*, but also pointed out that fundamental, empirical research is still lacking in this field.

A prerequisite for successful general mode design is that the question designer understands how differences between modes affect the question-answer process and how they affect the way respondents perceive the question, process the information and select and communicate the response. Christian and

Dillman (2004) give examples of the influence of visual presentation on question meaning, and show how using a different question format in a web survey produces responses that are equivalent to a telephone survey.

A recent study by Christian, Dillman, and Smyth (2005) provides additional insight into how and why different wordings across survey modes lead to similar results. In a telephone interview, the question, "When did you start attending Washington State University?" led to only 13% of the respondents reporting the desired month and year. Instead, most respondents gave comments like, "last spring semester," "Fall 2002," or "This is my first semester." As in any good telephone interview, these responses were followed-up by the interviewer to get the desired response format. For the web survey, the decision was made to ask for write-ins of the date information, which was justified by the desire of the creators of the survey to place many questions on a single screen in a common format. In the initial web survey only 45% of the respondents answered correctly to the question of what month and year they started school, which was asked in a format desired by the programmers (mm/yyyy; two digits for month and four digits for year). As web surveys are self-administered, no interviewer assistance or follow-up is available and all help and information should be communicated through the web. Therefore, a series of experiments was carried out to improve this question through a series of visual design manipulations. By decreasing the size of the month box relative to the year box, replacing month and year with the more precise language of symbols, and placing those symbols in natural reading order ahead of the appropriate response boxes, the percent of people responding in the desired way increased from 45% to 95%. These results clearly illustrate how different wording approaches of the question (telephone and web survey) can lead to the same result, but through different mechanisms. In the telephone survey, the interviewer served as an intelligent system that could easily convert the answer to the desired format required by the CATI programming, and if necessary ask for more information. In the web survey, the emphasis was on answer space labeling and layout in order to get the respondents to respond in the desired format and avoid error messages. Thus, different wording produced the same results. Although the same wording, "What month and year did you begin the studies?" could have been used for both web and telephone, the experiment showed that it would not have improved the accuracy of the recorded answers.

Just as in comparative research, in generalized-mode design the burden is on the researcher to demonstrate that these different questions do indeed elicit equivalent responses. This requires that at least some questions are kept identical across different modes, so they can be used to gauge the equivalence of other questions in the questionnaire. This is similar to the strategy used to adjust responses in different modes to make them equivalent, a topic that is discussed in the next section.

16.4.2 Empirically Based Adjustment

Designing for multiple modes is important, but even after careful multiple-mode design it is possible that differences between modes still remain. To cope with these, it is useful to collect additional data in the survey on possible mode effects. These auxiliary data are first used to investigate the mode effects, and may be used later in the analysis to correct for mode differences by statistical means. For instance, if in a longitudinal survey different modes are used in successive measurement occasions (e.g., face-to-face interviews in the first wave, followed by telephone interviews in the second wave), it is not possible to decide whether a change over time is a real change in the person surveyed or if it is caused by a change in mode. The reason is that time effects and mode effects are fully confounded in the data. If at each time point a random subsample of respondents is investigated with the initial mode of the previous wave, and the majority with the main mode of the wave (e.g., in the second wave a small subsample is interviewed face-to-face as a reference sample, and the majority is interviewed by telephone as the intended mode for this second wave is telephone interviews) a strict mode comparison is feasible and will provide the researcher with information about mode effects that can be used for statistical adjustment. Thus, if a longitudinal study is considered with telephone interview for follow-up waves (or mailed questionnaires) and a face-to-face interview is chosen for the first recruitment wave, the preferred design is to embed a mode experiment in the first follow-up and use this for adjustment.

If for practical reasons a random subsample is not possible, for instance in an international study where some countries use mail/phone, and other countries use face-to-face interviews, limited mode experiments in each country still provides valuable information. In these studies one concentrates on those who can be interviewed with both modes, which of course is not necessarily a random sample of the whole country, but a relatively selective group (for instance, those with telephone access). In this group persons are assigned at random to each mode and a mode comparison is being performed. Thus, in a country that is sparsely populated, a mode comparison is performed in an area where it is still feasible to do both a face-to-face and a telephone interview. Another example, for respondents with internet access, a small mode experiment (e.g., telephone vs. web) may be embedded; even if this group is not a random subsample of the whole population, the experiment provides information that can be extrapolated to assess the risk of mode effects.

Finally, if embedded experiments are not possible at all, matching is an option. For example, in a concurrent mixed-mode survey, subjects may be matched in both modes on important variables, such as age, and education, to see if the matched groups produce responses that are different across the modes. Preferably, the variables on which matching takes place are measured independent of mode (e.g., register, sampling frame), but even if this is not possible, basic demographic questions are less mode sensitive than attitudinal questions, as respondents know the answer before the question is even posed (Balden, 2004). A similar approach is to use propensity score matching: logistic regression or equivalent procedures are used to predict which respondents end up in which mode and they are then matched on the predicted values (the propensity scores). Of course, matching is a much weaker design than a fully randomized embedded experiment with sub-sampling, or a limited experiment on a special subgroup. Still it may provide some insight in potential mode effects, and any empirical data are better than no data at all.

When mode effects are totally confounded with selection effects, meaning that answers between the two modes may differ because of the mode or because of the fact that different subgroups responded in different modes, and there is no auxiliary information, it is as good as impossible to adjust for mode effects and one has to fall back to ad hoc justifications.

16.5 CONCLUSION

There are several types of mixed-mode survey systems, as described in section 16.3 and summarized in Figure 16.1. Sequential mixed-mode *contacts* within a single-mode data collection do not pose any problems from a data integrity point of view. When different modes are only used for precontact, screening, and reminders and not for the data collection *itself*, mixing modes has only advantages. The main data collection is carried out in a single mode with known characteristics and data quality implications, and the (pre)contacts and follow-ups can be used to their special advantages: a win-win situation. Conversely, when multiple modes are being used for the data collection itself, either sequentially or concurrently, the situation is more problematic. In a mixed-mode data collection, questions of data integrity do play a role; for example, can data that are collected with different modes be combined and can data be compared across surveys or time points? There is only one situation in which a concurrent multiple mode has well documented positive effects on data quality. This is the case in which a second more private mode is used for a *subset* of special questions to ensure more self-disclosure and less social desirability (see also Lensvelt-Mulders, Chapter 24). These expected mode differences between self-administered and interviewer-administered surveys for sensitive and attitudinal questions are precisely the reason why researchers combine these two methods in one survey. Here the combined effect ensures better data. Examples are an additional paper questionnaire within a face-to-face interview, or an additional (Audio-) CASI-module within a CAPI interview. In all other cases, be it sequential or concurrent, mixed-mode approaches for data collection can have negative consequences for data integrity.

GLOSSARY OF KEY CONCEPTS

Adjustment. When different modes are used to collect data, an appropriate survey design allows for adjustment (removing mode differences) via statistical procedures.

Generalized mode design. Purposively constructing questions and questionnaires to be different in different modes with the goal of achieving cognitive equivalence of the perceived stimuli, thereby resulting in equivalent answers across modes.

Mixed-mode survey. A survey where multiple modes are used to communicate with the respondents. Modes can be mixed in the contact phase and in the actual data collection phase.

Mode effect. The effect that using a specific mode has on the responses that are obtained in that mode. Mode effects may be interpreted as a form of measurement bias.

Mode specific design. Writing questions and implementing a questionnaire in the best way for a mode, regardless of what might be done in another mode. That is, the questionnaire is optimized for each mode separately in an effort to improve the performance of individual survey modes, even if that results in different question formats across modes.

Preferred-mode-specific design. Designing a mixed-mode study where one mode is the primary or preferred mode, and other modes are seen as auxiliary. In this design the questionnaire is optimized for the primary mode and the questionnaires for the other (auxiliary) modes are adapted to the optimal design for the main mode.

Uni-mode design. From **unified** mode design; designing questions and questionnaires to provide the same stimulus in all survey modes in order to reduce differences in the way respondents respond to the survey questions in the different modes.

Chapter 17

Weighting Survey Data

Paul P. Biemer
RTI International and University of North Carolina

Sharon L. Christ
University of North Carolina

17.1 INTRODUCTION

After the survey data have been collected and all the essential steps of data processing (data entry, coding, editing, etc.) have been completed, a critical step must be implemented before the data can be analyzed. The survey data must be appropriately weighted. The weighting process essentially involves creating a new variable, say w_i, for each respondent (labeled i) in the sample that will be referred to as the *weight* associated with the respondent. The weight can be interpreted as the number of individuals in the target population represented by the sample respondent. As an example, a weight of 100 indicates that the respondent represents himself/herself and 99 other persons in the target population. Except in special cases, $w_i \geq 1$ for all respondents, because at a minimum, a respondent represents himself/herself, and $w_i = 0$ for all nonrespondents. In most practical situations, the w_i are not all equal even when all the sample members were selected with equal probability. This is due to so-called *post-survey weight adjustments* which attempt to reduce the standard errors of the estimates and/or compensate for the effects on the estimates of survey nonresponse and frame noncoverage. These adjustments allocate additional weight to some survey respondents who are selected to represent persons missed due to an incomplete frame or nonresponse. Therefore, even though the sample may be selected with equal probability, the weights assigned to the survey respondents can vary considerably.

Sometimes a data analyst ignores the weights and treats the data as if they were a simple random sample with no nonresponse or coverage error. This is equivalent to setting $w_i = 1$ for all i which usually results in biased estimates because the biasing effects of unequal probability sampling and missing data have not been removed from the estimates. In some cases, ignoring the weights may be justified but often it is done as a matter of convenience or because the analysis package does not accommodate unequal probability sampling.

It is easy to demonstrate that, when the weights are not all equal, a very different estimate can result when the weights are ignored from when they are properly applied in an analysis. For example, let n_r denote the number of respondents in the sample and consider the estimation of the population mean, $\overline{Y}$. If the weights are ignored, the estimator of $\overline{Y}$ is the simple expansion mean of the sample,

$$\overline{y} = \frac{1}{n_r}\sum_{i=1}^{n_r} y_i \qquad (17.1)$$

where y_i is the observation on the ith sampled unit. The preferred estimator is the weighted estimator of $\overline{Y}$ given by

$$\overline{y}_w = \frac{\sum_{i=1}^{n_r} w_i y_i}{\sum_{i=1}^{n_r} w_i}. \qquad (17.2)$$

It can be shown that $\overline{y}_w$ is essentially unbiased, whereas $\overline{y}$ has bias given by $\frac{-Cov(y_i,w_i)}{\overline{w}}$ where $\overline{w}$ denotes the mean weight (Kish, 1987 & 1992). Therefore, unless the weights are uncorrelated with the observations, y_i, $\overline{y}$ produces biased estimates of $\overline{Y}$.

The goal of this chapter is to present the essential concepts and principles of weighting using illustrations from very elementary survey designs such as simple random sampling and stratified random sampling. However, as will be described, the basic ideas of weighting carry over to more complex survey designs and sampling situations. This chapter does not provide comprehensive coverage of all the techniques of survey weighting, but rather focuses on a few techniques and ideas that illustrate how survey weights are constructed and accomplish their vital role in survey inference.

17.2 BASIC CONCEPTS OF WEIGHTING

For the purposes of describing the goals and objectives of weighting, it is useful to define three populations: the *target population* (or *universe*), the *frame population*, and the *respondent population*. As shown in Figure 17.1, these populations are nested within one another with the target population encompassing the frame population which in turn encompasses the respondent population. As shown in the figure, the sample is a very small subset of the respondent population. Weighting attempts to take this tiny sample and enlarge it to the level of the target population (the largest rectangle).

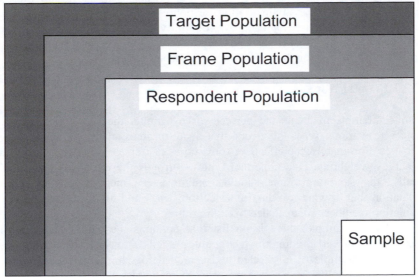

Figure 17.1. The correspondence among the Target, Frame and Respondent Populations, and the Sample

The target population is sometimes also referred to as the *inferential population*. It is the population to be studied in the survey and for which the basic inferences from the survey will be made. For example, a study of child health and well-being may infer to the population of all children in the country between the ages of 0 and 14 years of age. A study of biohazardous wastes may infer to all manufacturers and industrial establishments that produce such matter as by-products from their operations. The target population is regarded as the ideal population to be studied. In practice, this ideal is seldom achieved.

In order to select a sample from the population, one must compile a list (or frame) of all persons or units in the target population so that an appropriate sampling scheme can be implemented. For example, the sampling scheme may specify that every 120th unit on the frame be selected after sorting the list alphabetically. The subset of the target population that is represented by the sampling frame is referred to as the frame population.

Finally, the respondent population is a purely hypothetical concept because it is impossible to identify all the members of this population. It is defined as that subset of the frame population that is represented by units who would respond to the survey if selected. To illustrate the bias associated with survey nonresponse, Cochran (1977) supposed that the frame population were divided into two strata—the respondent stratum and the nonrespondent stratum. Persons selected for the survey who respond are assumed to be randomly selected from the respondent stratum and those that do not respond may be regarded as representing the nonrespondent stratum. Through this simple device, Cochran developed a formula for the bias due to nonresponse that we shall subsequently exploit in our discussion of nonresponse adjustment.

Understanding the motivation for the various components of the survey weights requires an understanding of the four primary reasons for weighting: reduction of frame error, compensation for nonresponse error, repairing sample misrepresentations caused by unequal probability sampling, and improving the precision of the estimates through the use of auxiliary information. The remainder of this section discusses four topics in some detail.

17.2.1 Frame Error

Despite attempts to create the perfect survey frame, the frame can still be subject to various types of errors that lead to inaccuracies in the survey estimates. Fortunately, the effects of some types of frame errors can be reduced by survey weighting. One important type of error is the erroneous exclusion. Ideally, the sampling frame should contain every member of the target population but, owing to the imperfections in building the frame, some population members are excluded from the frame.

As an example, there is no list that contains the names and contact information for all children in the country aged 0 to 14. To sample this population, a sample of is selected and screened for children within this age range. This sampling and screening process may miss both households and children that are part of the target population, resulting in noncoverage error because some children in the target population have a 0 probability of being selected for the survey.

In addition to noncoverage errors, other frame errors can introduce bias into the estimation process. As an example, the frame may include units that are not part of the target population (referred to as *erroneous inclusions*) or may include duplicate listings of the same persons or units (sometimes referred to generally as *frame multiplicity*). The effect on weighting of these errors will also be discussed subsequently. Initially, we assume that the only error arising from the sampling frame is noncoverage error and discuss how weighting can be used to compensate for this type of error.

Let N_F denote the number of eligible (nonduplicated) persons on the sampling frame and let N denote the number of eligible (nonduplicated) persons in the target population. When $N_F < N$, the frame is said to contain noncoverage error since the $N - N_F$ persons who are not on the frame have 0 probability of being selected.

To understand the nature of the noncoverage bias, assume that a SRS sample of size n is selected from the frame and ignore any nonresponse (i.e., assume the response rate is 100%). Let $\overline{Y}$ and $\overline{Y}_F$ denote the target population mean and the frame population mean, respectively. Note that the usual estimator of $\overline{Y}$, denoted by $\overline{y}$ in (17.1), is unbiased for $\overline{Y}_F$, but is a biased estimator of $\overline{Y}$ unless the difference between the means is 0, i.e. unless $B_F = \overline{Y}_F - \overline{Y} = 0$. B_F is referred to as the frame noncoverage bias in the estimate, $\overline{y}$ and is 0 if the frame and target population means are equal. It can be shown that the bias can also be written as

$$B_F = \gamma_{NF}(\overline{Y}_F - \overline{Y}_{NF}) \qquad (17.3)$$

(see, for example, Biemer & Lyberg, 2003) where $\gamma_{NF} = 1 - N_F/N$ is the noncoverage rate, i.e., the proportion of the target population that is not covered by the frame and $\overline{Y}_{NF}$ is the mean of the non-frame, population units, i.e., the mean of the units represented by the darkest shaded region in Figure 17.1.

As an example, in a random-digit-dialed (RDD) survey, persons living in non-telephone households are necessarily excluded even though they may be included in the target population. In the U.S., the proportion γ_{NF} is approximately 0.13—that is, 13% of the households in the U.S. have no working, land-line telephone in the household and therefore, have a 0 chance of being selected by an RDD survey. Inferences based on RDD samples are subject to a bias if they purport to apply to the total population including these nontelephone households.

To illustrate the potential noncoverage bias, suppose that the proportion of persons who smoke tobacco is 28.8% for persons in telephone households and 49.6% for persons in nontelephone households. The noncoverage bias for this characteristic when the target population includes both telephone and nontelephone households is $0.13 \times (0.288-0.496) = -0.027$ or -2.7 percentage points. Thus, estimates of the proportion of the total population that smokes tobacco will be underestimated from the RDD survey by almost 3 percentage points unless a weighting adjustment designed to reduce this bias is used. As we shall see, a noncoverage weighting adjustment is not likely to eliminate the noncoverage bias in an estimator but it reduces it to some extent. (For a discussion on the effectiveness of noncoverage adjustments for RDD surveys, see Massey & Botman, 1988.)

17.2.2 Nonresponse Error

To understand how survey weighting can partially compensate for nonrsponse error, we consider Cochran's (1977) two subpopulation model described earlier. Let $\overline{Y}_R$ denote the mean of the respondent subpopulation. The complement of this population within the frame is the nonrespondent subpopulation defined as the subset of the frame represented by the nonrespondents in the sample. This is the medium dark shaded region in Figure 1. Its mean is denoted by $\overline{Y}_{NR}$. Denote the proportion of the frame population that belongs to the respondent subpopulation as γ_R. For SRS, γ_R may be interpreted as the expected response rate for the survey because under SRS, $\gamma_R = E(n_r/n)$. In other words, if the same survey could be repeated many times under identical general conditions each time, the average response rate across the replicates would be γ_R.

Technically, estimates based only on survey respondents with no adjustment for nonresponse represent the respondent subpopulation only, not the entire frame population. Inferences to either the frame or target populations are, therefore, biased even though they may be unbiased for the respondent subpopulation. To see this, consider the expected value of the estimator in (17.1). Under SRS, the respondents in the sample may be considered to be an SRS of the respondent subpopulation and, thus, the expected value of $\bar{y}_r$ is

$\bar{Y}_R$; i.e., the sample mean is unbiased for the respondent subpopulation mean. For estimating the frame mean, the bias is $B_R = \bar{Y}_R - \bar{Y}_F$ which may be rewritten as

$$B_R = \gamma_{NR}(\bar{Y}_R - \bar{Y}_{NR}) \tag{17.4}$$

(Biemer & Lyberg, 2003) where $\gamma_{NR} = (1-\gamma_R)$ is the expected nonresponse rate for the survey; that is, the proportion of the frame population in the nonrespondent subpopulation. Note the similarity of equations (17.4) and (17.3). We will return to this point later in the chapter.

As an example, suppose n=5,000 individuals are selected with SRS and a total of 3200 persons responded to the survey for an overall response rate of n_r/n=0.64 or 64%. Suppose the mean income of the respondent subpopulation is $\bar{y}_R$=\$64,000. Suppose further that, using an external source such as administrative records, the mean income for the nonrespondent subpopulation was estimated to be $\bar{y}_{NR}$=\$51,000. We can estimate B_R by substituting these sample quantities for the population quantities in (4) which yields the estimate $\hat{B}_R$=0.36× (\$64,000-\$51,000) = \$4,680. Thus, we estimate that the mean income of the frame population will be overestimated by almost \$4,700 as a result of nonresponse. Through the use of post-survey weighting adjustments, it may be possible to eliminate this bias or at least reduce it.

Finally, we note that the noncoverage and nonresponse biases are additive; the overall bias is the sum of the noncoverage and nonresponse biases as follows:

$$B = B_F + B_R = \gamma_{NF}(\bar{Y}_F - \bar{Y}_{NF}) + \gamma_{NR}(\bar{Y}_R - \bar{Y}_{NR}) \tag{17.5}$$

(Biemer & Lyberg, 2003). The post-survey adjustments are designed to reduce the effects of each source of bias separately as well as cumulatively. For example, post-stratification adjustments that are designed to reduce the noncoverage bias can also reduce nonresponse bias to some extent. This point is also explored later in the chapter.

17.2.3 Unequal Selection Probabilities

Sample weights are needed to correct the sample for the effects of unequal probability sampling. Most surveys give higher probabilities of selection to some frame units than to others, a technique referred to as oversampling. For example, consider a survey of an area where 10% of the residents live in rural communities and 90% live in urban communities. An equal probability selection method (referred to as *epsem*) sample of size 5000 residents would yield approximately 500 residents from the rural communities and 4500 from the urban communities. To obtain a sample yielding estimates of approximately equal precision for both rural and urban characteristics, the population would be divided into rural and urban stratum and the 2500 residents would be selected in each stratum. This causes problems for estimates of the whole target population because now rural residents are over-represented in the sample at five times their rate in the population and urban residents are under-represented at 5/9 their rate in the population. Thus, inferences to the total population would be biased toward the rural residents due to the oversampling of this stratum. To correct for this, weights are introduced to ensure that the rural residents only contribute 10% of the estimate of the population and the urban residents contribute 90% of the estimate.

17.2.4 Sampling Variance Reduction

Finally, post-survey weighting often incorporates factors that result in substantial variance reduction through *ratio estimation* and *post-stratification*. A ratio estimator uses *auxiliary information* to form a weight that increases the efficiency of an estimator. An auxiliary variable is essentially another characteristic, X, of the sample units that are correlated with the characteristic of interest, Y. The population mean of the X's, denoted by $\overline{X}$ is assume to be known with certainty.

To illustrate, suppose we wish to estimate the average income of some population where we know the income of every member of a population as of five years ago. These data, denoted by X, constitute the auxiliary data because it is data obtained from sources outside of the survey. Suppose a SRS sample is drawn and the current income of each person in the sample, denoted by Y, is obtained. Let $\overline{x}$ denote the sample mean of the auxiliary data and let $\overline{y}$ denote the sample mean for the current survey data. Finally, let $\overline{X}$ denote the mean income for the entire population based upon the auxiliary data. The ratio estimator is then defined as

$$\overline{y}_R = \frac{\overline{y}}{\overline{x}}\overline{X} = \sum_{i=1}^{n} w_{Ri} y_i \tag{17.6}$$

where $w_{Ri} = \frac{1}{n\overline{x}}\overline{X}$ is a ratio weight. Because the previous income data, X, is expected to be highly correlated with the current income data, Y, (6) is likely to be a much more precise estimator of $\overline{Y}$ than $\overline{y}$. A proof of this and a comparison of simple expansion and ratio estimators can be found in many sampling theory textbooks; for examples, see Cochran, (1977), or Lohr, (1999).

Post-stratification is closely related to both ratio estimation and stratification. As the name implies, stratification involves stratifying the sample based upon characteristics of the units that are only known after data collection. Similar to ratio estimation, post-stratification requires that the post-strata totals are known with certainty.

For the previous illustration, suppose the number of households in the population is known for each of three household sizes—1, 2, and 3 or more— and denote these totals by N_h, h=1,2,3. The survey collections information on household income as well as household size. Denote the mean incomes for each household size by $\bar{y}_h$, h=1, 2, 3, and let n_h denote the number of households of each size in the sample. The post-stratification is estimator of income is

$$\bar{y}_{pst} = \sum_{h=1}^{3} \frac{N_h}{N} \bar{y}_h = \sum_{i=1}^{n} w_{pst,i} y_i \qquad (17.7)$$

where the post-stratification weight for unit i in stratum h is $w_{pst,i} = \dfrac{N_h}{N} \dfrac{1}{n_h}$.

These post-stratification weights as well as the ratio adjustment weights are often incorporated into the last stage of weighting.

17.3 CONSTRUCTING THE SAMPLE WEIGHTS

In this section, we describe a general approach to creating sampling weights for the purposes described in the previous section. Suppose a sample of n persons is selected with known selection probabilities, π_i, i=1,...,n. In most survey situations, the final survey weight, say w_i for observation i, is the product of three weight components. The first component, w_{Bi}, is often referred to as the *base* (or *design*) weight because it is the starting point for weight construction and derives from the survey design. It is simply the inverse of the probability of selection for unit i. The other weight components are regarded essentially as adjustments to the base weight.

There are two types of adjustments: one to compensate for nonresponse and one to compensate for noncoverage. The latter weight, referred to as a *post-stratification adjustment factor*, often does double duty in that it also incorporates ratio adjustment factors to reduce sampling variance. These weight adjustments are discussed in some detail subsequently. Thus, the final weight for the ith observation is the product of three components:

$$w_i = w_{Bi} \times w_{NRi} \times w_{NCi} \qquad (17.8)$$

where w_{NRi} is the nonresponse adjustment factor and w_{NCi} is the post-stratification adjustment factor.

For weights that are constructed using the principles in this chapter, the following properties hold:

1. The sum of the base weights over the sample respondents estimates N_R, the size of the respondent population; $\sum_{i=1}^{n_r} w_{Bi} = \hat{N}_R$.

2. The sum of the products of the base weight and the nonresponse adjustment factors over the sample observations estimates the size of the frame population: $\sum_{i=1}^{n_r} w_{Bi} w_{NRi} = \hat{N}_F$.

3. The sum of the final weights over the sample respondents estimates the target population size: $\sum_{i=1}^{n_r} w_i = \hat{N}$.

These three properties can be used to check the weights to identify errors in their computation. For example, if the sum of the base weights exceeds the known target population size, the calculation of the base weights should be checked for errors. In addition, these properties can serve as a guide in deriving the appropriate adjustment factors to apply to the base weights as we shall see.

17.3.1 Base Weights

Base weights are the simplest weights to construct since they are just the inverse of the probabilities of selection of the sample units (Horvitz and Thompson, 1952); i.e., $w_{Bi} - \dfrac{1}{\pi_i}$ where π_i is the selection probability for the ith sample observation. For many survey designs, π_i is fairly easy to compute. For epsem sampling, $\pi_i = n/N_F$ for every unit in the sample and thus $w_{Bi} = N_F/n$ for all i. Note that, consistent with Property 1,

$$\sum_{i=1}^{n_r} w_{Bi} = (n_r/n)N_F$$ is an estimate of N_R, the size of the respondent subpopulation.

For stratified sampling where epsem sampling occurs in each stratum, the selection probability for the ith unit sampled in stratum h is n_h/N_h where N_h is the population size and n_h is the sample size for the hth stratum. Thus, the weight for the ith unit sampled in stratum h is given by,

$$w_{Bhi} = \frac{N_h}{n_h} \tag{17.9}$$

For multi-stage sampling, the probability of selection is computed as the product of the selection probabilities for each stage of sampling. For example, for three stage sampling, the probability of selecting unit k in secondary j in primary i is:

$P(\text{unit } i, j, k \text{ selected}) = P(\text{primary } i \text{ selected})$
$\times P(\text{secondary } j \text{ selected}|\text{primary } i \text{ selected})$ $\tag{17.10}$
$\times P(\text{tertiary } k \text{ selected}|\text{secondary } j \text{ in primary } i \text{ selected})$

For example, primaries, secondaries and tertiaries are selected with equal probability with replacement at each stage, then

$$P(\text{unit } i, j, k \text{ selected}) = \frac{n \; n_i \; n_{ij}}{N \; N_i \; N_{ij}} \qquad (17.11)$$

where n is the number of primaries selected from N primaries, n_i is the number of secondaries selected from the N_i secondaries in primary i and n_{ij} is the number of tertiary units selected from N_{ij} tertiary units in secondary j. Therefore, the weight for this unit is given by

$$w_{Bijk} = \frac{N \; N_i \; N_{ij}}{n \; n_i \; n_{ij}} \qquad (17.12)$$

The probabilities of selection for many other basic sampling designs can be found in any sampling textbook (see, for example, Cochran, 1977 or more recently Lohr, 1999).

17.3.1.1 Example 1

To illustrate the basic principles for creating base weights, we use data from the National Survey of Child and Adolescent Well-Being (NSCAW) which is a survey of abused and neglected children in the U.S. (See Dowd, Kinsey, Wheeless, Suresh, & NSCAW, 2002, for a description of the survey.) The target population consists of all children in the United States who are subjects of child abuse or neglect investigations. The sampling frame is comprised of lists in each county of all children for whom an allegation of child abuse or neglect had been filed and investigated within the last month.

The sample design is essentially a stratified two stage design. The primary sampling units are counties and the second stage units are children within the counties who satisfy the survey eligibility criteria. For a given stratum h, the probability that the jth child, in the ith county is selected into the sample is the product of the county selection probability, denoted by π_{hi} and the probability that the child is selected given that the child's county is selected, denoted by π_{hij}. The inverse of this product is the base weight and is given by

$$w_{Bhidj} = \frac{1}{\pi_{hi}} \times \frac{1}{\pi_{hij}} \qquad (17.13)$$

The sum of the base weights for all sampled units within a stratum is an estimate of the total number of eligible children within that stratum. The sum of these stratum totals is an estimate of all eligible children in the population.

Counties were selected without replacement with probabilities proportional to size (referred to as πps sampling to distinguish it from *with* replacement with probability proportional to size or *pps* sampling). Thus, the selection probability for county (h, i) is $n_h N_{hi}/N_h$ where n_h is the number of PSU's selected from stratum h, N_{hi} is the number of eligible children in county (h,i) and N_h is the total number of eligible children in stratum h. Likewise, the selection probability for child (h, i, j) was computed as n_{hi}/N_{hi} where n_{hi} is the number of children selected in the ith county and as N_{hi} is the number of children in the in the county. With these definitions, the base weight in (11) becomes

$$w_{Bhij} = \frac{N_h}{n_h N_{hi}} \times \frac{N_{hi}}{n_{hi}} = \frac{N_h}{n_h} \times \frac{1}{n_{hi}} \qquad (17.14)$$

As an example, suppose that Stratum 4 contains 100 counties of which $n = 5$ counties were selected for the survey. One of the counties selected was county #57 with 810 eligible children. Of these, 20 children were selected. There are a total of 23,028 children in the entire stratum. The weights for these 20 children are the same and are equal to

$$w_{Bhidj} = \frac{23{,}028}{5} \times \frac{1}{20} = 230.28$$

17.3.2 Nonresponse adjustment

Little and Rubin (1987) consider a model for the response process that assigns a probability, π_{Ri} to the ith individual in the sample representing the propensity of the individual to respond to a given survey design and protocol. In their approach, the survey response is just another stage of *pps* sampling and can be treated as such in the nonresponse adjustment process. Thus, the probability that person i is (a) selected for the survey and, (b) when asked to participate in the survey, complies with the request is the product of two probabilities as follows:

$$P(i \text{ selected and responds}) = P(i \text{ selected}) \times P(i \text{ responds}|i \text{ selected}) \qquad (17.15)$$
$$= \pi_{Bi} \pi_{Ri}$$

Just as the base weight is the inverse of the probability of selection, the nonresponse adjustment can be viewed as the inverse of the estimated probability of responding to the survey or the response propensity. Thus, letting $w_{NRi} = (\pi_{Ri})^{-1}$, the nonresponse corrected weight is $w_{Bi} w_{NRi}$.

Failure to explicitly adjust the weights for nonresponse still implicitly adjusts them using a very crude estimate of the response propensity. The unadjusted estimator is essentially equivalent to assuming every unit in the sample has the same propensity to respond that is equal to the survey response rate. It is often possible to do much better than this crude adjustment if data are available on both respondents and nonrespondents that are correlated with the characteristics to be estimated.

17.3.2.1 Weighting class adjustments

There are several ways to compute the response propensity for each unit in the sample. The simplest approach is the weighting class adjustment (WCA) which divides the sample into groups based upon variables that are known for both respondents and nonrespondents and are thought to be related to response propensity. For example, response rates often vary by the age and gender of the sample members. If the ages and genders of nonrespondents are known, then all sample members can be classified into age by gender groups or weighting classes. The response rate for the weighting class (or WCA cell) is taken as the response propensity for each sample member in the class. The nonresponse adjustment for the ith respondent is simply his or her base weight, w_{Bi} divided by the response rate for the cell to which the ith respondent belongs. If the weighting classes are chosen so that the true response propensities do not vary much within each cell, the bias due to nonresponse will be very small. In fact, nonresponse bias will be completely eliminated if there is no variation in true response propensities within the WCA cells.

Consider a WCA table with C cells labeled $c = 1,..,C$. For some particular cell, say c^*, the weighted response rate is

$$RR_{Wc^*} = \frac{\sum_{i=1}^{n_{rc^*}} w_{Bi}}{\sum_{i=1}^{n_{c^*}} w_{Bi}} \tag{17.16}$$

where the sum in the numerator extends over the n_{rc^*} respondents in cell c^* and the denominator extends over all n_{c^*} sample members in cell c^*. Then for every respondent i in cell c^*, the adjustment factor is $w_{NRi} = (RR_{Wc^*})^{-1}$.

It can be shown that the contribution to total nonresponse bias for $\bar{y}_W$ from cell c^* is

$$B_{Rc^*} = P_{c^*} \gamma_{NRc^*} (\bar{Y}_{Rc^*} - \bar{Y}_{NRc^*}) \tag{17.17}$$

where P_{c^*} is the proportion of the frame population belonging to cell c^*, γ_{NRc^*} is the expected nonresponse rate for units in c^*, $\bar{Y}_{Rc^*}$ and $\bar{Y}_{NRc^*}$ are the means of the respondents and nonrespondents, respectively, in c^*. Thus, an equivalent way to view the WCA method is that it attempts to minimize the difference $\bar{Y}_R - \bar{Y}_{NR}$ within the weighting classes. Then it assigns the weighted mean of the respondents within a cell to all the nonrespondents in that cell. If the cells are chosen so that $(\bar{Y}_{Rc^*} - \bar{Y}_{NRc^*})$ is very small, especially when P_{c^*} is large, the overall nonresponse bias will also be small.

17.3.2.2 Example 2
To illustrate the WCA nonresponse adjustment procedure, we return to the NSCAW baseline interview data. The overall response rate for the NSCAW survey was 65%, which varied across subgroups of the populations. To correct for the potential bias due to nonresponse, the base weights can be adjusted using the WCA method.

For each investigated child, child welfare agencies recorded the age, gender, and race of the child, whether or not the allegation of child abuse or neglect was substantiated, and other child and family characteristics. The variables as well as urbanicity of the PSU, the size of the PSU and second stage sampling domain for the child can be used to form the weighting class cells for the nonresponse adjustment. For this illustration, we consider a simplified WCA based on only two variables: age and gender.

The WCA cells and their respective calculations are shown in Table 17.1. The response rate for each cell is computed using equation (16). For example, the sum of the respondent base weights for the category "males 11 years old and older" is 99,465. This may be interpreted as the number of males 11 years old and older in the respondent subpopulation that are represented by this category of respondents in the sample. The sum of the base weights for all sample members in this cell is 178,462. This may be interpreted as the total number of children in this class in the frame population. Thus, the weighted estimate of the response rate for this class is 0.557. This may be interpreted as the estimated response propensity for the NSCAW baseline survey for males 11 years old and older. The response propensities for the other five cells are computed in the same manner.

Table 17.1 NSCAW Response Propensities for Age by Gender Weighting Classes

	Female	Male
0–2 years	$\dfrac{121087.61}{165680.68} = 0.7308$	$\dfrac{122433.19}{169565.80} = 0.7220$
3–10 years	$\dfrac{278199.40}{439687.34} = 0.6327$	$\dfrac{302339.40}{465352.78} = 0.6497$
11+ years	$\dfrac{143090.47}{223206.41} = 0.6411$	$\dfrac{99465.01}{178461.88} = 0.5573$

The weighting class adjustment for a cell is the inverse of the cell response propensity, that is, for each child, i, in the $c*$, $w_{NRi} = (RR_{Wc*})^{-1}$. For example, to obtain the nonresponse adjusted weight for a child in the WCA cell corresponding to females aged 3–10 years old, the base weights for these children computed in Example 1 are multiplied by $w_{NRi} = 1/0.6327 = 1.58$.

17.3.2.3 Model-based adjustment methods

There are potentially more effective methods for estimating the response propensities for various subgroups of the population and using these estimates to adjust the data for nonresponse. One widely used method involves applying logistic regression to estimate the response propensity.

Let R_i be an indicator variable associated with every sample member which is 1 if sample member i responds and is 0 otherwise. Let X_{ji} for $j = 1$,

2,..., p denote p variables that are available on both respondents and nonrespondents and are believed to be correlated with R_i. The X_{ji} variables are analogous and may be identical to variables used to form the weighting classes in the WCA method.

The logistic regression of R_i on X_{1i}, ..., X_{pi} can be used to estimate the response propensity, $P(R_i=1| X_{ji})$. Then the nonresponse weight adjustment factor can be computed as $w_{NRi} = [\hat{P}(R_i = 1 | X_{ji})]^{-1}$ where $\hat{P}(R_i = 1 | X_{ji})$ is the logistic regression estimate of P $(R_i=1| X_{ji})$.

The advantage of the response propensity modeling method is that it combines dummy and continuous variables to fit a wide range of models that would be impossible to duplicate with the WCA scheme. This can lead to better fitting models and more effective nonresponse adjustments. Interactions among the indicator variables are analogous to the cross-classification cells used in the WCA method. In fact, the WCA method using classification cells formed by the classification variables X_{ji} is equivalent to using a fully saturated logistic regression model with these same predictor variables. The advantage of the logistic modeling approach is that unsaturated models can also be used which is a systematic way of collapsing cells that are too small to be used in a weighting class adjustment.

An important disadvantage of the modeling approach is that the adjustment factors, w_{NRi}, may be quite unstable which can lead to widely varying and extreme weights. One way to reduce this variation is to group the response propensities into classes and use an average value of $\hat{P}(R_i = 1 | X_{ji})$ in computing the w_{NRi}. This can diminish the effectiveness of the weighting adjustment for the nonresponse bias reduction (Vartivarian & Little, 2002).

17.3.3 Post-stratification Adjustments

Post-stratification shares several similarities with WCA but is aimed at and achieves somewhat different results. To post-stratify the sample, the respondents in the sample are divided into cross-classification cells similar to the weight class cells described earlier. There are two important differences, however. First, only the information on respondents is needed to form these cells, removing the restriction that the cross-classification variables be known for nonrespondents. Second, in forming the cells, the objective is to group together respondents who have very similar responses with regard to the key survey variables; that is, the within adjustment cell variance of the y_i's should be as small as possible. Third, we require accurate information on the total number of persons in the population (either the frame or target population) for each cell in the cross classification table. The post-stratification adjustment (PSA) multiplies the weight of each individual in an adjustment cell by a constant so that the weight total in each cell agrees with the population totals.

PSAs are used to address a number of deficiencies in the sampling and data collection process. If the known cell total are target population totals, PSA reduces the noncoverage bias; however, PSA factors can also reduce sampling variances. If the target population totals are not known, the PSAs can be performed using the frame totals to stabilize the sampling variances of the estimates. Moreover, if part of the original sampling frame was intentionally removed prior to sampling, adjusting to the original frame totals can reduce the noncoverage bias associated with the use of the reduced frame. Finally, PSAs can be used in lieu of or in combination with nonresponse adjustments to reduce nonresponse bias.

To implement the method, we begin by cross-classifying the respondents in the sample into L mutually exclusive and exhaustive PSA cell labeled $h = 1$, ..., L. These cells need not be the same as those used for nonresponse adjustment. For household surveys, cross-classifying into age, race and sex cells is common because the target population totals for these cells are available from the most recent population census. Let N_h, $h = 1,...,L$ denote these totals where $N_1 + \cdots + N_L = N$, the target population total. Then the noncoverage adjustment factor for the $i*$ unit in a particular cell of the table denoted by $h*$ is

$$w_{NCh*i*} = \frac{N_{h*}}{\sum_{i=1}^{n_{rh*}} w_{Bh*i} w_{NRh*i}}. \tag{17.18}$$

With this adjustment, the sum of the post-stratified adjusted weights for cell $h*$ will total N_{h*}:

$$\sum_{i=1}^{n_{rh*}} w_{Bh*i} w_{NRh*i} w_{NCh*i} = N_{h*} \tag{17.19}$$

When the totals N_h are target population totals, the PSA can reduce the noncoverage bias if the adjustment cells are suitably chosen. A formula similar to (17.17) applies for this adjustment. It can be shown that the contribution to total noncoverage bias of the $h*$ cell is

$$B_{NCh*} = W_{h*} \gamma_{NCh*} (\overline{Y}_{Ch*} - \overline{Y}_{NCh*}) \tag{17.20}$$

where $W_{h*} = N_{h*}/N$ is the proportion of the total population belonging to cell $h*$, γ_{NCh*} is the noncoverage rate for units in $h*$, $\overline{Y}_{Ch*}$ and $\overline{Y}_{NCh*}$ are the means of the covered and noncovered subpopulations, respectively, in $h*$. Thus, we see that, the most effective strategy in forming the PSA cells is to minimize $\overline{Y}_C - \overline{Y}_{NC}$ within adjustment cells; that is, to form PSA cells where the difference between the means of the frame and the non-frame units within the cells are approximately 0. In the same way the WCA method assigns the mean of the respondents to the nonrespondents within weighting class, the PSA assigns the weighted mean of the frame population to the nonframe population units in each cell. By defining the post-stratification strata so that $(\overline{Y}_{Ch*} - \overline{Y}_{NCh*})$ is small, especially when W_{h*} is large, the overall noncoverage bias will also be small.

As noted previously, post-stratification can also reduce the MSE of survey estimates by reducing the sampling variance. The principle is the same as ratio estimation. Quite often some variables that would be ideal for stratification prior to sampling are not available until after the sample has been drawn and the sample units have been contacted. Some of the gains in precision that would have been realized had these variables been used for stratification can be realized by post-stratifying by these variables. Cochran (1977) shows that the contribution to the variance of an estimator of the h^* cell is approximately

$$W_{h*}Var(y_{h*i}) \tag{17.21}$$

for large n_{rh*} where $Var(y_{h*i})$ is the within cell variance. Thus, to achieve the greatest reduction in variance, the PSA cells should be chosen to minimize the within cell variance, particularly for the largest cells. This can be accomplished by choosing post-stratification variables that are highly correlated with the y_i's. However, reducing $(\overline{Y}_{Ch*} - \overline{Y}_{NCh*})$ is best accomplished by choosing PSA variables that are highly correlated with the probability (or propensity) of being included on the frame. These two strategies may lead to different choices of post-stratification variables and both goals should be kept in mind in the selection of variables to use for adjustment.

For example, for an RDD health survey, post-stratifying by age, race, and sex may dramatically improve the precision of the estimates but may not be as effective for reducing noncoverage bias resulting from the exclusion of nontelephone households. For coverage adjustments, race, income, urbanicity, and education may be more effective. To achieve both goals, weighting classes could be formed using some of each type of variable. There is a danger in creating too many PSA cells as this will result in cells containing only a few observations. As a rule of thumb, n_{rh}, the number of respondents in cell h, should be at least 10 (see Kish, 1965). Cells that are too small can be combined to form larger cells but the effectiveness of the PSA will be reduced. A better strategy is to be judicious in the selection of post-stratification variables and choose one or two variables that address both bias and variance reduction.

Quite often, at least some of the variables that are well-suited for the nonresponse WCA also work quite well for reducing noncoverage bias as well as sampling variance. In such cases, the use of these variables will simultaneously reduce nonresponse bias, noncoverage bias and sampling variance. In the next example, we use the NSCAW survey data and an external data set that is described subsequently to illustrate the calculation of PSA adjustment factors.

17.3.3.1 Example 3
The NSCAW PSU frame was composed of all counties in the United States that were large enough to support at least one interviewer-workload, or about 60 cases or more per year. Counties smaller than this size were excluded from the sampling frame. The number of counties excluded was 710 out of a total or 3,141 counties or approximately 23%. However, because less than 3% of the

child welfare target population resides in these counties, the frame coverage rate is still quite high. Nevertheless, we want to adjust for this potential noncoverage bias using the PSA method.

Another source of noncoverage error in the survey is the possibility that some of the lists of children received from the CPS agencies may have been incomplete. Recall that lists were provided on a monthly basis. Investigations that closed out toward the end of the month may not have had adequate time to be keyed into the system. The use of monthly lists that accumulated cases from several prior months help to reduce this problem. In this manner, cases that were not keyed for one or two months could still show up in a subsequent month's listing. Still, it is possible that some investigations were missed for other reasons.

Fortunately, a reliable external source was available to help assess the accuracy of the sampling frame counts. A comparison of the NSCAW frame counts by state with the external counts suggested that frame noncoverage was almost 25% in some counties. The external data provided a means for computing PSA factors that partially account for this source of frame bias. Here we illustrate how to compute the PSA factors for this data set using two variables: state groups and substantiation status of an investigation.

Table 17.2 shows the computation of PSA factors for each post-stratum cell h using equation (18). The numerator of each ratio is the total count of cases in the cell from the DCDC file and the denominator is the sum of the nonresponse adjusted weights for all respondents in the cell as in equation (18). These adjustment values are multiplied by the base weight and nonresponse adjustment for each respondent i in stratum h. For example, the children with substantiated investigations living in California, Florida, or Texas have a target population estimate of 274,525 children, a frame population estimate of 199,579 children, and a PSA factor of 1.374.

Table 17.2. NSCAW Post-Stratification Adjustment Factors for State Group by Substantiation Post-strata

	Substantiated	Unsubstantiated
CA, FL, TX	$\dfrac{274252.20}{199579.49}=1.374$	$\dfrac{592310.28}{483039.94}=1.226$
IL, MI, NY, OH, PA	$\dfrac{192913.43}{177745.52}=1.085$	$\dfrac{469316.72}{260863.66}=1.799$
Remaining States	$\dfrac{403291.95}{263156.49}=1.533$	$\dfrac{982953.23}{611648.32}=1.607$

17.3.3.2 Raking

In developing the PSA factors, we assumed that the target population totals are known for all cells in the cross-classification of the post-stratification variables. For example, post-stratify by age and gender requires knowledge of the distribution of age separately for males and females in the population. Suppose the full cross-classification information is not available for one or more of the post-stratifying variables. For example, suppose we know the count of males and females and the number of persons in each age group, but we do not know the age-by-gender counts for the target population. Raking ratio estimation (Deming & Stephan, 1940) can be applied in these situations to fill in missing counts in the cross-classification table so that the weighted cell counts are consistent with the known marginal counts or control totals.

As an example, suppose we know only that the proportion male in the population is 0.47 and the proportion of persons aged 16–25 is 0.32, aged 26–45 is 0.41 and aged 46 or older is 0.27. We can still develop approximate gender-by-age post-stratification weights using the process of raking. Raking ratio estimation computes a distribution of the population using these marginal distributions and assumptions about the interactions among them. Iterative proportional fitting (IPF) is used to obtain the joint distribution from the marginal distributions.

The quality of the PSA factors relies on the accuracy of the external control data as well as the validity of the model implied by the IPF process. If the population controls used in the PSA process are inaccurate, it is possible that the adjusted estimates will have greater bias than the unadjusted estimates. Cochran (1977, p. 117) discusses the consequences of such inaccuracies on the estimates. In cases where the accuracy of the external data is suspect, raking should not be attempted.

17.3.3.3 Duplicate and extraneous units

Quite commonly, some population elements are listed multiple times on the sampling frame. As an example, a telephone directory may list two phone numbers that reach the same household and both numbers could be used to interview any member of the household. Such households would have twice the probability of being selected if a SRS sample of telephone numbers were drawn from the telephone directory. This problem is generally referred to as *frame multiplicity* in the survey research literature. Lessler and Kalsbeek (1992, p. 88f) provide a detailed discussion of the issue and its ramifications for survey error.

Ideally, the duplicate frame units can be identified and eliminated prior to sampling. If this is not feasible, it may still be possible to identify the units in the sample that are duplicated on the frame through the interview process. As an example, in an RDD survey, it is common practice to ask the respondent how many phone numbers can be dialed to reach the household. This information can then be used to correct the probabilities of selection and, thus, the base weights as follows. If the multiplicities are hidden and cannot be identified during data collection, the duplicated units will be oversampled and the estimates will be biased to some extent. The biases can be quite severe if the multiplicity is extensive.

An extraneous unit is nonpopulation (or ineligible) unit included on the frame. For example, in an RDD survey it may be impossible to identify all the business telephone numbers before they are sampled and dialed. Face to face surveys typically target housing units within its limited geographic area delineated by street boundaries. Interviewers may mistakenly list and interview units that fall outside these boundaries which introduces ineligible units in the sample. Ideally all extraneous units should be eliminated from the frame prior to sampling or interviewing, but that is not feasible in many practical situations. The next best solution is to include the identification of nonpopulation units as part of the data collection or subsequent stage of the survey process so that extraneous units can be removed post-data collection. Failure to do so will lead to biases in the estimates.

17.3.4 Computing Final Weights

We can now combine the results of Examples 1, 2, and 3 to form the final weights for each unit in the sample. Table 17.3 combines the results to obtain base weight adjustment factors for all cells used in the WCA and PSA computations. To compute the appropriate weight for a child, first classify the child into one of the cells in Table 4 to obtain the appropriate weighting adjustment factor. Multiply the base weight for the child by the weight adjustment factor to obtain the final child weight as shown in (17.8).

Table 17.3. Final Weight Adjustment Factors for NSCAW Sample

Nonresponse WCA Cells		PSA Cells Substantiated			Unsubstantiated		
		State Group 1	State Group 2	State Group 3	State Group 1	State Group 2	State Group 3
0-	Male	1.88	1.68	1.48	2.43	2.10	2.20
2	Female	1.90	1.70	1.50	2.46	2.12	2.23
3-	Male	2.17	1.94	1.71	2.81	2.42	2.54
10	Female	2.11	1.89	1.67	2.74	2.36	2.47
11	Male	2.14	1.91	1.69	2.78	2.39	2.51
+	Female	2.47	2.20	1.95	3.19	2.75	2.88

The final weights can be checked for accuracy using a variety of quality control checks. For example, properties 1–3 stated earlier can be applied to ensure the weight sums are consistent with the control totals used in the post-survey adjustments as well as other known external totals. If such external data are not available, the plausibility of the weight sums can still be assessed. It is also useful to view the distribution of the weights and to investigate any extremely small or large weights. Likewise the adjustment factors such as those in Table 5 should be checked for extreme values. Adjustment factors that exceed 6 are generally considered to be extreme. Weight trimming methods, which is discussed subsequently, offer a means reducing extreme weight problems.

The distribution of the final weights that were actually used for the NSCAW survey is shown in Figure 17.2. Note that the NSCAW weights range from 2 to 8175. The distribution is highly skewed to the right which is not atypical for unequal probability sample designs. This is because the units in the population that have higher probabilities of selection and consequently smaller base weights will dominate the sample. Some units with very small selection probabilities will still be selected in large samples and the weights for these units can be quite large as shown in the figure.

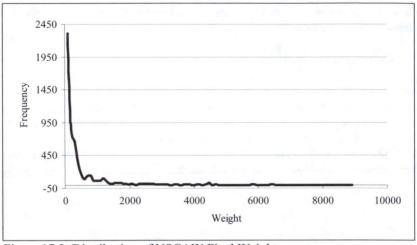

Figure 17.2. Distribution of NSCAW Final Weights

17.4 ESTIMATION AND ANALYSIS ISSUES

In this section, we discuss a few topics and issues related to estimation and analysis using survey weights. To avoid redundancy with the other chapters in this section of the book, our discussion is brief and directed toward a few key issues. Stapleton (Chapter 18 on 'Analysis of Data from Complex Surveys') addresses these issues in more detail. In Section 17.4.1, we discuss the effect of variation in the survey weights on the standard errors of the estimates. In cases where the weight variation is extreme, weight trimming, which is discussed in Section 17.4.2, may be necessary. Finally, we briefly discuss a few issues in the use of weights in analysis.

17.4.1 Effect of Weighting on the Variance

The estimator of the population mean given in equation (2) is fundamental to the analysis of survey data. When y_i is defined as an indicator variable denoting the absence or presence of some trait, (2) also provides an estimate of the population proportion. The numerator of (2) may be taken as an estimate of the population total. If the sum in both the numerator and denominator is restricted only to sample units belonging to particular class or domain (for e.g., defined by age, race, gender, education, etc.), then (2) also provides an estimate of the mean, proportion or total for virtually any analytic domains that a researcher wishes to define in an analysis. In this section, we consider the effect of weighting on the standard error of the estimator in (2).

Oversampling of some population subgroups and, to a smaller extent, the post-survey adjustments cause the weights to vary widely across the sample which often adversely affects the precision of the estimates. Because of their profound implications on precision, these *unequal weighting effects* should be considered at the design stage when it may be determined that the sample size should be increased to offset the variance inflation caused by unequal weighting. If the weight variation is too extreme, it may be necessary to reduce the amount of oversampling that is planned for the sample. Once the survey is conducted, there are very few options for dealing with extreme weight variation.

Kish (1965, p. 427) derived a formula for determining the maximum increase in the variance of an estimate of a population mean due to weight variation. His formula assumes there is no correlation between the survey weights and the characteristic whose mean is to be estimated. This may be a good approximation for many survey variables because the survey design and weight adjustments are optimized for only a few key characteristics out of hundreds that may be collected in a survey. The actual variance increase will vary across characteristics in the survey and will be smaller for characteristics where the covariance between the observations and the weights are larger. Under these assumptions, Kish obtained the following expression for the unequal weighting effect (*UWE*) defined as the ratio of the variance of the weighted mean to the variance of the unweighted mean:

$$UWE = 1 + cv^2 \tag{17.22}$$

where *cv* is the coefficient of variance of the weights or the sample standard deviation of the weights divided by the sample average weight. This formula may also be applied to determine the *UWE* for totals and proportions, by restricting the computations to subgroups of interest, for any population domain defined by the variables in the survey.

As an example, for the NSCAW sample the standard deviation of the final survey weights is 833 and the average weight is 434 yielding a weight *cv* of 833/434=1.92. Thus, *UWE* = $1+cv^2$ is 4.68 which implies that the standard errors of sample population means, totals and proportions may be doubled as a result of weighting. This is a rather large *UWE* which arises primarily from the high degree of oversampling done for the survey. However, for the key population domains that were oversampled, the *UWE* is much smaller, say between 1.5 and 2.0.

17.4.2 Weight Trimming

In cases where the *UWE* is quite large (say, greater than 5), the source of the extreme weight variation may be a relatively small number of extremely large or extremely small weights. One way to decrease the variance is to restrict the range of the weights through a process called *weight trimming*. Weight trimming reduces the variance in the estimates induced by weight variation, but it may also increase the nonsampling biases the weights were intended to reduce. In the end, the mean squared error of the estimates (defined as squared bias plus the variance of an estimator) may actually be larger after trimming the weights. For this reason, it is prudent to be quite conservative in use of weight trimming.

Weight trimming may be performed at any stage of the weight construction process: before or after applying the WCA nonresponse adjustment factors or after applying the PSA coverage adjustment factors. If the latter, the PSA process may need to be repeated so that trimmed weight sums will still equate to the control totals used in the PSA adjustment. Several iterations of trimming and readjusting the weights may be necessary to achieve the desired results.

Good survey practice dictates that the weights be trimmed once for all the variables in the survey and that the same trimmed weights be used in all subsequent analysis. It is not advisable to customize the trimming process in secondary data analysis or for specific survey characteristics in a primary analysis since this can lead to biased comparisons as well as researcher bias in the analytic results. If trimming is used for secondary data analysis, the analyst should provide the details on the process used for trimming and an evaluation of the impact of trimming on the estimates and their standard errors.

The first step in the weight trimming process is to determine which weights are considered extreme. As an example, weights that exceed the mean by three standard deviations may be considered too large and should be trimmed. This can be a subject process; however, Potter (1988, 1990) has provided a set of rules based on MSE optimization that are more objective. All weights above (or below) the cut-off values are set to this maximum (or minimum) value. In doing this, the weight sums for the untrimmed weights will need to be adjusted so that the weight totals after trimming still equate to the weight sums prior to trimming. The *UWE* is then re-evaluated for the trimmed weights and the process can repeated until the *UWE* reaches the desired level, all the weights fall with the desired range and the weight sums agree with all control totals. A number of schemes are available for determining the weight cut-offs and redistributing the trimmed weight remnants to the untrimmed weights. Potter (1988, 1990) provides a discussion of the issues and a comparison of several alternative schemes. Folsom and Singh (2000) describe a model-based process based on restricted maximum likelihood for simultaneously weighting and trimming the data.

17.4.3 Using Weights in the Analysis

In Section 17.4.1, we noted that equation (2) is theoretically an unbiased estimator of the population mean while (1) is biased where the bias is proportional to $-Cov(y_i, w_i)$. Thus, in cases where the weights are uncorrelated with the observations, why use them, especially because they may reduce the precision of the estimates. This point has been argued extensively in the literature (see a discussion of the arguments in Kish, 1992). Although there may be instances when (1) and (2) produce very nearly the same estimate, there may be many other instances when these estimators produce very different results. In cases where there is a difference the weighted estimate is preferred because it is unbiased.

Thus, there is general agreement in the statistical community that, for estimating description statistics, weights should always be used even though some estimates may not benefit from this practice. Presenting results in a report where some estimates use weights and others do not is confusing and may lead to yield inconsistent findings.

From statistical modeling and other types of multivariate analysis, the issue is less clear. If the effect of weights on an analysis is not large, some analysts may decide not to use the weighted results if the standard errors of the estimates are substantially smaller for the unweighted results. This practice is considered quite risky by many statisticians (e.g., see Hansen, Meadow, & Tepping, 1983) but may be accepted by some professional journals and peer-reviewed publications. There are situations where unweighted regression estimation may be preferable; for example, for very small samples where the ideal properties of weighted estimation may not be realized. The issues in the debate over whether to use sample weights in regression analysis are discussed by Little (2004) and Pfefferman (1996). DuMouchel and Duncan (1983) also discuss the alternatives and develop a test for the ignorability of weights in regression analysis that can be easily applied.

The use of weights in statistical analysis is greatly facilitated by the introduction of more and more statistical software packages of options for coping with complex survey designs and unequal probability weighting. Stapleton (Chapter 18) outlines several of the survey software packages. Standard statistical software packages do not handle sampling weights correctly and will produce erroneous results (Brogan, 1998).

Finally, it is important to note that this chapter has dealt exclusively for weights associated with a cross-sectional survey or the baseline data collection for a panel survey. Although many of the issues in weight construction and use are the same for cross-sectional and panel survey data, there are a number of important issues associated with the latter that are beyond the scope of this chapter. These issues are related to the nonresponse adjustments for panel attrition, dealing with temporary ineligible units in coverage adjustments and the appropriate weight to use for longitudinal data analysis. These issues are considered in Lepkowski (1988), Duncan and Kalton (1987) and Kalton (1986).

17.5 SUMMARY

To many researchers, the survey weighting process appears as a black box where, through some mysterious process, weights are derived that they are told must be used in the estimation process. They may be perplexed that some observations have a relatively small weight (say 20) whereas other observations receive a much larger weight (say, 3000). How is it that some observations are assigned so much more importance in the estimation process than others? They may complain when the weights have as much influence on their research findings as the survey data themselves and wonder whether the weights can be trusted. This chapter has attempted to illuminate this seeming black box by describing why survey weights are needed, what the weighting process entails and how each step of the weighting process should implement.

Clearly, the steps of the weighting process are quite subjective: whether to adjust or not adjust for nonresponse and noncoverage error, how to form weighting class and post-stratification cells, what data to use in the adjustment process, whether and how to trim the weights, and so forth. Even computing the base weights can be subjective; for example, in many RDD surveys, the number of telephones per household is not obtained and, thus, not used for computing selection probabilities.

Given the influence weights have on survey results, it is important that researchers understand enough about weighting process to be discerning users of the survey data. At a minimum, researchers should know whether post-survey adjustments were applied to the weights to reduce sampling variation and the effects of missing data. If no adjustments were applied, should they have been? If they were applied, what information was used in the adjustments, what is known about their quality, and what analyses have been performed to assess their effects on survey error? Were the weights trimmed and to what extent? We hope the information contained in this chapter prepares the data user to ask these questions and understand the answers.

GLOSSARY OF KEY CONCEPTS

Base (or design) weight. The starting point for weight construction and derives from the survey design. It is the inverse of the probability of selection for unit *i*.

Extraneous units (or erroneous inclusions). Refers to the inclusion of nonpopulation units on the frame.

Final weights. The weights used in analysis and are a multiplicative combination of the base weights and post-survey adjustments.

Frame multiplicity. Occurs when some population elements are listed multiple times on the sampling frame.

Frame noncoverage. Occurs when the frame population does not include all units in the target population.

Frame population. The subset of the target population that is represented by the sampling frame.

Noncoverage adjustment. An adjustment to the nonresponse adjusted base weight that is designed to partially correct for bias due to frame noncoverage.

Noncoverage bias. The bias in parameter estimates due to frame noncoverage.

Nonresponse adjustment. An adjustment to the base weight that is designed to partially correct the bias due to nonresponse.

Nonresponse bias. Defined as the expected nonresponse rate times the difference in the means of the respondent and nonrespondent populations.

Target (or inferential) population. The population to be studied in the survey and for which the basic inferences from the survey will be made.

Respondent population. That subset of the frame population that is represented by units who would respond to the survey if selected.

Post-stratification adjustment (PSA). A type of noncoverage adjustment that uses strata selected after sampling and target population counts to estimate and correct for noncoverage bias.

Post-survey weight adjustments. Multiplicative factors applied to the base weights to compensate for nonresponse, noncoverage and to reduce the variance through post-stratification and ratio estimation.

Probability proportional to size (PPS) sampling. Gives a greater probability of selection to larger units than to smaller units according to some size measure. If sampling is without replacement, it is referred to as πps sampling.

Raking (or raking ratio estimation). An iterative process of estimating cell counts from marginal counts for weighted class cells.

Weighted class adjustment (WCA). A type of nonresponse adjustment that uses weighted classes and nonresponse rates to estimate and correct for nonresponse bias.

Unequal weighting effect (UWE). The adverse effect of unequal weight variation on the precision of estimates.

Weight trimming. The process of moderating extreme weights for the purposes of improving the MSE of estimates.

Chapter 18

Analysis of Data from Complex Surveys

Laura M. Stapleton

University of Maryland, Baltimore County

18.1 INTRODUCTION AND GOALS OF THIS CHAPTER

With recent growth in the use of survey methods to obtain data for social science research and the many large-scale survey datasets available to secondary researchers, a vast array of research questions can be addressed. It is important, however, to understand the complexities of analyzing data from these complex sample datasets. There are two essential chapters in this text that a reader may want to consult prior to reading this chapter: Chapter 6 by Lohr on Coverage and Sampling and Chapter 17 by Biemer and Christ on Weighting Survey Data. This chapter on analyzing data from complex sample data sets builds on the information provided in those two chapters. The goals of this chapter are to introduce the reader to the problems associated with using traditional statistical procedures with data from complex samples, provide simple strategies to more appropriately estimate statistics and their sampling variances under some common sampling designs, and provide additional resources that can be accessed for further reading.

The layout of this chapter is as follows. First, in Section 18.2, a review of some of the sampling design characteristics that can affect analysis will be provided. In Section 18.3, a small example dataset will be introduced and analysis options will then be explained and a demonstration of each approach to analysis with the example dataset will be provided in Section 18.4. Applied analyses are then provided using data from an international survey on civics education in Section 18.5, and availability of software options for analysis of survey data will be discussed in Section 18.6. The final section outlines suggestions for practice and points the reader toward further sources of information on analysis for complex sample data.

18.2 ASPECTS OF SAMPLE DESIGNS THAT CAN AFFECT ESTIMATES

In most inferential statistical analyses, interest is on two distinct things: an estimate of a population parameter (such as a population mean or difference between two population means) and the sampling variance of that estimate (or how much we would expect the parameter estimate to fluctuate over repeated sampling; the square root of the sampling variance is termed the standard error). The accuracy of each of these estimates (of the population parameter and of the sampling variance) can be affected by the sampling design. The chapter on weighting (Biemer & Christ, Chapter 17) discusses some of the effects that the sampling design can have on estimates of population parameters and provides analytic procedures to accommodate the sampling design with the use of weights. This chapter focuses on effects of the sampling design on estimates of the sampling variance and assumes the researcher is using weights in the analysis to accommodate disproportional selection probabilities, when appropriate.

18.2.1 Sampling Variance and the Standard Error

The sampling variance of the parameter estimate informs the researcher how close to the true population parameter the sample estimate likely is. For example, suppose we have a *simple random sample* of 100 people from a population of one million and obtain each element's height in inches (y_i). The estimate of the population mean height, $\hat{\mu}$, would simply be determined as the mean height of the elements in the sample

$$\hat{\mu} = \frac{\sum_{i=1}^{n} y_i}{n} \tag{18.1}$$

where y_i is the height in inches of the ith individual and n is the number of observations in the sample (or 100 in this example). Suppose we find $\hat{\mu}$ to be 68 inches for our sample dataset. We know that 68 inches is not the actual population parameter—we have measurements for only 100 people out of a possible one million people—but the population parameter is probably somewhere near 68 inches, the question is "How near?" An estimate of the sampling variance gives us information about how near. Under an assumption of simple random sampling (SRS), the sampling variance for the estimate of a population mean is typically defined in most textbooks and in most software packages as

$$sv(\hat{\mu}) = \frac{s_y^2}{n} \tag{18.2}$$

where

$$s_y^2 = \frac{\sum_{i=1}^{n}(y_i - \hat{\mu})^2}{(n-1)} \tag{18.3}$$

The sampling variance of the estimate of the mean is therefore the variability of the y_i scores around the mean divided by the number of observations in the sample. It should be clear from this formula that the larger your sample, the smaller your estimate of the sampling variance of $\hat{\mu}$ (and the more *efficient* your estimate of $\hat{\mu}$). Technically, (18.2) assumes that observations were sampled with replacement, which is not typically the case. When sampling has been undertaken without replacement, use of (18.2) to obtain an estimate of the sampling variance is acceptable if the sampling fraction is small. If the sample is a large fraction of the population, formulas such as (18.2) should be corrected to reflect this fact, using something termed the *finite population correction factor* (or, *f.p.c.*). The f.p.c. is a multiplicative correction of $(1-\pi)$, where π is the selection probability for the elements in the sample. Suppose that our measure of the sampling variance of $\hat{\mu}$, $sv(\hat{\mu})$, using Equation 18.2 was found to be 4. What can we now say about the population mean? We can use this sampling variance estimate to create a confidence interval around our estimate of the mean, specifically an interval in which 95 out of 100 times our interval would be expected to contain the true population mean. To do this, however, we first need to calculate the standard error. Even though the procedure of determining the precision of our parameter estimate is usually referred to as variance estimation it is more typical in applied research to discuss standard errors around the parameter estimate (and not sampling variance) and the standard error is simply the square root of the sampling variance

$$se(\hat{\mu}) = \sqrt{sv(\hat{\mu})} = \frac{\sqrt{s_y^2}}{\sqrt{n}} \qquad (18.4)$$

and for our example, the standard error of the estimate of the population mean height would be 2. So, using the familiar 95% confidence interval formula

$$CI_{95\%} = \hat{\mu} \pm t_{crit} se(\hat{\mu})$$

we can state that the mean height in our population is estimated to be in the interval $CI_{95\%} = 68 \pm 1.98 \times 2$ or from 64.04 to 71.96 inches.

When analyzing data from complex sample data sets that have been collected through some sampling designs described by Lohr (Chapter 6), one of the main problems is that the estimates of sampling variances (and thus standard errors) will be *biased* when using the traditional formulas in (18.2) and (18.4).

18.2.2 Biased Sampling Variance and the Design Effect

What does it mean when an estimate is said to be *biased*? It means that even though the statistical formula that you (or the software) used in calculating your estimate provided you with a nice, neat number, that number is probably wrong. Every statistical formula is based on assumptions. And when the assumptions upon which the statistical formula was derived are violated, the statistical estimate is not necessarily accurate. The familiar formulas that are used to calculate estimates of sampling variances and standard errors (that are found in software and in textbooks) have a very important assumption: that observations are independent. Usually, when data have been collected using complex sampling designs, the observations are not independent. What happens when such assumptions are violated? Many people have studied the effects of the bias in sampling variance that occurs with various types of sampling designs and the effect depends on the type of sampling design that is used. I discuss these effects for some of the more popular sampling designs in the next sections.

18.2.2.1 Cluster and multistage sampling

When a sample has been collected with cluster or multistage sampling, the sampling variance estimates that you obtain from traditional statistical formulas will tend to be too small (or *negatively biased*). What is the effect of having negatively biased standard errors? Suppose in our example (where we determined that our mean estimate of the height was 68 and the 95% confidence interval was about 64.04 to 71.96 inches), the 100 people in the sample were not obtained with SRS but were obtained by randomly selecting 25 families and then surveying 4 adults from each family. It is likely that the height of people within one family is more similar than across families. Due to this dependence among observations, our estimate of the standard error might be too small and thus our estimate of the confidence interval—64.04 to 71.96 inches—might be too narrow. The true population mean height may lie outside that 95% confidence interval more than 5 times out of 100 – which represents an increase in the *Type I error* rate over the nominal α level of .05.

Suppose also that we were interested in testing whether means for two groups differ on height—perhaps people who live in the city as compared to people who live in rural areas. Again, given a sample obtained from a cluster sample of families, our estimate of the standard error of the difference of two means (city vs. rural), calculated using traditional formulas, will be too small and we will be more likely to proclaim that mean height is different in the two populations than we would have with an *unbiased* estimate of the standard error. It should be noted that standard error estimates from traditional formulas will be biased only when there is homogeneity (or likeness) of the individuals in the clusters on the response variable (y_i) as compared to across clusters.

18.2.2.2 Stratification

When a sample has been collected with stratification, and when the response variable is homogeneous within those strata, the sampling variance estimates that are obtained from the traditional statistical formulas will tend to be too large (or *positively biased*). Although the stratified sampling design may appear very similar to a cluster sampling design because individuals are placed into mutually exclusive strata or groups, the effect of these two designs on sampling variance estimates is quite different. What is the effect of having positively biased standard errors? Suppose now that we had not taken a cluster sample but instead had split our population into male and female groups then randomly selected 50 males and 50 females. We have stratified by gender. If we calculate the traditional standard error ignoring that we have explicitly sampled from these two groups (as if we have a simple random sample), then our estimates of the sampling variance and the standard error will likely be too large. The confidence interval that we draw around our estimate of the population mean height will contain the true population mean height more than 95 out of 100 times. Also, if we are comparing mean height for city versus rural populations, we may not see a statistical difference when there might be one. Thus, we lose *power* and are more likely to commit a *Type II error*.

18.2.2.3 Disproportionate sampling

As discussed by Biemer (Chapter 17), the use of disproportionate sampling can result in a non-optimal sample. Suppose we had sampled 90 men and 10 women in our sample of 100 people and the population was split evenly between men and women. We will have a fairly precise estimate of the mean height for men and a less precise estimate of the mean height for women. If we calculate the overall mean height of our sample, it would be biased because men tend to be taller than women, and our sample has a disproportionately high number of men. This bias can be removed by weighting. However, and importantly, our estimate of the overall mean height will be less precise with this design than if we had sampled 50 men and 50 women. Using traditional equations to estimate standard errors on weighted data will not capture this loss in efficiency and will lead to negatively biased standard error estimates (thus, type I error).

18.2.2.4 The design effect

What are the most typical effects or biases that are found with complex sample data? Usually, if a sample design includes cluster sampling (which most large scale survey designs do) the negative bias in standard error estimates attributed to using a cluster sample will outweigh any positive effect of using stratification. At this point, the reader might be interested in whether a measure can be obtained of how biased the traditional estimates will be. The answer is "yes," for certain statistics, for example, the sample mean. This measure is called the design effect; it is the ratio of the correct sampling variance of a statistic under the complex sampling design over the sampling variance that would have been obtained had SRS been used (Kish, 1965). If the complex sample design has no effect on the sampling variance, the value of the design effect would be 1.0. If the sample design improves the precision of the parameter estimate, the design effect will be less than 1.0, and if the design lessens the precision, the design effect will be greater than 1.0. The design effect and its calculation is discussed in more detail in Section 18.4, when we discuss analysis options.

18.2 Summary

When undertaking statistical analyses with data obtained from complex sampling designs, the traditional formulas for standard errors may yield biased estimates of the sampling variability. Cluster and multistage sampling and the use of disproportionate selection rates tend to result in negatively biased estimates whereas stratification tends to yield positively biased estimates. The design effect is a measure of the ratio of the sampling variance accounting for the sample design over the sampling variance when SRS is assumed. The design effect can be used as a measure of bias in the traditional estimates of sampling variance.

18.3 A SMALL EXAMPLE DATA SET

The remainder of this chapter is clearer when accompanied with a small example that can be used as each method for sampling variance estimation is introduced. Suppose that there are 450 students in our population of interest, with 30 students in each school, and five schools are in each of 3 locations. We sample from within each of these three location strata. Within the urban stratum, we randomly sample two schools; from the suburban location, we randomly sample two schools; and from the rural location, we randomly sample two schools. At the second stage of sampling, within each of our six selected schools, we randomly sample three students. We now have a total of 18 students in our sample and hypothesized data for these students are shown in Table 1. The values of *1*, *2*, and *3* under the stratum column refer to urban, suburban, and rural categories respectively. The value in the *y* column represents some measurement taken on each of the three randomly chosen students in each school, perhaps hours of TV watching on a typical weekend.

Table 18.1. Example Data Set

Stratum	School	Student	Y	W_{raw}	W_{norm}
1	1	1	9	25	1
1	1	2	7	25	1
1	1	3	8	25	1
1	2	4	4	25	1
1	2	5	4	25	1
1	2	6	5	25	1
2	3	7	2	25	1
2	3	8	3	25	1
2	3	9	2	25	1
2	4	10	6	25	1
2	4	11	5	25	1
2	4	12	4	25	1
3	5	13	1	25	1
3	5	14	0	25	1
3	5	15	1	25	1
3	6	16	4	25	1
3	6	17	4	25	1
3	6	18	3	25	1

The last two columns, w_{raw} and w_{norm}, contain the raw and normalized sampling weights that should be attributed to each student. The raw weights represent the number of people each subject is representing and these weights will sum to the population size. This raw weight (as described more fully by Biemer & Christ in Chapter 17), is a function of the selection probabilities at each stage of selection. For our specific example, it is equal to the inverse of the product of the probability of the school being selected, π_{sch}, and the conditional probability of the student being selected given selection of the school , $\pi_{stud \mid sch}$. Here,

$$w_{raw} = \frac{1}{\pi_{sch} \times \pi_{stud|sch}} = \frac{1}{\frac{2}{5} \times \frac{3}{30}} = 25$$

Each student in our sample represents 25 other students. The sum of these raw weights over our 18 students equals the total population size (450). To obtain a normalized weight, the raw weight is multiplied times the ratio of the sample size over the sum of the weights (in this case, 18/450) and thus the normalized weights will be 1 for all elements in our example dataset. The sampling design characteristics, and thus the observation weights, for this example are very simple. If differential selection probabilities were used, if our schools sizes differed, or if the number of schools per stratum differed in the population, the dataset would contain weights that differed across strata and schools.

This dataset is used in the next section to demonstrate the different approaches that can be employed to obtain estimates of sampling variances and standard errors for the estimate of the mean number of hours spent watching TV.

18.4 ANALYSIS OPTIONS FOR DATA FROM COMPLEX SAMPLING DESIGNS

In this section, I introduce four types of sampling variance estimation and demonstrate each of these approaches using our example dataset. These four types have been referred to by some as traditional, design-effect adjusted, linearization, and replication methods. The last three of these approaches are often termed design-based methods because they take the sampling design into account when an estimate of the sampling variance is calculated. A different approach, called a model-based or model-assisted analysis, actually includes sampling information in the statistical analysis model. These model-based methods are briefly discussed at the end of this chapter.

18.4.1 Traditional Analysis

A question we might pose with data from our simple example dataset is "What is the mean number of hours that students watch TV on a typical weekend?" Using traditional analysis and using the normalized weights for each observation, we can estimate the mean and standard error to be 4 and .572, respectively, using equations (18.5) and (18.6).

$$\hat{\mu} = \frac{\sum\limits_{i=1}^{n} w_i y_i}{\sum\limits_{i=1}^{n} w_i} \tag{18.5}$$

$$se(\hat{\mu}) = \sqrt{\frac{s_y^2}{\sum\limits_{i=1}^{n} w_i}} \qquad (18.6)$$

where

$$s_y^2 = \frac{\sum\limits_{i=1}^{n} w_i (y_i - \hat{\mu})^2}{(\sum\limits_{i=1}^{n} w_i - 1)} \qquad (18.7)$$

The confidence interval around this estimate is

$$CI_{95\%} = 4 \pm 2.11 \times .572$$

We therefore conclude that there is a 95% chance that the true population mean is within this interval of about 2.79 to 5.21 hours. This conclusion would be the typical interpretation by a researcher who does not realize that the data were collected using a stratified two-stage sample or who did not realize the importance of accounting for this complex sample design in the analysis.

18.4.2 Design-effect Adjusted Analysis

What is the effect of clustering and stratification in our sample design? If we could obtain a measure of how biased our traditional estimate of the sampling variance (and standard error) are expected to be given the complex sampling design, then we could use this design effect to inflate or deflate our standard error estimate from the traditional analysis. Under cluster sampling, a measure of the design effect of the sampling variance of the mean can be obtained, but one first needs to calculate the *intraclass correlation* (ICC). The ICC is a measure of the amount of variability in the response variable, y_i, that can be accounted for by the clustering. The ICC typically ranges from 0 to 1 (although it can be negative). A value close to 1 indicates that all of the elements in the cluster are nearly identical and therefore most variance is found between the cluster means (as opposed to within clusters). An ICC value near zero indicates that, within clusters, the individuals differ on the response variable and the cluster means do not differ greatly. An estimate of the ICC for a given sample, $\hat{\rho}$, can be obtained using components from an analysis of variance (ANOVA) on the variable of interest and using the cluster identifier (school in our example) as the between subjects factor,

$$\hat{\rho} = \frac{MS_B - MS_W}{MS_B + (n. - 1)MS_W} \qquad (18.8)$$

where MS_B is the model mean square, MS_W is the mean square error, and $n.$ is the sample size per group if balanced. Figure 18.1 contains the SPSS version 12.0 output for this ANOVA on our example dataset and using these results the estimate of the ICC .916. This is an extremely high ICC (the dataset was created to depict such a situation) and our interpretation of this ICC would be that over 90% of the variability in TV hours is accounted for by the school grouping and less than 10% by individual variability within the schools. Just by looking at Table 1 we might have guessed this; we can see that there are some schools in which all the students watch much TV (such as schools 1 and 4) and some schools in which all the students watch very little TV (such as school 5).

ANOVA

Y

	Sum of Squares	df	Mean Square	F	Sig.
Between Groups	93.333	5	18.667	33.600	.000
Within Groups	6.667	12	.556		
Total	100.000	17			

Figure 18.1 Analysis of Variance Table from Example Dataset with School as Between-Subjects Factor

How can we translate this knowledge of grouping dependency into an estimate of the design effect? It has been shown that with cluster sampling, the design effect (often referred to simply as *deff*) can be estimated as:

$$deff = 1 + \hat{\rho}(n - 1) \tag{18.9}$$

Note that if $\hat{\rho}$ =0, indicating no group dependency, the design effect estimate would be 1.0. For this example, the design effect is estimated as 2.831. Thus the sampling variance that we would estimate using a traditional analysis, ignoring the dependence among observations caused by the multistage sampling, would be nearly three times too small (and would need to be inflated by 2.831 to more accurately approximate the sampling variability). Note, however, that the estimate of the design effect in (9) did not take the stratification in our example dataset into account. Estimates of the *deff* are not as simply calculated for more complex sampling scenarios. Because the cluster effect has been typically found to have the most influence on variance estimates among all sampling design considerations (Kalton, 1983), equation (18.9) provides a fairly conservative *deff* estimate under a stratified cluster design. Another way to obtain estimates of *deff* is to consult technical manuals that accompany large datasets. Usually, these manuals will report on design effects for key variables in the dataset and these *deffs* have been estimated using statistical programs that were created to obtain unbiased estimates of the sampling variance under the complex sample design including all features of the design. One problem with relying on technical manuals to obtain *deff* information, however, is that the manuals usually only report on a few variables and generally do not report *deff* estimates for subgroups within the dataset.

The simplest method to obtain estimates of standard errors that have been adjusted for the complex sampling design is to use the design effect as an inflation (or deflation) factor. We can use our simple estimate of the design effect (that is not adjusted for stratification) in two ways to adjust a traditional analysis: (a) we can directly inflate the standard errors that resulted from our traditional analysis by a function of the design effect, or (b) we can adjust our case weights to reflect the design effect and create what can be termed an effective sample size weight.

To implement the first option, we can inflate the traditional standard error estimate by the square root of the design effect (sometimes called root design effect) of the response variable (Kalton, 1977; Kish, 1965). The standard error estimate from our traditional analysis was .572. Because the design effect is a measure of the inflation needed of the sampling variance, we must take the square root of the design effect (symbolized as *deft*) to determine the inflation needed in the standard error. We then can multiply the traditional estimate of the standard error by the *deft* to obtain a corrected standard error

$$se(\hat{\mu})_D = \sqrt{deff} \times se(\hat{\mu}) \qquad (18.10)$$

The square root of our estimate of *deff* is 1.683 and so our adjusted standard error would be .572×1.683, yielding .962. Our adjusted confidence interval could then be calculated and we would conclude that there is a 95% chance that the true population mean in TV watching hours is between about 1.97 to 6.03 hours. This interval is quite a bit wider than our original, traditional estimate of the confidence interval, suggesting that it is likely that there was more than a 5% chance that the true population mean would have fallen outside of our original interval of 2.79 to 5.21 (representing *Type I error*).

Using this manual approach of standard error inflation, a researcher needs only parameter estimates and standard errors from a traditional analysis, determine the square root of the design effect for the response variable and multiply that root design effect by the traditional standard error estimate to obtain a more appropriate standard error estimate. This procedure tends to result in fairly conservative estimates of the sampling errors in more complex statistical procedures (more complex than the simple mean we have examined here, such as regression coefficients) and can be rather unwieldy if used for complex models with many parameter estimates (Kish & Frankel, 1974).

A related approach, and one advocated in some national large-scale dataset training sessions (Rust, K., personal communication June 14, 2004) and in some technical manuals, is to create a design effect adjusted case weight by dividing the normalized sampling weight for each element by the average design effect for the variables of interest in the analysis.

$$w_{eff_i} = \frac{w_{norm_i}}{deff} \qquad (18.11)$$

When the design effect is greater than 1.0, dividing the normalized weight by the design effect will result in an average adjusted weight less than 1.0 and the sum of these adjusted weights will be less than the total sample size. For our small example dataset, the effective weights will be .353 for each student and the sum of these weights would be 6.354. So, instead of 18 people, our statistical analysis will be based on the assumption that there are only 6.354 people in the sample, which, as we saw from (4) will result in a larger estimate of the sampling variance and therefore the standard error. This new sum of adjusted weights has been termed the effective sample size. Use of these adjusted weights in traditional formulas will result in an inflation of standard errors and a subsequent decrease in power due to the smaller effective sample size (assuming the design effect is greater than 1.0). Using this procedure, statistics calculated by a statistical program such as SPSS or using equations (6) and (7) will reflect the reduction in effective sample size in the calculation of standard errors and degrees of freedom. For our example, using SPSS version 12.0 software and indicating that the data are weighted by the effective sample size weights (.353 for each student) or using (6) and (7), the standard error of the mean TV hours is estimated as 1.019. Typically, this case weight adjustment results in a standard error that is very close or identical to the standard error obtained by direct inflation of the standard error by the *deft*. Actually, the new standard error using the adjusted case weight method will always be $n/(n\text{-}1)$ larger than the standard error had the direct *deft* adjustment been used. Because we have a very small sample size (n=18), this difference is noticeable (in comparing our previous standard error estimate of .962 to 1.019).

It bears repeating that this design effect adjusted weight method only approximately captures the effect of the sample design on variance estimates. Although it does not provide a complete accounting of the sample design, the procedure is typically a better approach than conducting an analysis that assumes the observations are independent. It is very important, however, to determine whether the statistical software you are using treats weights in a way to produce effects as expected. Testing your program and the equations with our sample dataset should help to identify whether your statistical software is treating the weights as expected. Among the more popular statistical software used in the social sciences, current versions of SAS software do not treat the case weights in such a way to obtain this effective sample size adjustment, however current versions of SPSS do.

18.4.3 Linearization analysis

The approach of adjusting traditional standard errors by using the design effect (either manually or with case weight adjustments) is useful in two situations: you have a good estimate of the design effect (in the example above, we had a less than optimal estimate of the design effect–our estimate accounted for the clustering but ignored the stratification) and you only need to adjust the standard error for a simple univariate statistic. If you are estimating parameters for more complex models, this approach for adjustment of the standard error will tend to yield conservative estimates of the adjusted standard error (the standard error estimate will be positively biased—and you risk making a Type II error). A better approach to variance estimation for statistics from complex samples is to estimate standard errors using linearization. Sampling variance estimates for nonlinear functions (such as statistics from complex sample datasets) are often obtained by creating an approximate linear function, and then the variance of the new function is used as the variance estimate. This approach to variance estimation has several names in the literature, including the linearization method, the delta method, Taylor Series approximation, and propagation of variance (Kish, 1965; Lee, Forthofer, & Lorimor, 1989). In the specific case of complex sample data, linearization results in a variance estimate that typically is a weighted combination of the variation as assessed by the first order derivatives across *primary sampling units* (PSUs) within the same stratum (Kalton, 1983; Skinner, Holt and Smith, 1989). For our simple case of two-stage sampling with equal sizes from equally-sized strata, the approximation has been determined and the linearized standard error of the mean is estimated by the square root of summed stratum variances divided by the sample size

$$se_{\hat{\mu}_L} = \sqrt{\sum_{h=1}^{H} \frac{s_h^2}{n}} \tag{18.12}$$

where h represents the stratum, H is the total number of strata, n is the total sample size, and s_h^2 is the variance of cluster means within stratum h

$$s_h^2 = \frac{\sum_{\alpha=1}^{a}(\bar{y}_{h\alpha} - \bar{y}_h)^2}{a-1} \tag{18.13}$$

where α represents the cluster, a is the total number of clusters within the stratum, $\bar{y}_{h\alpha}$ is the mean on the response variable in cluster a within stratum h, and $\bar{y}_h$ is mean of the response variable within stratum h across all clusters.

Using (18.12), we obtain a standard error estimate of .906 for $\hat{\mu}$. Note that this estimate is somewhat smaller than our previous estimates using design effect adjustments due to the fact that we were ignoring the positive effects of stratification in our estimate of the design effect. There are many options to determine an approximate linear estimate and the choice of these depend on the complexity of the sampling design and the complexity of the parameter you are estimating; (18.12) is specific to estimating a standard error of the mean for a stratified, two-stage sample of equal cluster and stratum sizes. Most researchers who obtain linearized estimates with complex sample data approximate at the PSU level and ignore the sampling scheme within PSUs. Equations for linearized estimates for sampling variances for a range of different sampling schemes are available in Kalton (1983). Most researchers, however, use computer software that has been specially designed for complex sample data to provide these linearized estimates and more information on these software packages is provided in Section 18.6.

18.4.4 Replication Analysis

A final approach to estimation of sampling variances to be discussed here with our sample dataset is replication. Replication methods involve repeated sampling of elements from the original sample to create replicate samples. The statistic of interest is then computed in each of these replicate samples and the empirical distribution of the parameter estimate across these replicate samples is used to arrive at a measure of the sampling variance of the parameter estimate. The replication techniques that are most often used with complex sample data are Jackknife Repeated Replication (JRR), Balanced Repeated Replication (BRR) and bootstrapping. The choice of each of these methods depends on the complex sample design and the statistical software to be used. Perhaps the best way to understand these methods is to walk through examples.

Table 18.2 Example Dataset including Jackknife Replicate Weights

Stratum	School	Student	y	w'_1	w''_1	w'_2	w''_2	w'_3	w''_3
1	1	1	9	0	2	1	1	1	1
1	1	2	7	0	2	1	1	1	1
1	1	3	8	0	2	1	1	1	1
1	2	4	4	2	0	1	1	1	1
1	2	5	4	2	0	1	1	1	1
1	2	6	5	2	0	1	1	1	1
2	3	7	2	1	1	0	2	1	1
2	3	8	3	1	1	0	2	1	1
2	3	9	2	1	1	0	2	1	1
2	4	10	6	1	1	2	0	1	1
2	4	11	5	1	1	2	0	1	1
2	4	12	4	1	1	2	0	1	1
3	5	13	1	1	1	1	1	0	2
3	5	14	0	1	1	1	1	0	2
3	5	15	1	1	1	1	1	0	2
3	6	16	4	1	1	1	1	2	0
3	6	17	4	1	1	1	1	2	0
3	6	18	3	1	1	1	1	2	0

18.4.4.1 Jackknife repeated replication

JRR usually involves dropping one or more observations from the original dataset, rerunning the analysis, and repeating this process until each observation has been dropped once. Within our small dataset, we have six primary sampling units (our six schools) in three strata. We can drop each of these PSUs (and their respective student observations) one at a time to create six replicate samples. Note that because we have stratification, we need to maintain the weight of the stratum relative to the other strata when we drop a PSU from the stratum. Therefore, for each stratum, we can create a replicate by dropping a PSU (by reassigning all of the case weights in that PSU to be 0) and reweighting observations in the remaining PSU to account for that entire stratum. This set of new weights when we drop the first PSU in the first stratum is shown as w'_1 in Table 18.2. A complement replicate for the first stratum is created by dropping the second PSU in the stratum (by assigning all case weights to 0) and reweighting the observations in the first PSU to account for the entire stratum. This second set of new weights is shown as w''_1 in Table 18.2. This process is repeated for each stratum until two replicate samples are created for each stratum for a total number of six replicate samples. With this method of JRR, usually referred to as JR2 (Lee et al., 1989), the number of replicate samples will be the same as the number of PSUs. Table 18.2 displays the six replicate weights we obtain from using this procedure with our example dataset. Note that the sum of the each of the sets of jackknife weights will be equal to the original sum of weights, and in our case, the sum of each of the replicate weights is equal to 18. We can now run six pseudo analyses with each analysis using one of the sets of replicate weights.

For each pseudo analysis the weighted mean of y in each replicate is calculated as

$$\mu_h^* = \frac{\sum_{i=1}^{n} w_{hi}^* y_i}{\sum_{i=1}^{n} w_{hi}^*} \tag{18.14}$$

where * indicates either the pseudo replicate (') or complement replicate (''). For this example, our six replicate means (or pseudo values) are $\mu_1' = 3.39$, $\mu_1'' = 4.61$, $\mu_2' = 4.44$, $\mu_2'' = 3.56$, $\mu_3' = 4.50$, and $\mu_3'' = 3.50$, where the subscript refers to the stratum (with a dropped PSU) indicator and a single ' indicates the first replicate from the stratum and '' refers to the second replicate from the stratum. The jackknife estimate of the standard error for this paired selection design is determined by

$$se_{\hat{\mu}_J} = \sqrt{\frac{\sum_{h=1}^{H}\left[(\mu_h'-\hat{\mu})^2 + (\mu_h''-\hat{\mu})^2\right]}{2}} = \sqrt{\frac{\sum_{h=1}^{H}\left[(\mu_h'-\mu_h'')^2\right]}{4}} \tag{18.15}$$

and we again obtain an estimate of .906 for the standard error of the mean number of TV hours.

There are various ways to obtain jackknife replicate samples. Because we have paired selection in the sampling design (two PSUs are chosen from each stratum) we were able to undertake JR2 replication: the weights for one PSU are set to zero and the other PSU weights are inflated to represent the dropped PSU. This method can be simplified under this paired selection design by using the pseudo replicate only (and not utilizing the complement replicate) in variance estimation. The standard error is thus determined by

$$se_{\hat{\mu}_J} = \sqrt{\sum_{h=1}^{H}(\mu_h'-\hat{\mu})^2} \tag{18.16}$$

For this type of jackknife analysis and the three pseudo replicates, $\mu_1' = 3.39$, $\mu_2' = 4.44$, $\mu_3' = 4.50$, our estimate of the standard error of the mean is equivalent to the prior estimate, .906. The type of jackknife replication one can use depends on the sampling scheme. If the sample was obtained with a single stage (no selection of clusters) then jackknifing could be accomplished with one observation dropped (or its weight set to zero) at a time and the weights for the remaining observations in that stratum would be adjusted. If a single stage cluster sample was taken (with no stratification) the jackknifing could have been accomplished by dropping one cluster at a time and reweighting all clusters to account for the dropped cluster. Some large scale datasets include sets of jackknife weights so that specialized survey statistical software can accomplish these replicate analyses for you. These software packages are discussed in more detail in section 18.5.

18.4.4.2 Balanced repeated replication

Another type of replicate creation and sampling variance estimation is referred to as Balanced Repeated Replication (BRR) or half-sample replicates. In this approach each replicate is created using half of the PSUs in the sample, one from each stratum. A second replicate, the complement replicate, can then be created out of the remaining PSUs. BRR can only be accomplished when the sampling design has been undertaken with the selection of two PSUs from each stratum (as we have in our example dataset). If the sample design did not include two PSUs from each stratum, similar strata and/or PSUs can be grouped to obtain such a design (but such realignment must be done with caution).

Table 18.3 Example Dataset including Balanced Repeated Replicate Weights

Stratum	School	Student	y	w_1'	w_1''	w_2'	w_2''	w_3'	w_3''	w_4'	w_4''
1	1	1	9	0	2	2	0	0	2	2	0
1	1	2	7	0	2	2	0	0	2	2	0
1	1	3	8	0	2	2	0	0	2	2	0
1	2	4	4	2	0	0	2	2	0	0	2
1	2	5	4	2	0	0	2	2	0	0	2
1	2	6	5	2	0	0	2	2	0	0	2
2	3	7	2	0	2	0	2	2	0	2	0
2	3	8	3	0	2	0	2	2	0	2	0
2	3	9	2	0	2	0	2	2	0	2	0
2	4	10	6	2	0	2	0	0	2	0	2
2	4	11	5	2	0	2	0	0	2	0	2
2	4	12	4	2	0	2	0	0	2	0	2
3	5	13	1	0	2	0	2	0	2	0	2
3	5	14	0	0	2	0	2	0	2	0	2
3	5	15	1	0	2	0	2	0	2	0	2
3	6	16	4	2	0	2	0	2	0	2	0
3	6	17	4	2	0	2	0	2	0	2	0
3	6	18	3	2	0	2	0	2	0	2	0

The term Balanced in the name BRR refers to the need to choose orthogonal replicates. There is a complication creating replicates using half of the PSUs because dependent replicates can result, providing pseudo values that are correlated across replicates. For example, suppose we take School 1, 3 and 5 for our first replicate. Then, for our second replicate, we take 1, 3, and 6. A third replicate might be 2, 4, and 6. Our 2nd replicate is more similar to the 1st replicate than to our 3rd replicate. They share two-thirds of their observations. A solution to this problem is to balance the formation of replicates by using an orthogonal design matrix (Lee, et al., 1989) and these matrices are available from Wolter (1985). The weights associated with four BRR replicates (or half samples) are provided in Table 18.3, along with their complement BRR weights. This design matrix was taken from an example in Lohr (1999).

The half-sample replicate means for this example are estimated as $\mu_1' = 4.33$, $\mu_1'' = 3.67$, $\mu_2' = 5.56$, $\mu_2'' = 2.44$, $\mu_3' = 3.44$, $\mu_3'' = 4.56$, $\mu_4' = 4.67$, and $\mu_4'' = 3.33$. And the standard error is a measure of the variability across replicates

$$se_{\hat{\mu}_{BR}} = \sqrt{\frac{\sum_{r=1}^{R}\left[(\mu_r' - \hat{\mu})^2 + (\mu_r'' - \hat{\mu})^2\right]}{2R}} = \sqrt{\frac{\sum_{r=1}^{R}\left[(\mu_r' - \mu_r'')^2\right]}{4R}} \qquad (18.17)$$

where R represents the number of half-sample replicates. Again, we obtain an estimate of the standard error of the mean hours spent watching TV to be .906. Just as with jackknife repeated replicates, this process can be made computationally easier by dropping the complement half-sample replicates and estimating the standard error by

$$se_{\hat{\mu}_{BR}} = \frac{\sqrt{\sum_{r=1}^{R}(\mu_r' - \hat{\mu})^2}}{R} \qquad (18.18)$$

With larger datasets, BRR estimates of variance are seen less computationally taxing than JRR because they use only half samples.

18.4.4.3 Bootstrapping

Bootstrapping is similar to JRR and BRR in that the observations from the original sample are used to form replicate samples. In bootstrapping, however, observations from the original sample are sampled with replacement to obtain a dataset that is either the same size as the original dataset or is of a size that is a function of the number of selected elements minus 1 (Efron & Tibshirani, 1993). Although you might see bootstrapping procedures that use sampling with replacement of the same size of the original dataset, some researchers have found that more appropriate sampling variance estimates are obtained with selection of (n-1) units. Bootstrapping is not a simple task with complex sample data but it has been cited as being possibly the most flexible and efficient method of analyzing survey data because it can be used to solve a number of problems posed by the sample design (Lahiri, 2003). Developing an appropriate bootstrapping technique for a particular sampling design, however, is difficult.

The process of creating bootstrapped replicates will depend on the complex sampling design. For our dataset, because we have a two-stage design with strata and clusters, we bootstrap at the first stage of selection. Within strata, we randomly sample (a-1) schools (from the original sample) with replacement, where a represents the number of schools within the specific stratum. Because our sample design only included an original two PSUs in each stratum, we only select (2-1)=1 PSU at random. Once the school is selected for the bootstrap sample, all observations in the school are selected for inclusion. Each observation's sampling weight is adjusted to reflect its status in the replicate sample, using

$$w^*_{h\alpha i} = w_{h\alpha i_i} \frac{\alpha_h}{(\alpha_h - 1)} f_{h\alpha}$$

Where $w_{h\alpha i}$ represents the sampling weight for the ith person in the αth PSU in the hth stratum, and $f_{h\alpha}$ represents the number of times the PSU was randomly selected with replacement for the given Bootstrap replicate. Note that in our two-PSUs per stratum design, the maximum frequency of selection for any PSU is 1 and the formula results in the doubling of the weights for the selected observations and setting to 0 if not selected. This process is then repeated for each stratum. Table 18.4 contains frequency counts and adjusted weights for four example bootstrap replicates with our example dataset.

Table 18.4 Example Dataset including Bootstrap Frequency Counts and Weights for Four Sample Replicates

Stratum	School	Student	y	f^1	w^1	f^2	w^2	f^3	w^3	f^4	w^4
1	1	1	9	1	2	1	2	0	0	0	0
1	1	2	7	1	2	1	2	0	0	0	0
1	1	3	8	1	2	1	2	0	0	0	0
1	2	4	4	0	0	0	0	1	2	1	2
1	2	5	4	0	0	0	0	1	2	1	2
1	2	6	5	0	0	0	0	1	2	1	2
2	3	7	2	1	2	0	0	0	0	0	0
2	3	8	3	1	2	0	0	0	0	0	0
2	3	9	2	1	2	0	0	0	0	0	0
2	4	10	6	0	0	1	2	1	2	1	2
2	4	11	5	0	0	1	2	1	2	1	2
2	4	12	4	0	0	1	2	1	2	1	2
3	5	13	1	1	2	0	0	0	0	0	0
3	5	14	0	1	2	0	0	0	0	0	0
3	5	15	1	1	2	0	0	0	0	0	0
3	6	16	4	0	0	1	2	1	2	1	2
3	6	17	4	0	0	1	2	1	2	1	2
3	6	18	3	0	0	1	2	1	2	1	2

Note that with random selection of a PSU in each stratum, there is no control over the PSUs selected across the replicates; in our example in Table 4, replicates 3 and 4 contain exactly the same PSUs and therefore observations. In the case when α_h=2, this selection process reduces to the random half-sample replication as with BRR, but with BRR one can achieve the full precision possible for a linear estimate using slightly more than H replicates due to the orthogonal selection of pseudo replicates. The bootstrap, however, because of its random selection of PSUs, provides less precision for the same number of half samples and this means that for a design with two PSUs per stratum, there is probably no benefit of using the bootstrap over the BRR (Rao, Wu, & Yue 1992; Rust & Rao, 1996).

Unlike JRR and BRR, the number of bootstrap replicates does not depend on the number of PSUs in the sample. This bootstrap resampling process usually is repeated hundreds (or possibly thousands) of times and the empirical standard deviation of the parameter estimate across these replicates is considered the sampling error of the original parameter estimate

$$se_{\hat{\mu}_B} = \sqrt{\frac{\sum_{r=1}^{R}(\hat{\mu}_r - \overline{\hat{\mu}})^2}{R-1}} \tag{18.19}$$

where $\hat{\mu}_r$ is the estimate of the mean of the response variable in replicate r, and $\overline{\hat{\mu}}$ is the average estimate of the mean of the response variable across the R replicates. For this extremely small example with just four replicates with $\hat{\mu}_r$ equal to 3.67, 5.56, 4.33, and 4.33, respectively, our estimate of the standard error would be .788, slightly lower than the estimate obtained through linearization and jackknifing methods. An advantage to using bootstrap replication is that, if 1,000 bootstrap samples are generated, an empirical 95% confidence interval can be created by sorting the resulting 1,000 estimates and by taking the 25th and 975th estimates as the lower and upper bounds of the confidence interval.

18.4.4.4 Summary of replication methods

Three methods of resampling observations from the dataset to produce multiple replicates have been introduced here. The treatment has been very brief and readers are encouraged to consult other resources before undertaking a replication analysis. Which of the approaches is the best? All three are useful for a range of statistics. Bootstrap methods typically require many more replications than JRR or BRR. Additionally, JRR and BRR are available in most survey software packages already. Researchers have compared the robustness of variance estimates from JRR, BRR and linearization and none of the methods performed consistently better than the others and the decision to use either should depend on availability of programs and the type of statistic (Kish & Frankel, 1974). For statistics such as medians and percentiles, replication methods are found to be more robust than the linearization methods.

18.4.5 Model-based and Model-assisted Analysis

All of the methods discussed in the previous section for estimating robust standard errors assume that the interest is in the overall finite population parameter estimate and the sample design is a nuisance. The goal of the special analysis was to estimate correct standard errors for the overall parameter estimate of interest. Some researchers, however, desire to utilize some of the sample design in their analysis model and these analyses are considered model-assisted or model-based. Most often, clustering is considered to be part of the statistical model. For example, in our small dataset, it is possible that we might have been interested in whether differences in school means existed in hours of TV watching and, if so, whether these differences were related to school size. The school is seen as an additional level of analysis and not just an irritant in the sample design. For this type of analysis, multilevel models have been proposed and are of increasing popularity. Interested readers are referred to Hox (2002), and Raudenbush & Bryk (2002).

18.4 Summary

There are different methods available to estimate sampling variances, standard errors and test statistics when analyzing data collected through complex sampling designs. Design effect adjustments, linearization, and replication techniques are some of these methods. While design effect adjustments are simple to implement and do not require advanced software, they tend to yield conservative estimates as compared to linearization and replication.

18.5 APPLIED EXAMPLES USING IEA CIVIC EDUCATION SURVEY DATA

In the remainder of this chapter, I discuss an applied example using data from the 1999 Civic Education study conducted by the International Association for the Evaluation of Educational Achievement, known as the IEA. Some of the variance estimators discussed in Section 18.4 are applied to two types of analyses and any differences in interpretations that we would make given the estimates are addressed.

18.5.1 The IEA CIVED Data Set

The population of interest for IEA's survey on civic education in 28 countries was defined to be "all students enrolled on a full-time basis in that grade in which most students aged 14:00 to 14:11 [years; months] are found at the time of testing" (Schulz, & Sibberns, 2004, p. 42). It would be difficult to take a random sample of such a population. In many countries, a list of all students of specific ages enrolled full time just does not exist. The most cost efficient way to sample from this population is to draw a sample of schools and within those selected schools identify the students who are from the population of interest. The IEA study used a two-stage stratified cluster design but each of the 28 countries was able to determine the details of its own sampling scheme. In most of the countries, at the first stage of selection, schools were placed into strata and these strata might have been defined according to academic/vocational status, public/private status or school performance measures and school type (Schulz, & Sibberns, 2004). The schools were then sampled from each stratum with probability proportional to size, and within each school, one intact classroom was chosen from the target grade. In some countries, it was reported that disproportionate rates of sampling were used across the school strata.

Using this sampling procedure, during 1999, nearly 90,000 students took a test of civic knowledge and skills and a survey designed to measure demographic information, attitudes and participation behaviors related to civic activities. The types of questions on the test of civic knowledge and skills included multiple choice items assessing knowledge of the concepts of democracy, equality, and elected bodies and assessing skills in interpreting information, such as that provided in a political leaflet. The types of survey questions on attitudes and behaviors included questions on characteristics of the home (number of people living in the home, number of books in the home, parent educational levels) and information on participation in school organizations. Because we know that the sample design included multistage sampling and disproportionate rates of selection, the traditional estimate of the sampling variance will probably be too small. On the other hand, because the selection of schools was stratified the negative bias may be somewhat ameliorated. More information on this dataset (including procedures to access to the publicly-available data) can be obtained from the technical report (Schulz, & Sibberns, 2004) and from the study's website: http://www.wam.umd.edu/~iea/. Web links to each of the 28 national coordinators are also available on this website.

For this particular set of analyses, suppose we are undertaking research on the data from Sweden. In the international dataset, there are 3,073 students in the sample from 138 Swedish schools. Suppose that we had a couple of analytic goals. First, we wanted to estimate the mean and confidence interval for the item "number of people living in the home" (*BSGHOME*). And second, we wanted to compare the average civic skills score (*SKILSMLE*) of boys and girls. In this section of the chapter, we walk through our sample analyses, using the IEA data, and examine any differences in interpretation seen with the variance estimation techniques described in section 18.4. We first undertake a traditional analysis on the complex sample data. Then, we will undertake both design-effect adjusted analyses and a linearization analysis to obtain an estimate of the standard error, and finally we use a replication method, specifically JRR.

18.5.2 Confidence Interval for a Population Mean

Our first question might be "What is the mean number of people living in the home?" Using traditional analysis and using the normalized weights provided on the dataset (*HOUSEWGT*), we determine that the estimate of the mean and standard error, using (5) and (6) with weights incorporated are

$$\hat{\mu} = 4.274$$

$$se(\hat{\mu}) = 0.022$$

Our 95% confidence interval would then be 4.231 to 4.317—a fairly precise estimate of the number of people living in the home of 14-year old students in Sweden. Note that, for simplicity, 73 observations with missing data or outliers were removed from this analysis; how to model when data are missing is another issue that must be addressed when working with survey data and readers are encouraged to consult the chapter by Rässler, Rubin, and Schenker (Chapter 19) for an introduction to the issues and recommendations for practice.

Turning now to design-effect adjusted estimates of the standard error of the mean number of people living in the home, we need to obtain an estimate of the design effect. In the IEA technical manual (2004), only one design effect estimate is reported. Although many organizations often report the *deff*s for several key variables, IEA only reported the *deff* for the combined civics knowledge and skills total score. The value of this *deff* estimate was 4.8. Given that the number of people living in the home may show very different dependencies within school groups as compared to achievement scores, perhaps we should estimate our own design effect due to clustering. The results of an ANOVA run in SPSS version 12.0, with *IDSCHOOL* as the between-subjects factor is shown in Figure 18.2.

ANOVA

BSGHOME

	Sum of Squares	df	Mean Square	F	Sig.
Between Groups	518.871	137	3.787	2.278	.000
Within Groups	4757.784	2862	1.662		
Total	5276.655	2999			

Figure 18.2 Analysis of Variance Table from IEA Data with IDSCHOOL as a Between-Subjects Factor

The intraclass correlation, estimated using (18.8), is .056 and, in turn, the *deff* is estimated via (18.9) to be 2.152. This *deff* estimate is not entirely appropriate. We have ignored two things—stratification and disproportionate weighting. In selecting the sample, the administrators for Sweden divided schools into one of seven strata: large private schools, private schools, schools with many immigrants, and all remaining schools were categorized by their locations in big cities, suburbs, other cities, and rural areas. Additionally, because of varying school size, students are associated with differing sampling case weights. The size of the normalized weight for individuals ranges from 0.1 to 4.0 (with a mean of 1.0). Therefore, we must acknowledge that this estimate is only the design effect due to clustering and is only an approximate effect for the full sampling design. To undertake a manual standard error adjustment, we multiply our traditional estimate of the standard error by the square root of 2.152, or 1.467, obtaining a new standard error estimate of .033. This new estimate yields a new confidence interval of 4.210 to 4.338. Using SPSS, we could also create a new weight, by dividing *HOUSEWGT* by the design effect of 2.152. Using these new adjusted weights in an analysis we again obtain a mean of 4.274 and, again, an adjusted standard error of the mean of .033.

Linearized sampling variance estimates are available in SAS version 9.0 (and in SPSS since version 13.0). In SAS, with the use of *PROC SURVEYMEANS* and the specification that the *STRATA* variable is *IDSTRAT* and the *CLUSTER* variable is *IDSCHOOL* as shown in the syntax in Figure

18.3, we obtain the same estimate of the mean as from the traditional analysis (as we should), 4.27, but the estimate of the standard error is .036, a bit higher than our *deff* adjusted estimate and higher still than the traditional estimate.

```
PROC SURVEYMEANS;
STRATA IDSTRAT;
CLUSTER IDSCHOOL;
VAR BSGHOME;
WEIGHT HOUSEWGT;
RUN;
```

Figure 18.3 SAS Syntax for Obtaining a Linearized
Standard Error Estimate of the Mean

Although the IEA civic education data set does not include variables containing actual replicate weights (for JRR or BRR variance estimation), the technical manual includes information about how a user can create jackknife replicate weights using two variables included on the data set, *JKZONE* and *JKREP*. The manual indicates that, for Sweden, 70 sampling zones were created (much like our three strata in our example dataset) and in each of these zones two PSUs exist. The manual instructs that 70 replicates can be created by undertaking the following process for each zone: assign the weight of zero to all the observations in the PSU with *JKREP*=0 and for the observations in the PSU with *JKREP*=1, multiply the *HOUSEWGT* by a value of 2 (p. 135). It is possible that the reweighting could have been accomplished in a different way; instead of multiplying by 2, the original weight could have been multiplied by the ratio of the sum of the weights in the entire stratum over the sum of the weights in the PSU with *JKREP*=1. Although more difficult to program, this alternate strategy maintains the original stratum size in the replicate analyses.

Figure 18.4 contains the SAS syntax to generate the jackknife replicate weights as instructed in the IEA manual, subsequently run 70 analyses using these 70 weights. The syntax results in a dataset containing 70 records, with each record holding the pseudo value of the estimate of the mean.

Note that in the IEA proposed analysis, no complement replicate is created within the same sampling zone. The standard error can then be calculated as shown in (16) and for our analysis we obtain an estimate of 0.038, similar to the estimate obtained from the linearization process.

What have we learned from this? For all of the standard error estimation approaches that took the complex sample design into account, in relative terms the estimate of the standard error was quite a bit larger (.033, .036, .038) than the original estimate of the standard error from a traditional analysis (.022). For this example, however, the practical effects may not be astounding. For any of the methods, it appears that we have a precise measure of the average number of people living in the home (however, our confidence interval based on the traditional analysis is a bit too narrow).

```
%MACRO JACK;
 %DO I=1 %TO 70;
 IF JKZONE=&I THEN JACK&I=JKREP*2*HOUSEWGT;
 ELSE JACK&I=HOUSEWGT;
 %END;
%MEND;

%MACRO RUNJACK;
 %DO I=1 %TO 70;
PROC MEANS DATA=JACK; VAR BSGHOME; WEIGHT JACK&I;
 OUTPUT OUT=JACK_MEAN MEAN=BSGHOME_MN;
PROC DATASETS;
 APPEND BASE=ALL_JACK DATA=JACK_MEAN;
QUIT;
%END;
%MEND;

%JACK;
%RUNJACK;
```

Figure 18.4 SAS Syntax for the Generation of Jackknife Replicates
and Pseudo Estimates

18.5.3 Tests of Differences in Subgroup Means

Suppose we are also interested to determine whether, on average, boys and girls in Sweden have different amounts of civics skill, measured as a test scale score (*SKILSMLE*). Here we are interested in the difference between two population means. Using the traditional formula, we can calculate the means as shown in (5) and determine the test for a difference in the two means by the traditional independent samples *t*-test:

$$t = \frac{\left(\hat{\mu}_1 - \hat{\mu}_2 \right)}{\sqrt{\dfrac{s_p^2}{\displaystyle\sum_{i=1}^{n} w_{i1}} + \dfrac{s_p^2}{\displaystyle\sum_{i=1}^{n} w_{i2}}}} \tag{18.20}$$

where s_p^2 is an estimate of the pooled weighted variance across the two groups, defined as

$$s_p^2 = \frac{\displaystyle\sum_{i=1}^{n_1} w_{i1}(y_{i1} - \hat{\mu}_1)^2 + \sum_{i=1}^{n_2} w_{i2}(y_{i2} - \hat{\mu}_2)^2}{\displaystyle\sum_{i=1}^{n_1} w_{i1} + \sum_{i=1}^{n_2} w_{i2} - 2} \tag{18.21}$$

In SPSS, using an analysis tool to compare means, I obtain an estimate of the mean difference of 2.034 (girls in the sample scored about two points higher than boys, on average). The estimated standard error of this difference is .670, and the resulting value of the traditional t-statistic is 3.033 ($p<.05$). If we are choosing an α level of .05, we conclude that the mean civics skills scores for boys and girls are significantly different.

But we have undertaken a traditional analysis and know that, because the sample was obtained using multistage sampling, the estimate of the standard error of this difference in means may be too small. Calculating the design effect for the mean of *SKILSMLE*, using (18.8) and (18.9), we could make a manual adjustment to this standard error estimate. The design effect due to clustering for the estimate of the sampling variance of *SKILSMLE* is estimated in this example to be 4.231. Note that this design effect is more similar to the design effect reported in the IEA manual than the design effect for *BSGHOME*. Multiplying the traditional standard error for the difference in the boy and girl means (.670) by the *deft* (2.057) yields a new standard error of 1.379. Using *deff*-adjusted weights and running the analysis in SPSS, we obtain exactly the same standard error estimate of 1.379 and the new estimate of the t-statistic is reported as 1.474 ($p=.141$). In a traditional analysis, using an α of .05, we would have rejected the null hypothesis that the two population means are equal and would have concluded that girls have higher *SKILSLME* scores, on average, as compared to boys. Adjusting the standard error for the complex sample design using a *deff* adjustment leads us to retain the null hypothesis given the same α level and conclude that there is no evidence that allows us to reject the hypothesis that girls and boys score at the same level, on average.

Let us now obtain a linearized estimate of the standard error of the difference in *SKILSMLE* means for boys and girls. Using *PROC SURVEYREG* in SAS, the standard error is estimated as .896 and the subsequent t-value is 2.27 ($p<.05$). Note that this standard error estimate is quite a bit smaller than the estimate that we obtained with the design effect adjustment. This difference in estimates is due to the fact that we are now estimating the sampling variance of a bivariate statistic. As analyses become more complex, the design-effect adjustment will be too conservative. In fact, given this linearized estimation, we would have rejected the null hypothesis and concluded that there were statistically significant differences on *SKILSMLE* between boys and girls.

Using the same jackknife procedure as outlined in the previous analysis of the *BSGHOME* mean, I obtain a standard error estimate of .873, slightly smaller than the linearized estimate. The t-statistic is then 2.33 ($p<.05$) and again, we would be led to reject the null hypothesis of equivalent means.

The message here is that, depending on the variance estimation technique we use, we can come to different conclusions about parameters in the population. It is likely that traditional estimates of standard errors will be biased with data from complex survey designs, so we should look at other estimates. Although simple to apply, *deff* adjustments are really only appropriate for univariate statistics and when an accurate measure of *deff* is available to you. If linearized and replication methods are not feasible given the computing resources, it may be advisable to run both traditional and *deff*-adjusted analysis to understand the range of likely standard errors.

18.6 ANALYSIS OPTIONS AVAILABLE IN SOFTWARE PACKAGES

The more advanced approaches to variance estimation, linearization and replication, have been used with great success among statisticians who are very familiar with complex sample data issues. Procedures for statistical analysis with these approaches are available in several software packages that were developed expressly for survey data analysis, such as WESVAR and SUDAAN. The data analysis packages that are more familiar to most faculty and graduate students, SPSS and SAS, have only recently included variance estimation for complex sample data. The functions that are supported by a range of different software packages are described in the sections that follow.

18.6.1 SPSS

Until recently, SPSS software (www.spss.com) did not provide the option of modeling with complex sample data while taking into account the sampling design. However, starting with versions 12.0 and 13.0, SPSS has offered an add-on module, called CS, which can be purchased for analyzing data from complex sample designs. This add-on package provides appropriate standard error estimates for simple means, linear regression models, logistic models, and analysis of (co)variance. Users with access only to the BASE SPSS package will not be able to avail themselves of the functions available in the CS package. Thus, users should plan to use design effect adjustments (either manual inflation of the standard error or use of design effect adjusted weights), manually calculate estimates using equations provided in Kalton (1983), manually undertake replication analyses, or consider using some of the different software options discussed here.

18.6.2 SAS

Starting with version 8, SAS (www.sas.com) has included in its STAT module linearized sampling variance estimates for univariate means and linear regression parameter estimates, using the *PROC SURVEYMEANS* and *PROC SURVEYREG* procedures respectively. Starting with version 9, SAS included procedures to estimate appropriate standard errors for analyses involving categorical data: *PROC SURVEYFREQ* and *PROC SURVEYLOGISTIC*. Users with access to SAS/STAT can use any of these procedures for most typical analyses assuming the sampling design information is included on the dataset. Users with access only to the SAS/BASE module may want to consider using design effect adjustments. Note, however, that only the manual inflation of the standard error approach is possible in SAS; the design-effect adjusted weighting method will not provide estimates as expected. Additionally, a user may want to manually calculate estimates using equations provided in Kalton (1983), attempt manual replication analyses, or consider using some of the different software options discussed here.

18.6.3 WESVAR

The WESVAR software (www.westat.com/wesvar/) was developed specifically for analyzing complex sample data and focuses on replication techniques to variance estimation. A free 30-day download of the complete version 4 software package is available at the website. Also, for those students and users who do not have the resources to purchase version 4, an older version, version 2, is made available free of charge. Version 2 uses replicate weights and can compute appropriate variance estimates for frequency tables, means and multiple linear and logistic regression models. Version 4 provides the ability to create replicate weights and offers two types of BRR variance estimation and three types of JRR variance estimation.

18.6.4 Other software available: SUDAAN, STATA, Mplus, AM

SUDAAN (http://www.rti.org/sudaan/) is also devoted to analyzing complex sample data sets and supports both JRR and BRR replication methods, but also linearized variance estimates. It supports a broad range of analysis models, including loglinear and survival analysis modeling. SUDAAN can be called from SAS.

Stata (http://www.stata.com/), like SAS and SPSS, is a full data base management and statistical package that also includes a complex sample modeling component. Its focus is on regression modeling and provides Taylor Series linearization for variance estimation.

Mplus (http://www.statmodel.com) is a very flexible multivariate analysis software tool that can accommodate both design-based analysis (using the linearization approach to variance estimation) and model-based analysis for data from two-stage sampling designs. This software can be used for more complex statistical modeling, including structural equation modeling, latent class modeling, and hierarchical linear modeling.

A free statistical software program devoted to complex sample analysis has recently been developed, AM (am.air.org/). AM software was originally created to be used with large-scale assessment and survey programs in the United States, but grew into a general software package applicable to many complex sample data analyses. It is currently in a Beta version but interested users can try out its Taylor Series linearization and replication estimation methods.

18.7 SUMMARY OF IMPORTANT ISSUES AND RECOMMENDATIONS

There are two overarching recommendations that I have for any analyst working with complex sample data.

- *Understand the sampling design that was used to obtain the dataset.* If the dataset is accompanied with a technical manual, familiarize yourself with the sampling strategy used and any provided recommendations for variance estimation. Look to see if the dataset includes sampling information for each observation; this information would include a stratum indicator, a PSU indicator, and a sampling weight. Are jackknife or balanced repeated replicate weights provided on the data file? Also, determine whether the authors provide design effect estimates for key variables. Once you have all these questions answered, you can decide the best way to estimate sampling variances, given the software resources available to you. If you do have a multi-stage sample design and you do not have an accompanying technical manual (or the manual lacks such specificity), it may be instructive to estimate the design effects for yourself (at least the *deff* associated with the clustering) as shown in Section 18.4.
- *Choose an appropriate technique.* If you have access to survey data analysis software, use linearized or replication methods to estimate sampling variances. If you do not have access to such software, believe you have appropriate estimates of the design effect, and are mainly interested in univariate statistics, undertake a traditional analysis and inflate the resulting standard errors using the square root of the design effect or create an effective sample size weight and run a weighted traditional analysis with these new weights (assuming your software treats the weights as expected). If you are interested in bivariate or multivariate statistics or do not have an adequate estimate of the design effect, you might want to estimate traditional statistics, but then use a range of possible *deff* estimates to determine whether your interpretation from the analysis would change depending on the design effect. This type of sensitivity analysis would alert you to possible misinterpretation resulting from traditional analysis on data from a complex sample design.

GLOSSARY OF KEY CONCEPTS

Bias. How far the average statistic lies from the parameter it is estimating. Random errors cancel each other out in the long run, those from bias will not. Bias can be classified into negative and positive bias. Negatively-biased estimates are estimates that tend to be smaller than the true parameters and positively-biased estimates are estimates that tend to be larger than the true parameters.
Cluster or Multistage Sampling. A sampling technique where the entire population is divided into groups, or clusters, and a random sample of these clusters are selected. When all observations in the selected clusters are included in the sample, the sample is called a cluster sample and when only a sample within the cluster is selected, the sample is called a multistage sample.

Design Effect. The inflation or deflation in the sampling variance of a statistic due to the sampling design.

Intraclass Correlation (ICC). The amount of variance in a response variable that can be attributed to a clustering effect.

Linearization. A method by which sampling variances (and standard errors) are estimated under complex sample designs. Also referred to as Taylor Series approximation, variance propagation, and the Delta method.

Replication Techniques. Methods by which sampling variances (and standard errors) are estimated under complex sample designs. With these methods, replicate samples are created from the original sample and the empirical variability of the statistics across the replicate samples is used to create a measure of the sampling variability for parameter estimates from the original sample. These methods include Jackknife Repeated Replication, Balanced Repeated Replication, and Bootstrapping.

Sampling Variance. The variability in the sample estimates of a population parameter if all possible samples (of the same size) were drawn from a given population. It is the square of the standard error.

Standard Error. The average distance any single sample estimate of a population parameter is expected to be from the true value. It is the standard deviation of the sample estimates of a population parameter, over all possible samples of the same size. It is the square root of the sampling variance.

Stratified Sampling. A stratified sample is obtained by taking samples from each stratum or sub-group of a population.

Variance Estimation. The process by which the sampling variance (or standard error) is estimated. Usually when using complex sample data sets, traditional estimates of sampling variance are found to be biased.

Chapter 19

Incomplete Data:
Diagnosis, Imputation, and Estimation

Susanne Rässler
University of Erlangen-Nürnberg

Donald B. Rubin
Harvard University

Nathaniel Schenker[1]
University of Maryland

19.1 INTRODUCTION

Survey data can be imperfect in various ways. Sampling, noncoverage, interviewer error, and features of the survey design and administration can affect data quality. In particular, surveys typically have missing-data problems due to nonresponse. This can be in the form of unit nonresponse, which occurs when a selected unit (person, establishment, etc.) does not respond to any of the survey items, because of noncontact, refusal, or some other reason; or it can be in the form of item nonresponse, which occurs when a unit responds to some items but not to others. Discussions of several issues related to nonresponse in surveys are contained in the three volumes produced by the Panel on Incomplete Data of the Committee on National Statistics in 1983 (Madow, Nisselson, & Olkin, 1983; Madow, Olkin, & Rubin, 1983; and Madow & Olkin, 1983) as well as in the volume stimulated by the 1999 International Conference on Survey Nonresponse (Groves, Dillman, Eltinge & Little, 2002).

The standard textbook on statistical analysis with missing data, Little and Rubin (1987, 2002) categorizes methods proposed for analyzing incomplete data into four main groups. The first group is composed of simple procedures such as complete-case analysis (also known as listwise deletion) and available-case analysis, which discard the units with incomplete data in different ways and analyze only the units with complete data. Although these simple methods are relatively easy to implement, they can often lead to problems such as

---

[1] The findings and conclusions in this chapter are those of the authors and do not necessarily represent the views of the National Center for Health Statistics, Centers for Disease Control and Prevention

inefficient and/or biased estimates as well as estimates for different quantities that are based on different subsets of units. The second group of methods comprises weighting procedures, the standard approach for dealing with unit nonresponse. Weighting procedures essentially introduce a factor into the survey weight for each responding unit equal to the inverse of the estimated probability of response for that unit. The third group comprises imputation-based procedures, a standard approach for handling item nonresponse, especially in public-use databases. Imputation methods fill in values that are missing, and the resultant completed data are then analyzed as if there never were any missing values. Multiple imputation is a method for reflecting the added uncertainty due to the fact that imputed values are usually not the real values. The final group of methods comprises direct analyses using model-based procedures, in which models are specified for the observed data, and inferences are based on likelihood or Bayesian analyses.

This chapter reviews these four approaches to handling missing data. Simple approaches are discussed in Section 19.3, weighting methods are covered in Section 19.4, imputation and multiple imputation are discussed in Sections 19.5 and 19.6, respectively, and direct analysis using model-based procedures is treated in Section 19.7. This review of approaches is preceded in Section 19.2 by a basic discussion of missing-data mechanisms and ignorability, and the review is followed by a concluding discussion.

19.2 MISSING-DATA MECHANISMS AND IGNORABILITY

In any discussion of methods for handling missing data, it is useful to outline various missing-data mechanisms, which describe to what extent missingness depends on the observed and/or unobserved data values. Many methods are based, either implicitly or explicitly, on the assumption of a particularly simple missing-data mechanism, and thus their behavior can be influenced strongly by the true mechanism.

Key concepts about missing-data mechanisms were formalized by Rubin (1976), and accordingly, modern statistical literature (e.g., Little & Rubin, 2002, p. 12) distinguishes three cases: missing completely at random (MCAR), missing at random (MAR), and not missing at random (NMAR).

MCAR refers to missing data for which missingness does not depend on any of the data values, missing or observed. Thus, the probability of a unit responding to a particular survey item does not depend on the value of that item or any other item. The assumption of MCAR can be unrealistically restrictive, as discussed shortly.

Often, it is plausible to assume that missingness can be fully explained by the observed values in the dataset. For example, in a social survey, response behavior for certain variables might depend on completely observed variables such as gender, age group, living conditions, social status, and so forth. If the probability of a unit responding to an item depends only on such observed values but not on any missing values, then the missing data are MAR, but not MCAR because of this dependence.

If, given the observed values, missingness still depends on data values that are missing, the missing data are NMAR. This might be the case, for example, with income reporting, if people with higher incomes tend to be less likely to respond, even for units with the exact same observed values of race, education, last year's income, and other variables.

In addition to defining formally the concepts of MCAR, MAR, and NMAR, Rubin (1976) developed the notion of ignorability. Suppose that, in a situation with missing data, parametric models have been specified for: (a) the distribution of the data that would occur in the absence of missing values; and (b) the missing-data mechanism. Rubin (1976) showed that if the missing data are MAR and the parameters of the data distribution and the missing-data mechanism are distinct (which means, roughly, not functionally related), then valid inferences about the distribution of the data can be obtained using a likelihood function that does not contain a factor for the missing-data mechanism; that is, the missing-data mechanism may be ignored in likelihood inferences (see also Section 19.7). For Bayesian inference, the condition of distinctness of parameters is interpreted as a priori independence.

In many situations, it is reasonable to assume that the parameters of the data distribution and the missing-data mechanism are distinct, so that the question of whether the missing-data mechanism is ignorable often reduces to a question of whether the missing data are MAR. Moreover, even when the parameters are not distinct, if the missing data are MAR, then inferences based on the likelihood ignoring the missing-data mechanism are still valid in the sense of being approximately unbiased but not fully efficient. Thus, the MAR condition is typically regarded as the more important one in considerations of ignorability. Little and Rubin (2002, Section 6.2) includes further discussion of these ideas.

The assumption of ignorability is made often in analyses of incomplete data, and it can be advantageous for several reasons. First, it can simplify analyses greatly. Second, the MAR assumption is often reasonable, especially when there are fully observed covariates available in the analysis to explain the missingness; further, it cannot be contradicted by the observed data without the incorporation of external assumptions. Even when the missing data are NMAR, a method based on the assumption of MAR can be helpful in reducing bias by adjusting for differences between the respondents and the nonrespondents on variables that are observed for both. Finally, even if the missing data are NMAR, it is usually difficult to specify a correct nonignorable model, for the obvious reason that the relationship of missingness to the missing values cannot be observed (because the missing values are not observed).

19.3 SIMPLE APPROACHES TO HANDLING MISSING DATA

Perhaps the simplest treatment of missing data is to delete all cases with at least one missing item from the analysis, that is, to use complete-case analysis (listwise deletion). This approach is generally biased unless the missing data are MCAR, with the degree of bias depending on (a) the magnitude of the missing-data problem, (b) the degree to which the assumption of MCAR is violated, and (c) the particular analysis being implemented. Even when complete-case analysis is unbiased, it can be highly inefficient, especially in multivariate analysis problems. Consider, for example, a dataset with 10 variables, each of which has probability of missingness of .05, and suppose that missingness on each variable is independent of missingness on the other variables. Then, the probability of a case being complete is $(.95)^{10} = .60$, from which it follows that complete-case analysis would be expected to discard 40% ($= 1 - .60$) of the cases, many of them having a large fraction of their values observed.

An alternative to complete-case analysis, when a particular quantity is to be estimated, is to include in the analysis all of the cases that are complete on the variables that are needed for calculating the estimate. This approach, available-case analysis, might be regarded as complete-case analysis restricted to the variables of interest. Available-case analysis retains at least as many of the data values as does complete-case analysis. However, it can have problems when more than one quantity is estimated and the different estimates are compared or combined, due to the fact that the sample base changes from one quantity to the next. For example, if summaries of different variables are to be compared, the set of units for which each variable is summarized can differ across variables, and the summaries can be incomparable if the missing data are not MCAR; an extreme illustration would be if, say, last year's mean income were based on males, and this year's were based on females. As an example in the context of combining estimates, if the covariance of two variables as well as their individual standard deviations have been estimated using available-case analysis, and these estimates are to be used in estimating a correlation coefficient, the resulting estimated correlation can lie outside the range [-1, 1].

Complete-case analysis and available-case analysis are often the default treatments of missing data in older software packages, and they are relatively simple to implement, which is an undeniable advantage. However, as just discussed, they can have serious deficiencies, which can be overcome via the use of more sophisticated methods.

19.4 WEIGHTING ADJUSTMENTS

For the case of unit nonresponse in surveys, a modification of complete-case analysis that can help to remove bias when the missing data are not MCAR is to weight the complete cases (i.e., the respondents) based on background information that is available for all of the units in the survey. Such weighting adjustments traditionally have been the most commonly used procedures for handling unit nonresponse. This section provides a basic discussion of weighting methods. For further discussion of the procedures described here and related procedures, see Bethlehem (2002), Gelman and Carlin (2002), and Little & Rubin (2002, Section 3.3).

Typically, even if there were no adjustment for unit nonresponse in a survey, each sampled unit would already be weighted by the inverse of its probability of selection, so that unbiased estimates of population quantities, such as totals, under repeated sampling could be calculated using those weights. The basic idea underlying a weighting adjustment for unit nonresponse is to treat unit nonresponse as an extra layer of sampling, and then to weight each responding unit by the inverse of its probability of both selection *and* response.

Suppose that for unit i in a survey, the probability of selection is π_i, so that the design (inverse probability of selection) weight is $d_i = 1/\pi_i$. If the probability of response given selection for unit i is denoted by ϕ_i, then Pr(selection and response) = Pr(selection)×Pr(response | selection) = $\pi_i \phi_i$, and the unit's weight, accounting for both selection and response, is $w_i = 1/(\pi_i \phi_i) = d_i(1/\phi_i)$. Thus, if ϕ_i were known, the weighting adjustment for unit nonresponse would multiply each responding unit's design weight by the adjustment factor $1/\phi_i$, and unbiased estimation in the presence of nonresponse would be possible for the same population quantities as in the absence of nonresponse using these weights.

Usually, ϕ_i is unknown, and an estimated value $\hat{\phi}_i$ is substituted into the weighting adjustment factor. A simple technique of this type classifies the sampled units into weighting classes based on background variables that are available for both the respondents and the nonrespondents, and then estimates ϕ_i for units within each weighting class by the response rate in that weighting class. The resulting weighting adjustment removes biases to the extent that the missing data are MAR with the probability of response depending only on the weighting classes.

A generalization of the weighting class approach is to fit a model, such as a logistic or probit regression to predict response from background variables X that are available for both the respondents and the nonrespondents. The predicted probability of response for unit i, say $\hat{p}(X_i)$ (where X_i are the background variables for unit i), is then substituted for ϕ_i in the weighting adjustment. Such response propensity weighting removes biases to the extent that the missing data are MAR with the probability of response depending only on the predictors included in the response propensity model.

A mixture of the weighting class approach and the response propensity weighting approach is to fit a response propensity model and then form weighting classes composed of units with similar values of $\hat{p}(X_i)$. Within each such weighting class, each unit's value of ϕ_i is then estimated by the simple response rate. This hybrid approach can avoid extreme values for the adjustment factor $1/\hat{\phi}_i$ that can occur when ϕ_i is estimated by $\hat{p}(X_i)$ as in pure response propensity weighting, and can be less dependent on the correct specification of the response propensity model.

The weighting class approaches discussed earlier can be thought of as adjusting the weights so that the weighted proportion of complete cases in each weighting class is similar to the design-weighted proportion that would have been obtained from the full sample in the absence of nonresponse. If the proportion of the entire population in each weighting class is known from an external source, such as a census, however, an alternative is to adjust the weights so that the weighted proportion of complete cases in the weighting class is similar to the population proportion. Such a procedure, known as a post-stratification weighting adjustment, can often result in estimates that are more precise than those obtained using a weighting class adjustment.

Often in the production of data from a survey, a weighting adjustment for unit nonresponse based on one set of variables is combined with a post-stratification-type adjustment based on a different, sometimes more limited, set of variables. Thus, the final survey weight for each unit is calculated as the product of three factors: a design weight, an adjustment for unit nonresponse, and a post-stratification-type adjustment. Such a weighting procedure was used, for example, in the National Health Interview Survey (Botman, Moore, Moriarity, & Parsons, 2000).

Although the computation of point estimates following a weighting adjustment is often relatively straightforward, the valid estimation of standard errors is often far less straightforward because the weights are themselves estimates. Many statistical software packages have utilities available for estimating variances from complex survey data that include weighting, stratification, and clustering, but the weights are typically treated as known (as is the case with design weights) rather than estimated from observed data (as is typically the case with weighting adjustments for unit nonresponse). A computationally intensive approach that accounts for the estimation of the weights is to use a replication method such as balanced repeated replication, the jackknife, or the bootstrap, with the weighting adjustments recalculated separately for each replicate.

Weighting methods are relatively simple, and they are often a reasonable approach to the problem of unit nonresponse. Although they tend to decrease bias when the background variables used in weighting and the variables of interest in the analysis are both related to nonresponse, they also tend to increase variance, with the increase being related to the variability of the weights across the complete cases. Thus, they are most appropriate for surveys with large sample sizes, for which bias is a more serious issue than variance.

For dealing with item nonresponse, the use of weighting adjustments is typically problematic, in large part because discarding the incomplete cases discards additional observed data that are not used in creating the weighting adjustment. Therefore, the standard method for handling item nonresponse in surveys is imputation, discussed in the next two sections.

19.5 SINGLE IMPUTATION

Imputation refers to filling in a value for each missing datum based on other information (such as a fitted imputation model and variables that are observed for the nonrespondents). It is typically used for item nonresponse but can also be used for unit nonresponse (see for example, Rässler & Schnell, 2004). Imputation has the obvious benefit of completing the data matrix, so that standard analytic techniques designed for complete data can be applied. Moreover, in the context of a dataset produced for analysis by the public, imputation has two additional benefits. First, the missing data are handled in the same way across different analysts, thus helping to ensure comparability of analyses. Second, the data producer often has additional information that is not available to the public but that can be used in creating imputations.

Many intuitively appealing approaches have been developed for imputation. A naïve approach replaces each missing value on a variable with the unconditional sample mean of that variable from the respondents, or with the conditional sample mean after the cases are grouped on selected variables that are observed for both the respondents and the nonrespondents. An extension of conditional mean imputation is regression imputation, in which a regression of the variable with missing values on other observed variables is estimated from the complete cases, and then the resulting prediction equation is used to impute the estimated conditional mean for each missing value. Stochastic regression imputation adds a random error to the regression prediction, where the random error has variance equal to the estimated residual variance from the regression.

Another common imputation procedure is hot deck imputation, in which the missing values for an incomplete case are replaced by the observed values from a so-called donor case. A simple hot deck procedure is to define imputation cells based on a cross-classification of variables that are observed for both complete and incomplete cases, and then to impute the missing values for each incomplete case within an imputation cell using a randomly chosen complete case from the cell as the donor. Nearest neighbor imputation is a type of hot deck imputation in which a distance function (metric) is used to define the best donor cases for each incomplete case based on variables that are observed for all of the cases. When the distance is defined as the difference between cases on the predicted value of the variable to be imputed, the imputation procedure is termed predictive mean matching imputation.

Little (1988) gives a detailed discussion of issues in creating imputations. Two major considerations for imputation are that random draws rather than best predictions of the missing values should be used, and that all observed values should be taken into account to the extent possible. Replacing missing values by point estimates, such as means or regression predictions, tends to distort estimates of quantities that are not linear in the data, such as variances, covariances, and correlations. Failure to take into account observed variables can result in biases to the extent that missingness depends on such variables. In other words, accounting for all observed variables can help to ensure that the missing data are MAR and that procedures that are based on the MAR assumption are valid.

The considerations just discussed lead to the conclusion that techniques such as stochastic regression imputation and hot deck imputation are preferable to techniques such as mean imputation. However, although use of the more preferable techniques can lead to acceptable point estimates, special corrections are still needed for the resulting variance estimates. Imputing a single value for each missing datum and then analyzing the completed data using standard techniques designed for complete data generally results in standard error estimates that are too small, confidence intervals that undercover, and p-values that are too significant; this is true even if the modeling for imputation is conducted absolutely correctly.

Special methods for variance estimation following single imputation have been developed for specific imputation procedures and estimation problems; see, for example, Schafer and Schenker (2000) and Lee, Rancourt, and Särndal. (2002). However, such techniques need to be customized to the imputation method used and to the analysis methods at hand, and they often require the user to have information from the imputation model that is not typically available in public-use datasets. A more broadly applicable but computationally-intensive approach is to use a replication technique such as balanced repeated replication, the jackknife, or the bootstrap for variance estimation, with the imputation procedure repeated separately for each replicate; see for example, Efron (1994) and Shao (2002). Such an approach was also identified in Section 4 as a way to estimate variances following a weighting adjustment for unit nonresponse.

Multiple imputation, described in the next section, is an approach that is broadly applicable but less computationally intensive than the replication approach just mentioned, and it is thus particularly useful in the content of creating public-use data.

19.6 MULTIPLE IMPUTATION

Multiple imputation, introduced by Rubin (1978) and discussed in detail in Rubin (1987, 2004), is an approach that retains the advantages of imputation while allowing the uncertainty due to imputation to be directly assessed. With multiple imputation, the missing values in a dataset are replaced by $m > 1$ simulated versions, generated according to a probability distribution for the true values given the observed data. Typically, m is small, such as $m = 5$. Each of the imputed (and thus completed) datasets is first analyzed by standard methods designed for complete data; the results of the m analyses are then combined in a completely generic way to produce estimates, confidence intervals, and tests that reflect the missing-data uncertainty. Multiple imputations can be created under both ignorable and nonignorable models for nonresponse, although the use of ignorable models has been the norm, in part based on considerations of the type discussed in Section 19.2.

Procedures for inference about a scalar quantity, say Q, are described here. A review of procedures for more complicated problems, such as significance testing for multidimensional quantities, is given in Little and Rubin (2002, Section 10.2). Typically, if the data were complete, inferences for Q would be based on a point estimate $\hat{Q}$, its variance estimate, $\hat{V}$, and a normal or Student's t reference distribution. With multiple imputation and the subsequent analysis of the m completed datasets, there are m sets of completed-data statistics, say $\hat{Q}_l$ and $\hat{V}_l$, $l = 1, ..., m$. The m sets of statistics are combined to produce the final point estimate $\bar{Q} = m^{-1} \sum_{l=1}^{m} \hat{Q}_l$ and its estimated variance $T = \bar{V} + (1 + m^{-1})B$, where $\bar{V} = m^{-1} \sum_{l=1}^{m} \hat{V}_l$ is the "within-imputation" variance, $B = (m-1)^{-1} \sum_{l=1}^{m} (\hat{Q}_l - \bar{Q})^2$ is the "between-imputation" variance, and the factor $(1 + m^{-1})$ reflects the fact that only a finite number of completed-data estimates $\hat{Q}_l$, $l = 1, ..., m$ are averaged together to obtain the final point estimate. The quantity $\hat{\gamma} = (1 + m^{-1})B / T$ estimates the fraction of information about Q that is missing due to nonresponse.

Inferences from multiply imputed data are based on $\bar{Q}$, T, and a Student's t reference distribution. Thus, for example, interval estimates for Q have the form $\bar{Q} \pm t(1 - \alpha / 2)\sqrt{T}$, where $t(1 - \alpha / 2)$ is the $(1 - \alpha / 2)$ quantile of the t distribution. Rubin and Schenker (1986) provided the approximate value $v_{RS} = (m-1)\hat{\gamma}^{-2}$ for the degrees of freedom of the t distribution, under the assumption that with complete data, a normal reference distribution would have been appropriate (that is, the complete data would have had large degrees of freedom). Barnard and Rubin (1999) relaxed the assumption of Rubin and Schenker (1986) to allow for a t reference distribution with complete data, and suggested the value $v_{BR} = (v_{RS}^{-1} + \hat{v}_{obs}^{-1})^{-1}$ for the degrees of freedom in the multiple-imputation analysis, where $\hat{v}_{obs} = (1 - \hat{\gamma})(v_{com})(v_{com} + 1)/(v_{com} + 3)$, and v_{com} denotes the complete-data degrees of freedom.

The theoretical motivation for multiple imputation is Bayesian, although the resulting multiple-imputation inference is also usually approximately valid from a frequentist viewpoint. Let Y_{obs} and Y_{mis} denote, respectively, the observed and missing values in a dataset. Bayesian inferences for Q are based on the posterior distribution for Q given just the observed data. The posterior density, $p(Q | Y_{obs})$, can be related to that of the posterior distribution that would have been available with complete data, $p(Q | Y_{obs}, Y_{mis})$, as follows:

$$p(Q | Y_{obs}) = \int p(Q | Y_{obs}, Y_{mis}) p(Y_{mis} | Y_{obs}) dY_{mis}, \qquad (19.1)$$

where $p(Y_{mis} | Y_{obs})$ is the posterior predictive density of the missing data. Thus, the observed-data posterior distribution is just the average of the complete-data posterior distribution over the posterior predictive distribution of Y_{mis}. This average can be approximated by drawing several values of Y_{mis}

from its posterior predictive distribution, calculating the complete-data posterior distribution based on each draw, and then averaging the resultant complete-data posterior distributions. Multiple imputations are ideally multiple draws from an approximate posterior predictive distribution for Y_{mis}, and the multiple-imputation analysis procedures described in the preceding two paragraphs approximate the complete-data and observed-data posterior distributions in terms of point estimates, which are treated as approximate posterior means ($\hat{Q}$ and $\bar{Q}$ for the complete data and observed data, respectively), and variance estimates, which are treated as approximate posterior variances ($\hat{V}$ and T for the complete data and observed data, respectively).

A feature of imputation, either single or multiple, that gives such procedures great built-in flexibility and is especially attractive in the context of public-use data, is that the model used in imputation (underlying $p(Y_{mis} \mid Y_{obs})$ in the theoretical motivation), need not be the same as the model used in subsequent analyses of the completed data (underlying $p(Q \mid Y_{obs}, Y_{mis})$). Thus, for example, an organization distributing public-use data can do its best job at imputing for missing data, and then secondary analysts are free to explore a variety of models for analyzing the completed data. As implied by expression (19.1), however, the derivation of procedures for analyzing multiply imputed data is based on the assumption that the imputer's and analyst's models are compatible, in the sense that they can be derived from the same overall model for the data and the missing-data mechanism. Thus, formally, the imputer's and analyst's models must be compatible in order for the resulting analyses to be valid. Such compatibility can be enforced more easily when the imputer and analyst are the same entity or communicate with each other. In the context of public-use data, however, to promote near-compatibility of the two models so that multiple-imputation analyses will be approximately valid, the imputer should include as rich a set of variables in the imputation model as possible, to accommodate the variety of analyses that might be carried out by secondary analysts. When the data come from a complex sample survey, variables reflecting features of the sample design should be included as well. See Meng (1994) and Rubin (1996) for further discussion of such issues.

If a model with parameter θ has been specified for the data, the posterior predictive density for Y_{mis} can be expressed as $p(Y_{mis} \mid Y_{obs}) = \int p(Y_{mis} \mid Y_{obs}, \theta) \, p(\theta \mid Y_{obs}) \, d\theta$. This suggests that a draw with density $p(Y_{mis} \mid Y_{obs})$ can be created in two steps: (1) Draw a value, say θ^*, from the posterior distribution of θ with density $p(\theta \mid Y_{obs})$; and (2) draw a value from the posterior predictive distribution of Y_{mis} given the drawn value from step 1, that is, having density $p(Y_{mis} \mid Y_{obs}, \theta^*)$. Multiple imputations can be created by repeating steps 1 and 2 independently m times.

In the two-step procedure just described, step 1 reflects uncertainty due to estimating the parameter θ, and step 2 reflects variability of Y_{mis} given a specific value of θ. It is important to reflect both sources of variability in creating multiple imputations, so that variances will not be underestimated. Rubin (1987, Chapter 4) labeled imputation methods that do not account for all sources of variability as "improper." Thus, for example, fixing θ at a point estimate $\hat{\theta}$, and then drawing m imputations for Y_{mis} independently with density $p\left(Y_{mis} \mid Y_{obs}, \hat{\theta}\right)$, would constitute an improper procedure.

For simple patterns of missing data, the two-step paradigm is relatively straightforward to implement. For example, Rubin and Schenker (1987) described its use in the context of fully parametric imputation involving logistic regression models. Steps 1 and/or 2 can also incorporate more nonparametric analogues. For example, the simple hot-deck procedure that randomly draws imputations for incomplete cases from matching complete cases is not proper because it ignores the sampling variability due to the fact that the population distribution of complete cases is not known but rather is estimated from the complete cases in the sample. Rubin and Schenker (1986, 1991) described a two-step procedure, termed "approximate Bayesian bootstrap imputation," which first draws a bootstrap sample from the complete cases and then draws imputations randomly from the bootstrap sample. The initial bootstrap step is a nonparametric analogue to drawing a value θ^* with density $p\left(\theta \mid Y_{obs}\right)$, and the subsequent hot-deck step is a nonparametric analogue to drawing a value of Y_{mis} with density $p\left(Y_{mis} \mid Y_{obs}, \theta^*\right)$. Dorey, Little, and Schenker (1993) combined an initial bootstrap step with a fully parametric second step. Schenker and Taylor (1996) combined a fully parametric first step with predictive mean matching imputation at the second step. Finally, Heitjan and Little (1991) combined an initial bootstrap step with bivariate predictive mean matching imputation at the second step.

As a parametric example of the two-step procedure, consider the case of stochastic regression imputation for missing values of a variable. Even with each missing value being replaced by its predicted value plus a random error with variance equal to the estimated residual variance, the procedure is not proper because it fails to include the uncertainty in the regression coefficients and the residual variance that are used to create the imputed values. The proper procedure uses two steps: the first step draws random values of the regression coefficients and the error variance from their observed-data posterior distribution; and the second step uses these drawn values in imputing for the missing data. For details see Rubin (1987, p. 167).

For more complicated patterns of missing data, it is often infeasible to use the two-step paradigm to draw values with density $p\left(Y_{mis} \mid Y_{obs}\right)$, particularly because of difficulties with drawing parameter values with the observed-data posterior density, $p\left(\theta \mid Y_{obs}\right)$, in the first step. In such cases,

Bayesian iterative simulation methods, discussed in the next section, are often useful.

19.7 DIRECT ANALYSIS USING MODEL-BASED PROCEDURES

Direct analyses of the incomplete data can be implemented by specifying a model for the incomplete data and then basing inferences on the likelihood or posterior distribution under that model. Let $Y = (Y_{obs}, Y_{mis})$, and let R denote a matrix of indicators for whether the values in Y are observed or missing. In its full generality, modeling the incomplete data is accomplished by simultaneously modeling both Y and R, as mentioned when the notion of ignorability was introduced in Section 2. Selection models (e.g., Heckman, 1976) specify the marginal distribution of Y as well as how the distribution of R depends on Y, as follows:

$$p(Y, R \mid \theta, \xi) = p(Y \mid \theta) p(R \mid Y, \xi),\qquad(19.2)$$

where θ and ξ are unknown parameters. In contrast, pattern-mixture models (e.g., Rubin, 1977) specify the distribution of Y for each pattern of missing data (implied by R) as well as the probability of the various patterns occurring, as follows:

$$p(Y, R \mid \phi, \pi) = p(Y \mid R, \phi) p(R \mid \pi),$$

where ϕ and π are unknown parameters. When R is independent of Y, the missing data are MCAR, and the selection and pattern-mixture specifications are equivalent as long as $\theta = \phi$ and $\xi = \pi$. When the missing data are not MCAR and distributional assumptions are added, the two specifications can differ.

Little and Rubin (2002, Chapter 15) discuss use of the selection and pattern-mixture approaches in the context of nonignorable missingness for a variety of types of data. As discussed in Section 19.2, the correct specification of nonignorable models is usually difficult, due to lack of information in the data about the relationship between the missing-data mechanism and the missing values themselves. For this reason, selection models and pattern-mixture models for nonignorable missing data tend to depend strongly on assumptions about the specific distributions as well as identifying restrictions. Thus, although they offer different and interesting approaches to modeling nonignorable missing data, it is suggested that they be used primarily for sensitivity analyses; see, for example, Rubin (1977) and Little (1993).

Consider now the situation of ignorable missing data, which, for reasons discussed earlier and in Section 19.2, is a common assumption in missing-data problems. The observed data are Y_{obs} and R, and under the selection model specification given by expression (19.2), the likelihood function based on the observed data is

$$L(\theta,\xi \mid Y_{obs}, R) \propto \int p(Y_{obs}, Y_{mis} \mid \theta) p(R \mid Y_{obs}, Y_{mis}, \xi) dY_{mis} . \qquad (19.3)$$

As shown by Rubin (1976) and discussed in Section 19.2, if the missing data are MAR, that is, $p(R \mid Y_{obs}, Y_{mis}, \xi) = p(R \mid Y_{obs}, \xi)$, and if θ and ξ are distinct, then expression (19.3) is proportional to the likelihood ignoring the missing-data mechanism,

$$L(\theta \mid Y_{obs}) \propto \int p(Y_{obs}, Y_{mis} \mid \theta) dY_{mis}, \qquad (19.4)$$

and thus, inferences may be based on this simpler likelihood. Articles have appeared in the literature describing analyses of incomplete data under the assumption of ignorable missingness for a vast number of different analytic problems. Little and Rubin (2002, Chapters 11–14) review such examples.

The remainder of this section describes two techniques, the EM algorithm (Dempster, Laird, & Rubin, 1977) and Bayesian iterative simulation (e.g., Tanner & Wong, 1987; Gelfand & Smith, 1990), which have proven very useful for conducting such analyses when there are general patterns of missing data. These techniques can be applied in the context of nonignorable missing data as well as that of ignorable missing data, but the presentation here is in the latter context.

In many missing-data problems, even the observed-data likelihood (4) is complicated, and explicit expressions for maximum likelihood estimates of θ are difficult to derive. The EM algorithm, a technique for computing such maximum likelihood estimates iteratively, takes advantage of the facts that: (1) if θ were known, it would be relatively easy to impute values for Y_{mis}; and (2) if the data were complete, computation of maximum likelihood estimates would be relatively simple. Starting with an initial estimate of θ, the EM algorithm iterates between two steps, an E-step (E for expectation) and an M-step (M for maximization of the likelihood), until convergence. Given the estimate of θ at iteration t, $\theta^{(t)}$, the E-step computes the expected value of the complete-data loglikelihood $Q(\theta \mid \theta^{(t)}) = \int \log L(\theta \mid Y) p(Y_{mis} \mid Y_{obs}, \theta = \theta^{(t)}) dY_{mis}$ given Y_{obs} and $\theta = \theta^{(t)}$; this step often involves computing the expected values of the complete-data sufficient statistics, which sometimes are linear in the data. Then the M-step determines $\theta^{(t+1)}$ by maximizing the expected complete-data loglikelihood $Q(\theta \mid \theta^{(t)})$. For discussions of the theoretical properties of the EM algorithm, examples of its use, methods for obtaining standard errors based on the algorithm, and extensions, see Dempster et al. (1977), McLachlan and Krishnan (1997), Schafer (1997), and Little and Rubin (2002, Chapters 8, 9, and 11–15).

Bayesian inferences for θ are based on the observed-data posterior distribution with density $p(\theta \mid Y_{obs}) \propto p(\theta) L(\theta \mid Y_{obs})$, where $p(\theta)$ is the prior density for θ. As is the case with maximum likelihood estimation, working explicitly with the observed-data posterior distribution can be difficult.

Bayesian iterative simulation methods, which include data augmentation and Gibbs sampling, facilitate the creation of draws with density $p(\theta \mid Y_{obs})$ using steps that are analogous to those of the EM algorithm but that involve simulation. In a simple form, Bayesian iterative simulation methods begin with an initial approximation to $p(\theta \mid Y_{obs})$ and then iterate between two steps, an I-step, which imputes an updated value for Y_{mis}, and a P-step, which draws a value from an updated conditional posterior distribution for θ, until convergence of the distribution of draws of Y_{mis} and θ. Specifically, given the draw of θ at iteration t, $\theta^{(t)}$, the I-step draws a value $Y_{mis}^{(t+1)}$ with density $p(Y_{mis} \mid Y_{obs}, \theta^{(t)})$, and then the P-step draws a value $\theta^{(t+1)}$ with density $p(\theta \mid Y_{obs}, Y_{mis}^{(t+1)})$. As t increases, the draws $(Y_{mis}^{(t)}, \theta^{(t)})$ converge in distribution to draws with joint density $p(Y_{mis}, \theta \mid Y_{obs})$, and thus the draws $\theta^{(t)}$ converge in distribution to draws with density $p(\theta \mid Y_{obs})$. The empirical distribution of multiple such draws of θ can be used to approximate the observed-data posterior distribution of θ. The draws at successive iterations are serially associated with each other, however. Therefore, to obtain multiple independent draws from the observed-data posterior distribution of θ, it is standard practice either to independently repeat the entire iterative procedure until convergence multiple times and take one draw from each such run, or to implement the iterative procedure once until convergence and then take every k^{th} draw thereafter, with k chosen large enough to achieve approximate independence. For discussions of theoretical properties, variations, and examples of the use of Bayesian iterative simulation methods, see Tanner and Wong (1987), Gelfand and Smith (1990), Schafer (1997), and Little and Rubin (2002, Chapters 10–14).

Bayesian iterative simulation methods are not only useful for obtaining draws of θ for purposes of approximating $p(\theta \mid Y_{obs})$, but also for purposes of creating multiple imputations of Y_{mis} when the pattern of missing data is not simple and thus the two-step paradigm described in Section 6 cannot be implemented in a straightforward manner. Because, as just discussed, the draws $(Y_{mis}^{(t)}, \theta^{(t)})$ converge in distribution to draws with joint density $p(Y_{mis}, \theta \mid Y_{obs})$, it follows that the draws $Y_{mis}^{(t)}$ converge in distribution to draws with density $p(Y_{mis} \mid Y_{obs})$. Thus, multiple independent draws from the predictive distribution of Y_{mis} can be obtained and used as multiple imputations.

Consider an extension of the example of stochastic regression imputation given at the end of Section 19.6, and suppose there are several variables having a complicated pattern of missing data. Suppose further that the variables are approximately continuous, and that if there were no missing data, they would be assumed to have a multivariate normal distribution. The assumption of multivariate normality implies a multivariate linear regression for each subset of the variables on the remaining variables, where the parameters for the regression are functions of the parameters for the multivariate normal distribution. Whereas the two-step procedure discussed in Section 19.6 is difficult to implement in this situation, Bayesian iterative simulation is relatively straightforward. Given the current drawn values for the parameters of the multivariate normal distribution, the I-step uses a multivariate version of stochastic regression imputation to impute for the missing values. Then the P-step draws new values for the parameters of the multivariate normal distribution from their posterior distribution given the completed data (which, under standard prior distributions, is a normal inverted-Wishart distribution). For further details about imputation from the multivariate normal model, see Schafer (1997). For discussion of a recent and practical application of multivariate normal imputation to establishment data, along with estimation of a sophisticated econometric model, see Jensen and Rässler (2006).

19.8 SUMMARY AND DISCUSSION

Missing values are a common problem in data analyses. This entry has discussed concepts regarding mechanisms that create missing data, as well as strengths and weaknesses of four commonly used approaches to deal with missing data. Simple approaches, such as complete-case analysis and available-case analysis, are generally valid only when the missing data are missing completely at random. Even then, such approaches can have problems of inefficiency and incomparability. Weighting adjustments can help to eliminate biases inherent in complete-case analyses, and they are especially useful for handling unit nonresponse in large surveys.

Multiple imputation can be used to adjust for both unit and item nonresponse. It is especially useful in the context of public-use data, because of its general applicability and flexibility, as well as the fact that it allows the data producer to create one adjustment for missing data that can be used by all secondary data analysts. Multiple imputation is also a useful technique in the context of designed missing data, such as when split questionnaire designs (also known as matrix sampling designs) are used to reduce costs and respondent burden (e.g., Raghunathan & Grizzle, 1995). Moreover, it can offer new potential for analysis, e.g., in the context of censored data (see Gartner & Rässler, 2005 or Jensen, Gartner, & Rässler, 2006).

For specific analytic problems in the presence of missing data, especially when the data producer and data analyst are the same entity, direct analyses of the incomplete data can be conducted. Techniques such as the EM algorithm and Bayesian iterative simulation are very useful for handling the complexities caused by the missing data. For a given problem, if the sample is large, likelihood-based analyses and Bayesian analyses under diffuse prior distributions would be expected to give similar results, because the likelihood would be expected to dominate the prior. For small samples, however, Bayesian analyses have the advantage of avoiding assumptions such as asymptotic normality that are typically made with large-sample analyses. Moreover, results under various prior assumptions can be compared.

Multiple-imputation analyses and direct Bayesian analyses would also be expected to give similar results for a specific problem, as long as the imputer's and analyst's models are compatible with each other as well as with the model used for the Bayesian analyses. Multiple imputation has an advantage of flexibility over direct Bayesian analyses, in the sense that the imputer can use one model to fill in the missing data, whereas the analyst can use a different model to draw inferences from the completed data; however, incompatibility of the two models can degrade the approximations underlying multiple-imputation methods somewhat.

Bayesian iterative simulation methods also facilitate the creation of multiple imputations for general patterns of missing data. In fact, analogues to such methods for multiple imputation, in which variables are imputed sequentially using different regression models that are not necessarily derived from a joint distribution for all of the data, have been developed recently, and they provide very flexible tools for multiple imputation (Kennickel, 1991; Van Duuren & Oudohoorn, 2000; Raghunathan, Lepkowski, van Hoewijk, & Stenberger, 2001; Münnich & Rässler, 2005; Van Buuren, Brand, Oudshoorn, & Rubin, 2006). Further research should lead to greater understanding of the theoretical properties of such methods as well as to refinements of the methods. Because of uncertainties about correct models in the presence of missing data, it is useful to conduct sensitivity analyses under different modeling assumptions. In fact, this was one of the original motivations for multiple imputation. Rubin (1978; 1987, Chapter 1) recommended the creation of imputations under multiple models for purposes of sensitivity analysis, in addition to the creation of repeated imputations under a single model for assessments of variability due to missing data under that model. For examples of such sensitivity analyses, see Rubin (1977, 1986) and Rässler (2002).

Many of the approaches discussed herein can be applied under the assumption of either ignorable or nonignorable missing data. The assumption of ignorability cannot be contradicted directly by the observed data, and procedures that assume ignorability typically lead to at least partial corrections for bias due to missing data, especially if several variables are included in the analysis to explain missingness. Nonignorable models can be very difficult to specify, and their performance can be quite sensitive to the modeling assumptions. Therefore, a sensible approach is to use ignorability as a "baseline" assumption, and to conduct additional sensitivity analyses using nonignorable models. For comparisons of the performance of ignorable and nonignorable models, see Glynn, Laird, and Rubin (1986), Rubin, Stern, and Vehovar (1995), and Baker, Ko, and Grobard (2003).

GLOSSARY OF KEY CONCEPTS

Ignorable missingness. If the data are MAR (which includes MCAR), and if the parameter governing the distribution of the data is distinct from the parameter governing the missingness mechanism given the data, the missingness is said to be ignorable with respect to likelihood-based or Bayesian inference. In this case, the observed data observed-data likelihood does not depend on the missingness mechanism. Distinct means a priori independent for Bayesian inference and that the joint parameter space is the product of the individual disjoint parameter spaces for likelihood-based inference.

Item Nonresponse. A unit answers some items on the questionnaire but not other items.

Missing At Random (MAR). Data are missing at random if the missingness is possibly related to the observed data in the data set, but, conditional on these data is not related to any unknown values. In other words, the missing values are a random sample of all values within classes defined by observed values (i.e., conditional on the observed data, the missingness is completely at random).

Missing Completely At Random (MCAR). Data are missing completely at random if the missingness is unrelated to the (unknown) missing values of that variable as well as unrelated to the values of other variables. For example, the missing values are a random sample of all values. The rate that values are missing can vary across the different items in the questionnaire.

Multiple imputation. Each missing value is replaced by a set of m ($m>1$) values, resulting in m completed data sets. Each of these is analyzed as if it were the true data, and the results are combined to produce a single final point estimate and its associated sampling variability, which reflects both sampling variance if no data were missing and the uncertainty with which the missing data can be predicted from the observed data. Generally, valid procedures ae obtained without specialized equations.

Nonignorable missingness. When the missingness is not ignorable. In this case, a model for the missingness generally must be postulated and included in the analysis to allow valid inferences.

Not Missing At Random (NMAR). The missingness depends on some unobserved (missing) values, even after conditioning on all observed values.

Single imputation. Each missing value in a data set is filled in with one value, yielding one completed data set. To get valid inference from singly imputed data, in general, special variance estimators have to be used to account for the particular imputation method applied and for the particular point estimator used.

Unit Nonresponse. A unit fails to provide any data on the questionnaire.

Note: these definitions were established in Rubin (1976, Biometrika). Also see Little and Rubin (2002).

Chapter 20

Accommodating Measurement Errors

Joop J. Hox[1]

Department of Methodology & Statistics, Utrecht University

20.1 INTRODUCTION

Most if not all measures collected in survey research contain some amount of measurement error. Psychometric theory (e.g., Nunnally & Bernstein, 1994; Traub, 1994) makes clear that especially when only a few questions are used to measure a specific underlying concept, that concept will be measured with considerable measurement error. For that reason, psychological tests tend to use scales that consist of a large number if items (30–60 items are not uncommon in psychological measurement), in order to attain a sufficient reliability for the combined scale score. In contrast, the measures used in surveys are typically short, because there is limited room in the questionnaire. Faced with the choice between including fewer topics in the questionnaire, while having more questions for each topic, versus having more topics and fewer questions, most survey researchers opt for the latter (Heath & Martin, 1997).

This practice is unfortunate, because it implies that most measures used in surveys contain large measurement errors. Heath and Martin (1997) note that, in addition, most measures of social and political concepts do not undergo the thorough process of development and evaluation that psychological tests go through. The theoretical foundation is often weak (cf. Hox, 1997), and scales with no more than five or six questions are common in surveys. In some cases, there is only a single question available as indicator for a specific concept. Using only a single question effectively evades the issue of measurement error, because there is no information about its reliability or validity. However, this does not solve the problems associated with measuring instruments that have a relatively low reliability.

The remainder of this chapter mainly addresses problems associated with lack of reliability. Following classical psychometric theory, reliability is defined as absence of random measurement error. The related notion of validity, which is defined as absence of systematic measurement error, is discussed briefly.

Whether they are single survey questions or scales that consist of multiple questions, measurements that contain a sizeable amount of error involve two kinds of problems. Firstly, measurement error attenuates the strength of the relationships analyzed, which means that the statistical power of

---

[1] I thank Paul Biemer and Henk Kelderman for their comments.

significance tests decreases. Secondly, many analysis methods in fact assume that the explanatory or predictor variables are measured without measurement error. When the predictor variables do contain measurement errors, the results of such tests may be biased. The exact nature of the bias depends on the statistical test used; some possibilities are discussed in the next section of this chapter. When information about the reliability of measurement is available or can be estimated from the available data, one can take the measurement errors into account in the analysis. A powerful method to accomplish this is structural equation modeling. The next section discusses the consequences of measurement error in more detail. After that, accounting for measurement error using structural equation modeling is discussed in detail. Other approaches are described briefly. The discussion section summarizes the issue of measurement error and describes what is required in the design of the study to make such analysis possible.

20.2 EFFECTS OF MEASUREMENT ERROR

20.2.1 Measurement Error and Classical Reliability Theory

Classical reliability theory (cf. Nunnally & Bernstein, 1994; Traub, 1994) is a convenient model to discuss the problem of measurement error. In classical reliability theory, the observed score X is assumed to consist of two independent components, the true score T and the random error component e:

$$X = T + e.$$ (20.1)

The error component has a mean of zero and a variance indicated by σ_e^2. Because T and e are independent, the variance of the observed score X is given by:

$$\sigma_X^2 = \sigma_T^2 + \sigma_e^2.$$ (20.2)

The reliability of a measurement is defined as the proportion true score variance in the total score, which is given by:

$$\rho_{XX} = \frac{\sigma_T^2}{\sigma_T^2 + \sigma_e^2} = \frac{\sigma_T^2}{\sigma_X^2}.$$ (20.3)

Equation (20.3) is not useful for estimating the reliability ρ_{XX}, because the true scores T are unknown. The true scores T are a latent variable, meaning that it is a hypothetical construct that cannot be measured directly. The clue to estimating reliability is that the measurement is repeated. The simplest approach is to repeat the measurement using the same instrument, which allows calculating the correlation r_{XX} between the two measurement occasions. This correlation is an estimate for the reliability called the test-retest method. Because the error components are assumed random and independent between the two measurement occasions, the test-retest method implies no memory, or induction of total amnesia between the two measurement occasions. This assumption is in many applications implausible, and other ways to assess the reliability have been developed. One of these is the test-parallel test method.

Here, two versions of the measurement instrument are developed that are based on different questions but are exactly parallel, meaning that they have the same mean and variances for the true and error components. If these conditions are met, the correlation $r_{XX'}$ between the two parallel measurements is an estimate for the reliability based on the test-parallel test method. Because developing two parallel tests requires an extra effort, an often used variant of the parallel test method is the split half method. Here, an existing multiple-item instrument is split at random into two halves, and the correlation between the two halves is used as a reliability estimate. For example, an instrument that consists of ten items could be split in two halves, the first formed by item 1, 3, 5, 7 and 9, and the second formed by item 2, 4, 6, 8 and 10. The correlation between these two halves produces an estimate $\hat{\rho}$ of the reliability of each of the two halves. Because the total instrument contains twice as many questions, the reliability of the total instrument is estimated using the *Spearman-Brown* formula for increasing the test length with a factor k (to estimate the reliability for the split-half method, $k=2$):

$$\rho_{XX'} = \frac{k\hat{\rho}}{1+(k-1)\hat{\rho}}. \tag{20.4}$$

A popular method to assess the reliability of a multiple-question instrument is calculating coefficient alpha. Coefficient alpha, or Cronbach's alpha, is an estimate of the reliability of the instrument based on splitting the instrument into as many components as there are questions or items. Coefficient alpha is given by:

$$\alpha = \frac{k}{k-1}\left(1 - \frac{\sum \sigma_i^2}{\sigma_X^2}\right), \tag{20.5}$$

where σ_i^2 denotes the variance of item i, which is summated for all k items in the instrument, and σ_X^2 denotes the variance of the total score. Both the split-half method and coefficient alpha assume that the different components (the two halves or the k items) are parallel measures, meaning all have the same mean and true and error variances. If this assumption is not met, both estimate in general a lower boundary for the reliability $r_{XX'}$. A second assumption is that the measurement errors in the different components have a correlation of zero. This assumption is called the assumption of local independence. It is important, and it can easily be violated if there are two items that ask the same question in almost the same words.

20.2.2 The Effect of Measurement Error on Statistical Tests

The main effect of measurement error on statistical tests of relationships between variables is that it reduces the power of the test. The power of a statistical test is defined as the probability of rejecting the null-hypothesis of no effect if it is in fact not true. This effect can be demonstrated by examining the effect of measurement errors on a correlation. Assume that we have two constructs, which give rise to two true scores T_1 and T_2. The correlation ρ_{12}

between the true scores T_1 and T_2 depends on the covariance between the true scores σ_{12} and their variances σ_1^2 and σ_2^2:

$$cor\left(T_1 T_2\right) = \frac{\sigma_{12}}{\sqrt{\sigma_1^2 \sigma_2^2}}. \tag{20.6}$$

Because the measurement errors of T_1 and T_2 are uncorrelated, the correlation r_{12} between the observed variables X_1 and X_2 depends on the covariance between the true scores σ_{12} and the variances of the observed variables:

$$cor\left(X_1 X_2\right) = \frac{\sigma_{12}}{\sqrt{\left(\sigma_1^2 + \sigma_{e1}^2\right)\left(\sigma_2^2 + \sigma_{e2}^2\right)}}, \tag{20.7}$$

where the σ_e^2 represent the measurement error variance of variables X_1 and X_2. When equation (6) and (7) are compared, it is clear that they have the same numerator, and that the denominator of equation (7) is larger. As a consequence, $cor(X_1 X_2) \le cor(T_1 T_2)$, in other words: the presence of measurement error variance attenuates the correlation between the two measures. The significance of a correlation coefficient is commonly tested using a t-test with $t = r\sqrt{(n-2)/(1-r^2)}$. It is clear that with a larger r we obtain a larger t-value, which is why increasing the correlation leads to an increased probability of finding a statistically significant result given the same sample size n.

A similar argument can be given for other statistical tests such as the t-test for differences between group means and other tests. In all cases, measurement errors attenuate the estimate of the effect size and thereby decrease the power of the statistical tests. If the reliabilities of the measures are known, the correlation coefficient can be corrected for attenuation, to give an estimate of what that correlation would be if these measures had a perfect reliability. The equation is given by:

$$\hat{r}_{12} = \frac{r_{12}}{\sqrt{r_{11} r_{22}}}, \tag{20.8}$$

where r_{11} and r_{22} refer to the measurement reliability of X_1 and X_2. Similar equations can be given to correct other statistics for measurement error. The drawback is that all such corrections also affect the corresponding standard errors, so the calculations for the significance tests should also be changed. In addition, correction for measurement error is difficult in multivariate analysis. In general, statisticians prefer to make the correction for measurement errors an integral part of the analysis model.

20.3 INCLUDING MEASUREMENT ERROR IN THE ANALYSIS

A powerful approach to include measurement errors is to frame the analysis as a structural equation model (SEM). Structural equation modeling is a general data analysis model, which includes as special cases multiple regression analysis (mra), analysis of covariance (ancova), and multivariate ancova (mancova). This section starts with a brief introduction to structural equation modeling that shows how mra and (m)ancova can be cast in a SEM framework. Next, it is shown that the classical reliability model can be written as a structural model. This allows including measurement errors in two ways, depending on whether the data contain sufficient information to estimate the measurement error from the data themselves, or whether the information on the amount of measurement error must be taken from elsewhere. Both approaches are discussed, with an example of their use.

20.3.1 Structural Equation Modeling as a General Data Analytic Tool

Structural equation modeling is a very general and convenient framework for statistical analysis that includes several traditional multivariate procedures, for example factor analysis, regression analysis, discriminant analysis, and canonical correlation, as special cases (cf. Kline, 2005). Structural equation models are often visualized by a graphical *path diagram*. The statistical model is usually represented in a set of matrix equations. In the early seventies, when this technique was first introduced in social and behavioral research, the software usually required setups that specify the model in terms of these matrices. Thus, researchers had to distill the matrix representation from the path diagram, and provide the software with a series of matrices for the different sets of parameters, such as factor loadings and regression coefficients. A recent development is software that allows the researchers to specify the model directly as a path diagram. This works well with simple problems, but may get tedious with more complicated models. For that reason, current SEM software still supports the command- or matrix-style model specifications too.

A path diagram consists of boxes and circles, which are connected by arrows. Observed (or measured) variables are represented by a rectangle or square box, and latent (or unmeasured) factors by a circle or ellipse. Single headed arrows or paths are used to define regression coefficients (causal relationships) in the model, with the variable at the tail of the arrow having an effect on the variable at the point. Double headed arrows indicate covariances or correlations, without a directional or causal interpretation. Statistically, the single headed arrows or paths represent regression coefficients, and double-headed arrows covariances.

It is instructive to see how a familiar analysis procedure, such as multiple regression analysis, looks when represented as a path model. Figure 20.1 is a multiple regression model from Warren, White and Fuller (1974), who report a study of 98 farm managers. The dependent variable is the role behavior of the managers (rolbehav), to be predicted by knowledge of economics (knowledge), value orientation (valorien), role satisfaction (rolsatis) and degree of education (training).

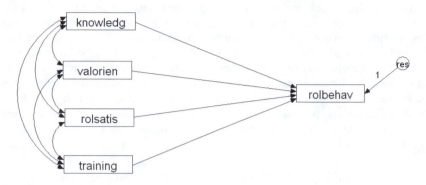

Figure 20.1. Multiple regression as a path diagram.

Figure 20.1 makes two things quite clear. Firstly, in multiple regression analysis, we generally assume that the independent variables are correlated; in Figure 20.1 we find that assumption as the two-headed arrows between the predictor variables. Secondly, the residual error in multiple regression analysis is actually an unobserved, latent variable. The regression coefficient of the residual error is constrained to one, to achieve identification. If we estimate the model in Figure 20.1, we obtain unstandardized and standardized regression weights, a variance estimate for the residual errors, and the squared multiple correlation of the dependent variable role behavior. Because SEM estimates are typically estimated using Maximum Likelihood estimation, and standard multiple regression uses least squares estimation, they may result in slightly different estimates, but these differences are very small. For all practical purposes, standard multiple regression and multiple regression using a SEM approach are identical.

20.3.2 Including Measurement Error in structural equation models

Using SEM to estimate multiple correlations has few advantages; we use this example only to show how a familiar analysis method looks when cast in the SEM framework. The real strength of SEM is, that we may specify and estimate more complicated path models, with intervening variables between the independent and dependent variables, and latent factor as well. In the context of measurement errors, it is important to note that the classical true score model can be formulated as a structural equation model, and embedded in a larger structural model. The true score model is given by equation (20.1), which is repeated here:

$$X = T + e.$$ (20.1, repeated)

It can be presented graphically by the path diagram in Figure 20.2.

Figure 20.2. Path diagram of the true score model.

If we have only one measure, as in Figure 20.2, we have observed a single variance, and it is not possible to estimate the variances of T and e. But if we have two parallel tests, as in the test-retest or the test-parallel test method, the path diagram is given by Figure 20.3 and we can estimate both σ_T^2 and σ_e^2.

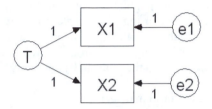

Figure 20.3. Path diagram for two parallel tests.

Since the error variances of $e1$ and $e2$ are assumed equal, we can estimate σ_T^2 and σ_e^2, and calculate the reliability of each measure using equation (20.3) as $\rho_{XX} = \sigma_T^2 / (\sigma_T^2 + \sigma_e^2)$. If $X1$ and $X2$ are split-halves, we obtain the reliability of half the test, and estimate the reliability of the total test using the Spearman-Brown formula in equation (4). More importantly, the latent variable T is an estimate for the true score and therefore contains no measurement error. By using the latent variable T instead of the observed variable X as dependent variable or predictor, we can estimate correlations, regression coefficients and explained variances after removing the measurement errors.

Thus, if replicate measurements of the same construct are available, measurement error variances and relationships between true score latent variables can be estimated. Figure 20.3 depicts the parallel test model, where all available measures have the same true score and measurement error variance. As stated earlier, if this assumption is not true, the parallel test model provides a lower bound for the reliability estimate. We can relax the assumptions of the parallel test model in two steps. Firstly, we can assume that the loadings for the true score are identical, but the error variances of the observed measures may be different. This leads to the so-called *tau-equivalent* test model. Secondly, we can constrain one loading for the true score to one and estimate the other. The resulting model is a *congeneric* test model (Jöreskog, 1971), which is a confirmatory factor analysis model where each observed variable has a loading only on the latent variable it is indicating. The congeneric test model is identified if there are at least three measures for the construct, or if there are at least two measures for each of a set of correlated constructs. If there are three or more replicate measurements we can even allow a small number of correlated measurement errors items, allowing for a violation of the assumption of uncorrelated measurement errors.

If we have only one observed variable, as in Figure 20.1, we can still estimate relationships between the true scores T provided that we can specify the variance of the measurement errors e using outside information. This is only possible if we know the reliability of the measure from an outside source (if our instrument is a psychological test, the test manual could provide information on its reliability) or if we can estimate this separately. In that case, we can specify the measurement error variance as:

$$\sigma_e^2 = \left(1 - \rho_{XX}\right)\sigma_X^2. \tag{20.9}$$

In equation (20.9), ρ_{XX} is the population value of the reliability of the measure X. Typically, it is estimated using the sample reliability r_{XX} which can be a split-half reliability, Cronbach's alpha, or another reliability estimate. As an example, we use the farm manager data from Warren et al. (1974). Table 20.1 gives the covariance matrix and the (split-half) reliability of the five variables.

Table 20.1. Covariances farm manager data

	rolbehav	knowledge	valorien	rolsatis	training
rolbehav	0.0209	0.0177	0.0245	0.0046	0.0187
knowledge	0.0177	0.0520	0.0280	0.0044	0.0192
valorien	0.0245	0.0280	0.1212	-0.0063	0.0353
rolsatis	0.0046	0.0044	-0.0063	0.0901	-0.0066
training	0.0187	0.0192	0.0353	-0.0066	0.0946
Reliability	0.8244	0.6201	0.6413	0.8018	1

The standard multiple regression model to predict role behavior from the other variables is given in Figure 20.1. To incorporate measurement error in the model, Rock, Werts, Lynn and Jöreskog (1977) divided each of the first four measures randomly in two halves. Table 20.2 provides the covariances and the number of items in each test half.

Table 20.2. Covariances farm manager data, split halves

	rolbh1	rolbh2	kno1	kno2	val1	val2	rolst1	rolst2	trainig
rolbeh1	.0271	.0172	.0219	.0164	.0284	.0217	.0083	.0074	.0180
rolbeh2	.0172	.0222	.0193	.0130	.0294	.0185	.0011	.0015	.0194
know1	.0219	.0193	.0876	.0317	.0383	.0356	-.0001	.0035	.0203
know2	.0164	.0130	.0317	.0568	.0151	.0230	.0055	.0089	.0182
val1	.0284	.0294	.0383	.0151	.1826	.0774	-.0087	-.0007	.0563
val2	.0217	.0185	.0356	.0230	.0774	.1473	-.0069	-.0088	.0142
rolsat1	.0083	.0011	-.0001	.0055	-0.008	-.0069	.1137	.0722	-.0056
rolsat2	.0074	.0015	.0035	.0089	-.0007	-.0088	.0722	.1024	-.0077
training	.0180	.0194	.0203	.0182	.0563	.0142	-.0056	-.0077	.0946
# items	12	12	13	13	15	15	5	6	1

Figure 20.4 shows the path diagram for a multiple regression analysis using a true score model for each of the four variables for which split halves are available. The path diagram merits close examination, because it presents many details of the setup for the model. In Figure 20.4, all loadings for the true score factors are constrained to one, except the loading of role satisfaction on the second role satisfaction variable. This is set to 1.2 to accommodate the fact that the second scale is based on six items and the first on five. All measurement errors for parallel split-halves are constrained to be equal (this is indicated in the path diagram by the labels k, v, r, and b which define the four equality constraints on the eight measurement error variances). Thus, Figure 20.4 specifies a parallel test model. The parallel test model fits the data reasonably well (Chi-square= 41.1, df= 26, p =.03; CFI= 0.94; RMSEA= .08). The congeneric test model however, which allows for different measurement error variances and different loadings, fits much better (Chi-square = 20.2, df= 19, p=0.38; CFI= 1.00; RMSEA= .03). The large p-value of the congeneric test model means that the model is not rejected, and the fit indices also indicate a good fit according to conventional SEM standards (cf. Kline, 2005).

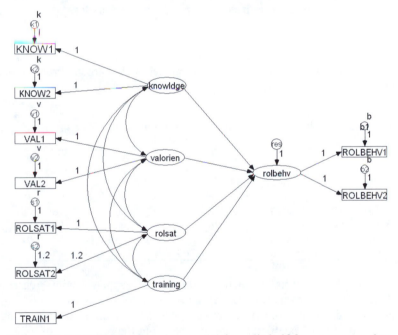

Figure 20.4. Multiple regression model for split-half farm manager data

Figure 20.5 shows the path model for the five variables in Table 20.1, and the measurement error variance calculated from the reliability also given in Table 20.2 as $\sigma_e^2 = \left(1 - r_{XX}\right)\sigma_X^2$.

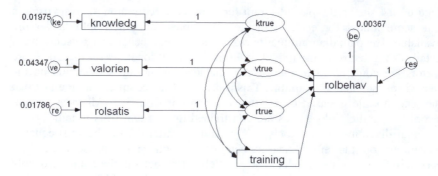

Figure 20.5. Multiple regression model with known error terms for variables

In the path diagram in Figure 20.5, each observed variable for which the reliability is known is replaced by a structure consisting of that observed variable, the measurement error term for which the variance is known, and a true score latent variable. Thus, the regression model estimates regression coefficients for the true scores instead of the observed variables.

   Table 20.3 presents the results of the multiple regression analysis. It contains four different models: the standard multiple regression model (Figure 20.1), the model based on the parallel tests assumptions (Figure 20.3), the congeneric model (not shown), and the model with known error variances (Figure 20.5).

Table 20.3. Results different multiple regression models for farm managers data

	standard mra			parallel tests			congeneric			known errors		
Variable	b	se	beta	B	se	beta	b	se	beta	b	se	beta
Knwldge	.23	.05	.36	.37	.14	.50	.36	.12	.54	.36	.12	.45
Valorien	.12	.04	.29	.16	.08	.33	.12	.06	.31	.16	.08	.31
Rolsatis	.06	.04	.12	.07	.06	.13	.06	.05	.12	.07	.05	.12
Training	.11	.04	.23	.07	.05	.16	.06	.05	.14	.07	.04	.15
R-square			.45			.69			.67			.75

Bollen (1989) explains mathematically what happens with regression coefficients when an analysis on variables with errors is compared to an analysis based on true scores. In brief: when an outcome variable contains errors, the regression coefficients are unbiased, but the proportion of explained variance goes down. When the predictor variable in a bivariate model contains errors, both the regression coefficients and the proportion of explained variance are biased toward zero. In a multivariate model, explained variance goes down, but regression coefficients changes unpredictably. Table 20.3 is a good example. In all models that model measurement error the proportion of explained variance is much higher than in the standard multiple regression analysis. The regression coefficients for the true scores tend to be higher than for the observed variables, but the corresponding standard errors also increase.

The variable training for which we assume a perfect reliability (actually there is no reliability information available for this variable) becomes less important when the other predictor variables are corrected for unreliability. In the standard multiple regression model, it has a significant effect, and in all three error-corrected models it is not significant. It is also clear that the precise way that errors are corrected has some impact on the resulting parameter estimates. Given that the congeneric model fits the data much better that the parallel tests model (which is estimated explicitly in the parallel tests model and assumed implicitly in the known errors model), the regression coefficients in the third congeneric tests model are probably the most accurate.

It should be noted that if there is a choice between including multiple indicators for each measure and using a measurement error variance based on a reliability estimate obtained from another sample (e.g., results from a calibration sample reported in a test manual), the first choice is preferred. If a reliability estimate is used to obtain an estimate for the error variance, the assumption is made that the assumptions for the specific reliability coefficient are fully met in the sample where it was calculated, and that our sample comes from the same or a comparable population. Parallel measures are assumed, independent errors and also true score and error variances tat are similar in both samples. If the measurement model is included in the analysis using SEM, we use only one sample, and we can test and possibly relax the assumptions of the measurement model.

20.4 OTHER APPROACHES TO ACCOMMODATING MEASUREMENT ERROR

In addition to the use of Structural Equation Modeling to include the measurement model in the analysis, other approaches are also used to cope with measurement error. Three other approaches are described in the following sections: latent class analysis, the instrumental variable method, and the plausible values method. Of these, latent class analysis and instrumental variables are described only briefly, and the plausible values approach is described in detail including an example.

20.4.1 Latent Class Analysis

The SEM approach properly assumes continuous variables. When the data are ordered categorical variables with a small number of categories, structural equation modeling can still be used. The estimation is then based on so-called polychoric correlations, which are estimates of the correlation between the continuous normal variables that are assumed to underlie the observed categorical variables. Because the sampling distribution of polychoric correlations is not the same as the sampling distribution of ordinary correlations, a different estimation method must be used, but otherwise the reasoning is the same. Unordered categorical data require a different but related approach: latent class analysis. In latent class analysis, the same general reasoning is followed as in SEM, but the precise model differs, because the latent variables are assumed to be unordered categorical, instead of continuous as in SEM. Biemer and Wiesen (2002) use latent class analysis to analyze responses from respondents who provide unreliable information on their marijuana use. The analysis model includes the assumption that the reported marijuana use is an imperfect indicator of actual use, which is an errors-in-variables model analogous to the structural equation models discussed in the previous section. One of the latent classes they found is indeed a class of probable users, who report high tendency for behaviors that strongly predict marijuana use, but deny using it.

20.4.2 Instrumental Variables

A very different approach to accommodating measurement errors in variables is the instrumental variable approach uses external information in additional *instrumental variables*. Instrumental variables are variables that are correlated with the variable that is measured with error but uncorrelated with the error term. For each variable in the regression equation that is measured with error, there should be at least one instrumental variable. Basically the instrumental variable method regresses the variable subject to measurement error on the instrumental variable(s), and estimates the original equation, replacing the variable that is measured with error with the predicted value from the first-stage regression. This results in consistent but biased estimates of model parameters. This procedure is also known as two-stage least squares (2SLS) estimation. Finding good instrumental variables is a difficult undertaking, and testing the assumptions for appropriate use of instrumental analysis is complex. The instrumental variable approach is used primarily in econometrics, for a detailed description see Fuller (1987).

20.4.3 Plausible Values

The plausible values method uses Item Response Theory (IRT) to estimate scores on multi-item scales. IRT was originally developed for the measurement of individual abilities, but it can also be applied to other measurement problems, such as measuring attitudes. In IRT measurement, each individual responds to a number of questions or items, sufficient to estimate the latent variable θ (e.g., the ability) with reasonable accuracy. In practice, often the sum of the item scores is used as an estimator for the latent variable. This is not a very good estimate, because the relationship between the latent variable θ and the observed sum score is nonlinear. In addition, if the number of items is small, the measurement is unreliable, and the uncertainty associated with individual estimates of θ is too large to ignore. The plausible values method was developed to deal with this issue.

      The basic idea behind the plausible values method is to generate imputed scores or plausible values from the empirically established distribution, based on an IRT analysis of the individual items plus all relevant background variables. These background variables are called conditioning variables.

Analyses of plausible values that involve variables not conditioned on when the plausible values were generated may produce biased results due to mis-specification. This is discussed by Mislevy (1991), who provides a detailed overview of the plausible values method. An example of scaling methods and plausible values in the context of educational research is given by Mislevy, Johnson, and Muraki (1992).

Plausible values are not the same as individual scores, but rather imputed values that can be used to estimate population characteristics correctly. The reasoning is analogous to the reasoning followed when missing values on observed variables are imputed using stochastic regression. The missing data are imputed using a statistical model, and in addition a random error is added from the appropriate error distribution. In multiple imputation this is performed several times, each time with a different value for the random error. When we measure a construct with imperfect reliability, the values of the latent variable θ are unknown and can be considered missing for *all* cases. But just like other missing values, they can be multiply imputed using an IRT model for the item scores plus the other observed variables. The multiply imputed values for the unobserved latent variable θ are called *plausible values*. When the IRT model is correct, these plausible values provide a way to obtain unbiased estimates and statistical tests. This requires some additional analyses.

In a manner analogous to multiple imputation for incomplete data, m multiple datasets are generated (with m typically being three or five) by taking random draws of plausible values from the appropriate distribution. The m multiple draws are different from each other in a way that quantifies the degree of uncertainty in the underlying distribution of possible latent trait values. Following Rubin (1987), the m plausible values give rise to m complete data sets. The mth data set contains all background variables plus the mth plausible value for the estimated score. Since there are m different data sets, all analyses must be replicated m times. The statistic t, based on the mth data set, is an estimate $t_{(m)}$ of the population value t. A better estimate of t is t_M, the mean of the m values for $t_{(m)}$. For statistical inference and significance testing, we need the standard error for the combined statistic t_M. The procedures used to combine the m results are exactly the same as the procedures used in multiple imputation for incomplete data. A detailed discussion is given in Rubin (1987), for an introduction see Chapter 19 by Raessler, Rubin, and Schenker in this book.

Plausible values share with multiple imputations the characteristic that generating plausible values is difficult and requires a high level of psychometrical expertise coupled with a good understanding of the data at hand, but once they have been made available using them in an applied setting is not very difficult. We illustrate the use of plausible values to cope with measurement error using a small example.

Table 20.4 presents a small data set with one explanatory variable gender and one dependent variable skill. The skill is a sum-score based on five items that are scored 0 for incorrect and 1 for correct. A reliability analysis produces a Cronbach alpha reliability of 0.77, which is rather high considering that we have only five items.

Table 20.4 Example data set with item scores and plausible values

gen-der	i1	i2	i3	i4	i5	skill	θ1	θ2	θ3	θ4	θ5
1	1	0	0	0	0	1	-1.03	-0.39	-0.21	-0.60	-0.49
1	1	1	1	0	0	3	0.62	0.18	0.90	0.35	0.35
1	1	1	1	0	0	3	0.47	-0.37	-1.04	0.50	0.70
0	1	1	1	0	0	3	0.43	-0.34	-0.10	1.26	-0.50
0	0	0	0	0	0	0	-1.62	-0.69	-0.88	-2.25	-0.80
0	1	0	0	0	0	1	-1.01	-1.32	-1.36	-0.91	-1.14
0	1	1	1	0	0	3	-0.90	0.78	-0.05	0.27	-0.08
1	1	1	1	1	1	5	1.55	1.97	1.93	1.61	1.10
0	1	1	1	0	0	3	0.81	0.02	-0.12	-0.32	-1.15
1	1	1	1	0	0	3	0.00	-0.71	-0.72	0.22	0.42
1	1	1	1	0	0	3	-0.07	0.22	1.05	0.03	0.41
0	1	0	0	0	0	1	-1.35	-1.00	-1.22	-1.01	-0.89
1	1	1	1	1	1	5	1.40	2.16	1.60	1.18	2.36
0	1	0	0	0	0	1	-0.20	-0.76	0.17	-0.68	-1.05
1	1	1	0	0	0	2	0.91	0.26	0.06	0.34	0.77

In addition to these observed variables, the table contains five plausible values for the unobserved latent variable theta, labeled theta1 to theta5. The research question is simply if males and females have different skill levels. If we carry out a *t*-test on the simple sum score *skill*, we find a mean skill level of 1.71 (s.d. 1.25) for males and 3.13 (s.d. 1.36) for females, with a *p*-value that just misses the conventional 0.05 significance level ($t=2.08$, $df=13$, $p=0.06$).

To use the five plausible values for the latent variable in the file we need to calculate five times the difference between male and female subjects plus their standard error. These statistics are given in table 20.5.

Table 20.5. Results from five analyses on plausible values theta1 to theta5

Dependent variable	Mean Difference	Standard Error	Sampling Variance
Theta1	1.028	0.4552	.2072
Theta2	0.888	0.4772	.2277
Theta3	0.954	0.4510	.2034
Theta4	0.972	0.4645	.2158
Theta5	1.503	0.3388	.1148

The best estimate of the real mean difference is simply the average of the five mean differences reported in Table20. 4. Thus, our best estimate for the difference between males and females is 1.069. The combined estimate of the sampling variance is more complicated. It is calculated as $T = \overline{V} + \left(1 + m^{-1}\right)B$, where the within imputation variance $\overline{V}$ is simply the mean of the five sampling variances, and the between imputation variance B is simply the variance of the five mean differences. For our data, the combined estimate of the sampling error is 0.267, whereas the standard error is 0.517. The *t*-ratio is 2.07 with 52 degrees of freedom. (The appropriate degrees of freedom are also estimated using the within and between imputation variances; for details see the formulas discussed by Raessler, Rubin, & Schanker in this book.) This leads to a *p*-value of 0.04 for the combined significance test. Thus, distinguishing between measurement error variance and sampling variance leads to a more powerful statistical test of out hypothesis.

20.5 CONCLUDING REMARKS

It is clear that measurement errors can have a strong effect on the results (parameter estimates and amount of explained variance) of an analysis that does not account for these errors. It should also be clear that in the error-corrected models the explained variance may be increased, but this is the explained variance in the corrected latent outcome variable. If we are interested in actually predicting the observed *outcome* variable, the error-corrected models do not improve on the standard multiple regression analysis. Thus, if actual measurement is intended, measurement error must be kept low, which implies more and better questions. If the goal is to test or estimate relationships, then including error terms in a structural equations model is a powerful and flexible approach. Even then, a certain minimum number of questions is desirable, for example at least three questions for each theoretical concept.

The advantage of using SEM to accommodate measurement errors is that the model is very general, so a range of specific analyses involving comparisons of means, variances and regression coefficients are possible. SEM software and handbooks are widely available. For unordered categorical variables, latent class models can be used in a way similar to SEM. Latent class modeling has also developed into a flexible analysis approach. However, the development of powerful software for latent class analysis is more recent than the development of SEM software, so the availability of software and introductory handbooks is smaller, and applications of latent class analysis in surveys is still uncommon.

Plausible value analysis is useful in those instances where analyses are made on large public data sets. Increasingly, large-scale studies make their data available for secondary analysis, and increasingly these data files include plausible values for the most important measurements. This means that these data can be multiply analyzed and the results combined using the standard procedures described, for example, by Raessler, Rubin, and Schenker in this book, or using freely available software such as Schafer's Norm.

Information about the reliability of measurements can be collected in different ways. All methods rely on replicating the measurement is some way, and subsequently analyzing the stability or consistency of measurement. The practice in survey research to administer short scales and use single questions makes it difficult to cope with measurement error. One option is to include measurement error as a known quantity in the analysis. If the is limited room in the questionnaire for extra questions to estimate the reliability of the measures, one approach is to do a follow-up study on a limited sample. Either a small subsample of respondents is re-interviewed so a test-retest reliability can be established, or a new sample is approached with a version of the questionnaire especially designed to estimate the reliability of important measures. Groves (1989) discusses some of the designs that can be used for the estimation of measurement error.

GLOSSARY OF KEY POINTS

Attenuation. The reduction of the estimated bivariate relationship between variables when one or both of these is measured with low reliability.

Classical true score theory. A measurement model that decomposes each measurement into a true score and an error component. The main object is to estimate the proportion of true score variance in a measure, which is defined as its reliability. The limitations of true score theory have led to the development of *item response theory*.

Item response theory (IRT). Statistical measurement models that assume a mathematical model for the probability that a given subject will respond correctly (positively, agree to) to a given question.

Latent variable. A characteristic that can not be observed or measured directly. It is hypothesized to exist in order to explain observed variables. Also called factor.

Measurement error. Lack of measurement precision due to flaws in the measurement instrument. If measurement errors are random they decrease the *reliability*, if they are systematic they decrease the *validity*.

Model fit. How closely the model-implied data match the observed data. In SEM model fit can be tested using a formal chi-square test (p-values >.5 indicate good fit), or it can be evaluated using model fit indices such as CFI (>0.9 indicates good fit) or RMSEA (<.05 indicates good fit).

Plausible values. Estimated latent score values drawn at random from a conditional distribution, given the responses to the items and a set of background variables (conditioning variables).

Reliability. Absence of random measurement errors.

Structural equation model. A multivariate model describing the relationships between multiple observed and/or latent variables. Often referred to as SEM.

Validity. Absence of systematic measurement errors.

Chapter 21

Survey Documentation:
Toward Professional Knowledge Management
in Sample Surveys

Peter Ph. Mohler
Director ZUMA Mannheim

Beth-Ellen Pennell
Survey Research Center, ISR, University of Michigan

Frost Hubbard
Research Associate, Survey Research Center, ISR, University of Michigan

21.1 INTRODUCTION

21.1.1 Purpose

Standards in survey documentation have evolved in parallel with the technological and methodological developments in survey research. In just a few decades, paper documents describing the contents of rectangular data files (i.e., codebooks) have been replaced with online access to documents that both describe and facilitate analysis of complex hierarchical and/or relational databases. Despite these advances, examples of complete or even adequate survey documentation remain surprisingly rare. This chapter discusses the barriers to collecting and publishing survey documentation, and makes practical recommendations for overcoming these barriers.

Some years ago, a debate arose in a meeting of the German General Social Survey (ALLBUS) Board about the use of the phrase working class as a descriptive category (see http://webapp.icpsr.umich.edu/GSS (General Social Survey) variables CLASS and CLASSY). Previous research had shown that marked differences could be obtained in the results of surveys with scales that included or excluded the phrase working class (Argyle, 1994). The debate became somewhat heated and went back and forth without much progress until Franz-Urban Pappi finally intervened. He pointed out that the working-class category is relevant for those researchers who are interested in the sociological concept of the working class. These researchers do not use such a scale as a standard subjective status self-classification, but as a specific tool to investigate respondents' self-classification as belonging to the working class as a societal concept. The debate ceased immediately and there was consensus that this difference should have been documented in the papers presented to the board. This debate gets to the heart of the purpose of this chapter.

21.1.2 Definitions

Documentation can be defined as material that is used to explain attributes of an object, system or process. When applied to surveys, this definition traditionally concentrates on the final product, typically the numeric data file as documented and published by a data archive (typically using SAS, SPSS, STATA, or some other statistical package). Increasingly, however, data producers and data archives are being asked to provide greater detail on the survey processes and survey context. Here, the concept of the survey life cycle is emphasized, especially as it relates to process quality. The survey life cycle, (i.e., the survey production processes) might be better covered by a definition such as: "the act or process of substantiating by recording actions and/or decisions" www.epa.gov/records/gloss/gloss03.htm). Thus, modern survey documentation must include both documentation of the product—the numeric data file—and documentation of the entire survey production process.

However, the survey life cycle is not the ultimate context into which the numerical data set is embedded. Surveys are also part of the general body of scientific literature in the classical sense: there is always literature that precedes (theory, publications on earlier studies, methodological findings) and follows the survey (published results). In this more general perspective, sample survey documentation is just a special kind of scientific literature with statements, references to other statements, and so on. Good scientific literature, in turn, is parsimonious by referring to others' works via bibliographical references thus avoiding lengthy imbedded texts from these other sources. From this viewpoint, modern sample survey documentation is the creation of a scientific body of literature serving as a reference for analysts, scholars, and survey practitioners.

21.2 THREE ELEMENTS OF SURVEY DATA DOCUMENTATION: NUMERICAL DATA, METADATA AND PARADATA

Survey documentation contains three components: (a) numerical data, (b) metadata and (c) paradata. Numerical data generally refers to rectangular data files that contain each respondent's answers to the survey questions in a row by column format, where the rows correspond to individual respondents and the columns contain the variables asked in the questionnaire plus derived variables. In the past, this numeric data file plus a list with references of locations on the punch cards/files and the items in a questionnaire was often the primary source of information that outside users of survey data received. However, the numeric data file does not contain enough information about the survey itself for an analyst or secondary data user to fully understand and analyze the quality of the statistical results of the numeric data. For this, users need the other two components of survey documentation: metadata and paradata.

Although the term metadata is used extensively in the context of documenting surveys, it is a vague concept whose meaning has evolved over time. The concept was first explicitly defined over three decades ago (Sundgren, 1973) and in its simplest form means "data that describe other data" (Dippo & Sundgren, 2000). In the early, premicrocomputer day of survey research, a codeplan (described later) was often the only standard form of metadata available. One prominent exception was Samuel Stouffer's (1963) seminal description, documentation, and presentation of the results of his 1954 study of the public's opinions on communism and civil liberties in the United States. Traditionally, metadata described the attributes of the numerical file representing the data of a survey, that is, the numerical representation or the text of the answers to the survey questions. Today, the term metadata is also used to encompass a broad spectrum of information about the survey, from study title to sample design to details such as interviewer briefing notes. Metadata can also refer to contextual data or information such as legal regulations, customs, economic indicators, and so on.

In terms of the documentation and organization of this broad spectrum of survey metadata via computers, significant progress began when preliminary metadata guidelines were developed (Sundgren, 1993). After these guidelines were developed, various groups began exploring ways to organize survey metadata electronically. These groups included national statistical agencies (e.g., Hert, Denn, & Haas, 2004; Bargmeyer & Gillman, 2003; LaPlant, Lestina, Gillman & Appe, 1996), the data archive community through the formation of the Data Documentation Initiative (DDI) (www.icpsr.umich.edu/DDI/), and the library and information science community which developed the Dublin Core Metadata Initiative (Stephens, 2003).

The third and final element of survey documentation, paradata, refers to "data on the process of collecting data" (Couper, 1998). Couper further breaks down paradata into two types: macro paradata and micro paradata. Macro paradata refers to all encompassing information such as response rates and coverage rates. Micro paradata, on the other hand, describes numerical information about the survey process itself like keystroke or audit trail files, time measures, and interviewer notes. Survey practitioners can use paradata to better understand the process of the survey, evaluate aspects of its quality and intervene during the survey process if necessary. Couper and Lyberg (2005) suggest that survey documentation should include such paradata.

Numerical data, metadata, and paradata comprise the information units of comprehensive survey documentation. Thus, documentation is the higher-level term that covers all three types of data and is how we refer to it throughout this chapter.

21.3 USES OF SURVEY DOCUMENTATION

Survey documentation essentially serves two purposes: (a) internal project documentation, that is, keeping track of the survey production process, which is necessary for data producers, and (b) survey documentation for secondary data analysis and/or replication used to inform others, mostly analysts. Without internal project documentation, it is nearly impossible to produce survey documentation for secondary data analysis and/or replication. The needs of the data users are targeted toward using data sets in various ways, while those of data producers are related to monitoring and managing the survey process, meeting disclosure or contractual requirements. Given the needs of both data users and producers, survey documentation should contain information about the:

- Theoretical concepts and their operationalization;
- Context in which the survey process has been implemented;
- Design and implementation of the survey;
- Quality indicators; and
- Content (i.e., the questions asked, in the order they are asked).

Although there is little debate as to the importance of each of these items in survey documentation, there is a question of balancing detail, relevance, and accessibility.

21.4 A CONCEPTUAL FRAMEWORK FOR SURVEY DOCUMENTATION

A first step routinely taken toward creating a conceptual framework for survey documentation is to list all the elements relevant for documentation as indicated above (cf. DDI, www.icpsr.umich.edu/DDI). Although these lists have a tendency to become extremely long, they still do not provide all possibilities. There is the danger that producing an exhaustive list deteriorates into a lifetime engagement instead of a by-product of a survey. To avoid this, one must distinguish between what is essential and time-sensitive. In other words, survey researchers must identify information that might be lost if not collected as part of the implementation of a process versus information that must be made more widely accessible. Furthermore, as in book references, what has already been documented elsewhere should not simply be inserted into the current documentation but appropriately referenced. The basic concept here, known more broadly as Knowledge Management, is the "process of collecting, organizing, classifying, and disseminating information ….so as to make it purposeful to those who need it" (Malhotra, 2001). The idea is to target the (different) users and provide the relevant data when it is needed.

The first task is to identify relevant items: what is needed, when, and by whom. Not all information about the survey needs to be documented in a handy and easily accessible way. What is used only once, or collected either because such information would be lost forever or because of data security, can simply be stored on any retrievable data storage platform or container. It can even be printed, to be accessed manually if necessary. This is crucial, because it costs much more to create a relational data base management system for specific documentation than simply to collect data or information and store it in a safe place. For example, a program detailing the selection algorithm used to select a specific sample from its frame is a critical document. It must be saved and stored, but it need not be readily accessible to a wide audience of data users.

In contrast, the information concerning Franz-Urban Pappi's working-class example earlier is essential, and must therefore be stored in a handy and easily accessible way. To demonstrate this, we list the relevant information for a proper documentation of a survey question in Figure 21.1. Figure 21.1 focuses on a specific survey question as the central organizing structure, but other perspectives could be chosen. Thus, we base our enumeration of relevant elements on the question text "Do you think that the law…" that is then linked to the numerical data set. Without knowing the answer categories, any statistical analysis would be useless. To access the answer categories one could either rely on the value labels given in the numerical data set, or review the entire text given in the original, the source questionnaire, which should include other relevant information such as filtering rules or interviewer instructions. In the case of international or cross-cultural surveys, inspection of culture-specific, or the translated questionnaires is important for obvious reasons. To avoid the working class problem mentioned previously, it is also essential to document the dimensions or latent constructs to be measured as well as to give a proper bibliography identifying the pedigree and previous use of the question.

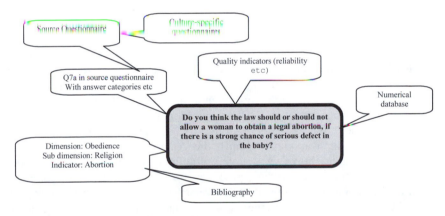

Adapted from Mohler & Uher, 2003

Figure 21.1: Relevant information for documenting a survey question/item

Illustrations such as Figure 21.1 serve as a good starting point for organizing the knowledge necessary for each intended user. To accomplish this, tools need to be designed that have a modularized, cascading structure, and above all, are relevant. Modular structure refers here to known concepts in computing and data base management. These structures avoid single, large chunks of text as shown above in Figure 21.1. Rather, smaller elements are identified (classes, sub-classes etc.) and interconnected or linked. In the example from the 1998 International Social Survey Program (ISSP), each sub-heading could serve as a modular element. Cascading refers to a network-like system that makes it possible for an item to build upon the information presented by a previous item. For example, many consumer products provide two sets of directions that constitute a cascade: a quick reference guide and a more comprehensive user manual that builds upon the information given in the brief reference. They also form a simple network, where references to the longer manual are given in the shorter reference guide. Similarly, there are cascades and networks for the processes that produce these products from the production of component parts to the final assembly of those components. The information must be cascaded and modularized because people who make the components may not need the same level of information as people who assemble those components. However, if one is interested in the whole production process and all types of users, all the different modules and their respective cascaded networks must be either at hand or at least retrievable (in the current example, for quality control purposes, training, or servicing the products).

Survey documentation is structured in much the same way. The information must be relevant, cascading, and modular. Relevance helps to determine the necessary elements for a specified purpose, cascading allows reference systems to build upon one element to the next, and modularization allows for to the addition, deletion, or editing of specific elements without changing the overall structure.

21. 5 EXAMPLES

Despite an ever-growing need to properly document and disseminate survey data collections, literature and guidance on how to do so is relatively scarce (Mohler & Uher, 2003). Formal frameworks have been developed for categorising elements of survey documentation, such as the framework of the Data Documentation Initiative (DDI) or guidelines of professional associations such as the World Association for Public Opinion Research (http://www.unl.edu/wapor/ethics.html), the American Association for Public Opinion Research (http://www.aapor.org/default.asp?page=survey_methods/-standards_and_best_practices/best_practices_for_survey_and_public_opinion_r esearch#best12) and the Council of American Survey Research Organizations (http://www.casro.org/codeofstandards.cfm/clipublic) (Mohler & Uher, 2003). However, several elements are missing from each of these guidelines: (a) the conceptual framework which allows data producers to identify relevant elements to document (i.e. to delineate the level of accessibility needed); (b) tools which support and integrate documentation into the survey production process; and (c) practical guidelines as to how to create the most basic document, namely, a codeplan that links the numbers or text associated with the respondent's answers with the survey questions.

In the following, we attempt to address these three shortcomings. As noted earlier, the literature on sample survey documentation is scarce. Often, unwritten tradition guides work in survey project teams and archives. In the rare case of written material (apart from the more recent DDI papers), topics focus on numerical data sets and editing of complex official data sets. The scientific community has generally ignored the survey production process (Mohler et al., 2003). To provide context and background, we first outline the current standards in survey documentation.

21.5.1 Standard survey documentation

The importance and relevance of documentation becomes evident if one imagines a survey with minimal documentation, namely a data file (e.g. SPSS or STATA) with variable names and value labels. The following examples illustrate this:

V12: Environment. Income
V13: Environment. Taxes
V14: Environment. No Cost
V15: Environment. Anxious
V16: Environment. Unemployment
V17: Environment. Not Urgent
(Where the attached values are: 0=deleted, 1=agree+, 2=agree,
3=disagree, 4=disagree+, 9=deleted, and 99=missing values)?

Figure 21.2: Minimal documentation *(Example taken from World Value Survey 2000 Data File)*

Upon review of this list, a number of questions immediately come to mind. For example,

- What were the actual questions that respondents were asked?
- Was English the only language used? If not, what were the other languages?
- What was the wording of the translations?
- What was the data collection mode or modes?
- Which questions preceded this item battery?
- Who were the respondents, and what was the sampling frame?
- Was the sample drawn using probability methods?
- How was the survey implemented?
- How was the quality of the data collection assessed, that is, response rate, measure of nonresponse bias, and so on?
- What was the substantive research question (concept) that these questions were intended to answer?
- How reliable or valid were the items measuring the latent concept?
- What was the pedigree or source of the questions?
- What were the outcomes of earlier research using these items (cited literature)?

Documentation that adequately answers these questions is more the exception than the rule. Machine readable codebooks, dating back to the 1960s (Mohler et al., 2003) are still the norm. Machine readable means that the marginals or frequencies of each variable are merged into the questionnaire text by a codebook program that reads the relevant data in from the numeric data file (not copied by typing).

Typically, machine readable codebooks contain very basic information, as described in the World Value Survey example, but may also include the actual question text (although in the order that the variables appear in the data file, not necessarily the order it appears in the questionnaire—an important distinction). In case of the World Values Study, additional textual information might look as follows:

I am now going to read out some statements about the environment. For each one I read out, can you tell me whether you agree strongly, agree, disagree or strongly disagree? (READ OUT EACH STATEMENT AND CODE AN ANSWER FOR EACH)

	Strongly Agree	Agree	Disagree	Strongly Disagree	DK
V12 A) I would give part of my income if I were certain that the money would be used to prevent environmental pollution	1	2	3	4	9
V13 B) I would agree to an increase in taxes if the extra money is used to prevent environmental pollution	1	2	3	4	9

Figure 21.3: Standard machine readable codebook documentation

Other information generally included in standard codebooks are the names of principal investigators, name and location of the institution conducting the survey, date of fielding, and possibly sample size. Little or no space is given to overall design, details of the sampling procedures, questionnaire design and pretesting methods or question pedigree. Figure 21.4, an example from the 1998 ISSP (International Social Survey Program), illustrates this lack of information quite well. In this example, the information on the principal investigators (titles given) is more complete than the minimal statement about the sampling frame[1]. For example, there is no information as to how the random route was actually executed, (e.g. was the starting address given to interviewers?) nor how it was monitored or controlled. Also of note is the reference to the ADM Master sample, an instance of cascading information. However, no reference is given, nor information as to where to find proper documentation of that master file (for documentation, see Hoffmeyer-Zlotnik, 1997). Other information not documented here concern the translation process (from English source to target German), and what, if any, pretest was conducted.

---

[1] Not documented are age limits (18 and above) or oversampling in East Germany of the ISSP

> "Study Description: Germany
>
> Study title: ISSP 1998 Germany—Religion II, Western and Eastern Germany
>
> Fieldwork dates: July 7th—September 24th, 1998
>
> Principal investigators: Dr. Janet Harkness, Prof. Dr. Peter Ph. Mohler
>
> Sample type: multi-stage with three stages; ADM (Working Group of German Market Researchers) Master Sample (the so-called random route ADM)
> Fieldwork methods: Self-completion questionnaire distributed by interviewer.
>
> Background variables were asked face-to-face.
>
> Context of ISSP questionnaire Self-completion questionnaire following on from a five minute face-to-face interview and followed by other questions and the background variables, all paper and pencil, face to face. The ISSP was the main topic of a ZUMA SOWI-BUS, as in Religion 1991
> Sample size: 2007 (West: 1000; East: 1007)" (ISSP 1998).

Figure 21.4: 1998 ISSP Codebook
(Source ISSP Codebook 1998, Zentralarchive Köln Codebook No. 3190, page I, 4)

In short, major parts of the survey life-cycle, identified earlier as being relevant for full survey documentation, cannot be found in standard codebooks provided by many data archives today.[2] Researchers often produce such information, but it does not become linked to the codebook. Even a simple step such as providing PDF-files of questionnaires in each target language is rarely done. This results in additional efforts by secondary analysts to find information relevant for their analyses. This can be time consuming, costly, and in almost all cases a haphazard and exceedingly frustrating effort, if undertaken at all.

21.5.2 Advances in Documentation

Two major advances in documentation were first introduced by the ISSP: (a) images of the questionnaires for all cultures/nations and languages and (b) standardized forms to gather metadata which allowed for the publication of a comprehensive report on methodology.

A major step forward to full documentation has been attempted by the European Social Survey (http://www.europeansocialsurvey.org). The ESS provides information about its protocols (e.g. field work, sampling, and translation), the national questionnaires, a comprehensive data report, national

---

[2] Some notable exceptions exist, such as the European Social Survey (ESS).

data sets, national additions/deviations, questionnaire images, and the like. (See Figures 21.5 and 21.6).

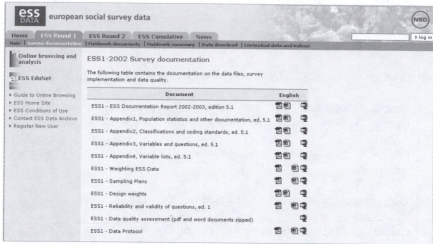

Figure 21.5: ESS Round 1 Survey documentation search page
(*NSD, Bergen http://www.europeansocialsurvey.org/*)

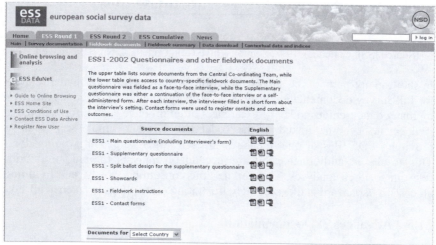

Figure 21.6: ESS Round 1 Fieldwork documentation search page
(*NSD, Bergen http://www.europeansocialsurvey.org/*)

Other information such as questionnaire development reports and event data (national events that occurred during the fieldwork period each country that might impact the context and results of the survey) are provided as well. To date, the ESS provides the most comprehensive documentation publicly available. Still, each category of documentation is presented separately. Thus, users must open several files to get the full set of information available. The ESS could benefit from a comprehensive review of the structure and usability of these data. The creation of cross-links and referencing is a valuable addition.

21.6 TOOLS FOR DOCUMENTATION

21.6.1 Codeplan

Creating an error-free link between the digits in the data file and the questions asked in the questionnaire is the most crucial part of survey documentation. If this link is lost or erroneous, the whole survey was in vain. A codeplan provides this link. We make a clear distinction here between a *codeplan* as the most basic document that establishes matches between items in a questionnaire and numbers in a data file and a *codebook* as provided by data archives. Codebooks contain additional information such as frequencies or study descriptions. There is hardly any systematic and coherent presentation easily available what actually constitutes a codeplan. Thus, we elaborate here this issue to some detail.

Four elements of information are most important in creating a codeplan:
- Location of text information in the questionnaire (item, answer scale, interviewer instruction, etc.) and location of the alphanumeric information in the data file or data base (position, length, field-name, relative position, etc);
- Properties of the numeric data field (width, decimals, alpha (character), or numeric);
- Definition of answer scale values, filters, refusals, don't knows, can't choose, and no information at all (often subsumed under the misleading headers of missing values and missing data); and
- Definition of derived variables, that is a re-arrangement of answers (data of birth re-arranged as age in years at interview, or coding of open ended answers into classifications such as the International Standard Classification of Operations or composite of several answers (educational level as a composite of school attended, degree at school and university degree).

How to achieve the first three elements in creating a codeplan can be best explained by example, (see also Groves et al. 2004). Another such example is in the codeplan of the 2002 ESS (Figure 21.7)[3].

The first step in linking data and questions is to link each question with a unique variable mnemonic (varname in SPSS, var in SAS). Here, *A1* is the question identifier in the questionnaire and *TvTOT* is the variable name in the data file. Next, the possible responses are identified and linked or set in the data file (response scale). In the previously mentioned case, the response None receives the code 00 in the data file. This response also serves also as a filter so that the following questions which all deal with watching television will not be asked of respondents who do not watch TV. This is the actual code in the ESS. However, this code does not indicate whether the respondent has access to a

---

[3] Note that the real ESS codebook does not exactly match the example provided in Figure 21.7.

TV. Consequently, one cannot distinguish between respondents who willingly do not watch TV and those who actually cannot. The ESS designers intentionally chose to use this single code to mean two different responses (which generally should not be done). This intentional choice is a demonstration of the ESS designers applying the relevance principle in *assuming* that the number of people who do not have access to a TV is extremely low.

Unique identifier of the question in the questionnaire
A1   TvTot →   *Unique identifier of the corresponding variable in the data file definition*

On an average weekday, how much time, in total,
do you spend watching television?

No time at all → *links value label in the data*
If answer is 00, go to question x   → *This is a filter marker*

Less than ½ hour	01	
½ hour to 1 hour	02	
More than 1 hour, up to 1 ½ hours	03	
More than 1 ½ hours, up to 2 hours	04	→ *Valid responses*
More than 2 hours, up to 2 ½ hours	05	
More than 2 ½ hours, up to 3 hours	06	
More than 3 hours	07	
(Don't know)	95	
Refused	96	→ *Other responses*
No mark in questionnaire (no answer)	**99**	→ *Worst case*

Variable in data file properties: numeric, two digits, no decimals

Figure 21.7: 2002 ESS Codeplan

The responses 00–07 can be used in statistical analyses (average time spent watching TV, for instance) and are thus sometimes called valid codes. However, this is misleading, because the response categories of don't know and refused also have substantive meanings. They can and should be used to identify groups in the population for whom the question has zero salience, to identify difficult or sensitive questions and/or specific response styles (refused and don't know). They are also helpful in identifying measurement errors due to nonresponse. To mix the last three categories up or to collapse them into one category is a serious mistake and should be avoided.

The last category, no mark in the questionnaire (99), actually should never appear in the data file. Nevertheless, survey reality proves to be different.

This code indicates that there is no trace in the questionnaire that the interviewer even asked the question. It is often labelled NA–no answer or even Not applicable, which is incorrect. A more proper name would be NM–no mark. If this happens in a paper-and-pencil survey, it points to an interviewer error. Consequently, it can be used as an interviewer quality indicator. If it happens to appear in a computer-assisted survey, it suggests a programming error occurred in sequencing or filtering. The properties of the numeric data file (two digits, no decimals, all numeric) were not provided in the ESS codeplan, as indicated in Figure 21.7. However, in a full-fledged codeplan this should always be the case.

21.6.2 Recent Developments in Creating Tools for Documentation

Much of the current accessibility of historical survey research data can be attributed to OSIRIS and SPSS, two computer software systems dedicated to facilitating statistical analysis and the handling of survey data. Both programs contain documentation tools that allow creating variable and value labels. In addition, OSIRIS has a special codebook routine that produces machine-readable codebooks. For many years, these were generally the only available, limited tools for project teams to generate survey documentation.

This situation changed with the advent of the DDI Alliance. The DDI is an international group of data archivists, producers and users, who have come together to develop the specifications for the content, presentation, transport, and preservation of technical documentation. The goal is to create document type definition for the mark-up of social science research community and related data documentation using the eXtensible Markup Language (XML). The DDI Alliance has recently taken a major step toward a concept-based scheme that adopts the survey life-cycle model. They recommend that major parts of the questionnaire documentation link to the survey process itself and not to abstract archival classifications. Figure 21.8 presents a visual picture of how the Inter-Consortium for Political and Social Research (ICPSR), a member of the DDI, suggests incorporating plans for survey documentation into each step of the survey life cycle. The ICPSR strongly urges researchers to plan for documentation early on in the survey life cycle, ideally in the Proposal Planning and Writing stage (Step 1), before the data even come into existence. Although the DDI and ICPSR realize that not all data collectors will be able to follow these steps, they currently that researchers incorporate steps 1–5, whereas steps 6 and 7 are more directed toward data archivists. For more in-depth coverage of each of the steps, please refer to "The Guide to Social Science Data Preparation and Archiving"(http://www.icpsr.umich.edu/access/dpm.html).

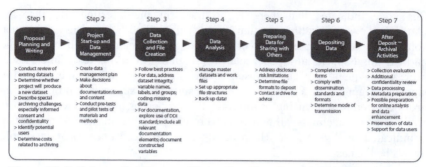

Figure 21.8: Schematic Diagram Illustrating Key Considerations Germane to Documentation at Each Step in the Data Creation Process .

However, providing a structure does not solve the problem. There remains the challenge of how to generate the documentation proper, that is, how to write and gather the necessary text parts on a day-to-day basis. As it is often the case, researchers faced with a specific problem found a proper solution. A 1995 monitoring study on the ISSP, systematically reported on the quality of this international survey (Park & Jowell, 1997). This report was based on a scheme of questions asked of each participating country. Since 1996, Janet Harkness and her colleagues at ZUMA (Harkness , Langfeldt, & Scholz, 2001) have built upon Park and Jowell's original scheme in a stepwise fashion and created a web-based form that provides comprehensive ISSP quality documentation.

A more generic and general approach was taken by Beth- Ellen Pennell and colleagues at the Institute for Social Research in Ann Arbor, Michigan. Pennell was first joined by ZUMA and later by the ICPSR in efforts to create comprehensive documentation forms as tools to collect information (primarily survey metadata) on a day-to-day basis following the survey life cycle model.

Figure 21.9: Survey Lifecycle Model of SMDS

The idea behind their form-approach is to develop a common tool that could help make survey documentation easier and more accessible. From a small first set of forms like in the ISSP, the Survey Metadata Documentation System (SMDS) grew to a Web-based generic tool covering all aspects of the survey production process in 11 Modules (see Figure 21.10). Each chapter is a module. Within each module, questions are hierarchically cascaded, that is, a chapter sets out with general questions followed by questions that are more detailed.

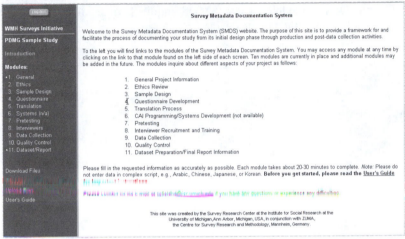

Figure 21.10: SMDS Opening

The logic of the forms is comparable to the logic in a standardized adaptive questionnaire where numerous filters provide automatic jumps, if a section does not apply to a respondent/study. For instance, as Figure 21.11 displays, the first two general questions in Module 3 on Sample Design ask about the target population of the sample.

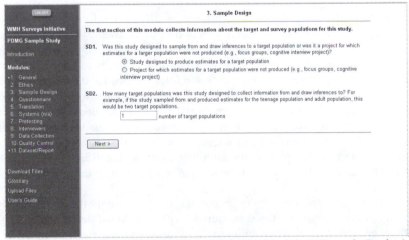

Figure 21.11: Opening two questions of SMDS Module 3 (Sample Design)

This example shows the basic properties of the SMDS form. First, a general question is asked and the researcher can answer by clicking one of the two boxes. If the researcher clicks the box Study designed to produce estimates for a target population, another window pops up asking for the number of target populations about which the study was designed to collection information.

However, the level of complexity increases considerably as more minute details of the sampling process are uncovered. The following example occurs later in the Sample Design module, where SMDS inquires in detail about different subsets or subsamples the sample design used.

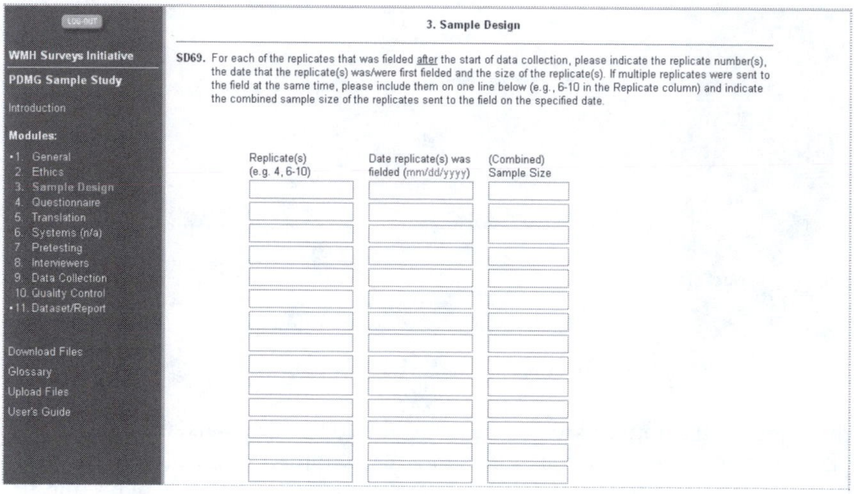

Figure 21.12: A complex, detailed item occurring later in SMDS Module 3
(Sample Design) questionnaire

As this example demonstrates, the number of different information elements grows rapidly with the number of filters and options asked. Relevance comes into play here. If the system is too fine, there will be too many elements in the resulting analysis that occur only once or not at all. If it is too crude, the one and only instance that counts is not detected (cf. Adorno, 1950; Züll, Weber, & Mohler, 1989). Turning back to the conceptual framework for survey documentation, this means that researchers have to make decisions about the relevance of items asked in the form. Relevance means, for instance, that the one and only national survey in an international study that used quota sampling instead of the required probability sampling must be identified. On the other hand, the details on the release of the sample replicates may only be of interest to the sampling statisticians.

From this follows a very important rule: although the tools can be refined without limits, on the substantive level there must be relevance. This will govern the level of accessibility to the information collected. Even the best tools cannot relieve researchers and archivists from making such decisions.

In summary, in addition to the long tradition of labeling and codebook routines of statistical programs, modern survey documentation needs tools which allow for documentation to take place during the survey process and become an integral part of everyday survey work. ISSP monitor forms and SMDS are prototypes of documentation that will serve the survey community in the years to come.

21.7 CONCLUSION

This chapter provided a tour d'horizon of survey documentation as it stands today and might develop in the near future. On this tour common or even now fashionable terms such as metadata or paradata were explained to some detail, a general framework for survey documentation is introduced which allows to expand the traditional or standard view on codebooks as the ultimate documentation format into new knowledge management systems. It also provided a view on recent developments in tools tailored for knowledge management based documentation. In focus were also the concepts and tools needed by survey producers to document their studies for themselves and future users. In addition to conceptual considerations, it provides a view toward modern documentation tools the survey research field can expect in the very near future. Examples given from the ESS and SMDS indicate the direction survey documentation will go in the near future.

It is important to note that study documentation needs to be exhaustive enough for others to evaluate findings, replicate the findings, or to be able to use the data for their own research. Secondary data analysts have none of the common ground and collective memory of the primary data producers. Therefore, the information required to be able to evaluate and replicate findings is considerable.

Unfortunately, comprehensive documentation appears to be low in data producers' priorities. Considering that science should rely on inter-subjectivity and replicability, this is somewhat counterintuitive. On the other hand, if one investigates the tools made available for statistical analyses (SPSS, SAS, etc.) and compares their usability and sophistication with toolboxes like the DDI, one feels quite sympathetic with research teams who do not want to spend their time in the "dungeons of data bookkeeping (aka documentation)".

To date, good and comprehensive documentation seems to be the realm of data archives only (ICPSR, ZA Cologne, NSD Norway). These archives and their sponsors invest many resources in professional data documentation (codebooks). Similarly, major studies such as the ESS provide end users with quite comprehensive documentation. However, there has been no standard tool available that allows research teams to account for documentation, stretching from the beginning of a study until the final publication of the data and the results (process documentation).

The need for process documentation becomes even more pressing for international studies. Here, almost all documents and data are multiples of a single culture study. Simple hierarchical categorical systems like the DDI schemes cannot handle these multiple sets of documentation units. They require intelligent database management systems (relational databases). Moreover, such surveys are embedded in several layers of contextual information. Among them are previous surveys, institutional and legal contexts, societal situations and the like. For a more complex survey such as a cross-cultural or cross-national survey or a time series, this information also must be incorporated in the study documentation. This chapter has noted that such a prerequisite might lead to an infinite amount of documentation units, including more and more layers. This tendency must be countered with structures offered by the concept of knowledge management, that is, the knowledge to produce goods.

From this perspective, documentation for social surveys requires three new concepts: (a) the data base management concept as the basic data and information structuring tool; (b), a clearly defined goal, namely the future usability of the information to produce (or reproduce) results obtained and their transformation into societal knowledge; and (c) a clearly defined audience or audiences for study documentation.

GLOSSARY OF KEY CONCEPTS

Cascading Structure. A network-like system that makes it possible for an documentation item to build upon the information presented by a previous item or even a chain of previous items.

Codebook. A document provided by data archives that is similar to a codeplan but contains additional information such as frequencies and a general description of the study.

Codeplan. The most basic document that establishes matches between items in a questionnaire and numbers in a data file.

Documentation. The act or process of substantiating by recording actions and/or decisions. www.epa.gov/records/gloss/gloss03.htm.

Flat File Data. Rectangular data files that contain each respondent's answers to the survey questions in a row by column format, where the rows correspond to each individual respondent's answers and the columns contain the variables asked in the questionnaire.

Knowledge Management. The process of collecting, organizing, classifying, and disseminating information so as to make it purposeful to those who need it.

Metadata. Data that describe other data. The term encompasses a broad spectrum of information about the survey, from study title to sample design to details such as interviewer briefing notes to contextual data or information such as legal regulations, customs, and economic indicators.

Modular Structure. A structure that avoids single, large chunks of text and instead identifies smaller elements (e.g. classes, sub-classes) that are interconnected or linked.

Paradata. Data on the process of collecting data.

Survey life cycle. A progression through a similar series of stages that characterize the course of production of a survey from design to publication.

Chapter 22

Quality Assurance and Quality Control in Surveys

Lars E. Lyberg
Statistics Sweden

Paul P. Biemer
RTI International and University of North Carolina

22.1 INTRODUCTION

A large-scale survey is a complex system of interrelated activities and processes that must be well-integrated and controlled in order to produce a quality product. If one component of the system performs poorly, the result may be poor quality no matter how well the other components perform. As an example, if interviewers are poorly trained or supervised, there may be numerous errors in the data regardless of how well the questionnaire is designed. For this reason, government statistical agencies and other survey organizations have developed methods for monitoring and controlling the performance of survey operations so that problems can be corrected before they have had a chance to affect survey quality. In this chapter, we review some of these methods and procedures, which are referred to collectively as quality assurance.

Quality assurance comprises a system of procedures, checks, audits, and corrective actions to ensure that the products produced by an organization are of the highest achievable quality. Quality control is part of the quality assurance system and refers to a set of procedures and techniques aimed at verifying the quality of outputs of various processes. Quality control occupies a central role in any quality assurance program because even well designed processes can occasionally produce deficient products. Therefore, quality control provides data on the quality of individual operations within a survey. Without these data, continuous quality improvement would not be possible.

The success of any quality assurance program is determined largely by the structure, culture and management practices of the survey organization. Organizations that have an appropriate organizational structure and a culture that embraces continual improvement of its products tend to produce outputs that are of very high quality. Organizations that are structured around stovepipes, isolated divisions that hamper free communication among survey staff, tend to produce poor quality surveys. In addition, organizations that do not develop detailed plans prior to conducting a survey, do not conduct routine project and technical reviews of all major surveys, do not follow standardized written procedures and do not evaluate and document the quality of their products will produce data that are deficient in quality. The best survey organizations adopt a systematic approach to continuous quality improvement that is guided by top management with involvement of staff at all levels of the organization. The principles and methods described in this chapter characterize what we believe are the most important elements of this systematic approach, comprising the three levels: product, process, and organizational quality. We begin with a discussion of some of the basic concepts of survey quality.

22.2 SURVEY QUALITY

22.2.1 The Survey Process

A survey can be viewed as a sequence of steps or stages as shown in the flow diagram of Figure 22.1 (Biemer & Lyberg, 2003). The initial stages constitute the design phase, which is largely iterative. During this phase, new information may be obtained regarding the feasibility and effectiveness of the design and, as a consequence, specific design elements such as the questionnaire, the sampling frame or the mode of data collection may be modified accordingly. For example, the questionnaire may prove to be too long which will require rethinking the mode of administration or even the research objectives.

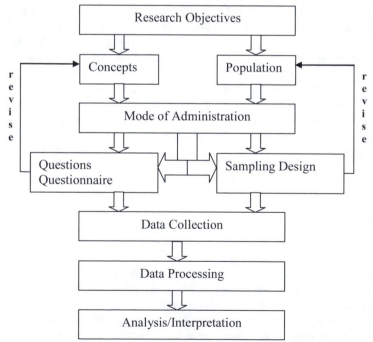

Figure 22.1. The Survey Process (Source: Biemer & Lyberg 2003, p. 27)

Errors can be introduced at each stage of the survey process (cf dfe Leeuw, Hox, & Dillman, Chapter 1) so safeguards must be in place for assessing and controlling them. At the planning stage it is important to select known dependable methods in accordance with a planning criterion such as minimizing the total survey error (the sum of all variance and squared bias terms) for a given budget or minimizing the cost of achieving a prespecified total survey error level. Because errors are highly interactive the planning might involve several revisions and trade-offs before an acceptable design can be established. Any revisions and tradeoffs are based on knowledge on how various methods work and their cost and error structures (cf, de Leeuw, Chapter 7). When information on the costs or errors of the possible design options is lacking, this planning phase may include pilot and pretesting activities (cf. Campanelli, Chapter 10) whose purposes are to check how the various approaches perform.

Once a design is specified and is being implemented, controls must be put in place to ensure that survey operations are performed according to specifications. This is done through a series of checks and verifications often using methods adapted from the statistical process control such as control charts and acceptance sampling schemes along with simpler forms of error identification (Mudryk, Bougle, Xias, & Yeung, 2001; Ryan, 2000). We call these measures quality control (QC), which is part of the more general concept of quality assurance (QA) to be discussed in some detail subsequently.

Another type of quality check that is often performed after the survey is conducted is the evaluation study. Here the purpose is to assess the magnitude of specific error components that make up the total survey error. Such studies add to our knowledge about error sources and error structures that can be used to inform users and producers of statistics. Ultimately this can lead to changes in future survey processes and design principles. The evaluation of specific error sources can sometimes be similar to quality control of the survey processes underlying the error source. For instance, quality control of a coding operation involves repeated estimation of coding process variables, such as the error rate for a particular coder's daily work. Such estimates can provide a means for evaluating of how the process is functioning during a specific time-period, or for individual coders, but the estimates are less suitable as means for an evaluation of the entire coding operation. In addition, such process statistics are unsuitable for continuous quality improvement. One would need a special evaluation study to do that where the finer points of the coding quality can be assessed and where issues such as magnitude of the total coding error, error on different nomenclature levels, expert coder variability, and differences between automated and manual coding are dealt with. An overview of evaluation methods is provided in Biemer and Lyberg (2003). With our definition Quality Control becomes part of evaluation.

22.2.2 Definitions of Quality and Survey Quality

Survey quality is a vague concept and has been used in varying ways. As pointed out by Morganstein and Marker (1997), ambiguous definitions of quality tend to undermine improvement work so one should try clarifying the concept to the extent possible. One of the most cited definitions of quality is attributed to Juran (Juran & Gryna, 1980), viz.; quality is "fitness for use." Under this definition, a survey product is of good quality if it meets the requirements established by the survey objectives. For example, if the objectives specify that an estimator should have a coefficient of variation of 20%, then a survey process that achieves only this level of precision has acceptable quality.

For many years, high quality was equated with small mean squared error (MSE), which is the sum of the variance and the squared bias. The smaller the MSE (i.e., the more accurate the estimates are), the better is survey quality. Deming (1944) recognized that quality should go beyond accurate estimates and should also encompass relevance (Deming 1944). Within the last 10–15 years, the definition of quality has been expanded further to encompass other dimensions that are important to data users such as timeliness and accessibility. During this period, we see the development of so-called quality frameworks for official statistics, which has been triggered, by the rapid technology development and other developments in society. For example, accessing data sets through the Internet is now commonplace and, for users, this is an important component of quality. Decision-making in society has become more complex and global resulting in demands for harmonized and comparable statistics across countries and surveys. Thus, quality frameworks for official statistics have been established to accommodate all these demands.

Several quality frameworks have been developed and they each consist of a number of quality dimensions. The quality framework developed by Eurostat (2000) consists of six dimensions: relevance, accuracy, timeliness and punctuality, accessibility and clarity, comparability, and coherence. Similar frameworks have been developed by, among others, Statistics Canada (Brackstone, 1999), Statistics Sweden (Rosén & Elvers, 1999), the U.K. Office for National Statistics, the Organization for Economic Cooperation and Development (OECD) and the International Monetary Fund (IMF). The Federal Statistical System of the United States has a strong tradition in emphasizing the accuracy component (U.S. Federal Committee on Statistical Methodology, 2001), viewing other dimensions as design constraints in the planning criterion.

Without sufficient accuracy, other dimensions are irrelevant but the opposite can also be true. Very accurate data can be useless if they are released too late to affect important decision-making or if they are presented in ways that are difficult for the user to access or interpret. As an example, the results from an exit poll to determine who won an election may prove useless if they are only available many weeks after election.

Quality dimensions are often in conflict. Typical conflicts exist between timeliness and accuracy because it takes time to get accurate data through for instance extensive nonresponse follow-up. Comparability and relevance may also conflict since introduction of new and more relevant survey measures can affect comparisons over time. Thus, providing a quality survey product is a balancing act where informed users should be key players.

Much remains to be done when it comes to user-orientation. For instance, most users have limited knowledge regarding concepts such as reliability, validity and bias and how measures of these psychometric properties of data might affect specific forms of data analysis. As a example, informing the user that the reliability of a variable is 0.50 may be useful for the more sophisticated users, but other users may not know what this means if the variable is to be used in a multiple regression analysis. Relatively little has been done to educate users and clients and it is not uncommon that users are most interested in the most visible quality indicators such as timeliness and nonresponse rates and rely on the producer when it comes to more complicated aspects such as interviewer errors. Even when statistical organizations try to be user-oriented, as with the advent of quality frameworks, it appears the attempts still tend to be producer-oriented. Most frameworks have been developed with minimal user interaction and very little is known about how users perceive and use quality reports and other metadata (Laiho, 2005).

In addition to fitness for use, there are also other quality definitions reported in the literature. Juran and Gryna (1980) distinguish between design quality and quality conformance, concepts that could be used in surveys. An example of design quality would then be the way data are presented. A multicolored booklet with graphics might be superior to a set of simple tables. Quality conformance is the degree to which the product conforms to its intended use. One might also say that quality conformance is fitness for use. Collins and Sykes (1999) discuss quality in market research and find it useful to distinguish between resource quality (organizational quality), design quality (the acceptable commodity), process management quality (how quality is managed in a particular survey), and service delivery quality (responsiveness to the needs of the customer).

As pointed out by Brackstone (1999) and Scheuren (2001), quality has become a buzzword in society. Any definition, sweeping or more distinct, can be challenged but it is probably true that any meaningful definition should be linked to user demands.

22.2.3 Measuring Survey Quality

All survey quality frameworks contain accuracy as well as other dimensions that are primarily qualitative. This raises the issue as to how quality can be measured so that it can be optimised. One way out of this dilemma is to view survey quality optimisation as minimizing the total survey error as measured by the MSE subject to constraints, which represent the other dimensions. This is view of the U.S. Federal Committee on Statistical Methodology. For example, we may specify that the MSE of some estimator is to be minimized subject to constraints on cost (the survey must be completed within a given budget) and timeliness (the data should be delivered to the client by a specified date).

In this regard, Hansen, Hurwitz, & Bershad (1961) developed the U.S. Census Bureau survey model, where the basic mean squared error (MSE) of an estimator is decomposed into a number of subcomponents, thereby allowing the designer to focus on the errors arising from a specific error source. For example, the effects of errors associated with interviewers, coders, editors, keyers and crew leaders can be measured by so-called correlated variance components. Respondent errors are reflected in the so-called simple response variance component as well as in the measurement bias components. Large agencies, such as the U.S. Census Bureau, have attempted to estimate these error components using special evaluation studies that might involve test-retest reinterviews, record check studies, latent class analysis and interpenetrated assignments (see Biemer & Lyberg, 2003 for a review). The problem with these post-survey analysis approaches is that estimates of MSE components are produced too late to be really useful for continuous improvement. Furthermore, just providing estimates without knowing the root causes of the errors does not facilitate continuous improvement. On the other hand, small evaluation studies are still very useful for designing future surveys since they can identify design options that result in smaller mean squared errors.

More recently, society has witnessed a quality revolution based on adherence and application of core values and approaches among businesses and organizations. Such approaches include decision-making based on data, strong customer or user orientation, employee empowerment, and committed leadership aiming for continuous improvement. In this respect a survey organization is no different from any other type of business. Some of these attempts have been labelled Total Quality Management (TQM), which is a term that is not used so much any more. To a large extent Quality Management that is a more neutral notion encompassing all kinds of quality strategies has replaced it.

The effect of the quality revolution in survey work manifests itself in various ways, most notably the acknowledgement of the users and other stakeholders, the fact that quality can be defined on three different levels: product, process and organization (that makes quality improvement easier to grasp) and that continuous improvement should be an important goal for every survey organization (Lyberg et al., 1997).

22.2.4 Quality Assurance and Quality Control

Given any definition of quality, preferably chosen together with user representatives, the survey organization must deliver the best quality possible given budget and other constraints. To be able to do that the organization needs a quality strategy consisting of programs for quality assurance and quality control (Bushery, Reichert, & Blass, 2003). As mentioned these terms tend to be used interchangeably but there is a distinction between the two. Quality assurance ensures that processes are capable of delivering good products, while quality control ensures that the product actually is good. Admittedly, there is a fine line between the two concepts. Examples of effective quality assurance systems include that appropriate methodologies are in place for all surveys, that established standards are adhered to, that reviews and audits are conducted, and that documentation is produced. Quality control is used to check that the quality assurance system actually performs according to requirements using methods such as verification, process control, and acceptance sampling (Biemer & Lyberg, 2003).

For instance, the organization might have a quality assurance system for coding in place, comprising ingredients such as a suitable mix of manual and automated coding, appropriate coding instructions, coder training, an independent verification system and a system for distinguishing between different kinds of coding errors. The quality control system may consist of process control or acceptance sampling that establishes whether the coding system actually delivers according to specifications, e.g., that an achieved error rate does not exceed a prespecified level. Typically quality control should focus on high-risk areas within processes that generate survey error, such as, sampling error, specification error, frame error, nonresponse error, measurement error, and processing error (see also de Leeuw, Hox, & Dillman, Chapter 1). For instance, considering frame errors, it is more serious if large companies are missing rather than small companies. Within data processing, coding errors are typically more serious than data capture errors. With this view quality control becomes part of the quality assurance system rather than a separate operation. However, the important thing is that the survey organization develops survey processes that are stable and predictable, and where these features can be controlled (Mudryk et al., 2001).

Quality level	Main stakeholders	Control instrument	Measures and indicators
Product	User	Product specifications Evaluation studies	Framework dimension indicators Estimates of MSE or its components Assessments of specific errors
Process	Survey designer	Selecting and analysing key process variables (Paradata) Statistical process control Acceptance sampling Current best methods Standard operating procedures Checklists Pretests and experiments	Measures associated with control charts Common cause variation Special cause variation Outcomes of methodological studies
Organization	Management Owner Society	Business excellence models Reviews Audits	Scores on excellence model criteria Identifying weak and strong points Customer satisfaction

Figure 22.2 Controlling Quality

22.3 SURVEY QUALITY ON THREE LEVELS

It is useful to consider survey quality as a three-level concept. The first level, product quality, is the set of product characteristics ideally established with the main users. The second level, process quality, actually determines the product quality. If the process is well-designed and tightly controlled during production, the product from the process should be of good quality. By this view, problems with the final product can be traced to flaws in the process design or controls. The third level, organizational quality, can be viewed as deciding the process quality. If organizational characteristics such as leadership, competence and innovation are lacking, then the organization is incapable of developing dependable processes that can deliver quality products. The three levels are intertwined but the process quality is at the core.

Figure 22.2 shows how the three levels of survey quality can be controlled, the control instruments that are commonly used and some measures and indicators for assessing quality at different levels.

22.3.1 Product Level

As previously noted, product specifications for a survey should be decided together with the main users. This step is usually a weak point in survey planning. Ideally a quality framework (Haworth & Signore, 2005) could be used as a planning instrument, where the user and the producer establish the required levels of the different framework dimensions given constraints on costs and the total survey error (MSE). In practice cost is the predominant constraint and standard errors or indicators of the magnitude of individual error sources often replace estimates of MSE or its components. An example of the latter is the use of the coder error rate as an indicator of coding reliability. The lesson to be learned is that producers must work more closely with the users so that the users know risks and shortcomings associated with processing methods. Also the issue of trade-offs should be emphasized at this stage. Quality dimensions may be in conflict and error sources frequently interact (Holt & Jones 1998).

As an example, the users may be very interested in producing estimates for specific rare subgroups of the population; this will require over sampling these groups. However, as a consequence, estimates at the total population-level will be less precise. Also, users who want these data three months sooner than scheduled need to understand that the accelerated schedule will reduce the time available for post-data collection processing. Still, it is important that producers and users learn to work more closely together, which could result in explicit service level agreement documents that could also serve as a basis for continuous improvement (Lyberg, 2001).

22.3.2 Process Level

Good processes are the key to good products. If processes are stable and deliver according to specifications we do not have to worry too much about the products. There are two main ways of controlling a process. One is to standardize it so that it performs in basically the same way across time and surveys. Examples of standards include Current Best Methods (CBM) documents (Morganstein & Marker, 1997) where attempts are made to streamline specific processes such as nonresponse adjustment, questionnaire development, and documentation so that they are performed in similar ways across an organization. If the process is creative, such as questionnaire development, a corresponding CBM should not be expected to provide a step-by-step prescription on how to do things. Instead the CBM should list all-important areas that have to be addressed in the questionnaire development process and advice on known dependable methods for each area. If the process is more repetitive in nature, such as documentation, the CBM takes the form of a checklist where each step is ticked off after completion. CBMs should be current in the sense that they should be adjusted when new knowledge is gained or when general circumstances change. The CBM is a good example of a quality assurance device. (See Mohler, Pennel, Hubbard, Chapter 21 for further discussion of the importance of survey documentation.)

The other main way of controlling the process is to check its actual performance via selecting, measuring, and analyzing key process variables. The resulting process data are sometimes called paradata (Couper, 1998). Paradata is part of the large family of survey quality concepts. Scheuren (2001) distinguishes between macro and micro paradata. Typical macro paradata include global process measures such as response rates, frame coverage rates and data imputation rates. As the name suggests micro paradata are process data that concern individual records. One example is the practice of flagging imputed data elements.

Micro paradata can also be at a lower level, such as item-level time-stamps or even keystroke data (e.g., Couper, Hansen, & Sadosky, 1997). An overwhelming portion of paradata are in macro form and often part of or a byproduct from quality control operations, such as process control, where paradata might be plotted on control charts to check if variation tends to be natural or has its origin in special causes. With the widespread adoption of computer assistance in survey data collection (CATI, CAPI, Web, etc.), paradata are increasingly produced at higher levels of detail as an automatic byproduct of the process itself. Paradata might also come from quality control operations using acceptance sampling. For example, when the purpose is to accept or reject work units based on the number of errors discovered, the number of errors in selected work units may be retained for later analysis. These so-called statistical quality control methods and theories are described in more detail in Montgomery (2005).

Statistical quality control theory has found applications in survey operations that resemble those in a factory assembly line, such as keying, coding and printing (for reviews see Biemer & Lyberg, 2003; Mudryk et al., 2001). Methods for identifying errors may vary between processes. Usually, some type of verification scheme is used; for example, two-way independent verification for keying and coding. For other survey processes the notion of paradata is much looser. During the last 20 years, however, with the advent of Total Quality Management and other quality management systems the statistical control chart (also known as the Shewhart chart) has seen a revival in survey work. Morganstein and Marker (1997) and Deming (1986) advocate the use of the control chart as a tool for distinguishing between different kinds of variation and for developing stable and predictable processes. Their line of thought is not confined to just survey processes, but rather to all processes of importance to the statistical organization. Examples of such processes are budgeting, recruiting, and training. So the paradata concept is important for achieving organizational quality as well. (For a discussion of paradata in survey research see Lyberg & Couper, 2005.)

A generic statistical control chart is displayed in Figure 22.3. Paradata are plotted on the chart that has upper and lower control limits. The control limits are a multiple of the standard deviation (denoted by σ) of the data points on the chart; usually +/- 3σ. The middle level is the process average for the time period under review. As long as observations fall inside the control limits the variation is considered to have *common causes*; that is, it is natural variation that requires no action to maintain statistical control of the process. When, on the other hand, observations fall outside the control limits we say that the variation has special causes; that is, variation which is unusual and should be traced to its source and corrected.

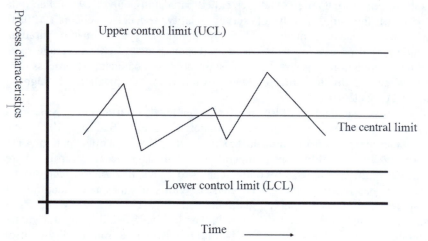

Figure 22.3. Typical Control Chart

Controls are needed in the process to prevent the occurrence of special cause variation. If the sources of special cause variation are eliminated, only common cause or natural variation remains and the process is said to be in *statistical control*.

If the process manager is not satisfied with the natural process variation at hand, that is, there is a need to decrease the common cause variation, a process improvement project must be conducted. Figure 22.4 shows fluctuations in response rates among interviewers in the Swedish part of the European Social Survey (Japec, 2005). In this control chart the control limits do not form straight lines due to variations in sizes of the workloads; that is, σ differs among data points or interviews. Survey managers should not intervene to affect interviewers with low response rates unless their rates fall below the lower control limit. As seen in the chart, three interviewers that have response rates that fall below the lower control limit indicating these response rates have special causes. The survey manager should intervene to discover why their response rates are so low.

It is important to distinguish between the common and special cause variation because they demand very different correction measures. Further, if the control limits were ignored and common cause variation were treated as if it were special cause variation, the result can be to increase the level of common cause variation in the process. In other words, instead of improving the process, the manager intervenes to make it behave even more erratically. Unfortunately, such practices occur all too often in survey management.

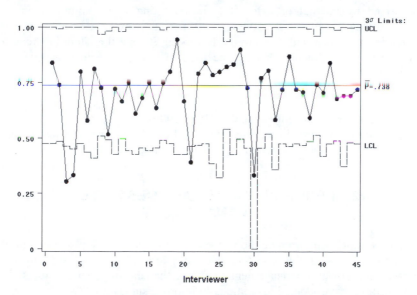

Figure 22.4. Control Chart for Monitoring Interviewer Response Rates in the Swedish ESS

22.3.3 Organization Level

To a large extent it is the organizational capability that decides process quality. Quality at the organization level can be assessed in various ways. There are business excellence models such as the European Foundation for Quality Management (EFQM) Excellence Model and the Malcolm Baldrige Award that can serve as assessment instruments. These models consist of criteria concerning areas such as leadership, competence development, processes, results, and customer relations. In applying for these awards, organizations are asked what approaches are in place for ensuring high quality in operations and practices, how widely spread the approaches are applied in the organization, and how compliance and effectiveness of the approaches are monitored and evaluated. Remarkably, across many organizations, the same pattern almost always emerges. Very good approaches are in place but only in some parts of the organization and approaches are very seldom evaluated systematically.

That the very best approaches will spread automatically in an organization is a very persistent myth that is rooted in many survey organizations. Quite the contrary: good practices are not automatically adopted in all parts of an organization. Rather, they need to be vigorously and consistently promoted. If the myth were true, all survey organizations would be nearly perfect by now, because in most organizations there are good procedures in place in each area somewhere in the organization or in similar organizations. Clearly, survey organizations are not perfect.

Recently, quality award assessments have been complemented by other more specialized survey-oriented self-assessment procedures based on audits performed by internal or external teams resulting in recommendations for improvements (Fellegi & Ryten, 2005). Such exercises have become increasingly popular and recently the European Statistical System has released its own Code of Practice that can be used to assess statistical organizations (Eurostat, 2005). Such assessments are able to identify not only good but also bad practices, which is important to note. Recently, a new standard for market, opinion and social surveys has been developed. Like other standards, it can be used to improve organizational quality (ISO, 2006).

The next section discusses some specific practices that separate the best performing organizations from the lesser performing ones.

22.4 RECOMMENDED PRACTICES FOR QUALITY MANAGEMENT

In this section, we examine how some of the principles discussed in the previous sections of this chapter have been applied to the management of surveys and consider management practices that the most successful survey organizations have adopted to continually improve survey quality.

The methods we consider can be applied to both public and private data collection organizations. We distinguish between public and private organizations because their organizational structures are somewhat different reflecting the differences in their missions and purposes. For example, national statistical institutes (NSI's) are responsible for collecting, compiling, analyzing and publishing statistical information. They may undertake massive data collection efforts on a routine basis to produce national statistics that describe the state of the economy and society. These tend to be recurring surveys that may have been conducted for years with periodic redesigns to achieve improvements in accuracy, contents, and efficiency. A substantial portion of the survey work of the institute is in some countries outsourced to private organizations who deliver data files to the institute for analysis and the reporting of findings. NSI's have a very diverse population of users within and outside the public sector who rely on these data for all sorts of policy and research purposes.

The nature of the work in private survey firms differs in several important ways. Private organizations acquire work through a highly competitive procurement process involving detailed planning and documentation of the proposed research. The scale of the data collections tends to be smaller and nonrecurring although some private organizations may conduct the same large-scale survey for many years. Survey firms quite often do not analyze the data they collect; rather data files are delivered to the sponsor (often a government agency) who then analyses the data and prepares a report. The sponsor may also disseminate the data to the research community at large through public use files. Further, private organizations must profit financially from the work to grow and prosper. Hence, the private organization may have very limited internal funds for conducting research on improving survey quality and must rely on external funding to progress in this area.

Much survey data collection is conducted in university research institutes as well. These entities share a number of features with private survey firms in that they may also bid for work through the competitive procurement process. However, the primary source of funding for university survey research is through federal and private foundation grants. This distinction is important because grant funds are usually much more flexible that contract research funds in providing for research in survey methodology and continuous quality improvement.

Despite these important distinctions, the public, private and university sectors have one critical common purpose, viz., to achieve the highest quality survey products within specified resource constraints for the survey. In this regard, there are a number of important issues that apply to all three types of organizations. These include:

- The structure and culture of the organization;
- Survey planning and resource allocation;
- Project management and quality monitoring;
- Documentation of quality.

These four commonalities are discussed in this section and together they constitute what might be termed quality assurance.

22.4.1 Organizational Structure and Culture

As noted in Section 22.3, excellence at the level of the organization drives process quality. Two critical components of an organization that can have dramatic effects on the quality of its outputs are the structure and culture of the organization.

Organizational structure is often defined by an organizational chart, which graphically displays the various divisions and units of an organization and their reporting responsibilities. The typical survey organization uses a functional structure, which aligns staff according to their specialty (e.g., statistics, survey methodology, survey management, IT, subject matter, customer relations, administration, etc.). Thus, survey projects draw staff across these functional units. One advantage of this structure is that specialists are concentrated in a group and can learn from one another and collaborate on difficult issues. One disadvantage is that the project manager has limited authority over project staffs that do not report directly to him or her. The matrix organization remedies these disadvantages by overlaying a project organizational structure over the functional structure. Thus, the project manager has authority over a staff member for some percentage of the time that staff member works on the project. A disadvantage of this approach is that staffs working on multiple surveys have multiple supervisors. Still, the matrix organizational structure is well suited for dealing with the complexities of survey work and is usually preferred over the purely functional structure.

Organizational culture refers to the shared assumptions, beliefs, and normal behaviors (or norms) of an organization. It can have a powerful effect on survey quality since it tends to govern what methods and practices are acceptable and considered as good practice versus poor or unacceptable survey practice within the organization. For example, the culture of an organization influences how sponsors and users get involved in the survey process, how questionnaires are pretested, what constitutes acceptable response rates, good versus bad methods of training and supervising interviewers, whether and how data quality is documented, and so on. It also includes presence of top management commitment to quality, good communication systems, self-supporting operations and teamwork. The culture of an organization will determine whether the organization continually evaluates and improves survey quality or simply maintains the status quo with little or no emphasis on continuous quality improvement. Organizational culture is extremely difficult to change but can be done provided top management is strongly committed to changing it (Conner, 1993; Marker & Morganstein, 2004; Saeboe, Byfuglien, & Johannessen, 2003; Collins 2001; Baldrige National Quality Program, 2006).

22.4.2 Survey Planning and Resource Allocation

The key objective of obtaining the highest quality data in most situations can be translated to minimizing total survey error subject to constraints on costs, timeliness, data availability and accessibility, and other quality dimensions depending on the quality framework used. The challenge in practice is to achieve an optimal balance between survey errors and costs when the relationships between them are largely unknown. For example, although it may be known that paying incentives to respondents may increase response rates by, say, 10 percentage points, it is usually not known whether and by how much the higher response rate will reduce nonresponse bias for particular characteristics of interest. Further, paying respondent incentives may require shifting resources away from other design features that also affect quality; for example, cutting the sample size or curtailing questionnaire pretesting. Predicting the total mean squared error (MSE) for a particular resource allocation model is often guesswork, albeit informed by organizational experience and intuition. Knowledge of the survey methods literature and the wisdom of a highly experience planning team will play a critical role in survey design optimization.

In private research organizations and some university research institutes, a highly competitive process is used to obtain government and other survey projects. In fact there are a few National Statistical Institutes that also compete for work on commission. The proposal writing process requires very detailed planning, specification and budgeting of all aspects of the survey design. For a given budget and deliverables timeline, the proposal team must make scores of decisions that will ultimately affect the MSE. These decisions concern the mode of data collection, the sampling frame, the sample size and sample design, how the questionnaire should be developed and tested, all aspects of the data collection protocol, the data processing requirements, methods for reducing the effects of missing data, the data release schedule and provisions to ensure confidentiality of responses, data quality evaluations, data file delivery, quality control requirements and finally, the plan for documenting the survey methodology used and the data quality achieved. The proposal writing process must consider the cost and error tradeoffs in conducting a survey. It also requires that every step of the survey process be specified and the roles of project staff well-defined. This level of planning and specification can dramatically improve survey quality.

In many public organizations, the process for acquiring survey work is noncompetitive, particularly for mandatory surveys. Nevertheless, a detailed planning process much like that of a competitive proposal must still be undertaken if near optimal survey quality is to be achieved. Moreover, it is important that the plan be routinely updated as the survey unfolds to gauge the effects of any deviations from the original plan to later stages of the process. If these steps are skipped, there is no guarantee that the resources required to achieve good process quality will be available for the key operations that occur later in the process.

22.4.3 Project Management and Quality Monitoring

As noted earlier, different sizes and types of organizations have different requirements when it comes to quality management. In most situations, the need for systematic, formal systems for quality monitoring is greater the larger the organization. This is because, in large organizations, responsibility for quality is often more defused and nebulous. In smaller organizations, the same principles apply; however, these can usually be accomplished with a less infrastructure and organizational formality. In this section, we assume a medium to large organization, such as a large private survey organization or an NSI.

A quality program in an organization may be viewed as consisting of three interrelated systems: (a) the compliance system, (b) the quality control system and (c) the management system (Moran & Biemer, 2004). Each system should also contain a feedback loop to drive continuous improvement. The compliance system ensures compliance with external regulations and standards, for example, the U.S. Office for Management of Budget (2005), and also with internal standards such as current best methods (CBMs). The role of the feedback loop for this system is to continually improve the system components, particularly the documented processes. The quality control system ensures the accuracy and completeness of the output of processes. Its feedback loops drive corrections to output and improvement of the processes, bringing them into alignment with client requirements. Finally, the management system integrates information across projects, providing management with information about the stability of quality processes, surfacing problems to be addressed and tracking the effectiveness of improvement initiatives. In terms of the three levels of survey quality discussed in Section 22.3, the compliance and quality control system focus on quality at the product and process levels while the management system focuses on quality at the organization level.

22.4.3.1 The Compliance System

Compliance audits are important to verify and correct staff performance on individual projects or surveys. This is typically a collaborative procedure where the auditor (or audit team) meets with the key project staff to review the design and execution of critical components of the survey process, check on the status of project deliverables, identify irregularities in the budget and assess client satisfaction with the progress of the work. The auditor also participates by ensuring that all audit findings are resolved. Corrective and preventive actions are used to correct staff performance—bringing it into alignment with regulations, external standards and written procedures. Sometimes, staff may deviate from written procedures because they have found a better way; in such cases, the corrective and preventive actions drive revisions to written procedures. Comments from staff who are applying these standardized approaches are extremely valuable for revising the written procedures by updating them for improved methodology as well as correcting or clarifying them. Regular evaluation of approaches in place is critical to any organization committed to continuous improvement.

22.4.3.2 The Quality Control System

As discussed in Sections 22.2.3 and 22.3.2, the quality control system collects data on key process variables (paradata) associated with various survey operations and provides feedback on processes that comprise an individual survey. In most organizations, the quality control system includes the verification of work units and other in-line quality checks associated with operations such as interviewing, keying, coding, and editing. Such checks are essential for monitoring quality at the product level (Biemer & Lyberg, 2003; Mudryk et al., 2001; Lyberg et al., 1997). However, as noted in Section 22.3.3, there needs to be a system to monitor compliance and to evaluate the effectiveness of the quality control approaches. Therefore, the quality control system should also include project reviews and technical reviews (audits) to monitoring quality at the product and process levels.

For example, quality control checks for field operations include interview verification checks to identify falsified interviews and the routine review of process statistics such as production rates, response rates, edit failure rates, missed deadlines, and so forth. They also consist of range checks that are performed in real time during data entry that identify potential errors early in processing, and prevent them from propagating, thus minimizing rework. Quality control checks include reviews of deliverables prior to sending them to the client in order to check for errors that may require a product to be returned for rework. Here the feedback loop includes client feedback and customer reviews regarding the quality and acceptability of the deliverables. This feedback can result in rework of product and/or revisions of the processes and quality control system so that future deliverables will be of progressively higher quality.

Routine internal project reviews are a key component of the quality control system and an important source of information for the management system. Every survey project should be subject to a periodic project review where the periodicity may be determined by a risk assessment taking into account such characteristics as budget, familiarity with client, and novelty of technology. During these reviews, survey managers may be required to submit items such as organizational charts, Gantt charts, financial summaries, and dates of key deliverables. A team of experts that provides guidance and makes recommendations to the survey manager reviews this information, along with a verbal discussion of issues on the project. Such reviews can dramatically reduce problems in surveys, particularly cost overruns or process inefficiencies.

The survey review teams may provide quantitative and qualitative assessments in a number of areas of concern:

- Technical. Technical problems include design, methodology, sample size/yield, processes and quality, and indicators thereof such as response rates.
- Fiscal. Fiscal problems include any anticipated and/or incurred cost issues.
- Schedule. Schedule problems include delays.
- Staff. Staff problems include issues with adequacy of staffing and other resources.
- Sponsors and users. Sponsor and user relations and management problems include issues of collaboration, expectations, use of data and associated documentation of quality, and dissatisfaction with products and services.
- Survey management. Survey management problems include issues with internal communications, dissemination of information, and meetings.
- Other. Other problems might include staff personal issues and working relationships.

The quality control system may also include a technical review which provides a more in-depth examination of the key technical aspects of a survey such as software development, statistical methodology and the data collection protocol. Like survey reviews, technical reviews typically use a risk-based approach to determine review frequency. At each review, a highly expert team of technical reviewers provides guidance and develops action items pertaining to methodological, documentation, and implementation issues. Mentoring is a less formal way for senior staff to act as consultants to help with survey planning and implementation with a focus on preventing problems. The presence of a deep bench of senior experts who act as mentors is one of the distinguishing features of successful organizations.

22.4.3.3 The Management System

The management system might consist of quality assurance staffs that integrate information from survey audits and technical reviews across surveys. This system may also include a formal customer feedback process to assess customer satisfaction with the product quality and organizational performance. The quality assurance staff summarizes information flowing from the compliance system, quality control system and customer feedback loops and provides reports to management for review and assessment. The integrated data provides information about the stability of quality processes, surfaces problems to be addressed at top management levels and tracks the effectiveness of improvement initiatives.

Management uses this integrated information, along with other metrics (such as revenue information from financial systems) to set goals and expectations for improvements. The quality assurance staff uses these goals and expectations to lead process improvement teams.

The management system might be developed in various ways depending on culture and other local circumstances. The important thing is to have a system in place that can convert information about quality in a broad sense into programs for continuous improvement (Biemer & Caspar, 1994).

22.4.3.4 Documentation of Quality

Documenting the survey practice and experience is an important activity for statistical organizations as well as for the field of survey methodology as a whole (cf. Mohler et al, Chapter 21). The primary purpose of documentation is to communicate the process, procedures and results from surveys to users of the data as well as other practitioners in the field. It is particularly important for data users because the methods used for collecting data and the limitations of the data will help to prevent misinterpreting the data. In addition, the documentation adds to our knowledge of survey methodology and will help to improve the quality of future surveys.

Documentation may take several forms: (a) documentation of best or recommended practices, (b) documentation of survey administrative processes, and (c) quality reporting. The first two of these have already been discussed in this chapter. A number of survey organizations are creating current best methods (CBMs) in an effort to achieve a higher degree of standardization of the statistical production process. These CBMs are a critical component of the quality assurance system. With regard to (b), we noted the importance of the survey plan in defining the quality-level of the survey because it describes the activities and levels of effort that will be devoted to each stage of the survey process. It is an essential device for balancing resources across the various operations in an optimal manner. Without it, more resources might be consumed during the early stages of the survey, leaving too few resources in the latter stages to achieve the intended quality levels. The plan also delineates the responsibilities of the staff involved and describes how the survey team will operate together. The documentation also serves the important role of informing new staff coming onto the survey as to the objectives and design of the survey.

It is also essential that survey organizations evaluate and document the quality of their surveys. We have previously discussed the dimensions of survey quality suggested by Eurostat; viz., relevance, accuracy, timeliness, accessibility, comparability, and coherence. Quality reporting refers to documents that are intended primarily to provide users of statistical products, surveys in particular, with information on these quality dimensions. Such documents are sometimes referred to as quality declarations, quality reports, or quality profiles.

A quality profile is a report that provides a comprehensive picture of the quality of a survey, addressing each potential source of error: specification, nonresponse, frame, measurement, and data processing. The quality profile is characterized by a review and synthesis of all the information that exists for a survey that has accumulated over the years that the survey has been conducted. As described in Biemer and Lyberg (2003), the goal of the survey quality profile is to:

- Describe in some detail the survey design, estimation and data collection procedures for the survey;
- Provide a comprehensive summary of what is known for the survey for all sources of error—both sampling as well as nonsampling error;
- Identify areas of the survey process where knowledge about nonsampling errors is limited;
- Recommend areas of the survey process for improvements to reduce survey error; and
- Suggest areas where further evaluation and methodological research are needed in order to extend and enhance knowledge of the total mean squared error of key survey estimates and data series.

The quality profile is supplemental to the regular survey documentation and should be based on information that is available in many different forms such as survey methodology reports, user manuals on how to use microdata files, and technical reports providing details about specifics. A continuing survey allows accumulation of this type of information over time and, hence, quality profiles are almost always restricted to continuing surveys.

In the United States, quality profiles have been developed in a number of surveys, including the Survey of Income and Program Participation (Jabine et al., 1990), U.S. Schools and Staffing Survey (SASS; Kalton, Winglee, Krawchuk & Levine, 2000), American Housing Survey (AHS; Chakrabarty & Torres, 1996), and the U.S Residential Energy Consumption Survey (RECS; U.S. Energy Information Administration, 1996). Kasprzyk and Kalton (2001) review the use of quality profiles in U.S. statistical agencies and discuss their strengths and weaknesses for survey improvement and quality declaration.

22.5 SUMMARY

More than just the absence of errors in the final data set, survey quality is a multi-dimensional concept that includes attributes that are defined by the user such as timeliness, accessibility, relevance, comparability and coherence. Because these dimensions are often competing, it is important for survey designers and practitioners to define the emphasis on each dimension carefully in concert with the main users of the data. Otherwise, the producer's perspective of quality (i.e., accurate data) may be the only dominant dimension.

Quality can be defined at three levels corresponding to the product, the process and the organization. Organizational quality is required for process quality and process quality is required for product quality. The structure and culture of an organization are two key determinants of organizational level quality. Usually a matrix organizational structure and a culture that fosters the open and honest pursuit excellence are ideal combinations for quality to flourish in an organization. Moreover, organizations must manage for quality by incorporating a quality assurance program consisting of good project management, a quality control system to ensure quality at the product and process levels and a compliance and monitoring system to ensure that the quality assurance program is being followed and is producing the desired results.

Finally, quality must be well-documented. This means that current best methods should be written and disseminated throughout the organization so that good practices will replace poor or inefficient ones. In addition, both the negative as well as the positive experiences of the quality assurance program should be disseminated. Too often, organizations widely report on their successes in survey quality while their failures are downplayed or even not discussed. In truth, there is much to be learned from both. Excellent organizations tend to have a culture where this important precept of quality assurance is frequently practiced.

GLOSSARY OF KEY CONCEPTS

Auditor. A person appointed and authorized to conduct the compliance audit and report the results.

Common cause variation. Arises from pphenomena that are constantly active within the system and is expected and predicable. Sometimes referred to as white noise.

Compliance audit. A collaborative procedure where the auditor (or audit team) meets with the key project staff to review the design and execution of critical components of the survey process, check on the status of project deliverables, identify irregularities in the budget and assess client satisfaction with the progress of the work.

Compliance system. A set of guidelines and procedures for conducting compliance audits.

Control chart. A statistical tool intended to assess the nature of variation in a process and to facilitate forecasting and management. It displays upper and lower control limits (usually three sigma limits) for distinguishing common and special cause variations. Sometimes referred to as a Shewhart chart after its inventor Walter A. Shewhart..

Current best method (CBM). Written documentation of a prefer way of conducting some type of operation such as imputation, nonresponse adjustment, editing or keying that represents the best practices of the field. See also Standard Operating Procedures (SOP).

Gantt chart. Named for Henry Laurence Gantt), it consists of a table of project task information and a bar chart that graphically displays project schedule, depicting progress in relation to time and often used in planning and tracking a project.

Management system. A set of guidelines and procedures for managing quality in an organization.

Metadata. Definitional data that provides information about or documentation of other data managed within an application or environment

Organizational culture. The assumptions, values, norms, and tangible signs (artifacts) of organization members and their behaviors.

Organizational structure. The way in which the interrelated groups of an organization are constructed, their inter-relationships and divisions of authority and responsibility.

Paradata. Data that provides information about how a process was conducted.

Quality assurance. A system of procedures, checks, audits, and corrective actions to ensure that the products produced by an organization are of the highest achievable quality.

Quality control. Part of the quality assurance system and refers to a set of procedures and techniques aimed at verifying the quality of outputs of various processes.

Quality control system. A set of procedures or guidelines for conducing quality control within an organization.

Quality framework. A specification that defines the various dimensions quality for an organization and how these dimensions will be interpreted.

Quality profile. A report that provides a comprehensive picture of the quality of a survey, addressing each potential source of error: specification, nonresponse, frame, measurement, and data processing. The quality profile is characterized by a review and synthesis of all the information that exists for a survey that has accumulated over the years that the survey has been conducted.

Resource allocation. The process of assigning a percentage of the budget and other resources to specific operations that together define a survey project.

Risk assessment. A systematic process for quantifying and describing the risk of error arising from the various operations, processes, actions, and events for a survey.

Special cause variation. Variation that is inherently unpredictable because it is outside the historical experience base and is evidence of some inherent change in the system or our knowledge of it.

Standard operating procedures (SOP). A prescribed procedure to be followed routinely for a given operation or situation.

Verification system. A set of guidelines or procedures for checking the accuracy of the output from some process or set of processes.

Chapter 23

Interviewer Training

Judith T. Lessler
Chatham Research Consultancy, LLC

Joe Eyerman
RTI International

Kevin Wang[1]
RTI International

23.1 INTRODUCTION AND PURPOSE OF THE CHAPTER

In many countries, face-to-face interviews are by far the most important, and in some cases, the only means of collecting survey data. In many other countries, where mail, the Internet, and telephone have become more important, the face-to-face interview persists but tends to be reserved for surveys where bias in the survey estimates of interest due to undercoverage is of great concern.

The face-to-face interview places enormous reliance on the interviewer for finding households or other appropriate sample units, identifying people in those units to be interviewed, gaining respondent permission, and asking questions in ways that obtain valid data. Training of face-to-face interviews, if poorly executed, can lead to unacceptable data quality in terms of biased and imprecise estimates due to undercoverage, unit and item nonresponse and additional measurement error.

In this chapter we discuss the nature of the interviewer task and how performance in that task relates to survey error. In particular, we focus on what has been learned about the relationship between interviewer training and subsequent performance. We then discuss skill acquisition and illustrate that current interviewer training methods do not do a good job of making sure that interviewers have acquired the skills that they need prior to beginning work on a particular study. Finally, we suggest a different model for interviewer training that focuses on tailoring and assessments of skills. Although most of this chapter focuses on face-to-face interviewing, we also mention some of the adaptations important to training interviews for the telephone.

---

[1] The authors gratefully acknowledge the assistance of NHIS representatives for providing access to CAPI Manuals with training instructions.

23.2 INTERVIEWER TASK

Interviewers are required to do a variety of tasks in most surveys. These tasks often require different sets of skills. Some, for example soliciting participation require adherence to the protocol, but permit behaviors that are highly adapted to the situation. Others, such as administering a questionnaire or making a measurement require strict adherence to a protocol. Failure of interviewers to complete tasks correctly can add to the cost of and increase the error in a survey. The tasks that interviewers must complete include:

1. Identification of sample elements and conduct of on site sampling activities;
2. Solicitation of participation;
3. Implementation of the measurement process;
4. Editing and transmission of data.

In the following, we briefly discuss the nature of these tasks and types of survey error that results from failure to complete the task successfully. A more detailed description of the interviewer's tasks in face-to-face surveys is presented by Loosveldt (Chapter 11).

23.2.1 Identifying the Sample Elements

Many surveys require interviewers to identify the sample elements (see also Lohr, Chapter 6). For example, consider a household survey in which a face-to-face interview is to be conducted with a household member who is at least 18 years of age. The interviewer must locate the housing unit, determine if it is occupied, contact someone who lives in the housing unit, determine the number of eligible persons within the household and then implement a sampling algorithm to select a potential respondent.

Some of these tasks require very careful execution of behaviors that are proscribed by the survey protocol and allow no deviation from these procedures. Others require the interviewer to use judgment and to adapt their behaviors to the particular situation that they encounter. For example, implementation of the sampling algorithm must be done exactly as specified for the probabilities of selection to be correct. In contrast, the interviewer has considerable discretion in determining how he or she will travel to the sample-housing-unit and usually determines the timing of attempts to contact an occupant of the housing unit. On the other hand, the timing of interview attempts may have implications for survey estimates if any tendencies for potential respondents to be at home are correlated with the survey items of interest and these visits must be done in accordance with the overall survey protocol. However, in most cases, specific training on how and when the interviewer should travel from his or her residence to the sample housing unit is not given and only general guidelines are provided.

Failure to complete these tasks correctly introduces coverage errors into the survey (cf. de Leeuw, Hox, & Dillman, Chapter 1). Although errors can often be detected in the aggregate by comparing population distributions obtained in the survey with other sources of data, detection of these errors for a specific interviewer often requires special efforts, such as, revisiting sample housing units and repetition of the initial activities. Also, inefficiencies in how the interviewer approaches these tasks increases the cost of a survey.

23.2.2 Soliciting Participation

Soliciting participation is one of the most complex tasks that an interviewer must conduct. It requires both strict adherence to the survey protocol and the ability to quickly adapt to situations that the interviewer may encounter. Often, as noted earlier in the case where household screening is required to construct a within housing unit sampling frame, the interviewer must obtain some level of participation to be able even to select the sample member.

Most surveys protocols require that introductions that describe the survey and the nature of the request for participation be read exactly directed by the protocol. Often this is required by an Institutional Review Board (IRB) or some other regulatory body to ensure that the rights of the sample members are protected (see also Singer, Chapter 5). However, within these constraints and a general constraint that requires the interviewer to not misrepresent the survey or its sponsors, interviewers have considerable latitude as to how they solicit the participation particularly as to what they say during the conversational exchange that occurs during the solicitation process. As an example, an interviewer might be required to inform the respondent that participation is voluntary, that any questions can be skipped without penalty, and that the purpose of the survey is to make the world a better place. But, interviewers may vary in their abilities to recognize underlying reasons for respondent noncooperation from visual and verbal cues. It is widely believed that the ability of the interviewer to recognize cues and tailor the approach by quickly adapting to what he or she encounters during this process is instrumental to the success of the survey (Groves, et al., 2004; see also Lynn, Chapter 3, section 3.3). However, the training the interviewers receive in these methods may be lacking or ineffective and, other than examining their overall response rates, it is not clear that we have ways to evaluate how well they are tailoring their responses and adapting to the conditions they encounter.

23.2.3 Implementing the Measurement Process

Implementation of the measurement process requires a combination of adherence to the exact measurement protocol and some ability to adapt to the situation. Most surveys require respondents to answer questions that are presented in a standardized manner. Interviewers are to read the questions exactly as written. However, few questionnaires are so well constructed that they do not require some intervention on the part of the interviewer to help the respondent with the response task. Many surveys provide the interviewers with question-by-question specifications that amplify the meaning of the questionnaire items by providing more detailed instructions as to what behaviors, activities, or items are to be included in the response. Because these are implicit rather than explicit instructions, the interviewer must determine whether or not these instructions should be conveyed to the respondent or the respondent must ask for clarification.

The interviewer often plays a key role in explicating the response task and establishing standards for the quality of the response. For example, the survey sponsor may wish to know the number of times the respondent has visited a dentist. A respondent may provide a range in response to the question—saying two to three times, not often, a lot, or so on. In these cases, the interviewer will ask the respondent to provide an exact number. Interviewers intervene when the person answering the questions provides elaborate or qualified responses, responses inconsistent with earlier responses, and responses that cannot be coded into the response categories that are provided in the questionnaire. For other examples of how the interviewer may affect the response process during the administration of the questionnaire, see Loosveldt, Chapter 11.

Measurement error results when the interviewer either fails to correctly administer the standardized portion of the interview or does not adequately judge the quality of the responses so that they can provide additional guidelines to the respondent. Interviewers are given general training on how to deal with situations in which the respondent is either uncertain of the meaning of the questions or of terms or gives poor quality responses. In addition, question-by-question specifications are often available to provide additional guidance to interviewers. It should be noted, that computerized interviews have greatly increased our ability to detect out-of-range and inconsistent responses; thus, the need to train interviewers on how to resolve inconsistencies has increased over the last decade. However, because of the difficulties associated with developing standardized questions that convey all of the information the respondent might need to answer the question (see also Schwarz et al., Chapter 2), some people have recommended that interviewers be given more freedom when eliciting information from the respondent. This is often referred to as nonstandardized or conversational interviewing. Conducting this type of interview will entail even more detailed training on the purpose of the survey and the information required meet these goals.

23.2.4 Transmission and Editing of Data

Interviewers may also be required to transmit data from field locations to central offices. This is a minor task in many modern surveys in which computers are used to assist in the performance of the survey tasks so that the interviewer does little editing and can transmit the data using simple procedures that are guided by the computer. In CATI-telephone surveys, this task is automatic because it is managed by the computer assisted interviewing system. However, in other cases where hard copy questionnaires or other types of data collection forms are still used, interviewers may edit data to detect and resolve inconsistencies before transmitting it to the central office. The editing and resolution process may also entail re-contacting the respondent to obtain missing information or to resolve inconsistencies; this is sometimes called data retrieval. The editing procedures are likely to be carefully specified by the survey protocol; however, the procedures that the interviewer is to use for data retrieval may be unscripted. Thus, similar to conversational interviewing, the success of the data retrieval activities may be highly dependent upon how well the interviewers understand the goals and purposes of the survey, and measurement error can result from failure to complete them correctly.

23.2.5 Summary

This brief review of the tasks that interviewers must complete clearly illustrates that interviewers are instrumental in the success of the survey, that they must possess a variety of skills, and that development of a skilled work interviewing work force is a key element in the success of the survey. However, as the next section shows, until very recently, there has been a paucity of research on training methods.

23.3 RESEARCH EXAMINING THE IMPACT OF TRAINING ON DATA QUALITY

In one of the earliest efforts to examine the effects on interviewer training on survey data quality, Guest (1954, p. 288) observed "Although relatively little *research* has been reported regarding methods of training opinion interviewers, there is a considerable body of *opinion* about how to do the job best." A cursory glance at the programs for the International Field Director's and Technologies Conference for the last several years suggests that survey practitioners have moved considerably beyond opinion about how to train interviewers. But Guest went on to add "In most cases, no attempt has been made to evaluate experimentally the results of differential training." Fifty years later, this remains a largely accurate assessment of the state of research on how interviewer training can affect survey data quality, although a sizable number of studies have emerged in the past few years.

Until recently, studies on the effects of interviewer training focused on how training methods and duration affected the interviewers' ability to administer standardized instruments. A study by Fowler and Mangione (1984, 1986) examined the effects of four training programs that with lengths of a half day, two days, five days, and ten days. The training programs also varied in terms of content and method of instruction. The half day training consisted mainly of a lecture and a demonstration interview. The two and five day training sessions included supervised role-playing, in-class interviewing exercises, practice interviews, and the use of tape recorded interviews. The ten day training included a practice interview conducted in a stranger's home with a supervisor present and also contained a component designed to provide interviewers with a general understanding of means by which interviewers can account for errors. After training, interviewers were randomly assigned to cases in the sample for an in-person interview on health. A sample of interviews were tape recorded and later evaluated with respect to interviewer behaviors that reflect on the ability to administer a standardized interview such as reading questions correctly, using directive probes, failing to probe inadequate answers, inaccurate recording of responses and providing inappropriate feedback. In general, the increased length of training was associated with fewer interviewer errors, although those in the ten day training session did not perform much better than the two and five day training groups. Billiet and Loosveldt (1988) reported on the results of a similar experiment in Belgium, comparing the effects of a three hour training session, which consisted of very little actual training versus five three-hour sessions. They found that for a series of items that were expected to have high item nonresponse rates, interviews conducted by interviewers with the more extensive training had lower item nonresponse rates than those with less training.

Regarding obtaining participation, Fowler and Mangione (1982) reported no statistically significant differences in response rates between the four training conditions. In fact, those given only a half day of training obtained the same response rate as those in the ten day training session (69%) whereas the two and five day sessions yielded 63% and 67% response rates. Billet and Looseveldt (1988) reported refusal rates of 23.3% for the trained group and 28.2% for the untrained group. Beyond those results, there were virtually no experiments on the effects of interviewer training on response rates until the emergence of recent research on so-called refusal avoidance training methods, pioneered by Morton-Williams (1993) and Groves and McGonagle (2001).

Groves and McGonagle (2001) present and test a training methodology designed to develop interviewer proficiency in "tailoring" interactions with respondents and maintaining interactions with the potential respondents Tailoring refers to the practice of adapting behavior to the respondent's concerns but the interviewer may also take into account other cues about the sample dwelling unit or the potential respondent in order to provide feedback to the respondent that addresses the respondent's reasons for not wanting to participate. Maintaining interaction with the respondent allows the interviewer the opportunity to gather additional information about why the respondent may not wish to participate and in turn, address those concerns in an effort to forestall a final refusal. As Groves and McGonagle (2001, p. 251) note, the principle behind maintaining interaction is not to necessarily to "…maximize the likelihood of obtaining a 'yes' answer in any given contact, but minimize[s] the likelihood of a 'no' answer in any given contact."

The training approach articulated by Groves and McGongale (2001) is based upon several related streams of evidence regarding interviewer effects on respondent cooperation. It is generally believed that more experienced interviewers have greater success in gaining cooperation from potential respondents due to greater experience in detecting reasons for unwillingness to participate and being able to address those reasons in a familiar, natural sounding response. Studies by Groves and Couper (1998), Snijkers, Hox, and de Leeuw (1999) and Kennickell (1999) have found interviewer attitudes and confidence to be predictive of success in gaining cooperation. Groves and Couper (1998) and Snijkers et al. (1999) report evidence that experienced interviewers consider tailoring of introductions to be one of the most effective means of gaining respondent cooperation. Thus, the training of relatively inexperienced interviewers should be designed to provide interviewers with the tailoring skills that experienced interviewers gain naturally over their tenure.

Development of the training protocol for soliciting participation consists of three steps. First, focus groups among interviewers or other means are used to gather information on respondent expressions for unwillingness to participate. For some in-person surveys, this has also involved suggestions about how environmental or non-verbal cues may signal respondent reluctance to participate (e.g. O'Brien, Mayer, Groves & O'Neil, 2002). Next, the training staff assembled this material into prominent themes or sets of themes for reasons for refusal along with suggested behaviors by interviewers to address the respondent's expressed concern. The final step consists of carrying out the training which consists of training in the following five skills (excerpted from Groves & McGonagle 2001, p. 253):

1. Learning the themes of sample persons' concerns,
2. Learning to classify sample persons' actual wording into those themes (the diagnosis step),
3. Learning desirable behaviors to address the concerns,
4. Learning to deliver to the sample person, in words compatible with their own, a set of statements relevant to their concerns,
5. Increasing the speed of performance on 2–4.

In the first step, interviewers are instructed on the various classes of concerns that sample persons may express, both general ones (e.g. concerns regarding time, burden, or privacy) as well as study-specific concerns. Interviewers are then trained to recognize different expressions for these concerns and classify them as such. For example, interviewers may take part in an exercise in which they are asked to match verbatim responses to the types of common concerns. In the third step, interviewers would be instructed on the importance of call preparation and initial contact protocols, including training on respondent concerns and sensitivity to the respondent's tone and nonverbal cues. In the fourth step, interviewers could listen to a particular type of scripted concern and practice responding to that concern. In the final step, interviewers take part in exercises in which they listen to objections/concerns voiced by a respondent and then must immediately deliver a rebuttal in their own words. In this step trainers deliver utterances exemplifying diverse themes, demanding that a trainee respond quickly, moving rapidly among the trainees at a progressively faster rate. Thus, this training regimen represents the practical application of the suggestion by Groves and Couper (1998) that interviewer training should be directed toward developing skills in tailoring and maintaining interaction; that interviewers should be trained in quickly identifying sources of respondent concern and quickly providing natural responses to address these concerns.

Groves and McGonagle (2001) performed two experiments. The first experiment was carried out within the Current Employment Statistics (CES) survey of the U.S. Bureau of Labor Statistics (BLS), a longitudinal survey of employers who are asked to provide monthly data on numbers and types of employees, payroll and paid hours. The request protocol consisted of an initial phone call to the employer to identify an appropriate contact person for the survey, an advance mail notification to the contact person and finally, a telephone call to the contact person to request participation in the survey. The experiment focused only on the last phase of the process. The design of the experiment was a pretest, posttest design in which sixteen interviewers contacted 320 employers prior to the specialized training and 329 after the training in a sample stratified by four U.S. states and eight employer sizes.

The cooperation rate prior to training was 62.8% and 72.8% after training, a statistically significant increase. Groves and McGonagle (2001) also examined cooperation rates before and after the training by whether that interviewer was above or below the median pretraining cooperation rate among interviewers. They found that among those with pre-training cooperation rates below the median, the cooperation rate increased by almost 24 percentage points. Among interviewers with pretraining cooperation rates above the median, there was no difference in cooperation rates before and after the training. The training apparently had a much greater effect on the less skilled interviewers than those with higher skills. However, as Groves and McGonagle noted, the absence of a control group of interviewers for this evaluation meant that the difference in the cooperation rate before and after the training could have occurred due to interviewers naturally improving their skills in gaining cooperation as they gained more experience.

The second experiment was carried out within the U.S. Census of Agriculture of the National Agricultural Statistics Service (NASS). The training method was applied to a telephone survey of nonrespondents from the initial phase of the survey, which was a self-administered questionnaire that was mailed to farm operators. In contrast to the first experiment, the design of the second experiment added a control group of interviewers who were not given the specialized refusal avoidance training. The specialized training was administered in five states (Michigan, Washington, South Dakota, Georgia, and Oklahoma) at a point when about half of the follow up surveys were completed. Five other states (California, Wisconsin, Arkansas, North Dakota, and Alabama) made up the control group with similarly defined pre- and post-training periods as those in the experimental group. The second experiment also contained much larger sample sizes than in the first experiment. In the control group, 99 interviewers were assigned a total of 12,596 cases while in the experimental group, 96 interviewers were assigned a total of 10,599 cases (across the pre- and post-training period).

For this experiment, Groves and McGonagle (2001) report a nine percentage point difference in the cooperation rate among those interviewers given the refusal avoidance training; a rise from 59.9% in the pre-training period to 69.3% in the post-training period. In the control group, the cooperation rate increased from 55.5% in the pre-training period to 58.2% in the post-training period, a 2.7 percentage point increase. As with the first experiment, Groves and McGonagle also report that the specialized training had a greater effect on the cooperation rates of lower performing interviewers than higher performing ones.

Studies by O'Brien, Mayer, Groves, and O'Neill (2002) and McConaghy and Carey (2004) examine the effectiveness of refusal aversion training in the area of in-person household surveys. Since much of the empirical evidence that Groves and McGonagle drew upon to develop their training methodology came from in-person surveys, it is not surprising that these studies have found the method to be effective in reducing nonresponse too. O'Brien et al. (2002) report on a test of the methodology within the National Health Interview Survey (NHIS), involving 40 interviewers in the New York and Dallas census regions. Interviewers in each of the regions were split into control and treatment groups and cooperation rates were computed before and after the introduction of the refusal aversion training. Overall and separately within the two census regions, the cooperation rates increased between the pre- and post-training periods in the experimental groups by about 6 percentage points, while declining in the control groups by about 3 percentage points. The reported differences between the experimental and control groups of the pre- and post-training differences, within each region and overall, are statistically significant.

McConaghy and Carey (2004) report on an application of the methodology, which they term Avoiding Refusal Training or ART, to the General Household Survey in the UK. As in the second Groves and McGonagle (2001) experiment and the NHIS example of O'Brien et al. (2002), the design consisted of comparing the cooperation rates for a group of interviewers before and after receiving the specialized training versus those for a control group of interviewers. Unlike the previously discussed studies, in this case, interviewers with lower cooperation rates were more likely to be assigned to the experimental group. That is, the historical level response rate for interviewers in the experimental group prior to ART was 60.7% whereas the response rate for the control group was 67.1%. After ART, the response rate for the experimental group was 69.8%. For the control group, the response rate was virtually the same in the post-ART period (67.3%). In contrast to the findings of Groves and McGonagle (2001), the effect of ART on response rates did not vary by prior response rate levels. That is, there was no evidence that the ART training had more of an effect on those below the median response rate than those above the median response rate (within the ART group).

In contrast to the successes of refusal aversion training for in-person household surveys, attempts to apply this method to household telephone surveys have been less successful. In their article, Groves and McGonagle (2001) expressed reservations about the use of refusal aversion training in telephone surveys. A large portion of the refusals in telephone surveys take place almost immediately, giving the interviewer almost no time to develop rapport with the potential respondent. Also, by its very nature, the telephone mode does not allow the interviewer to detect any visual cues on respondent concerns about participation.

Mayer and O'Brien (2001) report on results from an experiment from the Questionnaire Design Experimental Research Survey (QDERS), an omnibus random digit dial (RDD) telephone survey for the Center for Survey Methods Research (CMSR) of the United States Census Bureau. Two independent RDD samples of 4,000 telephone numbers each were fielded during two data collection periods, each for about two weeks. Three groups of eight interviewers were used for the experiment: a control group which did not receive the refusal aversion training, a before group that received the refusal aversion training prior to the first data collection period and a between group that received the training between the first and second data collection period.

For the first data collection period, the initial cooperation rate for the before group was 33% whereas the rates for the two groups that did not receive training prior to data collection were 27% for the between group and 25.5% for the control group. Although none of the pairwise differences were statistically significant, the difference between the cooperation rates of the before group and the combined between and control group was statistically significant. All three groups showed increases in the initial cooperation rate between the first and second data collection periods, but increases for the groups that received refusal aversion training were statistically significant whereas the increase for the control group was not. Mayer and O'Brien (2001) suggest that there may be a kick–in effect for refusal aversion training in which it takes interviewers a short time in the field applying techniques learned in refusal aversion training before effects on cooperation rates are realized.

In contrast, papers by Shuttles, Welch, Hoover, and Lavrakas (2002, 2003) find no effects of refusal aversion training on the ratio of completed interviews to "non-immediate hang up first-refusals" in three experiments conducted using the Nielsen Station Index, an RDD telephone survey that requests respondents to maintain seven day television diaries. In each experiment, groups of forty to sixty interviewers were randomly assigned to receive the Avoiding Refusals Training (ART) or were assigned to a control group. While interviewers who underwent the ART training provided positive feedback on the training protocol, in each case, the completes to first refusals (CFR) ratios for those receiving ART were no different than the CFR ratios for those who did not receive the specialized training.

Cantor, Allon, Schneider, Hagerty-Heller and Yuan (2004) examined the use of interactive voice response (IVR, see also Miller Steiger & Conroy, Chapter 15) along with a computer assisted telephone interviewing (CATI) system to provide a simulation tool for training interviewers to deal with respondent reasons for refusal. The Automated Refusal Avoidance (ARA) training module provided interviewers with a self-paced tool for practicing responses to respondent concerns. An experiment was carried out as a follow up CATI interview of mail survey nonrespondents from a list sample of elderly respondents. In general, there was little effect from the use of ARA training on cooperation rates. For the entire sample, the treatment (ARA) and control groups had identical cooperation rates. Also, the effect of ARA training on cooperation rates did not vary by interviewer experience. Interviewers were trained in two cohorts and technical difficulties may have impeded the effectiveness of the ARA training for the first cohort. Additional multilevel analyses revealed that the ARA training had a positive but not statistically significant effect on cooperation rates in the second cohort. Interviewers gave ARA training generally positive feedback but indicated that the computer responses were not realistic enough, ignoring what the interviewer said in response to any particular objection.

Overall then, experiments on the effectiveness of training interviewers in tailoring and refusal avoidance have shown some benefits in terms of higher cooperation rates from this training approach, which is quite different from interviewer training for the purpose of administering standardized questionnaires. However, from the experiments reviewed in this chapter, the benefits did not consistently emerge across all of the studies and the method appears to have more effect on cooperation rates in face-to-face surveys than in telephone surveys.

In contrast to the considerable amount of recent research on how different methods of training can affect cooperation rates, there has been less research on the effects of types of interviewer training on other aspects of survey process. An important exception has been research conducted by Fred Conrad and Michael Schober on the effects of flexible or conversational interviewing on data quality (Schober & Conrad, 1997, 1998; Conrad & Schober, 2000). Standardized interviewing calls for interviewers to ask a survey item in a neutral manner and only provide nondirective probes to respondents who ask for clarification of the question. In conversational interviewing, the interviewer reads the question as worded (as in standardized interviewing) but is allowed to use her own words to clarify the meaning of the question and resolve the respondent's uncertainty regarding how to answer the question. Conrad and Schober (2000) report on the results of an experiment in which interviewers in the experimental group were trained to read questions exactly as worded as in a control group but could say whatever they wanted to assure that the respondent had understood the question as the survey designers had intended. Respondents were asked an initial interview followed by a reinterview. Standardized interviewing was used in the initial interview. Conversational interviewing was used for one group of reinterviews and standardized interviewing was used in all the other reinterviews. Respondents were much more likely to give answers in the reinterview that were different from their answers to the same questions in the initial interview when the reinterview was conducted using conversational interviewing than standardized interviewing. In addition, the changed responses were more consistent with the intended meaning of the question in the conversational interview.

Research on training interviewers to tailor interactions with respondents in order to gain cooperation and training interviewers to conduct conversational interviewing both have implications for how interviewers are trained. As we shall see, the types of skills and knowledge required for these types of training are different from those usually employed in conducting standardized survey interviewing. Presently however, we just note that training interviewers to tailor their responses or to conduct flexible interviewing may increase training costs, depending on the extent to which these approaches are emphasized.

23.4 LEARNING MODEL

New approaches to interviewer training continue to evolve, one of which is illustrated in this section. We describe an approach based on a learning model that focuses on the transformation of acquired declarative knowledge, that is the knowledge of factual information into procedural knowledge, that is the knowledge of how to perform a task. We then relate the acquisition of these types of knowledge to the prescribed and adaptive behaviors that make up the interviewers task.

23.4.1 Acquiring Declarative Knowledge and Learning a Skill

It has long been recognized that there are stages in the learning process. Norman (1982) explicates a learning process that was developed by Robert Woodworth in 1938. This process consists of four major stages—chaos, analysis, synthesis, and automatization (Norman, 1982, p. 78). As the learner progresses through these steps, he first perceives an unorganized almost chaotic situation and has little conception of how the process is completed. At the analysis and synthesis stages, the task or process to be learned is perceived to be composed of separate parts that can be learned and then combined or synthesized. Considerable attention and focus is required during these two stages in order to complete the skill. Finally, the learner may subsequently develop a skill that can be performed automatically with little conscious thought or attention. The goal of a training program is to move people through these stages in an efficient manner.

Learning to become a survey interviewer involves both acquiring knowledge and developing skills. Anderson (1995) contrasts declarative knowledge (the knowledge of factual information) with procedural knowledge (knowledge of how to perform various tasks). Cognitive research has shown that how material is studied is important for acquiring *declarative knowledge*. People remember information better if they engage in semantic processing of the material. Anderson (2000) reviews the PQ4R approach to learning factual information from textual material that was developed by Thomas and Robinson (1972). The steps are *previewing* the textual material, asking oneself *questions* about it, *reading* the material, thinking about it *(reflecting* on it), *reciting* information from the text, and finally *reviewing* the material.

Skill acquisition entails the accumulation and refinement of *procedural knowledge* to the point that the cognitive effort required to complete the task is reduced. Anderson describes skill acquisition as moving through three stages of learning: a *cognitive* stage, an *associative* stage, and an *autonomous* stage. During the cognitive stage the learner uses declarative information about the task and takes a problem-solving approach to executing the task using general problem-solving skills. In the associative stage, the learner masters the many operations or production rules for performing the task and no longer needs to think through each step of the process. This stage of learning entails repeated practice of the multiple components of the overall task, use of procedural knowledge that is specific to the domain being learned, and less use of general skills. At the autonomous stage, the skill becomes automatic and the cognitive attention that is required is greatly reduced.

A key feature of these models of learning is that they posit that effective learning entails acquisition and knitting together of component skills. Gagné (1962), Gagne, Briggs, and Wager (1989) and Gagne, Yekovich, and Yekovich (1993) explicate a three step process for designing a training program, namely, (a) identifying the component tasks, (b) insuring that each component is achieved, and (c) designing a learning sequence that optimizes the transition from one component to another. Anderson (2000) notes that some early research appeared to show that this was not an effective way to design a training program; however, later research has shown that the key is the identification of the correct components of the cognitive task, that is, an analysis that stresses that a key to designing effective instructional programs is identifying "precisely the skills to be taught and allows effective programs of instruction to be pursued" (Anderson, 1995, p. 425).

In our experience, we have found that only selective parts of the standard interviewer training procedures are based on an adequate task analysis and instruction in component skills. The one exception is the training on administration of the questionnaire that, because of its sequential, step- by-step nature, provides the cognitive task analysis. By reviewing each item, its associated question-by-question instructions, and the appropriate probing techniques, it is expected that interviewers become proficient in the entire questionnaire administration task in a step-wise fashion. This item-by-item instructional approach, however, does not guarantee that learning has occurred and does not validate skill acquisition. Therefore, interviewers are often required to complete practice or certifying interviews during training to verify their skill at that task.

     Skill acquisition can be observed because it entails overt performance. Although, it is not now common practice, it would be possible to monitor the acquisition of other skills required for successful execution of the survey protocol by observing behaviors or administering tests. Verifying that learning has occurred requires formulating behavioral tests to assess whether of not the trainee has the knowledge to behave in new ways. In addition, it would provide learners with the feedback that can be used in their self-monitoring activities.

23.4.2 Application to the Survey Setting

The key to successful development of training protocols is conducting the cognitive task analysis of the steps involved in functioning as an interviewer. In order to perform their tasks well, interviewers must acquire both declarative and procedural knowledge. Declarative or factual knowledge includes, for example, information on the purposes, uses, and sponsor of the survey. Interviewers need develop two types of skills, based on procedural knowledge. First they must be able to effectively implement the *prescribed behaviors*, that is, those things that must be done exactly as specified by a standard protocol. Examples are administration of the questionnaire, reading of the informed consent, saving of files in computer assisted interviews, and transmission of data to the central office, among others. Second, the interviewer needs to learn *adaptive behaviors*, which are those behaviors that when tailored to the situations at hand, within the bounds of the standard protocol, maximize the success of the effort. Examples of adaptive behaviors are planning the travel route to the segment in a household survey, explaining the survey to the selected sample members and soliciting response, selecting the setting for administration of the interview—all of which require the interviewer to adapt the protocol to the situation that is actually encountered. Table 23.1 lists some of the knowledge and behaviors that interviewers must master to successfully contact and enlist cooperation from the sample members in an area household survey that involves screening. The various tasks that an interviewer must complete entail using factual knowledge, prescribed behaviors, and adaptive behaviors that are tailored to the situation at hand.

     This general classification of the knowledge required provides a framework for identifying the subtasks that must be learned and their associated behavioral objectives. The strength of the training application developed, however, depends on a careful cognitive analysis of the tasks and their associated subtasks. This analysis provides the information that is needed to develop the behavioral tests that assess if learning has taken place.

Table 23.1. Knowledge Required For Successfully Contacting and Enlisting Cooperation in an Area Household Survey

Type of learning	Components
Declarative knowledge	Goals of the survey, government sponsor, organization conducting the data collection, uses of the survey information, confidentiality of the data, types and number of people participating, eligibility requirements, where to get additional information, voluntary nature of the response, length of time required to participate, participation incentives, procedures for obtaining parental consent.
Prescribed behaviors: *contacting sample members*	Identifying sample dwelling units (must correspond exactly to the listed units selected for the sample), determining occupancy using specific occupancy rules, identifying type of living situation (institution, group quarters, or household), recording date and time of calls to neighborhood or dwelling unit, documenting results of attempted contacts with sample members, screening for eligibility, using sample selection tables to select sample person.
Prescribed behaviors: *enlisting cooperation*	Presenting introductions and informed consent, identifying a screening respondent, administering screening questions, recording screening responses, presenting lead letters and informed consent materials.
Adaptive behaviors: *contacting sample members*	Organizing assignment materials for trips to segments, determining the date and time of original calls and return visits, asking questions of neighbors and others in the community to determine types of living arrangements, scheduling appointments for the interview.
Adaptive behaviors: *enlisting cooperation*	Observing characteristics of the neighborhood and household; adapting dress, behavior, and speech to these characteristics; using introductions that are adapted to the concerns and situation of the sample members; providing answers in tailored language to questions from the household members.

Nearly all of the interviewers' tasks entail the use of prescribed and adaptive behaviors. The goal of identifying the component procedures should be to make the classification fine enough so that each individual component represents a single behavior, whether adaptive or prescribed. This will facilitate the task of developing the training materials because it specifies the component skills. Developing training programs that present and evaluate prescribed behaviors is, on the face of it, easier than developing those that make use of adaptive behaviors. However, as we saw in the previous section, current research in survey methods is emphasizing the need for providing interviewers with guidance and practice in adapting or tailoring their approaches to particular situations (Groves & McGonagle, 2001).

23.5 A LEARNING MODEL BASED ASSESMENT TOOL FOR EXISTING TRAINING MODULES

The Learning Model can be applied to existing and new studies by mapping the survey process and identifying which areas could benefit from adaptive skills training. This section demonstrates this process by mapping the interview process for the National Health Interview Survey (NHIS) and evaluating the types of training delivered to the field interviewers.

It should be noted that this assessment is limited and should be considered a pilot. A more detailed evaluation of the NHIS, or any survey, should include in-person observations of the actual training sessions in order to code the context and style of the training, as well as the amount of time dedicated to each activity. These are clearly relevant factors for assessing the learning model and cannot be coded by examining printed training materials.

We selected a relatively well known survey, both in the United States and internationally. The National Health Interview Survey (NHIS) is a household survey that has been conducted by the U.S. Census Bureau annually since 1957. It is supported by the National Center for Health Statistics (NCHS). The NHIS focuses on the civilian, noninstitutionalized population in the United States. Each year the NHIS randomly samples approximately 48,000 households with 108,000 members from 201 primary sampling units nationally. The survey addresses health issues and produces information that is used to analyze issues such as health care coverage, health education, and to collect injury and illness statistics. The interviews are conducted in-person and include both a screening and interviewing stage, with the interview being conducted using CAPI.

We contacted representatives of the NHIS, described our project, and requested access to training materials such as train-the-trainer guides, training manuals, interviewer manuals, training exercise guides. The NHIS representatives were able to provide access to the CAPI Manual for NHIS Field Representatives (available at ftp://ftp.cdc.gov/pub/Health_Statistics-/NCHS/Survey_Questionnaires/NHIS/2003/frmanual.pdf).

The project materials were coded using into training categories defined using the different elements the interviewing task. Each of these categories was further coded using the training styles defined in Section 4 as: *Declarative, Prescribed, Adaptive, or Topic Not Covered.* We coded task elements with more than one training style where appropriate. The coding scheme and the results of the coding are summarized in Table 23.2.

It should be noted that our coding process is prone to errors of exclusion. That is, we are more likely to code a task element as Topic Not Covered or fail to identify training procedures that should be coded as Prescribed or Adaptive.

This is due to the nature of the materials that we coded. For the NHIS, we were limited to coding only the CAPI Manual for Field Representatives. This document is an excellent summary of the requirements of the NHIS interviewing task, however, it does not capture all of the content and training methods (e.g., nonverbal communication, practices exercises, demonstrations, question and answer sessions, role playing, etc.) that occur during the training session. Furthermore, it does not cover all the stages of the interview process, such as counting and listing, which are explained in more detail other documents not available for review (see for example, the Listing and Coverage Manual). As a result, our coding table is illustrative rather than analytical. It demonstrates a method for coding training programs, but the information contained is limited by the materials coded. Ideally, this coding scheme should be applied through in-person observation of a full training program.

Table 23.2 supports the expectation that most of the training techniques employed on the NHIS reflect the Declarative and Prescribed training approaches. However, there were several categories that clearly relied on the Adaptive technique: initial contact, resolve noncontact, convert refusals, convert item nonresponse, addressing respondent questions, and methods for using the computer. With the exception of using the computer, the Adaptive training techniques were applied to those categories that cover the case-by-case interaction of the interviewer with a reluctant respondent. These areas require the most flexibility and draw the heaviest on interviewer skills. However, many of the other categories could benefit from Adaptive training procedures, such as locating strata or overcoming barriers.

Table 23.2. Coding Scheme for Training Materials Applied to the NHIS

Item	Interviewer Tasks	Declarative	Prescribed	Adaptive	Not Covered
1.0	Identify sample elements*				
1.1	Locate strata				NA
1.2	Count				NA
1.3	List				NA
1.4	Special cases (vacant DU, etc.)				NA
2.0	Contact sample members				
2.1	Initial contact		✓	✓	
2.2	Overcome barriers (controlled access, etc)	✓	✓		
2.3	Resolve noncontacts		✓	✓	
2.4	Rostering / Select sample member	✓	✓		
3.0	Screening				
3.1	Solicit participation	✓	✓		
3.2	Convert refusals	✓	✓	✓	

Item	Interviewer Tasks	Declarative	Prescribed	Adaptive	Not Covered
3.3	Resolve noncontacts	✔	✔		
3.4	Resolve barriers (language, culture, etc.)		✔		
3.5	Administer screening instrument				✔
4.0	Interview				
4.1	Informed consent		✔		
4.2	Solicit participation of selected person				✔
4.3	Convert refusals	✔			
4.4	Convert item NR		✔	✔	
4.5	Complete partial interviews				✔
4.6	Resolve noncontacts				✔
4.7	Resolve barriers (language, culture, etc.)	✔	✔		
4.8	Resolve barriers with instrument		✔		
4.9	Administer interview instrument	✔	✔		
4.10	Use support materials		✔		
4.11	Addressing SRs questions or confusion		✔	✔	
5.0	Manage data				
5.1	Field edits	✔	✔		
5.2	Case management	✔	✔		
5.3	Transmit completed cases				✔
5.4	Overcome barriers (hardware, etc.)				✔
5.5	Unusual cases				✔
6.0	Administrative activities				
6.1	Workload managing / scheduling				✔
6.2	Payroll	✔	✔		
6.3	Expenses	✔	✔		✔
6.4	Communication		✔		
7.0	Hardware / software				
7.1	How to use computer	✔	✔	✔	
7.2	Helping the SR with computer				NA
7.3	Troubleshooting		✔		

* Materials not provided by NCHS.   ** NHIS does not use CASI.

23.6 CURRENT STATE OF THE ART AND GUIDELINES FOR THE FUTURE

Field interviewers are required to employ sophisticated and complex planning and negotiation skills in order to meet the diverse and dynamic requirements of their work assignments. However, most interviewer training programs focus on the delivery of information about study protocols and methods, not on the acquisition of skills required to successfully locate, contact, and interview respondents in the field. This is due in part to the survey methods literature, which has focused on the aspects of interviewer training that reflect prescribed behaviors, providing little guidance to the research community on best practices for teaching adaptive behaviors. This chapter articulates a learning model that can be useful in helping to understand the requirements for teaching adaptive skills. When applied to the survey setting, the learning model can be used to develop training protocols that more completely address the complexity of field interviewing, including both prescribed and adaptive behaviors.

As indicated by literature review in Section 23.3, there is an awareness of the need for Adaptive training approaches, as highlighted in the refusal avoidance training literature. However, there is a clear need for replication and extension of these studies. Furthermore, there is little research that examines the application of Adaptive learning methods to other areas of interviewer training. Overall, there appears to be a strong trend in the literature to support adaptive training, however, additional work is required to facilitate the application of these techniques to the development of training materials and implementing in training sessions. As demonstrated in section 5, the interview process can be mapped and compared to existing training modules to identify areas that may require adaptive skills but that are not currently being addresses only through prescriptive techniques. Although the analysis of the NHIS system is far from conclusive, it does suggest a few directions for future research. First, additional research is required to determine if other areas of interviewer training can benefit from increased emphasis on the principles of Adaptive learning. Second, although the current coding scheme is a useful tool for future work, additional coding must be completed through in-person observation of training sessions. Third, additional work is needed to code the training sessions of more surveys in order to produce a more representative estimate of the current state of interviewer training. Finally, future discussions of training improvements should be tempered by the real world limitations of fixed budget and fixed schedule, which require all project managers to choose the best design given the available resources.

GLOSSARY OF KEY CONCEPTS

Adaptive behaviors. Behaviors that are tailored to the actual situations encountered.
Conversational interviewing. Interviewing style in which interviewers read questions as they are worded but are then allowed to use their own words to

clarify the meaning of the question and resolve the respondent's uncertainty regarding how to answer the question.

Declarative knowledge. Knowledge of factual information or of what is true, which can be communicated directly to others.

Prescribed behaviors. Interviewer behaviors that must be carried out exactly as specified by a standard protocol.

Procedural knowledge. Knowledge about how to do something, which involves a degree of skill that increases through repetition or practice. Not easily communicated directly from one individual to another.

Tailoring. The practice of adapting behavior to the respondent's expressed concerns as well as other cues about the sample dwelling unit or the potential respondent in order to provide feedback to the respondent that addresses the respondent's reasons for not wanting to participate.

Chapter 24

Surveying Sensitive Topics

Gerty Lensvelt-Mulders

Department of Methodology & Statistics, Utrecht University

24.1 INTRODUCTION

Many issues that are of interest to social and behavioral researchers are sensitive issues, often related to important problems like the increase in sexually transmittable diseases, the growing numbers of young drugs-users, the mounting number of violent crimes, and the growing lack of integrity and counterproductive behavior in organizations. Therefore an accurate measurement of the prevalence of these issues and their predictors is very important for scientific theory-building as well as for policy-making (Peeters, 2005). In view of the fact that sensitive information is not always available through secondary data sources, it has to be collected from individuals by means of surveys or face-to-face interviews.

The aim of this chapter is to introduce the special problems that researchers encounter when studying sensitive topics. The fact that a topic is sensitive will have repercussions on all stages of the research cycle: the sampling, the development of the questions for the questionnaire, the data collection, and the analysis and reporting of the results. These demands mean that a detailed knowledge of survey design is required when developing a survey on a sensitive topic or a survey including sensitive questions. For this reason, this chapter contains many references to topics that are dealt with more extensively in other chapters of this handbook. The specific goals of this chapter are threefold. First, I intend to focus the reader's attention on the problems that arise when dealing with sensitive topics, then point the reader to some straightforward solutions for these problems that can be employed in conventional surveys, and finally I introduce some methods and instruments developed specifically for the study of sensitive topics.

This approach determines the way the chapter has been designed: section 24.2 is about which topics are sensitive and why, section 24.3 deals with the problems related to surveying sensitive topics; 24.4 provides solutions that can easily be implemented in a regular survey; 24.5 presents methods and instruments designed specifically for the study of sensitive questions; and finally 24.6 introduces some alternative methods of data collection that should be considered when questioning on an individual level becomes too difficult.

24.2 DEFINING SENSITIVE TOPICS

24.2.1 What Are Sensitive Topics?

Although most people know intuitively what sensitive topics are, it is not easy to define them in a straightforward way. Sensitive topics cover a wide range of subjects, they may be perceived as being more or less threatening by respondents, and sensitivity to them can differ in magnitude across individuals, groups, ethnic groups, and cultures. In a meta-analysis on sensitive-survey studies we were able to define nine main domains where sensitive topics frequently occurred: namely studies about sexual behavior, drugs and alcohol abuse, criminal offences and fraud, ethical problems, and attitudes involving abortion, euthanasia and suicide, as well as charity, politics, medical compliance, psychological problems and a diverse miscellaneous category (Lensvelt-Mulders, Hox, Van der Heijden, & Maas, 2005).

24.2.2 Why Is a Topic Perceived to Be Sensitive?

For a better understanding of the factors that make a topic sensitive let us explore the definition provided for us by Sieber and Stanley: Research is considered sensitive when it has potential social and personal consequences or implications, either for the respondent or for the social group represented by the respondent (Sieber & Stanley, 1988, p. 49).

For the respondent, the consequences of answering a particular question can be very personal and threatening. Such threats are characterized as extrinsic or intrinsic. A threat is extrinsic when certain responses carry the risk of sanctions, for instance if the questions are about illegal or deviant actions. A threat is intrinsic when the questions concern topics that are very personal or stressful to a respondent, or when certain responses imply a negative adjustment of one's self-image and make a respondent feel guilty, ashamed, or embarrassed. Such feelings change the relation between respondent and interviewer, making them more guarded (Lee & Renzetti, 1993). Think for instance about a survey on the relation between HIV and sexual behavior. It is difficult for a respondent to explain to an interviewer that he or she is HIV-positive because of the strong social stigma this entails. This same stigma will make it even harder to admit engaging in unsafe sexual behavior later in the interview, because this will bring issues like blame and guilt into play. Sieber also asserts that a topic can be a threat to the social group represented by the respondent. An example of this threat comes from a survey on the fraudulent acquisition of social benefit allowances (Van der Heijden, Van Gils, Bouts, & Hox, 2000). It is not necessarily in the respondent's interest to cooperate in such a survey. If the outcome of the survey is that large numbers of recipients are committing fraud, the rules will be tightened, it will become more difficult to apply for a benefit allowance, and the rules will more strictly interpreted. Thus, innocent or not, the findings may be seen as a threat—not only for the respondent but also for the entire social group.

24.2.3 Cross-Group Differences on Sensitive Topics

There are systematic cross-cultural differences in the extent to which topics are perceived as sensitive. In cross-cultural research we can differentiate between societies, ethnic groups within these societies and intra-group differences to be found within these ethnic groups.

24.2.3.1 Differences in social attitudes

Intercultural research is always very difficult because although countries may seem to be comparable they still show small but important differences in their attitudes. For instance, in the Netherlands, smoking marijuana is a less threatening topic to ask questions about than in the United States. In Sweden, questions about education touch a delicate nerve and in the United States income is sometimes called the last taboo (Lyberg & Dean, 1992; de Leeuw, 1999). Schwarz and coauthors (Chapter 2, section 2.4.5),) conclude that social groups also differ in the extent to which they pay attention to any given behavior, thus their susceptibility to environmental cues may differ resulting in misleading substantial conclusions. In a sensitive study across countries it is important to be aware of these subtle differences (Johnson, 1998).

24.2.3.2 Differences between ethnic groups

Most societies nowadays are composed of different ethnic groups, and researchers doing sensitive surveys should be aware of this. Different groups within a society may have different norms and values. Important factors that define topic-sensitivity for a social group are for instance religious backgrounds, political preferences, or hierarchical status. In a Dutch study on housing and family planning, attitudes differed across social and ethnic groups and with the ethnic background of the interviewers. When young members of the Turkish minority were asked to state their preferences, the responses differed according to the ethnic background of the interviewers. When the interviewer was from a Turkish background the responses were more in line with the Turkish view (larger families, less use of contraception), when the interviewer was Dutch the responses were more in line with the Dutch view (small families and more use of contraception; CBS, 2005). Thus attitudes that differ across ethnic groups can lead to socially desirable responses.

For lower social-status groups, more topics are perceived as being sensitive, than for higher social-status groups, because lower social-status groups have more to loose. For instance African Americans, who have been discriminated against in the past, are less inclined to participate, which results in higher nonresponse rates for African-Americans compared to white Americans (Johnson & van de Vijver, 2003).

24.2.3.3 Differences between cohorts

Some topics are less sensitive for younger than for older people, this holds for topics concerning sexual behavior or drug use. For instance, cohort differences on underreporting as opposed to boasting were found in a survey on marijuana misuse, where younger respondents exaggerated and older respondents underreported their drug-use (Brewer, 1981).

Summarizing, I assert that topics and questions are sensitive when truthful responding poses an internal or external threat to the respondents. The magnitude of this threat can vary across populations. As a consequence, not all the solutions developed to obtain more valid estimates of sensitive behavior will perform equally well for all groups of respondents. Differentiation between populations and sub-populations, and tailor-made solutions are always recommendable, but in sensitive research area they are even more crucial. For a more extensive overview of designing cross-cultural surveys I recommend the chapter by Janet Harkness on international surveys (Chapter 4) and the Wiley handbook on cross cultural studies by Harkness, van den Vijver, and Mohler (2003).

24.3 WHAT ARE THE DIFFICULTIES ASSOCIATED WITH SURVEY RESEARCH ON SENSITIVE TOPICS?

Researchers should be aware that the reliability and validity of data on sensitive topics could become flawed due to sampling problems, increased nonresponse rates, and the evasive-answer bias.

24.3.1 Sampling Problems

Sensitive topics often involve the study of hard to contact populations. When studying sexual behavior related to the spread of HIV among homosexual people, it is necessary to select a sample of homosexual people. When studying drug misuse among students, one has to sample drug-using students. Equally, when the topic of the study is about the living conditions of illegal immigrants, the researcher has to find a way to contact illegal immigrants. When studying sensitive topics one often searches for a special population within a sample of the total population. Such populations are called hidden because there are no known lists of their members. As a consequence, simple random sampling becomes very difficult.

In Section 24.4.1, I briefly present two solutions to this problem, one for populations that are not too hard to reach, one for really hidden populations. For a far more thorough overview of sampling issues that can be helpful for the study of sensitive topics the reader is referred to Lohr (Chapter 6).

24.3.2 Increased Nonresponse Rates

When a survey asks sensitive questions, higher than usual levels of nonresponse can be expected. Respondents who expect negative consequences from participation in the survey will be inclined to refuse their cooperation, or they cooperate initially then drop out when the questions become too difficult to answer (partial nonresponse). And finally, respondents can skip the more sensitive questions. Completely random nonresponse will not by definition lead to biases in your results. However, because nonresponse in sensitive surveys is seldom completely random, it will cause biases, which in the case of sensitive topics tend to be the underestimation of the sensitive variable (Lang, 2004). For an overview on nonresponse issues and nonresponse computation in general, the reader is advised to (re)read Lynn (Chapter 3).

24.3.3 The Evasive Answer Bias

Research on individually sensitive or deviant behavior is difficult because researchers have to overcome a problem that is felt in all research on latent variables, but which becomes pressing when dealing with an individual's sensitive behavior, the evasive-answer bias or the socially desirable answer (Lobel & Teiber, 1994). When studying a sensitive topic a researcher always invades the privacy of a respondent, which may cause them to break off the interview completely, leading to partial nonresponse. If this is the case, the researcher *knows* that there will be an increased risk of bias in the results. However, if respondents try to show themselves in a better light by giving a socially acceptable answer, the researcher will not know which answers are biased and which are not. The bias may be major, when a respondent just denies the sensitive behavior. The bias may be minor, because if respondents have a tendency to play down their behavior they do so by reporting it as being a little less frequent than it is in reality. For instance, in a survey on drinking, respondents tend to drink two glasses less than they actually do. In a survey were weight was asked to compute BMI, the reported weight was always lower than the real weight, and in face-to-face studies this underreporting was less marked than in telephone studies.

This tendency to adjust the replies in order to present a positive image of oneself, either to please the interviewer or to be shown in a better light, is called the evasive-answer bias or socially desirable responding. When a topic is sensitive many respondents feel the need to engage in positive self-presentation, and this need will peak when they have to report their own deviant behavior (Lang, 2004).

There is a tendency to think that the evasive answer bias will always lead to underreporting. For instance, it is thought that it is not socially desirable to report drinking in excess. But not all sensitive issues lead to the underreporting of the incriminating behavior. Researchers should always be aware of this. Some sensitive topics, like excessive drinking, may in some groups encourage boasting and thus lead to an overestimation of the true population score (Zdep, Rhodes, Schwarz, & Kilkenny, 1979). Himmelfarb and Lickteig (1982) found that most respondents expressed a positive attitude toward a halfway house being installed in their neighborhood, but when there were concrete plans to establish a halfway house near them many people protested.

24.4 HOW DO SURVEY RESEARCHERS DEAL WITH THESE ISSUES?

If a topic is considered to be embarrassing, threatening or an assault on their self-image, eligible respondents may become reluctant to cooperate in sensitive surveys, and when they do they will show a tendency to distort their answers in a socially desirable way (Sudman & Bradburn, 1982).

Researchers can resort to different methods to lower the negative effects of higher nonresponse rates and the evasive-answer bias on the validity and reliability of the data. In a survey the most important methods are:

1. Emphasizing the importance of a respondent's cooperation.
2. Increasing the respondent's perceived privacy protection.
3. Adjusting the questionnaire and some specific questions so that they look less threatening.
4. If the topic is thought to be so threatening that a respondent is unlikely to give an honest answer, a researcher can opt for a special form of survey, designed to overcome these problems.
5. In really difficult situations collecting additional information from other sources, like registers, is recommended.

In this section I describe methods that can be used in conventional surveys without causing a large increase in costs. The best advice when conducting surveys on sensitive topics is to use a total quality design, carefully taking into consideration the effects of the topic at every step in the research cycle. In the following I will briefly outline the complete survey research design.

24.4.1 Sampling Eligible Respondents

Most of our statistics are based on random-sampling designs so researchers aim at taking random samples. When a hidden population is fairly easy to reach, but is not yet known to the survey researcher, prescreening can be used to identify eligible individuals. Prescreening can be done at the first contact by asking screening questions. A sample of eligible respondents is then selected based on the information gained from the screening questions, and these are approached in a second cycle of the study. When a random sample is taken from all eligible respondents this approach is considered to be a random-sampling design.

When a sub-population is very hard to reach because it is not to be found in any existing list, you may consider using link-tracing designs, which have been developed to sample elusive and hard-to-detect populations. The underlying assumption with all these designs is that people who share similar characteristics, backgrounds or behavior are likely to know each other. The best-known link-tracing design is the snowball sample. Access to one or two members of the hidden population is all that is necessary to start the snowball rolling. After every survey a respondent is asked to present names and /or addresses of other members of the selected group. This approach is very useful for contacting groups of homeless people, drug addicts or underground groups (Czaja & Blair, 2005). Other link-tracing designs include procedures like chain-referral sampling, random walks, web crawls, and adaptive sampling (Thompson, 2002; Tourangeau & Smith, 1996).

24.4.2 How to Persuade Reluctant Respondents to Cooperate?

Once a sample has been drawn, the following question arises: "Why should the intended respondents want to cooperate in this sensitive issue survey?" In regular surveys cooperation is thought to be opportune; respondents balance costs and benefits and when the benefits prevail they are more willing to participate (Groves & Couper, 1998). So the question becomes: how can researchers studying a sensitive and incriminating topic make the benefits of cooperation prevail? The researcher's only chance of success lies in making the topic salient to the respondent, and he must achieve this by establishing an atmosphere of social exchange or tit-for-tat, and use his powers of persuasion.

If you start to study sensitive topics it is important that you, as a researcher, can make it clear to the respondent why your study is important and useful to him or her, because only then can you give the eligible respondent a reason to cooperate. This is called making a topic *salient* to the respondent. An example of making a sensitive topic salient is the study by Daling, Malone, Voight, White, and Weiss (1994) on the modest relation between full term pregnancy, induced abortion and the likelihood of breast cancer later in life. For women, induced abortion is a sensitive topic and therefore vulnerable to reporting bias. Research on the relation between breast- cancer risks and induced abortion can make this topic more salient for women, because knowledge about the risks and the early detection of cancer is important to all women. This increased saliency is thought to reduce the level of response-bias when respondents are asked questions about (the number of) abortions undergone earlier in life.

Social exchange is related to incentives and rewards for cooperation. Incentives are small gifts or tokens of the researcher's appreciation that are sent to all eligible respondents *before* the study starts. Unlike rewards, respondents do not have to perform to receive the incentive. Incentives create a tit-for-tat atmosphere; respondents feel obliged to help the researcher because they have already received tokens of his appreciation. The Netherlands Official Statistics Office has experimented with gifts of booklets containing ten stamps to reduce the nonresponse in mail surveys and it worked very well, the nonresponse rate fell significantly.

In general, incentives seem to lower the initial nonresponse rates, but we have not found papers that presented a systematic study of the use of incentives and rewards to make respondents cooperate more honestly in sensitive studies (Singer, van Hoewijck, & Maher, 2000). It is possible that an incentive will lower the initial refusal rate in sensitive surveys, but it could also increase the evasive-answer bias, because it could combine a feeling of being pressurized with a lack of saliency.

A researcher does have some instruments that can be used to make the respondent change his mind: the advance letter, the introduction letter and the survey itself. A good survey design includes an advanced letter to all sampled respondents and an introduction letter accompanying the survey. These letters are often the only opportunity that researchers have to communicate the aim of the study to their respondents and to persuade them to cooperate. A meta-analysis on advanced letters to introduce telephone interviews showed that it is beneficial to use this opportunity to the full (de Leeuw, Calegaro, Hox, Korendijk, & Lensvelt-Mulders, 2007). When writing this letter it is important to include: (1) the aim of the study (saliency), (2) what will be done with the results of the study, (3) who is conducting the study (authority principle), (4) a very specific privacy statement (security), (5) the amount of time the survey will take, so that respondents can weigh up the benefits of their time-investment and (6) an address that can be contacted should any questions arise. If applicable, a reward can be promised (reciprocation) or an incentive can be mentioned in the advance letter. Mentioning that respondents were hard to recruit did not have a significant positive effect on the response rate.

We have to add a rider to the privacy statement. A respondent's privacy should always be protected and therefore privacy statements are a legal requirement. Many respondents know this, and too much emphasize on privacy protection can harm the bond of trust between the respondent and the researcher, resulting in a higher nonresponse rates. As an illustration: In one of our own studies we used respondents from an access panel and we wrote our own privacy statement for the sensitive questions. We received many worried comments from respondents who told us that until then they had fully trusted their panel organization and that this statement had made them doubtful about participating.

Face-to-face interviews are not always viewed as a valid method to measure sensitive topics, but when done adequately they can elicit very honest responses and much information about circumstances and backgrounds. When conducting face-to-face interviews it is important to train the interviewers extensively. Interviewers who are trained to show a professional, friendly and neutral attitude, and who show that they are convinced by the respondent's answers, for instance, have lower biases than less well-trained interviewers (Hoyle, Harris, & Judd, 2002).

24.4.3 Designing Questionnaires to Elicit Honest Answers

Several studies have demonstrated that small changes in methodological factors like framing, the wording of the question, survey format and the ordering of questions can alter the responses. These alterations are known to affect the validity as well as the reliability of the responses. This is especially true when the questions are normative (Hall & Roggenbuck, 2002). This insight can be used to help to design optimally acceptable questions when studying sensitive topics.

24.4.3.1 Framing and ordering questions
The retrieval of answers to questions works better if the questions are embedded in a framework, because memory is often linked to situations. This notion is related to the concept of state-dependent learning. Learning that occurs in a particular emotional state or in a particular environment can be retrieved more easily and effectively when a person is in the same state or environment. It is not (always) possible to create the same environment or emotional state when conducting a survey, but we can frame a question so that the right situation is recalled. In a study on sick leave, it became apparent that most employees knew that they had taken sick leave, but the predominant error was that they had forgotten when. By carefully defining and redefining the period of time the question covered the validity of the answers improved (Gray, 1955).

A different way to approach the framing of sensitive topics is to reframe the context of the questionnaire. Lee (cf. Lee, 1993) embedded questions on alcohol abuse in a survey on consumer habits, instead of in a survey on alcoholism, thereby changing the reference frame. This approach leads to higher estimates of daily alcohol intake.

A reference frame can also be achieved by ordering the questions in a specific way. Results can become distorted when questions are clustered together in a particular sequence. This problem became apparent in a questionnaire on social class in Great Britain. After answering 10 questions about social class, respondents were asked if they felt they belonged to a specific social class and if this membership was important to them. Sixty percent of the respondents claimed to belong to a certain class and 79% claimed that this was important to them. These results differed markedly from earlier studies on the salience of social class. Later, it became apparent that these high estimates were the consequence of the ordering and clustering of the questions. Due to this particular ordering and clustering of the questions respondents were made more aware of something that they normally would not consider a part of their identity, this led to over-reporting and a biased result (for more details see Marshall, Rose, Vogler, & Newby, 1988).

Questions should be ordered like a parabola, starting with simple, unthreatening and easy-to-answer questions, advancing to the more difficult and incriminating questions and ending with more easy and friendly questions. When many incriminating questions have to be asked, they should be offered to the respondents in blocks that follow the same parabola, from easy, to more difficult to easy. It is also important to introduce each new block. Don't forget to emphasize respondents' privacy, explain to them why you have to ask these questions, why the answers are important and motivate them to go on and answer honestly.

24.4.3.2 Content of questions/ wording of questions

Using surveys to collect data on sensitive topics is demanding. Researchers should have a thorough understanding of designing questionnaires using items of superior quality. For an extensive overview of writing questions, I refer the reader to Fowler and Cosenza (Chapter 8). In this section, I only deal with what I think is the most important feature of sensitive questions: their tone; one has to strike the right note. To enhance the validity of the responses, sensitive questions should always be stated in simple, non-incriminating non-emotive and neutral terms that all respondents can understand and they should refer to well-specified situations (Dillman, 1991; Scherpenzeel, 1995). The ideal question has a longer introduction, which should consist of short, clear sentences, followed by a short, clear, and straightforward question.

Research on the wording of questions shows that using a simple and conversational tone works better than using a more formal register. This is especially true when the survey is carried out using a computer. Writing a question in the form of a short story, in which the situation is explained and the respondent is cleared of the incriminating behavior is helpful in sensitive studies. For instance "Did you ever take home office equipment worth over $25?" is an incriminating question. One can also phrase it like this: "In every office everyone sometimes takes home some equipment for personal use. Who has never taken a pencil or some paper? Did you ever take home office equipment worth over $25?" This is an easier question to answer honestly, because the designer has presented the respondent with a more permissive frame of reference.

Properly wording questions can intensify the appeal to honesty and can be easily manipulated by the researcher. In a study on health-risk behaviors, differences in question-wording created statistical significant differences in the prevalence estimates for riskful behavior (Brener, Grunbaum, Kann, McManus, & Ross, 2004). Differences in wording were given as "On how many occasions (if any) have you used cocaine in any form" versus "Have you ever, even once, used any form of cocaine?" The first question resulted in significantly higher estimates of cocaine use than the second question. Some precautions have to be taken because these question-manipulations can also decrease the validity of the answers, as happened to Kinsey (in Buckingham & Saunders, 2004). In a survey on sexual behavior, Kinsey did not ask *if* people had engaged in certain sexual behaviors, but *how often* they had done so. It is easy to see how this changes the respondent's frame of reference. It is now thought that the estimates in the Kinsey report are overestimations of the true prevalence, because due to the wording of the question it became embarrassing to admit that one did *not* engage in these behaviors.

It is advisable to test the questionnaire extensively when the first draft is finished. For an overview of methods that can be used to test a questionnaire see Campanelli (Chapter 10).

24.4.4 Enhancing the Perceived Privacy of Respondents

When answering questions about sensitive topics, respondents may become concerned that their privacy is not sufficiently covered by standard confidentiality assurances. These concerns seriously affect truthful reporting (Rasinski, Willis, Baldwin, Yeh & Lee, 1999). One way to obtain more honest answers is to increase the respondents' perceived privacy-protection. Although there are clear rules for the protection of a respondent's privacy (see also Chapter 5 on ethical issues by Singer, or Sieber & Stanley, 1988), this has become an important topic again because technical advances are providing new opportunities to link data from different sources, which can result in problems with security. Respondents should be made aware of the fact that their privacy is protected. This should be mentioned to them (in a letter or at the beginning of the interview) before they give their consent. But as stated before, there are limits to just how much the protection of respondents' privacy should be stressed, when too much emphasis is laid on protecting privacy it can become counterproductive and make respondents suspicious.

24.4.4.1 Paper and pencil questionnaires
One way to increase the respondent's perceived privacy is the envelope or black-box method. The respondent obtains a questionnaire accompanied by a large envelope that can be sealed and posted. If you make it a white envelope without any marks on it other then the address the questionnaire has to be sent

to, and if the questionnaire does not contain any visible form of numbering, the respondent will feel freer to respond honestly to the questions. If the questionnaire is not to be answered at home, then the respondent should be asked to put the envelope in a large sealed box so the researcher cannot take the envelope out of the box and look at the questionnaire. This is a simple and inexpensive solution to increase a respondent's feeling of privacy.

24.4.4.2 CAI

Computer-assisted interviewing (CAI) has long been considered a valid and reliable alternative for measuring sensitive topics (Couper & Nichols, 1998; de Leeuw & Nichols, 1996). For researchers on sensitive topics, the use of CAI has the important advantage that it lacks the social-context cues that are assumed to increase the need to give socially desirable answers (Supple, Aquilino, & Wright, 1999). But a warning is in place: using a computer does not have a consistently positive effect on the validity of socially sensitive reporting. The advantages associated with computerization alone are less convincing than those associated with the mode of response, namely self-administration (Moon, 1998; Skinner & Allen, 1983). In their meta-analysis on computer-assisted interviewing, Weisband & Kiesler (1996; Richman, Kiesler, Weisband, & Drasgow, 1999) describe what they call a *year effect*: although still positive, the effect of using CAI to measure sensitive topics decreases over time. This decrease in the validity of data obtained with CAI is probably due to the fact that respondents become more acquainted with computers. Computers are no longer a magical thing, but a utensil for daily use. Furthermore the appearance of negative publications in the media on the misuse of computer data (hackers, linkage of different files by official statistics and the RSI) has increased respondents' distrust of computers as a way of collecting sensitive data. For a more thorough overview of survey methods, see the chapters by de Leeuw (Chapter 7) and by de Leeuw and Hox (Chapter 13), and the paper by Tourangeau and Smith (1996). For a more extensive treatment of computerized data collection and Internet surveys see also Lozar Manfreda and Vehovar (Chapter 14).

24.5 INSTRUMENTS DEVELOPED TO STUDY SENSITIVE TOPICS

24.5.1 The Randomized Response Technique

When surveying people on sensitive topics privacy protection becomes extra important, because it is easy to harm or embarrass respondents with painful questions. What is needed is an instrument that truly convinces respondents of privacy protection and that is absolutely immune to forced disclosure (Fox & Tracy, 1986).

The randomized response technique (RRT) was introduced by Warner (1965) as a method of studying sensitive topics more validly. The rationale behind Warner's randomized response method is that when a respondent's privacy can be absolutely guaranteed, the tendency to refuse co-operation or to give nonincriminating or socially acceptable answers will decrease, and thus the trustworthiness of the data will increase. In its original form the respondent has to answer one of two statements. For example, statement A is "I used hard drugs last year" and statement B is the complementary statement "I did not use hard drugs last year." The respondents use a randomizing device to decide whether statement A or B has to be answered. Because the interviewer does not know the outcome of the randomizer, he or she does not know to which statement the answer refers. Yes, or True, can mean that the respondents used hard drugs last year *but* it can also mean that the respondent did not use hard drugs last year. Thus the respondent's privacy is protected, yet the probability of hard-drug use can be estimated for the sample. Probability theory can be used to get a bias-free estimate ($\hat{\pi}$) of the population probability of A (used hard drugs last year) by

$$\hat{\pi} = (\hat{\lambda} + p - 1)/(2p - 1),\tag{24.1}$$

where $\hat{\lambda}$ is the observed sample proportion of yes-answers. The sampling variance of $\hat{\pi}$ is:

$$\text{vâr}(\hat{\pi}) = \left[\hat{\pi}(1-\hat{\pi})/n\right] + \left[p(1-p)/n(2p-1)^2\right]\tag{24.2}$$

In equation 24.2, $\hat{\pi}(1-\hat{\pi})/n$ is the conventional equation for the sampling variance of a proportion, and $p(1-p)/n(2p-1)^2$ is a term for extra error added by the randomized response technique. This extra term also makes clear the extra costs of using a RRT approach; more respondents are needed to obtain the same confidence intervals than when direct question-answer surveys are used. A closer look at equation 24.2 shows that this added variance decreases when p is further from 0.5.

Since Warner published his first paper on randomized response in 1965, many researchers have tried to improve on his technique. Some developments were aimed at improving the efficiency of the technique by reducing the variance and thereby the confidence intervals. The Forced Response (FR) technique originally developed by Boruch (1971) is at this moment the most efficient technique (Lensvelt-Mulders, Hox, & der Heijden, 2005). Van der Heijden, Van Gils, Bouts & Hox (2000) designed a large-scale RRT survey using the FR design. The questions were offered to the respondent together with two dice. When the dice roll 2, 3, or 4, with probability $P_1=1/6$, the respondent is forced to answer yes irrespective of his own true answer to the question. When the dice roll 11 or 12, with probability $P_2 = 1/12$, the respondent is forced to answer no, again irrespective of his own true answer, and when the dice roll 5–0 the respondent is asked to answer the question truthfully ($P_3 = 3/4$). The advantage of using two dice is that respondents underestimate the probability of their throwing of 5–0, and feel safer than they really are (Fox & Tracy, 1986).

Other developments have aimed at improving the psychological features of the randomized response technique with a view to enhancing the respondent's trust in the technique so that they would be more inclined to open up. An example of such a technique is Kuk's card method (Kuk, 1990). Here, the sensitive question has to be answered with the aid of two piles of cards. When the answer to the sensitive question is yes, respondents should take a card of the left stack and answer with the given color (red or black). When the answer is no, the respondent has to take a card from the right stack and again name the color of the card. As the distribution of colors is manipulated (for instance the left stack contains 70% red cards and the right stack contains 30% red cards), we can compute the point estimates for the relevant behavior, while avoiding the incriminating yes–answer.

Meta-analysis of 42 experimental studies that compared the results of RRT surveys to more conventional surveys showed that using an RRT design resulted in more valid point-estimates than using a direct question-answer format across different modes of data collection (telephone interviews, face-to-face interviews, computer-assisted interviews, and self-administered questionnaires; Lensvelt-Mulders et al., 2005).

For many researchers, a point estimate is the least interesting measure in a survey. This also counts for the study of sensitive topics. Of course, it is important for scientists and policymakers to have insight into the prevalence of unprotected sexual intercourse, or the prevalence of law-breaking, but for scientists as well as for policy-makers, it is often more interesting to understand the underlying processes and the relationships between the explanatory variables and the sensitive behavior. In the earlier mentioned study on breaches of the law by people who receive social benefit allowances, it was important to understand if the rules were broken because individuals did not know all the rules, or because they thought the advantages outweighed the risks, or because in their social environment this behavior was considered socially acceptable (van der Heijden et al, 2000). It is possible to link RRT estimates to such variables using a specially adapted form of logistic regression. This is not the place to explain this method in full, but interested readers are referred for further reading to Maddala, 1983, Scheers & Dayton, 1988, and to www.randomizedresponse.nl.

24.5.2 The Unmatched Count Technique

Another technique to obtain point-estimates of sensitive actions, while totally protecting the respondent's privacy is the unmatched count technique (UCT) (Dalton, Wimbush, & Daily, 1994). UCT divides the sample randomly into two groups. One group, the control group, gets a list of 5–9 actions. The respondents have to name the number of actions from the list that they were engaged in during a certain period of time. For example:

How many of the following actions have you been engaged during the last six-month?

a.	Went to a party
b.	Went to church
c.	Drove after drinking alcoholic beverages
d.	Went shopping for clothes
e.	Saw a physician
f.	Went abroad

The other group gets a list with the same actions *plus* one extra action: the sensitive behavior that the researcher is interested in.

> **How many** of the following actions have you been engaged in during the last six-month?
> a.   Went to a party
> b.   Went to church
> c.   Drove after drinking alcoholic beverages
> d.   Physically abused (hit) my partner in anger
> e.   Went shopping for clothes
> f.   Saw a physician
> g.   Went abroad

The difference between the mean number of actions reported in the control group and the number of actions in the experimental group is the estimate for the sensitive behavior physical abuse of partner in anger. The accompanying standard error is not larger than in direct question-answer surveys.

This is a very straightforward method to estimate the prevalence of all sorts of sensitive behavior. Compared to other instruments like face-to-face interviews, computer-assisted personal interviews, telephone interviews, paper-and-pencil interviews, and randomized response interviews, the unmatched count technique produced more valid results (Lensvelt-Mulders, van der Heijden, Hox & Maas, 2005; Tsuchiya, Hirai, & Ono, 2007). A problem with the UCT is that it is not yet possible to use the point-estimates in a regression analysis to identify explanatory variables. So if insight in the process behind the sensitive actions is important, this technique is not the best choice at present.

24.5.3 Network Scale-up Methods

The network scale-up method is designed to estimate the size of closed, non-accessible, unregistered subpopulations (Erikson & Nosanchuk, 1983; Killworth, Johnson, McCarthy, Shelley, & Bernard, 1998). These estimates are made using the respondent's knowledge of the appearance of certain behavior in his personal social network. Network scale-up is a so-called proxy method, related to snowball sampling (Hughes & Preski, 1997; Ahart & Sacket, 2004). All proxy methods have in common that the information is not directly obtained from those concerned, but from relevant others.

Network scale-up works as follows. Two questions are asked. The first question consists of 8–15 names (or professions, or traits), with a known level of distribution among the population. On the basis of the number of people recalled by the respondent with these names (professions or traits) the size of his personal network is estimated. The second question concerns the number of people that the respondent knows who are affected by the sensitive topic, for example, "How many people do you know that have ever done some moonlighting?" With these data and the use of an equal likelihood probability model, you can estimate the number of offenders in the population (prevalence). If necessary, a third question can be asked, to validate the estimates for the sensitive issue, for instance: "how many people do you know that were involved in a car accident last year?" The number of car accidents is known, and can be used to validate the estimate for the number of offenders (Killworth et al., 1998).

The validity of network scale-up methods has not yet been studied extensively, so we cannot say anything here about the quality of the results in comparison to other methods developed to measure sensitive issues. It is possible to link the outcomes of network scale-ups to demographic and explanatory variables using logistic regressions.

24.5.4 Vignette Method or Scenario Designs

The scenario or vignette method also achieved more valid results when compared to the more conventional question-answer surveys (Armacost, Hosseini, Morris, & Rehbein, 1991).

A vignette is a concrete and detailed description of a situation that should contain all the factors that are thought to be important situational motivators. A vignette as it is used in a survey is generally followed by a set of questions about the situation. Vignettes can be used to obtain information about the respondent's norms and beliefs (Lee, 1993). For instance, a vignette on driving under the influence (DUI) can explain where and how much the main character has been drinking, why he or she decided to take the car, and how they drove into a police trap and got themselves arrested. This vignette can be followed by questions on drinking behavior, the relation between alcohol and safety, fairness of police behavior, and so on. Thus many different aspects of this sensitive behavior can become clear as well as the relation between the different aspects presented in the vignette.

Vignette studies result in estimations of the prevalence of sensitive behavior and their standard errors, and relations between all variables can be established. The preparations for vignette studies are more complex than writing conventional survey questions, because writing a convincing vignette in sufficient detail, which proves to be applicable, and appealing to all respondents is very difficult.

24.6 FURTHER ISSUES

The survey is the most commonly used form of data collection in the social sciences. But if a topic becomes so sensitive that the researcher can expect socially desirable answers, and if unbiased results are of the utmost importance, then two other approaches are available. Firstly, the collection of new data using non-obtrusive methods like observations and secondly the re-analysis of existing data. It should be clear that some of these methods only provide us with point estimates for the prevalence of a specific type of sensitive behavior. To be able to explain behavior, to develop a theory about behavior or to link behavior to attributes that can be helpful in policy making, researchers have to rely on results collected from individuals in surveys, interviews and the like. It is not within the scope of this book to explain all possible nonsurvey methods in detail, but I will mention the most frequently used methods.

24.6.1 Using Nonobtrusive Approaches to Collect New Data

There are many ways to count and observe overt behavior in a way that does not affect the behavior and that does not involve an intrusion in the respondent's life. Three examples of such structured observations studies are given here to boost the reader's creativity.

1. You can count the number of wine and beer bottles thrown into the bottle bank or garbage-cans to estimate drinking behavior, or to validate the outcomes of surveys on drinking behavior
2. You can calculate the amount of dental floss and toothpaste sold at the pharmacy after an intervention program carried out at public schools to evaluate the results of the intervention program
3. In a museum you can count the number of fingerprints on showcases to see which items in the exhibition where the most popular.

Using such observation methods can be helpful when trying to gain insights into sensitive behavior and they can also be used as a validation tool for survey responses.

24.6.2 Capture-Recapture Methods

The form the capture-recapture method takes here is a combination: collecting new data and comparing new data to existing files and registers.

When a population is hard to contact and the only statistic of interest is the prevalence of a sensitive action, for instance in the case of deviant behavior like driving under influence (DUI), the capture-recapture method can be a good measuring instrument. Capture-recapture methods originate from the biological sciences and were developed to estimate the magnitude of animal populations (Nichols, 1992; Seber,1996). Over the past years, these methods have been adapted for research in different areas like the epidemiology of crime. Capture-recapture methods use the registered data on the number of times an offender is captured for a given misdemeanor and later recaptured to estimate the size of the group of offenders that is never arrested, the so-called dark number. If the police are interested in the prevalence of DUI, they can carry out two checks leaving one or two weeks in between the first and second check. Thus they obtain a matrix with two statistics: the frequency of individuals arrested for DUI during the first wave of police checks, and the frequency of individuals arrested for DUI during the second wave. By combining the numbers of people arrested once and twice for DUI, we can compute the numbers of individuals that were not arrested but should have been. There are many official listings and combinations of listings that lend themselves to this approach. For a comprehensive overview, we recommend the paper by the International Working Group for Disease Monitoring and Forecasting (1995).

24.6.3 Data-mining

Data-mining is the secondary analysis of existing data that does not demand the collection of new data. Data-mining is the exploration and statistical analysis of large amounts of data from accounts and registers, aiming at detecting meaningful patterns. Data-mining is used to search for apparent patterns in known data, for identifying clusters of data and for finding answers to new questions. Multiple regressions, cluster analysis, and latent class analysis are the most common statistical techniques used to mine data. Data-mining is mostly used to make classifications and to study pattern deviation.

Classification analysis is used to identify potential rule-breakers or people at risk. For instance, in a study on fraud researchers define classes of patterns that are shared by all known offenders in a register, and compare all the other people to these patterns. If certain people are shown to have suspicious patterns, then they are checked by carrying out audits.

In deviation studies, every person in a register is given a personal profile, and deviations from this profile are monitored. Banking organizations use deviation studies to monitor trading patterns of investors in order to prevent insider trading. Every investor has a unique profile that is shown in his or her trading. As soon as an investment does not follow this unique profile, for instance when a normally very careful investor suddenly invests in highly risky funds, this deal will be suspect, a possible case of insider trading, and an audit will be undertaken.

A very successful type of analysis, and much used in accountancy research on white-collar crimes, is the use of Benford's law, which is also known as the first digit law, first digit phenomenon, or leading digit phenomenon. Benford's law states that in listings, tables of statistics, etc., the digit 1 tends to occur with a probability of 30%, which is much larger than the expected 11.1% (1 out of 9 digits). Benford's law can be observed, for instance, by examining tables of logarithms and noting that the first pages are much more worn and smudged than later pages (Hill, 1998). Using Benford's algorithm when inspecting the financial results of organizations can reveal irregularities.

24.7 SUMMARY

Summarizing this chapter, the most important learning moment should be that surveys on sensitive topics are like regular surveys but with an added dimension. Everything that holds for regular surveys in every step of the survey process also holds for sensitive surveys, but you have to go the extra mile. When doing a sensitive survey it is important to anticipate the problems, the most important being:

1. Sampling problems due to hard-to-contact or unlisted populations.
2. Nonresponse problems because the topic is harmful and threatening to the (social group of the) respondent.
3. Problems with the quality of the answers due to socially desirable answering and memory problems.

Doing a sensitive study is not easy; it is a challenge even for experienced survey researchers. But obtaining reliable and valid data of high quality on sensitive topics is not impossible.

GLOSSARY OF KEY CONCEPTS

Evasive answer bias (or socially desirable responding). The tendency of a respondent to respond in a socially acceptable way in order to obtain social approval or to avoid personal disgrace and embarrassment.

Network scale-up. The network scale-up method is designed to obtain estimates of the size of hidden populations. These estimates are computed using the respondent's knowledge of the appearance of certain behavior in his personal social network. A random sample of respondents is collected. Every respondent receives two questions. The first question consists of 8–15 names (or professions, or traits), with known distribution in the population. The size of his or her personal network is estimated on the basis of the number of people with these names (professions) recalled by the respondent The second question concerns the number of people affected by the sensitive issue. Using both numbers, the number of offenders in the population can be estimated.

Randomized response technique. The randomized response technique was originally introduced by Warner (1965) to study sensitive topics. The rationale behind all randomized response designs is that the respondent's privacy is absolutely guaranteed by introducing an element of chance into the data. This is thought to enhance respondent's cooperation and honest reporting of sensitive information.

Sensitive questions. Questions are considered sensitive when they are about private, stressful or sacred issues, and when answering them tends to generate emotional responses, or potential fear of stigmatization on the part of the person or his/her social group.

Snowball designs. A snowball design is a so-called link-tracing design; social links are followed from one respondent to another to obtain a sample, by asking a respondent to name one or more people who could be eligible respondents. These designs are developed to gain access to hidden and hard-to-find human populations.

Unmatched count technique. A research method developed by Dalton and coworkers (1994) to ensure the anonymity of respondents. Respondents are randomly assigned to two groups. The first group receives blocks of 5 behavioral statements, the second group receives the same block of statements + 1: the sensitive one. All respondents are asked to indicate how many statements apply to him or her. The difference in mean numbers of behavioral statements between both groups is an indicator for the base-rate of individuals involved in the sensitive behavior.

Vignette (or scenario design). A vignette is a concrete and detailed description of a situation that should contain all the factors that are thought to be important situational motivators. In a survey, vignettes are followed by a set of questions about the situation they have presented. Vignettes can be used to find out about the respondent's, behavior, attitudes, norms and beliefs.

Chapter 25

Panel Surveys

Dirk Sikkel
Sixtat

Adriaan Hoogendoorn
Vrije Universiteit, Amsterdam

25.1 INTRODUCTION

To set up your own panel is very easy. Just write a questionnaire in HTML, publish it on the Internet and attract some visitors. Make sure that one of the questions is about the email address of the visitor. After a month you write a new questionnaire, publish it again on the Internet and send the previous respondents an email with the link to the questionnaire. That's it. Now you are the proud owner of your private panel. What if not every one of them responds? No problem. Based on the information of the first questionnaire you know so much of them that you can easily fill in the questions yourself. It's not only easy, it is also fun. And when you finally become bored of your panel you can also make a profit by selling the email addresses, along with the information, to a local direct marketing firm.

Unfortunately, when your have higher ambitions than doing quick-and-dirty research, panel research is far more complicated. It has all the problems of doing cross sectional research, plus an extra number of stumbling blocks. But one thing remains true: it is fun, especially for a methodologist, who can apply all his skills to the challenges posed by the panel. And fortunately for him, there are many compelling reasons to carry out panel research, not for quick-and-dirty projects but for serious projects that play a crucial role in public and private policy decisions.

In this chapter, we discuss the most important issues that are characteristic of panel research. In section 25.2 we start with the reasons for the use of panels. Section 25.3 describes the different types of panels. In section 25.4 the most important success factor of panel research is discussed: the practical recruitment and maintenance of a panel. Section 25.5 deals with bias issues: the sources of bias in panel research are more varied than in other types of surveys. Section 25.6 is about the most important mathematical reason for panels: the measurement of change; it is the only section that gradually builds up to some tough mathematics but it also shows why real good panel design is complicated.

25.2 WHY PANEL SURVEYS?

A panel survey is a survey in which similar measurements are made on the same sample at different points in time (cf. Kasprzyk, Duncan, Kalton, & Singh, 1989). Why would you stick to the same sample several times? The traditional motivation to prefer a panel survey to a simple cross-sectional survey is that it is a much better instrument to measure *trends*. Panel data do not only provide you with better estimates in terms of bias and variance for change (net change), they also give you the extra information about the amount of change at the individual level (gross change), where you would be left in the dark if you had used two cross sectional surveys.

Another reason to use a panel survey is to measure a certain *concept across time,* such as being unemployed. In employment studies the interesting question is not so much "Who is unemployed?", but rather "Will people who are unemployed ever find a job?", and if so "Will they be able to keep their job, or will they soon fall back into unemployment?". By asking respondents about their employment status on a regular basis, you can cumulate data over time and thus obtain accurate measurement of employment careers, much better than you would get from a cross-sectional survey, where you have to ask respondents about their past. In the latter case you would experience serious recall effects, because people may forget or misplace jobs they had in the past (see also Schwarz et al., Chapter 2). The reasons mentioned above make panel surveys an excellent tool for longitudinal analysis, such as in employment status, health, and financial behavior. It is in these research areas that panel designs are common. But a panel design is also attractive for product testing in commercial research. This enables you to find out if a respondent likes the product not only at first glance, but also after a period of using it. Because more frequent questioning not only reduces recall effects, but is also more costly, it is a methodological challenge to find the optimal time between two measurements in a panel design in terms of cost and precision of estimates. An example of such a problem is shown at the end of the chapter.

Cumulating data over time also provides information over *rare events*, such as being a victim of a crime, getting (grand) children, choosing a mortgage. For example, in a study on the impact of victimization (see Winkel & Vrij, 1998) the researchers chose a panel design where the respondents received a questionnaire at the start (t_0) with questions about their current state of psychological well being and about their past experiences in relation to crime. Then, every week, they were questioned whether they had been victimized. If so, the respondents received questionnaires at various post-victimization times. The first measurement of respondent i would be at time point t_{1i}, within 1 week of the victimization, at t_{2i} about 1 month after the incident, at t_{3i}, 2 months after, and so on. Such a design provides data that allows an analysis the short and long term effect of being victimized in terms of psychological well-being and psychological distress and in relationship with personal characteristics of the victim. In fact, the study in this example combines two benefits of panel designs: 1. it is a longitudinal study, and 2. it concerns rare events.

Besides the reasons mentioned earlier, there are *straightforward, practical reasons* to use a panel. Such a practical reason may be, that you, as a large scale user of statistical information, want to have respondents at your disposal that you can ask questions any time you like. This is the case if you were the owner of an Internet Access Panel (IAP). Such panels became quickly popular in marketing research, for many reasons. A first advantage is that they are fast. Either the information can be collected in a few days, or, it even may already be available from earlier research. Information that was collected in previous questionnaires can be used for efficient routing (e.g., ask questions about mortgages only to house owners), for targeted sampling of a specific subpopulation (e.g., if your questionnaire is only about mortgages). A second practical advantage of an Internet Access Panel is that you can return to the same sample of respondents in case the data analyses leads to new questions (or, when you have to admit that you forgot to ask a question). In fact, an IAP provides you with all the benefits of Computer Assisted Self Interviewing, such as the absence of interviewer effects, possibilities to check the values and consistencies of the respondents' answers, to use summary correction screens (where previous responses are summarized and the respondent is asked if he wants to make corrections), and, provided the respondents have adequate computers, to use graphics, sound and video.

A methodological advantage of a panel survey is that you can use the panel design to *test measurement instruments* in terms of test-retest reliability. For a respondent it may be somewhat strange when the same question is asked twice, but this may be less the case if this question is asked twice in two different questionnaires with some time in between. Especially in Internet Access Panels with frequent contact one may, depending on the subject, attribute the difference entirely to the unreliability of the instrument. Another example of using the panel structure for data quality purposes is to detect measurement errors when you expect correlated data. For example, in the CentER Savings Survey, a group of researchers was interested in measuring total assets.

Table 25.1 Some suspicious series of annual reports of estimated value of residence (in thousand guilders) in the CentER Savings Survey.

Case	Year 1996	1997	1998	1999	2000	2001	2002	2003
1	300	310	325	.	475	525	1212	551
2	.	.	.	.	.	900	1983	1102
3	350	40	400	.	.	.	.	.
4	200	200	425	450	450	.	.	.
5	290	360	400	950	.	.	1653	1488
6	325	350	400	410	450	550	1102	606
7	95	220	220	.	.	.	286	275
8	80	80	80	400	530	.	584	584

Notes: In 2002 & 2003 the reported values were in Euros, and are recalculated into guilders. A dot refers to a missing observation. A series of annual reports is considered suspicious if at least one relative change in value between two successive years exceeds 50%.

For house owners the total assets depend on the estimated value of the residence. If a respondent is able to provide good estimates, and reports several years about the same house, you will obtain a series of values that relate to the price movements in the real estate market. However, respondents may make mistakes, and some of these can be discovered using simple rules to identify suspicious reports, as illustrated in Table 25.1. Such data pose questions to the data analyst; did cases 4, 7, and 8 change residences in 1998, 1997, and 1999 respectively? Was there confusion to report values either in Euros or in guilders in 2002 for cases 1, 2, and 6? Was the reported value for case 3 in 1997 a typing error?

Discrepancies as in Table 25.1 can be prevented during the interview, using *dependent interviewing* (Mathiowetz & McGonagle, 2000). Prior information can be used to check the consistency of a new value. In case of a large change, the respondent would then be asked if the given answer is correct (reactive dependent interviewing). Alternatively previously gathered information could be used in advance, presented to the respondent before the respondent is asked to report the new value (proactive dependent interviewing).

Panel research is growing in popularity and there are many reasons to use panel surveys. We have summarized these in Table 25.2.

Table 25.2 Reasons to use panel surveys and Internet access panels (IAP)

Accurate measurement of change (net change)
Identification where the change comes from (gross change)
Following concepts across time
Detecting rare events
Previously collected background data
Efficient routing using previously collected information
Targeted sampling
Rapid data collection (fast)
Summary correction screens
Electronic checks on values and consistencies of respondents' answers
Graphics, sound and video
Evaluation of measurement instruments (test retest correlations)
Longitudinal check on data
Dependent interviewing

The popularity of panel research in marketing is illustrated by the database of ESOMAR, the international organization of marketing research agencies. In June 2004, 1035 organizations were listed that carry out panel research on a continuous basis; 43 of those organizations are based in the United States, 38 of them reside in the Netherlands. Those organizations do not include the countless small and larger businesses that use panels in varying degrees of sophistication. Large companies (like Philips) have their own client panels that help them design new products. Publishing companies have their own reader panels that are used to evaluate the contents of magazines on a highly competitive market. Broadcasting companies have their own consumer panels, which they use for research for their consumer programs. And so the list goes on, and will continue to expand. Then there are the governmental, semi-governmental and academic agencies that run their own panels, national statistical offices and universities. Whereas most commercial panels are based on the Internet, most noncommercial panels are not. Famous, trend-setting face-to-face panels in the United States are PSID (Panel Study of Income Dynamics), CPS (Current Population Survey, designed to keep track of the labor market) and SIPP (Survey of Income and Program Participation, one of its main research topics is the transfer of government money to individuals). For those interested in the intricate methodology of large representative panels, a visit to their websites is worthwhile.

25.3 WHAT TYPES OF PANELS DO EXIST?

In providing a typology of web surveys Couper (2000b) draws an important distinction between probability and non-probability surveys, and identifies three interesting categories of panel surveys. A *volunteer opt-in panel* refers to the situation that we discussed in the introduction of this chapter. Visitors of well-used web sites are asked to register for a panel, and leave basic demographic information that can be used to select respondents from the database in a later stage. Although the respondent selection is based on probability sampling, the initial panel consists of volunteers. The situation is slightly different in the case of the two types of prerecruited panels. Here the panelists are recruited using traditional sampling techniques (e.g. random digit dialing telephone surveys). During the telephone interview basis background information is collected, that is used to find eligible respondents. In *prerecruited panels of Internet users* one is interested in obtaining a probability sample of people that have access to the Internet. In *prerecruited panels of the total population* one recruits the panel from the full population that include people that do not have Internet access. Here one often needs to provide respondents with the technical equipment (computer and software) in return for their participation. Although this approach solves coverage problems and problems regarding browser compatibility, there are obvious consequences in terms of cost. The latter strategy is also used in *special purpose panels*, such as a people meter panel when television viewing behavior is measured, or in consumer panels and scatter panels to measure consumer behavior. *Internet access panels* can be any of the three types mentioned before. For a detailed discussion of Internet surveys, see Lozar Manfreda and Vehovar (Chapter 14).

Bailar (1989) discusses a typology of survey types from a perspective of information needs. She distinguishes single time surveys, repeated surveys (with and without overlap), and longitudinal surveys (with and without rotation). Longitudinal surveys are intended to follow a specific group over a longer period, as in cohort studies, and sometimes to study a changing population over a longer period of time. In the first case it is important to follow the same persons for a longer period of time; this is called a *cohort study*, as the National Child Development Study (NCDS) in the United Kingdom. In the latter case, it is important to have respondents rotate in and out (a *rotating panel*) in order to keep the sample reflecting the population. Figure 25.1 shows a simple rotation scheme. At t_1 measurements are based only on group g_1. At t_2 statistics are estimated using group g_1 and g_2. At t_4, four groups are being used: g_1, g_2, g_3 and g_4. Then group g_1 leaves the panel. At t_5 groups g_2, g_3, g_4 and g_5 are used for estimation. Note that an estimate for the difference between t_1 and t_5 is based on the dependent estimates on the groups g_2, g_3, g_4 and the independent estimates of groups g_1 and g_5. Rotation is also helpful to reduce response burden and time-in-sample bias.

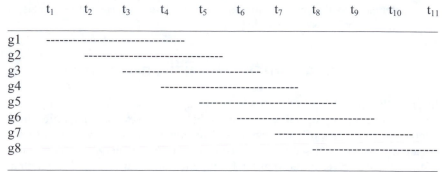

Figure 25.1 Scheme for a rotating panel

Different types of panel are, for example:
1. Volunteer opt-in panels (Harris Interactive, Greenfield, NFO)
2. Pre-recruited panels of Internet users (Pew Research Center)
3. Pre-recruited panels of full population (Knowledge Networks, CentERdata)
4. Direct access panels, Internet access panels
5. Special purpose panels: scatter panel, people-meter panel (AC Nielsen)
6. Rotating panels
7. Cohort studies

25.4 HOW TO SET UP AND MAINTAIN A PANEL SURVEY

Already in the planning stages, it is very important to realise that a panel needs maintenance. In fact, you will need some effective panel management tools to prevent you from drowning in management problems (if not in data). The panel management system becomes more critical as the time between waves gets shorter. Setting up a panel survey is basically not much different from setting up a cross-sectional survey, except that you need to keep the address of the respondent for a future contact. However, as soon as you collected the data in the first wave, the time until the next wave is ticking away, and you had better be prepared. Maintaining a panel survey requires that you are in control of the information flow and that you are able to react adequately if necessary.

To illustrate that controlling the information flow in a panel survey is not straightforward consider the simple question, "How many respondents are in the panel?" or "What is the response rate?" in the case of an Internet access panel. On one hand, due to ongoing refreshment of the sample, new respondents will be in various stages of entering the panel, and it will therefore not be completely clear how many people actually are in the panel. On the other hand it may not always be clear if a respondent has dropped out of the panel or whether he has for some reason failed to respond to several questionnaires. You need accurate definitions and an accurate up to date administration in order to answer this simple question. Your administration should cover topics like who did complete the questionnaires, who were reminded, or who can not participate due to technical problems, holidays, illnesses.

Also from a respondents' point of view, panel management is essential. Respondents will be less motivated to participate if a survey organization does not seem to care about the respondents' cooperation or their requests. Saris (1998) stresses that personal contact between panel households and survey staff is beneficial (if not essential) to maintain high response rates and continuing panel participation. Although this may seem trivial, this realization came after a period where different parts of the survey staff were strictly oriented towards their task, not to respondents' needs. Respondents were sent from pillar to post, and after some frustrating experiences dropped out of the panel. Respondent comments at the end of a questionnaire proved to be a good outlet for respondents' grieves, but require that the staff react adequately. What else can a survey organization do to stimulate respondents? Sometimes respondents receive incentives. If the incentive is not too cheap, respondents seem to appreciate it. In other cases they receive (summaries of) research. Although this may confirm the panel respondents that the bureau actually uses the information of the respondents, it may also influence them, with the possible consequence that they will respond more strategically. When respondents understand how the results are used, for example, for the development of health policy, they may perceive an interest to exaggerate their health problems or financial problems.

25.5 SOURCES OF BIAS IN A PANEL

There are many ways in which panel data may become biased, much more than in cross sectional research. Bias is not necessarily always a problem. There are many applications in panel research in which biased data may give perfectly usable results. Examples are

1. *Panels that are used for exploratory research.* When the research problem is to generate ideas in a certain substantive area, such as product development or commercial communication, the only requirement is that it can reasonably expected that the panel members constitute the full range of relevant consumers. Even testing ideas for products or advertising usually does not depend too much on the representativity of a panel, because results often are more affected by rapid market change than by the bias of the panel.

2. *Testing of scientific theories.* When a theory is formulated in terms of a general law, e.g., the linear model $\mathbf{y} = \boldsymbol{\beta}'\mathbf{x}$, then this law should apply to all cases, whether they are distributed according to some population distribution or not. A concrete example is the subjective experience of

noise (y) as a function of the distance one lives from the airport (x). As long as the bias is only in **x**, there is no problem in estimating β (for an interesting discussion of this example, see Groves, 1989 page 283ff.).

3. *The measurement of change in a population.* This example is a little trickier, because it depends on the assumption that the change itself is independent of the bias. At the end of this chapter a counter example is given. A plausible example is the reduction of subjective experience of noise after a reduction of flights in a neighboring airport.

These examples show that it is reasonable to not always pay the highest price and aim for perfectly unbiased estimates. But of course, there are also examples in which it is absolutely crucial to have representative estimators. The most notorious is election research, in which an error of a few tenths of percents can make a huge difference in the prediction of a country's political fate. For such situations, knowledge about the possible biases in a panel, and adequate weighting procedures are essential. For the theory of the technique of correcting bias by weighting we refer to Biemer and Christ (Chapter 17). In this chapter we restrict ourselves to general strategic considerations.

25.5.1 Recruitment Bias

Why does someone become member of a panel? Because of a legal obligation? A feeling of responsibility? Or because it's fun? In many instances, and for many persons, neither of these reasons apply, and for those it is likely that they refuse to take part in the panel. When there is no proper recruitment procedure, there is no cure for this type of bias. For example, with voluntary participation based on registration on a website, we have no way of knowing the inclusion probabilities of each of the participants. So they may be biased in the weirdest possible ways, for instance, eyesight, anger toward a dubious financial firm, or simply curiosity. When a well-documented selection procedure exists, as for example in the CentERpanel, the response rates are quite sobering, as can be deducted from Table 25.3.

Table 25.3 Response rates in different stages of recruitment in the CentERpanel

	%	Cumulative %
Phone number usable	98.2	98.2
Participation first contact interview	61.6	60.5
Prepared to take part in follow up interviews	51.2	31.0
Phone number correct in membership interview	98.6	30.5
Participation membership interview	82.4	25.2
Respondent qualifies as a member	91.9	23.1
Prepared to become a member	44.9	10.4

Here the response rates are described by stage. From all selected phone numbers, 98.2% was usable. From the potential respondents who were contacted, 38.4% refused the first contact interview. The data of those who did take part, and were prepared to take part in follow up interviews, were stored in a database and later retrieved when the respondents were asked to take part in the panel. In the end, 10.4% of the initial phone numbers became panel members. Most commercial research institutes do not keep track of the recruitment process in this detail. But when you have a selection procedure, for example, by a telephone survey, which brings you into contact with candidate members there is an attractive possibility to anticipate recruitment bias (and other types of bias as well). The trick is to use the telephone survey to establish population distributions of variables that are crucial for the substantive area for which the panel will have to provide information.

The Dutch CentERpanel is a general-purpose panel. The respondents are recruited by a telephone survey. To obtain a broad base for weighting with respect to relevant variables a set of 20 questions from the Quality of Life survey of Statistics Netherlands on a variety of topics was asked. Every household that was willing to participate in the panel was registered and stored in a basic sign up file. Every week new households are selected from this basic file. The chance of being selected for the panel depends on the following variables: urbanization, composition of household, income, age, and political preference. So by selection the panel was kept representative on these variables as good as possible. This, however, did not hold for the 20 Quality of Life variables. Table 25.4 shows the distribution of some variables in the different stages. The recruitment stage corresponds with the best possible estimation of the distribution in the Netherlands. The stage gives the distribution of those who entered the panel in 1999. The panel stage gives the distribution within the panel at the end of 1999. Table 25.4 shows that the panel sometimes seriously deviates from the recruitment distribution. Especially members of sport club are not inclined to become member of a panel. The recruitment distributions can be used according to needs. When the topic of a project is housing, the number of rooms in the house can be used for weighting. In a victimization survey, the data can be reweighted with respect to victimization of burglary and with respect to being afraid on the street.

Table 25.4 Distributions of some important variables with recruitment, entry and in the CentERpanel, 1999.

	Recruitment %	Entry %	Panel %
Number of rooms in the house			
1–3 rooms	13.1	12.1	17.7
4 rooms	37.3	42.9	31.8
5 rooms	28.3	27.3	30.9
6 or more rooms	21.3	17.6	19.5
Traveling time to work			
>20 minutes	40.7	52.0	49.3
<20 minutes	59.3	46.8	50.7
Satisfaction with health (1–10)			
1–5	6.0	2.9	7.3

	Recruitment %	Entry %	Panel %
6	6.3	5.9	10.8
7	22.6	21.7	27.5
8	40.0	46.9	36.3
9, 10	23.8	22.6	18.1
Visited the cinema last year			
yes	48.6	53.5	38.4
no	51.4	46.5	61.6
Member of sport club			
yes	54.7	60.2	35.6
no	45.3	39.8	64.4
Victim burglary (ever)			
yes	16.4	18.4	22.8
no	83.6	81.2	77.2
Afraid on the street			
yes	9.5	10.8	12.2
no	90.5	89.2	87.8

25.5.2 Nonresponse

To respond to questionnaires regularly can be a burden. When you are short of time or on a holiday, this may be a reason not to participate even though you have been selected for a particular questionnaire This is *wave nonresponse*. It may also happen that you are in the process of filling out a questionnaire and you decide to skip one or more questions, may be because they are too difficult (financial questions are notorious in this respect) or because you feel it's none of their business (e.g., if they are about sex and relationships). This is *item nonresponse*. Basically, nonresponse problems in a panel do not differ very much from those in a cross sectional survey (see also Lynn, Chapter 3). An important difference from the cross sectional case is that much more is known about the nonrespondents: information gathered in the recruitment stage and in previous waves. This makes it possible to use more sophisticated imputation models or weight with respect to a large choice of auxiliary variables.

Problems that are unique to panel research are (a) estimation of a process that evolves over time and (b) estimation of change between two or more moments in time. In the first case it makes sense that estimators are representative with respect to the average population distributions of auxiliary variables over time. In the second case estimators may be required to be representative to distributions at different points in time. For variables that vary with time, e.g. employment status, this can easily be achieved, because a weighting procedure can be devised where employment status at t_1 reflects the population distribution at t_1, employment status at t_2 reflects the population distribution at t_2, etc. For variables which are fixed in time, such as year of birth or gender, this may present a problem as one set of weights can not reflect different population distributions of such variables at different points in time.

25.5.3 Panel Attrition

What is it like to be in a panel? You respond to a questionnaire regularly. The first few times it is interesting. In the process of responding you are challenged to give opinions on a variety of subjects such as products, safety, public transport, and asylum seekers. But after a while it becomes boring. Being a busy person, you decide to stop responding to questionnaires and to quit the panel. This is called panel attrition. It can be described by the survival curve, which is the probability to stay in the panel longer than a given amount of time. Figure 25.2 shows the survival curves in the CentERpanel for member with a high and with a low education. The probability of surviving one year (52 weeks) of panel membership for members with a low education is 0.65; the probability of surviving two years is 0.48. For members with a high education these probabilities are 0.86 and 0.75 respectively. These survival curves clearly show that the composition of the panel changes when the process of replacement is not controlled.

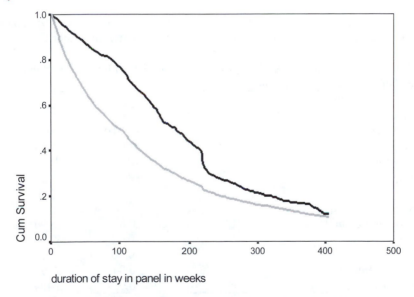

duration of stay in panel in weeks

Figure 25.2 Survival curves of respondents of the CentERpanel; black: high education, gray: low education.

Members decide to opt out or are no longer traceable, but they do not constitute a random sub-sample of the panel, but a group with specific features, for instance, very busy or easily bored. Even if the original panel was a well-behaved probability sample, after attrition it may be biased. This bias may occur with respect to two types of variables

1. Variables of which the population distribution is known. Usually these are standard variables such as age, sex, education, or region. By this we do not mean to say that this bias can always be ignored, but it can be handled in a standard way by weighting the sample with respect to the known population distributions.
2. Variables of which the population distribution is unknown. These are the really interesting variables, because they directly refer to subject matter of a given research project or to the psychological deviations of people who are willing to be a long time member of a panel. Are they lonely people? Do they have a high need for cognition? Are they nice? Do they have deviant personality traits?

A good thing about panels is that when participants enter the panel they fill in a questionnaire with questions for possible weighting variables to be used later if they happen to drop out. Then, a simple way of detection of the effects of panel attrition is to correlate the duration of stay in a panel with variables that are relevant for a given project. An example is given in Table 25.5, where some psychological characteristics are analyzed for a panel in the Netherlands. The maximum possible stay in a panel was 7 years. The first set of four variables was based on often heard prejudices of clients, who assumed that people who remained in a panel for a long time did so because they were lonely, because they were inclined to comply to others, because they liked thinking, or because they wanted to be modern by belonging to a panel. The second set of variables, the Big Five, represents a comprehensive set of personality dimensions.

Table 25.5 Correlation of psychological characteristics with duration of panel membership in the CentERpanel.

Psychological characteristics	r	n
Prejudices		
Loneliness	-0.010	1914
Social desirability	0.036	1714
Need for cognition	-0.071	1630
Innovativeness	-0.032	1638
Big Five personality traits		
Emotional Stability	0.017	2494
Extraversion	-0.025	2494
Agreeableness	-0.005	2494
Conscientiousness	0.049	2494
Openness to experience	0.024	2494

This type of research is the exceptional example where you want correlations to be negligibly small. Fortunately, they are. Duration of panel membership in the CentERpanel is hardly correlated with psychological variables. But what if the correlations are big? Then there are three options.

1. The no solution; ignore the problem, because your client will not notice anyway (although hard experience learned us that some do).
2. The rough solution: throw all older members out of the data set.

3.   The subtle solution: treat duration of panel membership as an explanatory variable and calculate all estimates conditional on duration = 0.

Option 3 is of course to be preferred, but it requires a statistical model and some nontrivial data processing that may be hard to execute in the time-pressured environment in which most research takes place.

25.5.4 Panel Effects

Panel attrition may cause a change in panel composition: the panel at t_2 is not the same as t_1. Unfortunately, there is another mechanism that may cause the panel at t_2 to be different from the panel at t_1, even if all responding panel members have the same identities. A question like "How much money do you spend on clothes on a monthly basis?" may make you think and finally convince you that you spend too much. Thus, answering this question may make you a different person, because you become aware of your silly spending habits. A person who answers on a weekly or monthly basis questions about products, psychology or politics cannot do so without learning something. Detection of this problem is difficult. Panel members may change their opinion because they are changed persons, but also because something in the world around them has changed (e.g., a product is improved, or some politician has made a blunder). An example of a rough detection procedure for measurement of change in the CentERpanel is the following.

The variable of interest is a dichotomous variable: 1 if a panel member agrees with a policy measure, 0 if he disagrees. These variables are observed at t_1 and t_2. At these moments we distinguish old panel members, who have stayed in the panel for more than a year, and new panel members, who have stayed for less than a year. Note that new panel members at t_1 may be old panel members at t_2 (see Figure 25.3). The four groups (old/new, t_1/t_2) are weighted such that they have the same distribution with respect to relevant demographic variables.

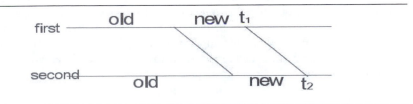

Figure 25.3 Old and new panel members at the first and second wave.

The difference in opinion between t_1 and t_2 for the old panel members may depend on the difference in the real situation and the panel effect, whereas the differences in opinion between the new members depend only on the difference in real situation.

In this example, the subject matter is policy with respect to asylum seekers. The research question is whether the Dutch people have changed their opinion between September 1996 and October 1998. The results with respect to different policy measures are given in Table 25.6. The percentages in the columns "old members" and "new members" are the differences in percentage in 1996 and 1998, respectively. So in 1998 the percentage of old panel members who were in favor of sharper border control was 6% higher than in 1996; among the new panel members the percentage in favor was 3% lower.

Table 25.6 Differences between percentages in opinion on asylum policy September 1996 and October 1998.

Item	Answer	Old members	New members	Panel effect
Sharper border control	yes	6	-3	9*
Better refugee centres	no	-3	-18	15*
General evaluation of policy	bad	10	26	-16*
Admission of number of foreigners	too many	15	7	8
Quicker processing of requests	yes	2	4	-2
Housing shortage as argument for refusal	agree	0	-11	11*
Unemployment as argument for refusal	agree	-4	-16	12*

*: $p < 0.05$.

The panel effect is equal to the difference between the percentages "old members" and "new members". In five out of seven cases the panel effect was statistically significant. The old panel members seem to have become stricter than the new ones, possibly because they have longer been stimulated to follow the news closely.

A clear example of a very strong panel effect is that of spontaneous brand or product awareness. In marketing research, a very common open type of question is "What beer brands do you know?" by which a manufacturer hopes to measure how easy his brand name springs to mind when the consumer thinks of beer. This question is often followed by aided awareness, where a respondent has to tick the brand names he knows from a given list of brands. Unfortunately, many beer manufacturers use this question, so after a while all panel members know all beer brands by heart. This makes Internet consumer panels very unsuitable for brand awareness questions.

25.6 MEASUREMENT OF CHANGE AND ACCURACY

This section is meant to show that there is more to panels than verbal reasoning. There is a lot of mathematics behind many topics in panel research. The measurement of change is such a topic. We start easy, but gradually things become more complicated. Congratulations if you can follow the mathematical argument to the very end, but don't be frustrated if you loose track at a certain stage. It will give you some intuitive ideas on when and where you can handle the problems yourself, and where you have to hand them over to a specialist.

25.6.1 Basics

Why is panel research so well suited for the measurement of change? The paradoxical answer is "because individuals hardly change," or at least the vast majority of them. Let X_1 and X_2 be two measurements on an individual at t_1 and t_2. Then the change between t_1 and t_2 is $X_2 - X_1$. The variance of $X_2 - X_1$ is the well-known formula

$$\text{var}(X_2 - X_1) = \text{var}(X_1) + \text{var}(X_2) - 2\,\text{cov}(X_1, X_2) \qquad (25.1)$$

where cov means covariance. In order to find out the meaning of this expression assume that the variances of X_1 and X_2 both are equal to σ^2, and the correlation between X_1 and X_2 is equal to ρ. Then cov $(X_1, X_2) = \rho\sigma^2$, hence

$$\text{var}(X_2 - X_1) = 2(1 - \rho)\sigma^2 \qquad (25.2)$$

Had the measurements on t_1 and t_2 been on different, independently drawn, individuals, the variance of $X_2 - X_1$ would have been $2\sigma^2$, so due to the panel design, the variance had been altered by a factor $(1 - \rho)$. Now, when ρ is close to 1, this can make a huge difference. You can save money by using a panel design, as the following realistic example will show. Let X_j be the employment status at t_j ($j = 1, 2$); $X_j = 0$ when unemployed and $X_j = 1$ when employed. Now assume that the Table 25.7 describes the joint distribution of X_1 and X_2

Table 25.7 Employment status at t_1 and t_2 (hypothetical example)

status at t_1	status at t_2	$X_2 = 0$ unemployed	$X_2 = 1$ employed
$X_1 = 0$	unemployed	0.19	0.01
$X_1 = 1$	employed	0.01	0.79

This is the situation when on both observations 80% of the population is employed and 1 out of 20 unemployed at t_1 has found a job at t_2; for a time difference of e.g. a month this is reasonably realistic. It is easily calculated that ρ is equal to 15/16, so $1 - \rho$ equals 1/6. In other words, the panel design reduces the variance of the change between t_1 and t_2 by a factor of 16. As a consequence, to measure the change with two cross sectional surveys requires 16 times as many respondents than with a panel.

25.6.2 Wave Nonresponse and Rotation

What happens when you measure change in a panel, but there is only partial overlap at the two time points? This may happen for two reasons. The first reason is that in both waves there is (unintended) nonresponse. The second reason is that you have designed the panel procedure in such a way that in each wave a proportion of the respondents is refreshed, a rotating panel. In both cases you loose some of the gains you have achieved by subtracting correlating observations, because the nonoverlapping observations are, of course, uncorrelated. In order to get some idea how nonresponse or refreshing the panel affects the variance of the change estimator we start out with a slightly more generalized situation.

Assume we have two independent unbiased estimators d_o and d_i of difference d. Their variances are σ_o^2 and σ_i^2, respectively. Now we want to make a linear combination $d_c = \alpha d_o + (1 - \alpha)d_i$ with minimum variance. Elementary algebra shows that we have to choose

$$\alpha = \frac{\sigma_i^2}{\sigma_o^2 + \sigma_i^2} \tag{25.3}$$

hence

$$d_c = \frac{\sigma_i^2 d_o + \sigma_o^2 d_i}{\sigma_o^2 + \sigma_i^2} \tag{25.4}$$

The estimator d_c is called the *composite estimator*. Its' variance is

$$\mathrm{var}(d_c) = \frac{1}{\dfrac{1}{\sigma_o^2} + \dfrac{1}{\sigma_i^2}} \tag{25.5}$$

Now d_o is, of course, the estimator of the difference based on the overlapping part of the panel, d_i the estimator based on the nonoverlapping independent samples. Now we make some assumptions to obtain formulas that give some insight in the effect of the nonoverlapping part. The total sample size at t_1 and t_2 is equal to n; the number of overlapping respondents is rn, so there are $(1 - r)n$ respondents in each non-overlapping sample. Then the formulas for the variances of the two estimators are

$$\sigma_o^2 = \frac{2(1-\rho)\sigma^2}{rn-1} \approx \frac{2(1-\rho)\sigma^2}{rn} \tag{25.6}$$

and

$$\sigma_i^2 = \frac{2\sigma^2}{(1-r)n-1} \approx \frac{2\sigma^2}{(1-r)n} \tag{25.7}$$

Substitution of (25.6) and (25.7) into (25.5) gives

$$\mathrm{var}(d_c) \approx \frac{2(1-\rho)\sigma^2}{n(r+(1-r)(1-\rho))} \tag{25.8}$$

Expression (25.8) shows the deteriorating effect of non response. For $r = 1$ (total response in both waves/complete overlap) the variance is $2(1-\rho)\sigma^2/n$. For $r = 0$ (independent surveys) we have the variance $2\sigma^2/n$. For $r = 0.5$ (50% overlap) we have

$$\mathrm{var}(d_c) \approx \frac{2(1-\rho)\sigma^2}{n(1-0.5\rho)} \tag{25.9}$$

so the gain of the panel design has partly been annihilated by the non-response/lack of overlap.

25.6.3 Response Burden and Incomplete Panel Designs

In certain types of panel surveys, the frequency of the data collection waves is so high that they experience serious panel attrition. A high attrition rate results into a low overlap and unreliable estimators for trends, as we saw in equation 25.8. It may be more efficient to change the panel design, use fewer measurements and paradoxically obtain more reliable estimates. We demonstrate this, using an important application of panel research for both official statistics and marketing research: expenditure surveys. In these surveys respondents register what products they bought, where and for what price. A panel design is appropriate for this purpose, both for theoretical reasons (from the interest in accurate measurement change, detecting rare events, following concepts across time), and for practical reasons (respondents need training or special electronic devices to report their purchases). Traditionally respondents report their purchases on a *continuous* basis. However, the task of reporting purchases is rather tedious and results into high attrition. Therefore one might consider an alternative design where respondents do not report all time, but at a sample of time points instead. Then, the question is: What effect does taking a sample of time points have with respect to the variance of *d*, estimators of the difference in consumption between to successive time periods? This question is treated in Hoogendoorn and Sikkel (1998). In order to answer this question, we will introduce some additional notation, for which we need a time unit of measurement (say a week) and a time period to report about (say a quarter). Define: X_{ij}^t to be the amount of purchases by household i in time unit j of

period t; $X_j^t = Nn^{-1}\sum_{i=1}^{n} X_{ij}^t$ the estimated population total for time unit j of

period t and $X^t = Nn^{-1}\sum_{i=1}^{n}\sum_{j=1}^{M} X_{ij}^t$ the estimated population total for period t.

Our quantity of interest is:

$$d = X^{t+1} - X^t \tag{25.10}$$

If we assume that the variances of X_{ij}^t are all equal to σ^2, that the correlation

between two reports is equal to ρ, i.e. $\mathrm{cov}(X_{ij}^u, X_{ik}^v) = \rho\sigma^2$, that the fraction

of sample overlap between two successive measurements is r (this means that the number of overlapping respondents is rn, and that less measurements leads to less attrition), then we find for the variance of $X^{t+1} - X^t$:

$$\mathrm{var}(X^{t+1} - X^t) = \mathrm{var}\left(\sum_{j=1}^{M} X_j^{t+1} - \sum_{j=1}^{M} X_j^t\right)$$

$$= \mathrm{var}(X^{t+1}) + \mathrm{var}(X^t) - 2\sum_{j=1}^{M}\sum_{k=1}^{M}\mathrm{cov}(X_j^{t+1}, X_k^t)$$

$$= \frac{2N^2\sigma^2}{n}\left(M + \frac{2\rho(M-1)r}{1-r} - \frac{2\rho r^2(1-r^{M-1})}{(1-r)^2} - \frac{\rho r(1-r^M)^2}{(1-r)^2}\right) \quad (25.11)$$

Suppose that in the alternative design, for each respondent reports purchases at m out of M weeks, such that the design is balanced, for example every week and every pair of weeks appears in the sample with the same frequency. We assume that the fraction overlap between two measurements is r. Note that due to fact that we have less measurements than in the case of continuously measurement, we also have less attrition. The alternative estimators for the estimated population totals for time unit j of period t and for time period t are

$$X_j^t = Mm^{-1}Nn^{-1}\sum_{i=1}^{n} X_{ij}^t, \text{ and}$$

$$X^t = Mm^{-1}Nn^{-1}\sum_{i=1}^{n} \sum_{j\in S(M,m)} X_{ij}^t$$

respectively. We find in the alternative design for the variance of $X^{t+1} - X^t$:

$$\text{var}(X^{t+1} - X^t) = \frac{2M^2N^2\sigma^2}{nm^2}\left(m + \frac{2\rho(m-1)r}{1-r} - \frac{2\rho r^2(1-r^{m-1})}{(1-r)^2} - \frac{\rho r(1-r^m)^2}{(1-r)^2}\right)$$

$$(25.12)$$

In practice the attrition $1-r$ is small enough to justify a Taylor approximation with respect to $1-r$. This leads to a formula that provides some insight. We find

$$\text{var}(X^{t+1} - X^t) \approx \frac{2N^2M^2\sigma^2}{nm}\left(1 - \rho + (2m^2 + 1)(1-r)\rho/3\right) \quad (25.13)$$

The second term on the right hand side represents the gain from correlations using panel data. The third term shows how these gains are reduced by attrition. Given the model assumptions (constant variance σ^2, constant correlation ρ, constant attrition rate of $1 - r$ between two measurements) we are able to determine the optimal design in terms of variance of the estimator. By differentiating equation 25.13 with respect to m, we find that the approximated variance is minimized by

$$m_{opt} = \sqrt{\frac{3}{2}\frac{(1-\rho)}{\rho(1-r)} + \frac{1}{2}} \quad (25.14)$$

Equation 25.14 shows that the optimal response burden m_{opt} decreases with both increasing correlation ρ and attrition rate $1 - r$. This makes sense, because, on one hand a high correlation ρ indicates that additional measurements do not provide much extra information. On the other hand, if there would be no attrition at all, it would be clearly optimal to take as many measurements as possible. This demonstrates that the higher the attrition, the lower the number of measurements should be. Figure 25.4 shows optimal values of m as a function of ρ for different values of r.

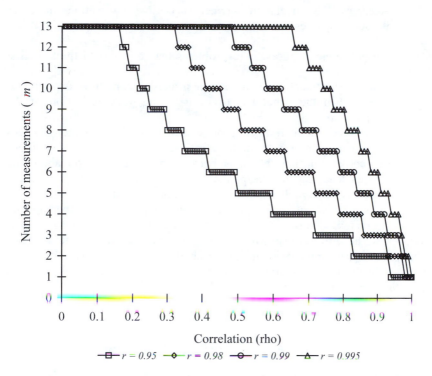

Figure 25.4 Optimal values of number of weekly measurement in a quarter as a function of the correlation ρ for different values of the fraction of sample overlap r. The optimal values correspond with minimal variance of difference estimator d.

Figure 25.4 shows that for many combinations of correlation and attrition the optimal design is not the traditional design of continuous measurement ($m = 13$). Especially when ρ is not too small, and there is some serious attrition ($r = 0.95$), it is recommended to reduce the response burden substantially. The example that we discussed here is just one illustration of many methodological issues around the topic of panel research.

25.7 SUMMARY

Panel research is here to stay for the following reasons:
1. Technology: information technology makes it easy and profitable to setup and maintain panels
2. Demand: the private sector, governmental institutions, and academic research will increasingly be supported by data
3. Substance: many concepts can, by definition, measured only by panel research

4.   Accuracy: the correlation between successive observations increases the accuracy of estimators, in particular estimators of change

However, panel research poses more problems than one should think at first glance:

1.   Panel recruitment and maintenance is a task that requires expertise, at least when the panel has to be a lasting good reflection of the population
2.   Even when the recruitment process is flawless, there are more sources of bias than in cross sectional surveys; there are also more solutions to correct for possible bias because more information about the respondents and non respondents is available but in fact the sheer quantity of possible solutions may be a problem in itself
3.   Optimal design of repeated measurements is mathematically complex, so know your limitations when advanced design is required

However, we hope to have shown what was stated in section 1: panel research is fun. Many problems are intellectually challenging, the issues that can be addressed with panel research are interesting and the panel itself is an incredibly rich source of information. A well-managed panel is therefore a valuable asset and very satisfying to work with.

GLOSSARY OF KEY CONCEPTS

Attrition. Loss of respondents from a panel. Panel participants may either drop out voluntarily or may be asked to leave.

Cohort study. A study in which a group of individuals are followed over time. These individuals usually share a certain condition (e.g., birth year, year of retirement).

Cross-sectional study. A study in which a single measurement is made on a sample of individuals at a single time point.

Gross change. The change at the individual level. Examples are changes in the status of economic activity, marital status etc. of individual persons. Measurement of gross change requires longitudinal studies.

Longitudinal study. A study in which the same group of individuals is interviewed at intervals over a period of time, such as Panel Study or Cohort Study.

Net change. The change at the aggregate level, with individual level changes in opposite directions cancelled out. Examples are month-to-month changes in rates of unemployment and other economic indicators. Net changes can be derived from cross-sectional studies and does not require panel designs, although the precision of the estimates in a panel study is usually higher.

Panel conditioning. The systematic error that occurs when panel participants change their (observed) behaviour as a result of being part of the panel.

Panel effect. See Time-In-Sample effect.

Panel maintenance. The process of maintaining contact with respondents, including administrative actions (e.g. address changes) and actions to stimulate cooperation.

Panel study. A study in which similar measurements are made on the same sample of individuals at different points in time (waves). The sample may change between waves in order to correct for changes in the population.

Response burden. The effort required to respond to a survey, usually quantified in terms of how long the survey takes. Other aspects of response burden are how difficult it is to provide the information, and how sensitive the respondent is about providing the information.

Time-in-sample bias. The effects from ongoing participation of panel participants. Given the experience with the survey over time, the responses of panel participants may increasingly begin to differ from the responses given by panel participants answering the same survey for the first time.

Wave. A distinct time point where data are collected in a panel survey.

Wave nonresponse. The type of nonresponse that occurs when one or more waves of panel data are missing for an individual that has provided data for at least one wave.

Chapter 26

Surveys Without Questions

Jelke Bethlehem
Statistics Netherlands

26.1 INTRODUCTION

Our society experiences an ever increasing demand for statistical information, but surveys are not the only way to collect such information. A survey is normally conducted to make inferences about a well-defined population. Such a population may consist of individuals, households, firms, schools, farms, or other economic or social institutions. Typically, a survey only collects data about a sample of objects from the population. It is implemented by asking questions about the current or past situation of the objects, historic events, habits, knowledge, or behavior. Data obtained in this way can be used to compute estimates of specific population parameters (totals, means, percentages, correlations, etc.).

Sample surveys are used widely by government agencies, market research organizations, social research institutions, and many others. They collect data for statistical purposes, that is, data are transformed in statistical information. Begeer, de Vries, & Dekker (1986) define the concept of *statistical information* to mean information about groups of objects, compiled from information about individual objects, and transformed in such a way that, in general, identification of specific objects is no longer possible.

The information about groups of objects usually takes the form of estimates of totals, means, percentages, and frequency distributions. This information can be computed for a population as a whole, or for specific sub-domains of the population Long years of practice have shown that surveys work. Nevertheless, survey researchers are often confronted with practical problems. Such problems may be resolved by using information from social registers, the topic of this chapter.

26.2 SURVEY PROBLEMS

One of the most important problems of conducting surveys is *nonresponse*, not obtaining requested answers to survey questions from sample individuals (see also Lynn, Chapter 3). They may refuse to participate, they may not be able to participate (e.g., because of illness or language problems), or it may not be possible to contact them (not at home). If a sample survey is affected by nonresponse, it may result in invalid estimates of population characteristics.

Refusal is an important cause for nonresponse. There are many reasons why people refuse. One reason is a high *response burden*. The response burden is indicated by several aspects of the survey questionnaire: (a) How long does it take to complete the questionnaire? (b) How difficult is it to provide the required information? (c) How sensitive are the questions asked?

The response burden is also increased by the growing number of surveys being conducted. This is particularly true for web surveys. Couper (2000) remarks that web surveys make it possible for many groups, other than traditional survey organizations, to conduct surveys. The abundance of good and bad web surveys has a negative effect on response rates. Potential respondents are busy and decline to respond. The effect is similar to that of telephone surveys, where the survey climate is spoiled by marketing activities.

Another problem a survey researcher may be confronted with is related to the questionnaire. It is a poor measuring instrument compared to measuring devices used in physics. It is easy and straightforward to accurately measure height, length, temperature or blood pressure of a person. But getting information about opinions, behavior and historic events is a different story. Asking questions and getting the right answer is not easy. Often *measurement errors* occur. Many things can happen: respondents do not understand a question, they understand the question but they do not know the right answer or they do not want to give the right answer. Also, they may think they know the right answer but forget some aspects (see also Schwarz et al., Chapter 2).

Surveys also have some practical disadvantages. Conducting surveys is time-consuming and expensive. Particularly if interviewers are used to collect data as in face-to-face surveys or telephone surveys, costs can be substantial. For large surveys, the fieldwork and subsequent data processing can take a significant amount of time. Usefulness of survey results often depends on timeliness. If it takes weeks or months to process a survey, value for money may be less than expected.

All these concerns about surveys lead to the question of whether there are alternative ways of getting information. Although a survey may be the only acceptable way to obtain certain information, sometimes the needed information is available from other sources. This means the researcher focuses on *secondary data analysis*, data collected by a different organization for different purposes, instead of *primary data analysis*, data collected just for his research project.

26.3 WHAT IS A REGISTER?

A register is a collection of data on a well-defined group of objects. The objects are defined by a precise set of rules such that it is always possible in practical situations to determine whether or not a specific object belongs to the group.

For each individual object, the register contains the values of the same well-defined set of variables. These variables describe the state of the objects at a specific moment in time. A register has facilities to update the information about objects contained in it. Updating can take place after an event has occurred that changes the values of one or more variables. Usually, there is a time-lag between the moment the event occurs, and the updating of the register.

Most registers can be called *administrative registers*. It means they are primarily used for administrative purposes. Begeer et al. (1986) describe administrative registers as registers containing information on objects that is required for administrative or other governmental action concerning individual objects.

In some cases, data on objects are always available, and can be used as needed. An example is a population register. In other cases, data are only partially available, and additional data have to be added before action can be undertaken. An example is a tax register, that lists names and addresses, but income information has to be included before tax payable can be computed for each person.

Registers can also be used for statistical purposes. It means information about groups of objects is compiled. Often, this information takes the form of values of parameters determining the distribution of variables. One can think of frequency distributions, means, percentages, and correlations. Such information should not allow identification of specific objects.

The statistical use of registers can take several forms. The first form is to use a register as a *sampling frame*. It is a list that unambiguously identifies every object in the population to be investigated. This list is used as the basis for selecting a sample from the population. The information in the register should be such that every selected object can be located and contacted. This means address, telephone number, email address, or other contact information should be available.

A typical example of such use of a register in The Netherlands is the GBA (Gemeentelijke Basis Administratie voor persoonsgegevens). It is a comprehensive and cohesive registration system for population data that was introduced in 1994. It is fully decentralised. Every municipality has its own population register containing basic data on all its inhabitants.

Statistics Netherlands, the national statistical institute of The Netherlands, uses the GBA as a sampling frame for its social surveys. An example is the Integrated Survey on Living Conditions. It is a large continuous survey. Every month, a sample is selected. Persons are selected by means of a stratified two-stage sample from the GBA. In the first stage, municipalities are selected within regional strata with probabilities proportional to the number of inhabitants. In the second stage, an equal probability sample is drawn in each selected municipality.

A second form of use of registers is for *weighting adjustment*. Many surveys are affected by nonresponse. If nonresponse leads to biased estimates, wrong conclusions are drawn from the survey results. To avoid this, some kind of correction procedure must be carried out. One of the most important correction techniques for nonresponse is *adjustment weighting*. It means that every observed object in the survey is assigned a weight, and estimates of population characteristics are obtained by processing weighted observations instead of the observations themselves.

Table 26.1 A simple example of weighting adjustment

Age	Sample count	Population count	Weight
Young	38	435	1.145
Middle	33	296	0.897
Old	29	269	0.926
Total	100	1000	

Table 26.1 shows a simple example of weighting adjustment. From a population of size 1000 a sample of size 100 is selected. The variable age has been measured in the sample, and it is also available in a population register. Thus, its distribution in the sample can be compared with its distribution in the population. The sample is not representative for the population. For example, the percentage of young people in the population is 43.5%, whereas in the sample the percentage is 38.0%. The sample contains too few young people. To correct this, young people in the sample get a weight equal to 54.5/38.0=1.145. For more information on weighting, see Bethlehem (2002).

A third form of using registers is, of course, is as a primary source of data for statistical analysis. If the register contains the right variables, their values are available for every element in the population. Population quantities can be computed directly, and without uncertainty due to sampling variance. A disadvantage of direct use of register data for statistical analysis is that data files can be very large, making computations cumbersome and time-consuming.

Going back to the GBA-example in The Netherlands, Statistics Netherlands uses this register for compiling demographic statistics. These data are also used to construct models for population forecasts.

The number of existing registers and their contents vary form country to country. Particularly, the Scandinavian countries seem to have progressed most in using register data for statistical analysis. As an example, Figure 26.1 contains the register-statistics model that has been developed by Statistics Sweden, see also Statistics Sweden (2001). Four statistical base registers form the basis of the system. These base registers differ by the type of object about which information is stored.

The *Population Register* contains data on persons. In fact, is composed of a large number of registers, all about persons. These registers can be linked to each other through a unique personal identification number.

The *Business Register* contains data on legal business units. Mostly, it includes financial data, but it also contains information such as the number of company owned vehicles. The information comes from several sources. Each legal unit has a unique identification number.

The *Activity Register* is the basic source for making labor market statistics. It not only contains data on employment (income, tax), but also on unemployment (looking for work), being off sick, pension, study, and so on. Key variables in this database link to persons in the population register, companies in the business register, and locations in real estate register.

The *Real Estate Register* contains data on the location (address), size and value of buildings, both houses and business premises. Key variables in this register link to owners and/or renters of properties.

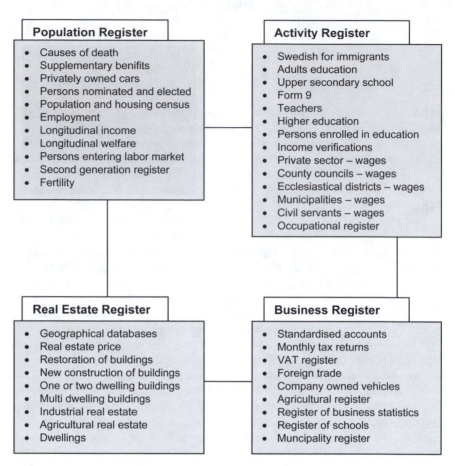

Figure 26.1 The register model of Statistics Sweden

26.4 USING REGISTER DATA

Statistical use of register data is a means of secondary data collection. This has some clear advantages. Because data are already available in electronic form, there is no response burden, and data collection costs are low compared to surveys. However, there are also disadvantages. Data are collected by different agencies for different purposes at different times. This gives rise to the question of whether register data is as useful as survey data. It is not unlikely that there is a discrepancy between register variables and the variables the researchers would like to use in their analysis. Sometimes, it is possible to derive research variables from the available register variables, but more often the researcher simply has to live with the variables as they are.

Another important aspect of the use of registers is data quality. One of the main dimensions of data quality is the accuracy. Estimates of population statistics should be as close as possible to the true values of these characteristics. In survey-based statistics, estimates are computed based on a sample from the population. Such estimates will never be exactly equal to the population characteristics to be estimated. There will always be some error. This error may have many causes. Two broad categories can be distinguished: sampling errors and nonsampling errors (For a more detailed discussion, see de Leeuw, Hox, & Dillman, Chapter 1).

1. *Sampling errors* are introduced by the sampling design. They are due to the fact that estimates are based on a sample and not on a complete enumeration of the population. The sample is selected by means of a random selection procedure. Every new selection of a sample results in different objects, and thus in a different value of the estimator. The magnitude of the sampling error can be controlled through the sampling design. For example, by increasing the sample size, or by taking selection probabilities proportional to some well-chosen auxiliary variable, the sampling-error of the estimate can be reduced.

2. *Nonsampling errors* occur even if the whole population is investigated. Non-sampling errors are errors made during the process of recording answers to questions. An important source of nonsampling errors is measurement errors. These errors occur when a respondent does not understand a question, or does not want to give the true answer, or if the interviewer makes an error in recording the answer. Also, interview effects, question wording effects, and memory effects belong to this group of errors. A measurement error causes a difference between the true value and the value processed in the survey. Another important source of nonsampling errors is *nonresponse*. There may be various reasons for this: refusal to co-operate, not at home at the time of the visit of the interviewer, or not able to cooperate due to illness or other circumstances.

Using register data substantially reduces sampling errors. Generally, the sample size is very large, if not equal to the size of the complete population. In the latter case, sampling errors vanish completely.

Nonsampling errors are not automatically reduced if register data are used. Substantial errors may still be caused by phenomena like lack of population coverage, missing data, and measurement errors. In practice most causes of nonsampling errors for surveys also play a role in registers. For example, the population register (maintained by municipalities) and business register (maintained by chambers of commerce) suffer from both over- and under-coverage due to the dynamics of these populations. Also registers containing information about jobs and allowances have measurement errors due to time delays in their registration of employment and unemployment. And the register of real estate values maintained by the land registry office does not contain information on new buildings.

Most administrative registers need to be edited and imputed before they can be used for statistical analysis. The degree to which these registers contain missing data and measurement errors differs from register to register. The quality of the data also depends on the objectives of the register owners and on their quality control systems. If some variables are of less importance to the register owner than others and the costs of monitoring the quality are high, the quality of the data can be very poor.

Probably one of the most important differences between registers and surveys is the almost complete absence of unit nonresponse. Unit nonresponse plays an important role in surveys, especially when it is related to the topic of the survey. This seems to be far less the case for registers, because participation in the data collection is often obligatory or beneficial to the data providers.

In general one can say that register-based statistics do not necessarily lead to estimates of higher quality than survey-based statistics. The quality of register-based statistics is largely determined by the measures undertaken by the register owners to reduce nonsampling errors.

26.5 COMBINING REGISTERS

Registers often contain many records (one for every member of the population), but not necessarily many variables. To have a richer data set it may be worthwhile considering merging two or more registers. In this section, the possibilities and problems of merging of registers are considered in some detail.

Merging two registers can only be successful if corresponding records in both registers can be uniquely identified. This is a very simple operation if both registers contain the same unique identification variable, like for example a personal identification number. Often such unique identifiers are not available in both data sets. They may simply be not there, or they may have been removed to protect the privacy of individuals. Then other techniques should be applied to merge both registers.

Successful matching of records in two data sets requires an overlap of variables in both data sets. These variables are called *key variables* or *identification variables*. The set of key variables should be such that all records in both data are unique with respect to the scores on these variables, that is, there are no two records in each data set with exactly the same set of values for the key variables.

An example of such a successful matching operation was carried out in a research project of Statistics Netherlands on the analysis of real income changes, see van der Stadt, Ten Cate, Hundepool, & Keller (1986). Tax data files from the Internal Revenue Service were used. Files for several years had to be combined. Legal restrictions prevented a unique identification number to be included in the files. Therefore, matching had to be carried out using a set of key variables. With address, sex and date of birth it was possible to match these files. The percentage of correct matches turned out to be higher than 99.7%.

Uniqueness cannot always be obtained. In an analysis of all households composed of father, mother and two children in a specific region of The Netherlands, it turned out that 68% of these households were unique on the set of key variables consisting of age father, age mother, and ages and sexes of the children, see Bethlehem, Keller, & Pannekoek (1990).

If the set of key variables is insufficient to obtain uniqueness, *synthetic matching* may be considered. It means records from both data sets are merged that not necessarily belong to the same individual. Nevertheless, it still may be possible to carry out proper analysis on such merged data sets. Let the situation be like that shown in Figure 26.2.

Data set 1		Data set 2			Merged data set		
X	Y	Y	Z	→	X	Y	Z

Figure 26.2 Synthetic matching

The first data file contains two sets of variables X and Y, and the second data file contains two sets of variables Y and Z. So, they have the set Y in common. They are the key variables. Suppose that Y is a set of categorical variables. By cross-classifying these variables, groups can be formed with the same values for the set. Two data sets are merged by randomly linking X-parts to Z-parts within each group. Now, the question is whether the tri-variate distribution of X, Y, and Z in the merged data set properly reflects the true distribution of these variables in the population. At first sight, this seems highly unlikely. The two data sets only contain information about the bi-variate distributions of X and Y and of Y and Z, and no information at all about the tri-variate distribution of X, Y and Z. However, it can be shown that under the assumption of *conditional independence* the obtained trivariate distribution is correct. Given the values of the set Y, the sets of variables X and Z must be independently distributed.

The covariance between X and Z can be written as

$$\text{Cov}(X, Z) = \text{Cov}\{E(X \mid Y), E(Z \mid Y)\} + E\{\text{Cov}(X, Z \mid Y)\}. \quad (26.1)$$

The first term on the right-hand side of this equation can be determined using the merged data sets. This is not the case for the second term. Therefore, Cov(X, Z) can only be determined under the assumption that the second term is equal to 0, and that is the conditional independence assumption.

In practical situations, it cannot be tested whether the conditional independence assumption holds. Analysis of a merged data set assuming conditional independence while it is not the case can lead to wrong conclusions. A simple example illustrates this. Suppose there are two data sets. The first data set contains data from a budget survey. One of the X-variables is expenditure on dog food. The second data set contains data from a survey on living conditions. One of the Z-variables measures ownership of a dog. Suppose these two data sets are merged using a set of Y-variables consisting of age, marital status, nationality, household composition and region. If the two variables expenditures on dog food and ownership of a dog are cross-tabulated after merging the data sets, it will turn out that a large amount of people buy dog food without having a dog. Apparently, they are very poor, and there will be a large number of people with a dog that do not buy dog food. These people also seem to be very poor.

The real correlation between dog food expenditure and dog ownership is almost equal to 1. However, this relationship is completely missed in the merged data set. There the correlation will be approximately equal to 0.

Sometimes it is argued that in practical cases the situation is not so bad as described in the example. The line of reasoning is that if the correlation R_{XY} between X and Y and the correlation R_{YZ} between Y and Z are strong, the correlation R_{XZ} between X and Z will not be disturbed too much. Indeed, if R_{XY} = 1 and R_{YZ} = 1, then there is no problem. However, for less perfect relationships, there is a wide band of possible values for R_{XZ} that may not properly be reflected in the merged data set. It can be shown, see e.g. De Jong (1991), that

$$\left| R_{XZ} - R_{YX}R_{YZ} \right| \le \sqrt{\left(1 - R_{YX}^2\right)\left(1 - R_{YZ}^2\right)}. \qquad (26.2)$$

So, if R_{YX} = 0.9 and R_{YZ} = 0.9, then R_{XZ} can still have any value between 0.62 and 1.00. Relationships are usually not that strong in social research. Correlations are often not much larger than 0.5. For relative strong correlations like R_{XY} = 0.6 and R_{YZ} = 0.8, the possible values of R_{XZ} are in the range from 0.00 to 0.96. This means anything between no relation at all and an almost perfect relationship between X and Z is possible.

The message is that researchers should be very careful in synthetic matching of data sets. To avoid wrong conclusions from their analysis, they should only consider merging data sets if exact matching is possible, that is, the key variables allow for unique identification in both data sets.

26.6 COMBINING REGISTERS AND SURVEYS

Another way to obtain a rich data set is by combining a register and a survey. A survey researcher can add register data to his survey data set, or he can make secondary use of someone else's survey data set by add this data to his own register data. In the previous section we have already seen that synthetic matching is no option, so we assume that exact matches of register records and survey records are possible. The situation obtained in this way, is displayed in Figure 26.3.

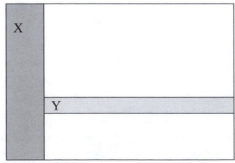

Figure 26.3 Matching a register and a survey

The set of X-variables has been retrieved from a register. The values of these variables are available for all individuals in the population. The set of Y-variables has been measured only in a survey. The values of these variables are just available for a sample of individuals from the population.

How to analyze such a combined data set full of holes? In the literature two approaches are discussed, which can be denoted by *mass imputation* and *weighting*.

Mass imputation comes down to filling in synthetic values for the missing data. These synthetic values are obtained by means of some imputation technique. There are many different imputation techniques, all having advantages and disadvantages, see Little and Rubin (1987), see also Rässler, Rubin and Schenker (Chapter 19). The most important ones are:

1. *Imputation of the mean.* A synthetic value is obtained by computing the mean of all available values. This technique is known to produce wrong estimates of standard errors of estimates in a subsequent analysis. The technique can be somewhat improved by imputation of the mean within groups formed by the combining values of X-variables.

2. *Random imputation.* A synthetic value is obtained by randomly selecting one from the set of available values. This technique introduces an extra variance component in the estimates. This technique can also be improved by applying it within groups.

3. *Regression imputation.* Using the cases for which both X-values and Y-values are available, a regression model is fitted explaining values of an Y-variable from the values of a set of X-variables. Then the model is used for predicting the missing Y-values.

Let X_1 denote the set of X-variables used in the imputation model, and let X_2 be the set of unused X-variables. Then the imputation approach assumes that the distribution of $(Y \mid X)$ of Y given X in the population can correctly be estimated using the available data with the distribution $(Y \mid X_1)$ of Y given X_1. In other words: the distribution of $(Y \mid X_1)$ is independent of X_2 (conditional independence). This means that estimated correlations using the imputed data set will be much weaker than the true correlations in the population. This is a serious drawback of the mass imputation procedure.

A second approach to analysis of the data set described in Figure 26.3 is *weighting* (see also Biemer and Christ, Chapter 17). By comparing the distribution of the X-variables in the register with the distribution of these variables in the sample survey, adjustment weights can be computed that compensate for under- or over-representation of specific groups. Each sample survey record will be assigned a weight. In the analysis only these records are used, but weights are taken into account (analysis of the weighted data).

The simplest weighting method is *post-stratification*. A high-dimensional table is formed by cross-classifying a number of (categorical) X-variables. All sample objects in a specific cell of this table are assigned the same weight. This weight is obtained by dividing the population percentage in the cell by the sample percentage in the cell.

More advanced weighting techniques (linear weighting, multiplicative weighting, or iterative proportional fitting) use only partial information from the table. They avoid the problem of empty cells. For more information on weighting, see Bethlehem (2002).

Many statistical packages (e.g., SPSS and Stata) are capable of carrying out a weighted analysis. However, one should be careful. Usually, consistent estimates can be computed of population parameters, but standard errors of these estimated may be wrong (see also Stapleton, Chapter 18).

26.7 CONCLUSION

Wherever possible, researchers should use existing data, and not bother people again with questions they have already answered in other surveys, or can be found in registers.

However, one should be careful in relying on existing data sets too much. Such data sets may haven been collected for different purposes, with different variables at different times. Also data quality may not been guaranteed.

It is sometimes possible to obtain richer data sets by combining data sets form various registers. If records from different data sets cannot be linked in a unique way, the correlation structure of the variables may be seriously affected.

Also combination of a survey with a register may not be without risk. Mass imputation should be avoided as much as possible. Preferably, an advanced weighting technique should be applied.

Although sample surveys are costly and time-consuming, it may turn out that they are in many situations simply the best instrument for collecting high quality, relevant data.

GLOSSARY OF KEY CONCEPTS

Administrative register. A register that is primarily used for administrative purposes, that is, a register containing information on objects that is required for administrative or other governmental action concerning individual objects.
Key variable/Identification variable. Variables that appear in different data sets, and that are used to link a record of an object in one data set to a record of the same object in another data set.
Mass imputation. A form of imputation in which a large amount of missing values for individuals are replaced by synthetic values, computed using nonmissing information for these objects.
Measurement error. An error that occurs when the respondent does not understand the question, or does not want to give the true answer, or if the interviewer makes an error in recording the answer. Also, interview effects, question wording effects, and memory effects belong to this group of errors. A measurement error causes a difference between the true value and the value processed in the survey.
Nonresponse. The phenomenon that individuals in the selected sample do not provide the requested information, or that the provided information is useless.

Nonsampling errors. Errors that even occur if the whole population is investigated. Nonsampling errors are errors made during the process of recording the answers to the questions.

Primary data analysis. Statistical analysis of a data set that has specifically been collected for the study at hand.

Register. A register is a collection of data on a well-defined group of objects. For each individual object, the register contains the values of the same well-defined set of variables. These variables describe the state of the objects at a specific moment in time. A register has facilities to update the information about objects contained in it.

Sampling errors. Errors introduced by the sampling design. They are due to the fact that estimates are based on a sample and not on a complete enumeration of the population. The sample is selected by means of a random selection procedure. Every new selection of a sample will result in different elements, and thus in a different value of the estimator.

Secondary data analysis. Statistical analysis of a data set that has been collected by others for other purposes.

Survey. A study that collects planned information from a sample of individuals in order to estimate particular population characteristics.

Synthetic matching. A form of matching records from two data sets. Records are grouped using the values of a set of identification variables. Within groups, records from both data sets are combined randomly.

Weighting adjustment/Adjustment weighting. The process of assigning weights to observed individuals in a survey. The weights are computed such that the weighted distribution of certain auxiliary variables is identical to the population distribution of these variables.

References

AAPOR (2007). *The problem with reporting margins of error and sampling error in online and other survey sof self-selected individuals.* Retrieved June, 2007, from www.aapor.org.

AAPOR. (2005). *Standard definitions: Final dispositions of case codes and outcome rates for surveys, online edition 3.1.* Retrieved November 2006, from: http://www.aapor.org/pdfs/standarddefs_3.1.pdf.

Adorno, T. W. (1950). Some aspects of religious ideology as revealed in the interview material. In T. W. Adorno, E. Frenkel-Brunswick, D. Levinson, & R. N. Sanford (Eds.), *The Authoritarian Personality.* New York: Harper.

Ahart, A. M., & Sacket, P. R. (2004). A new method of examining relationships between individual difference measures and sensitive behavior criteria: Evaluating the Unmatched Count Technique. *Organisational Research Methods, 7,* 101–114.

Alemagno, S.A., Cochran, D., Feucht, T.E., Stephens, R.C., & Wolfe, S.A. (1996). Assessing substance abuse treatment needs among the homeless: A telephone-based interactive voice response system. *American Journal of Public Health, 86,* 1626–1628.

American Psychological Association. (2003). *Psychological research online: Opportunities and challenges* (Working Paper Version 3/31/03). Washington, DC.: American Psychological Association.

Andary, L., Stolk, Y., & Klimidid, S. (2003). *Assessing mental health across cultures.* Bowen Hills, Australia: Australian Academic Press.

Anderson, J. R. (2000). *Learning and memory: An integrated approach.* New York: Wiley.

Anderson, J.R. (1995). *Cognitive psychology and its implications.* New York: Freeman.

Anderson, M., & Seltzer, W. (2004, March). *The challenges of taxation, investigation, and regulation: Statistical confidentiality and U.S. federal statistics, 1910–1965.* Paper prepared for Census Bureau Symposium, America's Scorecard: The Historic Role of the Census in an Ever-Changing Nation, Woodrow Wilson International Center for Scholars, Washington, DC.

Anderson, R. T., Aaronson, N. K., & Wilkin, D. (1993). Critical review of the international assessment of health-related quality of life. *Quality of Life Research, 2,* 369–395.

Andrews, F. M. (1984). Construct validity and error components of survey measures: A structural modeling approach. *Public Opinion Quarterly, 48,* 409–422.

Angus, V. C., Entwistle, V. A., Emslie, M. J., Walker, K. A., & Andrew, J. E. (2003). The requirement for prior consent to participate on survey response rates. *BMC Health Services Research, 3,* 21–30.

Aoki, K., & Elasmar, M. (2000, May). *Opportunities and challenges of a web survey: A field experiment.* Paper presented at the 55th Annual Conference of American Association for Public Opinion Research, Portland, OR.

Argyle, M. (1973). *Social interaction.* London: Tavistock

Argyle, M. (1994). *The psychology of social class.* London: Routledge.

Armacost R. L., Hosseini J. C., Morris S. A., & Rehbein K. A. (1991). An empirical comparison of direct questioning, scenario, and randomized response methods. *Decision Sciences, 22,* 1037–1060.

Armer, M. J., & Grimshaw, A. D. (1973). Methodological problems and possibilities in comparative research. In M. J. Armer & A. D. Grimshaw (Eds.), *Comparative social research: Methodological problems and strategies.* New York: Wiley.

Asch, S. E. (1951). The effects of group pressure on the modification and distortion of judgments. In H. Guetzkow (Ed.), *Groups, leadership, and men.* Pittsburgh, PA: Carnegie.

Bailar, B. A. (1989). Information needs, surveys, and measurement error. In D. Kasprzyk, G. Duncan, G. Kalton, & M. P. Singh (Eds.), *Panel Surveys.* New York: John Wiley and Sons.

Bailar, B. A., & Dalenius, T. (1969). Estimating the response variance components of the U.S. Bureau of the Census' survey model. *Sankhya, B,* 341–360.

Baker, R. (1999). Codes of ethics: Some history. *Perspectives on the Profession, 19.*

Balden, W. (2004, March). Multi-mode data collection: Benefits and downsides. Paper presented at the 2004 conference of the Great Lakes chapter of the Marketing Research Association, Cancun, Mexico. Retrieved April 15, 2004, from: http://glcmra.org/cancun. (full paper upon request from the author).

Baldrige National Quality Program (2006). Retrieved from: http://www.quality.nist.gov/

Bargmeyer, B., & Gillman, D. (2003). *Metadata Standards and Metadata Registries: An overview.*

Retrieved April 16, 2003, from: http://www.bls.gov/ore/pdf/st000010.pdf

Barnard, J., & Rubin, D. B. (1999). Small-sample degrees of freedom with multiple imputation. *Biometrika, 86,* 948–955.

Batagelj, Z., & Vehovar, V. (1998). WWW Surveys. In A. Ferligoj (Ed.), *Advances in methodology, data analysis, and statistics.* Ljubljana: Faculty of Social Sciences.

Bauman, S., Jobity, N., Airey, J. & Atak, H. (2000). *Invites, intros and incentives: Lessons from a web survey.* Paper presented at the 55th annual conference of American Association for Public Opinion Research, Portland, OR.

Baumgartner, H., & Steenkamp, J. E. M. (2001). Response styles in marketing research: A cross-national investigation. *Journal of Marketing Research, 38,* 143–156.

Beatty, P. (2004). The dynamics of cognitive interviewing. In S. Presser, J. M. Rothgeb, M. P. Couper, J. T. Lessler, E. Martin, J. Martin, et al. (Eds.), *Methods for testing and evaluating survey questionnaires.* New York: Wiley.

Beebe, T. J., Davern, M. E., McAlpine, D. D., Call, K. T., & Rockwood, T. H. (2005). Increasing response rates in a survey of Medicaid enrolees: The effect of a prepaid monetary incentive and mixed modes (mail and telephone). *Medical Care, 43,* 411–414.

Begeer, W., De Vries, W. F. M., & Dukker, H. D. (1986). Statistics and administration. *Netherlands Official Statistics, 1,* 7–17.

Belli, R. (1998). The structure of autobiographical memory and the event history calendar: Potential improvements in the quality of retrospective reports in surveys. *Memory, 6,* 383–406.

Belli, R., Schwarz, N., Singer, E., & Talarico, J. (2000). Decomposition can harm the accuracy of retrospective behavioral reports. *Applied Cognitive Psychology, 14,* 295–308.

Belson, W. A. (1981). *The design and understanding of survey questions.* Aldershot: Gower.

Bennett, M., & Trussel, N. (2001). *Return postage type as cooperation stimulant for a mail mode portion of a multi-mode survey.* Paper, 56th Annual AAPOR conference, Montreal, Canada,

Berlin, M. T., & Fleck, M. P. A. (2003). 'Quality of Life': a brand new concept for research and practice in psychiatry. *Revista Brasileira de Psiquiatria* [Brazilian Journal of Psychiatry], *25,* 249–252. Retrieved from http://www.scielo.br/scielo.php?script=sci_arttext&pid=S1516-44462003000400013&lng=en&nrm=iso, September 2006..

Berry, J. (1969). On cross-cultural comparability. *International Journal of Psychology, 4,* 119–128.

Berscheid, E., Baron, R., Dermer, M., & Libman, M. (1973). Anticipating informed consent: An empirical approach. *American Psychologist, 28,* 913–25.

Best, S., & Krueger, B. (2004). *Internet data collection.* Thousand Oaks, CA: Sage.

Bethlehem, J. G. (2002). Weighting nonresponse adjustments based on auxiliary information. In R. M. Groves, D. A. Dillman, J. L. Eltinge, & R. J. A. Little (Eds.), *Survey nonresponse.* New York: Wiley.

Bethlehem, J. G., Keller, W. J., & Pannekoek, J. (1990). Disclosure control of microdata. *Journal of the American Statistical Association, 85,* 38–45.

Biemer, P. P., & Caspar, R. A. (1994). Continuous quality improvement for survey operations: Some general principles and applications. *Journal of official statistics, 10,* 307–326.

Biemer, P. P., & Lyberg, L. E. (2003). *Introduction to survey quality.* New York: Wiley.

Biemer, P. P., & Wiesen. (2002). Latent class analysis of embedded repeated measurements: An application to the national household survey on drug abuse. *Journal of the Royal Statistical Society series A, 165,* 97–120.

Billiet, J. (2003). Cross-cultural equivalence with Structural Equation Modeling. In J. A. Harkness, F. J. R. Van De Vijver, & P. Mohler (Eds.), *Cross-cultural survey methods.* Hoboken, NJ: Wiley.

Billiet, J., & Loosveldt, G. (1988). Improvement of the quality of responses to factual survey questions by interviewer training. *Public Opinion Quarterly, 52,* 190–211.

Blair, E., & Burton, S. (1987). Cognitive processes used by survey respondents to answer behavioral frequency questions. *Journal of Consumer Research, 14,* 280 – 288.

Blazeby, J., Sprangers, M., Cull, A., Groenvold, M., & Bottomley, A. (2002). *Guidelines for developing questionnaire modules.* Retrieved August 28, 2006 from: http://www.eortc.be/home/ quality of life/Manuals/Module development% 20guidelines -2002.pdf

Bless, H., Igou, E. R., Schwarz, N., & Wänke, M. (2000). Reducing context effects by adding context information: The direction and size of context effects in political judgment. *Personality and Social Psychology Bulletin, 26,* 1036–1045.

Bless, H., Schwarz, N., & Wänke, M. (2003). The size of context effects in social judgment. In J. P. Forgas, K. D. Williams, & W. von Hippel (Eds.), *Social judgments: Implicit and explicit processes.* Cambridge, MA: Cambridge University Press.

Blohm, M., & Koch, A. (2004, August). *First contacts by phone or in person: Some evidence from*

ALLBUS 2000. Paper presented at the 15th Workshop on Household Survey Nonresponse, Maastricht, Netherlands.

Bollen, K. A. (1989). *Structural equations with latent variables.* New York: Wiley.

Bolton, P. (2001). Cross-cultural validity and reliability testing of a standard psychiatric assessment instrument without a Gold Standard. *Journal of Nervous & Mental Disease, 189,* 238–242.

Borgers, N., de Leeuw, E., & Hox, J. (2000). Children as respondents in survey research: Cognitive development and response quality. *Bulletin de Méthodologie Sociologique, 66,* 60–75.

Boruch, R. F. (1971). Assuring confidentiality of responses in social research: A note on strategies. *The American Sociologist, 6,* 308–311.

Botman, S. L., Moore, T. F., Moriarity, C. L., & Parsons, V. L. (2000). Design and estimation for the National Health Interview Survey, 1995–2004. *Vital and Health Statistics, 2,* 130.

Brackstone, G. (1999). Managing data quality in a statistical agency. *Survey Methodology, 25,* 139–149.

Bradburn, N. M., Sudman, S., Blair, E., & Locander, W. (Eds.). (1979). *Improving interview method and questionnaire.* San Francisco: Jossey Bass.

Bradburn, N. M., Sudman, S., & Wansink, B. (2004). *Asking questions* (2nd ed.). San Francisco: Jossey Bass.

Brambilla, D. J., & McKinlay, S. M. (1987). A comparison of responses to mailed questionnaires and telephone interviews in a mixed mode health survey. *American Journal of Epidemiology, 126,* 962–971.

Braun, M., & Harkness, J. A. (2005). Text and context: Challenges to comparability in survey questions. In J. H. P. Hoffmeyer-Zlotnik, & J. A. Harkness (Eds.), *ZUMA-Nachrichten spezial No. 11. Methodological aspects in cross-national research.* Mannheim, BRD: ZUMA.

Bremer, J., Terhanian, G., & Strange, P. (2004, August). *Propensity score matching as a bias correction method for internet-based studies.* Paper presented at the Joint Statistical Meeting, Toronto, Canada.

Brenner, M. (1981). Patterns of social structure in the research interview. In Brenner (Ed.), *Social method and social life.* London: Academic Press.

Bretschneider, M., & Schumacher, J. (1996). DEMOS eine Datenbank zum Nachweis Kommunaler Umfragen auf dem Weg zum Analyse instrument. *ZA-Information, 38,* 59–81.

Brewer, K. R. W. (1981). Estimating marijuana usage using randomized response: Some paradoxical findings. *Australian Journal of Statistics, 23,* 139–148.

Brick, M. J., Waksberg, J., Kulp, D., & Starer, A. (1995). Bias in list-assisted telephone samples. *Public Opinion Quarterly, 59,* 218–235.

Brogan, D. (1998). Software for sample survey data, misuse of standard packages. In P. Armitage & T. Colton (Eds.), *Encyclopedia of biostatistics, 5* (pp. 4167–4174). New York: Wiley.

Bruce, R., & Anderson, W. (1967). On the comparability of meaningful stimuli in cross-cultural research. *Sociometry, 30,* 124–136.

Buckingham, A., & Saunders, P. (2004). *The survey methods workbook.* Cambridge: Polity Press.

Bullinger, M. (2004). *The challenge of cross-cultural quality of life assessment.* Paper for the international workshop on researching well-being in developing countries. Retrieved June 20, 2006, from: http://www.welldev.org.uk/news/hanse-pdfs/bullinger-hanse-full.pdf.

Bushery, J., Reichert, J. W., & Blass, R. F. (2003). U.S. census 2010 quality assurance strategy. *ASA Proceedings of the Section of Government Statistics.*

Callegaro, M., Buskirk, T., Piekarski, L., Kuusela, V., Vehovar, V., & Steeh, C. (2004, August). *Calculating outcome rates for mobile phone surveys: A proposal for a modified AAPOR standard and its application to three case studies.* Paper presented at the RC33 Sixth Annual Conference on Social Science Methodology, Amsterdam, The Netherlands.

Campanelli, P. C. (1997). Testing survey questions: New directions in cognitive interviewing. *Bulletin de Méthodologie Sociologique, 55,* 5–17.

Campanelli, P. C., Martin, E. A.,& Rothgeb, J. M. (1991). The use of respondent and interviewer debriefing studies as a way to study response error in survey data. *The Statistician, 40,* 253–264.

Campanelli, P. C., Rothgeb, J., Esposito, J., & Polivka, A. (1991, May). *Methodologies for evaluating survey questions: An illustration from a CPS CATI/RDD test.* Paper presented at the annual meeting of the American Association for Public Opinion Research, Phoenix, AZ.

Cannell, C. F., Fisher, G., & Bakker, T. (1965). Reporting on hospitalization in the Health Interview Survey (PHS Publication No. 1000, Series 2, No. 6). Washington, D.C.: US Government Printing Office.

Cannell, C. F., Fowler F. J., & Marquis, K. H. (1968). The influence of interviewer and respondent psychological and behavioural variables on the reporting in household interviews. *Vital and*

Health Statistics, series 14, 26.

Cannell, C. F., & Kahn, R. (1968). Interviewing. In G. Lindzey, & E. Aronson (Eds.), *The handbook of social psychology, Vol 2*. Reading, MA: Addison-Wesley.

Cannell, C. F., Marquis, K., & Laurent, A. (1977). A summary of studies. *Vital & Health Statistics, Series 2, 69*. Washington, DC: Government Printing Office.

Cannell, C. F., Miller, P. V., & Oksenberg, L. (1981). Research on interviewing techniques. In S. Leinhardt (Ed.), *Sociological methodology 1981* (389–437). San Francisco: Jossey-Bass.

Cannell, C. F., Oksenberg, L., Kalton, G., Bischoping, K., & Fowler, F. J. (1989). *New techniques for pretesting survey questions* (Final Report). Bethesda, MD: National Information Center for Health Services Research and Health Care Technology Assessment (NICHSR).

Cannell, C.F., Oksenberg, L., & Converse, J.M. (1977). Strivin for response accuracy: experiments in new interviewing techniques. *Journal of Marketing Research, 14*, 306–315.

Cantor, D., Allen, B., Schneider, S., Hagerty-Heller, T., & Yuan, A. (2004). Testing an automated refusal avoidance training methodology. *ASA Proceedings of the Annual Meeting of the American Statistical Association*. Arlington, VA: ASA.

Casady, R. J., & Lepkowski J. M. (1991). Optimal allocation for stratified telephone survey design. *ASA Proceedings of the section on survey research methods*, 111–116.

Casady, R. J., & Lepkowski, J. M. (1993). Stratified telephone survey designs. *Survey Methodology, 19*, 103–113.

Caspar, R. (2004). *Material prepared by R. Caspar for Joint Program in Survey Methods (JPSM) course 2004 on "Questionnaire Design" conducted by Campanelli and Caspar*. College Park, MD: Joint Programme in Survey Methodology, University of Maryland, University of Michigan, Westat.

CBS. (2005). *Enquête-onderzoek onder allochtonen. Problemen en oplossingen*. [Surveying allochtonous respondents: problems and solutions] Heerlen/Voorburg, the Netherlands: Centraal Bureau voor de Statistiek.

Chakrabarty, R. P., & Torres, G. (1996). *American housing survey: A quality profile*. Washington, DC: U.S. Department of Housing and Urban Development and U.S. Department of Commerce.

Chambers, R. L., & Skinner, C. J. (Eds.) (2003). *Analysis of survey data*. Chichester, UK: Wiley.

Chen, C., Lee, S., & Stevenson, H. W. (1995). Response style and cross-cultural comparisons of rating scales among East Asian and North American students. *Psychological Science, 6*, 170–175.

Cheng, A. T. A. (2001). Case definition and culture: Are people all the same? *The British Journal of Psychiatry, 179*, 1–3.

Cheung, F. M. (2004). Use of western and indigenously developed personality tests in Asia. *Applied Psychology: An International Review, 53*, 173–191.

Christian, L. M., & Dillman, D. A. (2004). The influence of graphical and symbolic language manipulations on responses to self-administered questionnaires. *Public Opinion Quarterly, 68*, 57–80.

Christian, L. M., Dillman, D. A., and Smyth, J. D. (2007). The effects of aural vs. visual communication on answers to scalar questions in mixed-mode surveys. In James M Lepkowski, Clyde Tucker, J.Michael Brick, Edith D. de Leeuw, Lilli Japec, Paul J. Lavrakas, Michael W. Link, Roberta L. Sangster. *Advances in Telephone Survey Methodology*. New York: Wiley.

Christian, L. M., Dillman, D. A., & Smyth, J. D. (2005). *Instructing web and telephone respondents to report date answers in format desired by the surveyor* (Social and Economic Sciences Research Center Technical Report 05–067). Washington, DC: Washington State University.

Chrostowski, S. J., & Malak, B. (2003). Translation and cultural adaptation of the TIMSS 2003 Instruments. In M. O. Martin, I. V. S. Mullis, & S. J. Chrostowski (Eds.), *TIMSS 2003 Technical Report*. Chestnut Hill, MA: TIMSS & PIRLS International Study Center. Retrieved July 20, 2006 from: http://timss.bc.edu/PDF/ t03_download/T03_TR_Front.pdf.

Church, A. H. (1993). Estimating the effect of incentives on mail survey response rates: A meta-analysis. *Public Opinion Quarterly, 57*, 62–79.

Church, A. H. (2001). Is there a method to our madness? The impact of data collection methodology on organizational survey results. *Personnel Psychology, 54*, 937–969.

Citro, C. F., Cork, D. L., & Norwood, J. L. (Eds.). (2004). *The 2000 census: Counting under adversity*. Washington, D.C.: National Academies Press.

Clark, H. H., & Clark, E. V. (1977). *Psychology and language*. New York: Harcourt, Brace, Jovanovich.

Clark, H. H., & Schober, M. F. (1992). Asking questions and influencing answers. In J. M. Tanur (Ed.), *Questions about questions: Inquiries into the cognitive bases of surveys*. New York:

Russell Sage Foundation.

Coates, D. (2004, August). *On-line surveys: Does one size fit all?* Paper presented at the RC-33 6th International Conference on Social Methodology, Amsterdam, The Netherlands.

Cochran, W. G. (1977). *Sampling techniques* (3rd ed). New York: Wiley.

Coleman, M. P., Evans, B. G., & Barrett, G. (2005). Confidentiality and the public interest in medical research: Will we ever get it right? *Clinical Medicine, 3,* 219–28.

Collins, D. (2002). *Material prepared by D. Collins for Center for Applied Social Surveys (CASS) course 2002 on "Pretesting Survey Questionnaires" conducted by Campanelli, Collins, & Thomas.* Southampton, UK: University of Southampton, Southampton Statistical Science Research Institute, Center for Applied Social Surveys.

Collins, J. (2001). *Good to great.* New York: Harper Business.

Collins, M., & Sykes, W. (1999). Extending the definition of survey quality. *Journal of Official Statistics, 15,* 57–66.

Comley, P. (2000). Pop-up surveys. What works, what doesn't work and what will work in the future. *Proceedings of the ESOMAR Worldwide Internet Conference Net Effects, 237..* Retrieved November 21, 2001, from: http://www.virtualsurveys.com/papers/popup_paper.htm

Conner, D. R. (1993). *Managing at the speed of change.* New York: Villard Books.

Conrad, F. G., & Schober, M. F. (2000). Clarifying question meaning in a household telephone survey. *Public Opinion Quarterly, 64,* 1–28.

Conrad, F. G., Schober, M. F., Dijkstra, W. (in press). Cues of communication difficulty in telephone interviews. In J. Lepkowski, C. Tucker, M. Brick, E. de Leeuw, L. Japec, P. Lavrakas, et al. (Eds.), *Advances in telephone survey methodology.* New York: Wiley.

Converse, J. M. (1987). *Survey research in the united states.* Berkeley, CA: University of California Press.

Converse, J. M., & Presser, S. (1986). *Survey questions: Handcrafting the standardized questionnaire.* Beverly Hills, CA: Sage.

Cook, C., Heath, F., & Thompson, R. L. (2000). A meta-analysis of response rates in web- or Internet-based surveys. *Educational and Psychological Measurement, 60,* 821–836.

Cook, L. L., Schmitt-Cascallar, A. P., & Brown, C. (2005). Adapting achievement and aptitude tests: A review of methodological issues. In R. K. Hambleton, P. F. Merenda, & C. D. Spielberger (Eds.), *Adapting educational and psychological tests for cross-cultural assessment.* Mahwah, NJ: Erlbaum.

Cooley, P. C., Miller, H. G., Gribble, J. N., & Turner, C. F. (2000). Automating telephone surveys: Using T-ACASI to obtain data on sensitive topics. *Computers in Human Behavior, 16,* 1–11.

Council for Marketing and Opinion Research. (2001). *Highlights from CMOR's cooperation tracking system data.* Retrieved November 14, 2005, from: http://www.cmor.org/rc/rcnews.cfm?aID=0501

Couper, M. P. (1998, August). *Measuring survey quality in a CASIC environment.* Paper presented at the Joint Statistical Meetings of the American Statistical Association, Dallas, TA.

Couper, M. P. (2000). *The good, the bad, and the ugly* (Working paper series No. 077). Michigan, MI: University of Michigan, Institute for Social Research, Survey Methodology Program.

Couper, M. P. (2000). Web surveys: A review of issues and approaches. *Public Opinion Quarterly, 64,* 464–494.

Couper, M. P. (2001). The promises and perils of web surveys. *Paper presented at the ASC-conference on the challenge of the Internet.* Retrieved January 2006, from: http://www.asc.org.uk.

Couper, M. P. (2002). New technologies and survey data collection: Challenges and opportunities. *Invited paper presented at the International Conference on Improving Surveys.* Copenhagen, August 2002. Retrieved January 2006, from: http://www.icis.dk/ICIS_papers/Keynote1_0_3.pdf.

Couper, M. P., & de Leeuw, E. D. (2003). Nonresponse in cross-cultural and cross-national surveys. In J. A. Harkness, F. J. R. van de Vijver, & P. Mohler (Eds.), *Cross-cultural survey methods* (157–177). New York: Wiley, 2003.

Couper, M. P., Hansen, S. E., & Sadosky, S. A. (1997). Evaluating interviewer performance in a CAPI survey. In L. Lyberg, P. Biemer, M. Collins, E. de Leeuw, C. Dippo, N. Schwarz., et al. (Eds.), *Survey measurement and process quality.* New York: Wiley.

Couper, M. P., & Lyberg, L. (2005, April). The use of paradata in survey research. Proceedings of the 54th Session of the International Statistical Institute, Sydney, Australia.

Couper, M. P., & Nichols, J. D. I.. (1998). The history and development of computer-assisted survey information collection methods. In J. M. O'Reilly (Ed.), *Computer-assisted survey information collection.* New York: Wiley.

Couper, M. P., Singer, E., & Tourangeau, R. (2004). Does voice matter? An Interactive Voice Response (IVR) experiment. *Journal of Official Statistics, 20*, 551–570.

Couper, M. P., Singer, E., & Tourangeau, R. (2003).Understanding the effects of audio-CASI on self-reports of sensitive behavior. *Public Opinion Quarterly, 67,* 385–395.

Couper, M. P., Tourangeau, R., & Kenyon, K. (2004). Picture this! Exploring visual effects in web surveys. *Public Opinion Quarterly, 68*, 255–266.

Couper, M. P., Tourangeau, R., Conrad, F. G., & Singer, E. (2006). Evaluating the effectiveness of visual analog scales: A web experiment. *Social Science Computer Review, 24,* 227–245.

Couper, M. P., Traugott, M., & Lamias, M. (2001). Web survey design and administration. *Public Opinion Quarterly, 65*, 230–253.

Crawford, S., Couper, M. P., & Lamias, M. J. (2001). Web surveys: Perceptions of burden. *Social Science Computer Review, 19*, 146–162.

Crawford, S., McCabe, S. E., & Pope, D. (2005). Applying web-based survey design standards. *Journal of Prevention and Intervention in the Community, 29*, 43–66.

Cronbach, L., & Meehl, P. (1955). Construct validity in psychological tests. *Psychological Bulletin, 52,* 281–302.

Currivan, D. B., Nyman, A. L., Turner, C. F., & Biener, L. (2004). Does telephone audio computer-assisted self-interviewing improve the accuracy of prevalence estimates of youth smoking? Evidence from the Umass tobacco study. *Public Opinion Quarterly, 68*, 542–564.

Curtin, R., Presser, S. & Singer, E. (2005). Changes in telephone survey nonresponse over the past quarter century. *Public Opinion Quarterly, 69*, 87–98.

Czaja, R., & Blair, J. (2005). *Designing surveys: A guide to decisions and procedures* (2nd ed.). Thousand Oaks, CA: Sage.

Czaja, R., & Blair, J. (1996) *Designing surveys: A guide to decisions and procedures.* Thousand Oaks, CA: Sage, Pine Forge Press.

Dalenius, T. (1977). Strain at a gnat and swallow a camel: Or, the problem of measuring sampling and non-sampling errors. *ASA Proceedings of the Social Statistics Section, 20,* 21–25.

Daling J.R., Malone K. E., Voigt L.F., White E., Weiss N.S. (1994). Risk of breast cancer among young women: relationship to induced abortion. *Journal of the National Cancer Institute, 86*, 1584–1592.

Dalton, D. R., Wimbush, J. C., & Daily, C. M. (1994). Using the Unmatched Count Technique (UCT) to estimate base rates for sensitive behavior. *Personnel Psychology, 47*, 817–828.

Davis, D., & Silver, B. (2003). Stereotype threat and race of interviewer effects in a survey on political knowledge. *American Journal of Political Science, 47*, 33–45.

De Heer, W. (1999). International response trends: Results of an international survey. *Journal of Official Statistics, 15*, 129–142.

De Jong, W. A. M. (1991). Technieken voor het koppelen van bestanden. *Statistische Onderzoekingen, M41*.Voorburg: Statistics Netherlands.

De Leeuw, E. D. (2005). Surveying Children. In S.J. Best and B. Radcliff (Eds). Polling America: An Encyclopedia of Public Opinion. p. 831-835, Westport. CT. Greenwood Press.

De Leeuw, E. D. (2005). To mix or not to mix data collection modes in surveys. *Journal of Official Statistics, 21*, 233–255.

De Leeuw, E. D. (1999). De vraag naar gevoelige informatie: Een overzicht. [Questions on sensitive information: A Review] *Pedagogische Studiën, 76*, 92–103.

De Leeuw, E. D. (1992). *Data quality in mail, telephone and face-to-face surveys.* Amsterdam: TT-Publikaties. Retrieved from: http://www.xs4all.nl/~edithl.

De Leeuw, E., Borgers, N., & Smits, A. (2004). Pretesting questionnaires for children and adolescents. In S. Presser, J. Rothgeb, M. P. Couper, J. T. Lessler, E. Martin, J. Martin, & E. Singer (Eds.), *Methods for testing and evaluating survey questionnaires.* Hoboken, NJ: Wiley.

De Leeuw, E., Callegaro, M., Hox, J. J., Korendijk, E., & Lensvelt-Mulders, G. (2007). The influence of advance letters on response in telephone surveys: A meta-analysis. *Public Opinion Quarterly, 71*, 1–31.

De Leeuw, E. D., & De Heer, W. (2002). Trends in household survey nonresponse: A longitudinal and international comparison. In R. M. Groves, D. A. Dillman, J. L. Eltinghe, & R. J. A. Little (Eds.), *Survey nonresponse.* New York: Wiley.

De Leeuw, E. D. & Hox, J.J. (1988). The effects of response stimulating factors on response rates and data quality in mail surveys. *Journal of Official Statistics, 4*, 241–249.(also at www.jos.nu)

De Leeuw, E. D. & Hox, J. J. (2004). I am not selling anything: 29 Experiments in telephone introductions. *International Journal of Public Opinion Research, 16*, 464–473.

De Leeuw, E. D., Hox, J. J., & Huisman, M. (2003). Prevention and treatment of item nonresponse.

Journal of Official Statistics (JOS) 19, 153–176.

De Leeuw, E. D., Hox, J. J., & Kef, S. (2003). Computer-Assisted Self-Interviewing tailored for special populations and topics. *Field Methods, 15*, 223–251.

De Leeuw, E. D., Lepkowski, J., & Kim, S. W. (2002, August). *Have telephone surveys a future in the twenty-first century?* Paper presented at the 2002 International Conference on Information Systems, Copenhagen, Denmark.

De Leeuw, E. D., & Nichols, J. D. I. (1996). Technological innovations in data collection: Acceptance, data quality and costs. *Sociological Research on Line, 1.*

De Leeuw, E. D., & Van der Zouwen, J. (1988). Data quality in telephone and face-to-face surveys: A comparative meta-analysis. In R. Groves, P. Biemer, L. Lybert, J. Massey, W. Nicholls II, & J. Waksberg (Eds.), *Telephone survey methodology*. New York: Wiley.

DeMaio, T. J. (1984). Social desirability and survey measurement: A review. In C. F. Turner & E. Martin (Eds.), *Surveying subjective phenomena, volume two*. New York: Russell Sage.

DeMaio, T. J., & Landreth, A. (2004). Do different cognitive interview techniques produce different results? In S. Presser, J. M. Rothgeb, M. P. Couper, J. T. Lessler, E. Martin, J. Martin, et al. (Eds.), *Methods for testing and evaluating survey questionnaires.* New York: Wiley.

DeMaio, T. J. & Rothgeb, J. M. (1996). Cognitive interviewing techniques: In the lab and in the field. In N. Schwarz & S. Sudman (Eds.), *Answering questions: Methodology for determining cognitive and communicative processes in survey research* (p. 177–195). San Francisco: Jossey Bass.

Deming, W. E. (1986). *Out of the crisis*. Cambridge, MA: Cambridge University Press.

Deming, W. E. (1944). On errors in surveys. *American Sociological Review, 9*, 359–369.

Deming, W. E., & Stephan, F. F. (1940). On a least squares adjustment of a sample frequency table when the expected marginal totals are known. *Annals of Mathematical Statistics, 11*, 427–444.

Dempster, A. P., Laird, N. M., & Rubin, D. B. (1977). Maximum likelihood estimation from incomplete data via the EM algorithm (with discussion). *Journal of the Royal Statistical Society B, 39*, 1–38.

Denton, C. (2005). National representative report—Costa Rica/Central America. *First Quarter Newsletter of the World Association for Public Opinion Research*, 3–4.

de Rada, V.D. (2001). Mail Surveys Using Dillman's TDM in a Southern European Country: Spain. *International Journal of Public Opinion Research, 13*, 159–172

De Rouvray, C., & Couper, M. P. (2002). Designing a strategy for reducing 'no opinion' responses in web-based surveys. *Social Science Computer Review SSCREH, 20*, 3–9.

DeVellis, R. F. (2003). *Scale development: Theory and applications*. Thousand Oaks, CA: Sage.

Devore, J., & Peck R. (2005). *Statistics: The exploration and analysis of data*. Belmont: Brooks/Cole-Thomson Learning.

Dewar, A. (2006). Maximizing response to a postal survey on social capital. Office for national Statistics Survey Methodology Bulletin, 58, 29–33.

(also at www.statistics.gov.uk/about/services/dcm/reports_publications.asp)

Dillman, D. A. (2007). *Mail and internet surveys: The tailored design method* (2nd ed.). New York: Wiley.

Dillman, D. A. (2000). *Mail and internet surveys: The tailored design method*. New York: Wiley.

Dillman, D. A. (1991). The design and administration of mail surveys. *Annual Review of Sociology, 17*, 225–249.

Dillman, D. A. (1978). *Mail and telephone surveys. The Total Design Method*. New York: Wiley.

Dillman, D. A., & Bowker, D. K. (2001). The web questionnaire challenge to survey methodologists. In: U. D. Reips, & M. Bosnjak (Eds.), *Dimensions of internet science*. Lengerich: Pabst Science Publishers.

Dillman, D. A., Clark, J. R., & West, K. K. (1995). Influence of an invitation to answer by telephone on response to census questionnaires. *Public Opinion Quarterly, 51*, 201–219.

Dillman, D. A., & Christian, L. M. (2005). Survey mode as a source of instability across surveys. *Field Methods, 17,* 30–52.

Dillman, D. A., Dolson, D .E., Machlis, G. E. (1995). Increasing response to personally-delivered mail-back questionnaires. *Journal of Official Statistics, 11*, 129-139. (Also at www.jos.nu)

Dillman, D. A., Gertseva, A., & Mahon-Haft, T. (2005). Achieving usability in establishment surveys through the application of visual design principles. *Journal of Official Statistics, 21*, 183–214. (Also at www.jos.nu)

Dillman, D. A., Phelps, G., Tortorra, R., Swift, K., Kohrell, J., & Berck, J.(2002). Response rate and measurement differences in mixed mode surveys: Using mail, telephone, Interactive Voice Response and the Internet. Retrieved April 14, 2005, from: http://www.sesrc.wsu.edu/dillman/

papers/Mixed Mode ppr _with Gallup_ POQ.pdf.

Dillman, D. A., & Redline, C. (2004). Testing paper self-administered questionnaires: Cognitive interview and field test comparisons. In S. Presser, J. M. Rothgeb, M. P. Couper, J. T. Lessler, E. Martin, J. Martin, et al. (Eds.), *Methods for testing and evaluating survey questionnaires.* New York: Wiley.

Dillman, D. A., & Tarnai, J. (1988). Administrative issues in mixed mode surveys. In R. M. Groves, P. P. Biemer, L. E. Lyberg, J. T. Massey, W. L. Nicholls II, & J. Wakesberg (Eds.), *Telephone survey methodology.* New York: Wiley.

Dillman, D. A., Tortora, R. D., & Bowker, D. (1998). Influence of plain vs. fancy design on response rates for web surveys. *Proceedings of the section on survey methods research, 21.* Retrieved November 26, 2001, from: http://survey.sesrc.wsu.edu/dillman/papers/asa98ppr.pdf

Dillman, D. A., Tortora, R. D., & Bowker, D. (1998). *Principles for constructing Web surveys.* Retrieved from: http://survey.sesrc.wsu.edu/dillman/papers/websurveyppr.pdf.

Dippo, C. S. (1997). Survey measurement and process improvement: Concepts and integration. In L. Lyberg, P. Biemer, M.Collins, E. de Leeuw, C. Dippo, N. Schwarz, et al. (Eds.), *Survey measurement and process quality.* New York: Wiley.

Dippo, C. S., & Sundgren, B. (2000). The role of metadata in statistics. *Proceedings of ICES-2, the Second International Conference on Establishment Surveys.* Buffalo, NY.

Dorey, F. J., Little, R. J. A., & Schenker, N. (1993). Multiple imputation for threshold-crossing data with interval censoring. *Statistics in Medicine, 12,* 1589–1603.

Dornyei, Z. (2003). Questionnaires in second language research: Construction, administration, & processing. Mahwah, N.J.: Lawrence Erlbaum Associates.

Dowd, K., Kinsey, S., Wheeless, S., Suresh, S., & The NSCAW Research Group. (2002). *National survey of child and adolescent well-being: Wave I data file user's manual.* Research Triangle Park, NC: RTI International.

Doyle, P., Lane, J., Theeuwes, J. & Zayatz, T. (2001). *Confidentiality, disclosure, and data access: Theory and practical applications for statistical agencies.* Amsterdam etc.: Elsevier.

DuMouchel, W. H., & Duncan, G. I. (1983). Using sample survey weights in multiple regression analyses of stratified samples. *Journal of the American Statistical Association, 78,* 535–543.

Duncan, G. J., & Kalton, G. (1987). Issues of design and analysis of surveys across time. *International Statistical Review, 55,* 97–117.

Dunn, L. B., & Gordon, N. E. (2005). Improving informed consent and enhancing recruitment for research by understanding economic behavior. *Journal of the American Medical Association, 293,* 609–612.

Edwards, B., Schneider, C., & Dean Brick, P. (in press). Visual elements of questionnaire design: Experiments with a CATI establishment survey. In J. Lepkowski, C. Tucker, M. Brick, E. de Leeuw, L. Japec, P. Lavrakas, et al. (Eds.), *Advances in telephone survey methodology.* New York: Wiley.

Efron, B. (1994). Missing data, imputation, and the bootstrap. *Journal of the American Statistical Association, 89,* 463–479.

Efron, R., & Tibshirani, R. J. (1993). *An introduction to the bootstrap.* London: Chapman & Hall.

Eichman, C. (1999). Research methods on the web: Experiences and implications for market research. *Proceedings of the ESOMAR Worldwide Internet Conference Net Effects,* 69–76.

Enander, J., & Sajti, A. (1999, February). Online survey of online customers: Value-added market research through data collection on the Internet. *Proceedings of the ESOMAR Worldwide Internet Conference Net Effects,* 35–51.

Ericsson K. A., & Simon, H. A. (1984). *Protocol analysis: Verbal reports as data.* Cambridge, MA: MIT Press.

Erikson, B. H., & Nosanchuk, T. A. (1983). Applied network sampling. *Social Networks, 5,* 367–382.

Esposito, J. L., Campanelli, P. C., Rothgeb, J. M., & Polivka, A. E. (1991). Determining which questions are best: Methodologies for evaluating survey questions. *Proceedings of the Section of Survey Methods Research, 14.*

Eurostat. (2005). *European Statistics Code of Practice. For the national and community statistical authorities.* Retrieved from: http://epp.eurostat.cec.eu.int/pls/portal/docs/page/pgp_ds_quality/-tab47141301/versione_inglese_web.pdf.

Eurostat (2000, April). *Assessment of the Quality in Statistics* (Eurostat/A4/Quality/00/General/Standard report). Luxembourg. Retrieved August, 2006, from: http://www.unece.org/stats/documents/2000/11/metis/crp.2.e.pdf.

Ewing, M., Caruana, A., & Zinkhan, G. M. (2002). On the cross-national generalisability and equivalence of advertising response scales developed in the USA. *International Journal of Advertising, 21*, 323–343.

Faden, R.R. & Beauchamp, T.L. (1986). A history and theory of nformed consent. New York: Oxford University Press.

Fellegi, I., & Ryten, J. (2005). The effectiveness of a supranational statistical office: Pluses, minuses, and challenges viewed from the outside. *Journal of Official Statistics, 21*, 145–170.

Fisher, R.A. (1938). Quotation from address to the First Indian Statistical Congress.

Flaherty, D. H. (1989). *Protecting privacy in surveillance societies: the federal republic of Germany, Sweden, France, Canada, and the US.* Chapel Hill, NC: University of North Carolina Press.

Fienberg, S.E. & Willenborg, L.C.R.J. (1998). Special issue on confidentiality of statistical data. *Journal of Official Statistics*, 14, 4.

Folsom, R. E., & Singh, A. C. (2000). The general exponential model for sampling weight calibration for extreme values, nonresponse, and poststratification. *Proceedings of the Survey Research Methods Section, 23,* 598–603.

Forsyth, B. H., & Hubbard, M. L. (1992, August). *A method for identifying cognitive properties of survey items.* Paper presented at the annual meeting of the American Statistical Association, Boston, MA.

Forsyth, B. H., & Lessler, J. T. (1991). Cognitive laboratory methods: A taxonomy. In P. P. Biemer, R. M. Groves, & L. E. Lyberg (Eds.), *Measurement errors in surveys*. New York: Wiley.

Forsyth, B. H., Rothgeb, J., & Willis, G. (2004). Does pretesting make a difference? In S. Presser, J. M. Rothgeb, M. P. Couper, J. T. Lessler, E. Martin, J. Martin, et al. (Eds.), *Methods for testing and evaluating survey questionnaires.* New York: Wiley.

Fowler, F. J. (2004). Getting beyond pretesting and cognitive interviews: The case for more experimental pilot studies. In S. Presser, J. M. Rothgeb, M. P. Couper, J. T. Lessler, E. Martin, J. Martin, et al. (Eds.), *Methods for testing and evaluating survey questionnaires.* New York: Wiley.

Fowler, F. J. (2001). Why it is easy to write bad questions. *ZUMA-Nachrichten, 48*, 49–66.

Fowler, F. J. (1997). Choosing questions to measure the quality of experience with medical providers and health plans. *ASA Proceedings of the section on Survey Research Methods, 20*, 51–54.

Fowler, F. J. (1995). *Improving Survey Questions: Design and evaluation.* Thousands Oaks, CA: Sage.

Fowler, F. J. (1992). How unclear terms affect survey data. *Public Opinion Quarterly, 56*, 218–231.

Fowler, F. J., & Cannell, C. F. (1996). Using behavioral coding to identify cognitive problems with survey questions. In N. Schwarz, & S. Sudman (Eds.), *Answering questions: Methodology for determining cognitive and communicative processes in survey research* (pp. 15–36). San Francisco: Jossey-Bass.

Fowler, F .J., Gallagher, P. M., Stringfellow, V. L., Zalavsky, A. M., Thompson, J. W., & Cleary, P. D. (2002). Using telephone interviews to reduce nonresponse bias to mail surveys of health plan members. *Medical Care, 40*, 190–200.

Fowler, F. J., & Mangione, T. W. (1990). *Standardized survey interviewing: Minimizing interviewer-related error.* Beverly Hills, CA: Sage Publications.

Fowler, F. J., & Mangione, T. W. (1986). *Reducing interviewer effects on health survey data.* Washington, DC: National Center for Health Services Research.

Fowler, F. J., & Mangione, T. W. (1984). Standardized survey interviewing. *ASA Proceedings of the Annual Meeting of the American Statistical Association.* Arlington, VA: ASA.

Fowler, F. J., & Mangione, T. W. (1982). The effect of training and supervision on common measures of field interviewer performance. *NCHSR Research Proceedings Series Health Survey Research Methods.* Arlington, VA: ASA.

Fox, J. A., & Tracy, P. E. (1986). *Randomized response: A method for sensitive surveys.* Newbury Park, CA: Sage.

Frey, J. H. (1989). *Survey research by telephone* (2nd ed.). Thousand Oaks, CA: Sage.

Friedrich-Freksa, M., & Liebelt, M. (2005, March). *From short message service (SMS) questionnaires to mobile internet surveys: Integrating the mobile phone into market research.* Paper presented at the Seventh International General Online Research Conference (GOR '05), Zurich, Switzerland.

Fuchs, M. (2005). Children and adolescents as respondents: Experiments on question order, response order, scale effects and the effect of numeric values associated to response options. *Journal of Official Statistics, 21*, 701–725.

Fuller, W. A. (1987). *Measurement error models.* New York: Wiley.

Gabler, S. & Häder, S. (2000). Überlegungen zur Anwendung von RLD-Verfahren bei Telefonumfragen in Deutschland. Pp. 33–47 in: V. Hüfgen, (Ed..), *Methoden in Telefonumfragen.* Opladen, FRG: Westdeutscher Verlag GmbH,

Gagné R., Briggs, L. J., & Wager, W. W. (1989). *Principles of instructional design.* New York: Holt, Rinehart, & Winston.

Gagné, R. (1962). The acquisition of knowledge. *Psychological Review, 69,* 355–365.

Gagné, R., Yekovich, C. W, & Yekovich, F. R. (1993). *The cognitive psychology of school learning.* New York: Harper Collins.

Gauthier, A. H. (2000).*The promises of comparative research.* Paper prepared for the European Panel Analysis Group. Retrieved June 23, 2006, from: http://www.iser.essex.ac.uk/-epag/pubs/workpaps/ pdf/2000-16.pdf.

Gaziano, C. (2005). Comparative analysis of within-household respondent selection techniques. *Public Opinion Quarterly, 69,* 124–157.

Geisinger, K. F. (1994). Cross-cultural normative assessment: Translation and adaptation issues influencing the normative interpretation of assessment instruments. *Psychological Assessment, 6,* 304–312.

Gelfand, A. E. & Smith, A. F. M. (1990). Sampling-based approaches to calculating marginal densities. *Journal of the American Statistical Association, 85,* 398–409.

Gelman, A., & Carlin, J. B. (2002). Poststratification and weighting adjustment. In R. M. Groves, D. A. Dillman, J. L. Eltinge, & R. J. A. Little (Eds.), *Survey nonresponse.* New York: Wiley.

Glynn, R., Laird, N. M., & Rubin, D. B. (1986). Selection modeling versus mixture modeling with nonignorable nonresponse. In H. Wainer (Ed.), *Drawing inferences from self-selected samples.* New York: Springer.

Goerman, P. L. (2006). *Adapting cognitive interview techniques for use in pretesting Spanish language survey instruments* (U.S. Census Bureau Research Report Series, Survey Methodology No. 2006-3). Retrieved June 20, 2006, from: http://www.census.gov/srd/ papers/pdf/rsm2006-03.pdf

Gonier, D. E. (1999). The emperor gets new clothes. In: *Towards validation: Online research day: An ARF emerging issue workshop* (pp. 8–13). New York: Advertising Research Foundation. Retrieved January 9, 2001, from: http://www.dmsdallas.com/emporere/emporer.html

Goode, W. J. (1973). *Explorations in social theory.* New York, etc.: Oxford University Press.

Goodwin, C. J. (2005). *Research in psychology: Methods and design* (4th ed). New York: Wiley.

Göritz, A. (2005). *Incentives in web-based studies: What to consider and how to decide* (WebSM Guide No. 2). Web Survey Methodology Site. Retrieved December 29, 2005, from: http://www.websm.org/uploadi/editor/goeritz2005-incentives.pdf

Graesser, A., Bommareddy, S., Swamer, S., & Golding, J. (1996). Integrating questionnaires design with a cognitive computational model of human question answering. In N. Schwarz & S. Sudman (Eds.), *Answering questions: Methodology for determining cognitive and communicative processes in survey research.* San Francisco: Jossey Bass.

Graesser, A., Kennedy, T., Wiemer-Hastings, P., & Ottati, V. (1999). The use of computational cognitive models to improve questions on surveys and questionnaires. In M. Sirken, D. Herrmann, S. Schechter, N. Schwarz, J. Tanur, and R. Tourangeau (Eds.), *Cognition and survey research.* New York: Wiley.

Gräf, L. (2002). Assessing internet questionnaires: The online pretest lab. In: B. Batinic, U. D. Reips, M. Bosnjak, & A. Werner (Eds.), *Online social sciences* (73–93). Hogrefe & Huber, Seattle.

Gray, P. G. (1955). The memory factor in social surveys. *Journal of the American Statistical Association, 50,* 344–363.

Greenfield, P. M. (1997). You can't take it with you: Why ability assessments don't cross cultures. *American Psychologist, 52,* 1115–1124.

Grembowski, D., & Phillips, D. (2005). *Linking mother and child access to dental care: A multimode survey.* (NIH-funded study, grant # DE 14400. SESRC data report No. 05-023). Pullman, WA: WSU.

Gribble, J. N., Miller, H. G., Cooley, P. C., Catania, J. A., Pollack, L. & Turner, C. F. (2000). The impact of T-ACASI interviewing on reporting drug use among men who have sex with men. *Substance Use and Misuse, 80,* 869–90.

Grice, H. P. (1975). Logic and conversation. In P. Cole & J. L. Morgan (Eds.), *Syntax and semantics, vol. 3: Speech acts.* New York: Academic Press.

Grice, P. (1989). *Studies in the way of words.* Cambridge, MA: Harvard University Press.

Grimshaw, A. D. (1973). Comparative Sociology: In what ways different from other Sociologies? In M. Armer, & A. D. Grimshaw (Eds.), *Comparative social research: Methodological problems and strategies*. New York: Wiley.

Groves, R. M. (in press). Research synthesis: Nonresponse bias. *Public Opinion Quarterly.*

Groves, R. M. (1989). *Survey errors and survey costs: An introduction to survey errors*. New York: Wiley.

Groves, R.M., Cialdini, R.B. & Couper, M.P. (1992). Understanding the decision to participate in a survey. *Public Opinion Quarterly, 56, 475–495.*

Groves, R. M., & Couper, M. P. (1998). *Nonresponse in household interview surveys*. New York: Wiley.

Groves, R. M., Dillman, D. A., Eltinge, J. L., & Little, R. J. A. (2002). *Survey nonresponse*. New York: Wiley.

Groves, R. M., Fowler, F. J., Couper, M. P., Lepkowski, J. M., Singer, E., & Tourangeau, R. (2004). *Survey methodology*. New York: Wiley.

Groves, R. M., & Kahn, R. (1979). *Surveys by telephone: A national comparison with personal interviews*. New York: Academic Press.

Groves, R. M., & Lepkowski, J. M. (1985). Dual frame, mixed mode survey designs. *Journal of Official Statistics, 1, 263–286.*

Groves, R. M., & McGonagle, K. (2001). A theory-guided interviewer training protocol regarding survey participation. *Journal of Official Statistics, 17, 249–265.*

Groves, R. M., Singer, E., & Corning, A. (2000). Leverage-saliency theory of survey participation: Description and an illustration. *Public Opinion Quarterly, 64, 299–308.*

Guest, L. (1954). A new training method for opinion interviewers. *Public Opinion Quarterly, 18, 287–299.*

Haberstroh, S., Oyserman, D., Schwarz, N., Kühnen, U., & Ji, L. J. (2001). Is the interdependent self more sensitive to question context than the independent self? Self-construal and the observation of conversational norms. *Journal of Experimental Social Psychology, 38, 323–329.*

Häder, S., & Gabler, S. (2003). Sampling and estimation. In J. A. Harkness, F. J. R. Van de Vijver, & P. Mohler (Eds.), *Cross-cultural survey methods*. Hoboken, NJ: Wiley.

Hall, T.E., & Roggenbuck, J.W. (2002). Response format effects in questions about norms: Implications for the reliability and validity of the normative approach. *Leisure Sciences, 24, 325–38.*

Hambleton, R. K. (2005). Issues, designs, and technical guidelines for adapting tests into multiple languages and cultures. In R. K. Hambleton, P. F. Merenda, & C. D. Spielberger (Eds.), *Adapting educational and psychological tests for cross-cultural assessment*. Mahwah, NJ: Erlbaum.

Hambleton, R. K., Merenda, P. F. & Spielberger, C. D. (Eds.) (2005). *Adapting educational and psychological tests for cross-cultural assessment*. Mahwah, NJ: Erlbaum.

Haney, C., Banks, C., & Zimbardo, P. (1973). Interpersonal dynamics in a simulated prison. *International Journal of Criminology and Penology, 1, 69–97.*

Hanh, V. T. X., Guillemin, F., Cong, D. D., Parkerson, G. R. Jr., Thu, P. B., Quynh, P. T., & Briançon, S. (2005). Health related quality of life of adolescents in Vietnam: Cross-cultural adaptation and validation of the Adolescent Duke Health Profile. *Journal of Adolescence, 28, 127–146.*

Hansen, M. H., Hurwitz, W. N., & Bershad, M. A. (2001). Measurement error in censuses and surveys. *Landmark papers in survey statistics. The IASS Jubilee Commemorative Volume.* International association of survey statisticians of the International Statistical Institute. (Original work published 1961)

Hansen, M. H., Hurwitz, W. N., & Bershad, M. A. (1961). Measurement errors in censuses and surveys. *Bulletin of the International Statistical Institute, 38, 359–374.*

Hansen, M. H., Madow, W. G., & Tepping, B. J. (1983). An evaluation of model-dependent and probability-sampling inferences in sample surveys. *Journal of the American Statistical Association, 78, 776–793.*

Hantrais, L., & Mangen, S. (1996). *Cross-national research methods in the social sciences.* London: Pinter.

Harkness, J.A. (2002/2007). ESS Translation Strategies and Procedures. Retrieved July 25, 2007, from European Social Survey site: www.europeansocialsurvey.org

Harkness, J. A. (2006a). *Round 3 ESS translation strategies and procedures.* Retrieved June 16, 2006, from: http://naticent02.uuhost.uk.uu.net/ess_docs/R3/Methodology/r3_translation_guidelines.doc.

Harkness, J. A. (2006b, July). *What happens when you start working on guidelines.* Keynote presentation at the Fifth International Test Commission Conference, Brussels, Belgium.

Harkness, J. A. (1999). In pursuit of quality: Issues for cross-national survey research. *International Journal of Social Research Methodology, 2,* 125–140.

Harkness, J. A., Langfeldt, B., & Scholz, E. (2001). *International social survey programme study monitoring 1996–1998.* Reports to the International Social Survey Programme General Assembly on Monitoring Work Undertaken for the International Social Survey Programme by Zentrum für Umfragen, Methoden und Analysen, Germany.

Harkness, J.A., Mohler, P.Ph., and van de Vijver, F.J.R. (2003) in Harkness, J.A., van de Vijver, F.J.R. & Mohler, P.Ph. (Eds.). *Cross-Cultural Survey Methods.* Hoboken, New Jersey: Wiley. p. 3–16.

Harkness, J. A., Pennell, B. E. ,& Schoua-Glusberg, A. (2004). Survey questionnaire translation and assessment. In S. Presser, J. Rothgeb, M. P. Couper, J. T. Lessler, E. Martin, J. Martin, & E. Singer (Eds.), *Methods for testing and evaluating survey questionnaires.* Hoboken, NJ: Wiley.

Harkness, J. A., Schoebi, N., Joye, D., Mohler, P., Faass, T., Behr, D. (2007) Oral translation in telephone surveys (in press). J. Lepkowski, C. Tucker, M. Brick, E. de Leeuw, L. Japec, P. Lavrakas, et al. (Eds.), *Advances in telephone survey methodology.* New York: Wiley.

Harkness, J. A., & Schoua-Glusberg, A. (1998). Questionnaires in translation. In J. A. Harkness (Ed.), *ZUMA-Nachrichten Spezial No. 3. Cross-Cultural Survey Equivalence.* Mannheim: ZUMA.

Harkness, J. A., Van de Vijver, F. J. R., & Johnson, T. P. (2003). Questionnaire design in comparative research. In J. A. Harkness, F. J. R. van de Vijver & P. Mohler (Eds.), *Cross-cultural survey methods.* Hoboken, NJ: Wiley.

Harkness, J. A., Van de Vijver, F. J. R., & Mohler, P. (2003). *Cross-cultural survey methods.* New York: Wiley.

Harmon, M., Westin, E., & Levin, K. (2005, May). *Does type of pre-notification affect web survey response rates?* Paper presented at the American Association for Public Opinion Research 60th Annual Conference, Miami Beach, FL.

Harris-Kojetin, L. D., Fowler, F. J., Brown, J. A., Schnaier, J. A., & Sweeny, S. F. (1999). The use of cognitive testing to develop and evaluate CAHPS 1.0 core survey items. *Medical Care, 37,* Supplement, MS10-MS21.

Haworth, M., & Signore, M. (2005, April). *Quality measurement and reporting: Frameworks, guidelines and user needs.* Invited paper for the ISI meeting, Sydney, Australia.

Headland, T. N., Pike, K. L., & Harris, M. (1990). *Emics and etics: The insider / outsider debate.* Newbury Park, CA.: Sage.

Heath, A., & Martin, J. (1977). Why are there so few formal measuring instruments in social and political research?. In L. Lyberg, P., Biemer, M. Collins, E. de Leeuw, C. Dippo, N. Schwarz, & D. Trewin (Eds.), *Survey measurement and process quality* (71–86). New York: Wiley.

Heberlein, T. A., & Baumgartner, R. M. (1978). Factors affecting response rates to mailed questionnaires: A quantitative analysis of the published literature. *American Sociological Review, 43,* 447–462.

Heckman, J. J. (1976). The common structure of statistical models of truncation, sample selection and limited dependent variables and a simple estimator for such models. *Annals of Economic and Social Measurement, 5,* 475–492.

Heerwegh, D., & Loosveldt, G. (2002). Web surveys: The effect of controlling survey access using PIN numbers. *Social Science Computer Review, 20,* 10–21.

Heitjan, D. F., & Little, R. J. A. (1991). Multiple imputation for the fatal accident reporting system. *Journal of the Royal Statistical Society C, 40,* 13–29.

Herdman, M., Fox-Rushby, J., & Badia, X. (1997). 'Equivalence' and the translation and adaptation of health-related quality of life questionnaires. *Quality of Life Research, 6,* 237–247.

Herr, P. M. (1986). Consequences of priming: Judgment and behavior. *Journal of Personality and Social Psychology, 51,* 1106–1115.

Hert, C., Denn, S., & Haas, S. W. (2004). The role of metadata in the statistical knowledge network: An emerging research agenda. *Social Science Computer Review, 22,* 92–99.

Hess, J., Singer, E., & Bushery, J. (1999). Predicting test-retest reliability from behavior coding. *International Journal of Public Opinion Research, 11,* 346–360.

Hill, T. P. (1998). *The first digit phenomena.* Retrieved from: http://www.math.gatech.edu/~hill/-publications/cv.dir/1st-dig.pdf.

Himmelfarb, S., & Lickteig, C. (1982). Social desirability and the randomized response technique. *Journal of Personality and Social Psychology, 43,* 710–717.

Hippler, H.-J., & Seidel, K. (1985). Schriftliche Befragung bei algemeine Bevolkerungs-stichproben– Untersuchungen zur Dillman'schen 'Total Design Method'. *ZUMA-Nachrichten, 16*. Mannheim: ZUMA

Ho, D. (2003). *"Do-not-call" still a big hit.* Retrieved November 14, 2005, from: http://www.cbsnews.com/stories/2003/03/11/politics/main543573.shtml.

Hochstim, J. R. (1967). A critical comparison of three strategies of collecting data from households. *Journal of the American Statistical Association, 62,* 976–989.

Hoffmeyer-Zlotnik, J. H. P. (1997). Random Route Stichproben nach ADM. In S. Gabler & J. H. P. Hoffmeyer-Zlotnik (Eds.), *Stichproben in derUmfragepraxis*. Opladen: Westdeutscher Verlag.

Hoffmeyer-Zlotnik, J. H. P., & Harkness, J. A. (Eds.), (2005) *ZUMA-Nachrichten Spezial No. 11. Methodological aspects in cross-national research*. Mannheim: ZUMA.

Hoffmeyer-Zlotnik, J. H. P., & Wolf, C. (Eds.) (2003). *Advances in cross-national comparison. A European working book for demographic and socio-economic variables.* New York: Kluwer Academic/Plenum Publishers.

Holt, D., & Jones, T. (1998). *Quality work and conflicting quality objectives.* Paper prepared for DGINS meeting, Eurostat., May 2005.

Hoogendoorn, A. W. & Sikkel, D. (1998). Response burden and panel attrition. *Journal of Official Statistics, 14,* 189–205.

Hox, J. J. (2002). *Multilevel analysis: Techniques and applications*. Mahwah, N.J.: Erlbaum.

Hox, J. J. (1997). From theoretical concept to survey item. In: L. Lyberg, P. Biemer, M. Collins, E. de Leeuw, C. Dippo, N. Schwarz, & D. Trewin (Eds), *Survey Measurement and Process Quality* (47–71). New York: Wiley.

Hox, J. J., & De Jong-Gierveld, J. J. (Eds.) (1990). *Operationalization and research strategy.* Lisse, NL: Swets & Zeitlinger.

Hox, J. J. & De Leeuw, E. D. (1994). A comparison of nonresponse in mail, telephone, and face-to-face surveys. Applying multilevel modeling to meta-analysis. *Quality & Quantity,* 329-344.

Hox, J. J., De Leeuw, E. D., & Kreft, G. G. (1991). The effect of interviewer and respondent characteristics on the quality of survey data: a multilevel model. In P. P. Biemer, R. M. Groves, L. E. Lyberg, N. A. Mathiowetz, & S. Sudman (Eds.), *Measurement Errors in Surveys*. New York: Wiley.

Hoyle, R. H., Harris, M. J., & Judd, C. M. (2002). *Research methods in social relations.* London: Wadsworth.

http://news.com.com/Start-up+aims+to+join+telephone%2C+wireless+calls/2100-1033_3-5950752.html.

Hughes, L. C., & Preski, S. (1997). Using key informant methods in organizational survey research: Assessing for informant bias. *Research in Nursing and Health, 20,* 81–92.

Humphreys, L. (1970). *Tearoom trade: Impersonal sex in public places.* Chicago: Aldine.

Hunt, S. D., Sparkman, R. D. Jr., & Wilcox, J. B. (1982). The pretest in survey research: Issues and preliminary findings. *Journal of Marketing Research, 19,* 269–273.

Hyman, H. H. (1955). *Survey design and analysis.* Glencoe: Free Press.

International Standards Organization. (2006). *Standards for Marketing, Opinion and Social Research* (ISO Standard 20252: 2006). Retrieved from: http://www.iso.org/iso/-en/CatalogueDetailPage.CatalogueDetail?CSNUMBER=39339&ICS1=1&ICS2=40&ICS3=3.

International Working Group for Disease Monitoring and Forecasting, (1995). Capture-recapture and multiple-record systems estimation. *American Journal of Epidemiology, 142,* 1047–1058.

Jabine, T., King, K., & Petroni, R. (1990). *Quality profile for the Survey of Income and Program Participation (SIPP).* Washington, DC: U.S. Bureau of the Census.

Jabine, T., Straf, M., Tanur, J., & Tourangeau, R. (Eds.). (1984). *Cognitive aspects of survey methodology: Building a bridge between disciplines.* Washington, DC: National Academy Press.

Jackson, C. P., & Boyle, J. M. (1991). Mail response rate improvement in a mixed-mode survey. *Proceedings ASA-SMRS: American Statistical Association.* Retrieved April 14, 2005, from: www.amstat.org/sections/srms/proceedings/.

Japec, L. (2005). *Quality issues in interview surveys: some contributions*. Stockholm: Department of Statistics, University of Stockholm.

Javeline, D. (1999). Response effects in polite cultures: A test of acquiescence in Kazakhstan. *Public Opinion Quarterly, 63,* 1–28.

Jenkins, C., & Dillman, D. A. (1997). Towards a theory of self-administered questionnaire design. In L. Lyberg, P. Biemer, M. Collins, E. de Leeuw, K. Dippo, N. Schwarz, et al. (Eds.), *Survey measurement and process quality*. New York: Wiley.

Jensen, U., & Rässler, S. (2006). Stochastic production frontiers with multiply imputed German establishment data. *Zeitschrift für Arbeitsmarktforschung, 39*, 277–295..

Ji, L., Schwarz, N., & Nisbett, R. E. (2000). Culture, autobiographical memory, and behavioral frequency reports: Measurement issues in cross-cultural studies. *Personality and Social Psychology Bulletin, 26*, 586–594.

Johnson, T. P. (1998). Approaches to equivalence in cross-cultural and cross-national survey research. In J. A. Harkness (Ed.), *ZUMA-Nachrichten Spezial No. 3.: Cross-cultural survey equivalence*. Mannheim: ZUMA.

Johnson, T. P., & Van de Vijver, F. J. R. (2003). Social desirability in cross-cultural research. In J. A. Harkness, F. J. R. van de Vijver, & P. Mohler (Eds.), *Cross-cultural survey methods*. Hoboken, NJ: Wiley.

Johnson, T. P., Kulesa, P., Cho, Y. I., & Shavitt, S. (2005). The relation between culture and response styles: Evidence from 19 countries. *Journal of Cross-Cultural Psychology, 36*, 264–277.

Jöreskog, K. G. (1971). Statistical analysis of sets of congeneric tests. *Psychometrika, 34*, 183–202.

Jowell, R. (1998). How comparative is comparative research? *American Behavioral Scientist, 42*, 168–177.

Juran, J. M., & Gryna, F. M. Jr. (1980). *Quality planning and analysis: From product development through use*. New York,: McGraw-Hill.

Jussaume, R. A. & Yamada, Y. (1990). A comparison of the viability of mail surveys in Japan and the United States. *Public Opinion Quarterly, 54*, 219–228.

Kaczmirek, L., Neubarth, W., Bosnjak, M., & Bandilla, W. (2005, March). *Progress indicators in filter based surveys. Individual and dynamic calculation methods.* Paper presented at General Online Research Conference 2005, Zurich, Switzerland.

Kalton, G. (1977). Practical methods for estimating survey sampling errors. *Bulletin of the International Statistical Institute, 47*, 495–514.

Kalton, G. (1983). *Introduction to survey sampling*. Thousand Oaks, CA: Sage

Kalton, G. (1986). Handling wave nonresponse in panel surveys. *Journal of Official Statistics, 2*, 303–314.

Kalton, G. (2000). Developments in survey research in the past 25 years. *Survey Methodology, 26*, 3–10.

Kalton, G., & Anderson, D. W. (1986). Sampling rare populations. *Journal of the Royal Statistical Society, Series A, 149*, 65–82.

Kalton, G., Winglee, M., Krawchuk, S., & Levine, D. (2000). *Quality Profile for SASS: Rounds 1-3: 1987–1995* (NCES 2000-308). Washington, DC: U.S. Department of Education, National Center for Education Statistics.

Kanso, A. (2000). Mail surveys: key factors affecting response rates. *Journal of Promotion Management, 5, 2*, 3–16.

Kaplowitz, M. D., Hadlock, T. D., & Levine, R. (2004). A comparison of web and mail survey response rates. *Public Opinion Quarterly, 68*, 94–101.

Kasprzyk, D., Duncan, G., Kalton, G., & Singh, M. P. (1989). *Panel surveys*. New York: John Wiley and Sons.

Kasprzyk, D., & Kalton, G. (2001, May). *Quality profiles in U.S. statistical agencies.* Paper presented at the International Conference on Quality in Official Statistics, Stockholm, Sweden.

Katz, J. (1972). *Experimenting with human beings*. New York: Russell Sage.

Kennickell, A. B. (1991). Imputation of the 1989 survey of consumer finances: Stochastic relaxation and multiple imputation (with discussion). *Proceedings of the Section on Survey Research Methods, 14*, 1–10.

Kerlinger, F. N. (1986). *Foundations of behavioral research*. New York: Holt, Rinehart & Winston.

Killworth, P. D., Johnsen, E. C., McCarthy, C., Shelley, G. A., & Bernard, H. R. (1998). A social network approach to estimating seropositive prevalence in the US. *Social Networks, 18*, 289–312.

Kim, M. (1994). Cross-cultural comparisons of the perceived importance of conversational constraints. *Human communication Research, 21*, 128–151.

Kish, L (1995). *Survey sampling*. New York: Classic Wiley Paperback, Wiley (original work published 1965).

Kish, L. (1992). Weighting for unequal P_i. *Journal of Official Statistics, 8*, 183–200.

Kish, L. (1987). *Statistical design for research*. New York: Wiley.

Kish, L. (1965). *Survey sampling*. New York: Wiley.

Kish, L. (1962). Studies of interviewer variance for attitudinal variables. *Journal of the American Statistical Association, 57*, 92–115.

Kish, L. & Frankel, M.R. (1974). Inferences from complex samples. *Journal of the Royal Statistical Society (B)*, *36*, 1–37.

Kittleson, M. J. (1997). Determining effective follow-up of e-mail surveys. *American Journal of Health Behavior*, *21*, 193–196.

Kline, R. B. (2005). *Principles and practice of Structural Equation Modeling*. New York/London: The Guildford Press.

Knapp, F., & Heidingsfelder, M. (2001). Drop-out analysis: Effects of the survey design. In U. D. Reips, & M. Bosnjak (Eds.), *Dimensions of internet science*. Lengerich: Pabst Science Publishers.

Knäuper, B. (1999a). Age differences in question and response order effects. In N. Schwarz, D. Park, B. Knäuper, & S. Sudman (Eds.), *Cognition, aging, and self-reports* . Philadelphia: Psychology Press.

Knäuper, B. (1999b). The impact of age and education on response order effects in attitude measurement. *Public Opinion Quarterly, 63*, 347–370.

Knäuper, B., Schwarz, N., & Park, D. (2004). Frequency reports across age groups. *Journal of Official Statistics, 20*, 91–96.

Kohn, M. L. (1987). Cross-national research as an analytic strategy: American Sociological Association, 1987 Presidential Address. *American Sociological Review, 52*, 713–731.

Kripke, D. F., Garfinkel, L., Wingard, D. L., Klauber, M. R., & Marler, M. R. (2002). Mortality associated with sleep duration and insomnia. *Archives of General Psychiatry, 59*, 131–136.

Krosnick, J. A. (1991). Response strategies for coping with cognitive elements of attitude measures in surveys. *Applied Cognitive Psychology, 5*, 213–236.

Krosnick, J. A., & Alwin, D. F. (1987). An evaluation of a cognitive theory of response order effects in survey measurement. *Public Opinion Quarterly, 51*, 201–19.

Krosnick, J. A., & Fabrigar, L. (1997). Comparisons of party identification and policy preferences: The impact of survey question format. *American Journal of Political Science, 37*, 941–964.

Krotki, K. P. (2001, August). *Web-based surveys for a nationally representative sample*. Paper presented at Joint Statistical Meeting, Atlanta, GA.

Kuk, A.Y. S. (1990). Asking sensitive questions indirectly. *Biometrica, 77*, 436–438.

Kuusela, V. (2003, September). Mobile phones and telephone survey methods. In R. Banks, J. Currall, J. Francis, L. Gerrard, R. Kahn, T. Macer, et al. (2003). *Proceedings of the fourth ASC international conference*. Chesham, UK: ASC.

Kuusela, V., & Simpanen, M. (2002). *Effects of mobile phones on telephone survey practices and results*. Paper presented at the International Conference on Improving Surveys, Copenhagen, Denmark. Retrieved November 16, 2005, from: http://www.icis.dk/ICIS_papers/A_2_3.pdf.

Kvale, S. (1996). *Interviews: An introduction to qualitative research interviewing*. Thousand Oaks, CA: Sage.

Kwak, N., & Radler, B. T. (2002). A comparison between mail and web surveys: response pattern, respondent profile, and data quality. *Journal of Official Statistics, 18*, 257–274.

Kwak, N., & Radler, B. T. (1999, November). *A comparison between mail and web-based surveys: Response pattern, data quality, and characteristics of respondents*. Paper presented at 1999 Annual Research Conference, organised by Midwest Association for Public Opinion Research, Chicago, IL.

Lahiri, S.N. (2003). *Resampling methods for dependent data*. New York: Springer-Verlag.

Laiho, J. (2005, April). *Discussion of session on quality measurement and reporting for surveys*. Paper presented at the ISI meeting, Sydney, Australia.

Laiho, J., & Lynn, P. (1999, October). *Separating the stages of the survey co-operation process*. Paper presented at the International Conference on Household Survey Nonresponse, Portland Oregon.

Lang, S. (2004). Randomized response: Befragungstechniken zur vermeidung von verzerrungen by sensitiven fragen. Munchen: Universität München.

LaPlant, W. P. Jr., Lestina, G. J. Jr., Gillman, D. W., & Appel, M. V. (1996, March). *Proposal for a Statistical Metadata Standard*. Paper presented at the Census Annual Research Conference, Arlington, VA.

Lau, L. K. P. (2004, August). *Mobile phone surveys in Hong Kong: Methodological issues and comparisons with conventional telephone surveys*. Paper presented at the RC33 Sixth Annual Conference on Social Science Methodology, Amsterdam, The Netherlands.

Lavrakas, P. J. (2004, May). *Will a 'perfect storm' of cellular-linked forces sink RDD sampling?* Paper presented at the Fifty-Ninth Annual Conference of the American Association for Public Opinion Research, Phoenix, AZ.

Lavrakas, P. J. (1987). *Telephone survey methods: Sampling, selection and supervision*. Newbury

Park, CA: Sage Publications.

Lee, E. S., Forthofer, R. N., & Lorimor, R. J. (1989). *Analyzing complex survey data*. Newbury Park, CA: Sage Publications.

Lee, H., Rancourt, E, & Särndal, C. E. (2002). Variance estimation for survey data under single imputation. In R. M. Groves, D. A. Dillman, J. L. Eltinge, & R. J. A. Little (Eds.), *Survey nonresponse*. New York: Wiley.

Lee, R. M. (1993). *Doing research on sensitive topics*. London: Sage Publications.

Lee, R. M., & Renzetti, C. M. (1993). *The problems of researching sensitive topics: An overview and introduction*. In C. M. Renzetti & R. M. Lee (Eds.), *Researching sensitive topics*. Newbury Park, CA: Sage.

Lee, S. (2006). Propensity score adjustment as a weighting scheme for volunteer panel web surveys. *Journal of Official Statistics, 22*,2, 329–349. Also available at www.jos.nu.

Lehtonen, R., & Pahkinen, E. (2004). *Practical methods for design and analysis of complex surveys* (2nd ed.). New York: Wiley.

Lensvelt-Mulders, G. J. L. M., Hox, J. J., & Van der Heijden, P. G. M. (2005). How to improve the efficiency of randomized response designs. *Quality and Quantitiy, 39*, 253–265.

Lensvelt-Mulders, G. J. L. M., Hox, J. J., Van der Heijden, P. G. M., & Maas, C. J. M. (2005). Meta-analysis of randomized response research: 35 Years of validation studies. *Sociological methods and research, 33,* 319–348.

Lepkowski, J. M. (2005). Non-observation error in household surveys in developing countries. In United Nations, *Household sample surveys in developing transition countries* (pp.140-170). New York: United Nations. Retrieved July 21, 2006 from: http://unstats.un.org/unsd/hhsurveys/pdf/-Household_surveys.pdf.

Lepkowski, J. M. (1988). Telephone sampling methods in the United States. In R. M. Groves, P. P. Biemer, L. E. Lyberg, J. T. Massey, W. L. Nicholls II, & J. Waksberg (Eds.), *Telephone survey methodology*. New York: John Wiley and Sons.

Lesser, V. M., & Newton, L. (2001, May). *Mail, e-mail and web surveys: A cost and response rate comparison in a study of undergraduate research activity*. Paper presented at 2001 Association for Public Opinion Research Annual Conference, Montreal, Quebec, Canada.

Lessler, J. T., & Forsyth, B. H. (1996). A coding system for appraising questionnaires. In N. Schwarz & S. Sudman (Eds.), *Answering questions: Methodology for determining cognitive and communicative processes in survey research*. San Francisco: Jossey Bass.

Lessler, J. T., & Kalsbeek, W. (1992). *Nonsampling errors in surveys*. New York: Wiley.

Linacre, S. J., & Trewin, D. J. (1993). Total survey design: Application to a collection of the construction industry. *Journal of Official Statistics, 9*, 611–621.

Link, M. W., & Mokdad, A. H. (2004, May). *Responding to the national do not call registry: Evaluation of call attempt protocol changes in the BRFSS*. Paper presented at the fifty-ninth annual conference of the American Association for Public Opinion Research, Phoenix, AZ.

Link, M. W., & Oldendick, R. (1999). Call screening. *Public Opinion Quarterly, 63*, 577–589.

Linton, M. (1982). Transformations of memory in everyday life. In U. Neisser (Ed.), *Memory observed: Remembering in natural contexts*. San Francisco: Freeman.

Lipset, S. M. (1986). Historical traditions and national characteristics: A comparative analysis of Canada and the United States. *Canadian Journal of Sociology, 11*, 113–155.

Little, R. J. A. (2004). To model or not to model? Competing modes of inference for finite population sampling. *Journal of the American Statistical Association, 99*, 546–556.

Little, R. J. A. (1993). Pattern-mixture models for multivariate incomplete data. *Journal of the American Statistical Association, 88*, 125–134.

Little, R. J. A. (1988). Missing data adjustments in large surveys. *Journal of Business and Economic Statistics, 6,* 287–301.

Little, R. J. A., & Rubin, D. B. (2002). *Statistical analysis with missing data* (2nd ed.). New York: Wiley.

Little, R. J. A., & Rubin, D. B. (1987). *Statistical analysis with missing data*. New York: Wiley.

Lobel, T. E., & Teiber, A. (1994). Effect of self-esteem and need for approval on affective and cognitive reactions: Defense and true self-esteem. *Personality and Individual Differences, 16*, 315–321.

Loftus, E., Smith, K. D., Klinger, M. R., & Fiedler, J. (1991). Memory and mismemory for health events. In J. Tanur (Ed.), *Questions and questions* (102–137). New York: Russell Sage Foundation.

Lohr, S. L. (1999). *Sampling: Design and analysis*. Pacific Grove, CA: Duxbury Press.

Lohr, S. L., & Rao, J. N. K. (2000). Inference in dual frame surveys. *Journal of the American*

Statistical Association, 95, 271–280.

Lozar Manfreda, K. (1999, December). *Participation in web surveys*. Paper presented at 9th international meeting dissertation research in psychometrics and sociometrics. Oegstgeest, The Netherlands.

Lozar Manfreda, K., Bosjnak, M., Berzelak, J., Haas. I., Vehovar, V. (in press). Web surveys versus other survey modes: A meta-analysis comparing response rates. *International Journal of Market Research*.

Lozar Manfreda, K., Vehovar, V., & Batagelj, Z. (2001). Web versus mail questionnaire for an institutional survey. In A. Westlake, W. Sykes, T. Manners, & M. Rigg. (Eds.), *The Challenge of the Internet: Proceedings of the 2nd ASC International Conference on Survey Research Methods*. Berkeley, UK: Association for Survey Computing.

Luppes, M. (1995). A content analysis of advance letters from expenditure surveys of seven countries. *Journal of Official Statistics, 11*, 461–480.

Lyberg, L. E. (2006, August). *Quality assurance in comparative studies*. Paper presented at the 2006 Joint Statistical Meetings, Seattle, VA.

Lyberg, L. E., Biemer, P. P., Collins, M., De Leeuw, E. D., Dippo, C., Schwarz, N., & Trewin, D. (Eds) (1997). *Survey measurement and process quality*. New York: Wiley.

Lyberg, L. E., & Couper, M. (2005, April). *The use of paradata in survey research*. Invited paper presented at the ISI meeting in Sydney, Australia.

Lyberg, L. E., & Dean, P. (1992, May). *Methods of reducing nonresponse rates: A review*. Paper presented at the American Association for Public Opinion Research Conference (AAPOR), St. Petersburg, FL.

Lynn, P. (2003). Developing quality standards for cross-national survey research: Five approaches. *International Journal of Social Research Methodology, 6*, 323–336.

Lynn, P. (2003). PEDAKSI: Methodology for collecting data about survey non-respondents. *Quality and Quantity, 37*, 239–262.

Lynn, P. (1996). Weighting for nonresponse. In Association for Statistical Computing, *Survey and Statistical Computing 1996*. Berkeley, U.K.: Association for Statistical Computing.

Lynn, P., Beerten, R., Laiho, J., & Martin, J. (2002). Towards standardization of survey outcome categories and response rate calculations. *Research in Official Statistics, 9*, 61–85.

Lynn, P., Beerten, R., Laiho, J., & Martin, J. (2001). *Recommended standard final outcome categories and standard definitions of response rate for social surveys* (Working paper of the Institute for Social and Economic Research, 2001-23). Colchester: University of Essex. Retrieved from: http://www.iser.essex.ac.uk/pubs/workpaps/pdf/2001-23.pdf.

Lynn, P., Häder, S., Gabler, S., & Laaksonen, S. (2007). Methods for achieving equivalence of samples in cross-national surveys. *Journal of Official Statistics, 23*, 107-124.

Lynn, P., Lyberg, L., & Japec, L. (2006). What's so special about cross-national surveys? In J. A. Harkness (Ed.), *ZUMA-Nachrichten Spezial No. 12. Conducting cross-national and cross-cultural surveys*. Mannheim: ZUMA

Macer, T. (2003). We seek them here, we seek them there. How technological innovation in mixed mode survey software is responding to the challenges of finding elusive respondents. In R. Banks (Ed.), *Survey and statistical computing IV. The impact of technology on the survey process*. Association for Survey Computing. See also: Macer, T. (2004). CAWI and CATI: Software reviews. In *Quirks Marketing Review*. Retrieved April 15, 2005, from: www.meaning.uk.com.quirks/09.html.

Macer, T. (2001). Net development. *Research, the Magazine of the Market Research Society, 422*. Retrieved August 2006, from: http://www.meaning.uk.com/arts/55.html.

Maddala, G. S. (1983) *Limited dependent and qualitative variables in econometrics*. Cambridge, MA: Cambridge University Press.

Madow, W. G., Nisselson, H., & Olkin, I. (1983). *Incomplete data in sample surveys, volume 1: Report and case studies*. New York: Academic Press.

Madow, W. G. & Olkin, I. (1983). *Incomplete data in sample surveys, volume 3: Proceedings of the symposium*. New York: Academic Press.

Madow, W. G., Olkin, I., & Rubin, D. B. (1983). *Incomplete data in sample surveys, volume 2: Theory and bibliographies*. New York: Academic Press.

Malhotra, Y. (2001). Expert systems for knowledge management: Crossing the chasm between information processing and sense making. *Expert Systems with Applications, 20*, 7–16.

Mangione, T. W., Fowler, F. J., & Louis, T. A. (1992). Question characteristics and interviewer effects. *Journal of Official Statistics, 8*, 293–307.

Marquis, K. H., & Cannell, C. F. (1969). *A study of interviewer-respondent interaction in the urban employment survey*. Ann Arbor, MI: Survey Research Center, Institute for Social Research, University of Michigan.

Marshall G., Rose D., Vogler C., & Newby H.(1988). *Social class in modern Britain*. London: Hutchinson.

Mason, R., Carlson, J., & Tourangeau, R. (1994). Contrast effects and subtraction in part-whole questions. *Public Opinion Quarterly, 58*, 569–578.

Massey, J. T. (1995). Estimating the response rate in a telephone survey with screening. *Proceedings of the section on survey research methods, 18*, 673–677.

Massey, J. T., & Botman, S. (1988). Weighting adjustments for random digit dialed surveys. In R. Groves, P. P. Biemer, L. E. Lyberg, J. T. Massey, W. L. Nichols II, & J. Waksberg (Eds.), *Telephone survey methodology* (143–160). New York: Wiley.

Mathiowetz, N. A., & McGonagle, K. A. (2000). An assessment of the current state of dependent interviewing. *Journal of Official Statistics, 16*, 401–418.

Matsuo, H., McIntyre, K. P., Tomazic, T., & Katz, B. (2004). The online survey: Its contributions and potential problems. *ASA Proceedings of the Section on Survey Rersearch Methods, 27*, 3998–4000.

Mayer, C. E. (2004). In 1 year, do-not-call list passes 62 million: Complaints about telemarketers pile up. *Washington Post*, June 24, E05. Retrieved November 14, 2005, from: http://www.washingtonpost.com/wp-dyn/articles/A767-2004Jun23.html.

Mayer, T. S., & O'Brien, E. (2001). Interviewer refusal aversion training to increase survey participation. *ASA Proceedings of the Annual Meeting of the American Statistical Association.* Arlington, VA: ASA

McConaghy, M., & Carey, S (2004, May). *Training to help interviewers avoid refusals: Results of stage 1 of a pilot using Avoiding Refusal Training (ART) with interviewers at the Office for National Statistics, UK*. Paper presented at the 2004 Annual Meeting of the American Association for Public Opinion Research, Phoenix, AZ.

McKenna, S. P., Doward, L. C. (2005). The translation and cultural adaptation of patient-reported outcome measures. *Value in Health, 8*(2), 89–104.

McLachlan, G. J., & Krishnan, T. (1997). *The EM algorithm and extensions*. New York: Wiley.

McMahon, S. R., Iwamoto, M., Massoudi, M. S., Yusuf, H. R., Stevenson, J. M., Davod, F., Chu, S. Y., & Pickering, L. K. (2003). Comparison of e-mail, fax, and postal surveys of pediatricians. *Pediatrics, 111*, 299–303.

Medical Outcomes Trust Bulletin. (1997). Approaches to instrument translation: Issues to consider. *Medical Outcomes Trust Bulletin, 5*(4). Retrieved June 25, 2006 from: http://www.outcomes-trust.org/bulletin/0797blltn.htm.

Mehta, R., & Sivadas, E. (1995). Comparing response rates and response content in mail versus electronic mail surveys. *Journal of the Market Research Society, 37*, 429–439.

Mejer, L. (2003). Harmonization of socio-economic variables in EU statistics. In J. H. P. Hoffmeyer-Zlotnik, & C. Wolf (Eds.), *Advances in cross-national comparison. A European working book for demographic and socio-economic variables*. New York: Kluwer Academic / Plenum Publishers.

Meng, X. L. (1994). Multiple-imputation inferences with uncongenial sources of input (with discussion). *Statistical Science, 9*, 538–573.

Menon, G. (1994). Judgments of behavioral frequencies: Memory search and retrieval strategies. In N. Schwarz & S. Sudman, S. (Eds.), *Autobiographical memory and the validity of retrospective reports*. New York: Springer Verlag.

Menon, G., Rhagubir, P., & Schwarz, N. (1995). Behavioral frequency judgments: An accessibility-diagnosticity framework. *Journal of Consumer Research, 22*, 212–228.

Milgram, S. (1963). Behavioral study of obedience. *Journal of Abnormal and Social Psychology, 67*, :371–378.

Miller, K. (2003). Conducting cognitive interviews to understand question-response limitations among poorer and less educated respondents. *American Journal of Health Behavior, 27*, 264–272.

Mingay, D. J., & Kim, R. (1998). *Using cognitive and traditional methods to develop an automated telephone administered questionnaire*. Paper presented at the Annual Meeting of the American Association for Public Opinion Research, St. Louis, MO.

Mingay, D. M. (2000). Is telephone audio computer-assisted self-interviewing (T-ACASI) a method whose time has come? *Proceedings of the section on survey research methods, 23*, 1062–1067.

Mislevy, R. J. (1991). Randomization-based inference about latent variables from complex samples. *Psychometrika, 56*, 177–196.

Mislevy, R. J., Johnson, E. G., & Muraki, E. (1992). Scaling procedures in NAEP. *Journal of*

Educational Statistics, 17, 131–154.

Mohler, P., & Uher, R. (2003). Documenting comparative surveys for secondary analysis. In J. A. Harkness, F. J. R. van de Vijver & P. Mohler (Eds.), *Cross-cultural survey methods*. Hoboken, NJ: Wiley.

Molitor, F., Kravitz, R.L., To, Y.-Y., & Fink, A. (2001). Methods in survey research: Evidence for the reliability of group administration vs. personal interviews. *American Journal of Public Health, 91*, 826–827.

Montgomery, D. (2005). *Introduction to statistical quality control*. New York: Wiley.

Moon, Y. (1998). Impression management in computer-based interviews: The effects of input modality, output modality and distance. *Public Opinion Quarterly, 62,* 610–622

Moran, J., & Biemer, P. (2004, December). Quality assurance and quality management for survey research. *Proceedings of the Federal Committee on Survey Methodology Conference, Washington, D.C.*

Morgan, D. L. (1988). *Focus groups as qualitative research*. Thousand Oaks, CA: Sage.

Morganstein, D. R., & Marker, D. A. (1997). Continuous quality improvement in statistical agencies. In L. Lyberg, P. Biemer, M. Collins, E. de Leeuw, C. Dippo, N. Schwarz., et al. (Eds.), *Survey measurement and process quality*. New York: Wiley.

Morton-Williams, J. (1979). The use of "verbal interaction coding" for evaluating a questionnaire. *Quality and Quantity, 13*, 59–75.

Morton-Williams, J. (1993). *Interviewer approaches*. Aldershot, U.K.: Dartmouth Publishing.

Moskowitz, J. M. (2004). Assessment of cigarette smoking and smoking susceptibility among youth: Telephone computer-assisted self-interviews versus computer-assisted telephone interviews. *Public Opinion Quarterly, 68*, 565–587.

Mudryk, W., Bougie, B., Xiao, P., & Yeung, A. (2001). *Statistical methods in quality control at Statistics Canada*. Course Reference Materials, Statistics Canada, Ottawa.

Münnich, R., & Rässler, S. (2005). PRIMA: A new multiple imputation procedure for binary variables. *Journal of Official Statistics, 21*, 325–341.

Nathan, G. (2001). Telesurvey methodologies for household surveys—a review and some thoughts for the future? *Survey Methodology, 27*, 7–31.

National Center for Health Statistics. (1989). *Questionnaire design in the cognitive research laboratory, Series 6: Cognition and survey measurement, no 1* (DHHS Publication No. PHS 89-1076). Hyattsville, MD: US Department of Health and Human Services.

National Center for Social Research. (1999). *How to improve survey response rates: A guide for interviewers on the doorstep*. London, New Delhi: Sage Publications, Thousand Oaks.

National Research Council. (1979). *Privacy and confidentiality as factors in survey response*. Washington DC: National Academy Press.

National Research Council. (2005). *Expanding access to research data: Reconciling risks and opportunities*. Washington DC: National Academy.

Nichols, J. D. (1992). Capture-recapture models. *Bioscience, 42,* 94–102.

Nicholls, W. L II, Baker, R. P. Martin, J. (1997). The effect of new data collection technology on survey data quality. In: Lyberg, L., Biemer, P., Collins, M., De Leeuw, E., Trewin, D., Dippo, C., & Schwarz, N. (Eds) *Survey Measurement and Process Quality*. New York: Wiley.

Norenzayan, A., & Schwarz, N. (1999). Telling what they want to know: Participants tailor causal attributions to researchers' interests. *European Journal of Social Psychology, 29*, 1011–1020.

Norman, D. A. (1982). *Learning and memory*. New York: W. H. Freeman & Company.

NSDUH (2005). *Frequently Asked Questions*. Accessed 28 April 2005 at https://nsduhweb.rti.org.

Nunnally, J. C., & Bernstein, J. H. (1994). *Psychometric Theory*. New York: McGraw-Hill.

Nyman, A. M., Roman, A. M., & Turner, C. F. (2001, May). *Comparison of Computer-Assisted Telephone Survey Methodologies: CATI vs. T-ACASI*. Paper presented at annual meeting of American Association for Public Opinion Research, Montreal, Quebec, Canada.

O'Brien, E. M., Mayer, T. S., Groves, R. M., & O'Neill, G. E. (2002). Interviewer training to increase survey participation. *ASA Proceedings of the Annual Meeting of the American Statistical Association*. Arlington, VA: ASA

O'Muirchearteigh, C. (1991). Simple response variance: Estimation and determinants. In P. N. Beimer, R. M. Groves, L. E. Lyberg, N. A. Mathiewetz, & S. Sudman (Eds.), *Measurement errors in surveys* (pp. 287–310). New York: Wiley.

Oksenberg, L., & Cannell, C. (1989). *New methods for pretesting survey questionnaires*. Paper presented at the Annual Meeting of the American Association for Public Opinion Research, St. Petersburg, FL.

Oksenberg, L., Cannell, C., & Kalton, G. (1991). New strategies for pretesting survey questions.

Journal of Official Statistics, 7, 349–365.

Ongena, Y. (2005). *Interviewer and respondent interaction in survey interviews.* Amsterdam: Vrije Universiteit.

Ostrom, T. M., & Upshaw, H. S. (1968). Psychological perspective and attitude change. In A. C. Greenwald, T. C. Brock, & T. M. Ostrom (Eds.), *Psychological foundations of attitudes.* New York: Academic Press.

Øyen, E. (Ed.). (1990). *Comparative methodology: Theory and practice in international social research,* London: Sage.

Oyserman, D., Coon, H., & Kemmelmeier, M. (2002). Rethinking individualism and collectivism: Evaluation of theoretical assumptions and meta-analyses. *Psychological Bulletin, 128,* 3–73.

Paasche-Orlow, M. K., Taylor, H. A., & Brancati, F. L. (2003). Readability standards for informed consent forms as compared with actual readability. *New England Journal of Medicine, 348,* 721-726.

Pan, Y., & De la Puente, M. (2005). *Census Bureau guideline for the translation of data collection instruments and supporting materials: Documentation on how the guideline was developed* (U.S. Census Bureau Research Report Series, Survey Methodology #2005-06). Retrieved June 19, 2006, from: http://www.census.gov/srd/papers/pdf/rsm2005-06.pdf

Parackel, M. (2003). Internet-based and mail survey: A hybrid probabilistic survey approach. *Proceedings of the 2003 Australian Web Conference.* Retrieved April 15, 2005, from: http://ausweb.scu.edu.au/aw03/papers/parackal.html.

Parameswaran, R., & Yaprak, A. (1987). A cross-national comparison of consumer research measures. *Journal of International Business Studies, 18,* 35–49.

Park, A., & Jowell, R. (1997). *Consistencies and differences in a cross-national survey. The International Social Survey Programme (1995).* Retrieved from: www.za.uni-koeln.de/-data/en/issp/codebooks/c2880app.pdf).

Park, D. C. (1999). Cognitive aging, processing resources, and self-report. In N. Schwarz, D. C. Park, B. Knäuper, & S. Sudman (Eds.), *Aging, cognition, and self-reports.* Philadelphia: Psychology Press.

Paxson, M. C., Dillman, D. A., & Tarnai, J. (1995). Improving response to business mail surveys. In B. G. Cox, D. A. Binder, B. N. Chinappa, A. Christianson, M. J. Colledge, & P. S. Kott (Eds.), *Business survey methods.* New York: Wiley.

Payne, S. L. (1951). *The art of asking questions.* Princeton: Princeton University Press.

Peeters, C. F. W. (2005). *Measuring politically sensitive behavior.* Amsterdam: Vrije Universiteit.

Pepper, S. C. (1981). Problems in the quantification of frequency expressions. In D. W. Fiske (Ed.), *Problems with language imprecision: New directions for methodology of social and behavioral science, 9.* San Francisco: Jossey-Bass.

Peschar, J. (1982). Quantitative aspects in cross-national comparative research: Problems and issues. In M. Niessen, & J. Peschar (Eds.), *International Comparative Research.* Oxford: Pergamon Press.

Pew Research Center for the People and the Press. (2004). *Polls face growing resistance, but still representative survey experiment shows* (Survey Reports). Retrieved November 14, 2005, from: http://people-press.org/reports/print.php3?PageID=817.

Pfeffermann, D. (1996). The use of sampling weights for survey data analysis. *Statistical Methods in Medical Research, 5,* 239–261.

Phipps, P., & Tupek, A. (1991). Assessing measurement errors in a touchtone recognition survey. *Survey Methodology, 17,* 15–26.

Ponce, N. A., Lavarreda, S. A., Yen, W., Brown, E. R., DiSogra C., & Satter, D. (2004). The California health interview 2001. Translation of a major survey for California's multiethnic population. *Public Health Reports, 119,* 1–18.

Porst, R., & Jers, C. (2006). Die ALLBUS-"Gastarbeiter-Frage". Zur Geschichte eines Standard-Instruments in der Allgemeinen Bevölkerungsumfrage der Sozialwissenschaften (ALLBUS). Retrieved September 10, 2006 from: http://www.gesis.org/Publikationen/Berichte/ZUMA_Arbeitsberichte/2005.htm.

Porter, S. R., & Whitcomb, M. E. (2003). The impact of contact type on web survey response rates. *Public Opinion Quarterly, 67,* 579–589.

Potaka, L., & Cochrane, S. (2004). Developing bilingual questionnaires: Experiences from New Zealand in the development of the 2001 Maori Language Survey. *Journal of Official Statistics, 20,* 289–300.

Potter, F. (1990). A study of procedures to identify and trim extreme sampling weights. *Proceedings of the Survey Research Methods Section, 13,* 225–230.

Potter, F. (1988). Survey of procedures to control extreme sampling weights. *Proceedings of the Survey Research Methods Section, 11*, 453–458.

Presser, S. (1989). Pretesting: A neglected aspect of survey research. In F. J. Fowler Jr. (Ed.), *Conference Proceeding of Health Survey Research Methods* (pp. 35–38) (DHHS Pub. No. PHS 89–3447). Washington, DC: National Center for Health Services Research.

Presser, S., & Blair, J. (1994). Survey pretesting: Do different methods produce different results? *Sociological Methodology, 24*, 73–104.

Raghunathan, T. E., & Grizzle, J. E. (1995). A split questionnaire survey design. *Journal of the American Statistical Association, 90*, 54–63.

Raghunathan, T. E., Lepkowski, J. M., van Hoewyk, J., & Solenberger, P. (2001). A multivariate technique for multiply imputing missing values using a sequence of regression models. *Survey Methodology, 27*, 85–95.

Ramos, M., Sevedi, B. M., & Sweet, E. M. (1998). Computerized self-administered questionnaires. In M. P. Couper, R. P. Baker, J. Bethlehem, C. Z. F. Clark, J. Martin, W. L. Nicholls II, et al. (Eds.), *Computer assisted survey information collection* (398–408). New York: Wiley.

Rao, J. N. K., Wu, C. F. J., & Yue, K. (1992). Some recent work on resampling methods for complex surveys. *Survey Methodology, 18*, 209–217.

Rasinski, K. A., Rasinski, G. B., Baldwin, A. K., Yeh, W., & Lee, L. (1999). Methods of data collection: Perception of risks and losses, and motivation to give truthful answers to sensitive survey questions. *Applied Cognitive Psychology, 13*, 465–484.

Rässler, S. (2002). Statistical matching: A frequentist theory, practical applications, and alternative Bayesian approaches. *Lecture Notes in Statistics, 168*. New York: Springer.

Rässler, S., & Schnell, R. (2004). *Multiple imputations for unit nonresponse versus weighting including a comparison with a nonresponse follow-up study.* Diskussionspapier der Lehrstühle für Statistik 65/2004, Nürnberg, Germany.

Raudenbush, S. W. & Bryk, A. S. (2002). *Hierarchical linear models.* Newbury Park, CA: Sage.

Redline, C., & Dillman, D. A. (2002). The influence of alternative visual designs on respondents' performance with branching instructions in self-administered questionnaires. In R. Groves, D. Dillman, J. Eltinge, & R. Little (Eds.), *Survey nonresponse.* New York: Wiley.

Redline, C., Dillman, D. A., Dajani, A., & Scaggs, M. (2003). Improving navigational performance in U.S. Census 2000 by altering the visually administered languages of branching instructions. *Journal of Official Statistics, 19*, 403–20.

Reips, U. D. (2002). Context effects in web-surveys. In B. Batinic, U. D. Reips, M. Bosnjak & A. Werner (Eds.), *Online social sciences* (95–104). Seattle: Hogrefe & Huber.

Rice, S. A. (1929). Contagious bias in the interview. *American Journal of Sociology, 35*, 420–423.

Richman, W. L., Kiesler, S., Weisband, S., & Drasgow, F. (1999). A meta-analytic study of social desirability distortion in computer-administered questionnaires, traditional questionnaires and interviews. *Journal of Applied Psychology, 84*, 754–775.

Ritchie, J. & Lewis, J. (Eds.). (2003). Qualitative research practice. London: Sage.

Rizzo, L. J., Brick, M., & Park, I. (2004). A minimally intrusive method for sampling persons in random digit dial surveys. *Public Opinion Quarterly, 68*, 267–274.

Robert, C. P., & Casella, G. (1999). *Monte carlo statistical methods.* New York: Springer.

Rock, D. A., Werts, C. E., Linn, R. L., & Jöreskog, K. G. (1977). A maximum likelihood solution to the errors in variables and errors in equation models. *Multivariate Behavioral Research, 12*, 187–197.

Rogler, L. H. (1999). Methodological sources of cultural insensitivity in mental health research. *American Psychologist, 54*, 424–433.

Rokkan, S. (1962). The development of cross-national comparative research: A review of current problems and possibilities. *Social Science Information, 1*, 21–38.

Rokkan, S. (1969). Cross-national survey research: Historical, analytical and substantive contexts. In S. Rokkan, S. Verba, J. Viet, & E. Almasy (Eds.), *Comparative Survey analysis*. Paris: Mouton.

Rokkan, S., & Szczerba-Likiernik, (1968). Introduction. In S. Rokkan (Ed.), *Comparative research across cultures and nations*, Paris: Mouton.

Rosén, B., & Elvers, E. (1999). Quality concept for official statistics. *Encyclopedia of Statistical Sciences, Update 3*, 621–629. New York: Wiley.

Rosenthal, R., & Rosnow, R. (1975). *The volunteer subject.* New York: Wiley.

Ross, M. (1989). The relation of implicit theories to the construction of personal histories. *Psychological Review, 96*, 341–357.

Rubin, D. B. (1976). Inference and missing data. *Biometrika, 63*, 581–590.

Rubin, D. B. (1977). Formalizing subjective notions about the effect of nonrespondents in sample surveys. *Journal of the American Statistical Association, 72*, 538–543.

Rubin, D. B. (1978). Multiple imputation in sample surveys—a phenomenological Bayesian approach to nonresponse. *Proceedings of the Section on Survey Research Methods, 1,* 20–40.

Rubin, D. B. (1986). Statistical matching using file concatenation with adjusted weights and multiple imputations. *Journal of Business and Economic Statistics, 4*, 87–95.

Rubin, D. B. (1987). *Multiple imputation for nonresponse in surveys.* New York: Wiley.

Rubin, D. B. (1996). Multiple imputation after 18+ years. *Journal of the American Statistical Association, 91*, 473–489.

Rubin, D. B. (2004). The design of a general and flexible system for handling nonresponse in sample surveys. *The American Statistician, 58*, 298–302. (Original work published 1977)

Rubin, D. B., & Schenker, N. (1987). Interval estimation from multiply imputed data: A case study using census agriculture industry codes. *Journal of Official Statistics, 3*, 375–387.

Rubin, D. B., & Schenker, N. (1986). Multiple imputation for interval estimation from simple random samples with ignorable nonresponse. *Journal of the American Statistical Association, 81*, 366–374.

Rubin, D. B., Stern, H. S., & Vehovar, V. (1995). Handling `Don't know' survey responses: The case of the Slovenian Plebiscite. *Journal of the American Statistical Association, 90*, 822–828.

Rubin, H. J., & Rubin, I. S. (1995). *Qualitative interviewing: The art of hearing data.* Thousand Oaks, CA: Sage.

Rust, K. F., & Rao, J. N. K. (1996). Variance estimation for complex surveys using replication techniques. *Statistical Methods in Medical Research, 5,* 283–310.

Ryan, T. P. (2000). *Statistical methods for quality improvement.* New York: Wiley.

Saeboe, H. V., Byfuglien, J., & Johannessen, R. (2003). Quality issues at statistics Norway. *Journal of Official Statistics, 19,* 287–303.

Salant, P., & Dillman, D. A. (1994). *How to conduct your own survey.* New York: Wiley.

Saris, W. (1998). Ten years of interviewing without interviewers: The telepanel. In M. P. Couper, R. P. Baker, J. A. Harkness, Bethlehem, C. Z. F. Clark, J. R. van de Vijver, & P. MohlerMartin, W. L. Nicholls II, et al. (Eds.), *Cross-Cultural Survey Methods.* Hoboken, NJ: New York: Wiley.

Saris, W. (2003a). Multitrait-multimethod studies. In J. A. Harkness, F. J. R. van de Vijver, & P. Mohler (Eds.), *Cross-Cultural Survey Methods.* Hoboken, NJ: Wiley.

Saris, W. (2003b). Response function equality. In J. A. Harkness, F. J. R. van de Vijver, & P. Mohler (Eds.), *Cross-Cultural Survey Methods.* Hoboken, NJ: Wiley.

Schaefer, D. R., & Dillman, D. A. (1998). Development of a standard e-mail methodology: Results of an experiment. *Public Opinion Quarterly, 62*, 378–397.

Schaefer, N. (1991). Conversation with a purpose or conversation? Interaction in the standardized interview. In P. Biemer, R. Groves, L. Lyberger, N. Mathiowetz, & S. Sudman (Eds.), *Measurement errors in surveys* (367–393). New York: Wiley

Schafer, J. L. (1997). *Analysis of incomplete multivariate data.* New York: Chapman and Hall.

Schafer, J. L., & Schenker, N. (2000). Inference with imputed conditional means. *Journal of the American Statistical Association, 95*, 144–154.

Scheers, N. J., & Dayton, M. C. (1988) Covariate randomized response models. *Journal of the American Statistical Association, 83*, 969–974.

Scheers, N. J., & Mitchell, C.D. (1988). Covariate randomized response models. *Journal of the American Statistical Association 83*, 969–974.

Schenker, N. & Taylor, J. M. G. (1996). Partially parametric techniques for multiple imputation. *Computational Statistics & Data Analysis, 22*, 425–446.

Scherpenzeel, A. C. (1995). *A question of quality: Evaluating survey questions by multitrait-multimethod studies.* Leidschendam: KPN research.

Scheuch, E. K. (1990). The development of comparative research: Towards causal explanations. In E. Øyen (Ed.), *Comparative methodology: Theory and practice in international social research.* Wiltshire, U.K.: Sage.

Scheuren, F. (2004). *What is a survey?* Alexandria, VA: American Statistical Association. Retrieved July 24, 2006, from: http://www.whatisasurvey.info.

Scheuren, F. (2001). *How important is accuracy?* Proceedings of Statistics Canada Symposium, Statistics Canada, Ottawa, Canada.

Schillewaert, N., Langerak, F., & Duhamel, T. (1998). Non probability sampling for WWW surveys: A comparison of methods. *Journal of the Market Research Society, 40*, 307–313.

Schober, M. F., & Conrad, F. G. (2002). A collaborative view of standardized survey interviews. In

D. Maynard, H. Houtkoop-Steenstra, N. Schaeffer, & J. van der Zouwen (Eds.), *Standardization and tacit knowledge* (67–94). New York: Wiley.

Schober, M. F., & Conrad, F. G. (1998). Does conversational interviewing improve survey data quality beyond the laboratory? *ASA Proceedings of the Annual Meeting of the American Statistical Association.* Arlington, VA: ASA

Schober, M. F., & Conrad, F. G. (1997). Does conversational interviewing reduce survey measurement error? *Public Opinion Quarterly, 61,* 576–602.

Schonlau, M., Van Soest, A., Kapteyn, A., Couper, M. P., & Winter, J. (2004). Attempting to adjust for selection bias in web surveys with propensity scores: The case of the health and retirement survey (HRS). *Proceedings of the section on survey research methods, 24.*

Schuman, H., & Converse, J. (1971). The effect of black and white interviewers on black responses in 1968. *Public Opinion Quarterly, 35,* 44–68.

Schuman, H., & Ludwig, J. (1983). The norm of even-handedness in surveys as in life. *American Sociological Review, 48,* 112–120.

Schuman, H., & Presser, S. (1981). *Questions and answers in attitude surveys: Experiments in question form, wording, and context.* New York: Academic Press.

Schulz, W., & Sibberns, H. (Eds.). (2004). *IEA Civic Education Study technical report.* Amsterdam: IEA.

Schwarz, N. (1996). *Cognition and communication: Judgmental biases, research methods, and the logic of conversation.* Hillsdale: Erlbaum.

Schwarz, N. (1997). Questionnaire design: The rocky road from concepts to answers. In: L. Lyberg, P. Biemer, M.Collins, E. de Leeuw, C. Dippo, N. Schwarz, et al. (Eds.), *Survey measurement and process quality* (29–45). New York: Wiley.

Schwarz, N. (1999a). Self-reports: How the questions shape the answers. *American Psychologist, 54,* 93–105.

Schwarz, N. (1999b). Frequency reports of physical symptoms and health behaviors: How the questionnaire determines the results. In D. C. Park, R. W. Morrell & K. Shifren (Eds.), *Processing of medical information in aging patients: Cognitive and human factors perspectives.* Mahaw: Erlbaum.

Schwarz, N. (2003). Culture-sensitive context effects: A challenge for cross-cultural surveys. In J. A. Harkness, F. J. R. van de Vijver, & P. Mohler (Eds.), *Cross-cultural survey methods.* Hoboken, NJ: Wiley.

Schwarz, N., & Bless, H. (1992a). Constructing reality and its alternatives: Assimilation and contrast effects in social judgment. In L. L. Martin & A. Tesser (Eds.), *The construction of social judgments.* Hillsdale: Erlbaum.

Schwarz, N., & Bless, H. (1992b). Scandals and the public's trust in politicians: Assimilation and contrast effects. *Personality and Social Psychology Bulletin, 18,* 574–579.

Schwarz, N., & Bless, H. (2007). Mental construal processes: The inclusion/exclusion model. In D. A. Stapel and J. Suls (Eds.), *Assimilation and contrast in social psychology.* Philadelphia, PA: Psychology Press.

Schwarz, N., & Hippler, H. J. (1995). Subsequent questions may influence answers to preceding questions in mail surveys. *Public Opinion Quarterly, 59,* 93–97.

Schwarz, N., & Hippler, H. J. (1991). Response alternatives: The impact of their choice and ordering. In P. Biemer, R. Groves, N. Mathiowetz & S. Sudman (Eds.), *Measurement error in surveys.* New York: Wiley.

Schwarz, N., Hippler, H. J., Deutsch, B., & Strack, F. (1985). Response scales: Effects of category range on reported behavior and subsequent judgments. *Public Opinion Quarterly, 49,* 388 – 395.

Schwarz, N., Knäuper, B., Hippler, H. J., Noelle-Neumann, E., & Clark, F. (1991). Rating scales: Numeric values may change the meaning of scale labels. *Public Opinion Quarterly, 55,* 570–582.

Schwarz, N., & Oyserman, D. (2001). Asking questions about behavior: Cognition, communication, and questionnaire construction. *American Journal of Evaluation, 22,* 127–160.

Schwarz, N., Park, D. C., Knäuper, B., Davidson, N., & Smith, P. (1998, April). *Aging, cognition, and self-reports: Age-dependent context effects and misleading conclusions about age differences in attitudes and behavior.* Paper presented at the Cognitive Aging Conference, Atlanta, GA.

Schwarz, N., & Scheuring, B. (1992). Selbstberichtete Verhaltens- und Symptomhäufigkeiten: Was Befragte aus Anwortvorgaben des Fragebogens lernen. [Frequency-reports of psychosomatic symptoms: What respondents learn from response alternatives] *Zeitschrift für Klinische Psychologie, 22,* 197–208.

Schwarz, N., Strack, F., & Mai, H. P. (1991). Assimilation and contrast effects in part-whole question sequences: A conversational logic analysis. *Public Opinion Quarterly, 55,* 3–23.

Schwarz, N., Strack, F., Müller, G., & Chassein, B. (1988). The range of response alternatives may determine the meaning of the question: Further evidence on informative functions of response alternatives. *Social Cognition, 6,* 107–117.

Schwarz, N., & Sudman, S. (1996). *Answering questions: Methodology for determining cognitive and communicative processes in survey research.* San Francisco: Jossey-Bass.

Schwarz, N., & Sudman, S. (1994). *Autobiographical memory and the validity of retrospective reports.* New York: Springer Verlag.

Sears, D. O. (1986). College sophomores in the laboratory: Influences of a narrow data base on social psychology's view of human nature. *Journal of Personality and Social Psychology, 51,* 515–530.

Seber, G. A. F. (1996). A review of estimating animal abundance II. *International Statistical Review, 60,* 129–166.

Serpell, R. (1990). Audience, culture and psychological explanation: A reformulation of the emic-etic problem in cross-cultural psychology. *The quarterly newsletter of the Laboratory of Comparative Human Cognition, 12,* 99–132.

Shao, J. (2002). Replication methods for variance estimation in complex sample surveys with imputed data. In R. M. Groves, D. A. Dillman, J. L. Eltinge, & R. J. A. Little (Eds.), *Survey nonresponse.* New York: Wiley.

Sharma, D. C. (2005). *Net telephony set to surge, IDC says.* Retrieved November 14, 2005, from: http://news.com.com/Net+telephony+set+to+surge2C+IDC+says/2100-7352_3-5653437.html.

Sheatsley, P. (1983). Questionnaire construction and item writing. In P. Rossi, J. D. Wright, & A. B. Anderson (Eds.), *Handbook of survey research.* New York: Academic Press.

Shuttles, C. D., Welch, J. S., Hoover, J. G., & Lavrakas, P. J. (2002, May). *The Development and Experimental Testing of an Innovative Approach to Training Telephone Interviewers to Avoid Refusals.* Paper presented at the 2002 Annual Meeting of the American Association for Public Opinion Research, St. Petersburg, FL.

SIBIS (2003). *Towards the information society in Europe and the US.* Bonn, Germany: SIBIS. Retrieved November 14, 2005, from: http://www.empirica.biz/sibis/statistics/data/1-10.htm.

Sieber, J. E., & Stanley, B. (1988). Ethical and professional dimensions of socially sensitive research. *American Psychologist, 43,* 49–55.

Siemiatycki, J. (1979). A comparison of mail, telephone, and home interview strategies for household health surveys. *American Journal of Public Health, 69,* 238–245.

Singer, E. (1978). Informed consent: Consequences for response rate and response quality in social surveys. *American Sociological Review, 43,* 144–162.

Singer, E. (2003). Exploring the meaning of consent: Participation in research and beliefs about risks and benefits. *Journal of Official Statistics, 19,* 273–285.

Sirken, M., Hermann, D., Schechter, S., Schwarz, N., Tanur, J., & Tourangeau, R. (Eds.) (1999). *Cognition and survey research.* New York: Wiley.

Singer, E., Mathiowetz, N., & Couper, M. P. (1993). The impact of privacy and confidentiality concerns on census participation. *Public Opinion Quarterly, 57,* 465–82.

Singer, E., Van Hoewyk, J., Gebler, N., Raghunatan, T., & McGonagle, K. (1999). The effect of incentives on response rates in interviewer-mediated surveys. *Journal of Official Statistics, 15,* 217–230.

Singer, E., Van Hoewijck, J., & Maher, M. P. (2000). Experiments with incentives in telephone surveys. *Public Opinion Quarterly, 64,* 171–188.

Singer, E., Van Hoewyk, J., & Neugebauer, R. (2003). Attitudes and behavior: The impact of privacy and confidentiality concerns on participation in the 2000 census. *Public Opinion Quarterly, 65,* 368–384.

Skevington, S. M. (2002). Advancing cross-cultural research on quality of life: Observations drawn from the WHOQOL development. *Quality of Life Research, 11,* 135–144.

Skevington, S. M., Sartorius, N., Amir, M., & The WHOQOL-Group (2004). Developing methods for assessing quality of life in different cultural settings. The history of the WHOQOL instruments. *Social Psychiatry and Psychiatry Epidemiology, 39,* 1–8.

Skevington, S. M., & Tucker, C. (1999). Designing response scales for cross-cultural use: Data from the development of the UK WHOQOL. *British Journal of Medical Psychology, 72,* 51–61.

Skinner, C. J., Holt, D., & Smith, T. M. F. (1989). *Analysis of complex surveys.* Chichester: Wiley.

Skinner, H. A., & Allen, B. A. (1983). Does the computer make a difference? Computer versus face-to-face, versus self-report assessment of alcohol, drugs, and tobacco use. *Journal of Consulting and Clinical Psychology, 51,* 267–275.

Skjåk, K. K., & Harkness, J. (2003). Data collection methods. In J. A. Harkness, F. J. R. van de Vijver, & P. Mohler (Eds.), *Cross-cultural survey methods*. New York: Wiley.

Smid, M., & Hess, D. (2003). Harmonizing sampling frames and indicators in international market research: A German perspective. In J. H. P. Hoffmeyer-Zlotnik, & C. Wolf (Eds.), *Advances in cross-national comparison. A European working book for demographic and socio-economic variables*. New York: Kluwer Academic/Plenum Publishers.

Smith, A., Christopher, S., & McCormick, A. K. (2004). Development and implementation of a culturally sensitive cervical health survey: A community-based participatory approach. *Women and Health, 40*, 67–86.

Smith, P. J., Hoaglin, D. C., & Battaglia, M. P. (2005). Statistical methodology of the national immunization survey, 1994 – 2002. *Vital Health Statistics 2, 138*. National Center for Health Statistics. Retrieved November 14, 2005, from: http://www.cdc.gov/nchs/data/series/sr_02/sr02_138.pdf.

Smith, T. W. (1995, May). *Little Things Matter: How differences in questionnaire format can affect survey responses*. Paper presented at Annual Conference of the American Association for Public Opinion Research, Fort Lauderdale, FL.

Smith, T. W. (2003). Developing comparable questions in cross-national surveys. In J. A. Harkness, F. J. R. van de Vijver, & P. Mohler (Eds.), *Cross-cultural survey methods*. Hoboken, NJ: Wiley.

Smith, T. W. (2004). Developing and evaluating cross-national survey instruments. In S. Presser, J. Rothgeb, M. P. Couper, J. T. Lessler, E. Martin, J. Martin, & E. Singer (Eds.), *Methods for testing and evaluating survey questionnaires*. Hoboken, NJ: Wiley.

Smyth, J. D., Dillman, D. A., & Christian, L.M. (2006, January). *Does "yes or no" on the telephone mean the same as "check-all-that-apply" on the web?* Paper presented at Telephone Survey Methodology II, Miami, FL.

Smyth, J. D., Dillman, D. A., Christian, L. M., & Stern, M. F. (2006). Comparing check-all and forced-choice question formats in web surveys. *Public Opinion Quarterly 70*, 66–77.

Snell-Hornby, M. (1988). *Translation studies: An integrated approach*. Amsterdam: John Benjamins.

Snijkers, G. (2002). *Cognitive laboratory experiences on pre-testing computerised questionnaires and data quality*. Heerlen: Statistics Netherlands.

Snijkers, G., Hox, J., & De Leeuw, E. (1999). Interviewers' Tactics for Fighting Survey Nonresponse. *Journal of Official Statistics, 15,* 185–198. (Also on www.jos.nu)

Social and Economic Sciences Research Center. (2005). *Instructing web and telephone respondents to report date answers in format desired by the surveyor* (Technical Report 05-067). Washington, DC: Christian, L. M., Dillman, D. A., & Smyth, J. D.

Somers, H. (2005, December). Round-trip translation: What is it good for? *Proceedings of the Australasian Language Technology Workshop 2005*, Sydney, Australia. Retrieved September 6, 2006 from: http://www.alta.asn.au/events/altw2005/cdrom/pdf/ALTA200519.pdf#search=%22Round-Trip Translation%3A What Is It Good For%3F%22

Sperber, A. D., Devellis, R. F., & Boehlecke, B. (1994). Cross-cultural translation: Methodology and validation. *Journal of Cross-cultural Psychology, 25*, 501–524.

Srinivasan, R. & Hanway, S. (1999). A new kind of survey mode difference: Experimental results from a test of inbound voice recognition and mail surveys. Paper presented at the meeting of the American Association of Public Opinion Research, St. Pete Beach, FL.

Statistics Canada. (2003). *Survey methods and practices*. Ottawa: Ministry of Industry, Statistics Canada, Social Survey Division.

Statistics Sweden (2001). *The future development of the Swedish register system*. (R&D Report 2001:1). Stockholm: Statistics Sweden.

Steeh, C. (2004, May). *A new era for telephone interviewing*. Paper presented at the Fifty-ninth Annual Conference of the American Association for Public Opinion Research, Phoenix, AZ.

Steeh, C. (1981). Trends in nonresponse rates, 1952 – 1979. *Public Opinion Quarterly, 45*, 40–57.

Steeh, C., Kirgis, N., Cannon, B., & De Witt, J. (2001). Are they really as bad as they seem? Nonresponse rates at the end of the twentieth century. *Journal of Official Statistics, 17*, 227–247.

Steeh, C., & Piekarski, L. (2006, January). *Accommodating new technologies: The rejuvenation of telephone surveys*. Paper presented at the Second International Conference on Telephone Survey Methodology, Miami, FL.

Stephens, R. T. (2003). Utilizing Metadata as a knowledge communication tool. *Proceedings of the International Professional Communication Conference 2004, Minneapolis, MN*. Institute of Electrical and Electronics Engineers, Inc.

Stern, M. F., & Dillman, D. A. (2006). Community participation, social ties, and use of the internet. *City and Community*. 5, 409–424.

Stewart, D. W., & Shamdasani, P. N. (1990). *Focus groups: Theory and practice*. Thousand Oaks, CA: Sage.

Stouffer, S. A. (1963). *Communism, conformity, and civil liberties*. Gloucester, Mass: Peter Smith.

Strack, F. (1994). Response processes in social judgment. In R. S. Wyer, & T. K. Srull (Eds.), *Handbook of social cognition, volume 1* (2nd ed.). Hillsdale: Erlbaum.

Strack, F., & Martin, L. (1987). Thinking, judging, and communicating: A process account of context effects in attitude surveys. In H. J. Hippler, N. Schwarz, & S. Sudman (Eds.), *Social information processing and survey methodology*. New York: Springer Verlag.

Strack, F., Schwarz, N., & Gschneidinger, E. (1985). Happiness and reminiscing: The role of time perspective, mood, and mode of thinking. *Journal of Personality and Social Psychology, 49*, 1460 –1469.

Strack, F., Schwarz, N., & Wänke, M. (1991). Semantic and pragmatic aspects of context effects in social and psychological research. *Social Cognition, 9*, 111–125.

Strube, G. (1987). Answering survey questions: The role of memory. In H. J. Hippler, N. Schwarz, & S. Sudman (Eds.), *Social information processing and survey methodology*. New York: Springer Verlag.

Sturgeon, K., & Winter, S. (1999). International marketing on the world wide web. New opportunities for research: What works, what does not and what is next. *Proceedings of the ESOMAR Worldwide Internet Conference Net Effects, 191–200.*

Subcommittee on Disclosure Limitation Methodology (1994). *Federal committee on statistical methodology* (Statistical policy working paper No. 22). Washington DC: Statistical Policy Office, Office of Information and Regulatory Affairs, OMB.

Sudman, S. (1983). Applied sampling. In P. Rossi, J. D. Wright, & A. B. Anderson (Eds.), *Handbook of survey research*. New York: Academic Press.

Sudman, S., & Bradburn, N. M. (1974). *Response effects in surveys*. Chicago: Aldine.

Sudman, S., & Bradburn, N. M. (1982). *Asking questions: a practical guide to questionnaire design*. San Francisco: Jossey Bass.

Sudman, S., Bradburn, N. M., & Schwarz, N. (1996). *Thinking about answers: The application of cognitive processes to survey methodology*. San Francisco: Jossey-Bass.

Sudman, S., & Schwarz, N. (1989). Contributions of cognitive psychology to advertising research. *Journal of Advertising Research, 29*, 43–53.

Sundgren, B. (1993). Guidelines on the design and implementation of statistical metainformation systems. *R&D Report 4.* Stockholm: Statistics Sweden.

Sundgren, B. (1973). *An infological approach to data bases*. Unpublished doctoral thesis, University of Stockholm, Sweden.

Supple, A. J., Aquilino W. S., & Wright, D. L. (1999). Collecting sensitive self-report data with laptop computers: Impact on the response tendencies of adolescents in a home interview. *Journal of Research on Adolescence, 9*, 467–488.

Sykes, W., & Collins, M. (1992). Anatomy of the survey interview. *Journal of Official Statistics, 8*, 277–291.

Tafforeau, J., López Cobo, M., Tolonen, H., Scheidt-Nave, C., & Tinto, A. (2005). *Guidelines for the development and criteria for the adoption of health survey instruments*. European Commission. Retrieved June 23, 2006, from: http://forum.europa.eu.int/Public/irc/dsis/-health/library?l=/reports/healthsinterviewssurvey/guidelines_instruments/_EN_1.0_&a=d

Tanner, M. A., & Wong, W. H. (1987). The calculation of posterior distributions by data augmentation. *Journal of the American Statistical Association, 82*, 528–540.

Tanzer, N. K. (2005). Developing tests for use in multiple languages and cultures: A plea for simultaneous development. In R. K. Hambleton, P. F. Merenda, & C. D. Spielberger (Eds.), *Adapting educational and psychological tests for cross-cultural assessment*. Mahwah, NJ: Erlbaum.

Teune, H. (1990). Comparing countries: Lessons learned. In E. Øyen (Ed.), *Comparative methodology: Theory and practice in international social research*. London: Sage.

Thomas, E. L., & Robinson, H. A. (1972). *Improving reading in everyday class: A sourcebook for teachers*. Boston: Allyn and Bacon.

Thomas, R. (2002). *Material prepared by R. Thomas for Center for Applied Social Surveys (CASS) course 2002 on "Pretesting Survey Questionnaires" conducted by Campanelli, Collins, & Thomas.* Southampton, UK: University of Southampton, Southampton Statistical Science Research Institute, Center for Applied Social Surveys.

Thompson, S. K. (2002). *Sampling* (2nd ed.). New York: Wiley Interscience.

Thomson, K., Nicolaas, G., Bromley, C., & Park, A. (2001). *Welsh assembly election study 1999: Technical report.* London: National Center for Social Research.

Thornberry, J., Bhaskar, B., Wesley, B., Krulewitch, C.J., Wesley, B., Hubbard, M.L., Das, A., Foudin, L., Adamson, M. 2002. Audio computerized self-report interview use in prenatal clinics: Audio computer assisted self interview with touch screen to detect alcohol consumption in pregnant women application of a new technology to an old problem. *Computer Information Nursing 20*: 46-52.

Tjøstheim, I. (2005, April). *Mobile self-interviewing an opportunity for location-based market research. Are privacy concerns a showstopper?* Paper presented at the Association of Survey Computing Conference on Mobile Computing, London, UK.

Tjøstheim, I., & Thalberg, S. (2005). Are the mobile phone users ready for MCASI - mobile computer assisted self-interviewing? In *Excellence in international research 2005.* ESOMAR.

Tomas, R.K. (2004).

Tortora, R. (2004). Response trends in a national random digit dial survey. *Advances in Methodology and Statistics, 1*, 21–32.

Tourangeau, R. (1984). Cognitive science and survey methods: A cognitive perspective. In T. Jabine, M. Straf, J. Tanur, & R. Tourangeau (Eds.), *Cognitive aspects of survey methodology: Building a bridge between disciplines.* Washington, DC: National Academy Press.

Tourangeau, R., Couper, M.P., & Steiger, D.M. (2001). Social presence in web surveys. Federal Committee on Statistical Methodology conference, 2001. Retrieved August 2007 from http://www.websm.org.

Tourangeau, R., Rasinski, K., Jobe, J., Smith, T., & Pratt, W. (1997). Sources of error in a survey of sexual behaviour, *Journal of Official Statistics, 13*, 341–365.

Tourangeau, R., Rips, L. J., & Rasinski, K. (2000). *The psychology of survey response.* Cambridge: Cambridge University Press.

Tourangeau, R., & Smith, T. W. (1998). Collecting sensitive data with different modes of data collection. In M. P. Couper, R. P. Baker, J. Betlehem, C. Z. F. Clark, J. Martin, W. L. Nichols II, et al. (Eds.), *Computer assisted survey information collection* (431–453). New York: Wiley.

Tourangeau, R., & Smith, T. W. (1996). Asking sensitive questions. The impact of data collection, mode, question format, and question context. *Public Opinion Quarterly, 60*, 275–304.

Tourangeau, R., Steiger, D. M. & Wilson, D. (2002). Self-administered questions by telephone: Evaluating Interactive Voice Response. *Public Opinion Quarterly, 66*, 265–278.

Traub, R. E. (1994). *Reliability for the Social Sciences.* Thousand Oaks, CA: Sage.

Triandis, H. C. (1972). *The analysis of subjective culture.* Oxford, UK: Wiley-Interscience.

Trice, A. (1987). Informed consent: Biasing of sensitive self-report data by both consent and information. *Journal of Social Behavior and Personality, 2*, 369–374.

Trussell, N., & Lavrakas, P. J. (2004). The influence of incremental increases in token cash incentives on mail survey response: Is there an optimal amount? *Public Opinion Quarterly, 68*, 349–367.

Tsuchiya, T., Hiray, Y., & Ono, S. (2007). A study of the properties of the item count technique. *Public Opinion Quarterly, 71*, 253–272.

Tuckel, P., & O'Neill, H. (2002). The vanishing respondent in telephone surveys. *Journal of Advertising Research, 42*, 26–48.

Tucker, C. J., Brick, M., Meekins, B., & Esposito, J. (2005). *Household telephone service and usage patterns in the U.S. in 2004: Implications for telephone samples.* Bureau of Labor Statistics: Unpublished report.

Tucker, C., Casady, R., & Lepkowski, J. (1992). Sample allocation for stratified telephone sample designs. *Proceedings of the section on survey research methods, 15*, 291–296.

Tucker, C., Lepkowski, J. M., & Piekarski, L. (2002). The current efficiency of list-assisted telephone sampling designs. *Public Opinion Quarterly, 66*, 321–328.

Turner, C. F., Forsyth, B. H., O'Reilly, J. M , Cooley, P. C., Smith, T. K., Rogers, S. M., & Miller, H. G. (1998). Automated self-interviewing and the survey measurement of sensitive behaviors. In M. P. Couper, R. P. Baker, J. Betlehem, C. Z. F. Clark, J. Martin, W. L. Nichols II, et al. (Eds.), *Computer assisted survey information collection.* New York: Wiley.

Turner, C. F., Miller, H. G., Smith, T. K., Cooley, P. C., & Rogers, S. M. (1996). Telephone Audio Computer-Assisted Self-Interviewing (T-ACASI) and survey measurements of sensitive behaviors: Preliminary results. In R. Banks, J. Fairgrieve, L. Gerrard, T. Orchard, C. Payne, & A. Westlake (Eds.), *Survey and statistical computing 1996: Proceedings of the seconds ASC International Conference.* Chesham, Bucks, U.K.: Association for Survey Computing.

Tuskegee Syphilis Study Ad Hoc Advisory Panel. (1973). *Final report.* Washington, DC: US

Department of Health, Education, and Welfare.

Tuten, T. L., Bosnjak, M., & Bandilla, W. (1999/2000). Banner-advertised web-surveys. *Marketing Research, 11*, 16–21.

U.S. Energy Information Administration. (1996). *Residential energy consumption survey quality profile.* Washington, DC: U.S. Department of Energy.

U.S. Federal Committee on Statistical Methodology. (2001). *Measuring and reporting the quality of survey data* (Statistical Policy Working Paper 31). Washington, D.C.: U.S. Office of Management and Budget.

Van Buuren, S., Brand, J. P. L., Oudshoorn, C. G. M., & Rubin, D. B. (in press). Fully conditional specification in multivariate imputation. *Journal of Statistical Computation and Simulation, 76*, 1049–1064.

Van Buuren, S., & Oudshoorn, C. G. M. (2000). *Multivariate imputation by chained equations: MICE V1.0 User's Manual* (Report PG/VGZ/00.038). Leiden, The Netherlands: TNO Preventie en Gezondheid.

Van de Vijver, F. J. R. (2003). Bias and equivalence: Cross cultural perspectives. In J. A. Harkness, F. J. R. van de Vijver, & P. Mohler (Eds.), *Cross-cultural survey methods,* Hoboken, NJ: Wiley.

Van der Heijden, P. G. M., van Gils, G., Bouts, J., & Hox, J. J. (2000). A comparison of randomized response, computer-assisted self-interview and face-to-face direct questioning. *Sociological Methods and Research, 28*, 505–537.

Van der Stadt, H., Ten Cate, A., Hundepool, A. J. & Keller, W. J. (1986). Koopkracht in kaart gebracht: Een statistiek van de inkomensdynamiek. *Statistische Onderzoekingen, M28.* Voorburg: Statistics Netherlands.

Van der Zouwen, J., & Smit, J. H. (2004). Evaluating survey questions by analysing patterns of behaviour codes and question-answer sequences: A diagnostic approach. In S. Presser, J. M. Rothgeb, M. P. Couper, J. T. Lessler, E. Martin, J. Martin, et al. (Eds.), *Methods for testing and evaluating survey questionnaires.* New York: Wiley.

Van Deth, J. W. (1998). Equivalence in comparative political research. In J. W. van Deth (Ed.), *Comparative politic: The problem of equivalences.* London: Routledge.

Van Hattum, M. J. C. & de Leeuw, E .D. (1999). A disk-by-mail survey of pupils in primary schools: data quality and logistics. *Journal of Official Statistics, 15*, 413–429. (also at www.jos.nu)

Vartivarian S., & Little, R. (2002). On the formation of weighting adjustment cells for unit nonresponse. *Proceedings of the Survey Research Methods Section, 15.*

Vehovar, V., Batagelj, Z., Lozar Mnafreda, K., & Zaletel, M. (2002). Nonresponse in web surveys. In R. M. Groves, D. A. Dillman, J. L. Eltinge, R. J. A. Little (Eds), *Survey Nonresponse.* New York: Wiley.

Vehovar, V., Belak, E., Batagelj, Z., & Čikić, S. (2003). *Mobile phone surveys in Slovenia.* Unpublished manuscript.

Vehovar, V., Lozar Manfreda, K., & Batagelj, Z. (2000, May). *Design issues in WWW surveys.* Paper presented at the 55th Annual Conference of American Association for Public Opinion Research, Portland, OR.

Verba, S. (1971). Cross-national survey research: The problem of credibility. In I. Vallier (Ed.), *Comparative methodology on sociology: Essays on trends and applications.* Berkeley: University of California Press.

Wagenaar, W. A. (1986). My memory: A study of autobiographical memory over six years. *Cognitive Psychology, 18*, 225 – 252.

Wänke, M., & Schwarz, N. (1997). Reducing question order effects: The operation of buffer items. In L. Lyberg, P. Biemer, M. Collins, E. de Leeuw, C. Dippo & N. Schwarz (Eds.), *Survey measurement and process quality.* Chichester, UK: Wiley.

Ware, J. (1987). Standards for validating health measures: Definition and content. *Journal of Chronic Diseases, 40*, 473–480.

Warner, S.L. (1965). Randomized response: A technique for eliminating evasive response bias. *Journal of the American Statistical Association, 60*, 63–69.

Warren, R. D., White, J. K., & Fuller, W. A. (1974). An errors in variables analysis of managerial role performance. *Journal of the American Statistical Association, 69*, 886–893.

Weeks, M. F. (1992). Computer-Assisted Survey Information Collection: A review of CASIC methods and their implications for survey operations. *Journal of Official Statistics, 8*, 445–465.

Weir, P., Laurence, M., & Blessing, C. (2000). A comparison of the use of telephone interview to telephone audio CASI in a customer satisfaction survey. *Proceedings of the Survey Research Methods Section, 23*, 828–833.

Weisband, S., & Kiesler, S. (1996). *Self-disclosure on computer forms: Meta-analysis and implications.* Tucson   AR: University   of   Arizona.   Retrieved   from: www.al.arizona.ude/~weisbrand/chi/chi96.html.

Werking G., & Clayton, R. (1993). Automated telephone collection techniques for improving timeliness and data quality. Washington DC: Bureau of labour Statistics.

Whitcomb, M. E., & Porter, S. R. (2004). E-mail contacts: A test of complex graphical designs in survey research. *Social Science Computer Review, 22,* 370–376.

White, G. K. (1996). An on-line survey of food and beverage consumers on the Internet: An evaluation of the survey methodology. *Marketing Research On-line, 1,* 39–59. Retrieved November 11, 2001, from: http://mro.massey.ac.nz/online3.pdf

Widman, L., & Vogelius, L. (2002, June). *Daily reach using SMS: Measuring and reporting reach in real time.* Paper presented at the Week of Audience Measurement (WAM), Cannes, France.

Wilkins, J. R., Hueston, W. D., Crawford, J. M., Steele, L. L., & Gerken, D. F. (1997). Mixed-mode survey of female veterinarians yields high response rate. *Occupational Medicine, 47,* 458–462.

Wilkinson, R. K., & Hines, C. J. (1991). Data collection methods in the STPDS Surveys: Improving response   rates   in   mixed   mode   surveys.   Retrieved   April   15,   2005,   from: http://srsstats.sbe.nsf.gov/research/3-91.pdf.

Williams, M. D., & Hollan, J. D. (1981). The process of retrieval from very long term memory. *Cognitive Science, 5,* 87-119.

Willis, G. (2004). Overview of methods for developing equivalent measures across multiple cultural groups. In S. B. Cohen, & J. M. Lepkowski (Eds.), *Eighth Conference on Health Survey Research Methods,* Hyattsville, US. Department of Health and Human Services.

Willis, G. (1994). *Cognitive interviewing and questionnaire design: A training manual.* Washington, DC: Office of Research Methodology, National Center for Health Statistics.

Willis, G., & Lessler, J. (1999). *Questionnaire appraisal system-1999.* Research Triangle Park, NC: Research Triangle Institute.

Willke, J., Adams, C. O., & Girnius, Z. (1999). Internet testing: A landmark study of the differences between mall intercept and on-line interviewing in the United States. *Proceedings of the ESOMAR Worldwide Internet Conference Net Effects,* 145–157.

Winkel, F. W., & Vrij, A. (1998). Who is in need of victim support? The issue of accountable, empirically validated selection and victim referral. *Expert Evidence: The International Digest of Human Behaviour, Science and Law, 6,* 23–41.

Winkielman, P., Knäuper, B., & Schwarz, N. (1998). Looking back at anger: Reference periods change the interpretation of (emotion) frequency questions. *Journal of Personality and Social Psychology, 75,* 719–728.

Wolter, K. M. (1985). *Introduction to variance estimation.* New York: Springer-Verlag.

Woodall, G. (1998). *Market research on the Internet.* Great Falls, VA: Rockbridge Associates, Inc. Retrieved November 11, 2001, from: http://www.rockresearch.com/Articles/nmr01/nmr01.html

Zaller, J. R. (1992). *The nature and origins of mass opinion.* Cambridge: Cambridge University Press.

Zarkovich, S. (1966). *Quality of statistical data.* Rome: Food and Agricultural Organization of the United Nations.

Zdep, S. M., Rhodes, J. N., Schwartz, R. M., & Kilkenny, M. J. (1979). The validity of the Randomized Response Technique. *Public Opinion Quarterly, 43,* 544–549.

Zelditch, M. Jr. (1971). Intelligible comparisons. In I. Vallier (Ed.), *Comparative methods in sociology: Essays on trends and applications.* Berkeley: University of California Press.

Zukerberg, A., Nichols, E., & Tedesco, H. (1999, May). *Designing surveys for the next millennium: Internet questionnaire design issues.* Paper presented at the 1999 Association for Public Opinion Research Conference, St. Petersburg, FL.

Zull, C., Weber, R., & Mohler, P. (1989). *Computer aided text classification for the social ssciences: The general enquirer III.* Mannheim, BRD: ZUMA.

Index